PERGAMON GENERAL PSYCHOLOGY SERIES

Editors: Arnold P. Goldstein, Syracuse University
Leonard Krasner, SUNY, Stony Brook

CLASSROOM MANAGEMENT:

The Successful Use of Behavior Modification

PGPS-27

CLASSROOM MANAGEMENT:

The Successful Use of Behavior Modification

K. Daniel O'Leary and Susan G. O'Leary
State University of New York
Stony Brook, New York

PERGAMON PRESS INC.
New York · Toronto · Oxford · Sydney · Braunschweig

PERGAMON PRESS INC.
Maxwell House, Fairview Park, Elmsford, N.Y. 10523

PERGAMON OF CANADA LTD.
207 Queen's Quay West, Toronto 117, Ontario

PERGAMON PRESS LTD.
Headington Hill Hall, Oxford

PERGAMON PRESS (AUST.) PTY. LTD.
Rushcutters Bay, Sydney, N.S.W.

VIEWEG & SOHN GmbH
Burgplatz 1, Braunschweig

Printed in the United States of America

08 016789 6 (H)
08 016790 X (S)

To
Wesley Becker, Sidney Bijou and Leonard Ullmann
whose writing and teaching so significantly shaped our
behavior

Contributors

MELVIN E. ALLERHAND, PH.D.
Department of Psychology
Case Western Reserve University
Cleveland, Ohio 44106

CAROLE R. ARNOLD, PH.D.
Department of Psychology
Iowa State University
Ames, Iowa 50010

R. C. ATKINSON, PH.D.
Department of Psychology
Stanford University
Stanford, California 94305

SAUL AXELROD, PH.D.
Department of Education
University of Connecticut
Storrs, Connecticut 06268

BRUCE L. BAKER, PH.D.
Department of Social Relations
Harvard University
Cambridge, Massachusetts

ALBERT BANDURA, PH.D.
Department of Psychology
Stanford University
Stanford, California 94305

MRS. HARRIET H. BARRISH
Department of Human Development
University of Kansas
Lawrence, Kansas 66044

WESLEY C. BECKER, PH.D.
Department of Education
University of Oregon
Eugene, Oregon 97400

SANDRA L. BEM, PH.D.
Department of Psychology
Carnegie-Mellon University
Pittsburgh, Pennsylvania

CEDRIC BENSON, PH.D.
Director of Special Education
West Suburban Association
   for Special Education
Oak Park, Illinois 60300

HERSHEL BERKOWITZ, PH.D.
University of Colorado
Medical Center
Denver, Colorado

JAY S. BIRNBRAUER, PH.D.
Department of Psychology
University of North Carolina
Chapel Hill, N. Carolina 27514

MARCIA BRODEN
Department of Human Development
University of Kansas
Lawrence, Kansas 66044

CARL B. BRUCE
Northwest Jr. High School
Kansas City, Kansas

DONALD BUSHELL, PH.D.
Department of Human Development
University of Kansas
Lawrence, Kansas 66044

RICHARD A. CAMPBELL
Shawnee Mission Public School
1854 Topping
Kansas City, Missouri 64126

VALERIE A. CANE
Department of Psychology
University of Wisconsin
Madison, Wisconsin 53706

MRS. CONSTANCE CARLSON
2506 McDivitt Road
Madison, Wisconsin 53700

VIRGINIA CARTER
Department of Human Development
University of Kansas
Lawrence, Kansas 66044

MRS. MARILYN CLARK
Skyline School
Shawnee Mission, Kansas 66200

SHARON S. CRANSTON
Shawnee Mission North High School
Shawnee Mission, Kansas 66200

RONALD S. DRABMAN
Department of Psychology
State University of New York
Stony Brook, New York 11790

KAREN A. (CURTISS) ESVELDT
Neuropsychiatric Institute
University of California
Los Angeles, California

GARY W. EVANS
1906 S. Fifteenth Street
Rogers, Arkansas 72756

MICHAEL B. EVANS
Department of Psychology
University of Illinois
Urbana, Illinois 61801

MARLYN FOUNDOPOULOS
1938 North 46th Terrace
Kansas City, Kansas

A. S. GILMORE, PH.D.
University of South Florida
Tampa, Florida 33620

JOAN E. GRUSEC, PH.D.
Department of Psychology
University of Toronto
Toronto, Ontario

R. VANCE HALL, PH.D.
Department of Human Development
University of Kansas
Lawrence, Kansas

ROBERT P. HAWKINS, PH.D.
Department of Psychology
Western Michigan University
Kalamazoo, Michigan 49001

LORETTA (NIELSEN) JULIAN
1057 S. Westmore Avenue
Apt. 105
Lombard, Illinois 60148

RUTH E. KASS
Department of Psychology
State University of New York
Stony Brook, New York 11790

KENNETH F. KAUFMAN, PH.D.
Psychology Department
Sagamore Children's Center
Melville, New York

JOHN KIDDER, PH.D.
Child Development & Mental
  Retardation Center
Experimental Education Unit
University of Washington
Seattle, Washington

RICHARD J. KOTHERA
Superintendent of Schools
School District No. 15
Lombard, Illinois

DAVID S. KUYPERS, PH.D.
Leon County Mental Health
  Guidance Center
Tallahassee, Florida

EUGENE LEVITT, PH.D.
Indiana University
Medical Center
Department of Psychiatry
Indianapolis, Indiana 46202

THOMAS C. LOVITT, PH.D.
Mental Retardation & Child
  Development Center
University of Washington
4701 24th Avenue NE
Seattle, Washington 98105

CHARLES H. MADSEN, PH.D.
Department of Psychology
Florida State University
Tallahassee, Florida 32306

LESLIE F. MALPASS, PH.D.
Virginia Polytechnic Institute
  and State University
Blacksburg, Virginia 24061

HUGH S. MCKENZIE, PH.D.
Department of Education
University of Vermont
Burlington, Vermont 05401

FRANCES L. MENLOVE, PH.D.
Los Alamos Family Council
Los Alamos, New Mexico 87544

MARY LOUISE MICHAELIS
3412 Milam Lane
Lexington, Kentucky 40502

MARY ANN MITCHELL
Juniper Gardens Children's Project
2021 North Third Street
Kansas City, Kansas 66101

BRENDA S. MITTS
Department of Human Development
University of Kansas
Lawrence, Kansas 66044

CHARLES S. MORRILL, PH.D.
Department of Psychology
Northeastern University
Boston, Massachusetts

ROBERT D. O'CONNOR
Department of Psychology
University of Illinois
Urbana, Illinois 61801

K. DANIEL O'LEARY, PH.D.
Department of Psychology
State University of New York
Stony Brook, New York 11790

J. GRAYSON OSBORNE, PH.D.
Department of Psychology
Utah State University
Logan, Utah

GAYLON L. OSWALT, PH.D.
Parsons State Hospital
  & Training Center
Parsons, Kansas 67357

ROSS D. PARKE, PH.D.
Department of Psychology
University of Wisconsin
Madison, Wisconsin 53706

SIDNEY J. PARNES, PH.D.
Department of Psychology
State University of New York
Buffalo, New York

BERNARD PERLOFF, PH.D.
U.C.L.A. Urban Design Dept.
University of California
Los Angeles, California

H. W. REESE, PH.D.
Department of Psychology
West Virginia University
Morgantown, West Virginia

DOROTHEA ROSS, PH.D.
Department of Psychology
Stanford University School
  of Medicine
Stanford, California 94305

SHEILA ROSS, PH.D.
Palo Alto Medical Research
  Foundation
860 Bryant Street
Palo Alto, California 94301

DAVID RYBACK
Rohrer, Hibler, & Replogle
Suite 707
800 Place Victoria
Montreal 115

RICHARD A. SAUDARGAS
Department of Psychology
Florida State University
Tallahassee, Florida 32306

MRS. MURIEL SAUNDERS
Department of Human Development
University of Kansas
Lawrence, Kansas 66044

MRS. JESSICA (SHELLMAN) KIRK
Waianae Elementary School
Waianae, Hawaii 96792

B. F. SKINNER, PH.D.
Department of Psychology
Harvard University
Cambridge, Massachusetts 02138

ARTHUR W. STAATS, PH.D.
Department of Psychology
University of Hawaii
Honolulu, Hawaii 96822

PAUL R. SURRATT, PH.D.
Rehabilitation Institute
Southern Illinois University
Carbondale, Illinois 62901

MRS. CECILIA TAGUE
Rainier School
White River School District
Buckley, Washington 98321

DON A. THOMAS
Department of Human Development
University of Kansas
Lawrence, Kansas 66044

ROGER E. ULRICH, PH.D.
Department of Psychology
Western Michigan University
Kalamazoo, Michigan 49001

R. H. WALTERS, deceased

MICHAEL H. WARD
Harvard University
Cambridge, Massachusetts 02138

CAROL (KUPERS) WHALEN, PH.D.
Department of Psychology
University of California
Irvine, California 92664

CHARLES F. WILLIAMS, PH.D.
Department of Educational Technology
San Francisco State College
San Francisco, California

MONTROSE M. WOLF, PH.D.
Department of Human Development
University of Kansas
Lawrence, Kansas 66044

PATRICIA ANN WROBEL
Department of Human Development
University of Kansas
Lawrence, Kansas 66044

ELAINE H. ZIMMERMAN, PH.D.
c/o Joseph Zimmerman
Indiana University
Medical Center
Indianapolis, Indiana 46207

JOSEPH ZIMMERMAN, PH.D.
Indiana University
Medical Center
Indianapolis, Indiana 46207

Contents

Preface

The role of education in the development of today's youth is receiving increased attention and criticism by both parents and professionals. Clearly, the academic and social experiences during a child's twelve years in school are vital in determining the kind of life a child will or can have when he leaves school. Yet educators and psychologists have been remiss in providing the teacher with effective procedures for dealing with inappropriate social behavior and for developing useful and productive skills. Critiques of school procedures and policies are so bountiful that libraries could be built on such critiques alone. What is lacking is a positive solution to the problems facing schools and teachers. As Skinner noted in 1969, "There is nothing very new in prevailing educational theories .... Most teachers teach essentially as teachers have taught for centuries. The best of them are simply people who have a knack in getting along with others. All this must change, and the change will take time. But we are on the verge of a new educational 'method'—a new pedagogy—in which the teacher will emerge as a skilled behavioral engineer [pp. 6–7]." We feel that this new method is here and the present book presents both principles and data which we feel provide some clear solutions to the problems which teachers face daily. More importantly, the solutions presented have direct implications for what a teacher herself can do to solve some of the problems which she sees every day.

The purposes of this book are to

1. Supply the reader with a set of principles about changing behavior and to place those principles within the historical context of the development of treatment with children.

2. Present research evidence documenting the efficacy of such procedures in the classroom.
3. Discuss how teachers can implement such procedures for both preventing problems and for dealing with existing problems.
4. Influence the direction of research in the area of classroom management by making both educators and psychologists aware of a rapidly developing field, by describing both the advantages and disadvantages of some of the research in this book, and by pointing out directions which future research might take.

The articles in this book were selected because the research was conducted in the classroom or because they have direct relevance for classroom management. Greatest emphasis was placed on the former and 27 of the 37 articles include data from the classroom itself. Another criterion for selection of articles was the adequacy of design of the study; case studies were generally avoided. (In short, we included articles which have implications for teaching.) We have found that teachers enjoy reading studies in their original version. The teacher not only learns exactly what was done, she is also trained to evaluate research. Hopefully, the teacher of the future will serve as a master teacher whose job it will be to evaluate research about classroom management and curriculum materials, to supervise the student aides and paraprofessionals, and to help children individually who are having difficulty. It is our hope that the conceptual framework here presented and the research derived therefrom will provide teachers with the skills necessary to be effective for master teachers and behavior analysts.

The articles which are reprinted in full in the book are noted in the first chapter and elsewhere, and are designated by an italicized number in parentheses. References to any writing by O'Leary and O'Leary either in the first chapter, the commentaries, or the last chapter appear in the reference section at the end of the book. References for each article reprinted in the book appear directly at the end of each article.

This volume is intended for undergraduate students in education and psychology, for teachers who are currently in the field, and for clinical, educational, and school psychologists who consult with teachers about educational problems. The book contains explanations of basic terminology; it introduces the reader to the field of behavior modification with children in some detail; comments are made about each article in the book, and the concluding chapter discusses the implementation of the procedures discussed throughout the book. Consequently, the book could stand alone as an advanced undergraduate text. It might also be used, however, with basic experimental texts utilizing an operant learning framework since it well exemplifies many of the operant principles. Because of the emphasis on application of behavioral principles, we hope young teachers will find that this book serves as a guide for developing their repertoire of classroom skills. As importantly, we hope that the evidence and conceptual framework presented will be strong enough to change the behavior of the teachers and psychologists who have already been trained by mentors who had a different conception than the one here presented.

We wish to thank our colleagues Leonard Krasner, Alan Ross, Kenneth Kaufman, David Santogrossi, and Carol Whitehurst: a principal, William Kinnally; and two teachers, Lana Kaufman and Diane Santogrossi, who aided in the evaluation of various portions of this book. We are also appreciative of the suggestions of an undergraduate class who read an earlier version of this book. Special thanks goes to Frances DiNardo who cheerfully aided us in the typing of and the correspondence associated with this book. Thanks are due Leonard Krasner, Pergamon General Psychology Series Editor, for his editorial and administrative assistance in all phases of the publication of this book. Last, but certainly not least, we wish to thank the authors and publishers who permitted us to reproduce their articles for this book. Their research has given behavior modification the type of experimental basis so greatly needed in the field of education.

CHAPTER 1

Behavior Modification with Children

THE DEVELOPMENT OF TREATMENT PROCEDURES
FOR CHILDREN

Historical Introduction

Children have always had behavioral or emotional problems but until the early part of the twentieth century their problems were not considered worthy of any special attention. According to Despert (1965), the term "emotional disturbances" was not applied specifically to children until Sullivan used it in 1932. Despert noted that children with problem behaviors which are now called neurotic or psychotic were "variously labeled through the ages as possessed, wicked, guilty, insubordinate, incorrigible, unstable, maladjusted and problem children, roughly in that order [p. 38]." As one can see from such labels, there has been a fortunate change in attitude toward children's problems. However, this change in attitude has come slowly.

In the third century B.C., newborn children were examined by a council of elders to see if they were fit to live in the military state of Sparta. If they were too weak, they were left in the woods to die. This practice of abandoning physically unfit children or children with behavioral problems declined across the ages but other forms of infanticide or infant killing continued as a widespread practice even in the seventeenth and eighteenth centuries. In ancient Rome, children were treated as little more than animals. According to Roman Law as outlined in the Twelve Tables, children could be sold; the law specified that the buyer could make

1

extensive use of the physical and intellectual potentials of the child. Imprisonment of children with behavior problems was frequent in London in the 1800's, and child employment was extensively abused in the United States until the child labor laws were passed in 1916.

Some landmarks in the history of thought regarding the treatment of children's problems are found in the works of Witmer, Freud, Healy, Meyer, and Kanner. Though G. Stanley Hall is regarded as the pioneer in child psychology because of his historic work on the "content of children's minds" in 1883, psychological treatment of children did not begin until the turn of the century, and child psychiatry did not begin until the 1930's. In sum, prior to the late 19th century there was little compassion for children's problems, and as we shall see, treatment for children was not generally available until the 1930's.

The first psychological clinic in the United States was established by Leightner Witmer at the University of Pennsylvania in 1896. Witmer's clinic treated children who had learning difficulties and what were then referred to as "moral defects" (Reisman, 1966). Once a diagnosis was made, treatment consisted of retraining to alleviate the particular defect. Witmer was pragmatic in his outlook, and his assessments involved both a physical and a mental examination which included anthropometric measures, eye tests, and measures of reaction time. In his opinion, many social and academic difficulties were a function of undetected physical problems such as hearing loss and poor vision. Witmer pioneered the practices of collaborating with other disciplines such as social work, neurology, and education, but the teacher was always central in his collaborative efforts. His feeling that the teacher should be aware of many facets of the child's life is reflected in the following statement:

> There is a body of knowledge dealing with the out-of-school life of the child, with the child's father and mother, the food that he eats, the room in which he sleeps, his play, his life on the street which is not less important to the teacher than a knowledge of special methods of instruction [p. 270].

Using a very different but equally influential approach to treatment, Sigmund Freud applied psychoanalytic techniques to a child's problem in the frequently cited case of Little Hans in 1909. A Viennese physician who was a follower of Freud kept detailed anecdotal records concerning his four-year-old child's fear of going out of doors. The child purportedly was afraid to go outdoors because he feared that he would be bitten by horses. The child's father took Hans to see Freud once, and the remainder of the therapy or analysis was executed by the father who corresponded with Freud and who later interpreted the fear to the child. In brief, the child's fear was interpreted by Freud as a fear of his father. The child was particularly bothered by horses that "wore things in front of their eyes and have black things around their mouths." Freud felt that the description of the horses resembled the child's father because his father wore glasses (the things in front of the horses eyes) and his father had a mustache (the black things around his mouth). Through a series of discussions with the child, the father tried to give the child "insight" so that the child would see that his fear was really of the father and not of the horses. Freud was convinced that the treatment was successful when he was unexpectedly visited by a tall, sturdy, fourteen-year-old lad who presented himself with the words: "Ich bin der Kleine Hans" (I am little Hans). The case of Little Hans is significant since it is the first published account of a child analysis and since it was the first opportunity Freud had to verify his theories of infantile sexuality (Jones, 1955).[1]

During the period of the establishment of the Witmer clinic and the first child analyses made by Freud, another significant pioneering effort was begun with a psychiatric study of childhood disturbances at the Healy School in Chicago. In the early 1900's, delinquent behavior was assumed to be almost solely due to organic deficiencies, e.g., "bad heredity, enlarged tonsils, inflamed adenoids, uncorrected refractive errors, impacted teeth, cigarette smoking, intracranial pressure, systematic absorption of toxins from focal infections, phimosis (need for circumcision) and feeble mindedness (Reisman, 1966)." Fortunately, some people were disturbed by the fact that courts imposed penalties based solely on a physical exam, and they prompted an investigation into the causes of delinquency. William Healy established the Juvenile Psychopathic Institute in 1909. This institute was particularly significant because its researchers placed a much needed emphasis on environmental factors related to delinquency, such as neighborhoods, peers, school milieu, and general living conditions. Unlike the present behavior modification conceptualization of delinquency, however, Healy and his associates placed strong emphasis on unconscious motivation as a critical factor in delinquency.

In 1912 the Boston Psychopathic Hospital was the first mental hospital in the United States to establish an outpatient clinic which accepted children as patients. A year later the Phipps Psychiatric Clinic in Baltimore was opened under the direction of Adolph Meyer, and this clinic also accepted children as outpatients. Psychological clinics and clinical psychology courses at universities began to emerge rapidly during the first and second decade of the twentieth century—with Clark, Iowa,

---

[1]Wolpe and Rachman (1960) presented a detailed critique of this classic case which seriously questioned whether the case verified any of Freud's theories.

Minnesota, and Washington being among the first to follow Pennsylvania's lead. Interestingly, these clinics generally operated on the assumption that they were dealing with people who had *learning problems* — not people who were physically sick or mentally ill. For example, Meyer (whose views served as the basis for the practices of many of the first child guidance clinics) felt that "mental" disorders were generally maladjustments of personality and behavior rather than diseases of the nervous system. As Meyer (1908) noted, "The concrete conduct and behavior is the main thing deranged in our patients . . . . the mental facts we speak of are not mere thoughts but actual attitudes, affects, volitions and activities and possible disorders of discrimination." Meyer, like many psychologists today, felt that parents had to be involved in child treatment, and he proposed a rather straightforward approach to such treatment. He saw psychotherapy as the "regulation of action," and like current behavior modifiers, he felt that habit-training was the backbone of treatment programs.

By the early 1920's there were a number of psychoeducational approaches to child treatment. Such approaches did not offer very comprehensive treatment or explanatory systems, and consequently no single psychoeducational treatment approach was adopted by the majority of psychologists or psychiatrists. Psychoanalysis on the other hand, offered a comprehensive explanatory system for both normal and abnormal behavior and was adopted by the majority of practitioners. It explained behaviors such as dreams and slips of the tongue which previously were a mystery to most people. In addition, psychoanalysis had the blessings of G. Stanley Hall, one of the most prestigious psychologists of the early 1900's, who invited Freud to attend the twentieth anniversary of Clark University in 1909 (Jones, 1955). Despite many early schisms among followers of Freud concerning the ubiquitousness of sexual aspects of the problems and neuroses of clients, psychoanalysis began to pervade the conceptualizations of both normal personality development and clinical treatment. This psychoanalytic domination of the mental health field continued, and even at present, the preponderance of psychiatrists and psychologists regard the psychoanalytic notions or derivations thereof as their basis for treatment.

Psychoanalytic Psychotherapy with Children

In order to appreciate the intellectual climate in which behavior modification developed, let us now turn to discussion of the psychoanalytic or medical model approach to the treatment of children. The psychoanalytic approach to child treatment, sometimes referred to as the medical model has the following assumptions:

1. Problem behaviors are symptoms of an underlying cause.
2. Therapy should consist primarily of allowing the child to express his emotions.
3. A good relationship is a prime requisite for successful therapy, and the relationship between the therapist and the child is seen as the critical element in bringing about change in the child's behavior.

As Helen Witmer (1946) noted "child guidance clinics have as patients children who display a wide variety of behavior and personality disorders. The *symptoms*[2] that cause the parents concern are of many types: aggressive, uncontrollable behavior; nervousness, sensitivity, fears, excessive shyness, and other difficulties in relating to people; various kinds of school maladjustment; physical disorders without discoverable organic bases; delinquencies of various kinds; marked peculiarities of behavior and personality.... It is a fundamental tenet of dynamic psychiatry that these maladjustments in behavior and personality are but symptoms of some underlying disturbance ... [which] 'give no more specific information about the individual than would the terms fever or cough if they were similarly applied ....' 'psychic life is governed by psychic laws and follows its own course and rules,' and it is psychic life which must be studied if one is to discover what the behavior symptoms represent. Accordingly, in order to show to what kinds of problems child guidance is addressed, it is necessary to use a classification that is based on the nature of the disorder rather than on its symptoms [pp. 16–17]."*

Ullmann and Krasner (1969) have described the medical model of treatment as one in which "the individual's behavior is considered peculiar, abnormal, or diseased because of some underlying cause, usually physical in nature." As germs produce symptoms, people's inner problems produce abnormal behavior, and in order to alleviate or change the abnormal behavior one must find its cause. With adults, the search for such causes proceeds by having the client talk, free associate, and describe his dreams. However, since communication with children is difficult through the normal verbal means employed by therapists who are treating adults, expression of problems is thought to be encouraged by

---

*Reprinted with permission of The Commonwealth Fund and Harvard University Press, from Helen Witmer's (Ed.), *Psychiatric interviews with children.* Harvard University Press, Cambridge, Mass., 1946.
[2]Italics ours.

allowing a child to play with dolls and toys in the therapist's office. The therapist usually takes a warm, passive, or permissive role after establishing the setting with materials that are appropriate to the child's problem.

As Bakwin and Bakwin (1967) note "cars, soldiers, and electrical equipment could be useful for children preoccupied with problems of aggression or sexual excitement whereas a toy baby carriage, baby dolls, and the like, could be used with problems relating to the birth of a sibling or sibling rivalry." It is assumed that children will dramatize their own problems by their placement of the toys in the room and by their activity with them. It is also assumed that a child will release his emotions through catharsis or expression of feelings, and "as the bad feelings go out, the good feelings will sprout." The words and actions of the child during the play are "considered equivalent to the chain of free association" (Freud, A., 1964) which can later be interpreted by the therapist. Such interpretation may involve certain feelings the child has toward the therapist or toward his parents. Presumably through expression of feeling, there is a dissolution of some of the restraints or bottled-up feelings which the child has. Psychoanalysis of children's problems also proceeds in an educative sense by "exercising outward influence by modifying the relations with those who are bringing up the child, creating new impressions, and revising the demands made upon the child by the outside world" (Freud, A., 1964).

The importance of the conceptualization of disorders and its ramifications for treatment is reflected in the following statements of Helen Witmer (1946) regarding the significance of the therapeutic relationship in child psychotherapy.

> Dynamic psychiatry regards disorders of personality as disorders of personal relations; that is, as evidence of the difficulty the individual encountered in maintaining a feeling of security with the human beings who are emotionally important to him. It is highly logical, then, that chief reliance for therapy should be placed on the development of a satisfactory relationship between psychiatrist and patient and that numerous ways should be devised to use that relationship for therapeutic ends [p. 34].

Unfortunately, as will be seen in the article by Berkowitz (1968), (3), the relationship between the therapist and the child has been so stressed that traditional therapists rarely make contacts with or visit the child's school.

The conclusions generally made from evaluative research concerning the effectiveness of traditional psychotherapy offer little hope for teachers or parents. Levitt (1957, 1963), (1, 2), has been unable to detect any significant influence of psychotherapy with children. Similarly, Eysenck (1952) was unable to find any significant influence of psychotherapy with adults. While such research may have some shortcomings, the continued failure to find any consistent improvement or more than a small improvement in children or adults resulting from traditional psychotherapy should make one alert to alternative methods of dealing with human problems.

Partly associated with the psychoanalytic tradition was the development of various personality assessment batteries. These batteries consist of projective tests such as the Rorschach or Thematic Apperception Test (TAT). The Rorschach and the TAT consist of ambiguous ink blots and semi-ambiguous scenes. The child is instructed to tell a story about what he sees in the pictures. It is assumed that the child will *project* his personality in such a test since the vagueness of the ink blots or scenes will necessitate some elaboration which is presumably a function of one's personality. Evaluative research suggests that such tests are practically a waste of time for planning a treatment program for an individual (O'Leary, 1972). Although there are some projective tests which do differentiate "normal" children from children with many behavioral problems, they are usually not sensitive enough to differentiate "normal" children from those children usually referred to child clinics, and even if they did, one could probably make such distinctions more rapidly without such tests.

In sum, while many teachers may feel that referral to a psychologist for personality testing may be valuable, the tests themselves appear to contribute very little if anything in formulating a treatment plan for a child. On the other hand, there are a number of checklists which differentiate an average child from one with behavioral problems and which focus on classroom behaviors. The checklists alert one to particular problems which might have been missed in an interview with a teacher. Such checklists will be discussed in Chapter 12.

Behavior Modification with Children

In 1913 John B. Watson made a sharp break with the psychological and psychoanalytic conceptions of his time when he published a treatise, *Psychology as the behaviorist views it*. Reacting to what he felt was a psychology of little practical significance, Watson argued that the concept of consciousness and the method of introspection should be the domain of philosophers. He claimed that psychology is a purely objective experimental branch of natural science whose goal is the prediction and control of behavior.

The time seems to have come when psychology must discard all reference to conscious-ness; when it need no longer delude itself into thinking that it is making mental states the object of observation. We have become so enmeshed in speculative questions con-cerning the elements of mind, the nature of conscious content . . . that I, as an experi-mental student feel that something is wrong with our premises and the types of problems which develop from them . . . I believe we can write a psychology . . . and . . . never use the terms consciousness, mental states, mind, content, introspectively verifiable, imagery and the like . . . . Certain stimuli lead the organisms to make the responses. In a system of psychology completely worked out, given the response the stimuli can be predicted, given the stimuli the response can be predicted [pp. 163–167].*

Within such a framework, Watson and Rayner (1920) published a study which reported how a child could acquire fearful behavior through classical conditioning. Watson and Rayner chose a healthy, eleven-month-old infant who did not display any unusual fearful behavior. When a white rat was presented to Albert, he reached for it. When he touched the rat, a loud noise was made and Albert started to cry. After a number of soundings of the noise as Albert touched the rat, he became fearful not only of the rat but also of other furry objects. Thus, by pairing a neutral stimulus such as a white rat to which the child did not respond fearfully, with a stimulus such as a loud noise, which did elicit a fearful response, the neutral stimulus acquired fear-evoking properties. In short, Watson and Rayner reported that they had demonstrated one method of learning a fearful response.[3]

In 1924, Jones continued work with fears but in this case with their elimination. In a now classic study, Peter, a boy who was fearful of a white rabbit, was placed in a room with the rabbit that was some distance from him. The treatment proceeded as follows:

Peter was seated in a high chair and given food which he liked. The experimenter brought the rabbit in a wire cage as close as she could without arousing a response which would interfere with the eating. Through the presence of the pleasant stimulus (food) whenever the rabbit was shown, the fear was eliminated gradually in favor of a positive response (Jones, 1924).

Occasionally the experimenter also had children participate in the treat-ment to help with the "unconditioning." Such children were selected

---

*Reprinted with permission of the American Psychological Association, Inc., from J. B. Watson's "Psychology as a behaviorist views it," in *Psychological Review*, 1913, **20**, 158–177. Copyright © 1913 by the American Psychological Association, Inc.

[3]English (1929) followed the Watson & Rayner (1920) paradigm and failed to replicate the establish-ment of a conditioned fear response in a fourteen-month-old child when a large metal bar was struck as a wooden duck was lowered near the child. Bregman (1934) also failed to develop a conditioned response in infants of 8–16 months, and she concluded that conditioning could not be accepted as the explana-tion for the changes in emotional behavior of a young infant.

because of their fearless attitude toward the rabbit and because of their generally satisfactory adjustments. The modeling of the fearless behavior and the association of the originally fearful rabbit with a pleasant stimulus, food, presumably accounted for the reduction of Peter's fear. Most importantly, Jones felt that not only had one method of the acquisition of a normal fear been demonstrated but also the deconditioning of that fear.

In 1938 Mowrer and Mowrer devised an apparatus for the treatment of enuresis (bed wetting) which they viewed as a case of simple habit deficiency. The apparatus consists of a liquid-sensitive pad which is placed on the child's bed. When the child begins to urinate, a bell rings. The bell is loud enough to wake the child and his parents, and the parent takes the child to the bathroom to urinate in the toilet. The apparatus is then reset before the child returns to bed. Mowrer and Mowrer advocate the use of the pad and bell device until the child is dry for seven consecutive nights followed by seven additional dry nights with increased fluid intake before retiring. In the original 1938 study by the Mowrers, all 30 children who were treated by this method reached the criterion of 14 consecutive dry nights within two months after commencement of treatment.

Despite the successes of Watson and Rayner (1920) and the Mowrers (1938), behaviorally-oriented treatment procedures had little prominence until the 1960's, probably because the popular psychoanalytic conceptualization of abnormal behavior was almost antithetical to the use of such treatment. The conditioning principles like those of Watson and Mowrer were seen as mechanistic and as oversimplified models for the procedures that most therapists felt necessary for treatment of the total individual, i.e., his attitudes, habits, thoughts, and feelings. Furthermore, most of the basic principles of conditioning had been demonstrated with animals or rats, and practitioners saw conditioning therapy as synonymous with rat therapy and thus inadequate to solving problems of human concern. A critique of psychoanalytic procedures and a reconceptualization of learning principles with implications for many human problems was made by Skinner in 1953 in his book *Science and human behavior*. This book was a major impetus for a drastic reconceptualization of procedures for changing behavior in schools, hosptials, and outpatient facilities. In discussing psychotherapy, Skinner had the following to say:

> The field of psychotherapy is rich in explanatory fictions. Behavior itself has not been accepted as subject matter in its own right, but only as an indication of *something wrong somewhere else*. The task of therapy is said to be to remedy an inner illness of

which the behavioral manifestations are merely "symptoms"... the condition to be corrected is called "neurotic," and the thing to be attacked by psychotherapy is then identified as a "neurosis." The term no longer carries its original implication of a derangement of the nervous system, but it is nevertheless an unfortunate example of an explantory fiction. It has encouraged the therapist to avoid specifying the behavior to be corrected or showing why it is disadvantageous or dangerous. By suggesting a single cause for multiple disorders it has implied a uniformity which is not to be found in the data. Above all, it has encouraged the belief that psychotherapy consists of removing inner causes of mental illness, as the surgeon removes an inflammed appendix or cancerous growth or as indigestible food is purged from the body.... It is not an inner cause of behavior but the behavior itself which—in the medical analogy of catharsis—must be "got out of the system."

In emphasizing "neurotic" behavior itself rather than any inner condition said to explain it, it may be argued that we are committing the unforgiveable sin of "treating the symptom rather than the cause." This expression is often applied to attempts to remove objectionable features of behavior without attention to causal factors—for example, "curing" stammering by a course of vocal exercises, ["curing"] faulty posture by the application of shoulder braces, or ["curing"] thumb-sucking by coating the thumb with a bitter substance. Such therapy appears to disregard the underlying disorder of which these characteristics of behavior are symptoms.... [However], by accounting for a given example of disadvantageous behavior in terms of a personal history and by altering or supplementing that history as a form of therapy, we are considering the very variables to which the traditional theorist must ultimately turn for an explanation of his supposed inner causes [pp. 373–379].*

While the reconceptualization of behavior change and therapy was very important, the "proof of the pudding" rests in its product—that is, does such a reconceptualization lead to significant behavior change. In 1956 Azrin and Lindsley taught cooperative behavior to children seven to twelve years of age through the use of learning principles. They placed two children on either side of a table and demonstrated that cooperative behavior—defined as simultaneous placement of two metal pins in matching stimulus holes—could be developed, eliminated, and re-established without the use of specific instructions. Gewirtz and Baer (1958) investigated how depriving or satiating a child with adult attention affects adults' later reinforcing power. They found that when a child was deprived of adult attention by being left alone in an experimental room for 20 minutes, the adult's reinforcing power was greater than if the adult had interacted with the child in a friendly manner for 20 minutes. The assessment of the adult's reinforcing power was made by analyzing the extent to which the adult could change the frequency with which the child dropped marbles into different holes.

---

*Reprinted with permission of the Macmillan Company, from B. F. Skinner's *Science and human behavior.* Copyright © 1953 by Macmillan, New York.

In 1959 Williams reported that the tantrums of a 21-month-old child could be eliminated by ignoring or extinguishing the undesirable behavior. The child had developed tantrums after a long illness and would scream for as much as two hours when the parents left his bedroom. It was assumed that the parents had been reinforcing the tantrum behavior by attending to it (i.e., by remaining in the room when the child cried). After a medical examination which determined that there was no physical problem, the parents were told to put the child to bed in a "leisurely and relaxed" fashion, to close the door, and not to re-enter the room. The first night the child cried for 45 minutes, but by the tenth occasion the child no longer whimpered or fussed when the parents left the room. In short, the removal of the reinforcement for tantrum-like behavior led to the elimination of the tantrum behavior. The authors reported no unfortunate side-effects resulting from their treatment, and at 3 years of age, the child was reported to be a "friendly, expressive, outgoing child."

A number of applications of behavioral procedures which have direct relevance to classroom management were made in a nursery school at the University of Washington in the early 1960's. Regressed crawling, isolate behavior, and cooperative behavior were significantly altered by changing the behavior of the teachers. One of these studies published by Bijou, Baer, Wolf and a number of their associates is presented now to illustrate the type of behavioral changes they obtained. In 1964, Harris, Johnston, Kelley and Wolf reported that Dee, a 3½-year-old child, showed "unusually strong withdrawal behavior." More specifically they observed a great deal of crawling around the classroom which persisted after the first week of nursery school. The usual teacher attempts to change Dee's behavior (being warm and solicitous) were unsuccessful. The teachers made a conservative estimate that Dee spent at least 75% of her time in a crawling position (when she was expected to be on her feet). The teachers were told to ignore her crawling behavior and to give her attention for standing or for approximations to standing e.g., rising partially to her feet when she put her coat on a hook. Within a week after the change in the teacher's behavior, Dee's behavior was "indistinguishable" from that of the rest of the children, i.e., she was standing as frequently as all the other children. In order to be certain that the change in the teacher's behavior was related to the change in the child's behavior, the teachers were then asked to give attention to Dee whenever she was crawling and to withhold attention when she was standing. By the end of two days, Dee was spending nearly 82% of her time off-feet—she behaved just as she had earlier. The teachers were again told to ignore crawling and to attend to Dee when she was standing. Within several days Dee was standing as frequently as the rest of her classmates. This study, as well as many others conducted at the University of Washington preschool, clearly demonstrated the potential of the systematic application of learning principles to changing the behavior of children in a classroom.

Also in the early 1960's, Bandura and his associates conducted a series of experiments with modeling procedures. In some now classic studies, Bandura and his associates were able to demonstrate that simply having a child view a film of a child behaving aggressively was related to the subsequent aggressive behavior of the child who watched the film. More specifically, children who watched cartoons, adults, or peers behave aggressively on film displayed more aggressive behavior when subsequently placed in a playroom with a variety of toys than did children who observed non-aggressive films or no films at all (Bandura & Walters, 1963). The results of such studies cast serious doubt on the catharsis hypothesis and its application to psychotherapy and behavioral change procedures. That is, instead of decreasing aggressive behavior by a venting or drainage of aggressive feelings, viewing aggressive models appeared to increase aggressive behavior (Bandura, Ross, and Ross, 1963), (*11*).

The more deviant behaviors of autistic children were also modified through the systematic application of behavioral procedures by Ferster and Lovaas. An autistic child usually displays very severe forms of social withdrawal, some gross motoric abnormalities, a parrot-like speech pattern called echolalia, eating disturbances, and an intense desire for sameness (Bakwin & Bakwin, 1967). Ferster and DeMyer (1962) conducted an analysis of the behavioral repertoires of three autistic children. They demonstrated that these autistic children could learn to obtain tokens or coins by pressing a lever in a token dispensing machine and then later to insert the tokens or coins into other machines or reinforcing devices such as a T.V., a 35 mm viewer, or a record player. In addition, Ferster and DeMyer were able to develop more complex behavioral repertoires such as coin saving and simple discrimination learning. Most importantly, these investigators showed that the same learning principles which had proven effective in changing the behavior of animals and young normal children operated quite efficiently in changing the behavior of a child with a very unusual behavior pattern. Lovaas (1967) and his colleagues showed that by applying learning procedures for long periods of time (months or several years), the behavior of autistic children could be changed very dramatically. Self-destructive behavior could be eliminated, speech, self-help skills, and even reading, writing and arithmetic skills could be taught to these autistic children. Lovaas' work is exceptional in that he demonstrated not only that the behavior of autistic children could be changed but that the procedures could be taught to parents and university undergraduates who in turn could execute a continuing "treatment" program for the children.

Since the early 1960's, the application of learning principles to changing the social and academic behavior of children and adolescents has developed at an extremely rapid pace. Laboratories investigating the application of behavioral principles to children's problems have been in operation for approximately 5 years at the University of Kansas, the University of Illinois, and the University of Oregon. More recently, child behavior modification laboratories have developed from coast to coast in both the north and south with facilities in Maine, New York, Florida, Washington, Arizona, and Hawaii. In addition to the changes in a host of classroom behaviors which will be documented later in this book, hyperactive behaviors, which are often considered organic, have been modified by Patterson (1965). The behavior of delinquents at the former National Training School for boys was markedly changed by Cohen (1967), and Schwitzgebel (1964) significantly changed the frequency of arrests and incarceration of juvenile delinquents in Boston by using learning procedures. Barrett and Lindsley (1962), Barrett (1965), and Watson (1967, 1970) have developed environments for the assessment and significant alteration of the behavior of retarded children. Phillips (1968) devised a home-based treatment facility for young delinquent boys which offers great potential for dealing with a population often felt to be resistant to treatment. He trained foster parents to care for and change both the home and school behavior of the boys in their charge. Lazarus (1959) coupled the use of a gradual presentation of fearful stimuli with positive events to overcome a child's fear of cars. He desensitized or reduced the child's fear by reinforcing the child with candy whenever he (1) mentioned cars in a positive manner and (2) later when he sat in a car and (3) finally when he rode in the car.

In sum, the results of a decade or so of research have documented the effectiveness of the behavior modification approach in a wide variety of settings with very diverse child populations. As will be evidenced by the readings in this book, the behavior of children in classroom settings has been repeatedly altered by a variety of different procedures used by a number of investigators. In contrast to a host of other approaches applied to educational problems, most of the behavioral principles which appear in this book were first documented in laboratory settings, and thus there is evidence from both basic and applied research of the efficacy of such principles. Before analyzing the articles which apply such principles, however, let us look more closely at the conceptualizations which have guided the research and treatment of those people working in the behavior modification area.

CHARACTERISTICS OF BEHAVIOR MODIFICATION WITH CHILDREN

Focus on Observable Behavior

Behavior modification is a process in which some observable behavior is changed by the systematic application of techniques that are based on learning theory and experimental research. The rationale for insisting that the behavior selected for modification be observable is based on the assertion that the behavior modifier should be able to evaluate the effectiveness of his techniques, and that when the behavior to be modified is not observable or susceptible to evaluation in a manner such that more than one person would agree to the frequency, rate, intensity, duration, or pattern of behavior, evaluations become much less stringent. For example, while one might wish to evaluate the "mood" or emotional state of a depressed child, it is quite difficult to teach two people to evaluate mood in exactly the same manner. On the other hand it is relatively easy to teach observers to record the frequency with which the child talks to others, smiles, or gets out of his chair. These behaviors are often critical in helping one arrive at a conclusion about the degree of a child's depression.

The types of behaviors that have been evaluated in the behavior modification area range from precise and easily defined behaviors such as correct answers on a spelling test to broader and more conceptual categories such as information seeking (Krumboltz & Thoresen, 1964), and creative behavior (Reese & Parnes, 1970), (27). The behaviors may be verbal (talking out of turn) or motor (out of seat behavior) or a combination of verbal and motor behavior (throwing a temper tantrum). On the other hand, the behaviors may be internal or "inside the organism" yet made observable through various recording procedures. For example, one might record heart beat, blood pressure, or galvanic skin response. This emphasis on overt behavior means that one does not concern himself with intrapsychic conflicts (e.g., conflicts between the id and superego or between sexual and appetitive desires and the conscience). Similarly one does not concern himself with scales of ego strength of self-concept. Rather than having lengthy discussions with a child about his self-concept, the behavior modifier feels teaching the child new social or academic skills which will lead to more positive reactions from his environment may have the additional benefit of having the child think better of himself. That is, the child will acquire what many people term a better "self-concept" or greater "ego strength" as a consequence of learning new academic or social skills.

While it would be folly to say that no aspect of a person's behavior is controlled by unobservable factors, the behavior modifier generally assumes that a great deal of a child's behavior is controlled by observable antecedent and consequent events occurring in the external environment. That is, events which precede behaviors and events which follow behaviors are of utmost importance in determining the frequency of these behaviors. This emphasis on overt or observable factors which control a behavior implies that the behavior modifier—be he therapist, teacher, or parent—can alter antecedent and consequent events and hopefully in turn can alter the child's behavior. In contrast, a focus on intrapsychic conflicts, self-concept and ego strength renders treatment more difficult and certainly less explicit. Since such treatment is less explicit, the procedures generally available to traditional therapists to change psychic conflicts are not easily taught, and, equally important, they are seldom— if ever—explicit enough to allow someone other than the therapist himself to promote any behavioral change. As will become obvious in later sections of this chapter, if the treatment procedures cannot be made explicit, therapeutic procedures will remain an art; they will remain extremely difficult to evaluate; and their implementation will be possible by only a very select group. Most importantly, if parents and teachers cannot be taught critical aspects of behavior change, it is very likely that any changes brought about by a therapist will be reduced or eliminated when contact with the therapist ends.

Importance of Teacher and Parents as Behavior Modifiers

Techniques of behavior modification are usually most effective when they are employed by the very people who initially request that the behavior be changed and who are also the key people in the child's environment. If a problem existed in the home, the behavior modifier would work with the parent to help him change the child's behavior in the home. If problems existed both at home and at school, the behavior modifier would generally work on both fronts since, as will be emphasized later, one can change a child's behavior in one situation but have no effect in the other situation (Wahler, 1969). The parent or the teacher can exert a greater influence on the child than the psychologist himself since a psychologist could only see the child infrequently and often not in the critical situations where the problem behaviors exist. Consequently, the psychologist serves as a *consultant* to a parent or teacher concerning procedures for changing behavior, yet most frequently it is the parent or teacher himself who executes most of the behavior change procedures. Teachers and parents are the individuals who do in fact provide many of the antecedent and consequent events of the child's behavior and thus are in the most advantageous position to alter the child's behavior. The fact that the teacher implements the "treatment" or behavior change does not mean that the psychologist relinquishes responsibility with regard to the treatment. He is still responsible for seeing that appropriate procedures are executed and that the behavior is changed even though he himself does not deal directly with the child on a daily basis and may in fact see the child quite infrequently.

The Normality of "Abnormal" Behavior

Assuming there is a focus on observable behavior, what behaviors are considered "abnormal" and in turn worthy of modification? Every teacher is faced at some time with a child who seems different: a child who doesn't know how to mix well with others, a child who demands constant attention, a child who fidgets and chats incessantly with his neighbors, a child who misses school frequently, or a child who disrupts the class by jumping out of his seat and pinching other children. These children seem different and are often called abnormal. But what do we mean by abnormal? Abnormality can be conceptualized in a variety of ways, and in many respects one's view of abnormality determines one's approach to treatment. Consequently, it seems appropriate to describe the concept of abnormality in some detail and to emphasize the conceptual framework from which most of the articles in this book were derived.

Abnormal behavior can be conceived of as some deviation from a statistical norm. The very term abnormal suggests some deviation from a norm or an average. A deviant person then would be someone who is unlike everyone else—be he unusual in the sense that he has unusual problems or unusual intelligence. Unfortunately, the label, abnormality, then becomes almost synonymous with lack of conformity, and as a result, some professionals deem this definition inadequate. Abnormality may also be seen as a state of subjective unhappiness. However, there may be a plethora of people who would call a person abnormal yet they would not see that person as unhappy. On the other hand, Ullmann and Krasner (1965) in presenting a psychological formulation of maladaptive behavior within a behavior modification paradigm noted the following:

Maladaptive behaviors are learned behaviors, and the development and maintenance of a maladaptive behavior is no different from the development and maintenance of any other behavior. There is no discontinuity between desirable and undesirable modes of adjustment or between "healthy" and "sick" behavior. The first major implication of this view is the question of how a behavior is to be identified as desirable or undesirable, adaptive or maladaptive. The general answer proposed is that because there are no disease entities involved in the majority of subjects displaying maladaptive behavior, the designation of a behavior as pathological or not is dependent upon the individual's society.... Behavior that one culture might consider maladaptive, be it that of the Shaman or the paranoid, is adaptive in another culture if the person so behaving is responding to all the cues present in the situation in a manner likely to lead to his obtaining reinforcement [rewards] appropriate to his status in that society. Maladaptive behavior is behavior that is considered inappropriate by those key people in a person's life who control reinforcers [p. 20].*

More recently Ullmann and Krasner (1969) noted that "Behavior which is considered abnormal must be studied as the interaction of three variables: the behavior itself, its social context, and an observer who is in a position of power. No specific behavior is abnormal in itself. Rather an individual may do something (e.g., verbalize hallucinations... stare into space, dress sloppily) under a set of circumstances (e.g., during a school class...) which upsets, annoys, angers, or strongly disturbs somebody (e.g.,... teacher, parent, or the individual himself) sufficiently that some action results (e.g., a policeman is called, seeing a psychiatrist is recommended, commitment proceedings are started) so that society's professional labelers (e.g., physicians, psychiatrists, psychologists, judges, social workers) come into contact with the individual and determine which of the current set of labels (e.g., schizophrenic reaction, sociopathic personality, anxiety reaction) is most appropriate. Finally, there follow attempts to change the emission of the offending behavior (e.g., institutionalization, psychotherapy, medication) [p. 21]."†

---

*Reprinted with permission of Holt, Rinehart, & Winston, Inc., from Leonard P. Ullmann and Leonard Krasner's *Case studies in behavior modification.* Copyright © 1965 by Holt, Rinehart, & Winston, Inc., New York.

†Reprinted with permission of Prentice-Hall, Inc., from Leonard P. Ullmann and Leonard Krasner's *A psychological approach to abnormal behavior.* Copyright © 1969 by Prentice-Hall, Inc., Englewood Cliffs, New Jersey.

Before we go any farther, let us question more extensively whether it really makes any difference what concept of abnormality we use or whether we use one at all. Does it help to be able to say to a teacher or a parent, "Yes, this child is abnormal" or "No, this child is not abnormal." Frequently, though not always, a teacher or parent comes to a professional not to ask if a child is abnormal but to ask what can be done about a certain behavior or set of behaviors. They *already* have the feeling that the child is unusual in one way or another. That is, they are not able to deal with him as they have dealt with the other children in their family or their class. The job of the psychologist or psychiatrist is then to help the parent or teacher deal with the difficulty the child presents — not to worry about whether the child is abnormal or not. However, a parent with one child or a new teacher may not know for sure if the child she is discussing really is very different from the small number of children with whom she has come in contact. Consequently, their question may not be "What can I do with this child," but "Should I do anything with him to change his behavior?" In turn, they wish to know, "Does he deviate from the rest of the children of his own age? Is he abnormal or is he unusual? Do most children at this age display this behavior? Do most children talk at this age? What percentage of children walk at this age? Any attempt to answer such questions depends upon the culture in which one lives, and as Ullmann and Krasner (1969) noted, the consideration of abnormality must also take into account the observer or the person in power who is to to the labeling (the physician, psychologist, or psychiatrist).

Equally important, the labeling of a person will depend upon the kind of cutoff point the labeler uses in his implicit or explicit definition of abnormality. That is, some psychologists might call a person abnormal if he behaved differently from 95% of the population while another psychologist would call a person abnormal only if he behaved differently from 99% of the population. However, people differ on many behaviors and may be unusual in one sense and very normal in others. Consequently, if we are forced to deal with the issue of abnormality, we first must ask "Abnormal in what *specific* respect?" Yet even if we ask ourselves about a *particular* behavior of a child, how do we tell whether it is abnormal? For example, how should we answer a teacher who asks us whether a child who is out of his seat 15% of the time is abnormal? We would first have to know the grade of the child, his sex, the type of lesson in which the out-of-seat behavior is displayed (teacher-directed or seat work where the children are supposed to work independently), and the kind of school system in which the child resides (e.g., Southern, Northern, a school on an Indian Reservation, a city school in a ghetto, or a school in a wealthy suburb). Thus our answer must be qualified by the particular subpopulation in which the child lives or goes to school. To develop an objective recording system which would account for such variables relevant to particular populations might seem impossible, and one might again say, "Who cares whether one tells the teacher or parent if the child is abnormal or not, the question is, does the behavior of the child bother the parent or the teacher?" One might simply abandon the label abnormal, and tell the parent or the teacher that the issue of abnormality is irrelevant and a useless concern. However, what if the parent or the teacher is concerned about a behavior which is very common or what if the parent or teacher is not even aware of some behaviors which are unusual? As long as they are not concerned, perhaps we too should not be concerned.

While the issue of abnormality is a thorny one which might be abandoned for the sake of simplicity and parsimony, the present authors feel it cannot be ignored. Like it or not, the public will continue to ask us if their children are abnormal. If we admit that many of the undesirable classroom behaviors exhibited by particularly disruptive children are learned, that they are not different in quality but only in quantity from behavior exhibited by any child, and that such behavior can be unlearned, then how should we consider abnormality in a practical sense?

Let us examine more closely how a child might differ from his peers. All children seek their teacher's praise, but some children want more attention than usual. All children fidget and talk in class, but some children are more talkative or fidgety than others. Thus we can say that children differ from their peers in terms of the amount or *frequency* of the particular behaviors they display. Most children are occasionally annoyed with their teachers or their classmates. Usually children express their annoyance with a brief comment, a sudden look, or perhaps an occasional outburst. However, there are children who fly into tantrums at the slightest provocation and children who regularly lash out physically when other children call them names. Thus we can say that these children differ from other children in the *intensity* with which they react to situations. Some children learn very quickly while others learn so slowly that progress is barely discernible. Thus we can say that children differ according to the *rate* at which they acquire new behaviors. In summary, the children who are often labeled abnormal are not different from normal children in the sense that they display behaviors which are strangely unique to them. All children behave with varying frequencies and intensities and learn at varying rates. We tend to label or designate a child as abnormal when he exhibits some behavior or group of behaviors at unusually high or low frequencies and intensities and when he learns at an unusually high or low pace.

A child is often labeled abnormal primarily or solely on the basis of a professional's clinical experience in the absence of objective criteria. It seems that obtaining reliable objective indices of observable behavior will greatly aid the practitioner who is faced with parents and teachers who ask "Is this child abnormal?" While ultimately the questions posed by the parent and teacher will involve issues such as how do we *change* this behavior or that behavior, normative data and knowledge of deviation from that norm should prove useful. There is considerable research concerning behavioral assessment in classrooms, and detailed methods of obtaining such information will appear in the last chapter.

The articles which appear in this book approach the assessment problem or what was formerly called diagnosis by focusing on particular *target* behaviors. Most of the researchers have used frequency of certain observable behaviors as a focus for their studies though some researchers working within the general behavior modification framework have used intensity as a measure, or at least as a supplementary measure, in their evaluation of treatment effects. The reader should note that generally there is no systematic attempt by behavior modifiers to place the children who are described in this book in particular diagnostic categories such as delinquency, hyperkinetic reaction[4] or unsocialized aggressive reaction.[5] However, as will be seen, particular behaviors of children who were labeled by other professionals as emotionally disturbed, retarded, delinquent, and schizophrenic have been changed by a number of behavior modification techniques. There is a very distinct advantage to focusing on target behaviors: namely there is a specific focus for treatment. Instead of treating a disorder or a disease in a medical sense, a particular behavior or a series of behaviors is treated. The behavior modification approach argues that even if a child displays a behavior which is thought to have an organic origin like autism, retardation, or hyperactivity, the behavior itself can be treated as one would in any other behavior change program. As mentioned above, problem behaviors displayed by children

---

[4]Hyperkinetic reactions consist of "restlessness in the classroom, impulsive action, and a difficulty in concentration and intellectual development" (Ulett & Goodrich, 1969).

[5]Children with purported personality growth disturbances who have "extremely poor control over their aggressive and sexual impulses and who have usually been poorly socialized by their parents and even subtly encouraged by the pleasure of their parents in the expressions of aggression (Ulett & Goodrich, 1969).

described as autistic, retarded or hyperactive have been dramatically changed using a behavioral treatment approach. In contrast, when one views the child to be *mentally ill*, the child is considered to suffer from a sickness that is due to an organic factor which acts like a germ. The germ must be removed before a healthy state can be regained. In addition, if one considers a child to be mentally ill, it is often assumed that the "illness" can be classified, like many other diseases, without taking into account social factors (Ullmann & Krasner, 1969).

Treating Behaviors as Problems Not Symptoms

It is true that certain childhood behavior problems do have definite chemical or physiological bases which now imply that medical treatment is in order. For example, one form of retardation called phenylketonuria is clearly due to an enzyme deficiency in the liver, and if this deficiency is detected early, retardation can be avoided or arrested. Similarly, there is a form of mental retardation called Mongolism or Down's Syndrome which is caused by an extra chromosome. The childhood disorder, autism, which is characterized by severe social withdrawal, speech difficulties, eating problems, and a strange gait may be the result of genetic or biochemical problems. However, as mentioned earlier, the disruptive or unusual behaviors which children generally display in most classrooms are the result of a learning process and are not the symptoms of an underlying disease in a medical sense. Thus, the behavior is treated not as a *symptom* of a problem but as the problem itself. Some have said that direct treatment of a behavior is insufficient because the underlying causes of the problem are ignored. The disease or disorder will be expressed by a different symptom if one treats behaviors as the problem rather than treating "the underlying cause." Here again, one's conceptualization of abnormal is of critical importance for treatment. As Bandura (1968) aptly noted, all therapists—whether of a psychodynamic or behavior modification orientation—are searching for causes in that they are looking for determinants of behavior! It is in the conception of the determinants, however, where real differences exist. Traditional therapists focus on libidinal or intrapsychic conflicts as the determinants of behavior whereas behavior modifiers focus on eliciting stimuli and reinforcing events. Traditional therapists focus on early childhood factors whereas behavior modifiers focus on current factors. The focus of the behavior modifier on current factors which control a child's behavior and on changing target behavior has not led to undesirable side-effects or what many have called "symptom substitution." In fact, as will be discussed in the paper by Ward and Baker (1968) (7), having teachers reinforce appropriate classroom behavior, i.e., treat the disruptive behaviors as problems not symptoms has led to significant increases in appropriate classroom behavior, and no adverse effects were noticed after treatment when the children were tested with both overt behavioral indices as well as through assessment of fantasy.

Behavioral Insight

In the same way that argument has arisen over the types of causes of behavior that one should pursue, argument has arisen over the role of "insight" in behavior modification. As *all* therapists search for causes of behavior, *all* therapists are searching for insight into the problems of the people with whom they are dealing. However, the type or kind of insight may depend very heavily upon one's theoretical or conceptual framework. Insight in a traditional or psychodynamic sense refers to an understanding of the relationship between one's behavior and the conflicting forces in one's mind or psyche.

As will be seen from the forthcoming discussion, the behavior modifier uses a quite different conceptual framework from the traditional psychotherapist as he attempts to achieve insight or understanding of the case which will aid in his treatment plan. The behavior modifier tries to give his client insight into the factors which maintain his inappropriate or undesired behaviors in terms of specific reinforcing or rewarding stimuli, specific eliciting stimuli, and more global environmental factors called setting events. Since the articles in this book are generally based on principles of learning as espoused by behavior modifiers, analysis of the steps taken in assessment and treatment is now in order.

The Assessment of Target Behaviors and their Environmental Determinants

A teacher who refers a child to a psychologist describes "the problem" as she sees it in rather general terms. Assuming the psychologist is a behavior modifier, he would then ask the teacher to pinpoint the behaviors upon which she bases her conclusion. For example, if the teacher complained that a child was odd or unusual because of his inability to get along with peers, the behavior modifier would then ask the teacher to specify exactly what the child does and how frequently the behaviors which she regards as unusual occur. The behavior modifier usually asks the teacher to keep a daily log of these specific behaviors for at least a week. The manner in which the behavior is recorded may vary from simple anecdotal records to rather precise recording of the frequencies (and occasionally intensity) of certain behaviors during a specified time unit, e.g., a half-hour period, an hour period, or even during a morning. In short, the initial step after the teacher refers the child to the behavior modifier is to specify as clearly as possible the particular types of behavior which are of concern to the teacher and to measure their frequency. These behaviors are then called "target behaviors" because they serve as the targets for remediation. (A more detailed examination of methods of classroom assessment appears in Chapter 12.)

The second major step in target assessment is to identify the variables which are responsible for the behaviors in question. More specifically, the psychologist asks the teacher to note what factors immediately precede and what factors immediately follow the target behaviors. The rationale for assessing factors which immediately precede or immediately follow the target behaviors is that a great deal of a child's behavior is the result of learning and that such learning takes place through respondent or classical conditioning and operant conditioning. Respondent or classical conditioning refers to the learning where a stimulus *preceding* a behavior or group of behaviors controls these behaviors. However, this sort of control is of a special nature in that there is an almost invariable relationship between the behavior and the stimuli which precede the behavior. Such behaviors are often called *involuntary* because when the stimuli are presented, the behaviors almost invariably occur (e.g., salivation, pupil dilation, fright, increase in heart rate) and, it appears as if the organism had no choice in whether or not the behaviors occurred. A respondent behavior is generally not controlled by the stimuli which follow it. For example, pupil dilation (which occurs in response to a light) salivation (which occurs in response to food) are usually not influenced by stimuli following the behaviors.[6] Examples of fearful behavior seen in schools which are often assumed to be classically conditioned are fears of dogs or hamsters and fear of speaking in front of others. While some behaviors are controlled by stimuli preceding the behavior, other behaviors – called operant behaviors – are influenced by the stimuli which *follow* them. The teacher should be alert to fearful behavior which is controlled by preceding stimuli because it may be very difficult to eliminate such fearful

---

[6]However, Neal Miller (1969) has reported a series of studies which show that under special conditions behaviors such as stomach contractions, blood pressure, and heart rate can be significantly influenced by the stimuli which follow them.

behavior by some of the major methods of behavior modification to be described in this book. These methods focus on the *consequences* rather than the antecedents of behavior. When certain stimuli follow a behavior, the behaviors increase in frequency. Stimuli which increase the frequency of the behaviors they follow are called positive reinforcers. Part of the job of the teacher and the psychologist is to find out what stimuli do serve as positive reinforcers for the undesired or unwanted behaviors. Once this is known, the positive reinforcers can be removed and the frequency of the disruptive behavior should be reduced. For example, if the teacher unwillingly attends to some undesirable behavior by saying "Johnny, why do you do that?" it is very likely that the teacher's comment serves to reinforce the undesirable behavior. Consequently, the teacher can be asked to cease questioning Johnny about why he engages in such behavior. In addition, the teacher and psychologist should try to discover what stimuli could serve as positive reinforcers for behaviors which should be increased in frequency. For example, the psychologist will want to know if teachers' praise or approval, stars, or grades will serve to increase the frequency of desirable behavior or if on occasion more potent reinforcers such as prizes are necessary to increase certain behaviors. While the use of the more potent reinforcers just described is rare, several articles in this book will discuss the utilization of systematic and extensive uses of powerful incentives such as toys and comics. It is important to emphasize that these powerful incentive systems should be applied only after other possible reinforcers such as teacher attention are evaluated.

There are also certain stimuli which if made contingent upon behaviors will reduce the frequency of those behaviors. Such stimuli are called punishing stimuli, and the teacher should be aware of possible stimuli which could be used to punish or suppress behavior. As will be mentioned in the section on punishment, there are often very mild but interesting alternatives to criticism or to forms of physical punishment such as squeezing a child's arm or shaking a child which can be used to reduce disruptive behaviors in the classroom.

It has been stated that respondent behavior is controlled by stimuli which precede behavior and operant behavior is controlled by stimuli which follow behavior, and that the respondent behavior is often called involuntary while the operant behavior is called voluntary. However, operant behaviors and respondent behaviors often overlap, and the practical distinction between operants and respondents breaks down. For example, certain forms of anger and aggression may be elicited by a spanking or by a frustrating experience; but once the aggression is displayed, the reactions of the parent or teacher may further serve to maintain or reinforce the behavior. Thus, the distinction between operant and respondent behaviors should be seen as a convenient tool in conceptualizing behavior — not as a distinction which can be applied in every case. In fact, the present authors recommend that such a conceptualization be applied in general consideration of any case, but that particular types of behaviors may have peculiarities which must be considered, and as a result the particular kinds of behaviors to be changed should be given as much if not more consideration than the general operant-respondent classification. The authors would hope that in the future those scientists who are working on behavior change procedures will be able to concentrate on finding the best ways to deal with particular kinds of behavior. For example, the authors would hope that there will be much research directed at changing certain classes of behavior such as aggression, withdrawal, swearing, and lying, and that eventually we will be able to list a number of procedures which can best be used to decrease the frequency of each one of these groups of behaviors. At present however, there has been a greater emphasis on the evaluation of various treatment procedures than on changing particular classes of behavior, and consequently this book is organized around various treatment procedures rather than around target behaviors.

While the very name, behavior modifier, implies that there is going to be a focus on particular behaviors for amelioration, one should not disregard his "common sense" concerning problems which are referred to him. One can easily overlook physical or organic matters such as poor eyesight, vision or hearing. Most importantly, the psychologist who is consulting with a teacher has to know something about academic or achievement assessment since a large percentage of the children referred to child guidance clinics and psychological centers have reading and other academic difficulties. Many psychologists focus on "emotional" or behavioral problems of such children and argue that such difficulties preceded the reading problems, but it is impossible to tell whether the reading problem preceded the social problems (usually called emotional or behavior problems) or vice versa. It is very unlikely that a child who is doing poorly academically will evidence great gains socially without intellectual or academic improvement. As is noted by Thomas, Nielsen, Kuypers, and Becker (1968), (*31*), children with very poor academic skills who do not receive academic tutoring, are not greatly aided by lavish amounts of praise for good classroom behavior. Consequently, the psychologist and teacher should ask themselves "To what extent are any of the problem social behaviors such as daydreaming, walking around the room and talking to neighbors a result of not understanding what is going on in the classroom in academic matters?" If the child is not progressing well in reading, writing, arithmetic, or language development, a specific analysis of the problems in the particular subject matters where the child has problems is in order. If the psychologist or teacher does not feel that he or she has skills in the particular subject matter, he should ask for consultation from someone in that speciality area.

BEHAVIOR MODIFICATION PROCEDURES

There is a large variety of behavior modification procedures existing today but in general all such procedures can be viewed as concerted attempts either to increase or decrease behavior. Such a dichotomy is somewhat arbitrary, since certain procedures may be used to increase some behaviors while on other occasions the same procedures may be used to decrease behaviors. However, this method of classification whereby one looks at procedures to increase or decrease behaviors should be of use to those psychologists, teachers, or special educators who are faced with behavior change problems daily. Hopefully, they will be able to refer to such a classification and thus arrive at the particular procedure(s) best suited to their needs. Detailed analyses and discussions of many of these procedures are presented in later sections of this book.

Procedures to Increase Behaviors

Praise and Approval

If a child already shows some evidence of a certain behavior that one wishes to increase such as paying attention, a teacher might simply walk over to the child and enthusiastically praise him while he is paying attention. The teacher will find that the child will pay attention for longer and longer periods of time (Becker, Madsen, Arnold, & Thomas, 1967 (*4*); Madsen, Becker, & Thomas 1968 (*5*)). Approval may occur in many forms, e.g., a pat on the back, a smile, or saying, "That's good work!" While many teachers feel powerless in front of young children, research data clearly show that the positive words or gestures from a teacher which are made contingent upon a behavior can be extremely effective tools in changing a child's behavior. In addition the child will probably like school more as he receives more positive attention from the teacher.

Modeling
One of the simplest and most straightforward ways to establish a behavior is to show the child how to do something and then ask him to repeat what you did. Certain athletic skills such as riding a bicycle or throwing a baseball are taught primarily in this fashion. However, modeling can also be a very effective method of obtaining desired classroom behaviors. For example, a teacher may start teaching a child to print by showing him how to make certain movements with a pen and then asking the child to model her behavior. Similarly, a teacher may have one child perform a certain behavior and then ask another child to perform the behavior. The use of modeling to change a host of behaviors ranging from delay of gratification to aggression has been documented by Bandura (1969), (Bandura, Grusec, & Menlove, 1967 *(12)*; Broden, Bruce, Mitchell, Carter, & Hall, 1970, *(14)*; O'Connor, 1969, *(13)*).

Shaping
Shaping is the procedure of reinforcing successive approximations to some desired terminal behavior. For example, if a child answers in class but only at a whisper, a teacher can praise the child when he answers with just a little more volume than usual. Later she can reinforce answers that more closely approximate the terminal behavior she desires, i.e., answering in a manner audible to both the teacher and to her other students.

When a child or adolescent engages in behaviors which are particularly aversive or obnoxious such as back-talk, thumbing one's nose at a teacher, calling her names, or defying orders and requests, the teacher may find it very difficult to respond positively to any other appropriate behaviors the child makes during that class period or that particular day. While it is probably unwise to respond appropriately to good behavior which immediately follows a bad behavior, a teacher who "holds a grudge" against a child for a day and never responds to any of his positive behaviors may find it impossible to change his behavior. Simply put, holding a grudge for a long period is incompatible with shaping.

Passive Shaping
If a child does not display a behavior when requested to do so or when another child has modeled the behavior for him, it may be necessary to aid the child in performing the behavior by guiding him through the physical motions of the desired behavior. For example, if a child does not imitate any behavior—as some retarded children do not—the teacher can demonstrate raising her hand and then actually raise the child's hand

and subsequently praise the child or give him a gold star. The term passive shaping is used because the child is essentially passive while the teacher actively aids the child in displaying the behavior. Passive shaping has been especially effective in establishing a variety of imitative behaviors in retarded children (Baer, Peterson, & Sherman, 1967). It also may be used in helping a child learn to pour water from one container to another, to teach a child how to play a roll or a flam on a drum, or to teach a child certain ballet steps which are difficult to simply model.

Token Reinforcement Programs

A token reinforcement program generally involves three factors: (1) a set of instructions to the class about the behaviors that will be reinforced, (2) a means of making a potentially reinforcing stimulus — usually called a token — contingent upon behavior, and (3) a set of rules governing the exchange of tokens for back-up reinforcers such as prizes or opportunities to engage in special activities. Token reinforcement programs have been effectively utilized in mental hospitals with adult psychiatric patients (Ayllon & Azrin, 1968), with teenage children labeled childhood schizophrenic (Kaufman & O'Leary, 1971), with retarded children (Birnbrauer, Wolf, Kidder, & Tague, 1965), (17), emotionally disturbed children, (O'Leary & Becker, 1967), (15), and with disruptive children in a "normal" class (O'Leary, Becker, Evans, Saudargas, 1969), (16). While token reinforcement programs have proven very successful in changing both the academic and social behavior of children in classrooms (O'Leary & Drabman, 1971), the use of tangible reinforcers such as prizes or toys is often called bribery. As normal practice, the use of prizes in token reinforcement programs in classrooms is definitely not bribery in the usual sense, (i.e., trying to corrupt the conduct of a person). Nonetheless, the use of tangible reinforcers which are not natural to any classroom is not a procedure to be used in every class. They are extremely effective in changing behavior, but they should be utilized with care for their long range use with children has only begun to receive attention and the amateurish use of tangible extrinsic reinforcers may occasionally produce undesired behavioral effects.

While many token programs involve extrinsic reinforcers, i.e., reinforcers which are not usually found in a classroom or a hospital ward such as prizes, there are a number of token programs which have utilized intrinsic reinforcers or, as the term is used here, reinforcers which are natural to a classroom or hospital ward such as special privileges or special activities (Bushell, Wrobel, & Michaelis, 1968, (19); Osborne, 1969, (18); McKenzie, Clark, Wolf, Kothera, & Benson, 1968, (20)).

Programmed Instruction

Programmed instruction is a way of arranging academic materials in logically sequenced small steps. Each step or frame of the program generally provides information, requires the student to respond to the information, and gives feedback to the student regarding the correctness of his response (Morrill, 1961, (26); Skinner, 1963, (25)). With programmed instruction, a child can progress at his own rate, and the teacher can circulate among members of the class providing help where needed. The programmed instruction formats vary greatly from simple booklets with sequencing of materials (Holland & Skinner, 1961; Williams, Gilmore, & Malpass, 1968, (28)) to presentation of programmed mathematics material over television where a bed-ridden child can indicate his answer by dialing a phone which is connected to a central computer bank. In addition, some programmed instruction is presented via a machine which responds to a child's answers. If he gets an answer correct, the machine will type "correct" immediately following his answer. On the other hand, if he makes an error, the machine will go back into a sequence of materials and present the key concepts necessary for a child to advance (Atkinson, 1968), (29).

Self-Specification of Contingencies

Many of us occasionally say to ourselves that when and only when we finish a certain task, we will allow ourselves the privilege of purchasing a certain item or engaging in a certain behavior. This procedure of allowing oneself to engage in a certain behavior when one has finished a task has been discussed by Homme (1965). Homme utilized the Premack Principle which is as follows: If an organism is more likely to engage in behavior B than in behavior A, then behavior A can be made more probable by making the opportunity to engage in behavior B contingent upon displaying the behavior A. For example, if sitting in one's seat is a low probability behavior of a child, and drawing at the blackboard is a high probability behavior of the child, then if the teacher allows the child to draw at the blackboard only after the child has been sitting at his seat for a certain period of time, the probability of the child's in-seat behavior should increase (Homme, DeBaca, Devine, Steinhorst, & Rickert, 1963). Homme and his associates told three-year-old children who ran around the room a great deal that they should run and scream. He gave this instruction to the children after they had been in their seat sitting still and looking at the blackboard. In this case, the *teacher* specified that if and only if a child engaged in the low probability behavior (staying in-seat) could he engage in the high probability behavior (running around the room). However, there is some evidence to suggest that when *children* themselves specify that they should engage in certain academic tasks before allowing themselves to play in the free activity area of the room, the probability of their engaging in academic behavior increases (Lovitt & Curtiss, 1969), (*36*). It is possible that not all low probability behaviors can be increased by making high probability behaviors contingent upon them, and one must carefully choose the high probability behaviors he wishes to make contingent upon low probability behaviors. For example, if a child blurted out wisecracks in class but studied little it might be unwise to have the child make wisecracks every time he studied for a certain period of time. On the other hand allowing a child a few minutes of free time after he has correctly completed an assignment may well increase the speed and accuracy with which he does his assignments without increasing the frequency of inappropriate behavior.

Self-specification of contingencies need not be limited to the application of the Premack Principle. In token reinforcement programs it is probably wise to have children aid in the selection of the behaviors to be reinforced in the class; incentive programs in industry clearly show that involving the employees in the specification of behaviors to be reinforced and of the pay for such behaviors is better than simply having the management impose such a program on the employees (Lawler & Hackman, 1969).

Self-Reinforcement

The efficacy of self-reinforcement procedures in a classroom setting has received little attention, yet there are a number of studies with children in experimental settings which bear on this issue. Bandura and Perloff, (1967) (*33*), demonstrated that self-administered consequences can in fact serve a reinforcing function. A child was given complete control over tokens which were exchangeable for prizes; when the child made the tokens contingent upon his behavior, the tokens served to maintain his behavior. As will be seen in the section on modeling, modeling plays a very important role in the transmission of self-reinforcing behavior (Bandura & Kupers, 1964), (*35*). As summarized by Bandura (1969) the results of a series of modeling studies in the self-reinforcement area show that "people generally adopt the standards for self-reinforcement exhibited by exemplary models, they evaluate their own performances relative to that standard, and then they serve as their own reinforcing agents. For instance, those who have been exposed to models setting low standards tend to be highly self-rewarding and self-approving for comparatively mediocre performances. By contrast, persons who have observed models adhere to stringent performance demands display considerable self-denial and self-dissatisfaction for objectively identical accomplishments [pp. 33–34]." A teacher should bear such results in mind when she reinforces the behavior of children in her class, since presumably she can teach children to adopt high or low performance standards. That is, if the teacher reinforces only those behaviors which meet certain high standards it is likely that the child will later be self-approving of behaviors which meet high standards.

Establishment of Clear Rules and Directions

It is certainly true that simply making rules clear will not be effective in changing the behavior of many disruptive children (Madsen, Becker, & Thomas, 1968, (5), O'Leary, Becker, Evans, & Saudargas, 1969, (16)), but some children are aided by clear specification of the desired classroom behavior. The clear specification of classroom rules and occasional reviews of such rules can serve to prompt children to rehearse the rules themselves and, as observed in many classrooms, the children may remind others of the rules. Clear specification of rules is also an aid to classrooms where there is a great deal of change in the types of behaviors expected from one activity to another. For example, in the reading lesson, a teacher may expect much different behavior than during a science project. Not only do rules help a teacher to shift the kinds of classroom activities with ease, but allowing and expecting different behaviors during different lessons is probably good training for children. That is, they learn that certain behaviors are expected in one lesson but definitely prohibited in another. Such variation makes a classroom more interesting and pleasant for both the teacher and her students. Instead of learning to function in a completely unstructured classroom or a rigidly managed classroom, a child whose teacher expects and receives varying behaviors in different lessons is learning the type of self-control that will give him the greatest freedom and flexibility in the future.

When rules are made explicit, children must be reinforced for following them. Many children entering school have been reinforced by their parents for following a variety of instructions or rules made by their parents, and consequently such children exhibit general "rule-following behavior" with only infrequent praise. However, most children who are "behavior problems" probably have not been consistently reinforced in the past for following rules or instructions and it is incumbent upon the teacher to reinforce such children frequently when they do follow rules or instructions.

Procedures to Decrease Behavior

Extinction

When a teacher or parent stops making approval or some other form of her attention contingent upon behavior, the behavior will frequently extinguish or decrease in frequency (Bijou, 1965). Many behaviors have been decreased when the teacher stops attending to them. Among those behaviors which have been successfully extinguished are tantrums (Zimmerman & Zimmerman, 1962), (6), regressed crawling, vomiting, (Wolf, Birnbrauer, Williams & Lawler, 1965), and aggression in a classroom (Brown & Elliot, 1965). However, as will be emphasized repeatedly in this book, ignoring inappropriate behavior should be coupled with praise for appropriate behavior. Ignoring inappropriate behavior *without* praise for appropriate behavior is not only difficult for teachers to do but it may be ineffective in a number of instances (Madsen, Becker, & Thomas, 1968), (5). Consequently, alternatives to ignoring such behaviors are presented later.

Reinforcing Behavior Incompatible with Undesired Behavior

As just mentioned, when one extinguishes a behavior by not attending to that behavior, one should also reinforce or attend in a positive manner to the desired behavior. It is most helpful if one can reinforce a behavior which, if increased in frequency, would make the undesirable behavior less probable. For example, if a child is frequently talking and wandering around the classroom, it is helpful to reinforce academic behavior since the child cannot work on his academic material and at the same time talk and wander around the room. That is, the teacher will be reinforcing behaviors which are incompatible with the undesired behavior.

Soft Reprimands

When simply ignoring a certain behavior does not serve to reduce such behavior, a reprimand which is audible only to the child being reprimanded may prove very effective in reducing the behavior of especially disruptive children (O'Leary & Becker, 1968; O'Leary, Kaufman, Kass, & Drabman, 1970 (*10*)). In contrast, when the reprimand is audible to a number of children in the class, the loud reprimand will generally serve either to maintain the disruptive behavior or to increase it. As will be noted in the section on punishment, it probably is best to reprimand a child just as he begins to display an undesired behavior rather than reprimanding him after he has been misbehaving for some time (Walters,

Parke, & Cane, 1965), (8). Interesting alternatives to a verbal reprimand such as taking away a slip of paper on which a child's name is written are presented by Hall, Axelrod, Foundopoulos, Shellman, Campbell, & Cranston, (1971) (9).

Time-Out from Reinforcement

Teachers have long used the procedure of placing a child at the side of the room, in the back of a room, in a corner, or in a dunce's chair. Unfortunately, being placed in such a situation has a number of deleterious effects on the child, e.g., being the center of attention, being able to go through other children's pockets in the cloakroom, or getting out of doing an assignment. Time-out from reinforcement procedurally resembles the time-honored isolation procedures. However, time-out from positive reinforcement is a procedure in which some source of positive reinforcement is eliminated for a specific period of time. For example, if a child enjoys being with others and displays disruptive behavior, he may be placed somewhere in the room where there are no objects of interest and where it is difficult for others to see him. In certain laboratory schools, hospitals, or classrooms for very disruptive children he may even be placed in a small enclosed cubicle at the side of the room—called a time-out room. Isolation in a room adjacent to a classroom is not a feasible or even a suggested procedure for most teachers and should be used only with extremely disruptive children and then only when qualified consultants can supervise the treatment program. However, in classes where children are extremely disruptive, time-out from reinforcement presents an alternative to some of the usual methods of punishment such as restriction on a ward or withdrawal of some privilege. While the research evidence clearly documenting the effectiveness of this procedure is scanty, there are strong suggestions that time-out from reinforcement may be a very viable procedure for decreasing certain behavior (Pendergrass, 1970).

Relaxation

Certain forms of behavior which are generally considered emotional may be treated by teaching a child how to relax when he becomes frustrated, agitated, or angered. In 1938 Jacobsen introduced a method for obtaining muscle relaxation which has now been incorporated into a number of current treatment procedures for adults. Relaxation has merit for it can be taught like any other skill. If the relaxation exercises have been well practiced, the person becomes relaxed when he says to himself,

"Relax." Relaxation is thought to be incompatible with emotional behaviors such as fright, anger, or frustration. Since the verbal control of nonverbal behavior in children may be weak, and since controlled research on relaxation is almost nonexistent with children, at this point in time relaxation should simply be seen as a possible method by which a psychologist could aid a child in overcoming strong emotional reactions to fearful and frustrating situations. The use of relaxation is included here simply to alert teachers to a possible technique which a psychologist or psychiatrist might use with a child who exhibits extreme reaction to frustration or who displays fearful behavior; it is not included as a procedure to be implemented by teachers.

Gradual Presentation of Fearful Stimuli in Vivo

If a child has a fear of school, he may be placed in real-life (in vivo) situations which are quite unlike and distant from the classroom and then be brought gradually closer and closer to the actual fearful stimulus, the classroom. Lazarus, Davison and Polefka (1965) demonstrated the effectiveness of this procedure when it was combined with positive reinforcement for being in the classroom. Over a period of $4\frac{1}{2}$ months a nine-year-old school phobic boy was taken for a walk near the schoolhouse, went inside the schoolroom with the therapist, stayed in class with the therapist present and finally stayed in class in the absence of the therapist. Similarly, Ayllon, Smith, and Rogers (1970) successfully treated an eight-year-old school phobic girl in 45 days. Since it is very difficult to determine whether a child is staying away from school as a ploy for avoiding work when in fact the child is not at all frightened, one must carefully assess the extent to which the problem is one of truancy or fear of school. Yates (1970) presents an excellent discussion of the various types of school phobia and an evaluation of treatment results of various procedures designed to have the child return to school. A lengthy discussion of the treatment of school phobias will not be presented since such treatment is usually carried out by a psychologist and since primarily case studies and not experimental analyses of the treatment of school phobias are available.

Brain-damaged children with fears of a public bus or the sight of a live dog have been successfully treated by gradual exposure to such fear arousing stimuli (Obler & Terwilliger, 1970). As the child made an approach to the feared object he was immediately rewarded with candy, toys, or books. For example, if a child talked with the bus driver or put a token in the box on the bus he was reinforced both socially and with some prize. According to parental ratings before and after treatment, the treatment was quite successful when compared with children who received no treatment.

One example of fearful behavior which a teacher could treat by using a gradual presentation of the fearful situation is the fear of speaking in class. The teacher might first have the child read to her in private, then to a friend, to a group of close friends, to a group in the class, and finally to the entire class. As the child is able to progress from one step to the next without fear, the teacher should make certain that the child receives some form of reinforcement for his successes.

Desensitization

A widely practiced technique which is used with adults who have fears and anxiety is desensitization. After completely relaxing a client, the client is asked to imagine or visualize a series of scenes which he finds anxiety provoking. After many trials where the client visualizes the anxiety producing scenes in a relaxed state, the client finds that the instances in his daily life which he visualized while relaxed no longer produce anxiety (Paul, 1966; Wolpe, 1958). Obviously it would be difficult to have very young children visualize scenes which make them anxious, but desensitization has been used successfully with junior high school students.[7]

Response Cost

Response cost, point loss, or fines is a procedure often used in token programs. The usefulness of cost procedures in a classroom was suggested by McIntire, Jensen, and Davis (1968) in an after-school program for elementary and junior high school boys. Each child had a counter on which a teacher could either add or subtract points. The child gained points for correct answers and lost points for disruptive classroom behavior. "Whenever disruptive behavior occurred, the instructor could turn on the counter associated with that student's name and allow the counter to continue to subtract points until the instructor felt that the student had corrected himself [pp. 3–4]." The effectiveness of such cost procedures in a classroom setting was also documented by Kaufman and O'Leary (1971) in the children's unit of a psychiatric hospital. Children in the "cost" class received all their tokens (in the form of points) at the beginning of each rating period and then lost points when they were

---

[7]Desensitization, like relaxation, is not included here in the hope that teachers would attempt its use. It is included simply to alert teachers and psychologists of a procedure to be implemented by a psychologist which may be useful in decreasing fearful behavior.

rated by a teacher. In contrast, children in the "reward" class did not have any points at the beginning of the class period. At the end of a lesson the teacher placed a rating (points) in the child's booklet which reflected the extent to which he followed classroom rules. Thus the children in the reward group started with no points and earned them as the lesson progressed whereas the children in the cost class started with all the possible points and lost them as the lesson progressed. Although both token programs were very effective in reducing disruptive behavior of children labeled "behavior disorder" and "childhood schizophrenic," the results of the reward and cost procedures were not different from one another, and no undesirable side-effects of the cost procedures were noted. Response cost in many situations could be combined with reinforcement for good behavior. For example, a teacher might reduce the amount of time a child could spend at recess whenever he behaved inappropriately. In addition, she could allow him extra minutes in the free activity corner whenever he completed an assignment on time. Response cost or loss of privileges can also be combined with peer influence to decrease inappropriate behavior as exemplified by Barrish, Saunders, and Wolf (1969) *(22)*.

Medication

Drugs are used infrequently in the regular classroom but their use is almost ubiquitous in schools for "emotionally disturbed" children or in psychiatric units of children's hospitals. It is true that drugs are not generally considered within a learning framework, but occasionally they may be a useful adjunct in behavior therapy to prompt behaviors that would not ordinarily occur. For example, a physician can prescribe medication which might make it more likely that a hyperactive child will sit in his seat and thereby allow the teacher to praise him more frequently for sitting still (Conners, Eisenberg, & Barcai, 1967; Conners, 1969). Interestingly, many drugs that have sedating effects on adults have a stimulating effect on children and vice versa, e.g., amphetamines tend to calm the hyperactive child. The use of drugs has some disadvantages which are important. A number of drugs used with children have undesirable side-effects such as drousiness, dryness of mouth, and nausea. Furthermore, few, if any, studies have been done in a classroom which show that when a drug is removed, the behavior change produced by the medication is maintained. Unless special steps are taken to aid long range behavior change, the undesirable behavior will probably return when the drug is withdrawn. Such a result should not be surprising and the use of drugs should be seen simply as a method of prompting or artificially producing a behavior which can be further developed and maintained by methods available to the teacher. In contrast to drug treatment a behaviorally-oriented treatment approach actively teaches new behaviors and selectively increases or decreases the frequency of existing behaviors. Viewed as a prompting device, however, there is no reason why certain drugs could not be judiciously used in combination with behavior modification procedures to produce lasting behavior change.

Self-Instruction

The effects of self-instruction were investigated by Luria (1963) who found that children with a particular brain dysfunction could not press a balloon when an external signal such as light was flashed. When the children were taught to self-instruct (to say "Press" as they pressed the balloon), they could press the balloon without errors. Similarly, self-instruction has been shown to be of aid in both initiating and suppressing behavior (Bem 1967, (*34*); Meichenbaum & Goodman, 1969; O'Leary, 1969; Monohan, 1970). Some teachers have taught children to control their own behaviors by saying sentences to themselves such as "*i* before *e* except after *c*," "Stop, look, and listen," or "Count to ten," but self-instruction seems to be a relatively neglected area which should be of significance to anyone interested in teaching self-control.

Self-Evaluation

Before a child can be taught to reinforce himself for a behavior or set of behaviors, he must learn to evaluate his behavior correctly. For example, in learning how to print, a child cannot effectively improve his printing by saying "good" or giving himself a star if he does not know whether his printing is good or bad or if it is better than previous samples of his printing. To teach a child to properly evaluate his own behavior, he must be taught to use some sort of standard by which he can measure his own behavior. For example, in teaching printing one can use a standard which a child traces and which he later copies. In teaching a child to match a tone when he plays a musical instrument, he can use a strobotuner which tells him if he is playing on pitch. As he plays the instrument on pitch a certain signal would be seen on a screen, but if he plays off pitch another signal would appear. Similarly, machines are available which teach children "good sense of rhythm." Children learn to press a button in unison with a series of clicks presented in different rhythmic patterns. If the child presses in unison with the clicks or if he can remember and later produce the rhythmic pattern, a light flashes indicating the correctness of his responses (Skinner, 1968). Where the standards for behavior are not as objective as in printing or in playing on pitch, the child must be taught to evaluate more subtle aspects of his behavior as in the case of judging whether a sentence or a paragraph he wrote is good.

It should be emphasized that there is a difference between one's self-evaluative and one's self-reinforcing behavior. A person may realize that his performance on a task has been very poor but still reinforce himself by allowing himself to have a certain reward or by engaging in a certain pleasurable activity. On the other hand, a child may continually see that his behavior is very good relative to some external standard yet deny himself pleasurable things except on rare occasions. Also, a person may deny himself reinforcers and make many self-derogatory statements (either overtly or covertly) because he fails to see that his behavior is quite acceptable. One advantage of teaching self-evaluative skills is that such behavior should make a child less dependent upon adults (Broden, Hall, & Mitts, 1971, (37)). If a child learns to make self-evaluative statements, he need not continually run to the teacher's desk and ask "Is this good?" or "Is my paper nice?"

General Principles of Behavior Change

Schedules of Reinforcement

A schedule of reinforcement refers to the manner in which a reinforcer is made contingent upon a response. One can vary the number of responses between reinforcers or the time between reinforcers. A child may be rewarded for a fixed number of responses (e.g., 5 correct answers) or for a variable number of responses (e.g., on some occasions the child may be reinforced after three correct answers, while on other occasions he may be reinforced for five or eight correct answers). This difference between reinforcing a fixed number of behaviors and reinforcing a variable number of behaviors has led to the distinction fixed ratio vs. variable ratio schedule of reinforcement where the ratio refers to the number of reinforcers divided by the number of responses required to receive a reinforcer. Both animal research and research with young children in an experimental setting has demonstrated that when a child is reinforced on a variable ratio basis he will respond more rapidly than he will if he is reinforced on a fixed ratio basis. When the reinforcers are no longer made available to the child, the child who was trained on a variable ratio schedule of reinforcement will respond for longer periods of time (during extinction) than will a child who was trained on a fixed ratio schedule of reinforcement. One can also distinguish fixed vs. variable time or interval schedules of reinforcement. As the names imply, a fixed interval schedule of reinforcement refers to reinforcing a child for the first response just after a specified interval of time has passed. A variable interval schedule, on the other hand, refers to reinforcing a child for the first response after varying intervals of time, e.g., a teacher might reinforce the first correct answer of a child after 30 minutes, then after 15 minutes and finally after 40 minutes. If a teacher wishes to reinforce a child systematically she should probably do so on a variable ratio or variable interval schedule of reinforcement. In laymans terms, it appears better to "surprise" a child with reinforcers rather than to allow the child to predict that he will always get a reinforcer after a certain number of correct responses or after a certain number of minutes has passed if he were behaving appropriately.

Satiation and Deprivation

If one wishes to maximize the power of a reinforcer he should assure himself that the child does not have ready access to such reinforcers. For example, if one wishes to use M & M candies or raisins as reinforcers in a tutoring session with a small child, one should be sure that the child has not consumed any quantity of candy or raisins just before the tutoring sessions. If such candies or raisins were always available to the child he would be satiated with them and thus their reinforcing power would be minimized. Similarly, if a child is flooded with praise from a teacher or parent, the praise will lose its reinforcing value. While a teacher in a classroom of average size generally does not have to worry about too frequent delivery of praise, teachers who tutor children or who work with children in small groups should be attuned to the fact that their praise can lose its power if it is used too frequently. In order to make a tutor's praise most effective, it may even be possible to deprive a child of adult attention by having him wait outside the tutor's office for a five- or ten-minute period where he would have little to do. Gewirtz and Baer (1958) have demonstrated that deprivation can lead to strong adult reinforcing power whereas satiation will minimize such power.

PREVENTION

Considering the small number of psychologists and other "mental health" personnel who are involved in treatment of children's problems in school settings, it seems both financially unfeasible and practically impossible to ask professionals to deal with all the major problems that arise in a school. There are at least two possible approaches to the problem of providing adequate attention to problem children: (1) teachers, parents, paraprofessionals, and peers can be trained to handle problem situations which are currently dealt with by professionals, and (2) teachers, parents, paraprofessionals, and peers can be used more effectively to *prevent* problem situations from arising. Follow-Through programs which deal with children after they have been in Head Start are a step in the proper direction. Better teacher training with a focus on identification and remediation of problems in the classroom itself is certainly necessary. The use of peers to teach other children academic skills and the effective utilization of paraprofessions are additional answers to the manpower problem. Let us discuss each of the methods of preventing academic and social problems in the classroom.

Head Start and Follow-Through Programs

Head Start is an attempt by the federal government to give some children who are economically deprived an academic and social "head start" — to prevent academic failure and to prevent the development of inappropriate social behavior. Initial research evaluations of Head Start revealed that children who were in Head Start programs did score significantly better on measures of social and academic skills at the end of their Head Start experience than children who did not receive such experience. However, two years later the children who attended Head Start could not be distinguished from children who did not attend Head Start (Cicirelli, Cooper, & Granger, 1969). In an effort to capitalize on the gains made in Head Start, the federal government created Follow-Through, a first and second grade program for children who were in Head Start. Approximately 25 different approaches to Head Start and Follow-Through are now funded by the federal government, and these approaches will be evaluated in several years to assess what effects the various programs have. Two programs, with a heavy behavior modification orientation, seem to be having very significant effects with diverse racial and ethnic groups in a number of geographical regions in the United States. The Bushell program with headquarters at the University of Kansas and the Engelmann–Becker program at the University of Oregon both have a decided focus on academic programming and contingency management. Both programs are conducting workshops to teach the parents how to present some instruction to the children and how to reinforce the children for their efforts. That is, there is *follow-through* by the parents of what is taking place in the classroom. It is our impression that both the children and the parents are aided by such training, and it is likely that such training will reinforce or "follow-through" on those behaviors which were prompted by the Head Start program. If teachers and parents are not taught to follow-through by reinforcing desired academic and social behavior, the newly acquired academic and social behaviors will die. We can now optimistically say that most children can be "taught to be smart," and with this knowledge many legislators are arguing for the institution of educational programs for all children between the ages of three and five. In fact, a bill has already been introduced into Congress by Congressman John Tunney (H.R., 15433) which proposes that the U.S. Department of Health, Education and Welfare give money to communities who wish to start their children in school earlier than the traditional kindergarten age. In short, Tunney wants all children to start school at age three (Tunney, 1970). Because of the national political pressure for day care centers, it is likely that such legislative efforts will be passed within the next ten years. If so, many of the behavior problems currently seen in the classroom which are largely the result of poor academic skills may be prevented.

Teacher Training

Even if Head Start and Follow-Through programs accomplished most of their objectives, there presumably would still be a number of social and academic problems which a teacher would have to face. Undoubtedly there are a number of highly skilled teachers who already can change behavior very effectively, even though they may never have heard of behavior modification. Unfortunately, the skills of such teachers will remain an art if the precise manner by which they change behavior is not made explicit. The behavior modification approach represents a concrete attempt to make explicit those procedures by which a teacher can change behavior. Possibly the most important asset of the behavior modification approach is that it presents a conceptual framework for viewing the development of behavior and behavior change procedures. Since such a framework exists, the teacher herself can become a behavior analyst. She should learn a set of principles for observing and changing behaviors *on her own* in a systematic manner. If she learns a general approach to behavior change, she presumably could handle almost any problem as it arises in the classroom. Some of the principles presented in this book are so simple that one wonders why they are not already practiced throughout the country. It seems obvious that a teacher could (1) easily make the classroom rules clear, (2) give academic work that is commensurate with each child's skills, (3) frequently praise the children for their successes, (4) ignore children when they are involved in minor disruptions, (5) make explicit the consequences of severe disruptions, and (6) deal with each child consistently. Certainly, it is a waste of a psychologist's time and training to review such basic principles with individual teachers every time they have a problem. One method of eliminating this "irrational state of affairs" (Baer, 1970) where consultation is provided to individual teachers as problems arise is to provide in-service training programs for groups of teachers already in the field. More importantly, the principles of behavior modification should be included in all undergraduate education curricula. In short, there is a behavior modification project larger than any yet tackled which needs to be initiated—namely the changing of educational systems and curricula to include courses in behavioral principles and practical experience in the implementation of such principles.

Despite the occasional apparent simplicity of behavior modification procedures, one should be aware that the implementation of these procedures is not easy, and some of the effects of such procedures may seem counterintuitive. It is well known that some teachers upon hearing about behavior modification procedures say "I've always been doing that. I reward my students when they are good." Obviously such an answer reflects great naiveté since behavior modification procedures are much more complicated than that. Both the new teacher and the experienced teacher should recognize that research concerning the teacher's application of behavioral principles in the classroom has answered some questions quite definitively. However, in all of this research an emphasis has been placed not only on the implementation of behavioral principles but on very consistent implementation of such principles. It is hoped that the reader will sense the crucial importance of such consistency both conceptually and as it relates to the daily operations of a classroom.

Paraprofessionals

Our society is becoming increasingly aware of the fact that many functions of personnel with professional titles could be performed by people without such titles. The term "paraprofessional" describes the people who work beside or along with (para meaning beside) professional personnel but who are not trained in all aspects of the profession or who do not have a professional degree. Such an awareness has led to new schools for people working with professionals and new titles such as medical assistant, psychological assistant, and teacher assistant. For example, many functions of a physician can be performed by a physician's assistant who does not have a medical degree (M.D.) but who is trained to execute many technical tasks often done by physicians. Such functions might include performing preliminary medical examinations, maintaining patients' medical records, executing certain diagnostic tests, and performing resuscitation and other emergency procedures until a physician arrives.

Similarly, many functions of psychologists can be performed by someone without doctorate (Ph.D.) in psychology but who has been trained in specific technical tasks. For example, most testing functions and some teaching functions could be executed by a psychologist with a Masters degree in Psychology (M.A. or M.S.), or by a well-trained person without college training (Ryback & Staats, 1970, (*32*); Thomas, Nielsen, Kuypers, & Becker, 1968, (*31*)). Allerhand, (1967) (*30*), found that parents without high school degrees were as effective as psychology graduate students in administering two standard intelligence tests to Head Start children after three training sessions. Poser (1966) compared the effectiveness of psychiatrists (persons with medical degrees and additional psychiatric training), psychiatric social workers, and undergraduates in modifying the behavior of psychotic patients. Although the undergraduates had no special training in psychotherapy and although they were not told how to conduct their therapeutic sessions, patients seen by the undergraduates displayed greater gains than the untreated patients or the patients treated by the psychiatrists and psychiatric social workers. Rioch and her associates (1963) found that married women who received special training were able to change the behavior of their clients as well as professionals. The work of Allerhand, Poser, and Rioch should alert one to the possibility that paraprofessionals can definitely be used advantageously. If very specific procedures are found to deal with certain problems, trained housewives and undergraduates may perform a very useful function in psychological clinics, physical rehabilitation centers, and psychiatric hospitals.

Paraprofessionals in school systems have made the public aware that if they are properly trained they can perform certain skills as well as or better than permanently certified teachers. Paraprofessionals can grade papers, administer and score tests, record frequencies of behavior, dispense reinforcers, tutor children, and teach in circumscribed areas where the curriculum and its presentation are well defined. Such personnel if properly trained obviously could be of benefit to almost any classroom situation. If paraprofessionals were used in Head Start and Follow-Through programs as well as in the elementary school, the large numbers of children who lack academic and social skills when they arrive in third and fourth grade should be diminished greatly. The section on paraprofessionals in this book documents the effective use of such personnel, and with further documentation of their use, it is likely that they will find an entreé into almost all school systems in this country.

Utilization of Peers as Therapeutic Agents

The fact that children can significantly influence the behavior of other children has long been known by professionals and laymen alike. Unfortunately the therapeutic skills of children have not been used effectively by teachers. As will be evidenced in the section on peers as therapeutic agents, peers can successfully alter the behavior of other children in their classes. Surratt, Ulrich, and Hawkins (1969) (24), had a fifth grader record the amount of time four first graders were working appropriately. The first graders were reinforced with extra privileges for increasing amounts of time spent working and, as might be expected, the rate of studying or time spent working increased. Winett, Richards, Krasner, and Krasner (1971) had children rather than the teacher dispense tokens in a second grade classroom and found that attending to the reading assignment increased in four of five children selected for observation in a normal public school classroom. The child-monitored token program took place while the teacher was conducting reading conferences with individual children, and the use of peers during this period—often referred to as "independent seat work"—offers a practical method of implementing behavior change programs when a teacher could not easily evaluate the children's behavior. Ulrich, Wallace, and Dulaney (1970) had elementary school children teach 18–30-month-old children to identify the label objects. The elementary school children were taught to present stimuli to the infants in a particular manner, to reinforce the infant with a piece of sugar-coated cereal and to praise the infant when he made an appropriate vocalization or spoke correctly. All infants showed marked improvement following their instruction by the elementary students. While the utilization of children as behavior modifiers as described in the last example does not bear directly on classroom management, the utilization of young children as behavior modifiers is certainly a method of preventing children from entering elementary school without language or with extremely poor language skills. Even if adult teacher aides are used increasingly in the school system, using children can be both beneficial to other children and highly desirable for the child behavior modifier in an educational sense. As adults we know how much we ourselves learn when we are asked to explain or teach something to others. It should not be surprising that older students who teach younger students would also learn something about the subject they are teaching. The use of high school students as tutors for elementary school children is also desirable since the high school student may find out long before he enters college whether he would enjoy a teaching career.

The aid of peers can also be enlisted in a more indirect fashion by reinforcing them for ignoring the disruptive behaviors of a particular child (Carlson, Arnold, Becker, & Madsen, 1968, (23); Patterson, 1965). Carlson *et al.*, reinforced the class for ignoring the tantrum behavior of a child and points leading to a *class* party were made contingent upon the target child having no tantrums per half day of school. Evans and Oswalt, (1968) (21), reinforced the entire class when a single child answered questions correctly. They assumed that the class would reinforce the target child for his appropriate behavior and that as a consequence, the target child would show academic progress.

SOCIAL ISSUES RELATED TO BEHAVIOR CHANGE PROGRAMS

Before considering the evidence concerning behavior modification procedures, several issues should be discussed which are often of paramount concern to all when initially exposed to behavior modification. The issues include the topics of labeling, teacher expectations, control and responsibility, and the sensitivity of the behavior modifier.

Labeling

Special educators have worried about the influence on children of labels such as emotionally disturbed, retarded, schizophrenic, or delinquent. More specifically, they have been concerned that a child would be stigmatized by such a label, that people would react to him in accord with the label, and that the child in turn might continue to act the role de-picted by the label he received. That is, the child would tend to act the part of an emotionally disturbed child if he were so labeled. Because of this concern, many schools have wisely used euphemistic names for children often labeled retarded, emotionally disturbed or schizophrenic. For example, classroom labels are now Transitional Classes, Project Help, Community living and Community learning, Project Achieve, Project Learn, etc. Though there is little research on this important problem, the new labels are probably a good idea.

Teacher Expectations

The influence of teacher expectations on IQ scores was purportedly demonstrated by Rosenthal and Jacobsen (1966) who reported that simply telling a teacher that a child had potential for giftedness was related to a large IQ gain in one year—particularly in the first and second grades. This research has now been subjected to heavy criticism (Snow, 1969; Thorndike, 1969), and additional research has shown that giving a teacher differential expectancies about her children may influence her behavior in very diverse ways and that IQ scores of children do not always increase when the teacher is told that a child has a potential for being gifted. Given such an expectation, some teachers may spend more time with such a child while others appear to spend much less time with a child labeled gifted (Meichenbaum, Bowers, & Ross, 1969). Despite the absolute score a child receives on an intelligence test, it is probably always best to (1) present academic material to a child in a manner that enables him to succeed most of the time, (2) behave toward him in a manner that conveys the expectation that he can succeed, and (3) praise him heavily for his resulting good behavior.

Control and Responsibility

Because of the inherent power of some of the behavior modification procedures, people sometimes feel that they are very dangerous tools. Scientific advances always carry the potential for evil doings and psychological advances make some people feel particularly uneasy. On the other hand, principles of behavior control have the potential for a great amount of good. Psychological research will proceed in this country as well as in other countries, and as the potential for behavioral change becomes greater and greater, the scientific community must ask itself if the changes it is helping to make are really beneficial. That is, with greater control comes greater responsibility. Many of the behavioral changes effected in the articles in this book are reflective of general wishes of teachers. Changing children's behaviors such as being in one's seat and paying attention is occasionally criticized by educational philosophers because their change seems irrelevant to some educational goals. While being in one's seat and paying attention are not always inextricably related to learning, the child who is in his seat is more likely to receive effective help from the teacher. In short, having a child sit still and pay attention is but a first step in the progression toward many educational goals. As evidenced by the articles in this book children are taught more with greater precision in shorter periods of time than had formerly been possible. Yet one must question whether such goals are the critical aims of education. More importantly, just what behaviors should be taught? While many of the studies in behavior modification have focused on deviant children or adults, it is likely that future work will be addressed to enhancing diverse behaviors of normal children. For example, creativity, sensitivity to others, logical thinking, musical skills, and economic behavior are but a few of the behaviors which may well receive attention in the next decade by behavior modifiers. Sharing and cooperative behavior have already begun to be investigated by psychologists including those with an avowed behavior modification emphasis. Behavior modification can be a tool to maintain a poor educational system, it can be a tool for enhancing the positive aspects of our current system, or it can be helpful in creating new systems. Obviously it can only be a tool in creating new educational systems if teachers and researchers take a critical look at both the short term and long range results of existing systems. Whenever a powerful tool for rapidly changing behavior exists, such as behavior modification, it is imperative that the long term goals of our educational system be evaluated carefully.

Sensitivity

Shaping behavior requires a great deal of sensitivity to small nuances in behavior change and in environmental change. The teacher or therapist must notice and reinforce any small approximations to the desired terminal behavior. If one is to teach behaviors which will be maintained by the natural environment in which a child lives, a teacher or parent must be sensitive to the *actual* practices of the children's parents and peers instead of the *purported* practices of such persons. That is, one must be sensitive to the kinds of behaviors which really will receive rewards in the home and community—not just what parents say would be good for their children. Before one attempts to change a behavior of a client or a child in a classroom, a great deal of sensitivity is necessary to decide what the parent or teacher really desires. For example, a parent may come to a psychologist purportedly to seek aid for her child, but in reality she has come to discuss her own problems. Similarly, a teacher may come to a school psychologist purportedly to talk about a child with whom she is not making progress when in fact she may be most interested in finding out where she can get aid for herself about a personal problem. A parent may come to a teacher to discuss her child but may be even more interested in finding out how she can obtain state aid, welfare, or food stamps. Since some people are reticent to bring up such problems, a behavior modifier—be he psychologist, teacher, social worker, or psychiatrist—should be very careful to ascertain why his help is being sought lest he finds himself overzealously changing a behavior which was only of peripheral concern to the person seeking aid. In summary, while the behavior modifier must be aware of the experimental principles which he can apply to human problems, he must also be sensitive to the feelings and attitudes of his client or student and to be effective he must be warm and spontaneous. While teachers and therapists have always tried to be warm and loving, their love has often been rather haphazardly focused.

Another facet of sensitivity concerns a therapist's or teachers's warmth and emotional responses to a child. To be a good modifier of behavior one cannot simply dispense attention in a mechanical or machine-like fashion. One must give such attention in a spontaneous, warm manner. Equally important, one must be aware of a child's feelings and desires so that when the child is excited over success—be it ever so small—the teacher will respond immediately in a sincere fashion. That is, the teacher must have some empathy for the child. The teacher or therapist who is maximally effective probably frequently exhibits a variety of affective behaviors—she is soft and gentle on one occasion while on another she is ebullient and ecstatic with excitement about a child's progress. She probably reprimands occasionally but in a firm manner indicating or intimating that there will be some consequence if the child does not cease his activity. More importantly, when she is approving, she also acts as if she really means it. When such warmth and love are systematically channeled, their potential for changing behavior is enhanced immeasurably.

CHAPTER 2

Psychotherapy with Children: Evaluations

Psychotherapy is a term used to cover a wide variety of techniques which are generally designed to give a client relief from some problem. The Levitt articles in this section evaluate the results of psychotherapy with children, and the majority of the articles he evaluated reflect a psychoanalytic approach. Clearly, the wide range of procedures employed by various psychoanalytically-oriented psychotherapists prevents any precise description of such psychotherapy with children, but a brief description of psychotherapy should give the reader some general knowledge of the methods employed by the traditional or psychoanalytically-oriented therapist.

In traditional psychotherapy, the relationship between the therapist and the child is crucial. That is, the therapist is advised to establish a warm relationship with a child in order that the child can regain a sense of his own worth. In addition, there is often an emphasis on the release of emotion in the therapy session which is usually held in the therapist's office or an adjoining playroom. The release of emotions through catharsis or expression of feelings is seen as a method of draining off bad emotional feelings. In essence, it is felt that as the bad feelings flow out, the good feelings flow in. To provide a medium for the expression of feelings, many child therapists keep various toys in their office or playroom which might prompt expression of emotion. For example, to prompt aggressive feelings, therapists might have a dart board, a life-size doll which a child might hit or kick, or a hammer and a pegboard. Alternatively, a therapist might simply allow a child to describe his aggressive feelings toward his teacher or his parent. In almost all psychoanalytically-oriented child therapy, an attempt is made to give the child some insight into his problem by interpreting events, feelings, or the fantasy life of the child. Such interpretation might involve discussing with the child certain feelings he has toward the therapist or his parents.

The Levitt articles were selected for this section because they represent one of the few large scale attempts to critically evaluate the effects of psychotherapy with children. Despite many methodological problems associated with each of the Levitt articles, both raise questions about the very basis of the mental health movement. For example, the expansion of existing mental health centers is generally predicted upon the assumption that psychotherapy is effective. The mandatory therapeutic involvement which is required for some children by courts and schools is presumably even more inextricably based upon the assumption that psychotherapy works. However, Levitt's evaluations present no support for the assumption that psychotherapy is effective. Nonetheless, he is quick to warn that his research does not prove that psychotherapy with children is futile. Large scale evaluation studies like those of Levitt's are plagued with partial answers. However, considering the thousands of children involved in the Levitt studies, the large number of clinics and therapists, and the wide variety of children's problems, Levitt's failure to find any evidence that psychotherapy is effective should prompt us to look at alternatives to traditional psychotherapy for treating children's problems.

In the Levitt studies, children who received psychotherapy were compared with children who were accepted for treatment but who voluntarily broke off the clinic relationship without ever being treated. Combining data from two studies (Witmer & Keller, 1942; Lehrman, Sirluck, Black, & Glick, 1949), Levitt found a 72.5% improvement rate for those children who had been accepted for treatment but who had voluntarily broken off the clinic relationship. This 72.5% improvement rate for untreated children thus served as a baseline for evaluating the results of treatment with children. Although Levitt mentioned that some of the procedures used by therapists in his studies were based on learning theory, the behavior modification approaches which draw heavily from operant learning or conditioning principles were not evaluated by the Levitt studies. As mentioned previously, he was evaluating the effectiveness of traditional psychotherapy, not behavior modification.

The Berkowitz article concerning the interaction between child clinics and public schools documents the notion that therapists have generally not communicated with those persons who presumably should have essential information about a child's problems—namely, the teacher.

Almost no visits to the school were made by a therapist, and the frequency of contacts with the school were unrelated to the type of children's problems. The absence of such interaction between the therapist and the school clearly seems to be a poor practice if one's desire is to implement any change in the school since a child may behave very differently with the therapist than he does at school.

Readers not acquainted with statistical analyses should not concern themselves with the details of the statistics in the Levitt articles, but should read the articles for an understanding of the problem being addressed and the general conclusions reached.

ARTICLE 1

The Results of Psychotherapy with Children: An Evaluation*

EUGENE E. LEVITT

Illinois Institute for Juvenile Research

Abstract: A survey of eighteen reports of evaluations at close, and seventeen at follow-up, was compared with similar evaluations of untreated children. Two-thirds of the evaluations at close, and three-quarters at follow-up, showed improvement. Roughly the same percentages were found for the respective control groups. A crude analysis indicates that time is a factor in improvement in the follow-up studies; the rate of improvement with time is negatively accelerating. Further analysis contra-indicates the use of only two categories in evaluation. This scale tends to give much lower rates of improvement than three-, four-, and five-point scales.

It is concluded that the results of the present study fail to support the view that psychotherapy with "neurotic" children is effective.

A compendium of results of psychotherapy with adults was published a few years ago by Eysenck (1952). It included reports from 24 sources on more than 8,000 cases treated by an assortment of psychotherapeutic techniques. The average percentage of cases reported as improved (i.e., cured, improved, much improved, adjusted, well, etc.) is about 65.[1] Eysenck's control or baseline data estimating the remission rate in the absence of formal psychotherapy come from two sources. Those of Landis (1937) for hospitalized neurotics, and those of Denker (1946) for

---

*Reprinted from the *Journal of Consulting Psychology*, Vol. 21, No. 3, 1957, pp. 189–196, by permission of the American Psychological Association.

[1]The data, however, are not quite as "remarkably stable from one investigation to another" as Eysenck appears to believe. The 19 reports of the results of eclectic therapy differ significantly among themselves when frequencies of improvement and nonimprovement are compared. A chi square is 38.11 with a p beyond the 0.01 level for 18 degrees of freedom. Eysenck's point is nonetheless basically reasonable; the range of per cent improvement of from 41 to 77 represents considerable stability when one considers the differences in population, chronology, treatment, classification, and terminology among the studies.

neurotics treated at home by general practitioners, show similar remission rates of about 70% for a 2-year period. Comparing these figures with the average for the treated cases, Eysenck concluded, ". . . roughly two-thirds of a group of neurotic patients will recover or improve to a marked extent within about two years of the onset of their illness, whether they are treated by means of psychotherapy or not" (1952, p. 322). He concludes further that "the figures fail to support the hypothesis that psychotherapy facilitates recovery from neurotic disorder" (1952, p. 323).

The difficulties attending an evaluation of psychotherapy have been detailed many times, most recently by Rosenzweig (1954) in a critique of Eysenck's findings. Other thoughtful and well-organized delineations of evaluation problems include those of Thorne (1952), Zubin (1953a, b), and Greenhill (1955), among others. It is not within the province of the present paper to repeat these accounts.

The purpose of this paper is to summarize available reports of the results of psychotherapy with children using Eysenck's article (1952) as a model.[2] Certain departures will be necessitated by the nature of the data, but in the main, the form will follow that of Eysenck.

BASELINE AND UNIT OF MEASUREMENT

As in Eysenck's study, the "unit of measurement" used here will be evaluations of the degree of improvement of the patient by concerned clinicians. Individuals listed as "much improved, improved, partially improved, successful, partially successful, adjusted, partially adjusted, satisfactory," etc., will be grouped under the general heading of Improved. The Unimproved cases were found in groupings like "slightly improved, unimproved, unadjusted, failure, worse," etc.

The use of the discharge rate of children's wards in state hospitals as a baseline for evaluating the effects of psychotherapy is not recommended. It is most likely that hospitalized children are initially more disturbed than those brought to the child guidance clinics and family service agencies from which the data on treatment are drawn. Few guidance clinics or family service agencies accept psychotic children for treatment, tending

---

[2]Compendia similar to, and overlapping Eysenck's have been published by Zubin (1953b) and by Miles, Barrabee, and Finesinger (1951). These tend to be more detailed and descriptive. Eysenck's work is most concise; in it, descriptions and discussions of individual studies have been subordinated to the presentation of overall results. The present writer feels that this is the most provocative, and hence most fruitful, way of evaluating a collection of psychotherapeutic results.

instead to refer them to the state hospital. Furthermore, as Rosenzweig (1954) points out, the criteria for discharge from a state hospital are probably less stringent than those leading to an appraisal of Improved by other agencies. For these reasons, available statistics of state hospital populations such as those of Witmer (1935), McFie (1934), and Robins and O'Neal (1953) are not used as baseline data.

Follow-up evaluations of changes in behavior problems in normal children also do not furnish satisfactory control data. Studies such as those of McFie (1934) and Cummings (1946) report markedly conflicting results, probably as a function of differences in ages of the subjects, and of varying follow-up intervals. More importantly, behavior like nail biting and nose picking can hardly be regarded as comparable to the problems for which children are referred to guidance clinics.

The use of a follow-up control group of cases closed as unsuccessful, as in the study of Shirley, Baum, and Polsky (1940), suffers from obvious weaknesses. Such a group is not comparable to an untreated sample; it appears to represent the segment of the treatment population for which a poor prognosis has been already established.

A common phenomenon of the child guidance clinic is the patient who is accepted for treatment, but who voluntarily breaks off the clinic relationship without ever being treated. In institutions where the service load is heavy and the waiting period between acceptance and onset of treatment may range up to 6 months, this group of patients is often quite large. Theoretically, they have the characteristics of an adequate control group. So far as is known, they are similar to treated groups in every respect except for the factor of treatment itself.

Nevertheless, the use of this type of group as a control is not common in follow-up evaluations of the efficacy of treatment. Three studies report follow-up data on such groups. Of these, the data of Morris and Soroker (1953) are not suitable for the purposes of this paper. Of their 72 cases, at least 11 had treatment elsewhere between the last formal contact with the clinic and the point of evaluation, while an indeterminate number had problems too minor to warrant clinic treatment.

The samples in the remaining two studies appear satisfactory as sources of baseline data. Witmer and Keller (1942) appraised their group 8 to 13 years after clinic treatment, and reported that 78% were Improved. In the Lehrman study (1949), a one-year follow-up interval found 70% Improved. The overall rate of improvement for 160 cases in both reports is 72.5%. This figure will be used as the baseline for evaluating the results of treatment of children.

THE RESULTS OF PSYCHOTHERAPY

Studies showing outcome at close of treatment are not distinguished from follow-up studies in Eysenck's aggregation. The distinction seems logical, and is also meaningful in the predictive sense, as the analyses of this paper will indicate. Of the reports providing data for the present evaluation, thirteen present data at close, twelve give follow-up results, and five furnish both types, making a total of eighteen evaluations at close and seventeen at follow-up. The data of two reports (Jacobsen, 1948; Johnson & Reid, 1947) are based on a combined close-follow-up rating. Results for the three kinds of evaluations will be presented separately.

The age range covered by all studies is from preschool to 21 years at the time of original clinic contact, the customary juncture for the determination of age for the descriptive data. However, very few patients were over 18 years at that time, and not many were over 17. The median age, roughly estimated from the ranges, would be about 10 years.

The usual psychiatric classification of mental illnesses is not always appropriate for childhood disorders. The writer has attempted to include only cases which would crudely be termed neuroses, by eliminating the data on delinquents, mental defectives, and psychotics whenever possible. The latter two groups constituted a very small proportion of the clinic cases. The proportion of delinquent cases is also small at some clinics but fairly large at others. Since the data as presented were not always amenable to these excisions, an unknown number of delinquent cases are included. However, the outcomes for the separated delinquents are much the same as those for the entire included group.

As in Eysenck's study, a number of reports were excluded here for various reasons. The investigations of Healy and Bronner (1939), Feiker (1941), Ellis (1936), Mann (1942), and Giddings (1940) were eliminated because of overlap, partial overlap, or suspected overlap of the sample with samples of included reports. Those of Bennett and Rogers (1941), Rich (1948), Hunt, Blenkner, and Kogan (1950), Schiffmann and Olson (1939), and Heckman and Stone (1947) were not useable either because of peculiar or inadequate presentation of data, or because results for children and adults were inseparable.

The number of categories in which patients were classified varied from study to study. Most used either a three-, four- or five-point scale. A few used only two categories, while one had twelve. Classification systems with more than five points were compressed into smaller scales. The data are presented tabularly in their original form, but the totals are pooled into three categories, Much Improved, Partially Improved, and Unimproved. A summation of the former two categories gives the frequency of Improved Cases.

A summary of results at close is shown in Table 1.1. Results of follow-up evaluations are summarized in Table 1.2, while the results from two studies using a combined close-follow-up evaluation are presented in Table 1.3. In the latter two tables, the follow-up interval is given as a range of years, the usual form of presentation in the studies. An attempt has been made to compute an average interval per case, using the midpoint of the range as a median when necessary. These averages are tenuous since it cannot be safely assumed that the midpoint actually is the median value. For example, in the Healy-Bronner investigation (1929), the range of intevals is 1 to 20 years, but the median is given as $2\frac{1}{2}$ years. Since the proportion of cases which can be located is likely to vary inversely with the number of years of last clinic contact, the averages of

Table 1.1. Summary of Results of Psychotherapy with Children At Close

Study	N	Much Improved	Partially Improved		Unimproved		Per cent Improved
(11)	57	16	18	12	8	3	80.7
(26)	100	13	18	42	26	1	73.0
(28)	70	12	29	19	10		85.7
(44)	250	54	82	46	68		72.8
(34)	196	76	52		68		65.3
(31)	50	15	18		17		66.0
(10)	126	25	54		47		62.7
(53)	290	75	154		61		79.0
(2)	814	207	398		209		74.3
(43)	72	26	31		15		79.2
(33)	196	93	61		42		78.6
(6)	27	5	11		11		59.3
(9)	31	13	8		10		67.7
(8)	23	2	9		12		47.8
(7)	75	35	22		18		76.0
(1)	80	31	21		28		65.0
(35)	522	225			297		43.1
(13)	420	251			169		59.8
All cases	3,399	1,174	1,105		1,120		67.05
Per cent	100.00	34.54	32.51		32.95		

Table 1.2. Summary of Results of Psychotherapy with Children at Follow-up

Study	Interval in Years	N	Much Improved		Partially Improved		Unimproved		Per cent Improved
(33)	1–5	197	49		55	39	38	16	72.6
(5)	2	33	8		11	7	6	1	78.8
(11)	2–3	57	25		17	6	6	3	84.2
(52)[a]	1–10	366		81	78	106	101		72.4
(28)	2–3	70	21		30	13	6		91.4
(51)	5–8	17	7			3	4	3	58.8
(34)	1	196	99		46		51		74.0
(41)	16–27	34	22		11		1		97.1
(2)	1–20	705	358		225		122		82.7
(4)	5–18	650	355		181		114		82.5
(36)	3–15	484	111		264		109		77.5
(19)	1–4	732	179		398		155		78.8
(13)	5	359	228		80		51		85.8
(21)	1–2	25	6		12		7		72.0
(42)	1–2	25	10		6		9		64.0
(35)	½–1½	191	82				109		42.9
(23)	1–20	78	71				7		91.0
All cases	4.8[b]	4,219	1,712		1,588		919		78.22
Per cent		100.00	40.58		37.64		21.78		

[a]Data based on 13 studies originally reported in (54); results of 8 of these are included here.
[b]Estimated average follow-up interval per case.

Table 1.3. Summary of Results of Psychotherapy with Children Based on Combined Close–Follow-up Evaluation

Study	Interval in Years	N	Much Improved		Partially Improved		Unimproved		Per cent Improved
(29)	1–10	339	94		81	76	42	46	74.04
(30)	1–10	30		9	13		8		73.33
All cases	5.5[a]	369	103		170		96		73.98
Per cent		100.00	27.91		46.07		26.02		

[a]Estimated average follow-up interval per case.

4.8 years for the follow-up studies and 5.5 years for the close-follow-up studies and probably overestimates.

Table 1.1 shows that the average percentage of improvement, i.e., the combined percentages in the Much Improved and Partially Improved categories is 67.05 at close. It is not quite accurate to say that the data are consistent from study to study. A chi-square analysis of improvement and unimprovement yields a value of 230.37, which is significant beyond the 0.001 level for 17 *df.* However, as in the case of Eysenck's data, there is a considerable amount of consistency considering the interstudy differences in methodology, definition, etc.

The average percentage of improvement in the follow-up studies is given in Table 1.2 as 78.22. The percentage for the combined close-follow-up evaluations is 73.98, roughly between the other two. The percentage of improvement in the control studies was 72.5, slightly higher than the improvement at close and slightly lower than at follow-up. It would appear that treated children are no better off at close than untreated children, but that they continue to improve over the years and eventually surpass the untreated group.

This conclusion is probably specious, perhaps unfortunately. One of the two control studies was an evaluation one year after the last clinic contact, the other 8 to 13 years after. The former study reports only 70% improvement while the longer interval provided 78% improvement. The figure for the one-year interval is similar to the results at close, while the percentage of improvement for the control with the 8- to 13-year interval is almost identical with that for the follow-up studies.

The point of the analysis is more easily seen if the results at close and at follow-up are pooled. This combination gives the same sort of estimate as that furnished by the two control groups pooled since one of them is a long-interval follow-up while the other was examined only a short time after clinic contact. The pooled percentage of improvement based on 7,987 cases in both close and follow-up studies is 73.27, which is practically the same as the percentage of 72.5 for the controls.

It now appears that Eysenck's conclusion concerning the data for adult psychotherapy is applicable to children as well; the results do not support the hypothesis that recovery from neurotic disorder is facilitated by psychotherapy.

The discrepancy between results at close and at follow-up suggests that time is a factor in improvement. Denker's report (1946) also indicated the operation of a time factor. He found that 45% of the patients had recovered by the end of one year, 72% had recovered by the end of two years, 82% by three years, 87% by four years, and 91% by five years. The rate of improvement as a function of time in Denker's data is clearly negatively accelerating.

A Spearman rank-order correlation between estimated median follow-up interval and percentage of improvement in the 17 studies in Table 1.2 is 0.48, $p = 0.05$. This estimate of relationship should be viewed with caution because of the aforementioned difficulty in determining median intervals. However, it is uncorrected for tied ranks, which tends to make it a conservative null test. It is also, of course, insensitive to the curve of the bivariate distribution.

The percentage of improvement as a function of time interval is shown by the data of Table 1.4. The studies have been grouped at five time-interval points in the table. There are four studies with estimated median

Table 1.4. Improvement as a Function of the Interval Between Last Clinic Contact and Follow-up

Estimated Median Interval in Years	Number of Reports	Total N	N Improved	Per cent Improved
1–1½	4	437	261	59·73
2–2½	6	1,167	929	79.61
5–6½	3	742	583	78.57
10	2	1,189	958	80.57
12	2	684	569	83.19
All cases	17	4,219	3,300	78.22

intervals of 1–1½ years, six with intervals of 2–2½ years, three with 5–6½ years, two with 10 years, and two with 12 years.

The data of Table 1.4 indicate that most of the correlation between improvement and time-interval is accounted for by the studies with the shortest intervals, and those with the largest. The curve is more or less the same as that of Denker's data, negatively accelerating with most of the improvement accomplished by 2½ years. It is peculiar that the improvement after 1½ years is about 60%, less than the 67% improvement at close. However, the difference is not too great to attribute to variations in methodology and sampling among the concerned studies. Another potential explanation will be offered shortly.

This analysis suggests that improvement is in part a function of time, though the mechanisms involved remain purely speculative. Future comparisons of the results of psychotherapy should properly take this factor into consideration.

Inspection of the data in Table 1.1 discloses another potential factor in the improvement rate. The studies in which only two rating categories, improved and unimproved, have been used, appear to furnish lower percentages of improvement than the average. In the two reports of this kind in Table 1.1, the average improvement is only 50.5% compared with the overall 67%. A complete analysis of percentage of improvement as a function of number of categories is shown in Table 1.5.

Table 1.5. Improvement as a Function of the Number of Points on the Rating Scale in Evaluation at Close

Number of Points	Number of Reports	Total N	N Improved	Per cent Improved
2	2	942	476	50.53
3	12	1,980	1,442	72.83
4	2	320	242	75.63
5	2	157	119	75.80
All cases	18	3,399	2,279	67.05

Examination of Table 1.5 indicates that three-, four- and five-point rating scales produce about the same percentage of improvement. The use of a two-point scale, however, results in over 20% less improvement than the others.[3] This kind of analysis cannot be applied to the data in Table 1.2 since it will be confounded by the time factor.

Evidently, a certain proportion of the unimproved cases in the studies using two categories would have fallen in partially improved categories if they had been utilized. A number of cases in which a fair amount of improvement was manifested are forced into the unimproved category when central points are not available. A two-point scale thus seems to be overly coarse. It is desirable that finer scales be used in future evaluation studies.

The study of Maas, *et al.* (1955), which furnishes three-quarters of the cases in the 1–1½ year interval group in Table 1.4, used a two-point

---

[3]The marked difference between the two-point scale studies and those using finer scales is reflected in the consistency analysis. The chi square for 17 *df* was 230.37, but when the two-category studies are eliminated, it falls to 52.66 for 15 *df*. The value is significant beyond the 0.01 level, but the original chi square has been decreased by more than 75% with a loss of only two *df*.

scale. The percentage of improvement is only 43, which may account for the fact that this time-interval group has a lower percentage of improvement than in the studies at close.

There are a number of different kinds of therapies which have been used in the studies reported here. The therapists have been psychiatrists, social workers, and teams of clinicians operating at different points in the patient's milieu. Therapeutic approaches included counseling, guidance, placement, and recommendations to schools and parents, as well as deeper level therapies. In some instances the patient alone was the focus of attention. In others, parents and siblings were also treated. The studies apparently encompassed a variety of theoretical viewpoints, although these are not usually specified. Viewed as a body, the studies providing the data for Tables 1.1, 1.2, and 1.3 are therapeutically eclectic, a plurality, perhaps, reflecting psychoanalytic approaches.

Thus we may say that the therapeutic eclecticism, the number of subjects, the results, and the conclusions of this paper are markedly similar to those of Eysenck's study. Two-thirds of the patients examined at close and about three-quarters seen in follow-up have improved. Approximately the same percentages of improvement are found for comparable groups of untreated children.

As Eysenck pointed out (1955) in a sequel to his evaluation, such appraisal does not *prove* that psychotherapy is futile. The present evaluation of child psychotherapy, like its adult counterpart, fails to support the hypothesis that treatment is effective, but it *does not* force the acceptance of a contrary hypothesis. The distinction is an important one, especially in view of the differences among the concerned studies, and their generally poor caliber of methodology and analysis. Until additional evidence from well-planned investigations becomes available, a cautious, tongue-in-cheek attitude toward child psychotherapy is recommended.

REFERENCES*

Albright, Sue & Gambrell, Helen. Personality traits as criteria for the psychiatric treatment of adolsecents. *Smith Coll. Stud. soc. Wk*, 1938, **9**, 1–26. *1*.

Barbour, R. F. Selected surveys prepared for the inter-clinic conference. In J. F. Davidson (Chmn.), Follow-up on child guidance cases. Ninth Child Guidance Inter-Clinic Conference, London, 1951. Pp. 49–59. *2*.

---

*Italicized number at end of reference refers to study numbers in Tables.

Bennett, C. C., & Rogers, C. R. Predicting the outcome of treatment. *Amer. J. Orthopsychiat.*, 1941, **11**, 210–221. *3*.

Bronner, Augusta F. Treatment and what happened afterward. *Amer. J. Orthopsychiat.*, 1944, **14**, 28–35. *4*.

Brown, Jane L. The follow-up procedure of an intermittent child guidance clinic. Unpublished master's thesis, Smith Coll., 1931. *5*.

Brown, Marjorie. Adolescents treatable by a family agency. *Smith. Coll. Stud. soc. Wk*, 1947, **18**, 37–67. *6*.

Burlingham, Susan. A quantitative analysis of psychiatric social treatment carried out in seventy-five cases at the Institute for Juvenile Research. Unpublished master's thesis, Smith Coll., 1931. *7*.

Canaday, Louise J. A way of predicting the probable outcome of treatment of young children who run away. Unpublished master's thesis, Smith Coll., 1940. *8*.

Carpenter, Jean A. Some factors relating to the method and outcome of case-work treatment with the adolescent girl when the girl herself is the focus of treatment. Unpublished master's thesis, Smith Coll., 1939. *9*.

Christianson, Eva, Gates, Mary, & Coleman, Fay. A survey of the intake of a mental hygiene clinic with special reference to the outcome of treatment. *Smith Coll. Stud. soc. Wk*, 1934, **5**, 211–212. *10*.

Cohen, Marion, & Davis, Ellen. Factors related to the outcome of treatment in a child guidance clinic. *Smith Coll. Stud. soc. Wk*, 1934, **5**, 212–214. *11*.

Cummings, Jean D. A follow-up study of emotional symptoms in school children. *Brit. J. educ. Psychol.*, 1946, **16**, 163–177. *12*.

Cunningham, J. M., Westerman, Hester H., & Fischhoff, J. A follow-up study of children seen in a psychiatric clinic for children. Paper read at Amer. Orthopsychiat. Assn., Chicago, March, 1955. *13*.

Denker, P. G. Results of treatment of psychoneuroses by the general practitioner. *N.Y. State med. J.*, 1946, **46**, 2164–2166. *14*.

Ellis, Florine J. A study of one hundred children treated by the Northern New Jersey Mental Hygiene clinics. *Smith Coll. Stud. soc. Wk*, 1936, **6**, 277–278. *15*.

Eysenck, H. J. The effects of psychotherapy: an evaluation. *J. consult. Psychol.*, 1952, **16**, 319–324. *16*.

Eysenck, H. J. The effects of psychotherapy: a reply. *J. abnorm. soc. Psychol.*, 1955, **50**, 147–148. *17*.

Feiker, Hazel A. A comparative study of the methods of case work of adolescent boys in the years 1928–1930 and 1938–1940 at a child guidance clinic. Unpublished master's thesis, Smith Coll., 1941. *18*.

Fenton, N., & Wallace, Ramona. Child guidance in California communities, Part 6. Follow-up study of Bureau cases. *J. juv. Res.*, 1938, **22**, 43–60. *19*.

Giddings, Elizabeth R. Some factors affecting the outcome of treatment of Negro cases in a child guidance clinic. Unpublished master's thesis, Smith Coll., 1940. *20*.

Gollander, Barbara. A study of overinhibited and unsocialized aggressive children. III. Later adjustment. Unpublished master's thesis, Smith Coll., 1944. *21*.

Greenhill, M. H., *et al.* Evaluation in mental health. *Publ. Hlth Serv. Publ. No. 413*, Washington: U.S. Gov't Printing Off., 1955. *22*.

Healy, W., Bronner, Augusta F., Baylor, Edith M., & Murphy, J. P. *Reconstructing behavior in youth: a study of problem children in foster families.* New York: Knopf, 1929. *23.*

Healy, W., & Bronner, Augusta F. *Treatment and what happened afterward.* Boston: Judge Baker Guidance Clinic, 1939. *24.*

Heckman, A. A., & Stone, A. Testing casework results: forging new tools. *Surv. Midmonthly,* 1947, **83**, 267–270. *25.*

Hubbard, Ruth M., & Adams, Christine F. Factors affecting the success of child guidance treatment. *Amer. J. Orthopsychiat.,* 1936, **6**, 81–102. *26.*

Hunt, J. McV., Blenkner, Margaret, & Kogan, L. S. A field-test of the Movement Scale. *Soc. Casewk,* 1950, **31**, 267–277. *27.*

Irgens, Effie M. Must parents' attitudes become modified in order to bring about adjustment in problem children? *Smith Coll. Stud. soc. Wk,* 1936, **7**, 17–45. *28.*

Jacobsen, Virginia. Influential factors in the outcome of treatment of school phobia. *Smith Coll. Stud. soc. Wk,* 1948, **18**, 181–202. *29.*

Johnson, Lillian J., & Reid, J. H. An evaluation of ten years work with emotionally disturbed children. *Ryther Child Cent. Monogr.* IV, 1947. *30.*

La More, Mary T. An evaluation of a state hospital child guidance clinic. *Smith Coll. Stud. soc. Wk,* 1941, **12**, 137–164. *31.*

Landis, C. A statistical evaluation of psychotherapeutic methods. In L. E. Hinsie (Ed.), *Concepts and problems of psychotherapy.* New York: Columbia Univer. Press, 1937. *32.*

Lee, P. R., & Kenworthy, M. E. *Mental hygiene and social work.* New York: Commonwealth Fund, 1929. *33.*

Lehrman, L. J., Sirluck, Hilda, Black, B. J., & Glick, Selma J. Success and failure of treatment of children in the child guidance clinics of the Jewish Board of Guardians, New York City. *Jewish Bd. Guard. Res. Monogr.,* 1949, No. 1. *34.*

Maas, H. S., *et al.* Socio-cultural factors in psychiatric clinic services for children: a collaborative study in the New York and San Francisco metropolitan areas. *Smith Coll. Stud. soc. Wk,* 1955, **25**, 1–90. *35.*

Maberly, A., & Sturge, Brenda. After-results of child guidance. *Brit. med. J.,* 1939, **1**, 1130–1134. *36.*

Mann, Ida L. Results with child guidance patients diagnosed as psychoneurotic. *Smith Coll. Stud. soc. Wk,* 1942, **13**, 160–161. *37.*

McFie, Bernice S. Behavior and personality difficulties in school children. *Brit. J. educ. Psychol.,* 1934, **4**, 30–46. *38.*

Miles, H. H. W., Barrabee, Edna L., & Finesinger, J. E. Evaluation of psychotherapy. *Psychosom. Med.,* 1951, **8**, 83–105. *39.*

Morris, D. P., & Soroker, Eleanor. A follow-up study of a guidance-clinic waiting list. *Ment. Hyg. N.Y.,* 1953, **37**, 84–88. *40.*

Morris, D. P., Soroker, Eleanor, & Burress, Genette. Follow-up studies of shy, withdrawn children — I. Evaluation of later adjustment. *Amer. J. Orthopsychiat.,* 1954, **24**, 743–754. *41.*

Moses, Jane. A study of overinhibited and unsocialized aggressive children. Part IV: The later adjustment of unsocialized aggressive children. Unpublished master's thesis, Smith Coll., 1944. *42.*

Newell, N. W. The methods of child guidance adapted to a public school system. *Ment. Hyg. N.Y.*, 1934, **18**, 362–373. *43.*

Reid, J. H., & Hagan, Helen R. *Residential treatment of emotionally disturbed children.* New York: Child Welfare League of America, 1952. *44.*

Rich, G. J. Preschool clinic service and follow-up in a city health department. *Amer. J. Orthopsychiat.*, 1948, **18**, 134–139. *45.*

Robins, E., & O'Neal, Patricia. Clinical features of hysteria in children, with a note on prognosis. A two to seventeen year follow-up study of 41 patients. *Nerv. Child*, 1953, **10**, 246–271. *46.*

Rosenzweig, S. A transvaluation of psychotherapy—a reply to Hans Eysenck. *J. abnorm. soc. Psychol.*, 1954, **49**, 298–304. *47.*

Schiffmann, Frances, & Olson, Elma. *A study in family case work: an attempt to evaluate service.* Evanston, Ill.: Family Welfare Assoc., 1939. *48.*

Shirley, Mary, Baum, Betty, & Polsky, Sylvia. Outgrowing childhood's problems: a follow-up study of child guidance patients. *Smith Coll. Stud. soc. Wk*, 1940, **11**, 31–60. *49.*

Thorne, F. C. Rules of evidence in the evaluation of the effects of psychotherapy. *J. clin. psychol.*, 1952, **8**, 38–41. *50.*

Walcott, Esther. A study of the present adjustment made by solitary children who had withdrawn into an imaginary world. Unpublished master's thesis, Smith Coll., 1931. *51.*

Witmer, Helen L. A comparison of treatment results in various types of child guidance clinics. *Amer. J. Orthopsychiat.*, 1935, **5**, 351–360. *52.*

Witmer, Helen L., et al. The outcome of treatment in a child guidance clinic: a comparison and an evaluation. *Smith Coll. Stud. soc. Wk*, 1933, **3**, 339–399. *53.*

Witmer, Helen L., et al. The later adjustment of problem children. *Smith Coll. Stud. soc. Wk*, 1935, **6**, 1–98. *54.*

Witmer, Helen L., & Keller, Jane. Outgrowing childhood problems: a study in the value of child guidance treatment. *Smith Coll. Stud. soc. Wk*, 1942, **13**, 74–90. *55.*

Zubin, J. Design for the evaluation of therapy. *Res. Publ. Assoc. Res. nerv. ment. Dis.*, 1953, **31**, 10–15. a *56.*

Zubin, J. Evaluation of therapeutic outcome in mental disorders. *J. nerv. ment. Dis.*, 1953, **117**, 95–111. b *57.*

Psychotherapy with Children: A Further Evaluation*

EUGENE E. LEVITT

Indiana University Medical Center, Indianapolis, Indiana

Abstract: Evidence concerning the appropriateness of defector control groups is conflicting, but it is still probable that such a group yields a suitable baseline for the evaluation of psychotherapy. Twenty-two studies of outcome provided an overall improvement rate of 65.2 percent which is similar to the rate which was found in studies reviewed earlier, and also to the rate of improvement among defectors. It must still be concluded that there does not seem to be a sound basis for the contention that psychotherapy facilitates recovery from emotional illness in children. The data suggest that the improvement rate varies among psychiatric illnesses, and that future comparisons of treated and defector groups should be made within diagnostic categories.

PRELIMINARY CONSIDERATIONS

In 1957, the author reviewed articles involving the evaluation of the results of psychotherapy with children for the period 1929–1955 (Levitt, 1957a). A total of 18 reports of evaluations at close and 17 at follow-up were found. Of the total of nearly 8,000 child patients, two-thirds were rated as improved at close and three-quarters at follow-up. Using "defectors" from treatment (i.e., children who had been accepted for treatment but who never began treatment) as a control baseline, approximately the same percentages were found for respective control groups. It was concluded that the results failed to support the contention that psychotherapy with children is effective.

This conclusion was supported by the results of a long-range, follow-up

---

*Reprinted from *Behavior Research and Therapy*, Vol. 1, 1963, pp. 45–51.

study at the Institute for Juvenile Research in Chicago (Levitt, 1959), one of the largest community child guidance clinics in the United States. Treated groups were compared with defector controls from the same clinic population on 26 variables, and no differences were found.

The review has been criticized by Eisenberg and Gruenberg (1961), Heinicke (1960) and Hood-Williams (1960).[1] The major point is that defectors (alternatively "terminators" or "discontinuers") constitute an inappropriate control group because they may be less disturbed individuals who are able to respond favourably to the diagnostic procedure alone. The hypothesis certainly appears reasonable, though none of the critiques actually cite experimental findings which bear directly on it. There are, however, a number of investigations which do have direct bearing.

One study (Levitt, 1957b) shows that defector cases and those who have had some treatment do not differ on 61 factors, including two clinical estimates of severity of symptoms, and eight other factors relating to symptoms. Another study (Levitt, 1958a) found that experienced mental health professionals were unable to detect a difference in severity of symptoms between treated and defector child cases, based on case records. On a 5-point scale, the mean severity ratings were 3.02 for the defector children and 2.98 for the treated cases. Judgments of motivation for treatment also did not distinguish the two groups.

Ross and Lacey (1961) found that the defector cases had fewer histories of developmental difficulties, fewer "unusual behaviors" (confusion, disorientation, panic reactions, unpredictable, meaningless and self-destructive acts), a lower incidence of specific somatic complaints, and less parental "marital disharmony" (not including divorce and separation). The defectors also tended to have had shorter waiting periods between application and intake interview. There was no relationship to socio-economic status. Lake and Levinger (1960) did find a relationship with

---

[1] By restricting his analysis of data to only two studies, Heinicke was able to arrive at the conclusion that treated children at least showed a greater degree of "successful adjustments," while the control cases showed a greater percentage of "partial improvements." In addition to the obvious potential effect of selecting two investigations from many, those who are experienced psychotherapists cannot help but be struck by the greater difficulty in distinguishing among degrees of improvement, as opposed to distinguishing between any improvement and no improvement whatsoever. This suggests that the distinction between "successful" and "partial" will usually be relatively unreliable. Eisenberg classified neurosis in children as a "disorder for which there is reasonable likelihood of response to treatment," but admits that no definite conclusion concerning the efficacy of psychotherapy can be ventured at present. Despite his criticisms, Hood-Williams accepts the defectors as a control group, "albeit with reservations, whose very nature demands that conclusions drawn from them should be highly tentative." A detailed rebuttal of his critique has already appeared (Levitt, 1960).

⟩

socio-economic status, with the defectors tending to come from lower strata, but they found no relationship between continuing into therapy and the length of the waiting period. They report positive correlations between continuing into treatment and motivation of the parent for treatment.

A follow-up study of 142 defectors (Levitt, 1958b) disclosed that a family member was clearly resistant to treatment in 24 per cent of the cases, but 52 per cent attributed defection to deficiencies of the clinic, or to environmental circumstances.

Overall, the findings seem to be in conflict. Some of the studies appear to indicate that the defectors are less disturbed, but some appear to show no differences. One study shows a relationship to the socio-economic status, while another does not. The waiting period and parental motivation were found to be associated with termination in one study, but not in another.

The problem in attempting to reconcile these conflicting findings is that the definitions of "treated" and "defector" vary among studies. In the Levitt (1957b, 1958a) studies, a treated case was one which had at least 5 treatment interviews; in the Ross and Lacey study (1961) a minimum of 16 interviews. The term is not defined specifically in the Lake and Levinger investigation (1960). A defector in the Levitt studies is a case which had had a complete diagnostic work-up, had been accepted for therapy, and had failed the appropriate appointment when it was offered. For Ross and Lacey, a defector is one who had less than 5 treatment interviews, and terminated against clinic advice. In the Lake and Levinger study a defector is a case which broke contact with the clinic after a complete application procedure, including an interview, but no diagnostic work-up. It is entirely possible that these differences in definition lie at the root of the discrepancies in findings.

Ideally, the defector should be an individual who has been procedurally identical with the treated case except for the factor of formal treatment itself. In the Ross-Lacey investigation, the defectors could have had as many as 4 treatment interviews. In the Lake-Levinger study, the defectors had not been subjected to diagnostic evaluation, and had evidently, therefore, not actually been accepted for treatment. Only in the Levitt investigations does the handling of the defector case appear to satisfy the criterion. If we accept the results of these studies (Levitt, 1957b; Levitt, 1958a) then the conclusion is that there does not seem to be any basis for the view that the defector cases were more or less seriously disturbed than treated cases, at the time of diagnostic evaluation.

It is probably true that a defector group contains a percentage of cases which have noticeably improved in the interim between the diagnostic evaluation and the offer of therapy.[2] The critics of the 1957 review speculate that the defector group may be a poor control because it is likely to contain substantially more of such cases than will the group which eventually goes on to formal treatment.

There are several arguments against this contention. It has been pointed out (Levitt, 1960) that follow-up interviews with parents of defector cases suggest that about 18 per cent terminated contact with the clinic because of the interim symptomatic improvement. Only about 12 per cent offered this as the sole explanation for termination. This percentage could, of course, affect an inter-group comparison, but it hardly seems sufficient to account for an overall improvement rate of some 65 per cent.

The second point is simply that the treated group might also have an interim improvement rate, which would balance, or partly offset, this phenomenon in the defector group.

Interim improvement is usually a corollary of the hypothesis that the defectors are less seriously disturbed initially, since such a child is more apt to be improved by a brief contact. Another argument against the idea of interim improvement as a bias follows from the evidence which appears to suggest that the defectors are not, in fact, less seriously disturbed.

Summing up, we can say that the defectors may be a biased control group, though the available evidence appears to indicate otherwise. The need for such a control is undeniable and no one has yet suggested a superior method of establishing the baseline of spontaneous remission.

Eisenberg and Gruenberg (1961) and Eisenberg, Gilbert et al. (1961) believe that failure to distinguish among diagnostic categories tends to obfuscate an evaluation of outcome. They argue that it would be more revealing to match treated and defector control groups by diagnosis. The contention appears reasonable; spontaneous remission is usually variable among illnesses. Unfortunately, data on defector groups by diagnostic categories are not available. It is possible, however, to determine whether outcome varies by diagnosis among treated cases, which is the logical first step. The present review of evaluation studies will attempt to accomplish this.

---

[2]It is a common belief among clinic workers that this improvement is a function of therapeutic properties of the diagnostic procedure. If this is indeed true, then the amount of such improvement is likely to vary considerably from clinic to clinic, as the evidence (Filmer-Bennett and Hillson, 1959; Phillips, 1957) indicates that the diagnostic procedure varies. However, the etiology of the improvement is not relevant to the argument.

THE PRESENT REVIEW

The present review is based on 22 publications in which evaluative data are presented.[3] More than half of these are evaluations at follow-up rather than at close, but no distinction is made in this review. Some of the follow-up intervals are very short, and the interval is not stated in some studies. Furthermore, the combined breakdowns into diagnostic categories and into follow-up and close studies would fractionate the data to the point where comparisons would be unfeasible.

Data from the investigations are divided into five groups according to diagnostic criteria. Two groups are reasonably clearcut; psychotic children (Annesley, 1961; Bender and Gurevitz, 1955; Hamilton *et al.*, 1961; Kane and Chambers, 1961; Kaufman *et al.*, 1962), and those with special symptoms such as enuresis, tics, and school phobia (Hersov, 1960; Lazarus and Abramovitz, 1962; Phillips, 1961; Rodriguez *et al.*, 1959; Zausmer, 1954). A third group deals with cases of delinquency, aggressive behaviors, anti-social acting-out, etc. (Annesley, 1961; Cytryn *et al.*, 1960; Eisenberg *et al.*, 1958a; Morris *et al.*, 1956; Rexford *et al.*, 1956). The fourth group is roughly analogous to the adult neurotic (Annesley, 1961; Dorfman, 1958; Eisenberg *et al.*, 1961). The fifth group, which is by far the largest, is a mixed one in which a number of different diagnostic categories are represented, and includes accounts of general or unclassified child guidance clinic samples (Chess, 1957; LaVietes *et al.*, 1960; Miller, 1957; O'Neal and Robins, 1958a; Phillips, 1960; Seidman, 1957). The groupings are not entirely pure, but there is little overlap. By and large, cases of organicity have been excluded.

The establishment of a separate category for children with special symptoms does not imply that such a symptom may not be pathognomic of a more extensive psychological disorder. The distinction is required by the fact that the evaluation of therapy in these cases is based solely on outcome of treatment of the special symptom.

The therapy procedures which are represented in the studies cover a fairly broad range, including counselling with parents, environmental manipulation, techniques based on learning theory, nondirective coun-

---

[3]As in the earlier review, several studies have been excluded because of overlapping, and other reasons. Eisenberg's data (1958b) are included in the later study of Rodriguez *et al.* (1959). A second publication by O'Neal and Robins (1958b) includes data of an original publication (1958a). The latter is used because of its more complete presentation. The general improvement-nonimprovement findings are similar. Most of the results of the study by Cytryn *et al.* (1960) are included in the subsequent paper by Eisenberg *et al.* (1961). The article by Cunningham *et al.* (1956) appeared in the earlier review as an unpublished paper. The study of Michael *et al.* (1957) is inappropriate since only 25 of 606 treated cases were located at follow-up.

selling of children, and the use of adjuctive drugs. Shock therapies, chemotherapy as the exclusive approach, and other somatic treatments have been excluded. Several recent innovations in therapeutic methods are also excluded, largely because the numbers of cases are small, or because a systematic evaluation procedure does not appear in the study. Included in this category are Charny's "isolation treatment" (Charny, 1961), and the operant conditioning techniques of Ferster and DeMyer (1961).

RESULTS

The data from the 22 evaluation studies are summarized in Table 2.1. The customary trichotomous breakdown is employed: Much Improved includes any classification indicating great improvement, or "cured;" any classification indicating lesser degree of improvement, such as "partly," "moderately," or "slightly," is subsumed under Partly Improved; the No Improvement class also takes in "worse."

Table 2.1. Summary of Evaluation Data from Twenty-two Studies

Type of Disorder	Number of Studies	Much Improved		Partly Improved		Unimproved		Total	Overall Improved
		N	%	N	%	N	%	N	%
Neurosis	3	34	15	107	46	89	39	230	61
Acting-out	5	108	31	84	24	157	45	349	55
Special Symptoms	5	114	54	49	23	50	23	213	77
Psychosis	5	62	25	102	40	88	35	252	65
Mixed	6	138	20	337	48	222	32	697	68
Total	24*	456	26.2	679	39.0	606	34.8	1741	65.2

*The study of Annesley (1961) contributed data to three classifications.

The overall improvement rate for the 1741 cases in the present review is 65.2 per cent. Since evaluations at close and follow-up are not separated, the pooled defector rate of 72.5 per cent must be used as the baseline (Levitt, 1957a). This rate is significantly greater than the 65.2 per cent rate found in the present study. However, if we eliminate the psychotic and acting-out children (an attempt was made to do this in the earlier review) the adjusted figure becomes 68.3 per cent which does not differ significantly from the defector rate of 72.5 per cent.

If we pool all evaluation studies in the 1957 review, we find that 73.3 per cent of the cases show improvement. This is significantly higher than the improvement rate for studies in the present review. Again, an elimination of the psychotic and acting-out children from the present group makes the comparability more exact. We find, nonetheless, that the adjusted improvement rate of 68.3 per cent in the present study is still significantly lower than the rate for studies in the 1957 review. However, a difference of 5 per cent could easily be due to differences in sampling, treatment procedures, evaluation methods, and other sources of variation. Its clinical significance is certainly negligible.

The 3×5 matrix of frequencies of Table 2.1 yields a chi-square which is significant far beyond the 0.1 per cent level. It appears that much of the variation among diagnostic categories is a function of differences between the Much Improved and Partly Improved classifications. However, even if we aggregate the data for the two classifications of improvements, the 2×5 matrix still results in a chi-square which is significant beyond the 0.1 per cent level. If the two groups which seem to provide the greatest variation, the acting-out children and those with special symptoms, are eliminated, the resulting 2×3 matrix yields a nonsignificant chi-square.

DISCUSSION

The results of this second review of evaluations of outcome of therapy with children are similar to those of the earlier review, and like those earlier findings, do not differ markedly from results obtained with defector cases. And again, the inescapable conclusion is that available evaluation studies do not furnish a reasonable basis for the hypothesis that psychotherapy facilitates recovery from emotional illness in children.

Apart from this global inference, the data suggest that there is merit in Eisenberg's contention that comparisons of treated and defector cases ought to be made within diagnostic categories. It appears that the improvement rate with therapy is lowest for cases of deliquency and anti-social acting-out, and highest for identifiable behavioral symptoms, like enuresis and school phobia. However, until the required comparisons are actually made, it would be incautious to conclude that therapy is more or less successful with any diagnostic group. It is perfectly possible that the spontaneous remission rate, as indicated by appropriate defector control groups, is also lower for the deliquents and higher for the special symptoms, and that the differences which are found in Table 2.1 simply reflect these facts.

Strupp's statement (1962) that we have not yet arrived at the appropriate time for a definitive outcome study is probably quite true. It also appears true that in recent years, research attention has turned away from the evaluation of outcome *per se* and has taken up the therapist and the therapy process as phenomena for investigation. However, the study of therapeutic dyad or of the personality of the therapist as a variable, or other process phenomena, does not obviate the need for precise measurement of outcome. To find the personality or the process which makes for successful treatment, we must still have an appropriate evaluation of that treatment. As Strupp (1962) says, "Concerted effort is needed to develop meaningful and measurable criteria of therapeutic outcome." It is hard to see how this can be done without continuing to evaluate the outcome of therapy itself.

Indeed, the definitive investigation may already be in process. An evaluation study sponsored by the Jewish Board of Guardians in New York City (Bloch and Rosenfeld, 1962) is now entering its eighth year and will continue for at least two more years. The enormous care and attention to detail of this investigation makes it possible that it may evolve into Strupp's "missing link" of psychotherapy with children.

REFERENCES

Annesley, P. T. (1961) Psychiatric illness in adolescence: Presentation and prognosis. *J. Ment. Sci.,* **107,** 268–278.

Bender, L. & Gurevitz, S. (1955) The results of psychotherapy with young schizophrenic children. *Amer. J. Orthopsychiat.,* **25,** 162–170.

Bloch, D. A. & Rosenfeld, E. (1962) *Evaluation (process-outcome) studies of the psychiatric treatment of children.* Progress report and research plans for the years 1962–1964. Unpublished memorandum, Jewish Board of Guardians, New York.

Charny, I.W. (1961) *Regression and reorganization in the "isolation treatment" of children: A clinical contribution to sensory deprivation research.* Paper presented at the meeting of the American Psychological Association, New York.

Chess, S. (1957) *Evaluation of the effectiveness of an interracial child guidance clinic: diagnosis and treatment.* Unpublished paper, New York.

Cunningham, J. M., Westerman, H. H. & Fischhoff, J. (1956) A follow-up study of patients seen in a psychiatric clinic for children. *Amer. J. Ortho-psychiat.,* **26,** 602–611.

Cytryn, L., Gilbert, A. & Eisenberg, L. (1960) The effectiveness of tranquilizing drugs plus supportive psychotherapy in treating behavior disorders of children: A double blind study of 80 outpatients. *Amer. J. Orthopsychiat.*, **30**, 113-128.

Dorfman, E. (1958) Personality outcomes of client-centered child therapy. *Psychol. Monogr.*, **72**, No. 456.

Eisenberg, L., Marlowe, B. & Hastings, M. (1958a) Diagnostic services of maladjusted foster children: An orientation toward an acute need. *Amer. J. Orthopsychiat.*, **28**, 750-763.

Eisenberg, L. (1958b) School phobia: A study in the communication of anxiety. *Amer. J. Psychiat.*, **114**, 712-718.

Eisenberg, L. & Gruenberg, E. M. (1961) The current status of secondary prevention in child psychiatry. *Amer. J. Orthopsychiat.*, **31**, 355-367.

Eisenberg, L., Gilbert, A., Cytryn, L. & Molling, P. A. (1961) The effectiveness of psychotherapy alone and in conjunction with perphenazine or placebo in the treatment of neurotic and hyperkinetic children. *Amer. J. Psychiat.*, **117**, 1088-1093.

Ferster, C. B. & DeMyer, M. K. (1961) The development of performances in autistic children in an automatically controlled environment. *J. Chron. Dis.*, **13**, 312-345.

Filmer-Bennett, G. & Hillson, J. S. (1959) Some child therapy practices. *J. Clin. Psychol.*, **15**, 105-106.

Hamilton, D. M., McKinley, R. A., Moorhead, H. H. & Wall, J. H. (1961) Results of mental hospital treatment of troubled youth. *Amer. J. Psychiat.*, **117**, 811-816.

Heinicke, C. M. (1960) Research on psychotherapy with children: A review and suggestions for further study. *Amer. J. Orthopsychiat.*, **30**, 483-493.

Hersov, L. A. (1960) Refusal to go to school. *J. Child Psychol. Psychiat.*, **1**, 137-145.

Hood-Williams, J. (1960) The results of psychotherapy with children: A revaluation. *J. Cons. Psychol.*, **24**, 84-88.

Kane, R. P. & Chambers, G. S. (1961) Improvement: Real or apparent? A seven year follow-up of children hospitalized and discharged from a residential setting. *Amer. J. Psychiat.*, **117**, 1023-1026.

Kaufman, I., Frank, T., Friend, J., Heims, L. W. & Weiss, R. (1962) Success and failure in the treatment of childhood schizophrenia. *Amer. J. Psychiat.*, **118**, 909-913.

Lake, M. & Levinger, G. (1960) Continuance beyond application interviews in a child guidance clinic. *Soc. Casewk.*, **91**, 303-309.

LaVietes, R. L., Hulse, W. & Blau, A. (1960) A psychiatric day treatment center and school for young children and their parents. *Amer. J. Ortho-psychiat.*, **30**, 468-482.

Lazarus, A. A. & Abramovitz, A. (1962) The use of "emotive imagery" in the treatment of children's phobias. *J. Ment. Sci.*, **108**, 191-195.

Levitt, E. E. (1957a) Results of psychotherapy with children: An evaluation. *J. Cons. Psychol.*, **21**, 189-196.

Levitt, E. E. (1957b) A comparison of "remainers" and "defectors" among child clinic patients. *J. Cons. Psychol.*, **21**, 316.

Levitt, E. E. (1958a) A comparative judgmental study of "defection" from treatment at a child guidance clinic. *J. Clin. Psychol.*, **14**, 429-432.

Levitt, E. E. (1958b) Parents' reasons for defection from treatment at a child guidance clinic. *Ment. Hyg. N.Y.*, **42**, 521-524.

Levitt, E. E., Beiser, H. R. & Robertson, R. E. (1959) A follow-up evaluation of cases treated at a community child guidance clinic. *Amer. J. Ortho-psychiat.*, **29**, 337–347.

Levitt, E. E. (1960) Reply to Hood-Williams. *J. Cons. Psychol.*, **24**, 89–91.

Michael, C. M., Morris, H. H. & Soroker, E. (1957) Follow-up studies of shy, withdrawn children—II. Relative incidence of schizophrenia. *Amer. J. Orthopsychiat.*, **27**, 331–337.

Miller, D. H. (1957) The treatment of adolescents in an adult hospital: A preliminary report. *Bull. Menninger Clin.*, **21**, 189–198.

Morris, H. H., Escoli, P. J. & Wexler, R. (1956) Aggressive behavior disorders of childhood: A follow-up study. *Amer. J. Psychiat.*, **112**, 991–997.

O'Neal, P. & Robins, L. N. (1958a) The relation of childhood behavior problems to adult psychiatric status. *Amer. J. Psychiat.*, **114**, 961–969.

O'Neal, P. & Robins, L. N. (1958b) Childhood patterns predictive of adult schizophrenia. *Amer. J. Psychiat.*, **115**, 385–391.

Phillips, E. L. (1957) Some features of child guidance clinic practice in the U.S.A. *J. Clin. Psychol.*, **13**, 42–44.

Phillips, E. L. (1960) Parent-child psychotherapy: A follow-up study comparing two techniques. *J. Psychol.*, **49**, 195–202.

Phillips, E. L. (1961) Logical analysis of childhood behavior problems and their treatment. *Psychol. Rep.*, **9**, 705–712.

Rexford, E. N., Schleifer, M. & Van Amerongen, S. T. (1956) A follow-up of a psychiatric study of 57 antisocial young children. *Ment. Hyg. N.Y.*, **40**, 196–214.

Rodriguez, A., Rodriguez, M. & Eisenberg, L. (1959) The outcome of school phobia: A follow-up study based on 41 cases. *Amer. J. Psychiat.*, **116**, 540–544.

Ross, A. O. & Lacey, H. M. (1961) Characteristics of terminators and remainers in child guidance treatment. *J. Cons. Psychol.*, **25**, 420–424.

Seidman, F. (1957) *A study of some evaluation variables in a child guidance center.* Paper presented at the meeting of the American Association of Psychiatric Clinics for Children.

Strupp, H. (1962) Psychotherapy. *Annu. Rev. Psychol.*, **13**, 445–478.

Zausmer, D. M. (1954) The treatment of tics in childhood. *Arch. Dis. Childh.*, **29**, 537–542.

A Preliminary Assessment of the Extent of Interaction between Child Psychiatric Clinics and Public Schools*

HERSHEL BERKOWITZ

University of Colorado Medical Center

A great deal of attention has recently been focused on the role of the public school in the treatment and prevention of emotional disturbance in children. Public schools exert a significant impact upon the development of children, and have themselves become increasingly aware of the scope of this impact in recent years. The extent of their concern with the emotional as well as the educational development of their charges may, in part, be gathered from the large proportion of children whom they refer to treatment facilities each year.[1]

The Joint Commission on Mental Illness and Health (1961) has stressed the vital role which the public schools play in the general development of children, and has stressed the need for programs of primary prevention in the schools. The Commission's report calls for closer collaboration between treatment facilities and the schools. Other authors have also addressed this issue, directly or by implication stressing the benefits which might accrue from more contact and collaboration between educators and clinicians (Berkowitz, 1966; Caplan, 1961; Sanford, 1966; Sarason, Levine, Goldenberg, Cherlin & Bennet, 1966).

While there has been much agreement that closer contacts between clinics and schools would be useful, both in the areas of prevention and treatment of emotional disturbance in children, it is not clear to what

---

*Reprinted from *Psychology in the Schools*, Vol. V, No. 4, October 1968, pp. 291–295.

[1]Thirty percent of the children in treatment at the facility where the author is employed are referred directly by the schools. Additional children are brought to the clinic by their parents only after the schools have made them aware of their children's difficulties.

extent this principle has been implemented in actual practice. The present study is an attempt to assess the extent of contact and collaboration between the schools and four major child psychiatric treatment centers.

The most feasible way to begin such an assessment would be to examine the interaction between clinics and schools around cases referred for treatment by the schools. The most obvious question concerns the nature and number of contacts which are made between clinics and schools. A second question concerns the extent to which school contact varies in relationship to the kinds of difficulties which a child is experiencing in the school situation. One might expect, for example, that a school would require more support and assistance from a clinic if a child was an active behavior problem in the classroom than if he were more withdrawn and passive. Thus, the tendency for contacts between clinics and schools to vary in accordance with the nature of a child's symptomatology might be indicative of the amount of active collaborative interaction being maintained between the two involved institutions. An additional point of interest concerns the nature of treatment offered by the clinics. The work of Sarason *et al.* (1966) and of Sanford (1966) contains the implication that psychotherapy itself is not necessarily the only answer to children's difficulties and that a more flexible approach, emphasizing in some cases treatment, and in other cases the development of a growth-fostering environment might be more efficient and useful. It would thus be useful to consider the extent to which clinics vary the nature of treatment, and whether there is any relationship between such variation and possible variation in the contacts which they maintain with the schools.

METHOD

In order to answer these questions, each of four child psychiatric clinics, in locations ranging from the east coast, through the midwest, to the west coast, were asked to participate in the study. The clinics will be referred to as Clinics A, B, C, and D in the remainder of this report. All four clinics were members of the American Association of Psychiatric Clinics for Children (AAPCC) and were approved by the association for training in Child Psychiatry. The clinics' status as AAPCC training centers is taken as an indication that they are likely to provide models for practice in the child guidance area as a whole. Each clinic was asked to complete a data sheet on up to 25 children, in grades kindergarten through six who were in treatment at the clinic and whom had been referred there by the public schools. This information was to be extracted from case records by non-professional clinic personnel, and where possible supplemented by information from the children's therapists.

Subjects

Information was obtained on 63 boys and 16 girls, for a total of 79 children. Clinic A contributed information on 22, Clinic B on 18, Clinic C on 20, and Clinic D on 19 children. The mean age of the sample was 8.6 years, with a variance of 4.33, and there were no significant differences in age or sex between the children reported on by the four clinics.

Questionnaire

The data sheet questions relevant to the present report concerned the child's sex and age, the length of treatment in months, the nature of treatment, the nature of the child's difficulty as communicated by the school at time of referral, and the number of letter, telephone, and direct interpersonal contacts which occurred between clinic and school during the course of treatment. In addition, the clinics were asked to rate on a 3-point scale, the degree of urgency expressed by the school around the child's difficulties at the time of referral. This was apparently difficult to assess, however, and because almost all of the ratings were at the middle of the scale, it was not possible to evaluate the degree of urgency or to relate it to the other variables in the study.

In reporting on the nature of children's difficulties, four general primary problem areas were described, and it was requested that as many specific behaviors as were applicable to a given child's school reported difficulties be checked under each applicable category. Categories were selected on an empirical basis following a pilot study. They are as follows:

A. *Retardation* Mental retardation was seen as the primary problem by the school, and was a major area of concern.

B. *Primary Learning Problem* The school regarded the child's primary difficulty as one of not learning in one or more subject areas. No marked intellectual defect was noted, and social adjustment or behavior problems were either absent or were of only secondary concern to the school. The school may or may not have voiced concern about either brain damage or perceptual difficulties as being involved in this child's problem.

The child was described as being: (1) inattentive to material, (2) unable to concentrate, (3) unwilling or unable to master material, or (4) other (please specify).

C. *Primary Social Adjustment Problem* The school's primary complaint was of withdrawal, isolation, depression, or of some form of inappropriate affect or mood. Learning, behavior or intellectual problems, while perhaps present, were not strongly emphasized and were seen as of secondary importance and concern. The child was described as being: (1) withdrawn, (2) depressed, (3) isolated from peers, (4) frightened, (5) overly dependent, or (6) other (please specify).

D. *Primary Behavior Problem* The school's chief complaint was of disruptive behavior, impulsiveness, hyperactivity, aggression towards teachers or peers, or negativism. Problems in other areas were again seen by the school as secondary and the major concerns seem to be that the child was either unmanageable in the classroom or was disrupting the learning situation for other children. The child was described as being: (1) deliberately provocative, (2) disruptive of class, (3) impulsive, (4) hyperactive, (5) aggressive towards teachers, (6) aggressive towards peers, (7) negativistic and stubborn, (8) truant, (9) steals, or (10) other (please specify).

In many instances, problems were reported in more than one area. For the purposes of the study, a child's primary area of difficulty (primary symptom) was assessed by assigning him to that category in which the largest number of behaviors were checked. In nine cases, however, it was not possible to determine which of two areas was of primary concern, and in these instances, assignment to one or the other of the two categories was made at random.

FINDINGS AND DISCUSSION

The most striking finding obtained in this study concerns the paucity of contact between the clinics and schools involved. Clinics A and C, which had the greatest amount of contacts with the schools, averaged only around three such contacts for each child in treatment (*see* Table 3.1). While it is true that children in these clinics were seen in treatment for less than a year's time (*see* Table 3.2), short length of treatment alone does not account for this lack of contact. Clinic B, with the greatest length of treatment per child (*see* Table 3.2) had a total of only four contacts with the schools in the sample of 18 children reported upon.

Table 3.1. Total Contacts Between Clinics and Schools

Clinics	A	B	C	D
Mean	3.2227	0.222	3.25	0.737
Variance	9.994	0.183	10.092	1.208
N	22	18	20	19

Table 3.2. Length of Treatment in Months

Clinics	A	B	C	D
Mean	1.56	20.83	8.90	4.90
Variance	4.88	149.44	19.35	16.197
N	22	18	20	19

The lack of contact between clinics and schools is accentuated even further when one examines the kinds of contacts typically employed by the clinics involved. That is, the few contacts which did take place were typically in the form of letters or telephone calls; direct interpersonal contacts (school visits) between clinics and schools were extremely rare. While Clinic C averaged 3.25 contacts per child in treatment, the average number of school visits per child was only 0.91, the majority of contacts taking the form of telephone calls ($\bar{x}$ 1.95).[2] Similarly, Clinic A reported very few school visits ($\bar{x}$ 0.14), apparently relying heavily upon letters instead ($\bar{x}$ 2.72). Neither Clinic B nor D reported any school visits at all, except that two children in Clinic D's sample were attending a school at which the clinic maintained a program of consultation. These findings emphasize further the lack of close contact and communication between clinics and schools.

Adding further to this emphasis is the discovery that no relationship could be found between the number of contacts maintained with the school around a given child and the nature of the child's symptomatology. In no clinic did the difference in the number of contacts between any single symptom group and any other symptom group even approach

---

[2]Here, and elsewhere in this section, the comparisons cited are based upon *t* tests, significant to at least the 0.05 level of probability.

significance. Earlier in this paper the assumption was made that schools and clinics might interact more around the problems presented by certain kinds of children (e.g., behavior problems) than around those presented by other kinds of children (e.g., socially withdrawn children). The extent to which clinics and schools interacted differentially around children with different symptom pictures was thus viewed as a possible index of collaboration between the two institutions. The absence of such differential interaction, coupled with the dearth of over-all contacts between clinics and schools indicates that in fact, little if any meaningful collaboration is occurring between the clinics and the schools involved in this study. School contacts are few and seem to be determined by exigencies within each clinic rather than by any responsiveness to the problems presented by a given child in the school.

These conclusions lead to a consideration of another set of findings, findings which suggest that in general there seems to be little flexibility in the treatment programs maintained by the clinics under consideration. Despite large differences between clinics with respect to length of treatment (*see* Table 3.2), few differences occurred with respect to mode of treatment. All four clinics involved in the study relied almost exclusively upon individual treatment in their contacts with the children reported upon; 70 of the 79 children were seen in individual treatment, their parents being seen conjointly. In Clinic A, one child was placed in a nursery school, one received speech therapy, and one was seen jointly with a parent. In Clinic B, treatment was not specified for two children. In Clinic C, one child was seen in family treatment, and in D, only the parents were seen in two cases and a third child was placed in a nursery school. Only these 10 children, then, were involved in modalities other than individual treatment.

This heavy reliance upon individual treatment itself suggests a lack of flexibility in treatment program. Strongly supporting this impression is the finding that there is no relationship between length of treatment and children's symptomatology. While clear differences exist between clinics with regard to length of treatment, no such differences exist between different symptom groups within each clinic. Thus, Clinic A appears to rely upon short term treatment, regardless of a child's presenting symptomatology, Clinic B in long term treatment, etc.

Unless one assumes that neither length nor mode of treatment should be at all determined in relation to a child's symptomatology, these findings, together with the heavy reliance upon individual treatment mentioned earlier suggest a striking lack of flexibility in clinic treatment programs.

It appears that general clinic policy determines the nature and extent of treatment offered, and that little consideration is given to the nature of an individual child's difficulties in arriving at this determination.

On the basis of the findings discussed earlier it seems likely that such policy, in the clinics being considered here, does not include an emphasis upon collaboration with the public schools around children seen in treatment. Furthermore, it seems likely that such collaboration is not apt to occur so long as clinic policy, rather than the needs of individual cases determines treatment programming. The usefulness of such collaboration is an issue which requires a good deal of exploration. The kinds of cases in which such collaboration might be most useful have not been fully delineated, nor is the form of collaboration which would be most fruitful around a given kind of problem. These questions can best be answered on the basis of a flexible and innovative approach to treatment programming. If, as appears to be the case, treatment procedures within the clinics under consideration are governed largely by general clinic policy rather than by the exigencies of specific cases, such exploration becomes difficult indeed.

Only four clinics were involved in the present study, and clearly, there is a need for a more extensive investigation of the questions being addressed. However, the status of the participating clinics as AAPCC training centers suggests that the picture presented by them, in regard to psychoeducational collaboration and treatment programming, is probably a fairly accurate representation of practices among treatment centers in general. If this is the case then we are very far indeed from the close collaboration between clinics and educators which has been so strongly emphasized of late. If one accepts seriously the proposition that the school plays a vital role in a child's development in many areas of living, then this is an unfortunate situation indeed. Of even greater concern is the finding that even the exploration necessary to assess the possible value of such collaboration is apparently not encouraged in the clinics involved here.

REFERENCES

Berkowitz, H. Clinical child psychology in the schools. *Psychology in the Schools*, 1966, **3**, 223–229.

Caplan, G. *Prevention of mental disorders in children.* New York: Basic Books, 1961.

Joint Commission on Mental Illness and Health. *Action for mental health.* New York: Science Editions, 1961.

Sarason, S. B., Levine, M., Goldenberg, I. I., Cherlin, D. L., & Bennett, E. M. *Psychology in community settings: Clinical, educational, vocational, and social aspects.* New York: Wiley, 1966.

Sanford, N. *Self and society.* New York: Atherton, 1966.

COMMENT

The Levitt articles raise questions about the nature of the psychotherapy that the treated children received and the reasons for the improvement rates reported for the defectors or untreated children. For example, if two-thirds of all children who do not receive psychotherapy get better, what accounts for their improvement? If we assume that parents who have problems with their children ask advice from others concerning the management of such problems, it may be true that seeking advice from family, friends, or clergymen was beneficial in helping the parents of the children who were not treated by professionals. That is, there may be nothing special about traditional psychotherapy in prompting behavioral change which cannot be equaled or surpassed by general maturational factors and the varied though unsystematic parental attempts to deal with children's problems.

Another question raised by the Levitt articles concerns the referral of children to psychological or psychiatric clinics. That is, in the absence of any evidence that psychotherapy with children is effective, can one in clear conscience refer a parent to a traditional therapist? It should be emphasized again that Levitt's results do not prove that psychotherapy is futile. It may be that some children did benefit from psychotherapy but the measurement procedures were simply not precise enough to detect such changes. In addition, the improvement data presented by diagnostic categories suggest that different types of children improve at different rates. Children with special symptoms such as enuresis (bed wetting), tics, and school phobias seemed to improve at a much faster rate than children who exhibited deliquent, aggressive and anti-social problems. One cannot necessarily attribute the differences in improvement rates or even the improvement itself to the psychotherapy a child received; but the differing rates of improvement reported for the various diagnostic categories strongly suggest that future research should deal with particular types of treatments for particular types of problems. In addition, such results imply that the decision to refer a child to a clinic should—where possible—be based on the nature of the problem.

For example, if a child has a common problem such as thumbsucking, nail-biting, or enuresis which might change largely as a result of maturation or simple training procedures, the parent should probably first consult a close friend who has children and who would have dealt successfully with similar problems. It is important to reiterate that two-thirds of the children with problems improve without professional attention. However, if parents do not receive help from their friend's suggestions and if they are desirous of seeking professional advice, we would recommend that the teacher tell a parent to contact a therapist despite the results which question the efficacy of traditional psychotherapy. Problems such as aggressiveness and defiance of authority appear more resistant to change and in such cases professional help should probably be sought in all instances. Regardless of the absence of demonstrable behavior change, parents may benefit from simply receiving information about the nature of their children's problems.

The very term psychotherapy implies an almost mystical procedure whereby one deals with the psyche to effect change; and laymen and mental health professionals alike have tended to look to psychology and psychiatry for surprising, unexpected, and mysterious results. Unfortunately, straightforward, commonsense results generally do not have the appeal of intriguing mysterious phenomena. We feel that a return to some pragmatically-oriented treatment approaches that might have been advised by Grandma is in order. However, in contrast to the varied advice received from grandmothers and family friends, the treatment procedures evaluated in later sections of this book are generally based on a body of experimental literature and a conceptual framework which has demonstrated its potency in showing how behavior of children can be changed when certain psychological principles are applied systematically. The studies in this book will hopefully represent a clear and effective alternative to the kinds of traditional therapy described in the Levitt studies. Furthermore, if traditional therapists would adopt and aid teachers in the implementation of some of the procedures described in this book, they would not be plagued with the defense of a set of procedures whose efficacy remains equivocal.

CHAPTER 3

Praise and Positive Forms of Teacher Attention

Teacher attention in the form of a pat on the back, a hug, a smile, or a word of encouragement can be one of a teacher's most useful tools. By systematically using such teacher attention, the frequencies of a great variety of problem behaviors in pre-school and elementary school children have been successfully reduced. Fortunately, most teachers find the systematic use of praise natural and uncomplicated, and since teacher attention can be used to decrease a wide range of problem behaviors and to increase many appropriate behaviors, teachers should first attempt to handle most problems with teacher attention. Only when praise is ineffective should more complicated and powerful procedures, such as token reinforcement programs be employed.

One should not underestimate the skill required to maximize the effectiveness of praise. Let us consider the example of Sam, a child who is frequently out of his seat and engaging in activities which are very annoying to the rest of the class, e.g., wandering around the room and talking to others. We will assume that the teacher's goal is to increase the length of time Sam is in his chair working on his academic material. To maximize the effectiveness of her praise, the teacher must carefully consider variables such as the behaviors she selects to praise, the manner in which she shapes these behaviors, the temporal relationship between the desired behaviors and the praise, the content and variety of the praise.

The behaviors the teacher selects to praise should be behaviors compatible with learning, e.g., copying an assignment from the board. When possible, these behaviors should be incompatible with running around the room. Certainly one behavior she would choose to praise would be sitting on the chair. Although Sam will not automatically learn more if he is sitting down, sitting down is entirely incompatible with wandering around the room.

Next, the teacher should begin to shape the terminal behavior of sitting down. The importance of understanding "shaping" cannot be stressed enough since shaping is the central procedure in teaching any academic or social behavior. To shape a behavior, one must first establish what aspect of the terminal behavior the child is presently able to perform. Perhaps Sam is able to sit in his chair for only 1 minute. The teacher first praises him nearly every time he sits in his chair for 1 minute. After he begins to sit in his chair for 1 minute frequently, she praises him only when he is in his seat for approximately 1.5 minutes and continues to increase her requirement as he is able to sit for longer periods. As she does this, she also "thins" her schedule of praising, i.e., instead of praising him *every* time he is in his seat for 1.5 minutes, she praises him *every other* time, every third time, etc. Eventually, Sam will be sitting still for a 15–20 minute lesson along with the rest of the class. Thus, to shape a behavior, one should begin with a behavior the child displays, reinforce approximations to the desired terminal behavior, and as he improves, require his behavior to be more and more like the desired terminal behavior and begin to reduce the frequency of reinforcement.

The shaping procedure will proceed most quickly if the teacher can praise Sam immediately after he has met her criterion. Thus she should not wait until noon to tell him that he worked well and sat in his seat; rather, she should praise him immediately upon his completion of an assignment and while he is still sitting in his seat. In short, the teacher should "catch the child being good." Although other classroom responsibilities make this procedure an ideal not always attainable, the teacher should remember that immediate, frequent praise is most crucial early in the shaping process. In fact, she may find herself spending more time than usual with Sam initially, but careful shaping will result in her spending less and less time with him as he learns to sit in his seat.

Teacher attention of a positive nature should take many forms, e.g., a hug, a smile, a wink, a pat on the head, and statements like, "Good boy," "Sam, you're working so well today," and "I wish everyone were sitting as quietly as Sam." In addition, praise comments should often include a specification of exactly what behaviors the teacher likes. The clearer the teacher's requirements, the easier it will be for Sam to meet them. In order to make such requirements clear, the teacher should make comments like "Sam, I like the way you have been raising your hand to speak," "Your work is so much better when you pay attention," and "Sam, you're sitting and working very well!"

As will become apparent in the readings to follow, praising appropriate behavior is frequently accompanied by ignoring disruptive behavior. The rationale for using this combination of techniques is as follows. Ignoring disruptive behaviors will lead to their extinction, and the appropriate behaviors being shaped by praise will take the place of the inappropriate behaviors. Unfortunately, the experimental evidence for the effectiveness of ignoring disruptive behavior as an isolated procedure is not clear. There is some indication (Madsen, Becker, & Thomas, 1968), (5), that ignoring disruptive behavior without concommitant shaping of appropriate behavior can lead to an increase in disruptive behavior. This may be particularly true in the case of a whole classroom of disruptive children where peer reinforcement of disruptive behavior is frequent. However, in a class containing one or two problem children, ignoring disruptive behavior is probably an effective complement to praising appropriate behavior. It should be noted that "ignore" does not mean to ignore *all* disruptive behavior. Obviously, when children are being hurt, the teacher must intervene. (Methods of dealing with disruptive behavior which cannot be successfully ignored will be discussed in chapters dealing with punishment and token reinforcement programs.)

While careful, systematic use of teacher attention can be very effective, there are conditions under which teacher attention can increase the frequency of disruptive behavior. Disruptive behavior will increase in frequency if teacher attention follows or is contingent upon the disruptive behavior. For example, if every temper tantrum is followed by the teacher approaching the child, cuddling him, and making comments such as, "Everything will be all right," the frequency of tantrums is likely to increase. Disruptive behavior will increase in frequency if the child is punished by his peers when the teacher praises him for being good (O'Leary & Becker, 1967), (15). For example, the teacher says, "Sam, you've been so good today." Fred says, "Ha, ha, Sam's a goodie-good; Sam's teacher's pet!" If Fred's opinion is more important than the teacher's to Sam, he will probably stop displaying the behaviors that result in teacher praise and increase the frequency of peer-approved behaviors. One means by which the teacher may avoid this pitfall is to make her praise comments quietly and privately to Sam. A less likely but possible condition that may lead to an increase in disruptive behavior is illustrated by the following example. The teacher enthusiastically praises Alan, a very hyperactive and excitable child, for sitting quietly. The teacher's excitement may elicit or prompt excitement in Alan who may consequently bound from his seat, exactly the behavior the teacher wants to decrease in frequency. Again, quiet praise may be the technique of choice in such a case.

All of the articles in this chapter use a combination of praising appropriate behavior and ignoring disruptive behavior. Becker, Madsen, Arnold, and Thomas (1967) (4), provide an excellent description of the procedures for initiating a program in classroom behavior modification. They also include many informative comments by the five teachers who participated in the program. Madsen, Becker, and Thomas (1968) (5), expanded the work of Becker, Madsen, Arnold and Thomas (1967) with some experimental refinements. The precise instructions on how to praise and ignore are particularly useful. Zimmerman and Zimmerman (1962) (6), demonstrated how academic and tantrum behavior can be controlled with a praise and ignore procedure. Their example of the student with a spelling difficulty is especially interesting since they demonstrated that even the most well-meaning teacher can respond in ways that hinder rather than help the student.

In contrast to the first three studies which are concerned with demonstrating the effectiveness of the "praise and ignore" technique, Ward and Baker (1968) (7), addressed themselves to the question of possible side-effects of praise and ignoring. Specifically, they asked whether students whose disruptive behavior is reduced with a "praise and ignore" procedure improve in other areas, such as on psychological tests. A related question involved the possibility of symptom substitution, i.e., when one aspect of disruptive behavior is reduced in frequency, does the "illness" manifest itself by an increase in another disruptive behavior. Finally, Ward and Baker asked whether special attention to problem children leads to increased disruptive behavior in the rest of the class. They found no evidence for either generalization, symptom substitution, or adverse effects for the children who were not receiving special attention.

While the following articles will emphasize the control of classroom problems, praise and the complementary procedure of ignoring disruptive behaviors should be viewed as procedures for preventing the occurrence of problems. In short, the procedures discussed in this chapter should be a part of every teacher's repertoire and should be used on a *daily* basis with *both* normal and problem children.

ARTICLE 4

The Contingent Use of Teacher Attention and Praise in Reducing Classroom Behavior Problems*

WESLEY C. BECKER, Ph.D., CHARLES H. MADSEN, Jr., Ph.D.,
CAROLE REVELLE ARNOLD, M. A., and DON R. THOMAS, B. A.[1]

University of Illinois

The influence of the teacher's attention, praise, nearness and other social stimuli in maintaining deviant as well as positive social behavior in children has been repeatedly demonstrated with pre-school children (e.g., Allen, Hart, Buell, Harris & Wolf, 1964; Harris, Johnston, Kelley & Wolf, 1964). The expectancy that attention in almost any form may maintain deviant behaviors lies in the high probability that attentional responses from adults will be repeatedly followed by relief from aversive stimulation or the presentation of positive reinforcers in the history of most children. With such a history, stimuli produced by attentional responses are likely to become positive conditioned reinforcers which function to strengthen responses that are followed by such attentional stimuli. An essentially similar process is involved in the establishment of the effectiveness of praise comments such as "good boy," "that's fine," "you're doing great," which acquire conditioned reinforcement value through their repeated pairing with positively reinforcing stimuli.

Various forms of attention by nursery school teachers have been used

*Reprinted from *The Journal of Special Education*, Vol. 1. No. 3, 1967, pp. 287–307.

[1]We are extremely indebted to the principal of Hays School, Urbana, Ill., John M. Bustard, for his complete support of our work and to the teachers who made this research possible: Connie Carlson, Barbara Creinin, Joan Gusinow, Ozella Kelker and Mary Thomas. We also wish to acknowledge the assistance and support of Dr. Lowell M. Johnson, Director of Elementary Education, Urbana School District, Unit #116. This study was supported by grant HD-00881-04 from the National Institute of Child Health and Human Development.

to modify such behaviors as "regressive" crawling, isolate behavior, excessive orientation to adults, "aggressive" rather than cooperative peer interactions, and lethargy or passivity, among others. In addition, a similar procedure has been used to train mothers to modify the demanding-aggressive behavior of their children (Hawkins, Peterson, Schweid & Bijou, 1966). There is little question in the face of the extensive research by Sidney Bijou, Donald Baer and their students that a powerful principle for influencing the development of social behaviors has been isolated. The group of studies to be reported here demonstrate how the selective use of teacher attention and praise can be effectively applied in managing behavior problems in elementary classrooms; the studies also explore methods of training teachers to be more effective in this regard.

THE SETTING

The studies were carried out in Urbana, Illinois, in an elementary school whose population was 95% Negro. Our research group was invited into the school because it was believed that we could provide a service and they would provide us with a research laboratory. Seven teachers (half of those invited) agreed to participate in a workshop and seminar on the application of behavioral principles in the classroom. This report covers studies involving five of these teachers carried out between February and June, 1966.

The conduct of our research was guided to some extent by the necessity of establishing good relationships within the school system. Even though we had been invited by the school administration to see what we could do, there was still a need to convince teachers to participate, to keep them participating and to help them feel comfortable with observers in their classrooms. The comments of one of our teachers expresses better than we can the background into which the research had to be adapted.

> At one time few teachers wanted to work at our school, and only those who could not find a better position would teach. Suddenly the school found itself qualified under Title I of the Elementary and Secondary School Act to receive Federal aid. A large percent of its population was termed "culturally deprived" or perhaps more aptly, "deprived of middle-class culture." The school was bombarded with specialists, aids, volunteers, and experimental groups from the University of Illinois, all wanting to borrow the children or to help the children. By planning carefully, class interruptions were held to a minimum, but even then planning was done around a music teacher, an art teacher, a language teacher, special small group speech classes and language

classes. With all of this going on, plus many other items I shall leave unmentioned, it became increasingly more difficult to develop a continuous daily program. A self-contained classroom was a thing of the past. My attitude began to become very negative. I am not capable of judging the merits or demerits of this program, only time will measure this. I am merely attempting to describe briefly the setting, from my vantage point, into which a class in "behavior modification" was introduced. The enthusiasm held by some of the possibilities of behavior modification did not particularly excite me. The observing would interrupt my class and make it very difficult for me to function comfortably. The plan of the experiment was a bit nebulous, since too much knowledge of what was to be done would affect the results. To add to all this, these people were *psychologists!* My reinforcement history of working with psychologists need not be discussed here. I will simply state my relationship with them was inconsequential and negative; their reports were read carefully for some new information, but, finding none usually, the reports were filed as useless.

I vacillated for days on whether to take part in the class or not, finally deciding, despite my anxiety about the observation, that the only way to make educational psychology practical was to allow psychologists into the classroom to observe for themselves the classroom situation and problems.

Because of the need to sell ourselves to the teachers and maintain close contact with them, the seminar-workshop was initiated at the beginning of the second semester. At the same time we began to train observers, select target children and make baseline recordings of the children's behavior. This sequence of events is not ideal, since even though instructed otherwise the teachers were likely to try out the procedures they were learning in the workshop before we wished them to do so. The fact that they did this is suggested by an occasional decreasing baseline of problem behavior for a target child. Most changes, however, were dramatic enough that this potential loss in demonstrating an experimental effect did not grossly distort possible conclusions.

Most work in this area has used designs of the ABAB type. After baseline (A) an experimental effect is introduced (B), withdrawn (A), and reintroduced (B). We did not use this design (though we had an accidental counterpart to it in one room where the second (A) condition was provided by a student teacher) because: (a) we were afraid it might jeopardize the teacher's support; (b) the values of the experimental processes involved have been repeatedly confirmed; (c) "accidental" influences which might have produced changes in behavior would be unlikely to happen to ten children at the same time in five different classrooms; (d) we are unimpressed by arguments that Hawthorne effects, time alone or other "uncontrolled" variables such as the "weather" are causative in view of (b) and (c) above. By electing not to use an ABAB design we were also able to show the persistance of effects maintained by conditioned reinforcers over a longer period of time (nine weeks) than is usually the case. As a result of our caution and our success, we are now in a position where teachers and administrators in other schools are permitting us to establish controlled designs in return for our helping them with their problem children.

PROCEDURES

Selection of target children   The authors began by observing in the classrooms of the teachers who had volunteered for the project, and then discussing possible problem children with them. After tentative selection of two children in each class, explicit behavior coding categories were evolved and tested. The final selection was contingent upon demonstration that problem behavior did occur frequently enough to constitute a problem and could be reliably rated.

Rating categories   During the first four weeks the rating categories were repeatedly revised as reliability data demanded. Where it was not possible to get rater agreement for a category about 80%, a new definition was sought or a category abandoned. For example, in three classes (A, B & C) inappropriate talking and vocal noise were rated as separate categories (*see* Table 4.1). In two classes (D and E) the behavior patterns made it difficult to discriminate between these behaviors, so they were combined. The general rules followed in establishing categories were as follows:

1. They should reflect behaviors which interfered with classroom learning (time on task), and/or,
2. They should involve behaviors which violated the rules for permissible behavior established by the teacher and/or,
3. They should reflect particular behaviors a teacher wanted to change (e.g., thumbsucking).
4. The classes should be constituted by behaviors which were topographically similar in some important way.
5. The classes should be mutually exclusive.
6. The definitions must refer to observables and not involve inferences.
7. The number of classes should not exceed ten.

As Table 4.1 indicates, some codes were usable with all ten target children; others were devised especially for a particular child. For convenience we will speak of the Categories A and B in Table 4.1 as "deviant behaviors."

Table 4.1. Coding Categories for Children with Teachers A, B and C

Symbols	Class Label	Class Definitions

A. Behaviors Incompatible with Learning: General Categories

X	Gross Motor Behaviors	Getting out of seat; standing up; running; hopping; skipping; jumping; walking around; rocking in chair; disruptive movement without noise; moving chair to neighbor.
N	Disruptive noise with objects	Tapping pencil or other objects; clapping; tapping feet; rattling or tearing paper. *Be conservative, only rate if could hear noise with eyes closed. Do not include accidental dropping of objects or noise made while performing X above.*
A	Disturbing others directly and aggression	Grabbing objects or work; knocking neighbor's book off desk; destroying another's property; hitting; kicking; shoving; pinching; slapping; striking with object; throwing object at another person; poking with object; attempting to strike; biting; pulling hair.
O	Orienting responses	Turning head or head and body to look at another person, showing objects to another child, attending to another child. *Must be of 4 seconds duration to be rated. Not rated unless seated.*
!	Blurting Out, Commenting and Vocal Noise	Answering teacher without raising hand or without being called on; making comments or calling out remarks when no question has been asked; calling teacher's name to get her attention; crying; screaming; singing; whistling; laughing loudly; coughing loudly. *Must be undirected to another particular child, but may be directed to teacher.*
T	Talking	Carrying on conversations with other children when it is not permitted. *Must be directed to a particular child or children.*
‖	Other	Ignoring teacher's question or command; doing something different from that directed to do (includes minor motor behavior such as playing with pencil when supposed to be writing). *To be rated only when other ratings not appropriate.*

B. Special categories for children with teachers A, B and C (to be rated only for children indicated)

+	Improper position **Carole and Alice**	Not sitting with body and head oriented toward the front with feet on the floor, e.g., sitting on feet; standing at desk rather than sitting; sitting with body sideways but head facing front. *Do not rate if chair sideways but*

Table 4.1 *(continued)*

Symbols	Class Label	Class Definitions
		head and body both oriented toward the front with feet on the floor.
S	Sucking	Sucking fingers or other objects.
	Alice and Betty	
B	Bossing	Reading story out loud to self or other children *(do not rate ! in this case);* acting as teacher to other children, as showing flash cards.
	Carole	
‖	Ignoring	This category expanded to include playing with scissors, pencils, or crayons instead of doing something more constructive during free time.
	Charley	

C. Relevant Behavior

—— Relevant Behavior		Time on task, e.g., answers question, listening, raises hand, writing assignment. *Must include whole 20 seconds except for orienting responses of less than 4 seconds duration.*

Observer training and reliabilities Observers were obtained from undergraduate classes in psychology and education and were paid $1.50 an hour. Initially they worked in pairs, often in conjunction with one of the authors. After each rating session of 40 minutes, ratings were compared and discussed and reliability examined by category. Definitions were clarified and changes made when necessary. Reliabilities were above 80% before the baseline period was begun. Several reliability checks were made each week throughout baseline and periodically thereafter. As indicated in Figs. 4.1 to 4.5, reliability only occasionally fell below 80% when calculated by dividing the smaller estimate by the larger.

The observers were carefully trained not to respond to the children in the classes. They were to "fade into the walls." This procedure quickly extinguished the children's responses to the observers. Several incidents were reported where children were surprised to see the observers respond to a request from the teacher to move. After a while it was possible for other visitors to come into the class without distracting the children as they had in the past.

Rating procedure Except for a few occasional absences, target children were observed for 20 minutes a day, four days a week. In the experimental phase of the study frequency of reliability checks were reduced so that ratings of teacher behavior could also be obtained. Each observer had a clipboard with a stop watch taped to it. Observers would start their watches together and check for synchronization every five minutes (end of a row). They would observe for 20 seconds and then take ten seconds to record the classes of behavior which occurred during the 20-second period. All data are reported in terms of the percentages of the time intervals during which deviant behavior was observed to occur. The activities in which the children were involved varied considerably from day to day and contributed to daily fluctuation. For this reason only weekly averages are reported.

Ratings of teacher behavior At the beginning of the experimental phase for four teachers, and for a week prior to the experimental phase for teacher E, a 20-minute sample of the teacher's behavior was also obtained. The rating categories are given in Table 4.2. The main purpose of the ratings was to insure that the experimental program was being followed.

Experimental phase instructions Following a five-week baseline period (for most children) teachers were given instructions to follow for the nine-week experimental period. In all classes the teachers were given general rules for classroom management as follows (typed on a 5″ × 8″ card to be kept on their desks):

General Rules for Teachers
1. Make explicit rules as to what is expected of children for each period. (Remind of rules when needed.)
2. *Ignore* (do not attend to) behaviors which interfere with learning or teaching, unless a child is being hurt by another. Use punishment which seems appropriate, preferably withdrawal of some positive reinforcement.
3. Give *praise* and *attention* to behaviors which facilitate learning. Tell child what he is being praised for. Try to reinforce behaviors incompatible with those you wish to decrease.
   Examples of how to praise: "I like the way you're working quietly." "That's the way I like to see you work." "Good job, you are doing fine."
   Transition period. "I see Johnny is ready to work." "I'm calling on you because you raised your hand." "I wish everyone were working as nicely as X," etc. Use variety and expression.
   In general, give praise for achievement, prosocial behavior and following the group rules.

In addition to these general rules, teachers in classes A to D were given specific instructions with respect to their target children. An example follows:

Special Rules for Alice

Attempt to follow the general rules above, but try to give extra attention to Alice for the behavior noted below, but try not to overdo it to the extent that she is singled out by other children. Spread your attention around.

1. Praise sitting straight in chair with both feet and chair legs on floor and concentrating on own work.
2. Praise using hands for things other than sucking.
3. Praise attention to directions given by teacher or talks made by students.
4. Specify behavior you expect from her at beginning of day and new activity, such as sitting in chair facing front with feet on floor, attention to teacher and class members where appropriate, what she may do after assigned work is finished, raising hand to answer questions or get your attention.

The fifth teacher was given the general rules only and instructed not to give the target children any more special attention than was given the rest of the class. This procedure was decided upon because our observers

Table 4.2. Teacher Coding Categories

Symbols	Class Label	Class Definitions
C	Positive Contact	Positive physical contact must be included — such behaviors as embracing, kissing, patting (on head), holding arm, taking hand, sitting on lap, etc.
P	Verbal Praise	This category includes paying attention to appropriate behavior with verbal comments indicating approval, commendation or achievement such as: "That's good." "You're studying well." "Fine job." "I like you."
R	Recognition in Academic Sense	Calling on child when hand is raised. (Do not rate if child calls teacher's name or makes noises to get her attention.)
F	Facial Attention	Looking at child when smiling. (Teacher might nod her head or give other indication of approval — while smiling.)
A	Attention to Undesirable Behavior	This category includes the teacher's verbally calling attention to undesirable behavior and may be of high intensity (yelling, screaming, scolding or raising the voice) or of low intensity ("Go to the office." "You know what you are supposed to be doing." Etc.) Calling the child to the desk to talk things over should also be included, as well as threats of consequences. Score the following responses to deviant behavior separately:
L	Lights	Turning off the lights to achieve control.
W	Withdrawal of Positive Reinforcement	Keeping in for recess, sending to office, depriving child in the classroom.
/	Physical Restraint	Includes holding the child, pulling out into hall, grabbing, hitting, pushing, shaking.

felt that general classroom management was a problem for Mrs. E. She relied heavily on negative control procedures, and the general level of disruptive behaviors in the room was high. In view of this, we decided to see if the two target children in her class might not be used as barometers of a more general effect on the class of a change in control procedures.

When we first initiated the experimental phase of the study, we attempted to give the teachers hand signals to help them learn when to ignore and when to praise. This procedure was abandoned after the first week in favor of explicit instructions, as given above, and daily feedback on their progress. While hand signals and lights have been found to be effective in helping parents learn to discriminate when to respond or ignore (Hawkins, Peterson, Schweid & Bijou, 1966), the procedure is too disruptive when the teacher is in the middle of a lesson and is consequently placed in conflict about which response should come next.

At this point, the seminar was used to discuss and practice various ways of delivering positive comments. For some teachers, delivering positive comments was difficult, and their initial attempts came out in stilted, stereotyped form. With time, even our most negative teacher was smiling and more spontaneous in her praise (and enjoying her class more). Shortly after the experimental phase began, one teacher commented, "I have at least 15 minutes more every morning and afternoon in which to do other things."

The experimental phase was initiated March 30th and ended May 27th. A breakdown in the heating plant in part of the building for the week of April 8th (Week 7) accounts for the loss of data for some children that week.

RESULTS

The main results are presented in Figs. 4.1 to 4.5. The average "deviant" behavior for ten children in five classes was 62.13% during baseline and 29.19% during the experimental period. The t-test for the differences between correlated means was significant well beyond the 0.001 level. All children showed less deviant behavior during the experimental phase. However, differential teacher attention and praise were not very effective with Carole and did not produce much change in Dan until his reading skills were improved. Each child and class will be discussed in more detail and a breakdown of the behaviors which changed will be examined.

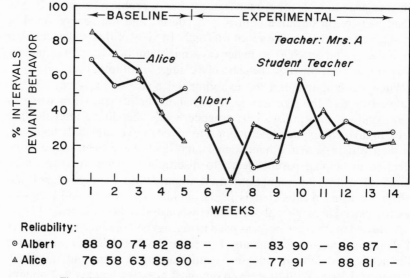

Reliability:

⊙ Albert	88	80	74	82	88	–	–	–	83	90	–	86	87	–
△ Alice	76	58	63	85	90	–	–	–	77	91	–	88	81	–

Fig. 4.1. Percentages of deviant behavior for two children in Class A.

Teacher A

Mrs. A is an anxious, sensitive person who expressed many doubts about her ability to learn to use "the approach" and about whether it would work with her middle-primary adjustment class. Both of the children on whom data were collected (Fig. 4.1) changed remarkably, as did Mrs. A and other members of her class. The teachers' views of what happened to themselves and to members of their classes are very instructive and will be presented elsewhere.

Albert (age 7–8) tested average on the Stanford-Binet, but was still on first-grade materials during his second year in school. He was selected because he showed many behaviors which made learning difficult. He talked, made other noises, did not attend to teacher and got in and out of his seat a lot. He loved to be "cute" and arouse laughter. In Mrs. A's words:

> He was a very noisy, disruptive child. He fought with others, blurted out, could not stay in his seat, and did very little required work. I had to check constantly to see that the minimum work was finished. He sulked and responded negatively to everything suggested to him. In addition, he was certain that he could not read. If I had planned it, I could not have reinforced this negative behavior more, for I caught him in every deviant act possible and often before it occurred. I lectured him and, as might be

expected, was making only backward motion. In November Albert came to me to tell me something and I was shocked by the intensity of his stuttering. He simply could not express his thought because his stuttering was so bad. I declared an "I like Albert Week." I gave him a great deal of attention, bragged about his efforts and was beginning to make some progress. This turned out to be the basis upon which an "ignore and praise" technique could be established. When the class began, I could see quickly what had happened to my relationship with Albert and had to fight to keep up my negative remarks until the baseline was established. Finally, I was free to use the technique. He quickly responded and his deviant behavior decreased to 10%, the lowest recorded. Along with the praising and ignoring, I attempted to establish a calmer atmosphere in which to work, and carefully reviewed class behavior rules. A good technique with Albert was to have him repeat the rule because "he was following it."

During Weeks 8 and 9 Albert showed less than 12% deviant behavior on the average. His worst performance out of seven observation days was 18.77% and he was under 5% deviant four out of seven days. Then an unplanned experimental reversal occurred.

Mrs. A relates what happened:

> As my student teacher gradually assumed more and more of the teaching load, the deviant behavior increased again. She made the same mistakes that I had. I deliberately planned her work so that I would be working with Albert most of the time. She felt the efficiency of the direct command, but she also realized that this was not modifying Albert's behavior in a lasting way. Gradually, she accepted the positive approach and in the last week or two of her work the deviant behavior began again to decrease. She had learned that with so negative a child as Albert, only building rapport by using positive reinforcement would succeed.
>
> Albert has improved delightfully. He still blurts out, but makes an effort to stop this. He is often seen holding his hand in the air, biting his lips. He completes his work on time, and it is done well. Often, when he has to re-do a paper, he takes it cheerfully and says, "I can do this myself." No sulking. He still finds it difficult to sit for a long period of time, but time on task has increased. He works very hard on his reading and has stated that he can read. His stuttering has decreased almost to zero. When the observers were questioned concerning this, they had detected little, if any stuttering. Most important to me, Albert has become a delightful child and an enthusiastic member of our class who feels his ideas are accepted and have merit.

Examination of the separate categories of behavior for Albert only serves to confirm the teacher's reports about which behaviors were most frequent and which changed the most.

The record of Mrs. A's behavior showed that she attended to and praised positive behaviors more than 90% of the time during the experimental period. Similar effective following of procedures was demonstrated for all five teachers.

Alice (age 7–8) scored 90 on the Stanford-Binet and was doing low first grade work. The data on Alice are less clear than those for Albert since her average deviant behavior showed a decline prior to the experimental phase. Mrs. A considered Alice a "sulking child." She would withdraw at times and not talk. She would sit inappropriately in her chair, suck her thumb, and make frequent movements of her hands and legs. Mrs. A said that Alice would report headaches after being scolded.

Mrs. A also indicated that two weeks before the end of baseline she told Alice that she was "disgusted with your sulking and would you please stop it." Mrs. A felt that this instruction in part accounted for the drop in deviant behavior prior to the experimental phase. Analysis of Alice's separate classes of behavior indicates, however, that the motor category declined from 45% to 25% to 8% the first three weeks of baseline and remained under 12% the rest of the experiment. Following this decline in "getting out of seat," frequency of odd sitting positions went from 0% to 25% to 18% over the first three weeks of baseline and declined to zero over the next two weeks. There was also a decline in talking during the first two weeks of baseline. In other words Mrs. A got Alice to stay in her seat, sit properly and talk less prior to the experimental change. The behaviors which show a correlation with the experimental change are decreases in *orienting, sucking* and *other* (ignoring teacher) response categories.

It is probable that the maintenance of Alice's improvement, except for the short lapse when the student teacher took over the class, can be attributed to the experimental program. Mrs. A reported at the end of the year as follows:

> Alice is a responsible, hard-working student who now smiles, makes jokes, and plays with others. When a bad day comes, or when she doesn't get her way and chooses to sulk, I simply ignore her until she shows signs of pleasantness. Through Alice I have learned a far simpler method of working with sulking behavior, the one most disagreeable kind of behavior to me. Alice is a child who responds well to physical contact. Often a squeeze, a pat, or an arm around her would keep her working for a long while. This is not enough, however. Alice is very anxious about problems at home. She must have opportunity to discuss these problems. Again through the class suggestions, I found it more profitable to discuss what she could do to improve her problems than to dwell on what went wrong. Alice's behavior is a good example of the effects of a calm, secure environment. Her time on task has lengthened and her academic work has improved.

Teacher B

Mrs. B had a lower intermediate class of 26 children. Before the experimental phase of the study, she tended to control her class through sharp commands, physical punishment and withholding privileges. The two children on whom observations were made (Fig. 4.2) showed consider-able change over the period of the experiment. Observers' comments indicate that Mrs. B was very effective in following the instructions of the experimental program. Only occasionally did she revert to a sharp com-mand or a hand slap.

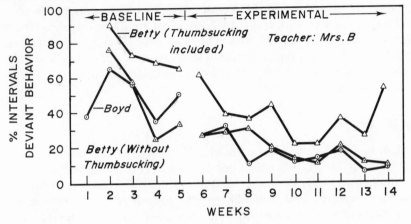

Reliability:

Boyd	80	86	85	92	95	93	–	–	–	94	–	93	–	–
Betty	–	91	63	85	90	91	–	100	90	93	93	89	–	93

Fig. 4.2. Percentages of deviant behavior for two children in Class B.

Betty (age 9–7) scored average on various assessments of intelligence and was doing middle third-grade work. Her initial problem behaviors included "pestering" other children, blurting out, sucking her thumb, making noises. She also occasionally hit other children. Often she said or did things that evoked laughter from others. As Fig. 4.2 shows, many of her problem behaviors showed a reduction during the baseline period (as happened with Alice), but thumbsucking did not. The experimental program brought thumbsucking under control for a while, but it increased markedly the last week of the experiment. Betty's other problem be-haviors showed continued improvement over the experimental period and remained at a level far below baseline for the last five weeks of the experimental period.

Boyd (age 9–7) was of average IQ. His achievement test placements varied between second- and third-grade levels. During baseline he was high on getting out of his seat and making other gross movements, talking out of turn and making noises. Mrs. B also reported that Boyd had difficulty "saying words he knows," giggled a lot and would not try to do things alone. He very much liked to be praised and tried not to do things which led to scolding. During this period Boyd was getting a great deal of teacher attention, but much of the attention was for the very behaviors Mrs. B wished to eliminate. Through a gradual shaping process Boyd learned to sit in his seat for longer periods of time working on task. He has learned to work longer by himself before asking for help. Mrs. B reports that he is less anxious and emotional, although we have no measure of this. Blurting out was not stopped entirely, but now he usually raises his hand, waits to be called on in full class activities and waits for his turn in reading.

Teacher C

Our biggest failure occurred in Mrs. C's middle primary class of about 20 children. Mrs. C was one of our most positive teachers, and we underestimated the severity of the many problems she was facing. With our present knowledge, we would likely have gone directly to a more potent token economy system for the whole class (*see* O'Leary & Becker, 1967). The above misjudgment notwithstanding, the experiment reported below is still of considerable value in pointing to one of the limits of "the approach," as our teachers came to call it. Besides focusing on Carole and Charley, as described below, we assisted Mrs. C in extinguishing tantrums in Donna (beginning Week 8), and in reducing swearing and hitting by Hope. The work with Donna was very successful.

Carole (age 7–5) scored from 78 to 106 on various intelligence tests. She was working at the mid first-grade level. Carole is an incessant beehive of activity. She scored high on response categories which indicate that she spent much time talking out of turn, turning in her seat, getting out of her seat, bossing other children and hitting others. Her most frequent behavior was talking when she should have been quiet. She was very responsive to peer attention. At times she would stand at the back of the room and read out loud to everyone. She liked to play teacher. She was also described as good at lying, cheating, stealing and smoking. Like most of the children in the study, Carole came from a deprived, unstable home. Descriptions of home backgrounds for most of the children in this study consist of sequences of tragic events (*see* Mrs. D).

The experimental phase of the program reduced Carole's average deviant behavior from about 75% during baseline to 55% for Weeks 7 to

9. A detailed analysis of Carole's responses shows that talking out of turn and blurting out still constituted over 30% of her deviant responses during Weeks 7 to 9. However Carole was in her seat more, sitting properly, responding more relevantly to teacher, and was on task 50% of the time. We were not satisfied with her improvement and felt that Charley (our other target child) while doing well, could also do better.

On April 25th (Week 9) we instituted a program in which ten cent notebooks were taped to Carole and Charley's desks. Mrs. C told the children that every 30 minutes she would put from one to ten points in their notebooks, depending on how hard they worked and how well they followed the class rules. At the end of the day if they had a certain number of points they could exchange the points for a treat. The initial reinforcer was candy. During this phase the rest of the class could earn a candy treat by helping Carole and Charley earn points. In this way they were not left out. The number of points required was based on a shifting criterion geared to Carole and Charley's progress. As noted below and in Fig. 4.3, Charley responded well to this added incentive and was gradually shifted to saving points over two, then three, then five days to earn puzzles. Carole still resisted. She worked for points for several days, but on May 3rd (Week 10) she announced she was not going to work for points today, and she didn't. She was a hellion all day. Over the following

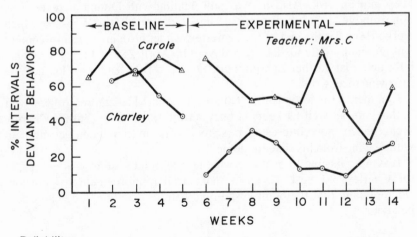

Fig. 4.3. Percentages of deviant behavior for two children in Class C.

two weeks Carole worked for a ring and then the components of a make-up kit. We were seeking stronger reinforcers and were stretching the delay of reinforcement.

On May 17th Mrs. C reported that Carole had earned points for three days in a row and was entitled to a component of the make-up kit. The 20% deviant behavior of that week showed that Carole could behave and work. The last week of May, Carole was back to talking and blurting out again. While some of our reinforcers were effective, Carole still needs a classroom where the structure would require her to depend on the teacher for praise and attention and where peer attention to her deviant behavior could be controlled.

Charley was presumed to be age 8 years and 2 months at the start of the study, but in fact was two years older. His IQ was given as 91, but with a proper CA was 73. He was doing mid-first-grade work in most subjects. Charley picked on the girls, hit other boys and bullied them (he was larger), got loud and angry if reprimanded, and at times he sulked and withdrew. No one was going to force him to do anything. Our ratings showed him highest in categories labeled *motor activities* (out of seat), *ignoring* teacher's requests, *turning in seat* and *talking* to peers.

Initially Charley responded very effectively to rules and praise. He loved to receive praise from Mrs. C. However, praise was not enough to keep him on task. Also he was still fighting with Donna at recess. As noted above, a point system was initiated April 25th (Week 9) which worked well for the rest of the semester, while the delay of reinforcement was gradually extended to five days. On April 25th Charley was also informed that further fighting with Donna would lead to a loss of the following recess.

Comments on May 10th: "Charley is great. He ignores others who bother him as well as keeping busy all the time." May 26th: "Charley seems much more interested in school work and has been getting help with reading from his sister at home."

It is not possible to evaluate whether the point system was necessary for Charley. At best we know that social reinforcement helped considerably and that the point system did help to maintain good classroom behavior.

Teacher D

Mrs. D teaches a lower intermediate class of about 25 children. One group of her children had been in a slow class where the teacher allowed them "to do what they wanted." A brighter group had been taught by a strict teacher who enforced her rules. Since September the class has been divided and subdivided six times and has had seven different teachers. Mrs. D describes the families of her two target children as follows:

> Don has average ability and achieves below the average of the class. The father works late afternoons and evenings. The mother, a possible alcoholic, has been known to do some petty shoplifting. She is frequently away from home in the evening. One older brother drowned at the age of seven. An older sister with above average ability left home at the age of fifteen. She later married. Her husband was killed this spring in an automobile accident. Another older sister lost an arm at a very early age and is an unwed mother at the age of fourteen. Another sister attends Junior High School.
>
> Dan's mother is of mixed parentage and has been in the hospital this year. The mother is divorced. The father remarried and it appears that there is a good relationship between the two families; however, the father has been in prison because of "dope."

Mrs. D was initially quite bothered about being observed, but quickly learned to look more carefully at the way in which her behavior affected that of her class.

Don was 10 years and 4 months old at the start of the study. In April of 1961 he was recommended for EMH placement. Since kindergarten his performance on intelligence tests had risen from 75 to 102. He was obviously of at least average ability. His level of school achievement was between grades two and three, except for arithmetic reasoning (4.3). Observations revealed a high frequency of moving around the room and talking when he should have been working. He was called "hyperactive" and said to have poor "attention." His talking to other children was quite annoying to his teacher and interfered with classwork. Don appeared to respond to teacher attention, but obtained such attention most often when he was acting up.

The experimental procedures quickly brought Don's level of deviant behavior down from about 40% to under 20%. He was particularly good at working when the task was specifically assigned. When he was left to his own devices (no stimulus control) he would start to play around. These observations suggest that Don would greatly profit from more individualized programming of activities. He was reported to show improved behavior in his afternoon classes involving several different teachers.

Danny was age 10 years, 6 months at the start of the study. He measured near 85 on several IQ tests. His classroom behavior was described as being generally disruptive and aggressive. During baseline he scored high on *motor, talking, orienting, ignoring* and *noise*. By all standards Danny was a serious behavior problem. He seldom completed work assignments and was in the slowest reading group. Because of the severity of his behavior and difficulty staying on task, an educational diagnosis was requested during the early part of baseline. The staffing at Week 2 indicated a two-year reading deficit and a one-year arithmetic deficit. The following comments from the psychological report which followed the staffing are of interest:

> Danny's lack of conscience development and other intrinsic controls still present a serious problem in controlling his behavior. His immediate impulsive aggressive reaction to threatening situations may hamper any educational remediation efforts. The evidence presented still suggests that Danny, in light of increasing accumulation of family difficulties, lack of consistent masculine identification, his irascible and changeable nature, and educational pressures will have a difficult time adjusting to the educational situation.
>
> It is our opinion that unless further action is implemented, i.e., school officials should attempt to refer this boy to an appropriate agency (Mental Health, Institute for Juvenile Research) for additional help and correction, he is likely to become a potentially serious acting out youngster.

The data on Danny presented in Fig. 4.4 are most interesting. They show a small improvement in his behavior the first two weeks of the experimental phase. Generally the observers felt the whole class was quieter and better behaved. Danny especially stayed in his seat more of the time. However, a most dramatic change occurs when tutoring sessions in reading were begun (Week 8 to 9). It would appear that unless the

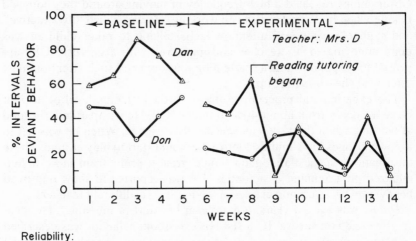

Fig. 4.4. Percentages of deviant behavior for two children in Class D.

child is capable of following the assigned activity, social reinforcement for "on task" behavior is not enough. In Danny's data this point is supported by an analysis of the kinds of activities where he showed the most improvement. Dan was averaging 80% deviant behavior when the activity was workbook assignments related to reading and language. In the reading group, where the teacher was there to help and direct activity, he averaged only 40% deviant behaviors. By early May (Week 11) the amount of deviant behavior during "seat work" activities had dropped to an average of 15%, with only an occasional bad day.

Well into April, Danny had not shown much improvement in his afternoon classes (with teachers not in our program). Several observations suggested that he would still show high rates of deviant behaviors on days when he was otherwise on task, if the activity shifted to something he could not do. For example, May 5th showed 25% deviant behavior during a period of seat work (*reading*), 30% during *spelling*, and 55% an hour later during *grammar* and *composition*. Danny was just beginning to move in reading, but was not ready for composition. The increase during Week 13 is due to one day where he was rated 40% off task. The rater comments indicate the basis for the "deviant" rating: "Danny should have been sitting quietly after doing his work, but, instead of just waiting for the next assignment, he was playing with clay with another child. However, he was very quiet." Comments from May 9th and 10th give some flavor of the changes which occurred.

> May 9th: Mrs. D reported that Danny, after he finished reading, immediately started on spelling. This is a highly unusual occurrence. Until now Danny has avoided spelling activities until made to work on them.
> May 10th: Danny completely surprised the observer when he was on task the whole observation period, except for one minor talking to neighbor.

In view of the rather dramatic changes Danny has made in classroom behavior through a combination of remediation and social reinforcement, perhaps it is necessary to question the assumptions implicit in the quotation from Danny's psychological report given earlier. It should be noted that no attempt was made to work on family problems, his conscience, his masculine identification, or his "irascible nature" in changing his adjustment to school.

Teacher E

We have saved until last the most dramatic of all the changes produced in teachers and children. Mrs. E had a lower primary class of 23 children.

Observation of February 1, 1966:

> Six children were in a reading group and 15 were working on individual projects. The noise level for the entire classroom was extremely high and went higher just before recess. Some behaviors noted included whistling, running around the room (5 occasions), yelling at another child (many times), loud incessant talk, hitting other children (7 times), pushing, shoving, and getting in front of each other in recess line. Mrs. E would re-establish quiet by counting to 10, after giving a threat.

Observations suggested that control was obtained mainly by shouting, scolding and the like in an attempt to suppress unwanted behaviors. This approach would work for a while, but there was then a gradual build up in noise until quiet was again demanded. Figure 4.5 shows that Mrs. E's responses on three days prior to a shift to positive reinforcement contained very few positive statements. Essentially, there was nothing to maintain appropriate classroom behaviors. The focus was on what not to do rather than what to do. There is a good possibility that the attention given deviant behavior in fact served to reinforce it.

Edward and *Elmer* were selected as barometers which might reflect changes for the whole class. Mrs. E was given the general instructions

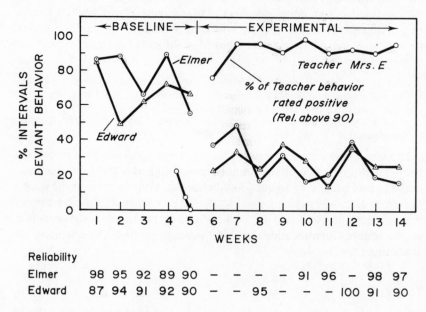

Reliability													
Elmer	98	95	92	89	90	–	–	–	–	91	96	–	98	97
Edward	87	94	91	92	90	–	–	95	–	–	–	100	91	90

Fig. 4.5. Percentages of deviant behavior for two children in Class E, and change in teacher E's behavior.

presented above but no special instructions for Edward and Elmer. They were not to receive more attention than other members of the class. She was to make her rules clear, repeat them as needed, ignore deviant behavior and give praise and attention to behavior which facilitated learning. We wanted to see if a general approach to classroom management would be effective with children showing a high level of deviant behavior. The rating of Mrs. E's behavior before and after the change clearly shows an effect of the experimental instructions and training on her behavior.

Edward (age 6–8) tested 95 on the Stanford-Binet. Mrs. E considered him to be "distractible," to have poor work habits, show poor attention and not to comprehend what he read. He never finished assignments. He could sight read and spell first grade words. The baseline observations showed a high incidence of wandering about the room, turning around in his seat, talking at the wrong time and making odd noises. He also showed little peer play.

A psychological examination in January of 1966 stressed Edward's poor social history (his parents had not talked to each other for three years), his lack of enthusiasm and emotional responsiveness, the apparent restriction on his peer interaction by his mother and his need for better listening and language skills. Edward received speech therapy while in kindergarten. Throughout the baseline and experimental phase of this study, Edward was seen by a social worker and continued in speech therapy. In view of the fact that his (and Elmer's) behavioral changes are found to be directly associated with the change in classroom procedures, rather than time per se, these other treatments do not offer convincing alternative explanations for the data.

Edward greatly reduced the time he spent in aimless wandering, twisting in his seat and talking. He responded well to praise in both the reading group and class activities. Mrs. E reports that he began to complete assignments. He also showed better give and take with his peers, and would laugh, cry and make jokes. While still "distractible," he has learned to work independently for longer periods of time.

Elmer (6 years, 10 months) scored 97 on a group IQ test. He apparently started out the school year working well, but his work deteriorated. He seemed "nervous," hyperactive and would not work. He threw several tantrums and would cry if his work was criticized. His twin sister was also in the class and was doing well. By comparison Elmer often lost out. The parents expected as much of Elmer as of his sister. During baseline he was rated as showing inappropriate gross motor behaviors as much as 70% of the time. *Talking* was as high as 50% at times. *Noise* and *turning* in seat were at about 10% each. Initially our observers thought he was brain damaged.

Elmer's rapid response to positive reinforcement and a better structured classroom made it possible for him to stay on task longer. However, he did not improve greatly in his reading group. When the children were silently reading, he would at times clown and make noises. More work on reading will be necessary for academic progress.

Elmer's father came to work as a teacher's aid in one of our other classes just after the shift off baseline. His work with Mrs. C and changes in Elmer led slowly to his accepting the value of a positive rather than a punitive approach. Very likely father's attempt to be more rewarding with Elmer contributed to the maintenance of Elmer's improved classroom behavior. More to the point, however, is the fact that Elmer's improved classroom behavior (we showed father the graph during Week 9) served to reinforce father's acceptance of a positive approach.

In her report at the end of the semester Mrs. E felt that 12 of 23 children in her class definitely profited from her change in behavior, that six children were unchanged, three somewhat improved and two more deviant. The children who were reported unchanged tended to be the quiet and submissive ones who escaped Mrs. E's attention much of the time. From her own comments, it is likely that those reported to be more deviant seem so only because they stand out from the group more now that Elmer and Edward are not such big problems.

IMPLICATIONS

The results of these investigations demonstrate that quite different kinds of teachers can learn to apply behavioral principles effectively to modify the behavior of problem children. These results extend to the elementary classroom, with normal teacher-pupil ratios, the importance of *differential* social reinforcement in developing effective social behaviors in children. Work now in progress suggests that rules alone do nothing and that simply ignoring deviant behavior actually increases such behavior. The combination of ignoring deviant behavior and reinforcing an incompatible behavior seems critical. Nearly all of our teachers found that the technique of praising a child who was showing an incompatible appropriate behavior, when another child was misbehaving, was especially effective. This action keeps the teacher from attending to the deviant act and at the same time provides vicarious reinforcement for an incompatible behavior. In the future we hope to bring together a group of techniques which various teachers found effective in implementing the general strategy of this project.

These findings add support to the proposition that much can be done by the classroom teacher to eliminate behaviors which interfere with learning without extensive changes in the home or intensive therapy.

REFERENCES

Allen, K. E., Hart, B. M., Buell, S. J., Harris, F. R., & Wolf, M. M. Effects of social reinforcement on isolate behavior of a nursery school child. *Child Development*, 1964, **35**, 511–518.

Harris, F. R., Johnston, M. K., Kelley, C. S., & Wolf, M. M. Effects of positive social reinforcement on regressed crawling of a nursery school child. *Journal of Educational Psychology*, 1964, **55**, 35–41.

Hawkins, R. P., Peterson, R. F., Schweid, E., & Bijou, S. W. Behavior therapy in the home: Amelioration of problem parent-child relations with the parent in a therapeutic role. *Journal of Experimental Child Psychology*, 1966, **4**, 99–107.

O'Leary, K. D., & Becker, W. C. Behavior modification in an adjustment class: A token reinforcement program. *Exceptional Children*, 1967, **33**, 637–642.

Wahler, R. G. Winkel, G. H., Peterson, R. F., & Morrison, D. C. Mothers as behavior therapists for their own children. *Behaviour Research and Therapy*, 1965, **3**, 2, 113–124.

ARTICLE 5

Rules, Praise, and Ignoring: Elements of Elementary Classroom Control*

CHARLES H. MADSEN, JR., WESLEY C. BECKER,
and DON R. THOMAS

Florida State University and University of Illinois

Abstract: An attempt was made to vary systematically the behavior of two elementary school teachers to determine the effects on classroom behavior of Rules, Ignoring Inappropriate Behaviors, and showing Approval for Appropriate Behavior. Behaviors of two children in one class and one child in the other class were recorded by observers, as were samples of the teachers' behavior. Following baseline recordings, Rules, Ignoring, and Approval conditions were introduced one at a time. In one class a reversal of conditions was carried out. The main conclusions were that: (a) Rules alone exerted little effect on classroom behavior, (b) Ignoring Inappropriate Behavior and showing Approval for Appropriate Behavior (in combination) were very effective in achieving better classroom behavior, and (c) showing Approval for Appropriate Behaviors is probably the key to effective classroom management.

Modern learning theory is slowly but surely increasing its potential for impact upon social problems. As problems in social development and interaction are more closely examined through the methods of experimental analysis, the importance of learning principles in everyday life becomes clearer. The potential contribution of these developments to

*Reprinted from the *Journal of Applied Behavior Analysis*, Vol. 1, No. 2, Summer 1968, pp. 139–150. Copyright 1968 by the Society for the Experimental Analysis of Behavior, Inc.

[1]We wish to express our appreciation to the teachers involved, Mrs. Barbara L. Weed and Mrs. Margaret Larson, for their cooperation in a study which involved using and applying procedures which at times made their teaching duties very difficult. Gratitude is expressed to the Director of Elementary Education, Unit District # 116, Urbana, Illinois, Dr. Lowell M. Johnson, and to the principals of Thomas Paine and Prairie Schools, Richard Sturgeon and Donald Holste. This study was supported by Grant HD-00881-05 from the National Institutes of Health. Reprints may be obtained from Wesley C. Becker, Bureau of Educational Research, 284 B Education Bldg., University of Illinois, Urbana, Illinois 61801.

childrearing and education appears to be especially significant. This report is a part of a series of studies aimed at demonstrating what the teacher can do to achieve a "happier", more effective classroom through the systematic use of learning principles. The study grows out of a body of laboratory and field research demonstrating the importance of social reinforcers (smiles, praise, contact, nearness, attention) in establishing and maintaining effective behaviors in children. Extensive field studies in experimental nursery schools by Wolf, Bijou, Baer, and their students (e.g., Hart, Reynolds, Baer, Brawley, and Harris, 1968; Allen, Hart, Buell, Harris, and Wolf, 1965; Bijou and Baer, 1963) provided a background for the extension of their work by the present authors to special and typical elementary classrooms. In general, we have found to date that teachers with various "personalities" and backgrounds can be trained systematically to control their own behavior in ways which will improve the behavior of the children they are teaching. (Becker, Madsen, Arnold, and Thomas, 1967). We have also found that teachers can "create" problem behaviors in the classroom by controlling the ways in which they respond to their pupils (Thomas, Becker, and Armstrong, 1968; Madsen, Becker, Thomas, Koser, and Plager, 1968). It is hoped that field studies of this sort will contribute to more effective teacher training.

The present study is a refinement of an earlier study of Becker *et al.* (1967), in which the behavior of two children in each of five classrooms was recorded and related to experimentally controlled changes in teacher behaviors. The teachers were instructed and guided to follow a program which involved making classroom rules explicit, ignoring disruptive behaviors unless someone was getting hurt, and praising appropriate classroom behaviors. Under this program, most of the severe problem children under study showed remarkable improvements in classroom behavior. However, that study lacked certain controls which the present study sought to correct. First, the teachers in the earlier study were in a seminar on behavior theory and practice during baseline conditions. Some target children improved during baseline, apparently because some teachers were beginning to apply what they were learning even though they had been requested not to do so. Second, public relations and time considerations did not make it possible to introduce the components of the experimental program one at a time (rules, ignoring, and praise) to better study their individual contributions. Third, a reversal of teacher behavior was not attempted. Such a reversal would more conclusively show the importance of teacher's behavior in producing the obtained changes. Fourth, extensive recordings of teacher behavior under all experimental conditions were not undertaken in the earlier study. The present study attempted to deal with each of these problems.

METHOD

Procedures

Teachers in a public elementary school volunteered to participate in the study. After consultation with teachers and observation of the children in the classroom, two children with a high frequency of problem behavior were selected for study in each class. Previously developed behavioral categories (Becker *et al.*, 1967) were modified for use with these particular children and baseline recordings were made to determine the frequency of problem behaviors. At the end of the baseline period the teachers entered a workshop on applications of behavioral principles in the classroom which provided them with the rationale and principles behind the procedures being introduced in their classes. Various experimental procedures were then introduced, one at a time, and the effects on the target children's behaviors observed. The experiments were begun in late November and continued to the end of the school year.

Subjects

Classroom A   There were 29 children in Mrs. A's middle-primary (second grade) room who ranged in school progress from mid-first-grade level to early-third-grade level. Cliff and Frank were chosen as the target children.

Cliff was chosen because he displayed no interest in school. In Mrs. A's words, "he would sit throughout entire work periods fiddling with objects in his desk, talking, doing nothing, or misbehaving by bothering others and walking around the room. Lately he has started hitting others for no apparent reason. When Cliff was required to stay in at recess to do his work, he would complete the work in a short time and it was usually completely accurate. I was unable to motivate him into working on any task during the regular work periods." Cliff is the son of a university professor who was born in Europe and immigrated when Cliff was 5-yr old. Cliff scored 91 on an early (CA 5-3) intelligence test. This score was discounted by the examiner because of language problems. His group IQ scores rose steadily (CA 5-9, IQ 103; CA 6-2, IQ 119; CA 7-1, IQ 123). His achievement scores indicated a low second-grade level at the beginning of the present study. Cliff was seen by the school social worker throughout the entire first grade and throughout this entire study.

Cliff was observed early in the year and it was noted that he did not respond once to teacher's questions. He played with his fingers, scratched himself repeatedly, played in his desk, paid no attention to the assignment and had to stay in at recess to finish his work. Almost continually he made blowing sounds and talked to himself. On occasions he was out of his seat making noises and talking. He would leave the room without permission. Before the study began the observers made the following notes: "What a silly kid, writing on the bottom of his shoes, writing on his arms, blowing kisses at the girls. He was vying for the attention of the girl behind him, but she ignored him. . . . Poor Cliff! he acts so silly for his age. He tried to talk to the other kids, but none of them would pay attention to him. . . . Cliff seems concerned with the little girl beside him (girl behind him last week). He has a sign on his desk which reads, 'Do you love me?'. . . ."

Frank was described by his teacher as a likable child. He had a record of misbehavior in the classroom and intense fighting on the playground. He was often out of his seat talking to other children and did not respond to "discipline". If someone was reprimanded for doing something, Frank would often do the same thing. Test scores indicated an IQ of 106 (Stanford-Binet) and achievement level just under beginning second grade at the start of school (average California Achievement Test scores 1.6 grades). The school psychologist noted that Frank's mother was a person "who willingly permitted others to make decisions for her and did not seem able to discipline Frank." Father was absent from the home during the entire year in the Air Force.

Classroom B   Twenty children were assigned to Mrs. B's kindergarten room. Two children were observed initially; one moved from the community shortly after baseline was taken, leaving only Stan for the study.

Stan was described as coming from a truly pathetic home environment. The mother was not married and the family of four children subsisted on state aid. One older brother was enrolled in a special class for the educable retarded. At the beginning of the year, Stan's behavior was characterized by the teacher as "wild". She reported that, "Stan would push and hit and grab at objects and at children. He had no respect for authority and apparently didn't even hear directions. He knew how to swear profusely, and I would have to check his pockets so I would know he wasn't taking home school equipment. He would wander around the room and it was difficult to get him to engage in constructive work. He would frequently destroy any work he did rather than take it home."

The difficult home situation was made manifest during the month of March. Stan had been absent for two weeks and it was reported that his mother was taking her children out of public school and placing them in a local parochial school. Investigation by school personnel indicated that Stan's mother had moved the children into a relative's home and had gone to the hospital to have another illegitimate baby. A truancy notice was filed for all four children including Stan. Following legal notice the children were returned to school.

Rating of Child Behavior

The same rating schedule was used in both classrooms except that Isolate Play was added to the list of Inappropriate Behaviors for the kindergarten. Since the children were expected to be involved in structured group activities during observation periods, going off by oneself to play with the many toys or materials in the room was considered inappropriate by the kindergarten teacher. Inappropriate Behavior was defined as the occurrence of one or more of the behaviors listed under Inappropriate Behavior in Table 5.1 during any observation interval.

Observers were trained in the reliable use of the rating schedule before baseline recordings began. Training consisted of practice in use of the rating schedule in the classroom. Two observers would each rate the same child for 20 min and then return to the research office to compare their ratings and discuss their differences with their supervisor. Training was continued until reliability was above 80% on each behavior code. Training lasted approximately two weeks. Reliability was determined periodically throughout the study by dividing the number of agreements by the number of agreements plus disagreements. An agreement was defined as a rating of the same behavior class in the same observation interval. Average reliability over children, behavior classes, and days for the 69 occasions (out of 238) on which it was checked was 81%. Single day reliabilities ranged from 68% to 96%. Reliabilities were checked in each phase of the study.

Instructions to observers followed those used by Becker *et al.* (1967). In essence, the observers were not to respond to the children, but to fade into the background as much as possible. Teachers, as well as children, quickly learned not to respond to the observers, although early in the study one observer was attacked by a kindergarten child. The observer did not respond to the behavior and it quickly disappeared. Experimental changes were initiated without informing observers in an attempt to control any observer bias. However, the changes were often dramatic enough

Table 5.1.   Behavioral Coding Categories for Children

I. Inappropriate Behaviors

A. *Gross Motor.* Getting out of seat, standing up, running, hopping, skipping, jumping, walking around, moving chair, *etc.*

B. *Object Noise.* Tapping pencil or other objects, clapping, tapping feet, rattling or tearing paper, throwing book on desk, slamming desk. Be conservative, only rate if you can hear the noise when eyes are closed. Do *not* include accidental dropping of objects.

C. *Disturbance of Other's Property.* Grabbing objects or work, knocking neighbor's books off desk, destroying another's property, pushing with desk (only rate if someone is there). Throwing objects at another person without hitting them.

D. *Contact (high and low intensity).* Hitting, kicking, shoving, pinching, slapping, striking with object, throwing object which hits another person, poking with object, biting, pulling hair, touching, patting, *etc.* Any physical contact is rated.

E. *Verbalization.* Carrying on conversations with other children when it is not permitted. Answers teacher without raising hand or without being called on; making comments or calling out remarks when no questions have been asked; calling teacher's name to get her attention; crying, screaming, singing, whistling, laughing, coughing, or blowing loudly. These responses may be directed to teacher or children.

F. *Turning Around.* Turning head or head and body to look at another person, showing objects to another child. Attending to another child.

Must be of 4-sec duration, or more than 90 degrees using desk as a reference. Not rated unless seated. If this response overlaps two time intervals and cannot be rated in the first because it is less than 4-sec duration, then rate in the interval in which the end of the response occurs.

G. *Other Inappropriate Behavior.* Ignores teacher's question or command. Does something different from that directed to do, including minor motor behavior such as playing with pencil or eraser when supposed to be writing, coloring while the record is on, doing spelling during the arithmetic lesson, playing with objects. *The child involves himself in a task that is not appropriate.* Not rated when other Inappropriate Behaviors are rated. Must be time off task.

H. *Mouthing Objects.* Bringing thumb, fingers, pencils, or any object in contact with the mouth.

I. *Isolate Play.* Limited to kindergarten free-play period. Child must be farther than 3 ft from any person, neither initiates or responds to verbalizations with other people, engages in no interaction of a nonverbal nature with other children for the entire 10-sec period.

II. Appropriate Behavior

Time on task; *e.g.*, answers question, listens, raises hand, works on assignment. Must include whole 10-sec interval except for Turning Around responses of less than 4-sec duration.

that observer comments clearly reflected programmed changes in teacher's behavior.

The target children were observed for 20 min per day, three days a week. In the middle-primary class, observations were taken when the children were engaged in seat work or group instruction. In the kindergarten class, observations were made when structured activities, rather than free play, were expected. Each observer had a clipboard, stopwatch, and rating sheet. The observer would watch for 10 sec and use symbols to record the occurrence of behaviors. In each minute, ratings would be made in five consecutive 10-sec intervals and the final 10 sec would be used for recording comments. Each behavior category could be rated only once in a 10-sec interval. The primary dependent variable was percentage of intervals in which an Inappropriate Behavior occurred. Since the varieties of Inappropriate Behavior permitted a more detailed analysis with the schedule used, the presentation of results is focussed on them, even though functionally their converse (Appropriate Behavior) was the main behavior being manipulated.

Ratings of Teacher Behavior

Ratings of teacher behavior were obtained to clarify relationships between changes in teacher behavior and changes in child behavior. Recordings of teacher behavior were also used by the experimenters to help the teachers learn the contingent use of Approval and Disapproval Behaviors. The teacher rating schedule is presented in Table 5.2. Teacher behaviors were recorded by subclasses in relation to child behaviors. That is, the record would show whether a teacher response followed Appropriate child classroom behavior or whether it followed one of the categories of Inappropriate Behavior. Responses to all children were rated. Teacher behavior was scored as the frequency of occurrence of a specified class of behavior during a 20-min interval. Teacher ratings were either recorded during one of the periods when a target child was being rated by another observer, or immediately thereafter when only one observer made both ratings. Teacher behavior was rated on the average of once a week, except during experimental transitions, when more frequent ratings were made. The number of days teacher behavior was rated under each condition is given in Table 5.3. Most recorded teacher behavior (about 85%) fell in the *Verbal* Approval or Disapproval categories. For this reason we have used the term *Praise* interchangeably with Approval Behaviors and *Criticism* interchangeably with Disapproval Behaviors.

Reliability of measures of teacher behavior were checked approximately every other rating day (21 of 42 occasions for the two teachers) by dividing the agreements as to time interval and behavior codes by the agreements plus disagreements. Average reliability over behavior classes,

Table 5.2. Coding Definitions for Teacher Behaviors

Appropriate child behavior is defined by the child rating categories. The teacher's rules for classroom behavior must be considered when judging whether the child's behavior is Appropriate or Inappropriate.

I. Teacher Approval following Appropriate Child Behavior
   A. *Contact*. Positive physical contact such as embracing, kissing, patting, holding arm or hand, sitting on lap.
   B. *Praise*. Verbal comments indicating approval, commendation or achievement. Examples: that's good, you are doing right, you are studying well, I like you, thank you, you make me happy.
   C. *Facial attention*. Smiling at child.

II. Teacher Approval following Inappropriate Child Behavior
   Same codes as under I.

III. Teacher Disapproval following Appropriate Child Behavior
   A. *Holding the child*. Forcibly holding the child, putting child out in the hall, grabbing, hitting, spanking, slapping, shaking the child.
   B. *Criticism*. Critical comments of high or low intensity, yelling, scolding,

raising voice. Examples: that's wrong, don't do that, stop talking, did I call on you, you are wasting your time, don't laugh, you know what you are supposed to do.
   C. *Threats*. Consequences mentioned by the teached to be used at a later time. If _____ then _____ comments.
   D. *Facial attention*. Frowning or grimacing at a child.

IV. Teacher Disapproval following Inappropriate Child Behavior
   Same codes as under III.

V. "Timeout" Procedures[a]
   A. The teacher turns out the lights and says nothing.
   B. The teacher turns her back and waits for silence.
   C. The teacher stops talking and waits for quiet.
   D. Keeping in for recess.
   E. Sending child to office.
   F. Depriving child in the classroom of some privilege.

VI. Academic Recognition
   Calling on a child for an answer. Giving "feed-back" for academic correctness.

[a]These are procedural definitions of teacher behaviors possibly involving the withdrawal of reinforcers as a consequence of disruptive behaviors which teacher could not ignore.

teachers, and days was 84% with a range from 70% to 96% for individual day measures.

Experimental Conditions

In the middle-primary class (Class A) the experimental conditions may be summarized as consisting of *Baseline*; introduction of *Rules*; *Rules* plus *Ignoring* deviant behavior; *Rules* plus *Ignoring* plus *Praise* for appropriate behavior; return to Baseline; and finally reinstatement of *Rules*, *Ignoring*, and *Praise*. In the kindergarten class (Class B) the experimental conditions consisted of *Baseline*; introduction of *Rules*;

Ignoring Inappropriate Behavior (without continuing to emphasize rules); and the combination of *Rules, Ignoring,* and *Praise.*

The various experimental procedures were to be used by the teachers for the classroom as a whole throughout the day, not just for the children whose behavior was being recorded, and not just when observers were present.

Baseline. During the Baseline period the teachers conducted their classes in their typical way. No attempt was made to influence their behavior.

Rules. Many people would argue that just telling children what is expected should have considerable effect on their behavior. We wished to explore this question empirically. Teachers were instructed individually and given written instructions as follows:

> The first phase of your participation in the use of behavioral principles to modify classroom behaviors is to specify explicit rules of classroom conduct. When this is done, there is no doubt as to what is expected of the children in your classroom. However, do not expect a dramatic shift in classroom control, as we all know that knowing the prohibitions does not always keep people from "sin". This is the first phase in the program and inappropriate behavior should be reduced, but perhaps not eliminated. The rules should be formulated with the class and posted in a conspicuous location (a chart in front of the room or a special place on the chalkboard where they will not be erased). Go over the rules three or four times asking the class to repeat them back to you when they are initially formulated and use the following guidelines:
>
> (a) Make the rules short and to the point so they can be easily memorized.
> (b) Five or six rules are adequate. Special instructions for specific occasions are best given when the occasion arises. Children will not remember long lists of rules.
> (c) Where possible phrase the rules in a positive not a negative manner (for example, "Sit quietly while working," rather than, "Don't talk to your neighbors"). We want to emphasize positive actions.
> (d) Keep a sheet on your desk and record the number of times you review the rules with the class (strive for at least four to six repetitions per day). Remember that young children do not have the retention span of an adult and frequent reminders are necessary. Let the children recite the rules as you ask them, rather than always enumerating them yourself.
> (e) Remind the class of the rules at times other than when someone has misbehaved.
> (f) Try to change no other aspects of your classroom conduct except for the presentation of the rules at appropriate times.

Teacher tally sheets indicated that these instructions were followed quite explicitly. The average number of presentations of rules was 5.2 per day.

Ignoring Inappropriate Behavior. The second experimental phase involved Ignoring Inappropriate Behavior. In Class A, repetition of rules was also continued. Individual conferences to explain written instructions were given both teachers. Both teachers were given the following instructions:

> The first aspect of the study was to make expectations explicit. This you have been doing over the past few weeks. During the next phase of the study you should learn to *ignore* (do not attend to) behaviors which interfere with learning or teaching, unless of course, a child is being hurt by another, in which case use a punishment which seems appropriate, preferably withdrawal of some positive reinforcement. Learning to ignore is rather difficult. Most of us pay attention to the violations. For example, instead of ignoring we often say such things as the following: "Johnny, you know you are supposed to be working"; "Sue, will you stop bothering your neighbors"; "Henrieta, you have been at that window for a long time"; "Jack, can you keep your hands off Bill"; "Susie, will you please sit down"; "Alex, stop running around and do your work"; "Jane, will you please stop rocking on your chair."
>
> Behaviors which are to be ignored include motor behaviors such as getting out of seat, standing up, running, walking around the room, moving chairs, or sitting in a contorted manner. Any verbal comment or noise not connected with the assignments should also be ignored, such as: carrying on conversations with other children when it is not permitted, answering questions without raising hands or being called on, making remarks when no questions have been asked, calling your name to get attention, and extraneous noises such as crying, whistling, laughing loudly, blowing noise, or coughing. An additional important group of behaviors to be ignored are those which the student engages in when he is supposed to be doing other things, e.g., when the child ignores your instructions you are to ignore him. Any noises made with objects, playing with pencils or other materials should be ignored, as well as, taking things from or disturbing another student by turning around and touching or grabbing him.
>
> The reason for this phase of the experiment is to test the possibility that attention to Inappropriate Behavior may serve to strengthen the very behavior that the attention is intended to diminish. Inappropriate Behavior may be strengthened by paying attention to it even though you may think that you are punishing the behavior.

Praise for Appropriate Behavior. The third phase of the experiment included individual contacts with teachers to encourage and train Praising of Appropriate Behavior. The Praise instructions to the teachers were as follows:

> The first phase included specifying explicit rules, writing them on the board and reviewing them 4–6 times per day. The second phase was designed to reduce the amount of attention paid to behaviors which were unwanted by ignoring them. This third phase is primarily directed toward *increasing* Appropriate Behaviors through praise and other forms of approval. Teachers are inclined to take good behavior for granted and pay attention only when a child acts up or misbehaves. We are now asking you to try something different. This procedure is characterized as "catching the child being good" and making a comment designed to reward the child for good behavior. Give praise, attention, or smile when the child is doing what is expected during the

particular class period in question. Inappropriate Behavior would not be a problem if all children were engaging in a great deal of study and school behavior, therefore, it is necessary to apply what you have learned in the workshop. Shape by successive approximations the behavior desired by using praise and attention. Start "small" by giving praise and attention at the first signs of Appropriate Behavior and work toward greater goals. Pay close attention to those children who normally engage in a great deal of misbehavior. Watch carefully and when the child begins to behave appropriately, make a comment such as, "You're doing a fine job, (name)." It is very important during the first few days to catch as many good behaviors as possible. Even though a child has just thrown an eraser at the teacher (one minute ago) and is now studying, you should praise the study behavior. (It might also decrease the rate of eraser throwing.) We are assuming that your commendation and praise are important to the child. This is generally the case, but sometimes it takes a while for praise to become effective. Persistence in catching children being good and delivering praise and attention should eventually pay off in a better behaved classroom.

Some examples of praise comments are as follows:

I like the way you're doing your work quietly (name).

That's the way I like to see you work _____.

That's a very good job _____.

You're doing fine _____.

You got two right _____, that's very good (if he generally gets no answers right).

In general, give praise for achievement, prosocial behavior, and following the group rules. Specifically, you can praise for concentrating on individual work, raising hand when appropriate, responding to questions, paying attention to directions and following through, sitting in desk and studying, sitting quietly if noise has been a problem. Try to use variety and expression in your comments. Stay away from sarcasm. Attempt to become spontaneous in your praise and smile when delivering praise. At first you will probably get the feeling that you are praising a great deal and it sounds a little phony to your ears. This is a typical reaction and it becomes more natural with the passage of time. Spread your praise and attention around. If comments sometimes might interfere with the ongoing class activities then use facial attention and smiles. Walk around the room during study time and pat or place your hand on the back of a child who is doing a good job. Praise quietly spoken to the children has been found effective in combination with some physical sign of approval.

General Rule: Give *praise* and *attention* to behaviors which facilitate learning. Tell the child what he is being praised for. Try to reinforce behaviors incompatible with those you wish to decrease.

The teachers were also instructed to continue to ignore deviant behavior and to repeat the rules several times a day.

Additional training given teachers consisted of: (a) discussion of problems with suggested solutions during weekly seminars on behavior analysis, and (b) specific suggestions from the experimenter on possible alternative responses in specific situations based on the experimenter's observations of the teachers during experimental transitions, or based on observer data and notes at other times when the data showed that the teachers were not on program.

Additional cues were provided to implement the program. Cards were placed on the teachers' desks containing the instructions for the experimental phase in which they were engaged.

Reversal. In Class A the final experimental conditions involved an attempt to return to Baseline, followed by a reinstatement of the *Rules*, *Praise*, and *Ignore* condition. On the basis of the earlier observations of Teacher A, we were able to specify to her how frequently she made disapproving and approving comments. The success of this procedure can be judged from the data.

RESULTS

Percentage of observation intervals in which Inappropriate Behaviors occurred as a function of conditions is graphed in Figs. 5.1 and 5.2. Major changes in Inappropriate Behaviors occurred only when Praise or

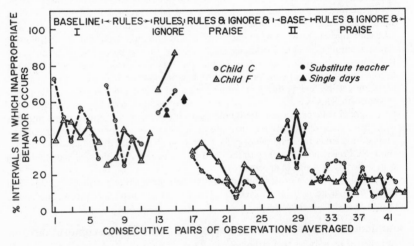

Fig. 5.1. Inappropriate behavior of two problem children in Classroom A as a function of experimental conditions.

Approval for Appropriate Behaviors was emphasized in the experimental procedures. A *t* test, comparing average Inappropriate Behavior in conditions where Praise was emphasized with those where Praise was not emphasized, was significant at the 0.05 level ($df = 2$).

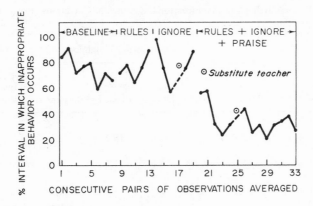

Fig. 5.2. Inappropriate behavior of one problem child in Classroom B as a function of experimental conditions.

Before examining the results more closely, it is necessary to inspect the data on teacher behavior. Table 5.3 gives the frequency of classes of teacher behaviors averaged within experimental conditions. Since day-to-day variability of teacher behavior was low for the measures used, these averages fairly reflect what went on.

Introduction of Rules into the classroom had no appreciable effect on Inappropriate Behavior.

Ignoring Inappropriate Behaviors produced inconsistent results. In Class A the children clearly became worse under this condition; in Class B little change was apparent. Both teachers had a difficult time adhering to this condition, and Teacher A found this phase of the experiment very unpleasant. Table 5.3 shows that Teacher A was only able to reduce critical comments from an average of one per 1 min to an average of three in 4 min. Teacher B cut her critical comments in half. In view of these difficulties, the present results cannot be taken as a clear test of the effects of responding with Disapproval to Inappropriate Behaviors.

The failure to eliminate Disapproval Reactions to Inappropriate Behaviors in Phase Three of the experiment, adds some ambiguities to the interpretation of the Phase Four data for Teacher A. The Rules, Ignore, and Praise condition for Teacher A involved both a reduction in critical comments (Ignoring) as well as a marked increase in Praise. As demonstrated previously (Becker *et al.*, 1967), this combination of procedures is very effective in reducing inappropriate classroom behaviors, but we

Table 5.3. Teacher Behavior—Averages for Experimental Conditions (Frequency per 20-min Observation)

Teacher A Behavior Classes	Experimental Conditions					
	Baseline I	Rules	Rules + Ignore	Rules + Ignore + Praise I	Baseline II	Rules + Ignore + Praise II
Approval to Appropriate	1.2	2.0	0.0	18.2	2.5	12.5
Approval to Inappropriate	8.7	0.8	2.0	1.2	4.0	5.1
Disapproval to Inappropriate	18.5	20.5	15.7	4.1	9.8	3.5
Disapproval to Appropriate	0.9	0.7	1.0	0.3	0.9	0.0
Timeout	3.3	1.4	1.7	0.4	0.0	0.1
Academic Recognition	26.5	23.6	46.3	52.4	45.4	45.6
Days observed	15	8	3	11	4	9

Teacher B Behavior Classes	Baseline	Rules	Ignore	Rules + Ignore + Praise
Approval to Appropriate	19.2	14.1	19.3	35.2
Approval to Inappropriate	1.9	0.9	0.3	0.0
Disapproval to Inappropriate	16.9	22.1	10.6	10.8
Disapproval to Appropriate	0.0	0.0	0.0	0.0
Timeout	1.5	1.5	0.3	0.4
Academic Recognition	14.5	5.1	6.5	35.6
Days observed	8	6	6	10

still lack a clear isolation of effects. The data for Teacher B are not confounded with a simultaneous shift in frequency of Disapproval and Approval Reactions, but they are made less interpretable by a marked shift in Academic Recognition (defined in Table 5.2) which occurred when the shift in Praise was made. Since Academic Recognition does not show any systematic relations to level of Appropriate Behaviors elsewhere in the study, we are not inclined to interpret this change as showing a causal effect. A best guess is that the effective use of Praise gave the teacher more time to focus on academic skills.

The reversal operation for Teacher A quite clearly shows that the combination of Praising and Ignoring exerts a strong control over Appropriate Behaviors.

As with Academic Recognition, no attempt was made to control how frequently the teacher used procedures labelled "Timeout" (defined in Table 5.2). The frequency data reported in Table 5.4 indicates that during Baseline, Teacher A, especially, used "Timeout" procedures to try to establish control (usually turning off the lights until the children were quiet). The changes in the frequency of use of "Timeout" procedures are not systematically related to the behavior changes graphed in Figs. 5.1 and 5.2.

In summary, the main results indicate: (a) that Rules alone had little effect in improving classroom behavior, (b) the functional status of Ignoring Inappropriate Behavior needs further clarification, (c) the combination of Ignoring and Praising was very effective in achieving

Table 5.4. Percentage of intervals in which behaviors occur: averages for two children in classroom A by experimental conditions.

Behavior Classes[1]	Baseline I	Rules	Rules + Ignore	Rules + Ignore + Praise I	Baseline II	Rules + Ignore + Praise II
Inappropriate Behavior[2]	46.8	39.8	68.5	20.5	37.6	15.1
Gross Motor	13.9	11.3	32.7	5.9	15.5	4.1
Object Noise	3.5	1.4	1.3	0.5	1.9	0.8
Disturbing Other's Property	3.3	1.8	1.9	0.7	0.7	0.3
Turning Around	21.6	9.9	11.4	9.1	12.8	7.6
Verbalizations	12.0	16.8	21.8	6.5	8.0	3.5
Other Inappropriate Behavior	10.9	7.8	16.5	3.9	7.8	2.6
Mouthing Objects	5.5	2.9	3.5	0.7	0.2	0.1

(The top of the table spans "Experimental Conditions" over all data columns.)

[1]*Contact* occurred less than 1% of the time and is not tabulated here.

[2]The sum of the separate problem behaviors will exceed that for Inappropriate Behavior, since the latter measure does not reflect the possibility that more than one class of problem behaviors may occur in an interval.

better classroom behavior, and (d) Praise for Appropriate Behaviors was probably the key teacher behavior in achieving effective classroom management.

The effects of the experimental procedures on individual classes of behavior for the two children in Class A are presented in Table 5.4. The data in Table 5.4 illustrate that with a few exceptions the effects on individual classes of behavior are similar to those for Inappropriate Behavior as a whole.

DISCUSSION

Technical Considerations

The problems of gaining good data and maintaining adequate experimental control in an ongoing classroom in a public school have not all been recognized as yet, much less solved. The greatest difficulty encountered was that of maintaining stable control over some important variables while others were being changed. When these variables involve aspects of teacher behavior, the problem becomes one of helping the teacher maintain discriminative control over her own behavior. Daily feedback from the experimenter, based on the observer ratings, can help in this task (i.e., show the teacher the up-to-date graph of her behavior). Also, providing the teacher with a small counter to help monitor her own behavior can be helpful (Thomas, *et al.*, 1968). Most difficult to control in the present study was teacher's Disapproving Reactions to Inappropriate Behaviors during the Ignore Phase of the experiment. Teacher A became very "upset" as her classroom became worse. One solution to this problem might be a pre-study in which the teacher is trained in effective management techniques, and then taken through a series of short periods where both Approval and Disapproval are eliminated and one or the other reinstated. The teacher would then have confidence that she can effectively handle her class and be better able to tolerate short periods of chaos (if such periods did occur). She would also have had sufficient training in monitoring her own behavior to permit more effective control.

No attempt was made to program the frequency of various classes of Academic Recognition behaviors. Since such behavior may be important in interpreting results, and was found to vary with some experimental conditions, future work should strive to hold this behavior constant also.

The present study emphasized the importance of contingencies between student and teacher behaviors, but did not measure them directly. While producing similar effects on two children in the same classroom and one child in another classroom, and showing correlated changes in teacher behaviors (including a reversal operation), more powerful data are potentially obtainable with a different technology. Video-tape recordings could enable the use of present coding techniques to obtain contingency data on all classroom members over longer observation periods. Just as the children adapted to the presence of observers, a class could be adapted to the presence of a TV camera man. Costs could be trimmed by saving only some sample tapes and reusing others after reliability ratings are obtained. The current observation procedures (short of having an observer for each child) cannot readily be extended to include simultaneous coding of teacher and child behavior without over-taxing the observers. The present findings, and related studies in this series, are sufficiently promising to warrant an investment in more powerful recording equipment.

Teacher Reactions

Teacher A. Initially, Mrs. A generally maintained control through scolding and loud critical comments. There were frequent periods of chaos, which she handled by various threats.

When praise was finally added to the program, Mrs. A had these reactions: "I was amazed at the difference the procedure made in the atmosphere of the classroom and even my own personal feelings. I realized that in praising the well-behaved children and ignoring the bad, I was finding myself looking for the good in the children. It was indeed rewarding to see the good rather than always criticizing. . . . I became convinced that a positive approach to discipline was the answer."

Teacher B. During Baseline Mrs. B was dispensing a great deal of praise and approval to her classroom, but it was not always contingent on Appropriate Behavior. Her timing was wrong and inconsistencies were apparent. For example, on one occasion two children were fighting with scissors. The instigator was placed under a table away from the rest of the class and left there for 3 min. After 3 min Mrs. B took the child in her arms and brought her back to the group even though she was still emitting occasional loud screams. Mrs. B would also ignore behavior for a period of time and then would revert to responding to Inappropriate Behavior with a negative comment; she occasionally gave Approval for Inappropriate Behavior. The training given in seminar and discussions with the experimenter led to an effective use of contingencies. Teacher B was also able to use this training to provide instructions and training for her aide to eliminate problems which arose in the final phase of study when the aide was continuing to respond to Disruptive Behaviors.

Changes in the Children

Cliff showed little change until Mrs. A started praising Appropriate Behavior, except to get worse during the Ignore phase. He was often doing no academic work, talking to peers, and just fiddling away his time. It took considerable effort by Mrs. A to catch Cliff showing praiseworthy behavior. As the use of praise continued, Cliff worked harder on his assigned tasks, learned to ignore other children who were misbehaving, and would raise his hand to get teacher's attention. He participated more in class discussions. He was moved up to the fastest arithmetic group.

Frank showed little change in his "hyperactive" and "inattentive" behaviors until praise was introduced. Frank responded rapidly to praise. After just two days in the "praise" phase, Frank was observed to clean his desk quietly and quickly after completing a handwriting assignment. He was able to finish a task and study on his own until the teacher initiated a new activity. He began to ask for extra assignments and volunteered to do things to help his teacher. He had learned to sit quietly (when appropriate), to listen, and to raise his hand to participate in class discussion, the latter occurring quite frequently.

Stan slowly improved after contingent praise was instituted, but some of the gains made by Mrs. B were in part undone by the teacher aide. The aide was described as playing policeman and it took special efforts by the teacher to get her to follow the program. Mrs. B summarized the changes in Stan as follows: "Stan has changed from a sullen, morose, muttering, angry individual into a boy whose smile seems to cover his whole face." He became very responsive to teacher praise and learned to follow classroom rules, to pay attention to teacher-directed activities for long periods of time, and to interact with his peers in a more friendly way.

Implications

This replication and refinement of an earlier study by Becker, *et al.* (1967) adds further confidence to the assertion that teachers can be taught systematic procedures and can use them to gain more effective behaviors from their students. Unless teachers are effective in getting children "ready to learn", their technical teaching skills are likely to be wasted. Knowledge of differential social reinforcement procedures, as well as other behavioral principles, can greatly enhance teachers' enjoyment of the profession and their contribution to effective development of the students.

The reader should note that while we formally recorded the behavior of a few target children, teacher and observer comments indicated dramatic changes in the whole "atmosphere" of the classroom and in the teachers' enjoyment of their classes.

REFERENCES

Allen, K. E., Hart, B. M., Buell, J. S., Harris, F. R., and Wolf, M. M. Effects of social reinforcement on isolate behavior of a nursery school child. In L. P. Ullmann and L. Krasner (Eds.), *Case studies in behavior modification.* New York: Holt, Rinehart, & Winston, 1965. Pp. 307–312.

Becker, W. C., Madsen, C. H., Jr., Arnold, Carole R., and Thomas, D. R. The contingent use of teacher attention and praise in reducing classroom behavior problems. *Journal of Special Education,* 1967, **1**, 287–307.

Bijou, S. W. and Baer, D. M. Some methodological contributions from a functional analysis of child development. In L. P. Lipsitt and C. S. Spiker (Eds.), *Advances in child development and behavior.* New York: Academic Press, 1963. Pp. 197–231.

Hart, Betty M., Reynolds, Nancy J., Baer, Donald M., Brawley, Eleanor R., and Harris, Florence R. Effect of contingent and non-contingent social reinforcement on the cooperative play of a preschool child. *Journal of Applied Behavior Analysis,* 1968, **1**, 73–76.

Thomas, D. R., Becker, W. C., and Armstrong, Marianne. Production and elimination of disruptive classroom behavior by systematically varying teacher's behavior. *Journal of Applied Behavior Analysis,* 1968, **1**, 35–45.

Madsen, C. H., Jr., Becker, W. C., Thomas, D. R., Koser, Linda, and Plager, Elaine. An analysis of the reinforcing function of "Sit Down" Commands. In Parker, R. K. (Ed.), *Readings in educational psychology.* Boston: Allyn and Bacon, 1968.

The Alteration of Behavior in a Special Classroom Situation*

ELAINE H. ZIMMERMAN and J. ZIMMERMAN

Indiana University Medical Center

Abstract: Unproductive classroom behavior was eliminated in two emotionally disturbed boys by removing social consequences of the behavior. Behavior which was more adequate and efficient with respect to social and scholastic adjustment was shaped and maintained with social reinforcers.

The classroom behavior of two emotionally disturbed boys was altered by arranging and manipulating its consequences.

The boys, in-patients in a residential treatment center (LaRue D. Carter Memorial Hospital), attended the first author's English class daily for 1 hr as part of an educational therapy program. There were three boys in the class, each receiving individual attention.

CASE I

Subject 1 (S-1) was 11 years old. He appeared to have no organic disorder and was of normal intelligence. In early class sessions, whenever S-1 was called upon to spell a word which had previously been studied and drilled, he would pause for several seconds, screw up his face, and mutter letters unrelated to the word. Following this, the instructor (E) consistently asked him to sound out the word, often giving him the first letter and other cues, encouraging him to spell the word correctly. Only after E had spent considerable time and attention would the boy emit a

---

*Reprinted from the *Journal of the Experimental Analysis of Behavior*, Vol. 5, No. 1, Jan. 1962, pp. 59–60. Copyright 1962 by the Society for the Experimental Analysis of Behavior, Inc.

correct response. The procedure was inefficient and profitless for improving the boy's spelling behavior. In fact, it may have been maintaining the undesirable pattern, since over the first 10 or 15 class sessions, consistently more time and attention were required of *E* to obtain a correct spelling response.

While "studying" in class, S-1 would obtain sheets of paper, wrinkle them, and throw them away, laughing as he caught *E*'s eye or that of one of the other students.

The Change in Approach

After several weeks in class, S-1 was quizzed via paper-and-pencil test on a lesson based on 10 spelling words, with time allotted for study and review. He handed in a paper with a muddled combination of barely legible letters. Immediately, *E* asked him to go to the blackboard. Her instructions were simply: "We will now have a quiz. I will read a word and you will spell it correctly on the board." She read the first word, and the subject misspelled it 10 or more times on the board. During this time, *E* sat at her desk, ignoring S-1, apparently busy reading or writing. Each time S-1 misspelled the word, he glanced at *E* but she did not respond. The boy erased the word and tried again, several times repeating "I can't spell it," or "I can't remember how," etc. Although ignored, the boy made no effort to sit down or leave the room. After approximately 10 min, he spelled the word correctly; *E* looked up at him immediately, smiled, and said, "Good, now we can go on." She read a second word; and after a similar series of errors and verbal responses, S-1 spelled the word correctly. With each successive word (through 10 words), the number of inappropriate (unreinforced) responses decreased, as did the latency of the correct response. At the end of the quiz, *E* took the boy's spelling chart, wrote an "A" on it, and praised him. She then asked the subject to help her color some Easter baskets. They sat down together, and chatted and worked.

Thereafter, attention in the form of smiling, chatting, and physical proximity was given only immediately after the emission of desired classroom behavior or some approximation of it in the desired direction. Undesirable behavior was consistently ignored. As a result of a month of this treatment, the frequency of bizarre spelling responses and other undesirable responses declined to a level close to zero per class session. At the conclusion of this study, the boy was working more efficiently, and was making adequate academic progress.

CASE II

Subject S-2 was an 11-year old boy, who, like S-1, had no apparent organic disorder and was also of normal intelligence. In initial class Sessions, S-2 emitted behavior considered undesirable in the classroom context with high frequency. He displayed temper tantrums (kicking, screaming, etc.), spoke baby-talk, and incessantly made irrelevant comments or posed irrelevant questions.

Several times a week, attendents dragged this boy down the hall to one of his classes as the boy screamed and buckled his knees. On several of these occasions, the boy threw himself on the floor in front of a classroom door. A crowd of staff members inevitably gathered around him. The group usually watched and commented as the boy sat or lay on the floor, kicking and screaming. Some members of the group hypothesized that such behavior seemed to appear after the boy was teased or frustrated in some way. However, the only observable in the situation was the consistent consequence of the behavior in terms of the formation of a group of staff members around the boy.

Observing one such situation which occurred before *E*'s class, *E* asked the attendant to put the boy in the classroom at his desk and to leave the room. Then *E* closed the door. The boy sat at his desk, kicking and screaming; *E* proceeded to her desk and worked there, ignoring S-2. After 2 or 3 min, the boy, crying softly, looked up at *E*. Then *E* announced that she would be ready to work with him as soon as he indicated that he was ready to work. He continued to cry and scream with diminishing loudness for the next 4 or 5 min. Finally, he lifted his head and stated that he was ready. Immediately, *E* looked up at him, smiled, went to his desk, and said, "Good, now let's get to work." The boy worked quietly and cooperatively with *E* for the remainder of the class period.

The Handling of Tantrums, Irrelevant Verbal Behavior, and Baby-talk

Each time a tantrum occurred, *E* consistently ignored S-2. When tantrum behavior was terminated, *E* conversed with the boy, placed herself in his proximity, or initiated an activity which was appealing to him. After several weeks, class tantrums disappeared entirely. Because the consequence of tantrum behavior varied in other situations, no generalization to situations outside the classroom has been observed.

Furthermore the frequency of irrelevant verbal behavior and of baby-talk declined almost to the point of elimination following the procedure of withholding attention after the emission of such behavior. On the other hand, when S-2 worked quietly or emitted desirable classroom behavior, *E* addressed him cordially and permitted some verbal interchange for several seconds. When a lesson was being presented to the class at large and S-2 listened attentively, *E* reinforced him by asking him a question he could answer or by looking at him, smiling at him, etc. The reinforcement was delivered intermittently rather than continuously because: (a) reinforcing every desired response of one student was impossible since *E*'s time was parcelled out among several students; and (b) intermittent reinforcement would probably be more effective than continuous reinforcement in terms of later resistance of the desired behavior to extinction. Like S-1, at the conclusion of the study this boy was working more efficiently in class and was making good progress. His speech was more generally characterized by relevancy and maturity.

ARTICLE 7

Reinforcement Therapy in The Classroom[1]

MICHAEL H. WARD and BRUCE L. BAKER

Harvard University

Abstract: Teachers were trained in the systematic use of attention and praise to reduce the disruptive classroom behavior of four first-grade children. Observation measures showed a significant improvement from baseline to treatment for these children and no significant changes for same-class controls. While the amount of teacher attention to target children remained the same from baseline to treatment, the proportion of attention to task-relevant behavior of these children increased. Psychological tests revealed no adverse changes after treatment.

Reinforcement techniques have been demonstrated to be quite effective in altering behavior in the laboratory situation (Krasner and Ullmann, 1965), and recently there have been increasing attempts to extend these methods to treatment in "real-life" situations. Of considerable importance is the potential usefulness of reinforcement therapy in the school classroom (e.g., Clarizo and Yelon, 1967; Hall, Lund, and Jackson, 1968; Woody, 1966).

Zimmerman and Zimmerman (1962) eliminated disruptive classroom behavior in two emotionally disturbed boys by removing the social consequences of maladaptive behavior. Quay, Werry, McQueen, and Sprague (1966) reported on the use of conditioning techniques in a small

[1]This research was supported in part by National Institute of Mental Health Grant No. 1-F1-MH-36, 634-01 (MTLH), and Harvard University Faculty Science Research Grant No. 33-493-68-1718. The authors wish to acknowledge the cooperation and assistance of Assistant Superintendent William Cannon of the Boston Public Schools, and Principal Gladys Wood and Assistant Principal Mary Lynch of the Aaron Davis School. Appreciation is expressed to the teachers, Carol Baumgardt, Sandra Napier, and Elaine Schivek, whose collaboration made this study possible. Our sincere thanks to Virginia Worcholick, Susan Hole, and Janet Ward, who served as observers, and to Sally Sanford, who did the testing. Reprints may be obtained from Michael H. Ward, Psychology Services, Menlo Park Division Palo Alto VAH, Miranda Drive, Palo Alto, California 94204.

Reprinted from the *Journal of Applied Behavior Analysis*, Vol. 1, No. 4, Winter 1968, pp. 323–328.

special class with conduct problem children. A program in which public school teachers were trained to manage classroom behavior problems by the contingent use of teacher attention and praise has been described by Becker, Madsen, Arnold, and Thomas (1967).

While these applications of reinforcement methods are certainly encouraging, several legitimate questions are often raised by psychologists and teachers concerned with treating disruptive classroom behavior. One critical area of concern is the generalization of treatment effects. First, when a child's disruptive behavior is successfully reduced, what are the effects on other aspects of his observable behavior and on his psychological test functioning? Second, how are other pupils in the class affected when the teacher concentrates on treating deviant behavior in one or two specific children?

The present study further explored the effectiveness of the teacher as a therapeutic agent, but it also attempted to assess the generalized effects of reinforcement therapy. Thus, teachers were trained to eliminate deviant behavior by differentially reinforcing the target children's desirable and undesirable classroom behavior. Control procedures were instituted to ascertain the effects of the reinforcement therapy procedures on the psychological adjustment of target and non-target children.

METHOD

Subjects

Twelve first-grade Negro children in an urban public school were assigned to three groups.

The Experimental Group (Group E) consisted of four behavior problem children. Three boys presented a high frequency of disruptive classroom behaviors, such as inappropriate talking and running around; one girl was highly withdrawn and inattentive. These target children were selected from three separate classrooms, on the basis of teachers' referrals and direct observations.

Control Group CI (Group CI) consisted of four children, matched for sex with the Group E children and selected at random from the three teachers' class lists. Thus, for each target child, a control child in the same classroom was also studied.

Control Group CII (Group CII) consisted of three boys and one girl, selected randomly from the classroom of a fourth first-grade teacher.

These pupils provided a baseline for test-retest changes in psychological test performance, independent of any experimental manipulations.

Apparatus

All treatment was carried out in the classroom. For two of the experimental subjects, two small (4-in.) electrically operated signal lights were used in six special-treatment sessions (after Patterson, 1965).

Procedure

For five weeks, the frequency of various deviant classroom behaviors of Group E and Group CI children was coded by trained observers. Deviant behavior was calculated as the percentage of 30-sec intervals in which the child exhibited any behavior which was not task-relevant. These observations constituted the baseline measure of deviant behavior.

At week six, the experimental treatment phase was instituted and continued for seven weeks (until the end of the school year). In the treatment phase, teachers systematically ignored deviant behavior and reinforced, with attention and praise, task-relevant productive behavior. Regular classroom observations of the Group E and Group CI children were continued throughout the study; the Group CII children were not observed at any time.

All three groups were administered a battery of psychological tests, both during baseline and at the conclusion of the seven-week experimental treatment phase.

Observers and observations   Three female undergraduates were trained to observe and record classroom behavior. The observers sat in the rear of the classroom; they did not interact with or respond to the children. Each Group E child was observed for four 15-min periods per week; each Group CI child was observed for two 15-min periods per week. During the observation period, the child was watched for the first 20 sec of each 30-sec interval of time; in the remaining 10 sec, the observers recorded the behaviors that had occurred. The observation periods were randomized throughout the school day to assure an adequate time-sampling. Inter-observer reliability checks were made periodically.

Table 7.1 shows the categories of behavior rated. These included gross and fine motor behaviors, aggression, deviant talking, non-attending, and disobeying, thumbsucking, and relevant appropriate behaviors such as hand-raising, task-oriented behavior, and so forth. In addition, the

Table 7.1. Classroom Behavior Rating Schedule (after Becker *et al.*, 1967)

Motor Behaviors (at seat)
Rocking in chair; moving chair in place; sitting out of position; standing while *touching* chair or desk.

Gross Motor Behaviors (not at desk)
Getting out of seat; running; jumping; skipping; *not touching* desk or chair.

Aggression
Hitting; punching; kicking; slapping; striking with object; throwing object at another person; pulling hair; disturbing another's books, desk, etc.; destroying another's property. Do *not* rate unless act is committed.

Deviant Talking
Carrying on conversation with other children; blurts out answer without being called upon; making comments or remarks; crying; screaming; laughing loudly; coughing loudly, singing, whistling; any vocal noise.

Non-Attending and Disobeying
Does something different from that which he has been directed to do or is supposed to do; includes "daydreaming"; *Note:* the above to be rated *only* when other classes are inappropriate (no other symbol may appear in interval). Note: Ignoring teacher's *direct* question or command may be rated in addition to other categories.

Thumb Sucking (and other objects)
Thumb or finger sucking; sucking such objects as a pencil, *etc.*

Relevant Behavior
Time-on-task; answering question; listening; following directions. Important: *Must* include *entire* 20-sec interval, except orienting response of less than 4-sec duration.

Hand Raising
Raises hand to ask or answer question; do *not* rate if child blurts out without being acknowledged. *Note:* may be rated with task-relevant behavior.

Teacher Attention
Teacher attends to the Subject *during* the 20-sec interval.

Positive Comments
"Good", "fine", "nice job" are said by teacher to Subject during the 20-sec interval.

General Reprimand
Teacher issues a *general* reprimand to the class or a group of students.

Negative Comments
"Shut up", "sit in your seat," "You're a bad boy," etc. are said by teacher to Subject during the 20 sec interval.

teacher's attention to children, as well as the nature of her comments, was coded.

Teachers and training sessions. Three female teachers were initially informed that their behavior problem children would be observed for five weeks, at which time the investigators would again meet with them to discuss some techniques for modifying these behavior problems.

None of the teachers was given any further information at this time. At no point were the teachers told that the same-class control children were being observed.

After baseline measurements had been completed, the investigators began a series of four weekly seminar-discussions with the three teachers. These sessions were devoted to discussions of behavior modification and the progress of the target children. The seminars included a general introduction to operant conditioning, reinforcement and punishment procedures, schedules of reinforcement, and selected aspects of the experimental literature relating to these and other topics (e.g., Ullmann and Krasner, 1965).

It was first necessary to help teachers identify and specify deviant behaviors. Throughout the treatment phase of the study, the investigators visited the classrooms and pointed out behavior problems. Thus, rather than: "He's always bad", teachers soon learned to define inappropriate behavior in more specific terms: "He is frequently out of his seat and he blurts out without being called on." It was also necessary to indicate to teachers which behaviors were to be reinforced when. Thus, for two of the behavior problem boys, six special 30-min treatment periods were conducted, in which an experimenter-controlled signal light on the child's desk was used as a reinforcer for sustained task-relevant behavior. The main purpose of this procedure was to bring the child's behavior under experimental control and allow the experimenter to indicate to the teacher the types of behaviors to be reinforced.

The principal therapeutic tool was the contingent use of teacher attention. The teachers were instructed to extinguish deviant behaviors by ignoring them, and to strengthen task-relevant behaviors by attending to and praising them. The need for immediacy, consistency, and contingency in reinforcement therapy was stressed. That is, the teacher was instructed to give *immediate* attention in a *consistent* manner, *contingent* upon the child's exhibiting task-relevant behavior.

A fourth female teacher, from whose classroom Group CII was chosen, did not participate in the seminar-discussions; at no time was she informed of the nature of the study.

Tests and measures. The measure of deviant classroom behavior was the direct observations described above; these included both the target behaviors and other types of deviant behavior.

In the baseline period, and again at the conclusion of the seven-week treatment period, each of the 12 children was tested individually by an independent examiner on the following battery of tests: four subtests of the WISC, the Draw-A-Person Test, and a projective questionnaire designed to measure attitudes toward school and feelings about self.

The Comprehension, Mazes, Digit Span, and Block Design subtests of the WISC were used to reflect the child's ability to pay attention to a task, and his general scholastic functioning. In the DAP Test, the child was asked to draw a picture of a person, using standard art paper and crayons provided by the tester. Such drawings have been used as measures of a child's adjustment, maturity, and self-image. Finally, the child was shown a photograph of a Negro child of the same sex and comparable age; the facial expressions in these pictures were judged by the authors to be "neutral". Twenty questions were asked about this child's feelings toward himself and toward school (e.g., "Is his teacher nice to him?" "Do the other kids in school like him?" "Does he like school?").

All children were given both sets of tests by the same examiner, who was not informed of experimental conditions.

RESULTS

Classroom Behavior

Reliability of observations. Inter-observer reliability of the observation periods was determined by the percentage of intervals in which the observers agreed perfectly as to whether deviant behavior had occurred. The mean percentage perfect agreement of the 31 reliability checks was 81% (SD = 21.6).

Behavior observations. Figure 7.1 shows the amount of deviant behavior in the behavior problem children and their same-class controls during baseline and during treatment. In the five-week baseline period, the Group E Children showed 74% deviant behavior, while the Group CI children showed 37% deviant behavior, a difference significant at $p = 0.002$ ($t = 5.14$; $df = 6$).[2] There was no overlap among subjects in the two groups.

For the last five weeks of treatment, Group E showed 57% deviant behavior, a decrease from baseline significant at $p = 0.03$ ($t = 3.91$; $df = 3$). During this same period, Group CI showed 41% deviant behav-

_____
[2] All statistical tests of significance are two-tailed.

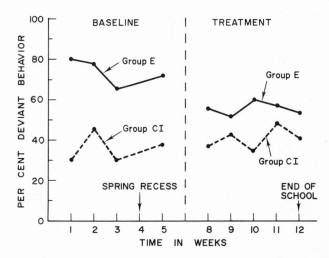

Fig. 7.1. Deviant behavior of Group E and Group CI.

ior, a slight, though not significant increase from baseline ($t = 0.32$; $df = 3$). The groups no longer differed significantly, although the deviant behavior in the target children was not decreased to the level of their controls by the end of school.

None of the specific categories of deviant behavior showed an increase in either Group E or Group CI, nor did teachers report any new behavior problems. Hence, the reduction in the target disruptive behavior was not followed by an increase in other classroom deviance.

Teacher attention. The principal therapeutic intervention used in the experiment was teacher attention to task-relevant behavior. However, as shown in Fig. 7.2, the observed improvement in the experimental children cannot be attributed simply to increased teacher attention, since there was no significant change from baseline to treatment in the *amount* of attention to target children ($t = 0.07$; $df = 3$). Teachers did increase significantly from baseline to treatment in the *proportion* of their attention to target children that was directed towards task-relevant behavior ($t = 3.46$; $df = 3$; $p = 0.04$).

Nevertheless, it appears that the teachers did not thoroughly master the contingent use of their attention to task-relevant behavior, and that further improvement in the target children might have been possible. For instance, the change in deviant behavior for Group E reported above did not include observations taken during the special treatment sessions

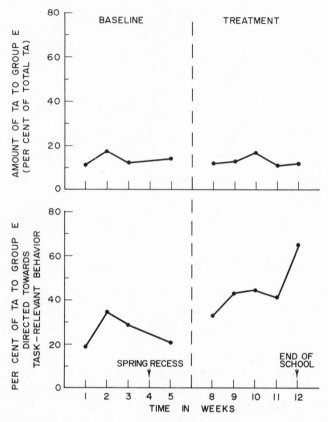

Fig. 7.2. Teacher attention to Group E: Amount of TA directed towards Group E and per cent of attention to Group E directed towards task-relevant behavior.

with two children. For these two experimental children, the deviant behavior during the special signal-light reinforcement periods decreased dramatically to an average of 18%. Yet there was apparently little generalization to other times.

Although the teachers did not increase their attention to target children, the data suggested that they decreased their attention somewhat to Group CI children; there was a slight, but not significant decrease in the amount of teacher attention from baseline to treatment ($t = 2.49$; $df = 3$, $p = 0.09$). The proportion of teachers' attention directed toward task-relevant behavior did not change from baseline to treatment for Group CI ($t = 0.11$; $df = 3$).

Psychological Tests

On the pre-treatment WISC, the behavior problem children were significantly lower than the controls on the Mazes subtest (t = 2.71; df = 10; p < 0.03); the groups did not differ on the other sub-scales. The changes in WISC scores after treatment were minimal and did not significantly differentiate the groups, although Group E tended to decrease on the Comprehension subtest relative to Group CII (t = 2.14; df = 6, p = 0.08).

The pre-treatment DAP drawings of the behavior problem children were generally like those of the control children, except that the Group E drawings were significantly smaller in size (t = 2.85; df = 10, p < 0.02). This variable has been considered an indicator of anxiety (Ward, 1968).

The pre and post-treatment drawings were scored on all those variables considered in the drawing literature to be suggestive of adjustment or maturity. No significant differences between groups in change scores were found on any single variable or on a combination score. Emotional adjustment, rated by two judges uninformed as to the order and conditions in which the drawings were produced, showed no consistent effects. Similarly, changes on the projective questionnaire did not differentiate the groups.

DISCUSSION

One focus of the present study was to ascertain the generalized effects on the target child of treating a specific behavior; especially studied were the deleterious effects on the child's classroom behavior and psychological test functioning. The data provide no evidence for adverse changes in the children as a consequence of teachers' employing reinforcement techniques or as a result of specific deviant behaviors being reduced.

On the other hand, the target children did not show the generalized improvement in psychological test functioning found by Baker (1968) with enuretic children treated by conditioning. Yet, the present treatment did not produce the distinctive cure which results with enuretics. Also, enuresis is usually an "involuntary" behavior, the alleviation of which is a considerable relief for the child. Deviant classroom behavior is in some sense "voluntary"; it is emitted for environmental gains, such as the teacher's attention, and may be more a discomfort to others than to the child himself. If attention is withdrawn from such an operant, the child will attempt other behaviors to regain attention. Whether the end result is new maladaptive behavior or generalized improvement may depend on what the teacher now reinforces.

A second focus was the generalized effects of reinforcement therapy on the class. No support was found for the argument that behavior of other pupils in a class deteriorates when the teacher's attention is somehow diverted from them in treating behavior problem children. Although teachers did slightly decrease the amount of attention given to control children, there was no significant increase in the control children's deviant behavior. This is particularly encouraging since the treatment was carried out in the last weeks of the school year when, according to teachers, disruption in the classroom typically rises. It appears, nonetheless, that in future treatment programs, more stress should be placed on the teacher maintaining normal relations with non-target children.

The principal reinforcer employed was contingent teacher attention. It is assumed that the decrease in deviant behavior in the target children resulted from the greater proportion of attention that teachers paid to these children's task-relevant behavior. It is recognized that the observed relationship between an increase in the proportion of teacher's attention to task-relevant behavior and an increase in such task-relevant behavior may have been artifactual; that is, if task-relevant behavior increased for some other undetermined reason and amount of teacher attention remained the same, then an increase in proportion of attention to task-relevant behavior would have also been found. Yet, it seems most likely that modified use of teacher attention was primary, especially in view of other reports indicating the functional role of teacher praise in increasing appropriate behavior in the classroom (Madsen, Becker, and Thomas, 1968).

The treatment procedures were not uniformly successful with all target children. Most notably, the withdrawn and inattentive behavior of one child changed very little. This behavior seems less under the control of teacher attention than more acting out behaviors; also, the latter are easier for the teacher to define, to notice, and to respond to correctly. Treating withdrawn behaviors may require better training in behavior shaping. In general it seems possible that more behavioral improvement could have been effected in all of the target children if the teachers had been more thoroughly trained. It is clear from the results of the special treatment sessions, in which the deviant behavior of two of the children dropped to 18%, that the full effectiveness of the reinforcement techniques was not realized at all times. It is likewise possible that a longer treatment period would have provided more time for the teachers' therapeutic skills to take effect.

Yet, the significant decrease in disruptive behavior in the target children, and the absence of adverse changes in these or other pupils, indicate that teachers can be trained as effective "therapists", using reinforcement techniques in the classroom. This finding, consistent with the conclusion reached by Becker *et al.* (1967), has important implications for in-classroom management of behavior problems. First, the availability to teachers of a set of techniques for controlling the disruptive behavior of students is of obvious advantage in terms of smoother classroom functioning. In addition, being taught to manifest productive task-relevant classroom behavior is worthwhile to the child himself. A child who is hyperactive or otherwise deviant in school necessarily misses many of the learning experiences which normally accrue to an attentive, actively participating pupil. A final consideration is that *in situ* amelioration of maladaptive behavior somewhat obviates the educational and financial disadvantages involved in removing a child from the classroom in order to attempt therapeutic rehabilitation.

While the results of this limited study are themselves encouraging, future research should continue to look beyond the specific behaviors being treated, and consider the generalized effects of reinforcement therapy.

REFERENCES

Baker, B. L. Symptom treatment and symptom substitution in enuresis. *Journal of Abnormal Psychology*, 1969, **74**, 42–49.

Becker, W. C., Madsen, C. H. Jr., Arnold, Carol, and Thomas, D. R. The contingent use of teacher attention and praise in reducing classroom behavior problems. *Journal of Special Education*, 1967, **1**, 287–307.

Clarizo, H. F. and Yelon, S. L. Learning theory approaches to classroom management: rationale and intervention techniques. *Journal of Special Education*, 1967, **1**, 267–274.

Hall, R. V., Lund, Diane, and Jackson, Deloris. Effects of teacher attention on study behavior. *Journal of Applied Behavior Analysis*, 1968, **1**, 1–12.

Krasner, L. and Ullmann, L. P. (Eds.) *Research in behavior modification.* New York: Holt, Rinehart & Winston, 1965.

Madsen, C. H. Jr., Becker, W. C., and Thomas, D. R. Rules, praise, and ignoring: elements of elementary classroom control. *Journal of Applied Behavior Analysis*, 1968, **1**, 139–150.

Patterson, G. R. An application of conditioning techniques to the control of a hyperactive child. In L. P. Ullmann and L. Krasner (Eds.), *Case studies in behavior modification.* New York: Holt, Rinehart & Winston, 1965. Pp. 370–375.

Quay, H. C., Werry, J. S., McQueen, Marjorie, and Sprague, R. L. Remediation of the conduct problem child in the special class setting. *Exceptional Children,* 1966, **32,** 509–515.

Ullmann, L. P. and Krasner, L. *Case studies in behavior modification.* New York: Holt, Rinehart & Winston, 1965.

Ward, Janet. *Integration and racial identification: a study of Negro children's drawings.* Unpublished bachelor honor's thesis, Radcliffe College, 1968.

Woody, R. H. Behavior therapy and school psychology. *Journal of Social Psychology,* 1966, **4,** 1–14.

Zimmerman, Elaine H. and Zimmerman, J. The alteration of behavior in a special classroom situation. *Journal of Experimental Analysis of Behavior,* 1962, **5,** 59–60.

CHAPTER 4

Classroom Punishment

Investigations of the effects of punishment in the classroom have been meagre. The dearth of experimentation has been partly due to the ethical concern of researchers and the practical limitations in the application of punishment to children. Also until very recently, psychologists have espoused the *legend* that punishment is an extremely ineffective means of controlling behavior (Solomon, 1964). In this respect, Walters, Parke, and Cane (1965) (8), note that parents have probably been wiser than the experts. We now know that punishment does suppress or weaken behavior and that the effectiveness of punishment is determined by factors such as the timing of punishment, the presence of an alternative to the punished response, the scheduling of punishment, and the relationship of the punishing agent to the one being punished.

Before considering the evidence regarding punishment, a definition of terms is in order. Punishment has been defined as a consequence of behavior which reduces the future probability of that behavior or as an operation in which an aversive stimulus is made contingent upon a response. The aversive stimulus is defined as one whose avoidance or termination is reinforcing. For example, children generally will do things to avoid being spanked and they will do things to terminate loud noises. The spanking and the loud noises are thus called aversive stimuli. In practice, however, few investigators have actually determined whether their subjects will work to escape or avoid a presumably aversive stimulus such as a loud tone or a mild shock before the investigators make the shock or tone contingent upon some response that they wish to suppress. They simply pick some stimulus such as shock or a tone which they *presume* a child would escape or avoid (and thus by definition would be aversive) and then make the shock or tone contingent upon some behavior they wish to weaken. Consequently, most research on punishment deals with testing various stimuli, which are assumed to be aversive, to see if they will weaken a response. In addition the withdrawal of a positive reinforcer is considered a form of punishment. That is, if one removes a child from a pleasant classroom or an activity which the child obviously likes when the child displays inappropriate behavior, the operation is called time-out from positive reinforcement. In summary, punishment here refers to the presentation of a stimulus assumed to be aversive or to the removal of a presumed positive reinforcer when the subject performs some response one wishes to weaken.

Though there now is considerable evidence indicating the effectiveness of punishment in weakening or suppressing a response (Cheyne & Walters, 1970), many investigators fear that there are adverse side-effects resulting from punishment. While it is true that certain applications of punishment may result in fearful and neurotic-like behavior (Masserman, 1943; Wolpe, 1948), one can avoid those applications of punishment which do produce negative side-effects. In order to avoid negative side-effects, one should (1) use punishment sparingly, (2) make clear to a child why he is being punished, (3) provide the child with an alternative means of obtaining some positive reinforcement, (4) reinforce the child for behaviors incompatible with those you wish to weaken, (5) avoid physical punishment if at all possible, (6) avoid punishing while you are in a very angry or emotional state, and (7) punish at the initiation of a behavior rather than at its completion.

Some of the reasons why punishment should be used sparingly need explication because teachers frequently use various forms of punishment. First, a teacher or parent who frequently uses punishment becomes a less effective modifier of behavior because he (1) loses positive reinforcing value and (2) his control through punishment weakens as the child adapts or becomes immune to punishment being used. A parent who spanks or slaps a child or a teacher who shakes a child or pulls his hair inadvertently provides an aggressive model for her children. For example, a parent who always uses physical punishment when she is angry provides her child with an example of what the child might do when he is angry—namely physically assault someone. Furthermore, a teacher or parent should be cautioned against the excessive use of punishment in a particular situation lest the situation itself become aversive. For example, a parent or teacher who continually criticizes a child on the basketball

court for his poor playing may find that the child quickly learns to avoid
the basketball court. Similarly, a child who receives repeated criticism
in school may learn to avoid school. Even if a child does not avoid school
altogether, there are many other subtle forms of avoiding school participation, e.g., not paying attention, day dreaming, and being restless. Even
worse, as Skinner (1968) notes, a child who receives a great deal of
punishment may counterattack.

> If the teacher is weak, the student may attack openly. He may be impertinent, impudent,
> rude or defiant. His verbal behavior may be obscene or profane. He may annoy the
> teacher and escape punishment by doing so surreptitiously – by groaning, shuffling
> his feet, or snapping his fingers . . . . Physical attacks on teachers are now common . . . .
> Vandalism is another form of counterattack which is growing steadily more serious . . . .
> A much less obvious but equally serious effect of aversive control is plain inaction.
> The student is sullen, stubborn, and unresponsive. He 'blocks'. He refuses to obey
> [p. 98].

Nonetheless, there are occasions in which punishment may be a necessary procedure in a classroom, and the following three studies document
the effectiveness of punishment under certain conditions.

Results indicating that punishment initiated early in a sequence of
behaviors is more effective than punishment administered late in the
sequence have come from numerous investigations both with animals and
humans (Aronfreed & Reber, 1965; Solomon, Turner, & Lessac, 1968).
The study by Walters, Parke, and Cane (1965) (8), did not take place in a
classroom, but the results of the study have several implications for
classroom management. The first critical finding by Walters *et al.*, is that
one can more easily suppress or weaken behavior if one punishes a child
as he begins to engage in an undesired behavior rather than if one waits
and punishes the child after he has spent considerable time engaging in the
disruptive behavior. For example, if one wishes to stop a young child
from playing with the dials on a T.V., it is best to tell him "no" as he
reaches for the dials rather than after the child has played with the dials
for some time. Similarly, if one wishes to reduce the frequency of talking
of a particular child in a classroom, it is best to watch the child and reprimand him just as the teacher sees him begin to talk to a neighbor rather
than wait until the child has talked with a neighbor for three or four
minutes. Naturally, it is not possible for a teacher to be constantly
surveillant and to reprimand a child each time he initiates disruptive
behavior, but punishment early in a sequence should probably be used by
teachers wherever possible. Walters *et al.*, also demonstrated that what
an adult does to a child who engages in an undesired behavior can have

important effects on children who observe the interaction between the child and the adult. In short, if one child watches another engage in undesired behavior and then receive punishment for engaging in that behavior, he will not engage in the undesired behavior as frequently as if there were no adult consequences for that behavior.

In a classroom, it would seem that if a child were allowed to engage in undesired behavior repeatedly, other children would view the teacher's nonreaction as a sign that engaging in such behavior is permissible. Consequently, a teacher should probably punish those behaviors which she finds particularly disruptive or significant behaviors which she does not want other children to model, e.g., swearing. As has been mentioned before, one should first try to ignore disruptive behavior and praise behaviors incompatible with the disruptive behavior. However, when the frequency of some disruptive behaviors is very high, and the peers reinforce it, some form of punishment may be in order.

The study by Hall and his associates, (9), depicts how various procedures such as pointing to the child and saying "no," taking away slips of paper on which a child's name is written, and requiring children to stay after school can serve as effective punishers. It may be surprising to some that a child's disruptive behavior was reduced when a slip of paper containing the child's name was withdrawn. Teachers should note that this article as well as others in this chapter demonstrate that there are effective suppressors of behavior which do not involve physical punishment. One should also be alerted to the possibility that retaining a child after school when he does poorly in an academic area may not function to increase his academic behavior in class. If the child likes the teacher he can obtain her undivided attention for a period each day after school and if he is not prevented from something he especially likes during the after-school period, it seems possible that he might maintain his poor academic behavior in order to receive the special attention. For example, Curry (1970) viewed the non-reading behavior of a bright young girl (Michelle), as a means of gaining extra attention. Consequently, he told the teacher and parents to discontinue any unusual attempts to help the child to read. Instead, Michelle was allowed to read at her regular time but if she made an error it was ignored. Similarly, to change the reinforcement for poor reading to good reading, she was allowed to read until she made a certain number of errors. Using these procedures, "in the course of three weeks Michelle's reading behavior progressed from a non-reading level to a satisfactory mid first grade level."

When teachers reprimand children, they usually do so in a manner that enables many of the children in the class to hear the reprimand. The study by O'Leary, Kaufman, Kass, and Drabman (1970) (*10*), documents the effectiveness of an alternative mode of reprimanding for reducing disruptive behavior, viz., soft reprimanding or reprimanding in a manner so that only the child concerned can hear the reprimand. The latter form works best in a class or during an activity where the teacher can move rather freely around the class, e.g., when correcting work, when using programmed instruction, or when the teacher is talking or lecturing as she walks around the classroom. Soft reprimands are probably most effective when combined with frequent praise for appropriate behavior and when the intensity of the teacher's emotional tone is low.

ARTICLE 8

Timing of Punishment and the Observation of Consequences to Others as Determinants of Response Inhibition*[1]

RICHARD H. WALTERS, ROSS D. PARKE, and VALERIE A. CANE

Abstract: Eighty Grade 1 and kindergarten children were assigned to one of eight conditions in a 2×4 factorial design involving two conditions of timing of punishment and four film conditions. Half the children under each film condition received punishment as they initiated a deviant response sequence; the remaining Ss were punished only after completing the deviation. After punishment training, Ss were assigned to one of four film conditions: film model rewarded for deviation; film model punished for deviation; no consequence to the film model; no film. Ss who received early punishment subsequently showed more resistance to deviation than Ss for whom punishment was delayed. There were significant differences among Ss under the four film conditions, with model-punished Ss showing relatively high resistance to deviation. A combination of early-punishment training and exposure to a punished model was most effective in producing inhibition. Subsequent tests with problem-solving tasks, the solution of which had been demonstrated in the films, revealed that Ss under model-rewarded and no-consequences conditions had learned from observation of the model; however, model-punished Ss did not perform significantly better in these tests than Ss who had not seen the film model.

The role of punishment in the socialization of children has received considerable emphasis in theoretical discussions but has seldom been explored in laboratory studies. Perhaps partly for humanitarian reasons and perhaps partly because ethical and practical considerations limit the

*Reprinted with abridgement from *Journal of Experimental Child Psychology*, Vol. 2, 1965, pp. 10–30, by permission of the authors and Academic Press.

[1]This study was supported by the Public Health research grant 605-5-293 of the (Canadian) National Health Grants Program, the Ontario Mental Health Foundation grant 42, and the Defense Research Board of Canada grant 9401-24. The authors are indebted to the Superintendent of Public Schools of Waterloo and to the Principles and Staff of Northdale and Brighton Schools. Thanks are due to Patsie Hutton and Keith Barnes for assisting as observers.

range of intensities of punishment that may be used in investigations with human subjects, psychologists have readily accepted the "legend" (Solomon, 1964) that punishment is an extremely ineffective means of controlling human behavior. In this respect most parents have probably been wiser than the "experts"; the renewed interest in punishment on the part of psychologists and the more cautious approach taken in recent theoretical discussions of this topic (e.g., Church, 1963; Solomon, 1964) are therefore welcome developments. The available research evidence strongly suggests that punishment may have very diverse (and sometimes very dramatic) effects, and that these effects are dependent on such parameters as the intensity and timing of punishment, the sequencing and scheduling of rewarding and punishing events, the strength and nature of the punished response, and the relative status of the agent and the recipient of punishment (Aronfreed, 1964; Bandura and Walters, 1963; Church, 1963; Martin, 1963; Mowrer, 1960a, b; Solomon and Brush, 1958; Solomon, 1964).

The purpose of this study was to investigate the effects of one of these parameters, the timing of punishment, on the resistance to deviation of children who, following direct punishment training, were exposed to a deviant model. Since the consequences of the responses to a social model have a considerable influence on the extent to which the model's behavior is imitated (Bandura, Ross, and Ross, 1963; Walters, Leat, and Mezei, 1963), consequences were varied in such a way as to permit an investigation, in a single experimental design, of some of the effects of both directly and vicariously experienced punishment.

TIMING OF PUNISHMENT

A theoretical basis for predicting the effects of timing of punishment has been offered by Mowrer (1960a, b). According to Mowrer, the execution of a prohibited act is accompanied by a sequence of response-produced cues, each providing sensory feedback. A punishment may be presented at any point during this sequence and result in a relatively direct association of a fear-motivated avoidance response with the response-produced cues occurring at the time that the punishment is administered. If the punishment occurs only when the deviant act has been completed, fear will be most strongly associated with the stimuli produced by the agent's preparatory responses. In contrast, punishment that occurs at or near the time that an act is initiated will result in a relatively strong association between the agent's preparatory responses and the emotion of fear; in this case, even the initiation of the deviant act will arouse fear that motivates incompatible prosocial or avoidance responses. Once an act has been initiated, secondary positive reinforcers associated with the instrumental behavior involved in the commission of the act may serve to maintain and facilitate the response sequence and thus to some extent counteract the inhibitory effect of punishment. Consequently, it may be argued, the earlier a punishment occurs in a deviant response sequence, the more effectively will it prevent the subsequent commission of the act.

Mowrer's account perhaps overemphasizes both the role of kinesthetic feedback and that of the emotion of fear, and underemphasizes the part played by perceptual-cognitive factors that are associated with the functioning of distance receptors. Visual and auditory cues accompanying the commission of a deviant act may be as closely associated with punishment experiences as kinesthetic feedback; since such cues are far more readily discriminable, they probably also play a more important role in the maintenance of behavioral control. This consideration does not, however, change the basic prediction generated by Mowrer's theory.

HYPOTHESIS 1 *Children who receive punishment as they begin to perform a class of responses will subsequently show greater resistance to deviation than children who receive punishment only on completion of responses of this class, provided that the deviant behavior falls in the same general category as the responses made during the punishment training session.*

CONSEQUENCES OF RESPONSES TO MODELS

Previous investigations (Bandura, 1965; Bandura *et al.*, 1963; Walters *et al.*, 1963; Walters and Parke, 1964) have demonstrated that the observation of a social model who receives punishment for a class of responses leads to response inhibition in the observer. The consequence of the model's response apparently serves as a cue signifying to the observer the nonpermissibility of the punished response within a given social context (Walters and Parke, 1964). Similarly, the observation of a reward to a model may signify the permissibility of a response class even if the rewarded response has previously been prohibited for the observer (Walters *et al.*, 1963; Walters and Parke, 1964). Under some circumstances, the observation of a model's performing a prohibited or socially disapproved act (for example, aggression) with no adverse consequences to himself may suffice as a cue to the observer that the act may be performed (Walters and Llewellyn-Thomas, 1963); the inhibitions created in the observer may thus be overcome either by rewarding a model who performs the disapproved responses or simply by not punishing the model's behavior (Walters and Parke, 1964).

HYPOTHESIS 2   *Children who observe a model punished for acts that they have been prohibited from performing will show greater resistance to deviation than children who see a model rewarded or receive no punishment for these acts.*

METHOD

Subjects   Eighty kindergarten and Grade I boys, with a mean age of 6 years, 5 months served as Ss. The boys were randomly assigned to one of eight conditions in a 2×4 factorial design involving two timing-of-punishment conditions (early vs. late punishment) and four film conditions. Under three of the four film conditions, the children were shown a colored film sequence depicting an interaction between a 6-year-old boy and a female adult who performed a mother role; the remainder of the children saw no film.

Equipment   For the timing-of-punishment manipulations, the equipment and procedures were similar in some respects to those used by Aronfreed and Reber (1964). Nine pairs of toys (one attractive, one unattractive) were used in a series of training trials. One toy in each pair was large, well detailed, and well made, and of interest to boys (e.g., cars, guns, and trucks); the other toy in each pair was smaller, less detailed, and in some cases sex-inappropriate (e.g., toy dishes, a bracelet, and a plastic doll).

Three film-sequences, similar to those used by Walters and Parke (1964), were prepared for the film manipulations. The sequences were identical, except for the addition of "endings" to two of the films. Complete correspondence was ensured through the use of copies of an original edited sequence. The film showed an adult female, presumably a mother, indicate to a child through a single gesture that he should not play with toys that had been set on a nearby table; the adult then sat the child in a chair beside the table, gave him a book to read, and left the room. After her departure, the child put the book aside and proceeded to play with the prohibited toys. Play continued for approximately 4 minutes. The play sequence displayed the child playing with a number of attractive toys similar to those used in the punishment-training sessions . . . .

Endings were added to two of the films. The reward-movie ending showed the adult return to the room, sit beside the child, hand him toys and play with him affectionately. For the punishment-movie ending, the adult, on returning, pulled the child up from the floor, where he was playing, snatched the toy from him, spanked him, and once again sat him on the chair with the book. In the no-consequences film, the mother did not re-enter. Because children are used to seeing sound-accompanied movies in school settings, a tape recording of background music was played during the showing of the films. The recording was identical for all children.

The children were tested in a mobile laboratory, divided into an experimental room and an observation room by a partition containing two one-way vision mirrors. A diagram of the experimental arrangements is provided in Fig. 8.1.

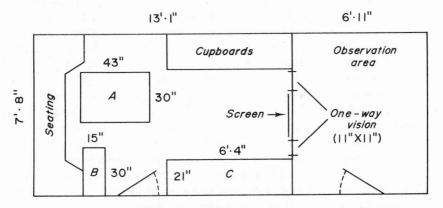

Fig. 8.1. Experimental arrangements.

On Table A were displayed three rows of toys, three toys in each row. When S was seated at one end of the table, the first row of the toys was readily accessible to him, the toys in the second row were accessible if he stood up in front of the table, while the third row could be reached only if S walked around the table. A folding table (B) was used to display toys during the punishment-training session; when not in use, these toys were placed on Table C, which also held a Bolex 18-5 projector and a Uher 4000-S portable tape recorder.

Procedure

The *E* brought *S* from his classroom to the mobile laboratory. She interacted with him in a relaxed and friendly manner and informed him that he was about to play a game with her. If *S* had been assigned to a film condition, he was also told that he would be shown a movie.

Punishment training   The *S* was seated behind Table B and instructed as follows:

> I'm going to put some toys out here on the table. Each time I'm going to put down two toys, and here is what I want you to do. I want you to pick the toy that you would like to play with. I want you to pick it up, hold it, and think about it for a while. Be sure you pick it up, hold it, and think about it. Now, if I ask you, I want you to tell me what the toy is or what it is used for. Do you understand?

After *S* indicated that he understood the nature of the task, *E* continued, "Now, some of these toys are for another boy, and you're not supposed to touch them. So if you touch a toy that is for the other boy, I'll tell you. O.K.?"

Following these instructions, *E* uncovered the toys on Table C and commenced the punishment training. On each of nine trials *E* placed a pair of toys before *S*. The order of presentation of pairs of toys was constant for all *S*s, and the position of the attractive toy was consistently alternated over the nine training trials, so that it appeared at *S*'s left on odd-numbered trials and on his right on even-numbered trials.

Each time *S* selected the attractive toy, *E* verbally punished him by saying, "No, that's for *the other boy*." For *S*s in the early-punishment condition, *E* administered the punishment as *S*'s hand neared the attractive toy, but before he touched it. As *E* spoke, she covered the forbidden toy and removed it from the table. The unattractive toy was left undisturbed for a few seconds to give *S* an opportunity to make the alternative choice. If he did so, he was asked to describe the toy. Almost all *S*s immediately selected the unattractive toy when rebuked for choosing the attractive toy.

For *S*s in the late-punishment condition, the punishment was presented only after *S* had picked up the attractive toy and held it for 2–3 seconds. The *E* took the toy from *S*'s hand while administering the same rebuke as was used for early-punished *S*s. Again *S* was given an opportunity to choose and describe the unattractive toy.

If, on any trial, *S* chose the unattractive toy first, *E* said, "What is it?" or "What is it used for?" Following *S*'s description of the toy, *E* acknowledged the response by a simple "O.K." and removed both the toys from the table.

Resistance-to-deviation test On completion of the punishment session the toys on Table C were covered. The *S* was then seated behind Table A, which contained three rows of toys, similar to, and in some cases identical with, those used in the punishment-training session. After removing the cloth covering these toys, *E* told all *S*s, "These toys are *for the other boy* so you had better not touch them." If *S* was under a film condition, *E* added, "Now, I'm going to show you a movie." She then switched on the projector and the tape-recorded music. As soon as the movie had ended, *E* gave the next set of instructions. *S*s under the no-film condition received these instructions immediately after being seated at Table A.

Then *E* said, "Before we play the game, I have to go and get something, so would you like to sit here and read this book while I am gone." (*E*, at this point, placed a dictionary on the table before *S*.) "I'm going to close the door when I go out so that nobody will come in and bother you. O.K.?"

Measures

An observer, who was seated behind the one-way vision screen, recorded *S*'s choices during the punishment-training session, thus providing a record of the number of punishments received by each *S*. In addition, during the test for resistance to deviation, the observer recorded on a specially prepared record sheet the times at which *S* touched and ceased to touch individual toys. The sheet was set up in such a way that, during the 15-minute period of *E*'s absence from the room, the observer's only task was to record times, read from a Heuer-Century Stopwatch, in the appropriate squares which designated specific toys.

From the observer's records, the following scores were calculated: the latency of *S*'s first deviant response, the number of times he deviated, and the total time for which he deviated. Weighted deviation scores were calculated in the following manner: a deviation involving one of the three most accessible toys was scored 1: a deviation involving one of the toys in the second row was scored 2; and *S*'s touching a toy in the third row was scored 3. A weighted-number-of-deviations and a weighted-time score were then obtained by multiplying the number of times *S* touched toys in each class, and the amount of time for which he handled them, by the appropriate weights. These scores had previously been employed by Walters *et al.* (1963) and Walters and Parke (1964). Since in both the earlier studies somewhat similar results were obtained and unweighted and weighted scores, only the weighted scores were utilized in this study. Weighted scores were preferred because they make use of more of the available information and reduce the number of ties in analyses based on ranking methods.

RESULTS

Reliability of measures

A second observer was present while 16 Ss were tested. Rank-order correlation coefficients were used as indices of interrater reliability for the resistance-to-deviation measures. These correlations were 1.00, 1.00, and 0.94 for the latency, number of deviations, and duration of deviations, respectively. Reliability of scoring was above 0.94 for all three classes of responses made by S during the test for observational learning.

Punishment-training data

A 2×4 analysis of variance indicated that there were no significant differences among the eight groups of Ss in respect to the number of punishments received ("incorrect" choices made) during the punishment-training session. Group differences in resistance to deviation cannot therefore be attributed to this variable. The mean number of punishments received by Ss under the early-punishment and late-punishment conditions were 4.1 and 3.8, respectively.

Over-all tests of predicted effects

The distributions of resistance-to-deviation data for some groups of Ss were markedly skewed; consequently, Table 8.1 gives both group medians and group means for the latency, weighted-deviations, and weighted-duration indices.

Most differences were in predicted directions. Model-rewarded and no-consequence Ss deviated more quickly, more often, and for longer periods of time than did model-punished Ss. Differences between early-punishment and late-punishment Ss were remarkably consistent across all film conditions; under each condition, the early-punishment Ss showed greater resistance to deviation.

Table 8.2 reports the results of nonparametric tests of main effects; it also presents the findings from over-all tests of the significance of differences among the eight groups of Ss. Eight of the nine comparisons yielded p-values of 0.05 or less; the remaining p-value fell between 0.10

Table 8.1. Group Means and Medians on Three Indices of Resistance to Deviation[a]

| | Film Conditions | | | | | | | |
| | Model Rewarded | | No Consequence | | Model Punished | | No Film | |
Punishment conditions	Mean	Median	Mean	Median	Mean	Median	Mean	Median
Early								
Latency (seconds)	590.1	750	333.2	144.5	697.0	900	624.5	900
Weighted deviations	5.2	1	3.7	4	2.5	0	2.9	0
Weighted duration	64.5[b]	2.5	15.3	12.5	0.7	0	16.4	0
Late								
Latency (seconds)	269.0	71.5	345.6	270.5	543.1	576	299.3	141
Weighted deviations	7.4	4.5	6.8	5.5	2.7	1.5	6.2	4.5
Weighted duration	33.7	11	32.7	131	9.5	2	30.9	14

[a]$n = 10$ in each group.
[b]Mean $= 11.3$, excluding one extreme case.

Table 8.2. Significance of Main and Overall Effects[a]

A. Model effects (Kruskal-Wallis H-tests; $df = 3$)
   Latency: $H = 6.54$; $p < 0.10$
   Weighted deviations: $H = 8.86$; $p < 0.05$
   Weighted duration: $H = 8.93$; $p < 0.05$
B. Punishment effects (Mann-Whitney U-tests)
   Latency: $z = 2.32$; $p < 0.02$
   Weighted deviations: $z = 2.67$; $p < 0.01$
   Weighted duration: $z = 2.27$; $p < 0.03$
C. Over-all effects (Kruskal-Wallis H-tests; $df = 7$)
   Latency: $H = 14.08$; $p < 0.05$
   Weighted deviations: $H = 16.74$; $p < 0.02$
   Weighted duration: $H = 14.69$; $p < 0.05$

[a]H and z corrected for ties.

and 0.05. Supplementary Mann-Whitney U-tests (Table 8.3) indicated that both model-rewarded and no-consequence Ss differed significantly from model-punished Ss. No-film Ss deviated to a greater extent, though not more quickly, than Ss who had seen the model punished.

Selected individual comparisons

The theoretical considerations advanced in the introduction to this paper would lead one to expect that Ss who were punished early and were

Table 8.3. Comparisons of Subjects Under Four Different Film Conditions (Mann-Whitney U-tests with corrections for ties).

Film Conditions Compared	Latency		Weighted Deviations		Weighted Duration	
	z	p	z	p	z	p
Model Rewarded vs.						
No. Consequence	0.89	n.s.	0.30	n.s.	0.72	n.s.
Model Rewarded vs.						
Model Punished	1.66	< 0.10	2.23	< 0.03	2.29	< 0.03
Model Rewarded vs. No. Film	0.33	n.s.	0.30	n.s.	0.11	n.s.
No. Consequence vs.						
Model Punished	2.53	< 0.02	2.82	< 0.005	2.81	< 0.01
No Consequence vs. No Film	1.06	n.s.	0.51	n.s.	0.33	n.s.
Model Punished vs. No Film	1.40	n.s.	2.19	< 0.05	2.13	< 0.05

also exposed to a punished model would show the greatest resistance to deviation and that Ss who were punished late and were exposed to a model who did not receive punishment would show the least resistance to deviation. Table 8.4, which summarizes the outcomes of individual comparisons between pairs of groups, indicates that early-punishment model-punished Ss were significantly more resistant to deviation not only than late-punishment model-rewarded and late-punishment no-consequence Ss but also than late-punishment no-film Ss. Differences between the early-punishment model-punished group and the early-punishment model-rewarded and no-consequences groups, respectively, also reached or approached an acceptable level of significance. Moreover, late-punishment model-punished Ss tended to be more resistant to deviation than any of the other three late-punishment groups. In addition, differences between the early-punishment no-film group and the late-punishment model-rewarded, no-consequence, and no-film groups, respectively, reached or approached significance. Since all the above differences would be predicted from the theoretical considerations advanced earlier, the benefit of one-tailed tests might be claimed; the findings concerning the efficacy of punishment procedures then become quite impressive.

DISCUSSION

The prediction concerning timing of punishment assumed that punishment occurring at the commencement of a response sequence more

	Early Punishment				Late Punishment			
	Model Rewarded A	No Consequence B	Model Punished C	No Film D	Model Rewarded E	No Consequence F	Model Punished G	No Film H
A[b] 1		1.31	0.99	0.57	1.57*	1.57*	0.23	1.75
2		0.55	1.58*	0.65	0.96	1.15	0.31	1.38
3		0.73	1.78**	0.48	1.00	1.23	0.31	1.49
B 1			2.14**	1.58*	0.19	0.19	1.31	0.19
2			2.39***	0.87	0.84	1.19	1.13	1.11
3			2.46**	0.52	0.23	0.69	1.16	0.65
C 1				0.53	2.38**	2.22**	1.24	2.38**
2				0.89	2.78****	2.74****	1.62*	3.33****
3				0.98	2.78****	2.78****	1.62*	3.25****
D 1					2.03**	1.64*	0.57	2.01***
2					1.72*	1.60*	0.40	1.82*
3					1.13	1.25	1.62*	1.20
E 1						0.15	1.57*	0.08
2						0.00	1.61*	0.08
3						0.27	1.61*	0.38
F 1							1.46	0.00
2							1.69*	0.11
3							1.53	0.08
G 1								1.52
2								2.14**
3								1.87*

*p = 0.12, **p = 0.05, ***p = 0.01.
Two-tailed p values.

[a]n = 10 in each group. In view of the small size of samples for individual comparisons and the necessity of using a nonparametric technique, significance levels as low as 0.12 (two-tailed p-value) are indicated.

[b]1 = latency; 2 = weighted deviations; 3 = weighted duration.

effectively inhibits the initiation of the sequence than does punishment that occurs only after the sequence has been completed. Confirmation of this prediction lends weight not only to previous findings of a similar nature (Aronfreed and Reber, 1964; Black, Solomon, and Whiting,[2] Walters and Demkow, 1963), but also to theories of punishment that hold that punishment is maximally effective as an inhibitory technique when it is closely associated with the response that it is designed to suppress (Church, 1963). These theories are also supported by experiments that provide evidence for the occurrence of delay-of-punishment gradients in animal and human learning (Banks and Vogel-Sprott, 1965; Bixtenstein, 1956; Coons and Miller, 1960; Kamin, 1959; Mowrer and Ullman, 1945; Sidman, 1953; Walters, 1964).

The study leaves little doubt that judiciously timed punishment can be extremely effective in controlling human behavior. More than half the children in the early-punishment model-punished and the early-punishment no-film groups did not deviate at all; under the former of these conditions no child deviated more than twice, and the deviations that occurred were all extremely brief. Moreover, the differences between early-punishment and late-punishment no-film *S*s in respect to latency and weighted number of deviations are clearly significant if the benefit of a one-tail test is claimed. Failure to find significant differences between early-punishment children under the individual film conditions can reasonably be attributed to the modifying effect of exposure to a deviant model whose behavior had a uniform outcome (reward, no consequence, or punishment).

In the present study, late-punishment *S*s were permitted to handle the attractive toys for a brief period before punishment was administered, whereas early-punished *S*s were never permitted to handle these toys. Consequently, predicted differences between early-punishment and late-punishment *S*s may be attributable to the classical conditioning of the approach responses of the latter *S*s rather than to the establishing of avoidance responses associated with temporally and topologically different components of *S*s' deviant response sequences.

In order to test the plausibility of a very similar alternative explanation of timing-of-punishment effects, Aronfreed and Reber employed a control condition. Children under this condition were asked to indicate their choice from each pair of toys merely by pointing; if the child pointed to an attractive toy, the experimenter removed both toys. The absence of a

---

[2]Cited in Mowrer (1960b).

significant difference between control Ss and Ss under a late-punishment condition, in respect to proportion of deviators, permitted Aronfreed and Reber to conclude that the relatively high incidence of deviation among late-punishment Ss was not due to habituation. The classical-conditioning interpretation might be more satisfactorily investigated by permitting control children briefly to handle attractive toys without rebuke or punishment, provided that control and late-punishment Ss were equated for the number of occasions on which they handled attractive toys. The presence of a difference between control and late-punishment Ss would then strongly favor an interpretation of the reported timing-of-punishment effects in terms of avoidance learning, whereas an absence of such a difference would be consistent with an interpretation in terms of the classical conditioning of approach responses.

Comparisons of children under the model-rewarded, no-consequence, and model-punished conditions supported previous findings concerning the influence of the consequences of responses of social models on the behavior of observers. No-consequence Ss, as in the experiments of Walters and Parke (1964) and Bandura (1965), deviated as readily and as often as model-rewarded Ss, a finding that again suggests that observing a model deviate without punishment may have a disinhibitory effect on the observer.

The occurrence of disinhibitory effects under the no-consequence condition superficially resembles findings from Virginia Crandall's (1963) study of the sequencing of reinforcements. In her study, nonreward that followed direct punishment was found to function like a positive reinforcer (Bandura, 1965; Walters and Parke, 1964). However, under Crandall's non-reward condition, a nonreacting adult experimenter remained in the room with the child subjects. Moreover, a follow-up study (Crandall, Good, and Crandall, 1964) demonstrated that the omission of punishment functioned like a positive reinforcer only when the nonreacting adult was present in the room.

In child-training situations parental nonreactions to a child's misdemeanours does not inevitably serve as a cue that the behavior may continue; in fact, many parents effectively utilize nonreaction as a means of inhibiting behavior of which they disapprove. In such situations, however, parents rarely avoid displaying some emotional reaction; consequently, the child's behavior is guided by emotional-intensity cues that parents, sometimes unwittingly, provide. In other words, "nonreaction" usually implies only that parents do not employ the customary methods of overtly rewarding or punishing a child.

Crandall's findings, together with the above considerations, suggested that it would be profitable to examine the responses of children following a film sequence identical to that used in the no-consequence condition, with the addition of a clip that displayed the mother reentering the room and standing beside the child in an impassive manner. Consequently, as a supplementary procedure, a sample of 20 children was shown a film of this kind, ten following early-punishment training and ten following late-punishment training.

After these children had been tested, they were again shown the film and questioned concerning the response of the mother to the model's playing with the toys in order to determine how the mother's nonreaction had been interpreted. The children's answers were recorded on tape and later independently classified by two raters who were not otherwise involved in the study. A third independent rating was secured in order to resolve any disagreements that occurred. If a child changed his description of the mother's behavior during questioning, his initial reaction was used for classification purposes.

Fourteen children were classified as seeing the mother as punitive, five as seeing her as rewarding or at least as not punishing the behavior, while the remaining child refused to respond during the interview. Eight of the children who saw the mother as punitive did not deviate at all, whereas all five of the children who saw the mother as nonpunitive deviated. Mann Whitney U-tests indicated that the two groups differed significantly on all measures of resistance to deviation ($p < 0.05$). While the mother-returns Ss could not be used as an intact group for comparisons with the samples used under other film conditions, the above findings lend weight to the hypothesis that observed consequences to a model may have an inhibitory or disinhibitory effect on the observers.

In this pilot investigation into the influence of nonreaction, the punishing and prohibiting experimenter did not serve as the mother in the film. It is consequently probable that the film-mother's nonresponsiveness was interpreted by the observers in terms of their own prior experiences of maternal nonreaction. In contrast, in Crandall's study, the experimenter who had administered punishments served also as the nonreacting adult; under these circumstances her nonreaction probably provided an explicit cue for the children that, within the social context of the experiment, punishment was no longer forthcoming.

Studies of the consequences of responses to a model (Bandura, 1965; Walters and Parke, 1964) seem, in general, to indicate that these consequences serve as cues indicating the permissibility or nonpermissibility of reproducing the model's behavior in a given social context. They thus can alter the probabilities of occurrence both of responses that existed in the observer's repertory prior to his observation of the performance of these responses by the model and of responses that he has acquired while observing the model. These probabilities can presumably be changed through alterations in the social context brought about by the provision of new incentives and deterrents, the creation or removal of a prohibition, or by subsequent observation of consequences to others who make the responses in question.

REFERENCES

Aronfreed, J. Conscience and conduct: A natural history of the internalization of values. In M. L. Hoffman (Ed.), *Character development.* New York: Soc. Sci. Res. Council, in press.

Aronfreed, J., & Reber, A. Internalized behavioral suppression and the timing of social punishment. *J. person. soc. Psychol.*, 1965, **1**, 3–16.

Bandura, A. Influence of models' reinforcement contingencies on the acquisition of imitative responses. *J. person. soc. Psychol.*, 1965, **1**, 589–595.

Bandura, A., Ross, Dorothea, & Ross, Sheila A. Vicarious reinforcement and imitative learning. *J. abnorm. soc. Psychol.*, 1963, **67**, 601–607.

Bandura, A., & Walters, R. H. *Social learning and personality development.* New York: Holt, 1963.

Banks, R. K., & Vogel-Sprott, Muriel D. The effect of delayed punishment on an immediately rewarded response in humans. *J. exp. Psychol.*, 1965, **70**, 357–359.

Bixtenstein, V. E. Secondary drive as a neutralizer of time in integrative problem solving. *J. comp. physiol. Psychol.*, 1965, **49**, 161–166.

Church, R. M. The varied effects of punishment on behavior. *Psychol. Rev.*, 1963, **70**, 369–402.

Coons, E. E., & Miller, N. E. Conflict versus consolidation of memory traces to explain "retrograde amnesia" produced by ECS. *J. comp. physiol. Psychol.*, 1960, **53**, 524–531.

Crandall, Virginia C. The reinforcement effects of adult reactions and non-reactions on children's achievement expectations. *Child Develpm.*, 1963, **34**, 335–354.

Crandall, Virginia C., Good, Suzanne, & Crandall, V. J. The reinforcement effects of adult reactions and non-reactions on children's achievement expectations: A replication. *Child Develpm.*, 1964, **35**, 485–497.

Kamin, L. J. The delay-of-punishment gradient. *J. comp. physiol. Psychol.*, 1959, **52**, 434–437.

Martin, B. Reward and punishment associated with the same goal response: A factor in the learning of motives. *Psychol. Bull.*, 1963, **60**, 441–451.

Mowrer, O. H. *Learning theory and behavior.* New York: Wiley, 1960. (a)

Mowrer, O. H. *Learning theory and the symbolic processes.* New York: Wiley, 1960. (b)

Mowrer, O. H., & Ullman, A. D. Time as a determinant in integrative learning. *Psychol. Rev.*, 1945, **52**, 61–90.

Sidman, M. Two temporal patterns of the maintenance of avoidance behavior by the white rat. *J. comp. physiol. Psychol.*, 1953, **46**, 253–261.

Solomon, R. L. Punishment. *Amer. Psychol.*, 1964, **19**, 239–253.

Solomon, R. L., & Brush, Elinor S. Experimentally derived conceptions of anxiety and aversion. In M. R. Jones (Ed.), *Nebraska symposium on motivation*. Lincoln: Univer. Nebraska Press, 1956. Pp. 212–305.

Walters, R. H. Delay-of-reinforcement effects in children's learning. *Psychonom. Sci.*, 1964, **1**, 307–308.

Walters, R. H., & Demkow, Lillian F. Timing of punishment as a determinant of response inhibition. *Child Develpm.*, 1963, **34**, 207–214.

Walters, R. H., & Llewellyn-Thomas, E. Enhancement of punitiveness through visual and audiovisual displays. *Canad. J. Psychol.*, 1963, **17**, 244–255.

Walters, R. H., & Parke, R. D. Influence of the response consequences to a social model on resistance to deviation. *J. exp. child Psychol.*, 1964, **1**, 269–280.

Walters, R. H., Leat, Marion, & Mezei, L. Response inhibition and disinhibition through empathetic learning. *Canad. J. Psychol.*, 1963, **17**, 235–243.

ARTICLE 9

The Effective Use of Punishment to Modify Behavior in the Classroom[1]

R.VANCE HALL[2], SAUL AXELROD, MARLYN FOUNDOPOULOS,
JESSICA SHELLMAN, RICHARD A. CAMPBELL, and SHARON S. CRANSTON

University of Kansas

Few topics in education elicit as many emotional responses as the mention of the use of punishment in the classroom. Many educators assert that punishment is ineffective, unnecessary, and inhumane. School boards have increasingly passed laws which limit the type of punishment and the circumstances under which it can be used. Therefore, when the use of punishment is suggested as a means for managing behavior in the classroom it would not be too surprising if many educators would immediately register protest.

Punishment as used in this paper, however, is a technical term which describes a behavioral procedure and will be defined as "any consequence of behavior that reduces the future probability of that behavior (Azrin & Holz, 1966, p. 381)." One can readily recognize that procedures designed to function as punishment are widely used in the schools if this definition is accepted, for teachers *do* give student detentions for being too noisy, *do* send students to the principal's office for fighting, or require that they do extra work for disturbing the class in attempting to reduce the strength of these behaviors.

Even though these procedures are widely used, many educators would

---

[1]This research supported in part by the National Institute of Child Health and Human Development and the Public Health Service (HD-03144-03 Bureau of Child Research and Department of Human Development and Family Life). Reprints may be obtained from R. Vance Hall, Juniper Gardens Children's Project, 2021 North Third Street, Kansas City, Kansas 66101.

Reprinted from *Educational Technology*, Vol. 11, No. 4, April 1971, pp. 24–26.

[2]Post-Doctoral Research Fellow with the Kansas Center in Mental Retardation and Human Development Grant #HD 00183 from the U.S. Public Health Service Department of Health Education and Welfare, National Institute of Child Health and Human Development.

173

question them as good teaching practices. There is also some controversy among the proponents of behavior modification regarding the use of punishment. Azrin and Holz (1966, pp. 438–441) claimed that punishment will produce undesirable side effects, such as social withdrawal and aggression. A study by Risley (1968), however, found no evidence to support this notion.

The present studies focus on the effects of punishment procedures on specific behaviors the classroom teacher wished to reduce or eliminate and which did not result in strong emotional responses.

EXPERIMENT ONE

Subject and Setting

Andrea was a seven-year-old deaf girl enrolled in a public school classroom for the trainable mentally retarded in Kansas City, Kansas. At the beginning of the study, she pinched and bit herself, her peers, the teacher, and visitors to the classroom at every opportunity and was so disruptive the teacher reported that academic instruction was impossible.

Observations

An outside observer tallied the number of times per school day that Andrea bit or pinched herself, or someone else in the classroom. As a check on the reliability of the scoring, the teacher also kept a record of the number of pinches and bites on six different days during the study. The average agreement of their records was 86 percent.

Experimental Phases

Baseline$_1$ A record of the number of bites and pinches under normal conditions was tabulated. Figure 9.1 shows that during this six-day baseline period, the average frequency was 71.8 per day, which indicates that Andrea was very busy indeed.

Pointed Finger and "No" for Bites and Pinches$_1$ During this phase whenever Andrea bit or pinched anyone, the teacher pointed at her with an outstretched arm and shouted "no!" Over the next 18 days the average number of bites and pinches dropped to 5.44 per day.

Baseline₂ To make certain that the decrease in bites and pinches had resulted from the punishment procedure, and not from other factors, baseline conditions were reinstated for three sessions. Once again Andrea could bite and pinch without having the teacher point at her or shout "no!" Immediately, the frequency of bites and pinches rose to a mean of about 30 per day.

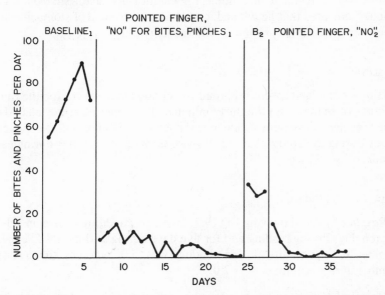

Fig. 9.1. The number of bites and pinches emitted by Andrea during the school day. *Baseline₁* – Prior to the punishment procedure. *Pointed Finger, "No" for Bites and Pinches₁* – Teacher pointing and shouting "no!" at Andrea contingent on bites and pinches. *Baseline₂* – Return to Baseline₁ conditions. *Pointed Finger, "No"₂* – Reinstatement of punishment procedures.

Pointed Finger and "No" for Bites and Pinches₂ When the teacher began pointing and shouting at Andrea for pinching and biting, the mean number of these deviant behaviors decreased to 3.1 per day. The teacher also reported that Andrea had begun to interact with her peers more frequently. Perhaps this was due to the fact that other students were less often punished with bites and pinches when they approached her.

EXPERIMENT TWO

(Taken from Hall, R. V., 1970)

Subject and Setting

Billy was a resident in a home for emotionally disturbed boys. The teacher indicated that he whined, cried, and complained of stomach aches when he was assigned arithmetic and reading tasks.

Observations

Billy's complaints were recorded by an outside observer for the thirty minutes of reading and the thirty minutes of arithmetic periods each day. The regular classroom teacher conducted reliability checks several times during the study. Agreement was 83 percent or better during each check.

Experimental Phases

Baseline$_1$ As shown in Fig. 9.2, baseline conditions were in effect for ten days during reading and for five days during arithmetic. The mean number of complaints during reading was 5.0, whereas the average number during arithmetic was 7.0.

Removal of Name Slips Contingent on Cries, Whines and Complaints$_1$ Beginning on the sixth day, at the start of each reading period the teacher gave Billy five colored slips of paper bearing his name. She informed him that she would take one slip away from him each time he complained during reading. The same procedure was put into effect during arithmetic starting on the eleventh day. The mean number of complaints decreased to 1.6 for the 10 reading sessions and to 2.0 for the five arithmetic sessions.

Baseline$_2$ In order to confirm that the punishment procedures accounted for the decrease in complaints, the teacher removed the contingency on complaining for five sessions. The rate of complaining quickly increased to 2.4 during reading and to 2.8 during arithmetic.

Removal of Slips for Cries, Whines and Complaints$_2$ For five sessions, the teacher once again gave five slips of paper to Bill containing his

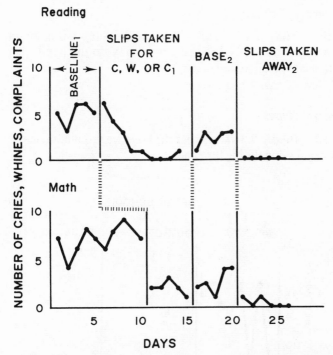

Fig. 9.2. The frequency of Billy's complaints during the 30 minute reading and arithmetic periods. *Baseline*₁ – Prior to experimental conditions. *Slips Taken Away for Crying, Whines, or Complaints*₁ – Teacher removes slips bearing child's name following complaining behaviors. *Baseline*₂ – Return to baseline conditions. *Slips Taken Away*₂ – Same as Slips Taken Away for Crying, Whines, or Complaints₁.

name. One slip was taken away for each complaint during reading and arithmetic. The mean frequency of Bill's complaining dropped to near zero during both subjects.

EXPERIMENT THREE

Subjects and Setting

According to their teacher, the ten boys enrolled in a class for the emotionally disturbed, "roamed around the room" so much that it interfered with their academic development. These boys were the subjects for the third experiment.

Observations

Each time a boy left his seat without permission during the math and reading periods the teacher placed a mark next to the pupil's name on a paper attached to a clipboard.

Experimental Phases

Baseline₁   Figure 9.3 shows that the boys were out of their seats about 23 times per session during baseline.

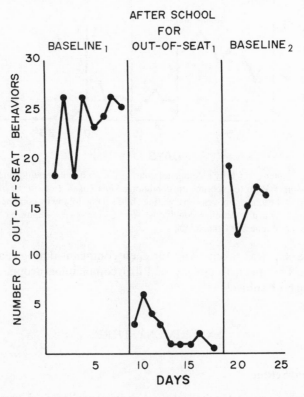

Fig. 9.3. The number of out-of-seat behaviors exhibited by the entire class during the mathematics and reading periods. *Baseline₁* – Prior to experimental procedures. *After School for Out-of-Seat₁* – Student had to remain after school five minutes for each out-of-seat behavior. *Baseline₂* – Return to baseline conditions.

After School Contingent on Out-of-Seat$_1$ During this stage, each boy was told to remain after school for five minutes every time he got out of his seat without permission. During the 10 sessions that this contingency was in effect, the mean number of out-of-seat incidents dropped to 2.2 for the entire class.

Baseline$_2$ Following the punishment phase, a five-day reversal phase was instituted. The boys were no longer given five-minute detentions for getting out of their seats and the behavior quickly increased to 15.8. (Following Baseline$_2$ a punishment procedure was instituted which again reduced out-of-seat behavior to low levels. These results are not included, however, since they were obtained over the entire school day and are therefore not comparable to the previous data.)

EXPERIMENT FOUR

(Taken from Hall, Cristler, Cranston & Tucker, 1970)

Subjects and Setting

The subjects of this experiment were three tenth-grade students in a French class that met daily for 45 minutes in Shawnee Mission, Kansas. At the beginning of the study, the students, two boys and a girl, had been receiving grades that were usually D's or F's on quizzes over homework and class lecture which were given three or four times a week.

Observations

The teacher scored the quizzes. As a check on the reliability of scoring, the teacher had an outstanding student independently score the quizzes. Agreement was 100 percent.

Experimental Phases

Baseline No contingencies were programmed during this stage of the study. Baseline conditions were in effect for 10 days for Dave, 15 days for Roy, and 20 days for Debbie. Grade scores were translated to a four-point scale as follows: $A = 4$, $B = 3$, $C = 2$, $D = 1$, $F = 0$. During this period, Dave's mean score was 0.4 with his median score equal to 0.

Roy's median and mean scores were 0 and 0.74, whereas Debbie had a median of 0 and a mean of 0.35. Figure 9.4 indicates that all three students were almost always getting D's or F's.

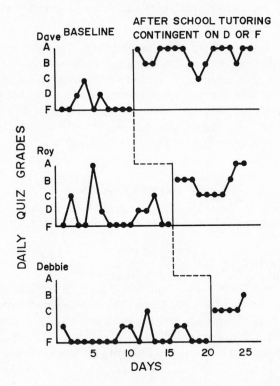

Fig. 9.4. A record of quiz grades for three high school French class students. *Baseline –* Prior to experimental procedures. *After School Tutoring Contingent on Grades of D or F –* Pupils required to stay after school for tutoring if they scored D or F on daily quizzes.

After School Tutoring for Low Grades   After the tenth session, the teacher told Dave that since he was having difficulty with his French lessons, he should come in after school whenever he scored a D or an F and that she would work with him until he knew the lesson well. From that point on Dave's average increased to 3.6 out of a possible 4.0 as can be seen in Fig. 9.4. He received no more D's or F's, in fact began earning A's.

Similar contingencies were programmed for Roy after Session 15 and for Debbie after Session 20. Roy's average increased to 2.8, whereas

Debbie's was 2.2. Neither Roy nor Debbie received any D's or F's from then on.

DISCUSSION

The use of punishment in the classroom is anything but novel. Hitting misbehaving students with rulers or making students sit in a corner with a dunce cap on their heads were common practices in the early days of American education. One of the main differences between these practices and the procedures used here, however, is that the punishment procedures did not involve corporal harm and did not attempt to hold the pupil up to ridicule.

In Experiment One the teacher pointed and shouted "no!" when Andrea bit or pinched. It is open to conjecture whether the teacher's expression, the pointed finger or the shouted "no!" were the punishing stimuli. The important thing is that all or part of these stimuli were punishing and therefore resulted in a decrease in Andrea's inappropriate behaviors. It is also important to note that the teacher reported that Andrea was no longer avoided by her peers after pinching and biting decreased. Hopefully this indicated that she would receive increased reinforcement from her peers so that eventually punishment would be unnecessary in maintaining low rates of pinching and biting.

In Experiment Two, taking away a slip of paper on which Bill's name was written also proved to be punishing since it decreased the rate of his complaining behaviors. (We cannot know why taking the slips was punishing. Perhaps, like the authors of this article, he too liked seeing his name in print.) At any rate, removal of the slips effectively decreased complaining behavior without any apparent adverse emotional responses.

Experiments Three and Four required that pupils stay after school if they violated the criteria for punishment. That these procedures were effective is indicated by the decreases seen in out-of-seat behaviors and poor grades on French quizzes.

Although some of these experiments are more easily recognizable as punishment procedures than others, they all demonstrate that punishment is not synonymous with physical pain or bodily harm and does not necessarily result in emotional responses.

Another important feature of these experiments is that the teachers were *systematic* in the application of the punishing consequences. Rather than depending on their own whims or until "they had had enough" the teachers devised certain behavioral criteria for the application of punishment. Only when pupils violated the criteria were they punished. Perhaps the reason that pupils exhibited little if any emotional behavior in this and in previous research where punishment was used systematically (e.g., Hall, Panyan, Rabon & Broden, 1968) is that they recognized the fairness of systematic procedures.

With few exceptions (Hall, Cristler, Cranston & Tucker, 1970; Hall, Fox, *et al.*, 1970) most published studies in behavior modification have been conducted by researchers sophisticated in the application of learning principles. Often their usefulness has been limited because of the nature and number of personnel required to conduct the studies. In contrast, however, the experiments reported here were designed and carried out by classroom teachers initially unsophisticated in the application of learning theory principles but who reported that the procedures were easy to apply. Furthermore, the studies involved both individual pupils and an entire classroom group, special class settings, and a regular class, and pupils ranging from primary age levels to seniors in high school. The combination of these studies, therefore, implies the general applicability of systematic punishment procedures which do not result in strong emotional behavior to classroom problems.

REFERENCES

Azrin, N. H. & Holz, W. C. Punishment. In W. K. Honig (Ed.), *Operant behavior: Areas of research and application.* New York: Appleton-Century-Crofts, 1966, 213–270.

Hall, R. V. Training teachers in classroom use of contingency management. *Educational Technology*, 1970.

Hall, R. V., Cristler, C., Cranston, S. S., & Tucker, B. Teachers and parents as researchers using multiple-baseline tactics. *Journal of Applied Behavior Analysis*, 1970, 3, 247–255.

Hall, R. V., Fox, R., Willard, D., Goldsmith, L., Emerson, M., Owen, M., Porcia, E., & Davis, R. Modification of disputing and talking out behaviors with the teacher as observer and experimenter. Paper presented at American Educational Research Association Convention, Minneapolis, 1970.

Hall, R. V., Panyan, M., Rabon, D., & Broden, M. Instructing beginning teachers in reinforcement procedures which improve classroom control. *Journal of Applied Behavior Analysis*, 1968, 1, 315–322.

Risley, T. R. The effects and side effects of punishing the autistic behaviors of a deviant child. *Journal of Applied Behavior Analysis*, 1968, 1, 21–34.

The Effects of Loud and Soft Reprimands on the Behavior of Disruptive Students*

K. DANIEL O'LEARY, KENNETH F. KAUFMAN, RUTH E. KASS, and
RONALD S. DRABMAN[1]

State University of New York

Abstract: Two children in each of five classes were selected for a 4 month study because of their high rates of disruptive behavior. During a baseline condition the frequency of disruptive behaviors and teacher reprimands was assessed. Almost all teacher reprimands were found to be of a loud nature and could be heard by many other children in the class. During the second phase of the study, teachers were asked to use primarily soft reprimands which were audible only to the child being reprimanded. With the institution of the soft reprimands, the frequency of disruptive behavior declined in most of the children. Then the teachers were asked to return to the loud reprimand and a consequent increase in disruptive behavior was observed. Finally, the teachers were asked to again use soft reprimands, and again disruptive behavior declined.

A number of studies demonstrate that teacher attention in the form of praise can reduce disruptive classroom behavior (Becker, Madsen, Arnold, & Thomas, 1967; Hall, Lund, & Jackson, 1968; Madsen, Becker, & Thomas, 1968; Walker & Buckley, 1968). In these studies, praising appropriate behavior was usually concomitant with ignoring disruptive behavior. In addition, shaping appropriate behavior or reinforcing successive approximations to some desired terminal behavior was stressed. Despite the generally positive results obtained when a teacher used these procedures, a closer examination of the studies reveals

---

*Reprinted from *Exceptional Children*, Vol. 37, October 1970, pp. 145–155.

[1]K. Daniel O'Leary is Associate Professor of Psychology, State University of New York, Stony Brook, and Kenneth F. Kaufman, Ruth E. Kass, and Ronald S. Drabman are Graduate Students in Psychology, State University of New York, Stony Brook. The research reported herein was performed in part pursuant to Biomedical Sciences Support Grant No. 31-8200-C, US Public Health Service, 1967–69.

that (a) they were not always effective (Hall *et al.*, 1968), (b) the teacher did not actually ignore all disruptive behavior (Madsen *et al.*, 1968), and (c) in one class of disruptive children, praising appropriate behavior and ignoring disruptive behavior resulted in classroom pandemonium (O'Leary, Becker, Evans, & Saudargas, 1969).

One might argue that where praising appropriate behavior and ignoring disruptive behavior prove ineffectual, the teacher is not appropriately shaping the children's behavior. Although such an argument is theoretically rational, it is of little solace to a teacher who unsuccessfully attempts to reinforce approximations to desired terminal behaviors. Furthermore, the supposition that the teacher is not appropriately shaping ignores the power of peers to reinforce disruptive behavior. Disregard of disruptive behavior is based on two premises — that it will extinguish if it is not reinforced and that praising appropriate behavior which is incompatible with disruptive behavior will reduce the frequency of the latter. However, even when a teacher ignores disruptive behavior, other children may reinforce it by giggling and smiling. These peer reactions may occur only occasionally, but they may make the disruptive behavior highly resistant to extinction. Thus, the teacher may ask what she can do when praise and ignoring are not effective. The present studies were designed to assess one alternative to ignoring disruptive behavior: reprimanding the child in a soft manner so that other children in the classroom could not hear the reprimand.

The effectiveness of punishment in suppressing behavior of animals has been amply documented (Solomon, 1964). Similarly, the effectiveness of punishment with children in experimental settings has been repeatedly demonstrated (Parke & Walters, 1967). However, experimental manipulations of punishment or reprimands with disruptive children have not often been investigated in applied settings. One attempt to manipulate teacher reprimands was made by O'Leary and Becker (1968) who varied aspects of teacher attention and found that soft reprimands were effective in reducing disruptive behavior of a class of first-grade children during a rest period. Since soft reprimands seemed to have no adverse side effects in the study and since ignoring disruptive behavior is not always effective, further analyses of the effects of soft reprimands seemed promising.

Soft reprimands offer several interesting advantages over loud ones. First of all, a soft reprimand does not single out the child so that his disruptive behavior is made noticeable to others. Second, a soft reprimand is presumably different from the reprimands that disruptive children ordinarily receive at home or in school, and, consequently, it should minimize the possibility of triggering conditioned emotional reactions to reprimands. Third, teachers consider soft reprimands a viable alternative to the usual methods of dealing with disruptive behavior. Two experiments are presented here which assessed the effects of soft reprimands.

EXPERIMENT I

Two children in a second-grade class were selected for observation because of their high rates of disruptive behavior. During a baseline condition, the frequency of disruptive behaviors and teacher reprimands was assessed. Almost all reprimands were loud, i.e., many children in the class could hear them. During the second phase of the study, the teacher was asked to voice her reprimands so that they would be audible only to the child to whom they were directed. The third phase of the study constituted a return to the teacher's former loud reprimand. Finally, during the fourth condition, the teacher was requested to again use soft reprimands.

Subjects Child D was described as nervous and restless. He bit his nails, drummed his fingers on his desk, and stuttered. He was often out of his seat talking and bothering other children. D avoided any challenging work. He was quick to argue and was known to get into trouble in the neighborhood.

Child S was described as uncooperative and silly. He paid little attention to his work, and he would often giggle and say things out loud. His teacher said that he enjoyed having other children laugh at him and that he acted in this manner to gain attention.

Observation Before base period data were collected, college undergraduates were trained over a 3-week period to observe in the classroom. During this time, the observers obtained reliabilities of child observations exceeding 70 percent agreement. There were two undergraduate observers. One observed daily, and the other observed less frequently, serving as a reliability checker. The observers were instructed to neither talk nor make any differential responses in order to minimize their effect on the children's behavior.

Each child was observed for 20 minutes a day during the arithmetic lesson. Observations were made on a 20-second observe, 10-second record basis: The observer would watch the child for 20 seconds and then record in 10 seconds the disruptive behaviors which had occurred during that 20-second period. The disruptive behaviors were categorized according to nine classes modified from the O'Leary and Becker study (1967). The nine classes of disruptive behavior and their associated general definitions are:

1. *Out-of-chair*: Movement of the child from his chair when not permitted or requested by teacher. No part of the child's body is to be touching the chair.
2. *Modified out-of-chair*: Movement of the child from his chair with some part of the body still touching the chair (exclude sitting on feet).
3. *Touching others' property*: Child comes into contact with another's property without permission to do so. Includes grabbing, rearranging, destroying the property of another, and touching the desk of another.
4. *Vocalization*: Any unpermitted audible behavior emanating from the mouth.
5. *Playing*: Child uses his hands to play with his own or community property so that such behavior is incompatible with learning.
6. *Orienting*: The turning or orienting response is not rated unless the child is seated and the turn must be more than 90 degrees, using the desk as a reference point.
7. *Noise*: Child creating any audible noise other than vocalization without permission.
8. *Aggression*: Child makes movement toward another person to come into contact with him (exclude brushing against another).
9. *Time off task*: Child does not do assigned work for entire 20-second interval. For example, child does not write or read when so assigned.

The dependent measure, mean frequency of disruptive behavior, was calculated by dividing the total number of disruptive behaviors by the number of intervals observed. A mean frequency measure was obtained rather than frequency of disruptive behavior per day since the length of observations varied due to unavoidable circumstances such as assemblies. Nonetheless, only three of the 27 observations for child D lasted less than 20 minutes and only four of the 28 observations for child S were less than 20 minutes. Observations of less than 10 minutes were not included.

Reliability The reliabilities of child observations were calculated according to the following procedure. A perfect agreement was scored if both observers recorded the same disruptive behavior within a 20-second interval. The reliabilities were then calculated by dividing the number of perfect agreements by the number of different disruptive behaviors observed providing a measure of percent agreement. There were three reliability checks during the base period (Loud I) and one during the first soft period for child D. There were two reliability checks during the base period and one reliability check during the first soft period for child S. The four reliability checks for child D yielded the following results: 81, 72, 64, and 92 percent agreement; the three for child S resulted in: 88, 93, and 84 percent agreement.

The reliability of the observations of the teacher's loud and soft reprimands to the target children was also checked. On two different days these observations were taken simultaneously with the observation of the target children. One reliability check was made during the base period and one check was made during the first soft period. A perfect agreement was scored if both observers agreed that the reprimand was loud or soft and if both observers scored the reprimand in the same 20-second interval. The consequent reliabilities were 100 percent and 75 percent during the base period and first soft period respectively.

Procedures

Base Period (Loud I) During the base period the teacher was asked to handle the children as she normally would. Since few, if any, soft reprimands occurred during the base period, this period was considered a loud reprimand phase.

Soft Reprimands I During this phase the following instructions were given to the teacher:

1. Make reprimands soft all day, i.e., speak so that only the child being reprimanded can hear you.
2. Approximately one-half hour before the observers come into your room, concentrate on using soft reprimands so that the observers' entrance does not signal a change in teacher behavior.
3. While the observers are in the room, use only soft reprimands with the target children.
4. Do not increase the frequency of reprimands. Reprimand as frequently as you have always done and vary only the intensity.
5. Use soft reprimands with all the children, not just the target children.

Loud Reprimands II During this phase the teacher was asked to return to loud reprimands, and the five instructions above for the soft period were repeated with a substitution of loud reprimands for soft ones.

Soft Reprimands II   During this final period, the teacher was asked to return to the soft reprimand procedures.

Results

Child D   Child D displayed a marked reaction to soft reprimands. The mean frequency of disruptive behavior during the four conditions was: Loud I, 1.1; Soft I, 0.8; Loud II, 1.3; Soft II, 0.9. A reversal of effects was evident. When the loud reprimands were reinstated disruptive behavior increased while disruptive behavior declined during the second soft period (Fig. 10.1). In addition, in order to more closely examine the effects of the two types of reprimands, there was an assessment of the frequency of disruptive behaviors in the two 20-second intervals after a reprimand, when another reprimand had not occurred in one of the two intervals. The results revealed that the average number of disruptive behaviors in these two intervals during the four conditions was: Loud I, 2.8; Soft I, 1.2; Loud II, 2.6; and Soft II, 1.6.

Child S   Child S also displayed a marked reaction to soft reprimands. The mean frequency of his disruptive behavior during the four conditions was Loud I, 1.4; Soft I, 0.6; Loud II, 1.1; Soft II, 0.5. Again a reversal of effects was evident when the loud reprimands were reinstated. The average number of disruptive behaviors in the two 20-second intervals just after a reprimand was made was as follows during the four conditions: Loud I, 2.9; Soft I, 1.5; Loud II, 2.1; Soft II, 0.9.

Teacher   Although teacher A was asked to hold constant the incidence of her reprimands across conditions, the mean frequency of her reprimands to child D during the four conditions was: Loud I, 7; Soft I, 5;

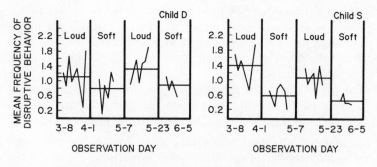

Fig. 10.1. Disruptive behavior of children D and S in Class A.

Loud II, 12; Soft II, 6. Similarly, she also had difficulty in holding constant her reprimands to child S across conditions as the following data show: Loud I, 6; Soft I, 4; Loud II, 8; Soft II, 3. Thus, there is some possibility that the increase in disruptive behavior during the second loud phase was a consequence of increased attention to the behavior per se, rather than the consequence of the kind of attention given whether loud or soft. As the disruptive behavior increased, teacher A felt it impossible to use the same number of reprimands that she had used during the soft period.

Because the frequency of loud reprimands was greater than the frequency of soft reprimands, one could not conclude from Experiment I that the loudness or softness of the reprimands was the key factor in reducing disruptive behavior. It was clear, however, that if a teacher used soft reprimands, she could use fewer reprimands and obtain better behavior than if she used loud reprimands.

EXPERIMENT II

Experiment II was conducted to assess the effects of loud and soft reprimands with the frequency held constant and to test whether all the children's disruptive behavior decreased when the teacher used soft reprimands. Experiment II is divided into three parts. Part I followed the same ABAB paradigm described in Experiment I (Loud, Soft, Loud, Soft), but Parts II and III involved variations which will be described later.

Part I

Subjects   Class B, Grade 2: Child Z was a large boy who said that he wanted to be a bully when he grew up. He was the only child in the class who deliberately hurt other children. He constantly called out answers without raising his hand and his work habits were poor. Child V was extremely talkative. He loved to be with other children and he was always bursting with something to say. He was also mischievous, but never intentionally hurt anyone. His work habits were poor and his papers were never completed.

Class C, Grade 3: Child E was an extremely nervous child. When she directed all her energy to her studies she could perform well. However, she was very undependable and rarely did her work. She was in and out of her seat and talked endlessly. Child W was a disruptive child whose reaction to most situations was to punch, kick, throw things, and to shove others out of his way. He did little work and devoted his time to such activities as chewing his pencils and punching holes in his papers.

↘ *Observation* The observational procedures described earlier in Experiment I were identical to those used in Experiment II. Each target child was observed during a structured academic lesson for 20 minutes each day on a 20-second observe, 10-second record basis. The nine classes of disruptive behavior were the same as those in Experiment I with some definitial extensions and a slight change in the definition of aggression. The dependent measure was calculated in the same manner as described in Experiment I.

To minimize the possibility of distance as the key factor in reprimanding the children, the target children in both classes were moved near the front of the room so that the teacher could administer soft reprimands without walking a great distance. This seating arrangement made it easier for the teacher to reprimand the target children either loudly or softly and decreased the possibility of the teacher's serving as a cue for appropriate behavior by her walking to the child.

The occurrence of loud and soft reprimands was recorded throughout the study by a teacher-observer. As mentioned previously, the teachers were asked to hold the frequency of reprimands constant both to the target children and to the class throughout the study. The teacher was also asked to hold other behaviors as constant as possible so that behaviors such as praise, "eyeing down" a child, and reprimands to the class as a whole would not confound the results. A graduate student observed almost daily and gave the teachers feedback to ensure adherence to these requirements.

In addition to observations on target children, daily observations of disruptive behavior were taken on all the other children by a sampling procedure for one hour each day. Each nontarget child was observed consecutively for 2 minutes. The observer watched the children in a predetermined order each day, looking for the disruptive behaviors that had been observed in the target children.

Reliability The reliabilities of child observations for both the target children and the class samples were calculated according to the procedures discussed in Experiment I. There were three reliability checks during the base period for both target children and the class sample. The average reliability for the target children was 84 percent and for the class sample was 79 percent. Nine additional reliability checks of the observations averaged 79 percent for the target children and 82 percent for the class sample.

The reliability of the observations during the base period of loud and soft reprimands used by Teacher B was 79 percent and 80 percent respectively. The reliability of the observation of loud and soft reprimands used by Teacher C was 82 percent and 72 percent respectively.

Results Because there were definite decreasing trends of disruptive behavior during both soft conditions for three of the four target children, the average of the mean levels of disruptive behavior during the last five days of each condition for the target children are reported in Table 10.1.

Table 10.1. The Average of the Mean Levels of Disruptive Behavior During the Last Five Days of Each Condition for the Target Children

Subjects	Loud I	Soft I	Loud II	Soft II
	Condition			
	($\times = 1.3$)	($\times = 0.9$)	($\times = 1.2$)	($\times = 0.5$)
Child Z	1.0	0.9	1.3	0.8
Child V	1.7	1.4	1.3	0.6
Child E	0.9	0.6	1.1	0.4
Child W	1.6	0.8	0.9	0.3

There were changes in children's behavior associated with changes in teacher behavior (*see* Fig. 10.2). There was a decrease in the children's disruptive behavior in the soft reprimand phase and then an increase in the disruptive behavior of three of the four children during the reinstatement of loud reprimands. Finally, the second soft period was marked by a decrease in disruptive behavior. Although the disruptive behavior of child V did not increase during the reinstitution of loud reprimands, a reduction of disruptive behavior was associated with each introduction of soft reprimands — particularly during the second soft phase. Consequently soft reprimands seemed to influence the reduction of disruptive behavior of each of the four children. A mean reduction of 0.4 and 0.7 disruptive behaviors was associated with each introduction of soft reprimands for these children.

In order to demonstrate that the reduction of disruptive behavior was not a function of changes in frequency of reprimands, the frequencies of

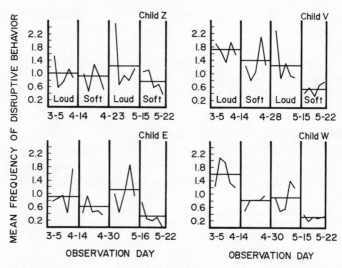

Fig. 10.2. Disruptive behavior of children Z and V in Class B and children E and W in Class C.

loud and soft reprimands are provided in Table 10.2. Although there was some slight reduction of reprimands for individual children during the soft reprimand phases, the teachers were able to hold the frequency of reprimands relatively constant across days and conditions, despite an obvious change in the children's behavior. The mean total reprimands, loud and soft, during the four conditions were as follows: Loud I, 5.7; Soft I, 4.6; Loud II, 5.3; Soft II, 3.7. Also of particular significance was the constancy of praise comments across conditions. There was an average of less than one praise comment per day given to each child in each of the four conditions. It can be inferred from these data that soft reprimands can be influential in modifying classroom behavior of particularly disruptive children.

The data from the class samples taken during the last five days of each condition did not show that soft reprimands reduced disruptive behavior for the whole class. Because of the variability within conditions and the lack of any clear relationship between type of reprimands and level of disruptive behavior, those data are not presented here. However, the changes in the behavior of the target children are evident when one considers that the mean frequency of disruptive behavior for the class sample B was 0.9 throughout the experiment and 0.8 during the second soft condition. The mean frequency of disruptive behavior for the class

Table 10.2. Average Frequency of Loud and Soft Reprimands Per Day

Condition	Type of Reprimand to Child Z		Condition	Type of Reprimand to Child V	
	Loud	Soft		Loud	Soft
Loud I	3.8	2.0	Loud	6.8	2.2
Soft I	0.6	2.6	Soft	0.5	6.7
Loud II	3.0	1.7	Loud	3.5	1.0
Soft II	0.1	2.6	Soft	0.1	3.6

Condition	Reprimand to Child E		Condition	Reprimand to Child W	
	Loud	Soft		Loud	Soft
Loud I	3.5	0.6	Loud	3.3	0.7
Soft I	0.4	5.0	Soft	0.4	2.3
Loud II	5.7	0.9	Loud	5.3	0.3
Soft II	0.2	3.4	Soft	0.1	4.6

sample C was 0.6 throughout the experiment and 0.5 during the second soft condition. Thus one should note that the disruptive behavior of the four target children during the second soft period was less than the level of disruptive behavior for the class.

Part II

Two target children and a class sample were observed in the class of a third-grade teacher. A baseline (Loud I) of disruptive behavior was obtained in this class during a structured academic lesson using the procedures described in Experiment I. In the second phase of the study (Soft I) the teacher was asked to use soft reprimands, just as the other teachers had done. Because of the infrequency of her reprimands in the second phase, the teacher was asked to double her use of soft reprimands in phase three (Soft II-Double). During phase four (Loud II), she was asked to maintain her more frequent use of reprimands but to make them loud. Both child and teacher observations were made in accord with the procedures described in Part I of Experiment II.

Subjects Child B was reported to be a happy extrovert who was a compulsive talker. Child R was described by his teacher as a clown with a very short attention span.

Reliability   The reliability of child observations was obtained for the target children on seven occasions, and the reliability of the class sample on five occasions. The resultant average reliabilities were 87 percent and 87 percent, respectively.

The reliability of the observations of teacher behavior was checked on two occasions during the base period and once during the first soft period. The average reliability of the observations of loud and soft reprimands was 82 percent and 72 percent, respectively.

Results   Child B's disruptive behavior declined from 1.6 during the last five days of baseline (loud reprimands) to 1.3 during the last five days of soft reprimands. In contrast, child R's disruptive behavior increased from 1.5 in the last five days of baseline to 1.9 during the last five days of soft reprimands (*see* Fig. 10.3). With the instructions to increase the use of soft reprimands during phase three (Soft II-Double), child B's disruptive behavior showed a slight drop to 1.1 while child R's increased slightly to 2.0. The return to loud reprimands was associated with an increase to 1.8 for child B and almost no change for child R.

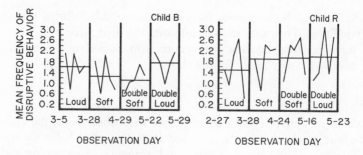

Fig. 10.3. Disruptive behavior of children B and R in Class D.

The increase in child R's disruptive behavior from the loud to the first soft condition cannot be attributed to the soft reprimands. In fact, the change appeared to be due to a decrease in both loud and soft reprimands. Even with the instructions to double the use of soft reprimands, the teacher observations reported in Table 10.3 indicate that the frequency of total reprimands during the double soft phase was less than during baseline. However, since child R's disruptive behavior did not increase with the return to loud reprimands, the experimental control over R's behavior was minimal or nonexistent. On the other hand, child B's disruptive behavior appeared to lessen with the use of soft reprimands.

Table 10.3. Average Frequency of Loud and Soft Reprimands Per Day

Condition	Type of Reprimand to Child B		Condition	Type of Reprimand to Child R	
	Loud	Soft		Loud	Soft
Loud I	2.0	0.4	Loud	1.5	0.2
Soft I	0.5	1.0	Soft	0.2	0.0
Soft II			Double		
(Double)	1.8	1.1	soft	0.0	0.8
Loud II	3.1	2.3	Loud	2.5	0.0

Condition	Reprimand to Child D		Condition	Reprimand to Child J	
	Loud	Soft		Loud	Soft
Loud	4.5	1.3	Loud	1.3	0.2
Soft	0.2	3.2	Soft	0.0	2.2

Again, the data from the class sample did not show that soft reprimands reduced disruptive behavior for the whole class. Those data will not be presented here in detail. The mean frequency of disruptive behavior for the class sample throughout the experiment was 0.62.

Discussion   The failure to decrease child R's disruptive behavior by soft reprimands may have been due to his very deficient academic repertoire. He was so far behind his classmates that group instruction was almost meaningless for him. It is also possible that the teacher felt frustrated because of increases in child R's disruptive behavior when she used soft reprimands; teacher D found them particularly difficult to use. She stated, "It was difficult for me to give soft reprimands as I feared they were a sign of weakness. The walking and whispering necessary to administer soft reprimands to the disruptive child were especially strenuous for me. As the day wore on, I found that my patience became exhausted and my natural tendency to shout like a general took over." Also of particular note was an observer's comment that when verbal reprimands were administered, whether in a loud or soft phase, they were rarely if ever soft in intensity. In summary, teacher D's data showed that soft reprimands did reduce disruptive behavior in one child. Because of lack of evidence for any consistent use of soft reprimands to the second child, nothing can be said conclusively about its use with him.

Part III

In a third-grade class of a fourth teacher, two target children and a class sample were observed during a structured academic activity. A baseline of disruptive behavior was obtained in the class with procedures identical to those of Experiment I. In the second phase of the study, the teacher was asked to use soft reprimands, just as the other teachers had done. Because of some unexpected results following this second phase, the general nature of the study was then changed and those results will not be presented here. Both child and teacher observations were made according to the procedures described in Part I of Experiment II.

Subjects   Child D was a very intelligent boy (135 IQ) who scored in the seventh-grade range on the reading part of the Metropolitan Achievement Test but he was only slightly above grade level in mathematics. His relations with his peers were very antagonistic.

Child J was occasionally considered disruptive by his teacher. However, he did not perform assigned tasks and would often pretend to be working while he actually was not.

Reliability   The reliability of child observations was obtained for the target children on 15 occasions, and the reliability of the class sample was obtained on three occasions. The resultant average reliabilities were 88 percent for the observations of the target children and 91 percent for the observations of the class sample.

The reliability of the observations of teacher behavior was checked on two occasions during the base period and once during the soft period. The average reliability of the observations of loud and soft reprimands on these three occasions was 78 percent and 79 percent respectively.

Results   Child D's disruptive behavior increased from 0.9 during the last five days of baseline (loud reprimands) to 1.0 during the last five days of soft reprimands. Child J's disruptive behavior increased from 0.4 to 0.8 from baseline to the soft reprimand period (*see* Fig. 10.4). There was no change in the class sample from baseline to the soft reprimand period. The mean frequency of disruptive behavior for the class sample during the loud and soft phase was 0.6 and 0.5 respectively.

As can be seen in Table 10.3, teacher E's behavior with child D and child J did appear to have been influenced by the experimental instructions.

Discussion   The reasons that soft reprimands failed to decrease disruptive behavior in this class are not clear. Several factors may have been

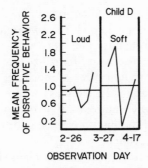 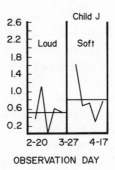

Fig. 10.4. Disruptive behavior of children D and J in Class E.

important. First of all, teacher E was always very skeptical about the possibility that soft reprimands could influence disruptive behavior whereas the other teachers were willing to acknowledge the probability of their influence. Second, it is possible that the children learned to control the teacher's behavior since a soft reprimand had to be made while the teacher was close to the child. That is, a child might realize that he could draw the teacher to his side each time he misbehaved during the soft reprimand period. In addition, this teacher tolerated more disruptive behavior than the other teachers, and her class was much less structured. Probably more important, she wished to investigate the effectiveness of various types of instructional programs rather than soft reprimands.

CONCLUSIONS

These two experiments demonstrated that when teachers used soft reprimands, they were effective in modifying behavior in seven of nine disruptive children. Because of a failure to document the proper use of soft reprimands by one teacher (D) to one child, it is impossible to assess the effectiveness on that child. Of particular significance was the finding that soft reprimands seemed to be associated with an increase in disruptive behavior of one – and possibly two – target children in one teacher's class although the soft reprimands did not influence the level of disruptive behavior for the class as a whole. The results of Experiments I and II lead to the conclusion that with particularly disruptive children a teacher can generally use fewer soft reprimands than loud ones and obtain less disruptive behavior than when loud reprimands are used.

The authors wish to make clear that they do not recommend soft reprimands as an alternative to praise. An ideal combination would probably be frequent praise, some soft reprimands, and very occasional loud reprimands. Furthermore, it is always necessary to realize that classroom management procedures such as praise and types of reprimanding are no substitute for a good academic program. In the class where soft reprimands were ineffective for both target children, a type of individualized instruction was later introduced, and the disruptive behavior of both the target children and the class sample declined.

Because soft reprimands are delivered by a teacher when she is close to a child it is possible that a soft reprimand differs from a loud one in other dimensions than audibility to many children. Although observations of teachers in this study did not reveal that teachers made their soft reprimands in a less harsh, firm, or intense manner than their loud reprimands, it might be possible for a teacher to utilize soft reprimands in such a manner. If the latter were true, soft reprimands might require less teacher effort than loud reprimands. Ultimately soft reprimands might prove more reinforcing for the teacher both because of the relatively small expenditure of effort and the generally positive and sometimes dramatic changes in the children's behavior. The inherent nature of the soft reprimand makes its use impossible at all times, particularly when a teacher has to remain at the blackboard or with a small group in one part of the room. As one teacher mentioned, "I had to do more moving around, but there appeared to be less restlessness in the class."

In sum, it is the authors' opinion that soft reprimands can be a useful method of dealing with disruptive children in a classroom. Combined with praise, soft reprimands might be very helpful in reducing disruptive behavior. In contrast, it appears that loud reprimands lead one into a vicious cycle of more and more reprimands resulting in even more disruptive behavior.

REFERENCES

Becker, W. C., Madsen, C. H., Jr., Arnold, C. & Thomas, D. R. The contingent use of attention and praise in reducing classroom behavior problems. *Journal of Special Education*, 1967, 1, 287–307.

Hall, R. V., Lund, D., & Jackson, D. Effects of teacher attention on study behavior. *Journal of Applied Behavior Analysis*, 1968, 1, 1–12.

Madsen, C. H., Becker, W. C., & Thomas, D. R. Rules, praise, and ignoring: Elements of elementary classroom control. *Journal of Applied Behavior Analysis*, 1968, 1, 139–150.

O'Leary, K. D., & Becker, W. C. Behavior modification of an adjustment class: A token reinforcement program. *Exceptional Children*, 1967, **33**, 637–642.

O'Leary, K. D., & Becker, W. C. The effects of a teacher's reprimands on children's behavior. *Journal of School Psychology*, 1968, **7**, 8–11.

O'Leary, K. D., Becker, W. C., Evans, M. B., & Saudargas, R. A. A token reinforcement program in a public school: A replication and systematic analysis. *Journal of Applied Behavior Analysis*, 1969, **2**, 3–13.

Parke, R. D., & Walters, R. H. Some factors influencing the efficacy of punishment training for inducing response inhibition. *Monographs of the Society for Research in Child Development*, 1967, **32**, (1, Serial No. 109).

Solomon, R. L. Punishment. *American Psychologist*, 1964, **19**, 239–253.

Walker, H. M., & Buckley, N. K. The use of positive reinforcement in conditioning attending behavior. *Journal of Applied Behavior Analysis*, 1968, **1**, 245–250.

CHAPTER 5

Modeling

The phenomenon discussed in this chapter has been variously described in psychology as modeling, copying, vicarious reinforcement, and imitation. There are many everyday examples of modeling. Little girls model their mothers when they "dress up" in high heels and wear lipstick. Children left alone in a car may imitate what they have seen their parents do many times and try to start the car themselves. Children may learn to swear partly as a result of listening to their parents swearing. Modeling is probably important in learning to tie shoes or to be polite. Children whose friends are aggressive might become more aggressive themselves by observing a high frequency of verbal and motor aggression. Television characters may also be modeled as evidenced by the many eight-year-old "Bat Men" using bathroom towels as capes. More specifically, modeling occurs when the probability of a child's response increases as a consequence of the child having observed a "model" exhibit the same or similar behavior.

Experimental studies concerning the effect of films upon the aggressive behavior of the observer have increased the public's awareness of the modeling phenomenon (Eron, 1963). The television industry in particular has initiated research into the influence of television violence and aggression. There are two schools of thought regarding how observing violence affects one's own aggressive or violent behavior. The traditional psychoanalytic catharsis hypothesis contends that participation in aggressive activities or viewing aggressive television programs will release aggressive impulses and thereby reduce the likelihood of future inappropriate aggressive behavior. In contrast ". . . evidence from controlled research

201

studies of children indicates that far from producing a cathartic reduction of aggression, direct or vicarious participation in aggressive activities within a permissive setting maintains the behavior at its original level and may actually increase it (Bandura & Walters, 1963, p. 256)." Because of such findings it would be worthwhile for all educators to pay special attention to the results of experimentation on the effects of television and movies—especially since there is increasing use of audio-visual aids in the schools.

While there is general agreement that modeling is a real and important phenomenon, there is less certainty regarding the nature and development of modeling behavior. We do know that the model may be another child, an adult, a child on a film, a cartoon figure, a puppet, or anything capable of emitting a particular response. The extent to which modeling occurs varies according to the sex, status, humanness, likeability, and age of the model; the observed consequences of the model's behavior; the behavior to be modeled; the behavior the child is engaged in while the model is being observed; and perhaps most important, the consequences to the child's modeling behavior.

The articles in this chapter illustrate the effectiveness of modeling for altering behaviors such as aggression, social isolation, fear of dogs, and disruptive classroom behavior. A discussion of the research on modeling and suggestions for the use of modeling by teachers follows the articles.

ARTICLE 11

Imitation of Film-Mediated Aggressive Models*[1]

ALBERT BANDURA, DOROTHEA ROSS,[2] and SHEILA A. ROSS

Stanford University

Abstract: In a test of the hypothesis that exposure of children to film-mediated aggressive models would increase the probability of Ss' aggression to subsequent frustration, 1 group of experimental Ss observed real-life aggressive models, a 2nd observed these same models portraying aggression on film, while a 3rd group viewed a film depicting an aggressive cartoon character. Following the exposure treatment, Ss were mildly frustrated and tested for the amount of imitative and nonimitative aggression in a different experimental setting. The overall results provide evidence for both the facilitating and the modeling influence of film-mediated aggressive stimulation. In addition, the findings reveal that the effects of such exposure are to some extent a function of the sex of the model, sex of the child, and the reality cues of the model.

Most of the research on the possible effects of film-mediated stimulation upon subsequent aggressive behavior has focused primarily on the drive reducing function of fantasy. While the experimental evidence for the catharsis or drive reduction theory is equivocal (Albert, 1957; Berkowitz, 1962; Emery, 1959; Feshbach, 1955, 1958; Kenny, 1952; Lövaas, 1961; Siegel, 1956), the modeling influence of pictorial stimuli has received little research attention.

A recent incident (San Francisco Chronicle, 1961) in which a boy was

*Reprinted from the *Journal of Abnormal and Social Psychology*, Vol. 66, No. 1, 1963, pp. 3–11, by permission of the American Psychological Association.

[1]This investigation was supported in part by Research Grants M-4398 and M-5162 from the National Institute of Health, United States Public Health Service, and the Lewis S. Haas Child Development Research Fund, Stanford University.

The authors are indebted to David J. Hicks for his generous assistance with the photography and to John Steinbruner who assisted with various phases of this study.

[2]This research was carried out while the junior author was the recipient of an American Association of University Women International Fellowship for postdoctoral research.

seriously knifed during a re-enactment of a switchblade knife fight the boys had seen the previous evening on a televised rerun of the James Dean movie, *Rebel Without a Cause*, is a dramatic illustration of the possible imitative influence of film stimulation. Indeed, anecdotal data suggest that portrayal of aggression through pictorial media may be more influential in shaping the form aggression will take when a person is instigated on later occasions, than in altering the level of instigation to aggression.

In an earlier experiment (Bandura & Huston, 1961), it was shown that children readily imitated aggressive behavior exhibited by a model in the presence of the model. A succeeding investigation (Bandura, Ross, & Ross, 1961), demonstrated that children exposed to aggressive models generalized aggressive responses to a new setting in which the model was absent. The present study sought to determine the extent to which film-mediated aggressive models may serve as an important source of imitative behavior.

Aggressive models can be ordered on a reality-fictional stimulus dimension with real-life models located at the reality end of the continuum, nonhuman cartoon characters at the fictional end, and films portraying human models occupying an intermediate position. It was predicted, on the basis of saliency and similarity of cues, that the more remote the model was from reality, the weaker would be the tendency for subjects to imitate the behavior of the model.

Of the various interpretations of imitative learning, the sensory feedback theory of imitation recently proposed by Mowrer (1960) is elaborated in greatest detail. According to this theory, if certain responses have been repeatedly positively reinforced, proprioceptive stimuli associated with these responses acquire secondary reinforcing properties and thus the individual is predisposed to perform the behavior for the positive feedback. Similarly, if responses have been negatively reinforced, response correlated stimuli acquire the capacity to arouse anxiety which, in turn, inhibit the occurrence of the negatively valenced behavior. On the basis of these considerations, it was predicted subjects who manifest high aggression anxiety would perform significantly less imitative and nonimitative aggression than subjects who display little anxiety over aggression. Since aggression is generally considered female inappropriate behavior, and therefore likely to be negatively reinforced in girls (Sears, Maccoby, & Levin, 1957), it was also predicted that male subjects would be more imitative of aggression than females.

To the extent that observation of adults displaying aggression conveys a certain degree of permissiveness for aggressive behavior, it may be assumed that such exposure not only facilitates the learning of new aggressive responses but also weakens competing inhibitory responses in subjects and thereby increases the probability of occurrence of previously learned patterns of aggression. It was predicted, therefore, that subjects who observed aggressive models would display significantly more aggression when subsequently frustrated than subjects who were equally frustrated but who had no prior exposure to models exhibiting aggression.

METHOD

Subjects

The subjects were 48 boys and 48 girls enrolled in the Stanford University Nursery School. They ranged in age from 35 to 69 months, with a mean age of 52 months.

Two adults, a male and a female, served in the role of models both in the real-life and the human film-aggression condition, and one female experimenter conducted the study for all 96 children.

General Procedure

Subjects were divided into three experimental groups and one control group of 24 subjects each. One group of experimental subjects observed real-life aggressive models, a second group observed these same models portraying aggression on film, while a third group viewed a film depicting an aggressive cartoon character. The experimental groups were further subdivided into male and female subjects so that half the subjects in the two conditions involving human models were exposed to same-sex models, while the remaining subjects viewed models of the opposite sex.

Following the exposure experience, subjects were tested for the amount of imitative and nonimitative aggression in a different experimental setting in the absence of the models.

The control group subjects had no exposure to the aggressive models and were tested only in the generalization situation.

Subjects in the experimental and control groups were matched individually on the basis of ratings of their aggressive behavior in social interactions in the nursery school. The experimenter and a nursery school teacher rated the subjects on four five-point rating scales which measured the extent to which subjects displayed physical aggression, verbal aggression, aggression toward inanimate objects, and aggression inhibition. The latter scale, which dealt with the subjects' tendency to inhibit aggressive reactions in the face of high instigation, provided the measure of aggression anxiety. Seventy-one percent of the subjects were rated independently by both judges so as to permit an assessment of interrater agreement. The reliability of the composite aggression score, estimated by means of the Pearson product-moment correlation, was 0.80.

Data for subjects in the real-life aggression condition and in the control group were collected as part of a previous experiment (Bandura *et al.*, 1961). Since the procedure is described in detail in the earlier report, only a brief description of it will be presented here.

Experimental Conditions

Subjects in the Real-Life Aggressive condition were brought individually by the experimenter to the experimental room and the model, who was in the hallway outside the room, was invited by the experimenter to come and join in the game. The subject was then escorted to one corner of the room and seated at a small table which contained potato prints, multicolor picture stickers, and colored paper. After demonstrating how the subject could design pictures with the materials provided, the experimenter escorted the model to the opposite corner of the room which contained a small table and chair, a tinker toy set, a mallet, and a 5-foot inflated Bobo doll. The experimenter explained that this was the model's play area and after the model was seated, the experimenter left the experimental room.

The model began the session by assembling the tinker toys but after approximately a minute had elapsed, the model turned to the Bobo doll and spent the remainder of the period aggressing toward it with highly novel responses which are unlikely to be performed by children independently of the observation of the model's behavior. Thus, in addition to punching the Bobo doll, the model exhibited the following distinctive aggressive acts which were to be scored as imitative responses.

The model sat on the Bobo doll and punched it repeatedly in the nose.

The model then raised the Bobo doll and pommeled it on the head with a mallet.

Following the mallet aggression, the model tossed the doll up in the air aggressively and kicked it about the room. This sequence of physically aggressive acts was repeated approximately three times, interspersed with verbally aggressive responses such as, "Sock him in the nose...," "Hit him down...," "Throw him in the air...," "Kick him...," and "Pow."

Subjects in the Human Film-Aggression condition were brought by the experimenter to the semi-darkened experimental room, introduced to the picture materials, and informed that while the subjects worked on potato prints, a movie would be shown on a screen, positioned approximately 6 feet from the subject's table. The movie projector was located in a distant corner of the room and was screened from the subject's view by large wooden panels.

The color movie and a tape recording of the sound track was begun by a male projectionist as soon as the experimenter left the experimental room and was shown for a duration of 10 minutes. The models in the film presentations were the same adult males and females who participated in the Real-Life condition of the experiment. Similarly, the aggressive behavior they portrayed in the film was identical with their real-life performances.

For subjects in the Cartoon Film-Aggression condition, after seating the subject at the table with the picture construction material, the experimenter walked over to a television console approximately 3 feet in front of the subject's table, remarked, "I guess I'll turn on the color TV," and ostensibly tuned in a cartoon program. The experimenter then left the experimental room. The cartoon was shown on a glass lens screen in the television set by means of a rear projection arrangement screened from the subject's view by large panels.

The sequence of aggressive acts in the cartoon was performed by the female model costumed as a black cat similar to the many cartoon cats. In order to heighten the level of irreality of the cartoon, the floor area was covered with artificial grass and the walls forming the backdrop were adorned with brightly colored trees, birds, and butterflies creating a fantasyland setting. The cartoon began with a close-up of a stage on which the curtains were slowly drawn revealing a picture of a cartoon cat along with the title, *Herman the Cat*. The remainder of the film showed the cat pommeling the Bobo doll on the head with a mallet, sitting on the doll and punching it in the nose, tossing the doll in the air, and kicking it about the room in a manner identical with the performance in the other experimental conditions except that the cat's movements were characteristically feline. To induce further a cartoon set, the program was introduced and concluded with appropriate cartoon music, and the cat's verbal aggression was repeated in a high-pitched, animated voice.

In both film conditions, at the conclusion of the movie the experimenter entered the room and then escorted the subject to the test room.

Aggression Instigation

In order to differentiate clearly the exposure and test situations subjects were tested for the amount of imitative learning in a different experimental room which was set off from the main nursery school building.

The degree to which a child has learned aggressive patterns of behavior through imitation becomes most evident when the child is instigated to aggression on later occasions. Thus, for example, the effects of viewing the movie, *Rebel Without a Cause*, were not evident until the boys were instigated to aggression the following day, at which time they re-enacted the televised switchblade knife fight in considerable detail. For this reason, the children in the experiment, both those in the control group, and those who were exposed to the aggressive models were mildly frustrated before they were brought to the test room.

Following the exposure experience, the experimenter brought the subject to an anteroom which contained a varied array of highly attractive toys. The experimenter explained that the toys were for the subject to play with, but, as soon as the subject became sufficiently involved with the play material, the experimenter remarked that these were her very best toys, that she did not let just anyone play with them, and that she had decided to reserve these toys for some other children. However, the subject could play with any of the toys in the next room. The experimenter and the subject then entered the adjoining experimental room.

It was necessary for the experimenter to remain in the room during the experimental session; otherwise, a number of the children would either refuse to remain alone or would leave before the termination of the session. In order to minimize any influence her presence might have on the subject's behavior, the experimenter remained as inconspicuous as possible by busying herself with paper work at a desk in the far corner of the room and avoiding any interaction with the child.

Test for Delayed Imitation

The experimental room contained a variety of toys, some of which could be used in imitative or nonimitative aggression, and others which tended to elicit predominantly nonaggressive forms of behavior. The aggressive toys included a 3-foot Bobo doll, a mallet and peg board, two dart guns, and a tether ball with a face painted on it which hung from the ceiling. The nonaggressive toys, on the other hand, included a tea set, crayons and coloring paper, a ball, two dolls, three bears, cars and trucks, and plastic farm animals.

In order to eliminate any variation in behavior due to mere placement of the toys in the room, the play material was arranged in a fixed order for each of the sessions.

The subject spent 20 minutes in the experimental room during which time his behavior was rated in terms of predetermined response categories by judges who observed the session through a one-way mirror in an adjoining observation room. The 20-minute session was divided in 5-second intervals by means of an electric interval timer, thus yielding a total number of 240 response units for each subject.

The male model scored the experimental sessions for all subjects. In order to provide an estimate of interjudge agreement, the performances of 40% of the subjects were scored independently by a second observer. The responses scored involved highly specific concrete classes of behavior, and yielded high interscorer reliabilities, the product-moment coefficients being in the 0.90s.

Response Measures

The following response measures were obtained:

Imitative aggression   This category included acts of striking the Bobo doll with the mallet, sitting on the doll and punching it in the nose, kicking the doll, tossing it in the air, and the verbally aggressive responses, "Sock him," "Hit him down," "Kick him," "Throw him in the air," and "Pow."

Partially imitative responses   A number of subjects imitated the essential components of the model's behavior but did not perform the complete act, or they directed the imitative aggressive response to some object other than the Bobo doll. Two responses of this type were scored and were interpreted as partially imitative behavior:

Mallet aggression   The subject strikes objects other than the Bobo doll aggressively with the mallet.

Sits on Bobo doll   The subject lays the Bobo doll on its side and sits on it, but does not aggress toward it.

Nonimitative aggression   This category included acts of punching, slapping, or pushing the doll, physically aggressive acts directed toward objects other than the Bobo doll, and any hostile remarks except for those in the verbal imitation category; for example, "Shoot the Bobo," "Cut him" "Stupid ball," "Knock over people," "Horses fighting, biting."

Aggressive gun play   The subject shoots darts or aims the guns and fires imaginary shots at objects in the room.

Ratings were also made of the number of behavior units in which subjects played nonaggressively or sat quietly and did not play with any of the material at all.

RESULTS

The mean imitative and nonimitative aggression scores for subjects in the various experimental and control groups are presented in Table 11.1.

Since the distributions of scores departed from normality and the assumption of homogeneity of variance could not be made for most of the measures, the Freidman two-way analysis of variance by ranks was employed for testing the significance of the obtained differences.

Total Aggression

The mean total aggression scores for subjects in the real-life, human film, cartoon film, and the control groups are 83, 92, 99, and 54, respectively. The results of the analysis of variance performed on these scores reveal that the main effect of treatment conditions is significant ($\chi_r^2 = 9.06$, $p < 0.05$), confirming the prediction that exposure of subjects to aggressive models increases the probability that subjects will respond aggressively when instigated on later occasions. Further analyses of pairs of scores by means of the Wilcoxon matched-pairs signed-ranks test show that subjects who viewed the real-life models and the film-mediated models do not differ from each other in total aggressiveness but all three experimental groups expressed significantly more aggressive behavior than the control subjects (Table 11.2).

Imitative Aggressive Responses

The Freidman analysis reveals that exposure of subjects to aggressive models is also a highly effective method for shaping subjects' aggressive

Table 11.1. Mean aggression scores for subgroups of experimental and control subjects

Response category	Experimental groups					
	Real-life aggressive		Human film-aggressive		Cartoon film-aggressive	Control group
	F Model	M Model	F Model	M Model		
Total aggression						
Girls	65.8	57.3	87.0	79.5	80.9	36.4
Boys	76.8	131.8	114.5	85.0	117.2	72.2
Imitative aggression						
Girls	19.2	9.2	10.0	8.0	7.8	1.8
Boys	18.4	38.4	34.3	13.3	16.2	3.9
Mallet aggression						
Girls	17.2	18.7	49.2	19.5	36.8	13.1
Boys	15.5	28.8	20.5	16.3	12.5	13.5
Sits on Bobo doll[a]						
Girls	10.4	5.6	10.3	4.5	15.3	3.3
Boys	1.3	0.7	7.7	0.0	5.6	0.6
Nonimitative aggression						
Girls	27.6	24.9	24.0	34.3	27.5	17.8
Boys	35.5	48.6	46.8	31.8	71.8	40.4
Aggressive gun play						
Girls	1.8	4.5	3.8	17.6	8.8	3.7
Boys	7.3	15.9	12.8	23.7	16.6	14.3

[a]This response category was not included in the total aggression score.

responses ($\chi_r^2 = 23.88$, $p < 0.001$). Comparisons of treatment conditions by the Wilcoxon test reveal that subjects who observed the real-life models and the film-mediated models, relative to subjects in the control group, performed considerably more imitative physical and verbal aggression (Table 11.2).

Illustrations of the extent to which some of the subjects became virtually "carbon copies" of their models in aggressive behavior are presented in Fig. 11.1. The top frame shows the female model performing the four novel aggressive responses; the lower frames depict a male and a female subject reproducing the behavior of the female model they had observed earlier on film.

The prediction that imitation is positively related to the reality cues of the model was only partially supported. While subjects who observed the

Table 11.2. Significance of the Differences between Experimental and Control Groups in the Expression of Aggression

Response category	χ_r^2	p	Comparison of treatment conditions[a]					
			Live vs. Film p	Live vs. Cartoon p	Film vs. Cartoon p	Live vs. Control p	Film vs. Control p	Cartoon vs. Control p
Total aggression	9.06	< 0.05	ns	ns	ns	< 0.01	< 0.01	< 0.005
Imitative aggression	23.88	< 0.001	ns	< 0·05	ns	< 0.001	< 0.001	< 0.005
Partial imitation								
Mallet aggression	7.36	0.10 > p > 0.05						
Sits on Bobo doll	8.05	< 0.05	ns	ns	ns	ns	< 0.05	< 0.005
Nonimitative aggression	7.28	0.10 > p > 0.05						
Aggressive gun play	8.06	< 0.05	< 0.01[b]	ns	ns	ns	< 0.05	ns

[a]The probability values are based on the Wilcoxon test.
[b]This probability value is based on a two-tailed test of significance.

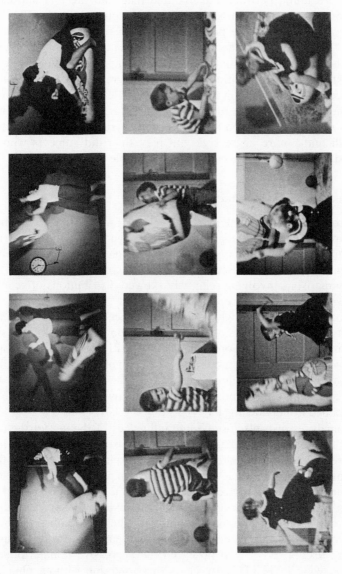

Fig. 11.1. Photographs from the film, *Social Learning of Aggression through Imitation of Aggressive Models.*

real-life aggressive models exhibited significantly more imitative aggression than subjects who viewed the cartoon model, no significant differences were found between the live and film, and the film and cartoon conditions, nor did the three experimental groups differ significantly in total aggression or in the performances of partially imitative behavior (Table 11.2). Indeed, the available data suggest that, of the three experimental conditions, exposure to humans on film portraying aggression was the most influential in eliciting and shaping aggressive behavior. Subjects in this condition, in relation to the control subjects, exhibited more total aggression, more imitative aggression, more partially imitative behavior, such as sitting on the Bobo doll and mallet aggression, and they engaged in significantly more aggressive gun play than did subjects who were exposed to the real-life aggressive models (Table 11.2).

Influence of Sex of Model and Sex of Child

In order to determine the influence of sex of model and sex of child on the expression of imitative and nonimitative aggression, the data from the experimental groups were combined and the significance of the differences between groups was assessed by t tests for uncorrelated means. In statistical comparisons involving relatively skewed distributions of scores the Mann-Whitney U test was employed.

Sex of subjects had a highly significant effect on both the learning and the performance of aggression. Boys, in relation to girls, exhibited significantly more total aggression ($t = 2.69$, $p < 0.01$), more imitative aggression ($t = 2.82$, $p < 0.005$), more aggressive gun play ($z = 3.38$, $p < 0.001$), and more nonimitative aggressive behavior ($t = 2.98$, $p < 0.005$). Girls, on the other hand, were more inclined than boys to sit on the Bobo doll but refrained from punching it ($z = 3.47$, $p < 0.001$).

The analyses also disclosed some influences of the sex of the model. Subjects exposed to the male model, as compared to the female model, expressed significantly more aggressive gun play ($z = 2.83$, $p < 0.005$). The most marked differences in aggressive gun play ($U = 9.5$, $p < 0.001$), however, were found between girls exposed to the female model ($M = 2.9$) and males who observed the male model ($M = 19.8$). Although the overall model difference in partially imitative behavior, Sits on Bobo, was not significant, Sex × Model subgroup comparisons yielded some interesting results. Boys who observed the aggressive female model, for example, were more likely to sit on the Bobo doll without punching it than boys who viewed the male model ($U = 33$, $p < 0.05$). Girls reproduced the nonaggressive component of the male model's aggressive pattern of behavior (i.e., sat on the doll without punching it) with considerably higher frequency than did boys who observed the same model ($U = 21.5$, $p < 0.02$). The highest incidence of partially imitative responses was yielded by the group of girls who viewed the aggressive female model ($M = 10.4$), and the lowest values by the boys who were exposed to the male model ($M = 0.3$). This difference was significant beyond the 0.05 significance level. These findings, along with the sex of child and sex of model differences reported in the preceding sections, provide further support for the view that the influence of models in promoting social learning is determined, in part, by the sex appropriateness of the model's behavior (Bandura *et al.*, 1961).

Aggressive Predisposition and Imitation

Since the correlations between ratings of aggression and the measures of imitative and total aggressive behavior, calculated separately for boys and girls in each of the experimental conditions, did not differ significantly, the data were combined. The correlational analyses performed on these pooled data failed to yield any significant relationships between ratings of aggression anxiety, frequency of aggressive behavior, and the experimental aggression measures. In fact, the array means suggested nonlinear regressions although the departures from linearity were not of sufficient magnitude to be statistically significant.

DISCUSSION

The results of the present study provide strong evidence that exposure to filmed aggression heightens aggressive reactions in children. Subjects who viewed the aggressive human and cartoon models on film exhibited nearly twice as much aggression than did subjects in the control group who were not exposed to the aggressive film content.

In the experimental design typically employed for testing the possible cathartic function of vicarious aggression, subjects are first frustrated, then provided with an opportunity to view an aggressive film following which their overt or fantasy aggression is measured. While this procedure yields some information on the immediate influence of film-mediated aggression, the full effects of such exposure may not be revealed until subjects are instigated to aggression on a later occasion. Thus, the present study, and one recently reported by Lövaas (1961), both utilizing a design in which subjects first observed filmed aggression and then were frustrated, clearly reveal that observation of models portraying aggression on film substantially increases rather than decreases the probability of aggressive reactions to subsequent frustrations.

Filmed aggression, not only facilitated the expression of aggression, but also effectively shaped the form of the subjects' aggressive behavior. The finding that children modeled their behavior to some extent after the film characters suggests that pictorial mass media, particularly television, may serve as an important source of social behavior. In fact, a possible generalization of responses originally learned in the television situation to the experimental film may account for the significantly greater amount of aggressive gun play displayed by subjects in the film condition as compared to subjects in the real-life and control groups. It is unfortunate that the qualitative features of the gun behavior were not scored since subjects in the film condition, unlike those in the other two groups, developed interesting elaborations in gun play (for example, stalking the imaginary opponent, quick drawing, and rapid firing), characteristic of the Western gun fighter.

The view that the social learning of aggression through exposure to aggressive film content is confined to deviant children (Schramm, Lyle, & Parker, 1961), finds little support in our data. The children who participated in the experiment are by no means a deviant sample, nevertheless, 88% of the subjects in the Real-Life and in the Human Film condition, and 79% of the subjects in the Cartoon Film condition, exhibited varying degrees of imitative aggression. In assessing the possible influence of televised stimulation on viewers' behavior, however, it is important to distinguish between learning and overt performance. Although the results of the present experiment demonstrate that the vast majority of children *learn* patterns of social behavior through pictorial stimulation, nevertheless, informal observation suggests that children do not, as a rule, *perform* indiscriminately the behavior of televised characters, even those they regard as highly attractive models. The replies of parents whose children participated in the present study to an open-end questionnaire item concerning their handling of imitative behavior suggest that this may be in part a function of negative reinforcement, as most parents were quick to discourage their children's overt imitation of television characters by prohibiting certain programs or by labeling the imitative behavior in a disapproving manner. From our knowledge of the effects of punishment on behavior, the responses in question would be expected to retain their original strength and could reappear on later occasions in the presence of appropriate eliciting stimuli, particularly if instigation is high, the instruments for aggression are available, and the threat of noxious consequences is reduced.

The absence of any relationships between ratings of the children's predisposition to aggression and their aggressive behavior in the experimental setting may simply reflect the inadequacy of the predictor measures. It may be pointed out, however, that the reliability of the ratings was relatively high. While this does not assure validity of the measures, it does at least indicate there was consistency in the raters estimates of the children's aggressive tendencies.

A second, and perhaps more probable, explanation is that proprioceptive feedback alone is not sufficient to account for response inhibition or facilitation. For example, the proprioceptive cues arising from hitting responses directed toward parents and toward peers may differ little, if any; nevertheless, tendencies to aggress toward parents are apt to be strongly inhibited while peer aggression may be readily expressed (Bandura, 1960; Bandura & Walters, 1959). In most social interaction sequences, proprioceptive cues make up only a small part of the total stimulus complex and, therefore, it is necessary to take into consideration additional stimulus components, for the most part external, which probably serve as important discriminative cues for the expression of aggression. Consequently, prediction of the occurrence or inhibition of specific classes of responses would be expected to depend upon the presence of a certain pattern of proprioceptive or introceptive stimulation together with relevant discriminative external stimuli.

According to this line of reasoning, failure to obtain the expected positive relationships between the measures of aggression may be due primarily to the fact that permissiveness for aggression, conveyed by situational cues in the form of aggressive film content and play material, was sufficient to override the influence of internal stimuli generated by the commission of aggressive responses. If, in fact, the behavior of young children, as compared to that of adults, is less likely to be under internal stimulus control, one might expect environmental cues to play a relatively important role in eliciting or inhibiting aggressive behavior.

A question may be raised as to whether the aggressive acts studied in the present experiment constitute "genuine" aggressive responses. Aggression is typically defined as behavior, the goal or intent of which is injury to a person, or destruction of an object (Bandura & Walters, 1959; Dollard, Doob, Miller, Mowrer, & Sears, 1939; Sears, Maccoby,

& Levin, 1957). Since intentionality is not a property of behavior but primarily an inference concerning antecedent events, the categorization of an act as "aggressive" involves a consideration of both stimulus and mediating or terminal response events.

According to a social learning theory of aggression recently proposed by Bandura and Walters (1963), most of the responses utilized to hurt or to injure others (for example, striking, kicking, and other responses of high magnitude), are probably learned for prosocial purposes under nonfrustration conditions. Since frustration generally elicits responses of high magnitude, the latter classes of responses, once acquired, may be called out in social interactions for the purpose of injuring others. On the basis of this theory it would be predicted that the aggressive responses acquired imitatively, while not necessarily mediating aggressive goals in the experimental situation, would be utilized to serve such purposes in other social settings with higher frequency by children in the experimental conditions than by children in the control group.

The present study involved primarily vicarious or emphatic learning (Mowrer, 1960) in that subjects acquired a relatively complex repertoire of aggressive responses by the mere sight of a model's behavior. It has been generally assumed that the necessary conditions for the occurrence of such learning is that the model perform certain responses followed by positive reinforcement to the model (Hill, 1960; Mowrer, 1960). According to this theory, to the extent that the observer experiences the model's reinforcement vicariously, the observer will be prone to reproduce the model's behavior. While there is some evidence from experiments involving both human (Lewis & Duncan, 1958; McBrearty, Marston, & Kanfer, 1961; Sechrest, 1961) and animal subjects (Darby & Riopelle, 1959; Warden, Fjeld, & Koch, 1940), that vicarious reinforcement may in fact increase the probability of the behavior in question, it is apparent from the results of the experiment reported in this paper that a good deal of human imitative learning can occur without any reinforcers delivered either to the model or to the observer. In order to test systematically the influence of vicarious reinforcement on imitation, however, a study is planned in which the degree of imitative learning will be compared in situations in which the model's behavior is paired with reinforcement with those in which the model's responses go unrewarded.

REFERENCES

Albert, R. S. The role of mass media and the effect of aggressive film content upon children's aggressive responses and identification choices. *Genet. psychol. Monogr.*, 1957, **55**, 221–285.

Bandura, A. Relationship of family patterns to child behavior disorders. Progress Report, 1960, Stanford University, Project No. M-1734, United States Public Health Service.

Bandura, A., & Huston, Aletha C. Identification as a process of incidental learning. *J. abnorm. soc. Psychol.*, 1961, **63**, 311–318.

Bandura, A., Ross, Dorothea, & Ross, Sheila A. Transmission of aggression through imitation of aggressive models. *J. abnorm. soc. Psychol.*, 1961, **63**, 575–582.

Bandura, A., & Walters, R. H. *Adolescent aggression*. New York: Ronald, 1959.

Bandura, A., & Walters, R. H. *Social learning and personality development*. New York: Holt, Rinehart, & Winston, 1963.

Berkowitz, L. *Aggression: A social psychological analysis*. New York: McGraw-Hill, 1962.

Darby, C. L., & Riopelle, A. J. Observational learning in the Rhesus monkey. *J. comp. physiol. Psychol.*, 1959, **52**, 94–98.

Dollard, J., Doob, L. W., Miller, N. E., Mowrer, O. H., & Sears, R. R. *Frustration and aggression*. New Haven: Yale Univer. Press, 1939.

Emery, F. E. Psychological effects of the Western film: A study in television viewing: II. The experimental study. *Hum. Relat.*, 1959, **12**, 215–232.

Feshbach, S. The drive-reducing function of fantasy behavior. *J. abnorm. soc. Psychol.*, 1955, **50**, 3–11.

Feshbach, S. The stimulating versus cathartic effects of a vicarious aggressive activity. Paper read at the Eastern Psychological Association, 1958.

Hill, W. F. Learning theory and the acquisition of values. *Psychol. Rev.*, 1960, **67**, 317–331.

Kenny, D. T. An experimental test of the catharsis theory of aggression. Unpublished doctoral dissertation, University of Washington, 1952.

Lewis, D. J., & Duncan, C. P. Vicarious experience and partial reinforcement. *J. abnorm. soc. Psychol.*, 1958, **57**, 321–326.

Lövaas, O. J. Effect of exposure to symbolic aggression on aggressive behavior. *Child Develpm.*, 1961, **32**, 37–44.

McBrearty, J. F., Marston, A. R., & Kanfer, F. H. Conditioning a verbal operant in a group setting: Direct vs. vicarious reinforcement. *Amer. Psychologist*, 1961, **16**, 425. (Abstract).

Mowrer, O. H. *Learning theory and the symbolic processes*. New York: Wiley, 1960.

San Francisco Chronicle. "James Dean" knifing in South City. *San Francisco Chron.*, March 1, 1961, 6.

Schramm, W., Lyle, J., & Parker, E. B. *Television in the lives of our children*. Stanford: Stanford Univer. Press, 1961.

Sears, R. R., Maccoby, Eleanor E., & Levin, H. *Patterns of child rearing*. Evanston: Row, Peterson, 1957.

Sechrest, L. Vicarious reinforcement of responses. *Amer. Psychologist*, 1961, **16**, 356. (Abstract)

Siegel, Alberta E. Film-mediated fantasy aggression and strength of aggressive drive. *Child Develpm.*, 1956, **27**, 365–378.

Warden, C. J., Fjeld, H. A., & Koch, A. M. Imitative behavior in cebus and Rhesus monkeys. *J. Genet. Psychol.*, 1940, **56**, 311–322.

ARTICLE 12

Vicarious Extinction of Avoidance Behavior*[1]

ALBERT BANDURA, JOAN E. GRUSEC, and FRANCES L. MENLOVE

Stanford University

Abstract: This experiment was designed to investigate the extinction of avoidance responses through observation of modeled approach behavior directed toward a feared stimulus without any adverse consequences accruing to the model. Children who displayed fearful and avoidant behavior toward dogs were assigned to 1 of the following treatment conditions: 1 group of children participated in a series of brief modeling sessions in which they observed, within a highly positive context, a fearless peer model exhibit progressively stronger approach responses toward a dog; a 2nd group of Ss observed the same graduated modeling stimuli, but in a neutral context; a 3rd group merely observed the dog in the positive context, with the model absent; while a 4th group of Ss participated in the positive activities without any exposure to either the dog or the modeled displays. The 2 groups of children who had observed the model interact nonanxiously with the dog displayed stable and generalized reduction in avoidance behavior and differed significantly in this respect from children in the dog-exposure and the positive-context conditions. However, the positive context, which was designed to induce anxiety-competing responses, did not enhance the extinction effects produced through modeling.

Recent investigations have shown that behavioral inhibitions (Bandura, 1965a; Bandura, Ross, & Ross, 1963; Walters & Parke, 1964) and conditioned emotional responses (Bandura & Rosenthal, 1966; Berger, 1962) can be acquired by observers as a function of witnessing aversive stimuli administered to performing subjects. The present experiment was primarily designed to determine whether preexisting avoidance behavior can similarly be extinguished on a vicarious basis. The latter phenomenon

*This research was supported by Public Health Research Grant M-5162 from the National Institute of Mental Health.

[1]The authors are indebted to Janet Brewer, Edith Dowley, Doris Grant, and Mary Lewis for their generous assistance in various phases of this research.

Reprinted from the *Journal of Personality and Social Psychology*, Vol. 5, No. 1, 1967, pp. 16–23, by permission of the American Psychological Association.

221

requires exposing observers to modeled stimulus events in which a performing subject repeatedly exhibits approach responses toward the feared object without incurring any aversive consequences.

Some suggestive evidence that avoidance responses can be extinguished vicariously is furnished by Masserman (1943) and Jones (1924) in exploratory studies of the relative efficacy of various psychotherapeutic procedures. Masserman produced strong feeding inhibitions in cats, following which the inhibited animals observed a cage mate, that had never been negatively conditioned, exhibit prompt approach and feeding responses. The observing subjects initially cowered at the presentation of the conditioned stimulus, but with continued exposure to their fearless companion they advanced, at first hesitantly and then more boldly, to the goal box and consumed the food. Some of the animals, however, showed little reduction in avoidance behavior despite prolonged food deprivation and numerous modeling trials. Moreover, avoidance responses reappeared in a few of the animals after the normal cat was removed, suggesting that in the latter cases the modeling stimuli served merely as temporary external inhibitors of avoidance responses. Jones (1924) similarly obtained variable results in extinguishing children's phobic responses by having them observe their peers behave in a nonanxious manner in the presence of the avoided objects.

If a person is to be influenced by modeling stimuli and the accompanying consequences, then the necessary observing responses must be elicited and maintained. In the foregoing case studies, the models responded to the most feared stimulus situation at the outset, a modeling procedure that is likely to generate high levels of emotional arousal in observers. Under these conditions any avoidance responses designed to reduce vicariously instigated aversive stimulation, such as subjects withdrawing or looking away, would impede vicarious extinction. Therefore, the manner in which modeling stimuli are presented may be an important determinant of the course of vicarious extinction.

Results from psychotherapeutic studies (Bandura[2]) and experiments with infrahuman subjects (Kimble & Kendall, 1953) reveal that avoidance responses can be rapidly extinguished if subjects are exposed to a graduated series of aversive stimuli that progressively approximate the original intensity of the conditioned fear stimulus. For the above reasons it would seem advisable to conduct vicarious extinction by exposing observers to

---

[2]A. Bandura, "Principles of Behavioral Modification," unpublished manuscript, Stanford University, 1966.

a graduated sequence of modeling activities beginning with presentations that can be easily tolerated; as observers' emotional reactions to displays of attenuated approach responses are extinguished, the fear-provoking properties of the modeled displays might be gradually increased, concluding with interactions capable of arousing relatively strong emotional responses.

If emotion-eliciting stimuli occur in association with positively reinforcing events, the former cues are likely to lose their conditioned aversive properties more rapidly (Farber, 1948) than through mere repeated nonreinforced presentation. It might therefore be supposed that vicarious extinction would likewise be hastened and more adequately controlled by presenting the modeling stimuli within a favorable context designed to evoke simultaneously competing positive responses.

The principles discussed above were applied in the present experiment, which explored the vicarious extinction of children's fearful and avoidant responses toward dogs. One group of children participated in a series of modeling sessions in which they observed a fearless peer model exhibit progressively longer, closer, and more active interactions with a dog. For these subjects, the modeled approach behavior was presented within a highly positive context. A second group of children was presented the same modeling stimuli, but in a neutral context.

Exposure to the behavior of the model contains two important stimulus events, that is, the occurrence of approach responses without any adverse consequences to the performer, and repeated observation of the feared animal. Therefore, in order to control for the effects of exposure to the dog per se, children assigned to a third group observed the dog in the positive context but with the model absent. A fourth group of children participated in the positive activities, but they were never exposed to either the dog or the model.

In order to assess both the generality and the stability of vicarious extinction effects, the children were readministered tests for avoidance behavior toward different dogs following completion of the treatment series, and approximately 1 month later. It was predicted that children who had observed the peer model interact nonanxiously with the dog would display significantly less avoidance behavior than subjects who had no exposure to the modeling stimuli. The largest decrements were expected to occur among children in the modeling-positive context condition. It was also expected that repeated behavioral assessments and the general disinhibitory effects of participation in a series of highly positive activities might in themselves produce some decrease in avoidance behavior.

METHOD

Subjects

The subjects were 24 boys and 24 girls selected from three nursery schools. The children ranged in age from 3 to 5 years.

Pretreatment Assessment of Avoidance Behavior

As a preliminary step in the selection procedure, parents were asked to rate the magnitude of their children's fearful and avoidant behavior toward dogs. Children who received high fear ratings were administered a standardized performance test on the basis of which the final selection was made.

The strength of avoidance responses was measured by means of a graded sequence of 14 performance tasks in which the children were required to engage in increasingly intimate interactions with a dog. A female experimenter brought the children individually to the test room, which contained a brown cocker spaniel confined in a modified play-pen. In the initial tasks the children were asked, in the following order, to walk up to the playpen and look down at the dog, to touch her fur, and to pet her. Following the assessment of avoidance responses to the dog in the protective enclosure, the children were instructed to open a hinged door on the side of the playpen, to walk the dog on a leash to a throw rug, to remove the leash, and to turn the dog over and scratch her stomach. Although a number of the subjects were unable to perform all of the latter tasks, they were nevertheless administered the remaining test items to avoid any assumption of a perfectly ordered scale for all cases. In subsequent items the children were asked to remain alone in the room with the animal and to feed her dog biscuits. The final and most difficult set of tasks required the children to climb into the playpen with the dog, to pet her, to scratch her stomach, and to remain alone in the room with the dog under the exceedingly confined and fear-provoking conditions.

The strength of the children's avoidant tendencies was reflected not only in the items completed, but also in the degree of vacillation, reluctance, and fearfulness that preceded and accompanied each approach response. Consequently, children were credited 2 points if they executed a given task either spontaneously or willingly, and 1 point when they carried out the task minimally after considerable hesitancy and reluctance. Thus, for example, children who promptly stroked the dog's fur repeatedly when requested to do so received 2 points, whereas subjects who held back but then touched the dog's fur briefly obtained 1 point. In the item requiring the children to remain alone in the room with the dog, they received 2 points if they approached the animal and played with her, and 1 point if they were willing to remain in the room but avoided any contact with the dog. Similarly, in the feeding situation children were credited 2 points if they fed the dog by hand, but a single point if they tossed the biscuits on the floor and thereby avoided close contact with the animal. The maximum approach score that a subject could attain was 28 points.

On the basis of the pretreatment assessment, the children in each nursery school were grouped into three levels of avoidance behavior, with the corresponding scores ranging from 0 to 7, 8 to 17, and 18 to 20 points. There were approximately the same number of children, equally divided between boys and girls, at each of the three avoidance levels. The subjects from each of these groups were then assigned randomly to one of four conditions.

Treatment Conditions

Children who participated in the *modeling-positive context* condition observed a fearless peer model display approach responses toward a cocker spaniel within the context of a highly enjoyable party atmosphere.

There were eight 10-minute treatment sessions conducted on 4 consecutive days. Each session, which was attended by a group of four children, commenced with a jovial party. The children were furnished with brightly colored hats, cookie treats, and given small prizes. In addition, the experimenter read stories, blew large plastic balloons for the children to play with, and engaged in other party activities designed to produce strong positive affective responses.

After the party was well under way, a second experimenter entered the room carrying the dog, followed by a 4-year-old male model who was unknown to most of the children. The dog was placed in a playpen located across the room from a large table at which the children were seated. The model, who had been chosen because of his complete lack of fear of dogs, then performed prearranged sequences of interactions with the dog for approximately 3 minutes during each session. One boy served as the model for children drawn from two of the nursery schools, and a second boy functioned in the same role at the third school.

The fear-provoking properties of the modeled displays were gradually increased from session to session by varying simultaneously the physical restraints on the dog, the directness and intimacy of the modeled approach responses, and the duration of interaction between the model and his canine companion. Initially, the experimenter carried the dog into the room and confined her to the playpen, and the model's behavior was limited to friendly verbal responses ("Hi, Chloe") and occasional petting. During the following three sessions the dog remained confined to the playpen, but the model exhibited progressively longer and more active interactions in the form of petting the dog with his hands and feet, and feeding her wieners and milk from a baby bottle. Beginning with the fifth session, the dog was walked into the room on a leash, and the modeled tasks were mainly performed outside the playpen. For example, in addition to repeating the feeding routines, the model walked the dog around the room, petted her, and scratched her stomach while the leash was removed. In the last two sessions the model climbed into the playpen with the dog where he petted her, hugged her, and fed her wieners and milk from the baby bottle.

It would have been of interest to compare the relative efficacy of the graduated modeling technique with bold displays of approach behavior from the outset. However, pretest findings showed that when modeled displays are too fear provoking, children actively avoid looking at the performances and are reluctant to participate in subsequent sessions. The latter approach would therefore require additional procedures designed to maintain strong attending behavior to highly aversive modeling stimuli.

Children assigned to the *modeling-neutral context* condition observed the same sequence of approach responses performed by the same peer model except that the parties were omitted. In each of the eight sessions the subjects were merely seated at the table and observed the modeled performances.

In order to control for the influence of repeated exposure to the positive atmosphere and to the dog per se, children in the *exposure-positive context* group attended the series of parties in the presence of the dog with the model absent. As in the two modeling conditions, the dog was introduced into the room in the same manner for the identical length of time; similarly, the dog was confined in the playpen during the first four sessions and placed on a leash outside the enclosure in the remaining sessions.

Children in the *positive-context* group participated in the parties, but they were never exposed to either the dog or the model. The main purpose of this condition was to determine whether the mere presence of a dog had an adverse or a beneficial effect on the children. Like the third condition, it also provided a control for the possible therapeutic effects of positive experiences and increased familiarity with amiable experimenters, which may be particularly influential in reducing inhibitions in very young children. In addition, repeated behavioral assessments in which subjects perform a graded series of approach responses toward a feared object without any aversive consequences would be expected to produce some direct extinction of avoidance behavior. The inclusion of the latter two control groups thus makes it possible to evaluate the changes effected by exposure to modeling stimuli over and above those resulting from general disinhibition, direct extinction, and repeated observation of the feared object.

Posttreatment Assessment of Avoidance Behavior

On the day following completion of the treatment series, the children were readministered the performance test consisting of the graded sequence of interaction tasks with the dog. In order to determine the generality of vicarious extinction effects, half the children in each of the four groups were tested initially with the experimental animal and then with an unfamiliar dog; the remaining children were presented with the two dogs in the reverse order.[3] The testing sessions were separated by an interval of $1\frac{1}{2}$ hours so as to minimize any transfer of emotional reactions generated by one animal to the other.

The unfamiliar animal was a white mongrel, predominantly terrier, and of approximately the same size and activity level as the cocker spaniel. Two groups of 15 children, drawn from the same nursery-school population, were tested with either the mongrel or the spaniel in order to determine the aversiveness of the two animals. The mean approach scores with the spaniel ($M = 16.47$) and the mongrel ($M = 15.80$) were virtually identical ($t = 0.21$).

Follow-Up Assessment

A follow-up evaluation was conducted approximately 1 month after the posttreatment assessment in order to determine the stability of modeling-induced changes in approach behavior. The children's responses were

---

[3]The authors are especially indebted to Chloe and Jenny for their invaluable and steadfast assistance with a task that, at times, must have been most perplexing to them.

tested with the same performance tasks toward both animals, presented in the identical order.

After the experiment was completed, the children were told that, while most dogs are friendly, before petting an unfamiliar dog they should ask the owner. This precautionary instruction was designed to reduce indiscriminate approach behavior by children who were in the modeling conditions toward strange dogs which they would undoubtedly encounter.

Measurement Procedure

The same female experimenter administered the pretreatment, post-treatment, and follow-up behavioral tests. To prevent any possible bias, the experimenter was given minimal information about the details of the study and had no knowledge of the conditions to which the children were assigned. The treatment and assessment procedures were further separated by the use of different rooms for each activity.

In order to provide an estimate of interscorer reliability, the performances of 25% of the children, randomly selected from pretreatment, posttreatment, and follow-up phases of the experiment, were scored simultaneously but independently by another rater who observed the test sessions through a one-way mirror from an adjoining observation room. The two raters were in perfect agreement on 97% of the specific approach responses that were scored.

A dog's activity level may partly determine the degree of fear and avoidance exhibited by the children; conversely, timorous or unrestrained approach responses might differentially affect the animals' reactivity. Therefore, during the administration of each test item, the animals' behavior was rated as either passive, moderately active, or vigorous. The raters were in perfect agreement in categorizing the dogs' activity levels on 81% of the performance tests.

Changes in children's approach-response scores across the different phases of the experiment, and the number of subjects in each treatment condition who were able to carry out the terminal performance task served as the dependent measures.

RESULTS

The percentages of test items in which the animals behaved in a passive, moderately active, or vigorous manner were 55, 43, and 2, respectively, for the model-positive context group; 53, 44, and 2 for children in the model-neutral context condition; 52, 45, and 3 for the exposure-positive context group; and 57, 41, and 2 for the positive-context subjects. Thus, the test animals did not differ in their behavior during the administration of performance tasks to children in the various treatment conditions.

Approach Responses

Table 12.1 presents the mean increases in approach behavior achieved by children in each of the treatment conditions in different phases of the experiment with each of the test animals.

The children's approach responses toward the two dogs did not differ either in the posttreatment assessment ($t = 1.35$) or in the follow-up phase ($t = 0.91$) of the study. Nor were there any significant effects ($t = 1.68$) due to the order in which the test animals were presented following completion of the treatment series. A t-test analysis also disclosed no significant change ($t = 1.50$) in mean approach scores between measurements conducted in the posttreatment and the follow-up phases of the experiment. Moreover, analysis of variance of the posttreatment scores revealed no significant Treatment × Dogs ($F = 2.15$) or Treatment × Order ($F = 0.30$) interaction effects. The data were therefore combined across phases and test animals in evaluating the major hypotheses.

An analysis of covariance, in which adjustments were made for differences in initial level of avoidance, was computed for mean approach responses performed by children in the various groups. The results reveal

Table 12.1. Mean increases in approach responses as a function of treatment conditions, assessment phases, and test animals

Phases	Treatment conditions			
	Modeling–positive context	Modeling–neutral context	Exposure–positive context	Positive context
Posttreatment				
Spaniel	10.83	9.83	2.67	6.08
Mongrel	5.83	10.25	3.17	4.17
Follow-Up				
Spaniel	10.83	9.33	4.67	5.83
Mongrel	12.59	9.67	4.75	6.67
Combined data	10.02	9.77	3.81	5.69

that the treatment conditions had a highly significant effect on the children's behavior ($F = 5.09$, $p < 0.01$). Tests of the differences between the various pairs of treatments indicate that subjects in the modeling-positive context condition displayed significantly more approach behavior than subjects in either the exposure ($F = 9.32$, $p < 0.01$) or the positive-context ($F = 8.96$, $p < 0.01$) groups. Similarly, children who had observed the model within the neutral setting exceeded both the exposure ($F = 6.57$, $p < 0.05$) and positive-context groups ($F = 4.91$, $p < 0.05$) in approach behavior. However, the data yielded no significant differences between either the two modeling conditions ($F = 0.04$) or the two control groups ($F = 0.76$).

Within-Group Analysis of Approach Responses

The approach scores obtained by the different groups of children in preexperimental and subsequent tests are summarized graphically in Fig. 12.1. Within-group analyses of changes between initial performance and mean level of approach behavior following treatment disclose significant increases in approach behavior for children in the modeling-positive context group ($t = 7.71$, $p < 0.001$) and for those who observed the modeling performance within the neutral setting ($t = 5.80$, $p < 0.001$). Although the positive-context group showed an increment in approach behavior ($t = 5.78$, $p < 0.001$), children who were merely exposed to the dog in the positive context achieved a small, but nonsignificant ($t = 1.98$), reduction in avoidance responses.

Terminal Performances

Another measure of the efficacy of modelling procedures is provided by comparisons of the number of children in each condition who performed the terminal approach behavior at least once during the post-treatment assessment. Since the frequencies within the two modeling conditions did not differ, and the two control groups were essentially the same, the data for each of the two sets of subgroups were combined. The findings show that 67% of the children in the modeling treatment were able to remain alone in the room confined with the dog in the playpen, whereas the corresponding figure for the control subjects is 33%. The χ^2 value for these data is 4.08, which is significant beyond the 0.025 level.

Within the control groups, the terminal performances were attained

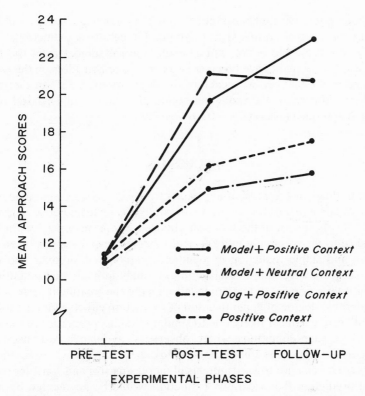

Fig. 12.1. Mean approach scores achieved by children in each of the treatment conditions on the three different periods of assessment.

primarily by subjects who initially showed the weakest level of avoidance behavior. The differences between the two groups are, therefore, even more pronounced if the analysis is conducted on the subjects whose pretreatment performances reflected extreme or moderately high levels of avoidance behavior. Of the most avoidant subjects in each of the two pooled groups, 55% of the children in the modeling conditions were able to perform the terminal approach behavior following the experimental sessions, while only 13% of the control subjects successfully completed the final task. The one-tailed probability for the obtained $\chi^2 = 4.74$ is slightly below the 0.01 level of significance.

The relative superiority of the modeling groups is also evident in the follow-up phase of the experiment. Based on the stringent criterion in which the most fearful task is successfully performed with *both* animals, a significantly larger number of children in the modeling conditions (42%) than in the control groups (12%) exhibited generalized extinction ($\chi^2 = 4.22$, $p < 0.025$). Moreover, not a single control subject from the two highest levels of avoidance behavior was able to remain alone in the room confined in the playpen with each of the dogs, whereas 33% of the most avoidant children in the modeling conditions successfully passed both terminal approach tasks ($\chi^2 = 4.02$, $p < 0.025$).

DISCUSSION

The findings of the present experiment provide considerable evidence that avoidance responses can be successfully extinguished on a vicarious basis. This is shown in the fact that children who experienced a gradual exposure to progressively more fearful modeled responses displayed extensive and stable reduction in avoidance behavior. Moreover, most of these subjects were able to engage in extremely intimate and potentially fearful interactions with test animals following the treatment series. The considerable degree of generalization of extinction effects obtained to the unfamiliar dog is most likely due to similar stimulus properties of the test animals. Under conditions where observers' avoidance responses are extinguished to a single animal, one would expect a progressive decrement in approach behavior toward animals of increasing size and fearfulness.

The prediction that vicarious extinction would be augmented by presenting the modeling stimuli within a highly positive context was not confirmed, although subjects in the latter condition differed more significantly from the controls than children who observed approach behavior under neutral conditions. It is entirely possible that a different temporal ordering of emotion-provoking modeling stimuli and events designed to induce anxiety-inhibiting responses would facilitate the vicarious extinction process. On the basis of evidence from conditioning studies (Melvin & Brown, 1964) the optimal treatment procedure might require repeated observational trials, in each of which aversive modeling stimuli are immediately followed by positively reinforcing experiences for the observers. These temporal prerequisites depend upon the abrupt presentation and termination of the two sets of stimulus events that cannot be readily achieved with live demonstrations. It would be possible, however, to study the effects of systematic variations in the temporal spacing of critical variables if modeling stimuli were presented pictorially. Apart from issues of economy and control, if pictorial stimulus material proved equally as efficacious as live modeling, then skillfully designed therapeutic films could be developed and employed in preventive programs for eliminating common fears and anxieties before they become well established and widely generalized.

Although children in both the exposure and the positive-context groups showed some increment in approach behavior, only the changes in the latter group were of statistically significant magnitude. Apparently the mere presence of a dog had some mild negative consequences that counteracted the facilitative effects resulting from highly rewarding interactions with amiable experimenters, increased familiarity with the person conducting the numerous tests of avoidance behavior, and any inevitable direct extinction produced by the repeated performance of some approach responses toward the test animals without any adverse consequences. As might be expected, the general disinhibitory effects arising from these multiple sources occurred only in the early phase of the experiment, and no significant increases in approach behavior appeared between the posttreatment and follow-up assessments.

The data obtained in this experiment demonstrate that the fearless behavior of a model can substantially reduce avoidance responses in observers, but the findings do not establish the nature of the mechanism by which vicarious extinction occurs. There are several possible explanations of vicariously produced effects (Bandura, 1965b; Kanfer, 1965). One interpretation is in terms of the informative value of modeling stimuli. That is, the repeated evocation of approach responses without any adverse consequences to another person undoubtedly conveys information to the observer about the probable outcomes of close interactions with dogs. In the present study, however, an attempt was made to minimize the contribution of purely cognitive factors by informing children in all groups beforehand that the test animals were harmless.

The nonoccurrence of anticipated aversive consequences to a model accompanied by positive affective reactions on his part can also extinguish in observers previously established emotional responses that are vicariously aroused by the modeled displays (Bandura & Rosenthal, 1966). It is therefore possible that reduction in avoidance behavior is partly mediated by the elimination of conditioned emotionality.

Further research is needed to separate the relative contribution of cognitive, emotional, and other factors governing vicarious processes. It would also be of interest to study the effects upon vicarious extinction exercised by such variables as number of modeling trials, distribution of extinction sessions, mode of model presentation, and variations in the characteristics of the models and the feared stimuli. For example, with extensive sampling in the modeled displays of both girls and boys exhibiting approach responses to dogs ranging from diminutive breeds to larger specimens, it may be possible to achieve widely generalized extinction effects. Once approach behaviors have been restored through modeling, their maintenance and further generalization can be effectively controlled by response-contingent reinforcement administered directly to the subject. The combined use of modeling and reinforcement procedures may thus serve as a highly efficacious mode of therapy for eliminating severe behavioral inhibitions.

REFERENCES

Bandura, A. Influence of models' reinforcement contingencies on the acquisition of imitative responses. *Journal of Personality and Social Psychology*, 1965, **1**, 589–595. (a)

Bandura, A. Vicarious processes: A case of no-trial learning. In L. Berkowitz (Ed.), *Advances in experimental social psychology*. Vol. 2. New York: Academic Press, 1965. Pp. 1–55. (b)

Bandura, A., & Rosenthal, T. L. Vicarious classical conditioning as a function of arousal level. *Journal of Personality and Social Psychology*, 1966, **3**, 54–62.

Bandura, A., Ross, D., & Ross, S. A. Vicarious reinforcement and imitative learning. *Journal of Abnormal and Social Psychology*, 1963, **67**, 601–607.

Berger, S. M. Conditioning through vicarious instigation. *Psychological Review*, 1962, **69**, 450–466.

Farber, I. E. Response fixation under anxiety and non-anxiety conditions. *Journal of Experimental Psychology*, 1948, **38**, 111–131.

Jones, M. C. The elimination of children's fears. *Journal of Experimental Psychology*, 1924, **7**, 383–390.

Kanfer, F. H. Vicarious human reinforcement: A glimpse into the black box. In L. Krasner & L. P. Ullmann (Eds.), *Research in behavior modification*. New York: Holt, Rinehart & Winston, 1965. Pp. 244–267.

Kimble, G. A., & Kendall, J. W., Jr. A comparison of two methods of producing experimental extinction. *Journal of Experimental Psychology*, 1953, **45**, 87–90.

Masserman, J. H. *Behavior and neurosis*. Chicago: University of Chicago Press, 1943.

Melvin, K. B., & Brown, J. S. Neutralization of an aversive light stimulus as a function of number of paired presentations with food. *Journal of Comparative and Physiological Psychology*, 1964, **58**, 350–353.

Walters, R. H., & Parke, R. D. Influence of response consequences to a social model on resistance to deviation. *Journal of Experimental Child Psychology*, 1964, **1**, 269–280.

ARTICLE 13

Modification of Social Withdrawal Through Symbolic Modeling*[1]

ROBERT D. O'CONNOR

Stanford University[2]

Abstract: The present experiment was designed to test the efficacy of symbolic modeling as a treatment to enhance social behavior in preschool isolates. Nursery school children who displayed marked social withdrawal were assigned to one of two conditions. One group observed a film depicting increasingly more active social interactions between children with positive consequences ensuing in each scene, while a narrative soundtrack emphasized the appropriate behavior of the models. A control group observed a film that contained no social interaction. Control children displayed no change in withdrawal behavior, whereas those who had the benefit of symbolic modeling increased their level of social interaction to that of non-isolate nursery school children.

Recent years have witnessed increasing applications of principles of learning to psychopathology. Ample evidence has accumulated to indicate that behavioral approaches hold considerable promise for the treatment of diverse psychological conditions (Bandura, 1969; Eysenck, 1964; Krasner and Ullmann, 1967; Wolpe and Lazarus, 1967). Many of these applications, however, have been concerned with the treatment of highly circumscribed disorders. Only recently have researchers begun to investigate the modifications of interpersonal modes of behavior.

*Reprinted from the *Journal of Applied Behavior Analysis*, Vol. 2, No. 1, Spring 1969, pp. 15–22. Copyright 1969 by the Society for the Experimental Analysis of Behavior, Inc.

[1]This research was supported by Public Health Research Grant M-5162 from the National Institute of Mental Health to Albert Bandura, and by the Louis Haas Research Fund, Stanford University. The author is grateful to Professor Bandura, whose enthusiastic assistance and many suggestions were invaluable during all phases of this project, and to Professor Eleanor E. Maccoby, who provided support and helpful comments during the initial stages of the experiment. Professors Robert R. Sears and Edith Dowley generously assisted in the design and implementation of observational procedures, and Marian O'Connor collaborated on numerous resources which insured the success of the program.

[2]Reprints may be obtained from the author, Dept. of Psychology, University of Illinois, Urbana, Illinois 61801.

Social interaction, an obviously important factor in personality development, has become the focus of much attention among social-learning
theorists, developmentalists, and therapists. There are several reasons
for high-lighting the role of interpersonal behavior in personality development. First, a child who is grossly deficient in social skills will be seriously
handicapped in acquiring many of the complex behavioral repertoires
necessary for effective social functioning. Second, children who are
unable to relate skillfully to others are likely to experience rejection,
harrassment, and generally hostile treatment from peers. Such negative
experiences would be expected to reinforce interpersonal avoidance responses which, in turn, further impede the development of competencies
that are socially mediated. Current theories concerning the determinants
of personality patterns (Bandura, 1969; Bandura and Walters, 1963;
Mischel, 1968; Peterson, 1968) emphasize social variables and underscore the general importance of social interaction.

Several attempts have been made to enhance the social behavior of
isolate children (Allen, Hart, Buell, Harris, and Wolf, 1964; Hart, Reynolds, Baer, Brawley, and Harris, 1968; Hartup, 1964; Patterson and
Anderson, 1964) through differential reinforcement. These studies have
shown that if peer interaction is reinforced, either socially or otherwise,
and isolate play is either punished or ignored, children eventually display
a higher level of social behavior. The utilization of a treatment program
based solely on reinforcement procedures may encounter difficulties in
the development of social responsiveness in extreme isolates. However,
while a series of preliminary observations which served as a pilot for the
present study found 20% or more of nursery school children exhibiting
relatively low levels of social responsiveness, many of whom could be
helped by arranging favorable response consequences; a smaller percentage of children either perform no social interaction response or provide
only rare opportunities for the application of reinforcement. When such
gross deficits exist, the reinforcing agent must either introduce a rather
laborious set of "shaping" procedures, which requires waiting for the
emission of a reinforceable social response, or resort to more active
means of establishing the desired behavior.

Lovaas (1966) showed that relatively complex repertoires can be
established to replace gross deficits through a combination of modeling
and reinforcement procedures. Of greater interest and relevance to the
approach used in the present study is evidence that children can acquire
new patterns of behavior on the basis of observation alone (Bandura and
Huston, 1961; Bandura and McDonald, 1963; Bandura and Mischel,

1965; Bandura, Ross, and Ross, 1963; Hicks, 1965). Since repertoires can thus be learned on a non-response basis, with no reinforcement to the observer, a modeling program may be particularly effective in the case of gross behavior deficits.

It was noted earlier that in most cases, severe withdrawal reflects both deficits in social skills and avoidance of interpersonal situations. An optimal treatment, therefore, should transmit new social competencies and also extinguish social fears. Modeling procedures are also ideally suited for this purpose. A series of studies by Bandura (1968a) demonstrated that various patterns of avoidance behavior can be successfully eliminated through modeling, and that such procedures are readily applicable to therapeutic situations.

By devising a carefully constructed film sequence, the therapist can stage rather complicated situations and events in a dramatic manner that controls the viewer's attention to relevant cues. While the exclusion of extraneous events provides much of this attention control, the enthusiastic and emotionally expressive behavior of models can further enhance attention and vicarious learning in the viewer (Bandura, 1962; Berger, 1962; Berger and Johansson, 1968). Once the observer's attention has thus been directed toward the filmed events, the therapist may introduce repeated exposure to clearly defined stimuli.

Positive response consequences to the model, such as social praise or material reinforcements for modeled behaviors, which have been shown to increase the performance of similar behavior in observers (Bandura, 1965; Bandura, 1968b), can also be incorporated into filmed events. Symbolic modeling processes employing such principles have effectively extinguished severe avoidance behavior in children (Bandura and Menlove, 1968).

The present experiment sought to extend the use of symbolic modeling to the modification of social withdrawal. This approach appears particularly well suited for achieving both of the desired outcomes indicated in the pathology described above; i.e., the transmission of social skills and the extinction of social fears. These two modeling processes, along with the facilitation of interpersonal behaviors which may exist in the observers' repertoire, provided the rationale for the manipulation of social interaction behavior, which in fact comprised the focus of the experimental change assessment.

Children who displayed extreme social withdrawal were shown a sound-film depicting peers engaged in progressively more active social interaction. The viewers were children who not only had very low base-rates of social interaction, according to the dual assessment procedure (below), but whose frequent retreats into corners, closets, and lockers gave observers and teachers a similar impression of active, purposive withdrawal in many instances. The filmed behavior of peers presented to these "isolates" was actively followed by reinforcing outcomes such as peer approval, either verbal or expressional (smiling, nodding, etc.); peer acceptance of the model into a game or a conversation, i.e., invitations to join or offering play materials or reaching out to take the model's hand, etc.; in most scenes the model behavior resulted in some tangible reinforcement such as a block or other toy, a book to read together with the peers, a dish to wash or dry in a cooperative homemaking activity; and so on. A second group of equally withdrawn children viewed a film that contained no human characters. After exposure to their respective films, the children's social behavior was observed in the nursery school situation. It was predicted that children having the benefits of symbolic modeling would display a significant increase in social interaction with their peers.

METHOD

Selection of Isolates

Head teachers in each of nine nursery school classes were asked to choose from their enrollment lists the five most socially withdrawn children in their class. Each teacher was to rank order these five children "who interact the least with their peers". Of the 365 children enrolled, the 45 nominated in this preliminary selection and 26 children randomly chosen from the remaining non-isolates were then observed in the nursery school setting at randomly selected times throughout the day.

Each child was observed for a total of 32 intervals, each interval consisting of 15 sec, over a period of eight days (with the time of day counterbalanced on consecutive days). During each 15-sec interval, the children's behavior was scored in terms of five separate response categories; one every 3 sec. These included physical proximity, verbal interaction, "looking at", "interacting with", and the size of the group involved in any interaction sequence. Although the first three response categories, considered social orienting responses, were scored, the measure of social behavior was based entirely on the frequency with which the children interacted with their peers (i.e., category four). The three categories of "orienting" responses and the "size of group" category were included in the observations for intra-sample reliability checks and for possible assessment purposes in case the primary "interacts" category had not reflected such notable change in the children's behavior. Obviously, a score in the "interaction" category necessitated "proximity and looking at" responses, and increases in the less critical "verbalizes" and "number in group" categories had to accompany most interactions performed by these former isolates. The major emphasis of the experimental manipulation, therefore, was on the interaction scores, and the changes assessed were in this category alone, although changes in the other behavioral categories were at least as significant as those reported in the response class of interest here. A social interaction was defined as any behavior directed toward another child which involved a reciprocal quality. Neither parallel play nor solitary verbalizations qualified. The two-way nature of a scorable interaction necessitated not only the output of the subject child, but some indication of recognition and attention from the second child in the interaction. Thus, if a subject spoke to or otherwise directed his behavior to another child, but the second child did not respond in any way, at least appearing to be aware of the intended interaction, no score was given for an interaction.

Six trained observers performed the ratings. During a randomly chosen 50% of the sessions, these observers were paired and observed a given child independently but simultaneously. Inter-scorer reliability on each of these sessions was $r = > 0.92$ (# of agreements/the 32 possible agreements on a given child's interactions), which allowed for matched observer correlations across subjects of $r = 0.90 +$ (product-moment) in all pairs of observers.

Children who scored fewer than five of 32 possible interactions and who had been rated by teachers as isolates were selected as subjects and randomly assigned to either the modeling or the control film conditions. Thus, to qualify for the experiment, children had to meet the dual criteria of having exhibited extreme withdrawal over a long period of time as judged by their teachers, and to have displayed isolate behavior as measured by objective behavioral observations. Of the 20 "isolates" who met these criteria, 13 were included in the experiment; four of the remaining seven were omitted because they were frequently absent from school; and three of the children vigorously refused to leave the nursery room.

The 26 non-isolate children were primarily included to furnish an additional base line for evaluating any changes produced by the treatment program. These children displayed a mean of 9.1 social interactions, while the means for children assigned to the modeling and control conditions were 1.75 and 1.50 respectively, with the scores in both groups ranging from 0 to 5. The modeling group contained four girls and two boys and the control group, four girls and three boys.

Treatment Conditions

Children in both conditions were brought individually to the experimental room where they were told they could watch a television program. Each child was seated before a large TV console while the experimenter plugged in the set and ostensibly tuned in the picture. The films were shown on a glass lenscreen by means of a rear projector arrangement. As the apparatus was plugged in, the hidden projector and tape recorder were activated simultaneously. An extension speaker directed the sound through the TV set.

The experimenter left the child alone in the room to view the film on the pretext that he had some work to complete and would return before the film had ended. The experimenter then observed the session through a one-way mirror from an adjoining room. All children appeared to be highly attentive to the "TV show" throughout the film. The attention apparently commanded by the television presentation was quite impressive and obviously advantageous to the experimental procedure.

Children in the modeling condition saw a sound-color film lasting approximately 23 min. The film portrayed a sequence of 11 scenes in which children interacted in a nursery school setting. In each of these episodes, a child is shown first observing the interaction of others and then joining in the social activities, with reinforcing consequences ensuing. The other children, for example, offer him play material, talk to him, smile and generally respond in a positive manner to his advances into the activity. The scenes were graduated on a dimension of threat in terms of the vigor of the social activity and the size of the group. The initial scenes involve very calm activities such as sharing a book or toy while two children are seated at a table. In the terminal scenes, as many as six children are shown gleefully tossing play equipment around the room.

Multiple modeling has been shown to be more efficacious than single modeling (Bandura and Menlove, 1968). Also, a second pilot study conducted as a preliminary to the present experiment suggested a powerful effect on social behavior of subjects as a result of multiple, live peer-modeling; the child displaying the social approach behavior was varied from scene to scene in terms of age and sex, including a total of six different models, four girls and two boys, with their ages ranging from 4 to 7 yr.

To accent further the modeling cues and the positive consequences associated with the social behavior of the approaching child, a narrative sound track was prepared in which a woman's voice, judged by the experimenter to be very soothing, described the actions of the model and the other children in the ongoing sequence. The script consisted entirely of descriptions of ongoing social responses and outcomes and was a further attempt to focus the viewers' attention to relevant cues.

The control film depicted 20 min of the acrobatic performances of Marineland dolphins and was accompanied by a musical soundtrack. Since the film contained no human characters, it provided a control for any effects which might have been derived solely from the presentation of a film in the experimental procedure and contact with experimenters. The control group further provided a basis on which to measure any change in the social behavior of isolate subjects which might have occurred as a result of nursery school participation during the course of the project.[3]

Post-Treatment Assessment

Immediately after being shown their respective films, the children were returned to their regular classrooms. They were given 2 min to adapt to the classroom situation, after which they were observed for 32 consecutive intervals, each lasting 15 sec, according to the same observation procedure employed in the pretreatment assessment. The social interaction score was again the number of 15-sec intervals in which the child displayed a direct social interchange (defined according to the "reciprocal quality" criteria mentioned earlier) with one or more children. In order to control for any bias in ratings, observers were kept unaware of condition assignments, and each observed a random combination of treated and control subjects. Aside from the usual "blind assessment" control, this randomizing technique was thought to reduce further any possible observer bias.

RESULTS

Figure 13.1 represents the mean number of social interaction responses performed by children in the modeling and control conditions during the pretest and immediately after the experimental session.

---

[3]A copy of the 400 ft super-8-mm film and sound-track can be obtained from the author for approximately $66.00 (cost) plus $6.00 for packing and mailing.

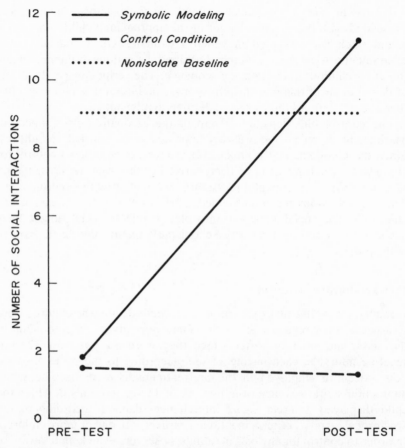

Fig. 13.1. Mean number of social interactions displayed by subjects in the modeling and control conditions, before and after the experimental sessions. The dotted line represents the level of interactions manifested by 26 non-isolate children who were observed at the pretest phase of the study.

An analysis of within-group changes showed that the seven control children remained essentially unchanged, whereas the six children who had viewed the modeling film markedly increased their level of social interaction ($t = 2.29$; $p < 0.03$). The post-test interaction scores of treated subjects were in fact similar to those of non-isolates who had been observed during the pretest period.

A between-groups analysis revealed the change in social interaction to be significantly greater for subjects in the modeling treatment than for controls ($t = 2.53$; $p = 0.015$). A between-groups comparison of the levels of social interaction achieved at post-test indicated significant differences as evaluated by either the t-test (t = 2.70; p = 0.01) or the Mann Whitney U-test (U = 3.0; p < 0.004).

Having measured the powerful effects of the modeling film in terms of the group comparisons above, data for the individual subjects in the modeling condition were found to indicate consistent positive changes across subjects. All six children in the modeling condition exhibited increased social interaction behavior in the post-film assessment. Children in the control condition performed essentially the same number of interactions before and after viewing the control film, with only slight increases or decreases in the behavior.

DISCUSSION

The present results established symbolic modeling as a highly efficacious procedure for modifying social withdrawal. Children who did not receive the modeling treatment remained socially withdrawn, whereas those who observed a systematic filmed presentation of peer interactions associated with reinforcing consequences displayed a significant increase in social responsiveness.

Follow-up observations could not be made because the nursery school term was completed. However, a second set of teachers' ratings was obtained at the end of the school year. The teachers, who were kept uninformed as to which conditions children had been assigned, again rated the five most withdrawn children from their enrollment lists as they had done in the preliminary selection. Only one of the six subjects who had been in the modeling condition was still rated as an isolate. It is interesting to note that this child, who also improved the least as measured by behavior observation, viewed the modeling film with the sound track 20-sec behind the picture due to a mechanical failure. Four of the seven control subjects were again judged to be extreme isolates. Although these findings have some suggestive value, they should be accepted with reservations because of the global nature of the ratings and the fact that changes in classroom enrollment may affect their comparability.

Immediate treatment effects achieved by symbolic modeling may produce lasting changes in social interaction without the need of additional procedures, provided that the children's initial social behavior is favorably received by peers. However, the application of systematic reinforcement of appropriate social responses would ensure the maintenance of

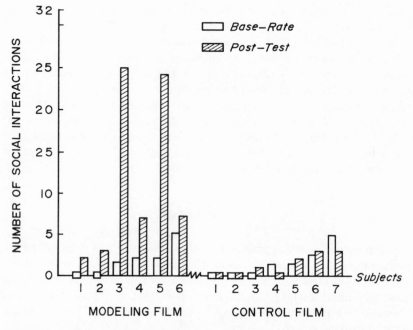

Fig. 13.2. Actual number of social interactions displayed by each child in either condition, before and after exposure to the modeling or control film.

the induced behavioral changes. Bandura has suggested "the combined use of modeling and reinforcement procedures" as the most efficacious mode of therapy in "eliminating severe behavioral inhibitions" (Bandura, Grusec, and Menlove, 1967). In order to substantiate this hypothesis a study needs to be conducted which extends the design of the present experiment to include durational (follow-up) assessment periods, as well as a comparison of modeling, shaping, and combined treatment procedures. In the present study, social inhibitions were reduced and appropriate social responses were facilitated through symbolic modeling with built-in reinforcement to the model. New responses to familiar social stimuli which were formerly assumed to have elicited avoidance behavior were acquired vicariously within one treatment session.

The subsequent performance of these newly acquired behaviors is seen as primarily resulting from the facilitation and extinction effects which derive from the observation of models performing the target behaviors with no aversive consequences ensuing. This theoretical explanation of the modeling effects achieved is based on the same set of experimental data which guided the construction of the treatment film (an important point in the comparison of differential treatment outcomes). A distinction is drawn between response *acquisition* and response *performance* according to experimental data derived from a recent experiment (Bandura, 1965*b*) which suggested that novel behaviors may be acquired by observers, even though the models are punished, but that these responses may not be performed readily without the addition of strong incentives beyond those of the situational stimuli in the modeling presentation. The conclusion from this study is theoretically relevant to the present discussion, in that it suggests that a model's reinforcement contingencies may be negative enough to inhibit performance of newly acquired responses, but have little or no effect on their acquisition. Other data, such as the Berger (1962, 1968) studies mentioned earlier and a recent demonstration of arousal reduction in snake phobics through live modeling (Blanchard, 1968), provide support for the additional modeling effects of disinhibition and the facilitation of responses existing in the observer's repertoire, which complete the three-fold theory of modeling effects incorporated into the design of the present film and the theoretical explanation of its effects.

An alternative explanation for the increased social behavior of children who observed the modeling film might be based strictly on the principles of reinforcement theory. Since the data here indicate only changes in the rate of social interaction responses, it might be argued that the simplest behavioral description would identify the filmed presentation as a discriminative stimulus for appropriate matching responses. (Baer and Sherman, 1964; Peterson, 1968). This approach would be based upon what is often considered the most parsimonious behavioral analysis of observable events, i.e., the performance of measurable behaviors and a description of the stimulus situation in which the matching behaviors, as a "functional response class", occurred. The rationale for such a description might be based upon the observer's prior history of reinforcement for matching models' behavior, or similar conceptions of "imitation", *per se*, with emphasis on the change in reinforcement value of models' behavior, the controlling power of modeled behavior as a discriminative stimulus, etc. (Staats, 1963, 1968). Aside from recent suggestions concerning the presumptive nature of these "heavyweight" reinforcement-theory explanations (Glucksberg, 1968); the parsimony deriving from reinforcement approaches, in terms of therapeutic efficiency, has not yet been demonstrated in instances where gross behavior deficits are identified as the changeworthy phenomena. The expense of "shaping time" must be compared to a treatment which may provide for the acquisition of possibly novel skills according to principles of associative learning (contiguous presentation of modeling stimuli), as well as facilitating the performance of modeled responses and other appropriate behaviors in the observer's repertoire (discriminative stimulus function of non-aversive modeled behavioral outcomes), while reducing negative arousal responses to feared stimuli, all in one treatment session. The explanatory value of reinforcement principles may thus be relevant to performance variables, while an approach that is intended to effect input (learning) variables as well may provide treatment procedures with markedly greater applicability to behavior deficit conditions. The allowance for possible *learning deficits* in treatment strategies designed to modify *behavior deficits*, i.e., attention to input as well as output deficits, may be much more than a theoretical distinction. The powerful effects of the modeling presentation reported here underscore what appears to be a very practical, therapeutically useful reason to allow for the notion of mediational processes as well as reinforcement principles when these factors may be relevant to the therapeutic strategy.

This brief discussion of two possible explanations of the modeling effects achieved in the present study may serve to direct the reader's attention to further analyses of the modeling process in general. Thoroughly detailed presentations may be found in more appropriate publications (Bandura, 1968c; Bandura, 1969; Mischel, 1968; O'Connor, 1969; Staats, 1968; Ullmann, 1968).

It should be noted in passing that the present experiment achieved significant changes in social behavior among children with relatively severe deficits without developing a therapeutic relationship. Until recently, a fairly intimate client-therapist relationship and the attainment of insight have been considered necessary conditions for personality change. In contrast, the results and discussion above indicate that the social behavior of children can be effectively enhanced by efforts to arrange social stimulus conditions which may ensure the acquisition of requisite competencies, the reduction of inhibiting fears, and the facilitation of appropriate responses. It should also be apparent that attention to learning variables provides for treatment procedures which can optimistically be applied to any program of behavior change. Teachers and other social agents might greatly increase the efficacy of their work with individual children, as well as in group procedures, by employing some of the principles of social learning and symbolic modeling presented here. The use of carefully designed therapeutic films in classroom and experimental situations alike may provide significantly more efficient modification of various behavior deficits and other deviant behaviors.

REFERENCES

Allen, K. E., Hart, B. M., Buell, J. S., Harris, F. R., and Wolf, M. M. Effects of social reinforcement on isolate behavior of a nursery school child. *Child Development*, 1964, **35**, 511–518.

Bandura, A. Influence of models' reinforcement contingencies on the acquisition of imitative responses. *Journal of Personality and Social Psychology*, 1965, **1**, 589–595. *(b)*

Bandura, A. Modeling approaches to the modification of phobic disorders. *Ciba Foundation symposium: The role of learning in psychotherapy*. London: Churchill, 1968. *(a)*

Bandura, A. *Principles of behavior modification*. New York: Holt, Rinehart & Winston, 1969.

Bandura, A. A social learning interpretation of psychological dysfunctions. In P. London and D. Rosehan (Eds.) *Foundations of abnormal psychology*. New York; Holt, Rinehart & Winston, 1968. Pp. 293–344.

Bandura, A. Social learning theory of identificatory processes. In D. A. Goslin (Ed.), *Handbook of socialization theory and research*. Chicago: Rand McNally, 1968. Pp. 213–262 *(b)*

Bandura, A. Social learning through imitation. In M. R. Jones (Ed.), *Nebraska Symposium of Motivation: 1962*. Lincoln: University of Nebraska Press, 1962. Pp. 211–269.

Bandura, A. Vicarious processes: A case of no-trial learning. In L. Berkowitz (Ed.), *Advances in experimental social psychology*. Vol. II. New York: Academic Press, 1965. Pp. 1–55.

Bandura, A., Grusec, J., and Menlove, F. L. Vicarious extinction of avoidance behavior. *Journal of Personality and Social Psychology*, 1967, **5**, 16–23.

Bandura, A. and Huston, Aletha C. Identification as a process of incidental learning. *Journal of Abnormal and Social Psychology*, 1961, **63**, 311–318.

Bandura, A. and McDonald, F. J. Influence of social reinforcement and the behavior of models in shaping children's moral judgments. *Journal of Abnormal and Social Psychology*, 1963, **67**, 274–281.

Bandura, A. and Menlove, F. L. Factors determining vicarious extinction of avoidance behavior through symbolic modeling. *Journal of Personality and Social Psychology*, 1968, **8**, 99–108.

Bandura, A. and Mischel, W. Modification of self-imposed delay of reward through exposure to live and symbolic models. *Journal of Personality and Social Psychology*, 1965, **2**, 698–705.

Bandura, A., Ross, D., and Ross, S. A. Transmission of aggression through imitation of aggressive models. *Journal of Abnormal and Social Psychology*, 1961, **64**, 575–582.

Bandura, A. and Walters, R. *Social learning and personality development*. New York: Holt, Rinehart & Winston, 1963.

Baer, D. M. and Sherman, J. A. Reinforcement control of generalized imitation in young children. *Journal of Experimental Child Psychology*, 1964, **1**, 37–49.

Baer, D. M., Peterson, R. F., and Sherman, J. A. The development of imitation by reinforcing behavioral similarity to a model. *Journal of the Experimental Analysis of Behavior*, 1967, **10**, 405–416.

Berger, S. M. Conditioning through vicarious instigation. *Psychological Review*, 1962, **69**, 450–466.

Berger, S. M. and Johansson, S. L. Effect of model's expressed emotions on an observer's resistance to extinction. *Journal of Personality and Social Psychology*, 1968, **10**, 53–58.

Blanchard, E. B. *Relative contributions of modeling, informational influences, and physical contact in the extinction of phobic behavior.* Unpublished doctoral dissertation. Stanford University, 1968.

Eysenck, H. J. *Experiments in behavior therapy.* New York: Macmillan, 1964.

Glucksberg, S. A self-made straw man. *Contemporary Psychology*, 1968, **13**, 624–625.

Hart, B. M., Reynolds, N. H., Baer, D. M., Brawley, E. R., and Harris, F. R. Effect of contingent and non-contingent social reinforcement on the cooperative play of a preschool child. *Journal of Applied Behavior Analysis*, 1968, **1**, 73–76.

Hartup, W. W. Peers as agents of social reinforcement. *Young Children*, **20**, 1965.

Hicks, D. J. Imitation and retention of film-mediated aggressive peer and adult models. *Journal of Personality and Social Psychology*, 1965, **2**, 97–100.

Krasner, L. and Ullmann, L. P. *Research in behavior therapy.* New York: Macmillan, 1964.

Lovaas, I., Berberich, J. P., Perlof, B. F., and Schaeffer, B. Acquisition of imitative speech by schizophrenic children. *Science*, 1966, **151**, 705–707.

Mischel, W. *Personality and assessment.* New York: Wiley & Sons, 1968.

O'Connor, R. D. *Modeling treatment of non-behavior disorders.* Paper presented at 41st annual meeting of the Midwestern Psychological Association, Chicago, March 1969.

Patterson, G. R. and Anderson, D. Peers as social reinforcers. *Child Development*, 1964, **35**, 951–960.

Peterson, D. R. *The clinical study of social behavior.* New York: Appleton, Century, Crofts, 1968.

Peterson, R. F. Some experiments on the organization of a class of imitative behaviors. *Journal of Applied Behavior Analysis*, 1968, **3**, 225–235.

Staats, A. W. *Learning, language, and cognition.* New York, Holt, Rinehart & Winston, 1968.

Staats, A. W. and Staats, C. K. *Complex human behavior.* New York, Holt, Rinehart & Winston, 1963.

Ullmann, L. P. Making use of modeling in the therapeutic interview. Paper read at A.A.B.T. meetings, San Francisco, 1968.

Wolpe, J. and Lazarus, A. A. *Behavior therapy techniques.* London: Pergamon Press, 1966.

Effects of Teacher Attention on Attending Behavior of Two Boys at Adjacent Desks*

MARCIA BRODEN, CARL BRUCE, MARY ANN MITCHELL,
VIRGINIA CARTER, and R. VANCE HALL[1]

University of Kansas

Abstract: The effects of teacher attention on the attending behavior of two boys seated at adjacent desks were investigated. Baseline records were obtained of the appropriate attending behavior of two boys who were described as the most disruptive pupils in a second-grade classroom of a poverty area school. During the first experimental phase, the teacher systematically increased the amount of attention for appropriate attending in one of the pair, Edwin. This resulted in a dramatic increase in his attending rate and a lesser, though significant, increase in attending behavior of the second boy, Greg. During the second experimental phase, systematic attention for attending was instituted for Greg and was discontinued for Edwin. This resulted in further increases in attending by Greg and a reduction in attending by Edwin. A brief withdrawal of reinforcement for attending in both Greg and Edwin reduced attending levels for both. Following this reversal appropriate attending for both boys was systematically reinforced and attending returned to high levels.

A number of studies have demonstrated that contingent teacher attention can be used to modify pupil study behavior in regular school classrooms (Hall, Lund, and Jackson, 1968; Hall, Panyan, Rabon, and Broden, 1968; Thomas, Becker, and Armstrong, 1968; Broden and Hall, 1968).

*Reprinted from the *Journal of Applied Behavior Analysis*, Vol. 3, No. 3, Fall 1970, pp. 199–203. Copyright 1970 by the Society for the Experimental Analysis of Behavior, Inc.

[1]The authors wish to express appreciation to Anita Glover, Clarence Glasse, Dr. Bertram Carruthers, and Dr. O. L. Plucker of the Kansas City Public Schools; Deloris Rabon of the Project Staff; and Marion Panyan of Wheatridge Colorado State Training School without whose cooperation and active participation this study would not have been possible. Reprints may be obtained from R. Vance Hall, 2021 North Third Street, Kansas City, Kansas 66101. This research was carried out as a part of the Juniper Gardens Children's Project, a program of research on the development of culturally deprived children and was partially supported by the National Institute of Child Health and Human Development: (HD 03144) and the Office of Economic Opportunity (CG 8180) Bureau of Child Research, University of Kansas.

In carrying out reinforcement procedures to improve study behavior of individual disruptive pupils such as those reported by Hall *et al.* (1968), both the teachers and observers had noted increases in appropriate study of pupils sitting near the primary subjects of these studies. This observation was consonant with the often repeated opinion of teachers that one disruptive pupil increases the inappropriate behavior of his neighbors, and if his behavior is controlled it positively affects that of those around him.

The present study investigated the behavior of a pair of boys who were seated at adjacent desks in a second-grade classroom. The effect of providing social reinforcement contingent on appropriate attending behavior of one, the other, and finally both seatmates was investigated.

Subjects and Setting

The subjects were two boys enrolled in the second grade of an elementary school located in the most economically deprived area of Kansas City, Kansas. One of the pair, Greg, had been retained in the first grade due to poor classroom behavior and academic performance. An individual Stanford Binet given to Greg the previous year indicated an I.Q. of 60. Greg was referred to the experimenters by the teacher and principal because of a high level of disruptive and non-study behaviors, which included talking out to the teacher, talking to neighbors, waving papers in the air, looking around the room, getting out of seat without permission, and playing with various toys.

The second boy, Edwin, sat next to Greg. A Stanford Binet test administered to Edwin yielded an I.Q. of 72. He, like Greg, came from a poverty area home. Although less disruptive than his seat partner, he often talked to Greg, laughed at him, stared out the window, and usually failed to do assigned classwork. Edwin and Greg had been referred by the teacher and principal and were considered the most disruptive pupils in the class.

METHOD

Observation

Observations of Edwin and Greg were made daily from 10:00 to 10:30 a.m. during the spelling and writing period. The method of observation was time sample recording similar to that reported by Hall *et al.* (1968) except that instead of recording the behavior of one pupil during every

10 sec, the behavior of Edwin was recorded at the end of the first 5 sec and that of Greg at the end of the next 5 sec. This procedure was repeated throughout the observation session so that each of the boys was observed once during each 10-sec interval. Thus, the observer recorded whether or not each subject appeared to be appropriately attending to a teacher-assigned task 180 times per 30-min session. Attending behaviors included writing if writing had been assigned, looking toward pages in the appropriate book if reading had been assigned, and looking toward the teacher if she was talking. Non-attending behaviors included being out of seat without permission, talking without prior teacher permission, looking toward peers, and other behaviors incompatible with attending to assigned tasks. Teacher attention was recorded if the teacher spoke to a subject during any 5-sec interval he was being observed. In addition a record was also kept of glances (whether or not the subject looked at his seat partner).

The observer entered and left the room quietly and avoided eye contact or any other interaction with the teacher or pupils. Seventeen times and at least twice during each phase of the experiment a second observer made an independent simultaneous observational record. These records were compared by dividing the number of intervals of agreement by the number of intervals observed and multiplying by 100. The agreement of records for attending behavior, teacher attention and glances were computed independently. Agreement ranged from a low of 82% to a high of 93% for all behavior.

Baseline$_1$ During the first phase (Baseline$_1$), no attempt was made to change the conditions that existed before time observations were begun.

Increased Attention to Edwin's Attending Behavior After the Baseline phase, a conference was held with the teacher and the basic principles of positive reinforcement were explained. In addition, the results of previous classroom studies (Hall *et al.*, 1968) in which teacher attention had been used to modify study behavior were presented. The teacher was then asked to begin attending to and praising Edwin whenever she noticed he was attending appropriately in class and to ignore all his inappropriate behaviors. No change was to be made in her approach to Greg, that is, no increased attention contingent on attending behavior was to be given.

Increased Attention to Greg's Attending Behavior Beginning on the twenty-third day of observation, a second experimental phase was instituted. During this phase, the teacher was asked to discontinue systematic attention to Edwin's appropriate attending but to increase her attention to Greg whenever she noticed him attending to assigned tasks.

Baseline₂   During the next experimental phase (Baseline$_2$) the teacher was asked to return to Baseline$_1$ conditions in which she essentially ignored the appropriate attending behavior of both boys and spoke to them only to give instructions and reprimand them for nonattending behaviors.

Increased Attention to Attending Behavior of Both Boys   In the final experimental phase, the teacher was asked to provide both boys with increased attention contingent to appropriate attending behavior.

RESULTS

Baseline₁   Figure 14.1 presents a record of appropriate attending behavior for Edwin and Greg. Each data point represents the combined data for two observation sessions. Since not all the phases had an even number of sessions, however, the last data point in the first four phases of the experiment (designated by the circled data points) represents the combined data for three of the sessions rather than two sessions.

During the seven Baseline sessions, the mean of Edwin's appropriate attending behavior was 31%. The mean recorded for Greg was 33%. On the average, Edwin received teacher attention 2.6 times per session during intervals when he was appropriately attending. Teacher attention to Greg during appropriate attending intervals averaged 1.4 per session.

Increased Attention to Edwin's Attending Behavior   During the first experimental phase, when the teacher was asked to give increased attention to Edwin's appropriate attending, his mean rate of attending increased to 73% per session. His mean rate of attending for the last seven sessions of this phase, as indicated by the horizontal line, was 81% compared to the mean of 31% during the seven Baseline sessions. Teacher attention to Edwin while attending appropriately occurred on the average of 7.9 intervals per session.

There was a more moderate, though substantial, increase in Greg's appropriate attending in this phase. Greg's mean rate of appropriate attending for the entire phase was 47%. The mean rate in the final seven sessions was 58%, compared to 33% in the seven Baseline sessions.

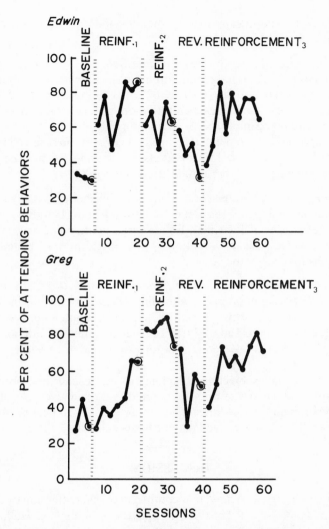

Fig. 14.1. A record of Edwin's and Greg's study behavior: *Baseline₁* — prior to experimental procedures. *Increased Attention to Edwin's Attending Behavior* — systematic teacher attention to attending to task behaviors of Edwin only. *Increased Attention to Greg's Attending Behavior* — systematic teacher attention to attending behaviors of Greg only. *Baseline₂* — withdrawal of systematic teacher attention to attending to task behaviors for both boys. *Increased Attention to Attending Behavior of Both Boys* — reinstatement of teacher attention to attending to tasks for both Edwin and Greg.

Teacher attention during appropriate attending intervals increased slightly to 2.9 intervals per session for Greg.

Increased Attention to Greg's Attending Behavior   When the teacher discontinued providing increased attention to Edwin for appropriate attending his mean rate dropped to 62%, as is indicated by the horizontal line in Fig. 14.1. Teacher attention was recorded in only 1.6 appropriate attending intervals per session for Edwin.

Greg's appropriate attending increased however, as he received teacher attention for attending in 15.2 intervals per session. In the last seven sessions his mean rate of appropriate attending was 82%.

Baseline₂   During the Baseline$_2$ phase, the Teacher essentially ignored appropriate attending and this decreased attending for both boys. By the final seven sessions of Baseline$_2$, Edwin's rate of attending was 41% and Greg's was 48%. Teacher attention was recorded in only 1.7 intervals per sessions for each of the boys.

Increased Attention to Attending Behavior of Both Boys   In the final experimental phase, appropriate attending increased once again. By the final seven sessions, Edwin's rate of appropriate attending was 71%, while Greg's had increased to 74%. Teacher attention for attending was recorded in 11.3 intervals per session for Edwin and in 12.3 intervals per session for Greg.

According to the subjective judgments of the teacher and observers, the disruptive behaviors of both Edwin and Greg had also been affected by the experimental procedures. They reported marked decreases in the amount of talking, laughing, and playing with each other.

DISCUSSION

Earlier studies had indicated that contingent teacher attention can effectively modify classroom behavior of individual pupils (e.g. Hall, *et al.*, 1968). The present study indicated that increasing the appropriate attending behavior of one of two pupils seated at adjacent desks may be correlated with an increase in the attending behavior of the second pupil as well.

One possible explanation of why the second pupil's attending behavior increased when a neighboring pupil received increased teacher attention for attending might be that the second got some "spillover" of reinforcement from the teacher. This possibility should be considered, for while the teacher was reinforcing attending in one of the pair of pupils, she often moved in close proximity to his desk, which placed her close to the other pupil. Proximity of an adult has been considered a reinforcing consequence by some authors and researchers (Bijou and Baer, 1961). There was in fact a slight increase in the amount of teacher attention to Greg's appropriate attending in the first experimental phase even though the teacher had been asked not to increase her attention to him. Therefore, without intending to do so, the teacher may have provided more reinforcement to the behavior of the second pupil when she reinforced the behavior of his neighbor.

Another possibility is that teacher proximity acted as a cue or discriminative stimulus (S^D) for appropriate attending. This could occur due to the fact that when the teacher was nearby, a pupil would be more likely to receive reinforcement for appropriate behavior and/or punishment for inappropriate behavior than if she were at a relatively greater distance.

Another possible explanation for increased study in the second pupil might be that when study behavior for one of the pair increased, he was less likely to look at, laugh at, talk to, or otherwise provide social reinforcement for the behavior of this neighbor. These behaviors were incompatible with appropriate attending and were less probable when high rates of appropriate attending were being maintained. In an effort to check this possibility, a record was kept of the number of times the boys looked at each other during the various phases of the experiment. Table 14.1 presents the mean number of intervals in which Edwin looked at Greg and Greg looked at Edwin in the final seven sessions of each phase of the experiment. Since no attempt was made to manipulate looking behavior, no casual relationship was demonstrated. Generally, however, each boy tended to look at his neighbor at a decreased rate during intervals when

Table 14.1. A record of the number of times Edwin and Greg looked at each other (glances) during the various experimental phases.

	Edwin to Greg	Greg to Edwin
Baseline$_1$	17	19
Increased Attention to Edwin's Attending Behavior	8	7
Increased Attention to Greg's Attending Behavior	17	8
Baseline$_2$	28	20
Increased Attention to Attending Behavior of Both Boys	8	14.5

his behavior was being reinforced. Further research in which this and/or other peer behaviors are systematically manipulated will be necessary to establish whether a functional relationship actually exists between peer behavior and appropriate attending.

Another possible explanation for increased study of the second pupil might be to attribute it to imitation or modeling. Research in a number of studies has indicated that children may imitate behaviors that they see others perform, though they never receive extrinsic reinforcement for those behaviors themselves (Bandura, 1962; Baer and Sherman, 1964; Baer, Peterson, and Sherman, 1967).

Further research will be necessary to determine whether any or all of these explanations are valid. The present study does indicate that as teachers have long surmised, increasing the appropriate behavior of one pupil tends to be associated with increased appropriate behavior of a pupil seated at an adjacent desk.

REFERENCES

Baer, D. M., Peterson, R. F., and Sherman, J. A. The development of imitation by reinforcing behavioral similarity to a model. *Journal of Experimental Analysis of Behavior*, 1967, **10**, 405–416.

Baer, D. M. and Sherman, J. A. Reinforcement control of generalized imitation in young children. *Journal of Experimental Child Psychology*, 1964, **1**, 37–49.

Bandura, A. Social Learning Through Imitation. In M. R. Jones (Ed.), *Nebraska Symposium on Motivation*. Lincoln: University of Nebraska Press. 1962. Pp. 211–269.

Bijou, S. W. and Baer, D. M. *Child development: I a systematic and empirical theory*. New York: Appleton-Century-Crofts, 1961.

Broden, M., Hall, R. V., Dunlap, A., and Clark, R. Effects of teacher attention and a token reinforcement system in a junior high school education class. *Exceptional Children*, 1970, 341–349.

Hall, R. V., Lund, D., and Jackson, D. Effects of teacher attention on study behavior. *Journal of Applied Behavior Analysis*, 1968, **1**, 1–12.

Hall, R. V., Panyan, M., Rabon, D., and Broden, M. Instructing beginning teachers in reinforcement procedures which improve classroom control. *Journal of Applied Behavior Analysis*, 1968, **1**, 315–322.

Thomas, D. R., Becker, W. C., and Armstrong, M. Production and elimination of disruptive classroom behavior by systematically varying teacher's behavior. *Journal of Applied Behavior Analysis*, 1968, **1**, 35–45.

COMMENT

The preceding four articles illustrate ways in which aggression, avoidance behavior, social withdrawal, and study behavior can be influenced by having the child observe a model. The Bandura, Ross, and Ross (1963) study is a classic example of how a child's aggressive behavior is increased by observing both live and film-mediated aggressive models. This study along with that of O'Connor (1969) suggests that movies and television can have both negative and positive effects on children's behavior. Unfortunately, the evaluation of the treatment effect in the O'Connor study occurred only two minutes after treatment. Before general use of the O'Connor technique could be advised, more long term assessment of the treatment effect is necessary. The Bandura, Grusec, and Menlove (1967) vicarious extinction procedures could also be adapted to deal with school related problems such as fear of speaking in front of the class, walking to school alone, taking books out of the library, or asking a girl to dance.

The Broden *et al.* paper differs from the first three articles. As you may have noticed, the term "modeling" is used only once. However, the situation in which the children were observed is clearly similar to the situations described in the previous articles. Broden *et al.* suggest that factors other than "modeling" may be important for producing what are typically referred to as modeling behaviors. For example, if both children are behaving appropriately, the proximity of the teacher while she is praising one child may serve as a reinforcer for the child sitting in the adjacent seat. Also, if the majority of the children are studying, a disruptive child will receive little peer reinforcement for his inappropriate behavior. Thus, children may become less disruptive not because they are modeling appropriate behavior but because the teacher's proximity serves as a reinforcer or because the children's peers no longer reinforce the disruptive behavior. The Broden paper is also significant because it evaluates a technique used by many teachers — that of praising one child with the hope that other children will observe and improve. While Broden *et al.* demonstrated that this technique can be effective when the two children are sitting in adjacent seats, Becker, Thomas, and Carnine (1969) cite evidence that the technique is not effective in all situations. To be specific, when half the class was praised for appropriate behavior, their behavior improved. However, the half of the class that was not praised did not improve.

In addition to the research presented here, Bryan and Walbek (1970) describe some findings which may have relevance to the classroom situation. They exposed children to one of several kinds of models. The model either kept all of his winnings from a game or donated some to charity. In addition, the models either verbalized charitable feelings, greedy feelings, or neutral feelings. The children's post-experimental verbalizations corresponded to the verbalizations of the model; but the children's own charitable behavior, or the lack of it, conformed to the model's behavior regardless of the moral position preached by the model. That is, the actions of the model spoke louder than his words. Thus, the teacher should pay attention to her own behavior since it serves as a model for her children and she should attempt to maintain consistency between what she says and what she does. For example, a teacher who encourages politeness will be most successful if she is careful to say "Please" and "Thank you." If an adult or peer practices one thing but preaches another, the child is more apt to model the practiced behavior than the behavior which is verbally advocated.

Modeling seems to be most effective in altering the frequency of behaviors which the child already has in his repertoire or for producing new combinations of existing behaviors. For example, the children in the O'Connor study almost certainly had the necessary behaviors in their repertoire for social interaction, e.g., verbal and play skills. Modeling as a single technique would undoubtely be less effective in teaching a mute child to talk. Consider the example of a child learning to play the piano. If the child has acquired a fair amount of skill, he may easily model the phrasing demonstrated by his teacher even though he has never exhibited that particular set of behaviors himself. A beginner would have considerably more difficulty in modeling a phrasing technique because he does not have the requisite behavioral components in his repertoire. Thus, modeling may be a useful way to help a child assemble behaviors he has into new combinations. A combination of individualized shaping procedures and modeling will be required to teach behaviors which he has not yet acquired or which are in early stages of development.

CHAPTER 6

Token Reinforcement Programs:
Extrinsic Reinforcers

The use of reinforcers to influence academic behavior is certainly not new. Giving stars for academic achievement and extra recess for "being good" is familiar to most of us. On the other hand, the *frequent* and *systematic* use of prizes such as candy, kites, money, perfume, plants, and comics is generally not common in schools. Approximately a decade ago, Staats initiated a token program for children with reading difficulties. (This early program was discussed in a 1969 paper), and Ayllon and Azrin (1968) initiated a token program for hospitalized psychiatric patients. Since then, token reinforcement programs have developed at a very rapid pace and can be found in Head Start centers, physical rehabilitation centers, alcoholic units, and in schools for the blind, retarded, and emotionally disturbed. The basic ingredients of a token program usually include (1) a set of instructions to the class about the behaviors that will be reinforced, (2) a means of making a potentially reinforcing stimulus — usually called a token — contingent upon behavior, and (3) a set of rules governing the exchange of tokens for back-up reinforcers such as prizes or opportunities to engage in special activities. In almost all settings where token programs are initiated, they are instituted in order to bring about rapid behavior change in people who for various reasons appear "unmotivated." The token program with its prizes or back-up reinforcers often serves as an effective "priming" device or means of dramatically increasing the probability of appropriate behaviors. Thus, the token program is in a sense artificial — or to use Ogden Lindsley's description (1964) — a prosthetic device. However, it is artificial only in that the reinforcers are ordinarily not available to most classroom teachers. As will be emphasized in some of the articles to follow, it is possible to gradually replace the extrinsic reinforcers such as kites, candy, and comics, with reinforcers that are available to any teacher, such as stars and extra recess. More importantly, there are occasions when a teacher can implement a token program using reinforcers natural or intrinsic to the classroom without ever relying on extrinsic reinforcers. Because of important recent work with token programs using extrinsic and natural reinforcers, the articles concerning token reinforcement programs have been divided into two sections, viz., programs utilizing reinforcers extrinsic to the usual classroom and programs utilizing reinforcers intrinsic to the usual classroom. As mentioned earlier, intrinsic reinforcers refer to reinforcers which are *natural* to the classroom such as privileges and extra recess; the use of the term "intrinsic" does not refer to mastery of material or pride in one's work. While such factors may reinforce behavior, they cannot be easily observed or manipulated by a teacher.

This chapter will deal only with programs using extrinsic reinforcers. One of the most frequent objections to token reinforcement programs is that they are merely a system of bribes. Unfortunately, the word "bribe" has several accepted meanings (Webster, 1967), and whether one considers a token system a form of bribes or not depends upon the meaning of bribe referred to. If a bribe is considered as a method of influencing someone's behavior in a corrupt or dishonest manner, then the token programs exemplified in this book clearly do not deserve the term "bribery." On the other hand, if one accepts the secondary dictionary definition of a bribe — to dispense gifts for the purpose of influencing another's judgement or behavior — the token programs presented here clearly would be termed bribery systems. That is, token and back-up reinforcers are purposely made contingent upon appropriate behavior for the purpose of influencing the child's behavior. However, the use of such reinforcement procedures should not be deemed bribery in the sense that they are dishonest or immoral when they are used to establish behavior which is beneficial for the receiver of those reinforcement procedures. The only way one can legitimately regard such token reinforcement systems as methods of bribery is in recognition of the fact that reinforcement is a definite influencing process. A detailed discussion of the issue of bribery is provided by O'Leary, Poulos, and Devine (1971) dealing with both moral and methodological concerns related to tangible reinforcement. For anyone who is involved in the implementation of token programs, the consideration of a host of objections to tangible reinforcers by O'Leary *et al.* (1971) should be useful.

O'Leary and Becker's (1967) (*15*), token program is included because it effectively demonstrates how a token program involving a rating procedure can be used by one teacher with a relatively large class ($N = 17$) of emotionally disturbed children. It should be noted that some children who had not completed a paper for two years (and, we should add, who were diagnosed "minimal brain damage") repeatedly received perfect scores in their academic work. O'Leary, Becker, Evans, and Saudargas (1969) (*16*), designed a token program to assess some of the processes involved in token programs. The effects of rules were not particularly significant as was seen in the earlier study of Madsen, Becker, and Thomas (1968) (*5*). Similarly, having the afternoon divided into four structured lessons did not influence the behavior of most children; and, in contrast to some of the earlier studies presented in this book, praise and ignoring were not effective in reducing disruptive behavior. It should be emphasized, however, that the earlier studies in the "praise and ignore" chapter were not dealing with a whole class of disruptive children but rather with one or two disruptive children in an otherwise normal class. When a token program was combined with Rules, Structure, and Praise and Ignoring, the frequency of disruptive behavior was significantly decreased. Lastly, it should be noted that the reinforcers were gradually changed from prizes to stars and one or two pieces of candy per week without a significant increase in inappropriate behavior.

The study by Birnbrauer, Wolf, Kidder, and Tague (1965) (*17*), was one of the first to demonstrate the effective use of a token reinforcement program with retarded children in a classroom. The tokens used were check marks which were exchangeable for candy and prizes after the student completed his work. The token reinforcement system is described in detail, and for those interested in applying such procedures, this description should prove very useful. The reader should also note (1) that the usual method of motivating these retarded pupils to study, such as presenting material in an interesting and meaningful manner, using materials combining interest value and high probability of success (e.g., Montessori methods and programmed instruction), and social reinforcers such as teacher approval, stars and grades were not effective; (2) that it was not until the token reinforcement program was introduced that the study behavior of the pupils increased; (3) that paraprofessionals (high school graduates) were trained in the performance of classroom duties by the teacher and appeared to execute their duties skillfully; and (4) that there was an emphasis on analyzing the results for individuals as well as the group.

ARTICLE 15

Behavior Modification of an Adjustment Class: A Token Reinforcement Program*

K. DANIEL O'LEARY and WESLEY C. BECKER[1]

University of Illinois, Urbana

Abstract: A base rate of deviant behavior was obtained for the eight most disruptive children in a third grade adjustment class. In a token reinforcement program, the children received teacher's ratings which were exchangeable for reinforcers such as candy and trinkets. With the introduction of the token reinforcement program, an abrupt reduction in deviant behavior occurred. Delay of reinforcement was gradually increased to four days without increase in deviant behavior. The program was equally successful for all children observed, and anecdotal evidence suggests that the children's appropriate behavior generalized to other school situations.

Praise, teacher attention, stars, and grades provide adequate incentive for most pupils to behave in a socially approved way. However, for some students — notably school dropouts, aggressive children, and some retarded children — these methods are relatively ineffective. Where the usual methods of social approval have failed, token reinforcement systems have proven effective (Birnbrauer, Bijou, Wolf, and Kidder, 1965; Birnbrauer and Lawler, 1964; Birnbrauer, Wolf, Kidder, and Tague, 1965; Quay, Werry, McQueen, and Sprague, 1966). Token reinforcers are tangible objects or symbols which attain reinforcing power by being exchanged for a variety of other objects such as candy and trinkets which are back up reinforcers. Tokens acquire generalized reinforcing properties when they are paired with many different reinforcers. The generalized reinforcer is especially useful since it is effective regardless of the momentary condition of the organism.

*Reprinted from *Exceptional Children*, Vol. 33, May 1967, pp. 637–642.

[1]K. Daniel O'Leary is Instructor, and Wesley C. Becker is Professor, Psychology Department, University of Illinois, Urbana. This study was supported in part by Research Grant HD 00881-04 from the National Institutes of Health.

For the children in this study, generalized reinforcers such as verbal responses ("That's right" or "Good!") and token reinforcers such as grades had not maintained appropriate behavior. In fact, their teacher noted that prior to the introduction of the token system, being called "bad" increased the children's inappropriate behavior. "They had the attitude that it was smart to be called bad . . . . When I tried to compliment them or tell them that they had done something well, they would look around the room and make faces at each other." It is a moot question whether the poor academic performance of these children was caused by their disruptive social behavior or vice versa. It was obvious, however, that the disruptive behaviors had to be eliminated before an academic program could proceed.

Although classroom token reinforcement programs have proved effective in modifying behavior, the pupil teacher ratio has usually been small. In the study by Birnbrauer, Wolf *et al.* (1965), a classroom of 17 retarded pupils had four teachers in the classroom at all times. Quay (1966) had one teacher in a behavior modification classroom of five children. One purpose of this project was to devise a token reinforcement program which could be used by one teacher in an average classroom; a second purpose was to see if a token system could be withdrawn gradually without an increase in disruptive behavior by transferring control to teacher attention, praise, and grades, with less frequent exchange of back up reinforcers.

SUBJECTS

The subjects for this study were 17 nine year old children described as emotionally disturbed. They had IQ scores (Kuhlmann-Anderson) ranging from 80 to 107. They had been placed in the adjustment class primarily because they exhibited undesirable classroom behaviors such as temper tantrums, crying, uncontrolled laughter, and fighting. The children were in the classroom throughout the day with the exception of some remedial speech and reading work. Although the token reinforcement system was in effect for the whole class, the study focused on the eight most disruptive children.

METHOD

The children's deviant behaviors were observed by two students in the classroom from 12:30 to 2:10 three days a week. A third student made reliability checks two days a week. Among the behaviors recorded as deviant were the following: pushing, answering without raising one's hand, chewing gum, eating, name calling, making disruptive noise, and talking. Each student observed four children in random order for 22 minutes each session. Observations were made on a 20 second observe/ 10 second record basis. Deviant behaviors were recorded on observation sheets. During the observations, the children had three structured activities: listening to records or stories, arithmetic, and group reading. During these activities, instruction was directed to the whole class, and the children were expected to be quiet and in their seats.

Base Period The teacher was asked to handle the children as she normally did. To obtain data which reflected the frequency of deviant pupil behavior under usual classroom procedures, a base period was used. The observers were in the classroom for three weeks before any baseline data were recorded. At first the children walked up to the observers and tried to initiate conversation with them. As the observers consistently ignored the children, the children's approach behaviors diminished. Thus, it is likely that initial show-off behavior was reduced before baseline measures were obtained.

The average interobserver reliability for individual children during the four week base period, calculated on the basis of exact agreement for time interval and category of behavior, ranged from 75 to 100 percent agreement (Table 15.1). A perfect agreement was scored if both observers recorded the same behavior within a 20 second interval. The reliabilities

Table 15.1. Average Interobserver Reliabilities during Base and Token Reinforcement Periods.

Subject	Base Period		Token Reinforcement Period	
	Percentage of Perfect Agreement	Number of Reliability Checks	Percentage of Perfect Agreement	Number of Reliability Checks
1	85	3	88	9
2	82	2	94	9
3	92	3	96	9
4	100	1	93	5
5	77	3	87	9
6	75	4	87	9
7	80	4	80	8
8	75	3	88	8

were calculated by dividing the number of perfect agreements by the number of different responses observed. The percentage of each child's deviant behavior for any one day was calculated by dividing the number of intervals in which one or more deviant behaviors occurred by the number of observed intervals for that day. As can be seen from Fig. 15.1, there was a fairly stable base rate of deviant behavior with a slight increasing trend.

Token Reinforcement Period   On the first day of the token period the experimenter placed the following instructions on the blackboard: In Seat, Face Front, Raise Hand, Working, Pay Attention, and Desk Clear. The experimenter then explained the token procedure to the children. The tokens were ratings placed in small booklets on each child's desk. The children were told that they would receive ratings from 1 to 10 and that the ratings would reflect the extent to which they followed the instructions. The points or ratings could be exchanged for a variety of back up reinforcers. The reinforcers consisted of small prizes ranging in value from 1 to 29 cents, such as candy, pennants, comics, perfume, and kites. The total cost of the reinforcers used during the two months was $80.76. All the pupils received reinforcers in the same manner during class, but individual preferences were considered by providing a variety of items, thus maximizing the probability that at least one of the items would be a reinforcer for a given child at a given time.

The experimenter repeated the instructions at the beginning of the token period each day for one week and rated the children to provide a norm for the teacher. It was the teacher, however, who placed the ratings in the children's booklets during the short pause at the end of a lesson period. The ratings reflected the extent to which the child exhibited the appropriate behaviors listed on the blackboard. Where possible, these ratings also reflected the accuracy of the child's arithmetic work.

The number of ratings made each day was gradually decreased from five to three, and the number of points required to obtain a prize gradually increased. For the first three days, the tokens were exchanged for reinforcers at the end of the token period. For the next four days, points were accumulated for two days and exchanged at the end of the token period on the second day. Then, for the next 15 days, a three day delay between token and reinforcers was used. Four day delays were employed for the remaining 24 school days. During the three and four day delay periods, tokens were exchanged for reinforcers at the end of the school day. By requiring more appropriate behavior to receive a prize and increasing the delay of reinforcement it was hoped that transfer of con-

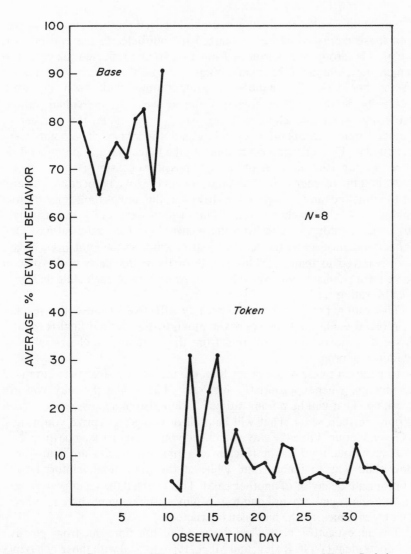

Fig. 15.1. Average Percentages of Deviant Behavior during the Base and Token Periods.

trol from the token reinforcers to the more traditional methods of teacher praise and attention would occur.

After the first week, the teacher made the ratings and executed the token system without aid. Procedures were never discussed when the children were present.

The children also received group points based on total class behavior, and these points could be exchanged for popsicles at the end of each week. The group points ranged from 1 to 10 and reflected the extent to which the children were quiet during the time the ratings were placed in the booklets. The number of group ratings made each day were gradually decreased from five to three as were the individual ratings. However, since the children were usually very quiet, the number of points required to obtain a popsicle was not increased. The points were accumulated on a thermometer chart on the blackboard, and the children received popsicles on seven of the eight possible occasions.

At first the teacher was reluctant to accept the token procedure because of the time the ratings might take. However, the ratings took at most three minutes. As the teacher noted, "The class is very quiet and usually I give them a story to read from the board while I give the ratings. One model student acts as the teacher and he calls on the students who are well-behaved to read.... This is one of the better parts of the day. It gave me a chance to go around and say something to each child as I gave him his rating...."

The rating procedure was especially effective because the teacher reinforced each child for approximations to the desired final response. Instead of demanding perfection from the start, the teacher reinforced evidence of progress.

In addition to the token procedure, the teacher was instructed to make comments, when appropriate, such as: "Pat, I like the way you are working. That will help your rating." "I am glad to see everyone turned around in their seats. That will help all of you get the prize you want." "Good, Gerald. I like the way you raised your hand to ask a question."

A technique used by the teacher to extinguish the deviant behavior of one child was to ignore him, while at the same time reinforcing the appropriate behavior of another child. This enabled the teacher to refrain from using social censure and to rely almost solely on positive reinforcement techniques, as she had been instructed.

The investigators also were prepared to use time out from positive reinforcement (Wolf, Risley, and Mees, 1964) to deal with those behaviors which were especially disruptive. The time out procedure involves isolating the child for deviant behavior for a specified period of time. This procedure was not used, however, since the frequency of disruptive behavior was very low at the end of the year.

The average interobserver reliability for individual children during the token period ranged from 80 to 96 percent. As indicated in Table 15.1, the reliabilities were recorded separately for the base and token periods because reliabilities were higher during the token period when the frequency of deviant behavior was low.

RESULTS

As can be seen from Fig. 15.1, the average percentage of deviant behavior at the end of the year was very low. The daily mean of deviant behavior during the token procedure ranged from 3 to 32 percent, while the daily mean of deviant behavior during the base period ranged from 66 to 91 percent. The average of deviant behavior for all children during the base period was 76 percent as contrasted with 10 percent during the token procedure. As can be seen from the F ratio (Table 15.2), the change from the base period to the token period was highly significant ($p < 0.001$). Using an omega squared, it was estimated that the treatment accounted for 96 percent of the variance of the observed deviant behavior.

Table 15.2. Analysis of Variance on Deviant Behavior Scores (N = 8).

Source	df	MS	F
Between Subjects	7	72.86	
Within Subjects	8	2203.00	
Treatment	1	17424.00	609.87*
Residual	7	28.57	

*$p < 0.001$

An examination of the individual records (Fig. 15.2) shows the small degree of individual variation and differences in deviant behavior from the base to the token period. Although subjects 2 and 7 exhibited more deviant behavior than others during the token period, the percentage of deviant behavior was obviously less than during the base period. The percentage of deviant behavior declined for all pupils from the base to the token period.

DISCUSSION

At least two variables in addition to the token procedure and social reinforcement possibly contributed to the change in the children's be-

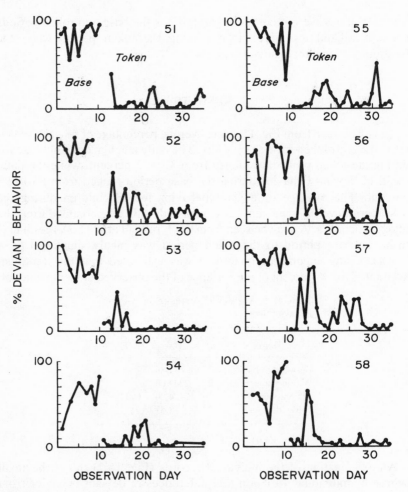

Fig. 15.2. Percentages of Deviant Behavior for Individual Children during Base and Token Periods.

havior. First, during the baseline and token phases of this demonstration, the teacher was enrolled in a psychology class which emphasized operant and social learning principles. The influence of this class cannot be assessed, although the dramatic and abrupt change from the base to the token phase of the demonstration makes it seem highly implausible that the psychology class was the major variable accounting for the change. However, in a replication of this study now being planned, the teacher will receive only a short introduction to the basic principles and subsequent instruction by the experimenter throughout the procedure.

Secondly, the reduction in deviant behavior enabled the teacher to spend more time giving children individual attention during the token phase of the experiment. She had time to correct and return the children's work promptly, thus giving them immediate feedback. She was also able to use teaching materials not previously used. Some children who had not completed a paper for two years repeatedly received perfect scores. The immediate feedback and new materials probably contributed to the maintenance of appropriate behavior.

An experiment within the Skinnerian paradigm involves the establishment of a stable base rate of behavior; next, environmental contingencies are applied and the maladaptive behavior is reduced. The contingencies are then withdrawn and there is a return to base conditions. Finally, the environmental contingencies are again instituted and the maladaptive behavior decreased. This procedure of operant decrease, increase, and finally decrease of maladaptive behavior in association with specific environmental conditions demonstrates the degree of stimulus control obtained by the technique.

A return to base conditions early in the treatment period of this study was not carried out because of a concern that the enthusiasm and cooperation generated by the program throughout the school system might be severely reduced. There is little doubt that a return to base conditions following three or four weeks of the token procedure would have resulted in an increase in disruptive behavior. When a reversal was used by Birnbrauer, Wolf, *et al.* (1965), a number of children showed a decline in the amount of studying and an increase in disruptive behavior. As an alternative, it was planned to return gradually to baseline conditions during the following fall, but radical changes in pupil population prevented this reversal.

Without a reversal or a return to baseline conditions it cannot be stated that the token system and not other factors, such as the changes that ordinarily occur during the school year, accounted for the observed reduction of deviant behavior. To demonstrate clearly the crucial significance of the token procedure itself, a systematic replication with different children and a different teacher is planned. As Sidman (1960) noted, "An investigator may, on the basis of experience, have great confidence in the adequacy of his methodology, but other experimenters cannot be expected to share his confidence without convincing evidence (p. 75)."

Two interesting implications of this study are the effects of delay of reinforcement and generalization. The use of tokens provides a procedure which is intermediate between immediate and delayed tangible reinforcement. In Birnbrauer, Wolf, *et al.*'s (1965) class of severely retarded children this delay was extended from a few seconds to over an hour. Some educable children studied for many days for check marks only and, presumably, the knowledge that they were approaching a goal. All the children in the present study worked for four days without receiving a back up reinforcer. In addition, more than one child made the comment toward the end of school that next year they would be old enough to behave and work well without the prizes.

Anecdotal records indicate that after the token procedure was put into effect, the children behaved better during the morning session, music, and library periods. These reports suggest that a transfer to normal classroom control using social reinforcement and grades would not be very difficult. Also, the gang behavior of frowning upon "doing well" disappeared. Some children even helped enforce the token system by going to the blackboard just before class began and reading the instructions to the class.

REFERENCES

Birnbrauer, J. S., Bijou, S. W., Wolf, M. M., and Kidder, J. D. Programmed instruction in the classroom. In L. P. Ullman and L. Krasner (Eds.), *Case studies in behavior modification.* New York: Holt, Rinehart and Winston, 1965. Pp. 358–363.

Birnbrauer, J. S., and Lawler, Julia. Token reinforcement for learning. *Mental Retardation*, 1964, 2, 275–279.

Birnbrauer, J. S., Wolf, M. M., Kidder, J. D., and Tague, Cecilia E. Classroom behavior of retarded pupils with token reinforcement. *Journal of Experimental Child Psychology*, 1965, 2, 219–235.

Quay, H. C., Werry, J. S., McQueen, Marjorie, and Sprague, R. L. Remediation of the conduct problem child in the special class setting. *Exceptional Children*, 1966, 32, 509–515.

Sidman, M. *Tactics of scientific research.* New York: Basic Books, 1960.

Wolf, M. M., Risley, T. R., and Mees, H. L. Application of operant conditioning procedures to the behavioral problems of an autistic child. *Behavior Research and Therapy*, 1964, 1, 305–312.

ARTICLE 16

A Token Reinforcement Program in a Public School: A Replication and Systematic Analysis*[1]

K. D. O'LEARY, W. C. BECKER, M. B. EVANS and R. A. SAUDARGAS

State University of New York at Stony Brook,
University of Illinois, and Florida State University

Abstract: A base rate of disruptive behavior was obtained for seven children in a second-grade class of 21 children. Rules, Educational Structure, and Praising Appropriate Behavior while Ignoring Disruptive Behavior were introduced successively; none of these procedures consistently reduced disruptive behavior. However, a combination of Rules, Educational Structure, and Praise and Ignoring nearly eliminated disruptive behavior of one child. When the Token Reinforcement Program was introduced, the frequency of disruptive behavior declined in five of the six remaining children. Withdrawal of the Token Reinforcement Program increased disruptive behavior in these five children, and reinstatement of the Token Reinforcement Program reduced disruptive behavior in four of these five. Follow-up data indicated that the teacher was able to transfer control from the token and back-up reinforcers to the reinforcers existing within the educational setting, such as stars and occasional pieces of candy. Improvements in academic achievement

---

*Reprinted from the *Journal of Applied Behavior Analysis*, Vol. 2, No. 1, Spring 1969, pp. 3–13. Copyright 1969 by the Society for the Experimental Analysis of Behavior, Inc.

[1]Portions of this paper were presented to the American Psychological Association, September, 1968, San Francisco, California. This research was supported primarily by Research Grant HD 0081-05 to Wesley C. Becker from the National Institutes of Health and secondarily by a Biomedical Science Grant 31-8200 to K. Daniel O'Leary from the State University of New York at Stony Brook. The authors are grateful to Nancy Brown, Connie Dockterman, Pearl Dorfmann, Jeanne Kappauf, Margery Lewy, Stanley Madsen, and Darlene Zientarski who were the major observers in this study. Appreciation for support of this study is expressed to Dr. Lowell Johnson, Director of Instruction, Urbana Public Schools, and to Mr. Richard Sturgeon, elementary school principal. The greatest thanks goes to Mrs. Linda Alsberg, the teacher who executed the Token Reinforcement Program and tolerated the presence of observers both morning and afternoon for eight months. Her patience and self-control during the Praise and Withdrawal Phases of the program were especially appreciated. Reprints may be obtained from K. Daniel O'Leary, Dept. of Psychology, State University of New York at Stony Brook, Stony Brook, N.Y. 11790.

during the year may have been related to the Token Program, and attendance records appeared to be enhanced during the Token phases. The Token Program was utilized only in the afternoon, and the data did not indicate any generalization of appropriate behavior from the afternoon to the morning.

Praise and other social stimuli connected with the teacher's behavior have been established as effective controllers of children's behavior (Allen, Hart, Buell, Harris, and Wolf, 1964; Becker, Madsen, Arnold, and Thomas, 1967; Brown and Elliot, 1965; Hall, Lund, and Jackson, 1968; Harris, Johnston, Kelley and Wolf, 1964; Harris, Wolf, and Baer, 1964; Scott, Burton, and Yarrow, 1967; Zimmerman and Zimmerman, 1962). When the teacher's use of praise and social censure is not effective, token reinforcement programs are often successful in controlling children (Birnbrauer, Wolf, Kidder, and Tague, 1965; Kuypers, Becker, and O'Leary, 1968; O'Leary and Becker, 1967; Quay, Werry, McQueen, and Sprague, 1966; Wolf, Giles, and Hall, 1968).

The token reinforcement program utilized by O'Leary and Becker (1967) in a third-grade adjustment class dramatically reduced disruptive behavior. In order to maximize the possibility of reducing the disruptive behavior of the children. O'Leary and Becker used several major variables simultaneously. The first objective of the present study was to analyze the separate effects of some of the variables utilized in the former study. More specifically, the aim was to examine the separate effects of Classroom Rules, Educational Structure, Teacher Praise, and a Token Reinforcement Program on children's disruptive behavior. Rules consisted of a list of appropriate behaviors that were reviewed daily. Educational Structure was the organization of an academic program into specified 30-min lessons such as spelling and arithmetic. The second objective was to assess whether a Token Reinforcement Program used only in the afternoon had any effect on the children's behavior in the morning. Third, the present study sought to examine the extent to which the effects of the Token Reinforcement Program persisted when the Token Program was discontinued.

METHOD

Subjects

Seven members of a second-grade class of 21 children from lower-middle class homes served. At the beginning of the school year, the class had a mean age of 7 yr, 5 months, a mean IQ score of 95 (range 80 to 115) on the California Test of Mental Maturity, and a mean grade level of 1.5 on the California Achievement Test. The class was very heterogeneous with regard to social behaviors. According to the teacher, three of the children were quite well behaved but at least eight exhibited a great deal of undesirable behavior. The teacher, Mrs. A., had a master's degree in counseling but had only student teaching experience. She was invited to participate in a research project involving her class and received four graduate credits for participating in the project.

Observation

Children   Mrs. A. selected seven children for observation. All seven children were observed in the afternoon and four of the seven (S1, S2, S4, and S6) were also observed in the morning. Morning observations were made by a regular observer and a reliability checker from 9:30 to 11:30 every Monday, Wednesday, and Friday. Afternoon observations were made by two regular observers and a reliability checker from 12:30 to 2:30 every Monday, Wednesday, and Friday. Observations were made by undergraduate students who were instructed never to talk to the children or to make any differential responses to them in order to minimize the effect of the observers on the children's behavior. Before Base Period data were collected, the undergraduates were trained to observe the children over a three-week period in the classroom, and attention-seeking behaviors of the children directed at the observers were effectively eliminated before the Base Period.

Each child was observed for 20 min each day. The observers watched the children in a random order. Observations were made on a 20-sec observe, 10-sec record basis; i.e., the observer would watch the child for 20 sec and then take 10 sec to record the disruptive behaviors which had occurred during that 20-sec period. The categories of behavior selected for observation were identical to those used by O'Leary and Becker (1967). Briefly, the seven general categories of disruptive behavior were as follows: (1) *motor behaviors:* wandering around the room; (2) *aggressive behaviors:* hitting, kicking, striking another child with an object; (3) *disturbing another's property:* grabbing another's book, tearing up another's paper; (4) *disruptive noise:* clapping, stamping feet; (5) *turning around:* turning to the person behind or looking to the rear of the room when Mrs. A. was in the front of the class; (6) *verbalization:* talking to others when not permitted by teacher, blurting out answers, name-calling; and (7) *inappropriate tasks:* doing arithmetic during the spelling lesson.

The present study was a systematic replication of O'Leary and Becker (1967). To facilitate comparison of the two studies, the dependent measure reported is the percentage of intervals in which one or more disruptive behaviors was recorded. Percentages rather than frequencies were used because the length of the observations varied due to un-avoidable circumstances such as assemblies and snow storms. Nonethe-less, most observations lasted the full 20 min, and no observation lasting less than 15 min was included.

Teacher   In order to estimate the degree to which the teacher followed the experimental instructions, Mrs. A. was observed by two undergra-duates for 90 min on Tuesday and Thursday afternoons. Teacher behav-ior was not observed on Monday, Wednesday, and Friday when the children were observed because Mrs. A. understandably did not wish to have as many as five observers in the room at one time. Furthermore, because Mrs. A. was somewhat reluctant to have three regular observers and one or two graduate students in the room at most times, she was informed of the need for this observational intrusion and the mechanics thereof. This explanation made it impossible to assess the teacher's behavior without her knowledge, but it was felt that deception about teacher observation could have been harmful both to this project and future projects in the school. Nonetheless, frequent teacher observa-tions by two graduate students who were often in the room the entire week ensured some uniformity of her behavior throughout the week. The graduate students frequently met with Mrs. A. to alert her to any deviations from the experimental instructions, and equally important, to reinforce her "appropriate" behavior. Observations of the teacher's behavior were made on a 20-sec observe, 10-sec record basis. The cate-gories of teacher behavior selected for observation were as follows:

I. Comments *preceding* responses.

  A. *Academic instruction:* "Now we will do arithmetic"; "Put everything in your desk"; "Sound out the words."
  B. *Social instruction:* "I'd like you to say 'please' and 'thank you'"; "Let me see a quiet hand"; "Let's sit up."

II. Comments *following* responses.

  A. *Praise:* "Good"; "Fine"; "You're right"; "I like the way I have your attention."

B. *Criticism:* "Don't do that"; "Be quiet"; "Sit in your seat!"
C. *Threats:* "If you're not quiet by the time I count three . . . ."; "If you don't get to work you will stay after school"; "Do you want to stay in this group?"

The teacher's praise, criticism, and threats to individual children were differentiated from praise, criticism, and threats to the class as a whole. For example, "Johnny, be quiet!" was differentiated from "Class, be quiet!". Thus, eight different classes of teacher behavior were recorded: two classes of comments preceding responses and six classes following responses.

Procedure

The eight phases of the study were as follows: (1) Base Period, (2) Classroom Rules, (3) Educational Structure, (4) Praising Appropriate Behavior and Ignoring Disruptive Behavior, (5) Tokens and Back-up Reinforcement, (6) Praising Appropriate Behavior and Ignoring Disruptive Behavior (Withdrawal), (7) Tokens and Back-up Reinforcement, and (8) Follow-up. Three procedures, Educational Structure and both of the Token Reinforcement Phases, were instituted for a 2-hr period during the afternoon. The remainder of the procedures were in effect for the entire day. The eight procedures were in effect for all 21 children. The first four conditions were instituted in the order of hypothesized increasing effectiveness. For example, it was thought that Rules would have less effect on the children's behavior than the use of Praise. In addition, it was thought that the combination of Rules and Praise would have less effect than the Tokens and Back-up Reinforcers.

Base Period After the initial three-week observer training period, the children were observed on eight days over a six-week Base Period to estimate the frequency of disruptive pupil behavior under usual classroom conditions.[2] The teacher was asked to handle the children in whatever way she felt appropriate. During the Base Period, Mrs. A. instructed all the children in subjects like science and arithmetic or took several students to small reading groups in the back of the room while the rest of the class engaged in independent work at their seats. Neither the

---

[2]Ten of the 18 observations during the Base Period were eliminated because movies were shown on those days, and disruptive behavior on those days was significantly less than on days when movies were not shown. Although movies were seldom used after Base Period, the seven subsequent observations when movies occurred were eliminated.

particular type of activity nor the duration was the same each day. Stars and various forms of peer pressure were sporadically used as classroom control techniques, but they usually had little effect and were discontinued until experimentally reintroduced during the Follow-up Phase.

Classroom Rules   There were seven observations over a three-week period during the second phase of the study. The following rules or instructions were placed on the blackboard by the teacher: "We sit in our seats; we raise our hands to talk; we do not talk out of turn; we keep our desks clear; we face the front of the room; we will work very hard; we do not talk in the hall; we do not run; and, we do not disturb reading groups." Mrs. A. was asked to review the rules at least once every morning and afternoon, and frequent observations and discussions with Mrs. A. guaranteed that this was done on most occasions. The classroom activities again consisted of reading groups and independent seat work.

Educational Structure   It has been stated that a great deal of the success in token reinforcement programs may be a function of the highly structured regimen of the program and not a function of reinforcement contingencies. Since the Token Phase of the program was designed to be used during structured activities that the teacher directed, Mrs. A. was asked to reorganize her program into four 30-min sessions in the afternoon in which the whole class participated, e.g., spelling, reading, arithmetic, and science. Thus, the purpose of the Educational Structure Phase was to assess the importance of structure *per se*. Mrs. A. continued to review the rules twice a day during this phase and all succeeding phases. During this phase there were five observations over a two-week period.

Praise and Ignore   In addition to Rules and Educational Structure, Mrs. A. was asked to praise appropriate behavior and to ignore disruptive behavior as much as possible. For example, she was asked to ignore children who did not raise their hands before answering questions and to praise children who raised their hands before speaking. In addition, she was asked to discontinue her use of threats. During this phase there were five observations over a two-week period.

Token 1   Classroom Rules, Educational Structure, and Praise and Ignoring remained in effect. The experimenter told the children that they would receive points or ratings four times each afternoon. The points which the children received on these four occasions ranged from 1 to 10, and the children were told that the points would reflect the extent to which they followed the rules placed on the blackboard by Mrs. A. Where possible, these points also reflected the quality of the children's participation in class discussion and the accuracy of their arithmetic or spelling. The children's behavior in the morning did not influence their ratings in the afternoon. If a child was absent, he received no points. The points or tokens were placed in small booklets on each child's desk. The points were exchangeable for back-up reinforcers such as candy, pennants, dolls, comics, barrettes, and toy trucks, ranging in value from 2 to 30 cents. The variety of prizes made it likely that at least one of the items would be a reinforcer for each child. The prizes were on display every afternoon, and the teacher asked each child to select the prize he wished to earn before the rating period started.

During the initial four days, the children were eligible for prizes just after their fourth rating at approximately 2:30. Thereafter, all prizes were distributed at the end of the day. For the first 10 school days the children could receive prizes each day. There were always two levels of prizes. During the first 10 days, a child had to receive at least 25 points to receive a 2 to 5¢ prize (level one prize) or 35 points to receive a 10¢ prize (level two prize). For the next six days, points were accumulated for two days and exchanged at the end of the second day. When children saved their points for two days, a child had to receive 55 points to receive a 10¢ prize or 70 points to receive a 20¢ prize. Then, a six-day period occurred in which points were accumulated for three days and exchanged at the end of the third day. During this period, a child had to receive 85 points to receive a 20¢ prize or 105 points to receive a 30¢ prize. Whenever the prizes were distributed, the children relinquished all their points. During Token I, there were 13 observations over a five-week period.

For the first week, the experimenter repeated the instructions to the class at the beginning of each afternoon session. Both the experimenter and Mrs. A. rated the children each day for the first week in order to teach Mrs. A. how to rate the children. The experimenter sat in the back of the room and handed his ratings to Mrs. A. in a surreptitious manner after each rating period. Mrs. A. utilized both ratings in arriving at a final rating which she put in the children's booklets at the end of each lesson period. The method of arriving at a number or rating to be placed in the child's booklet was to be based on the child's improvement in behavior. That is, if a child showed any daily improvement he could receive a rating of approximately 5 to 7 so that he could usually earn at least a small prize. Marked improvement in behavior or repeated displays of relatively good behavior usually warranted ratings from 8 to 10. Ratings from 1 to 5 were given when a child was disruptive and did not evidence any daily improvement. Although such a rating system involves much subjective judgment on the part of the teacher, it is relatively easy to implement, and a subsidiary aim of the study was to assess whether a token system could be implemented by one teacher in a class of average size. After the first week, the teacher administered the Token Program herself, and the experimenter was never present when the children were being observed. If the experimenter had been present during the Token Phases but not during Withdrawal, any effects of the Token Program would have been confounded by the experimenter's presence.

Withdrawal   To demonstrate that the token and back-up reinforcers and not other factors, such as the changes that ordinarily occur during the school year, accounted for the observed reduction in disruptive behavior, the token and back-up reinforcers were withdrawn during this phase. There were seven observations over a five-week period. When the prizes and the booklets were removed from the room, Mrs. A. told the children that she still hoped that they would behave as well as they had during the Token Period and emphasized how happy she was with their recent improvement. Rules, Educational Structure, and Praise and Ignoring remained in effect.

Token II   When the tokens and back-up reinforcers were reinstated, the children obtained a prize on the first day if they received 25 to 35 points. For the next four days, there was a one-day delay between token and back-up reinforcement; the remainder of the Token Reinstatement Period involved a two-day delay of reinforcement. The prize and point system was identical to that during Token I. During this phase, there were five observations over a two-week period.

Follow-up   The token and back-up reinforcers were again withdrawn in order to see if the appropriate behavior could be maintained under more normal classroom conditions. In addition to the continued use of Praise, Rules, and Educational Structure, it was suggested that Mrs. A. initiate the use of a systematic star system. Children could receive from one to three stars for good behavior twice during the morning and once during the afternoon. In addition, the children received extra stars for better behavior during the morning restroom break and for displaying appropriate behavior upon entering the room at 9:15 and 12:30. At times, extra stars were given to the best behaved row of children. The children counted their stars at the end of the day; if they had 10 or more stars, they received a gold star that was placed on a permanent wall chart. If a child received 7 to 9 stars, he received a green star that was placed on the chart. The boys' gold stars and the girls' gold stars were counted each day; and each member of the group with the greater number of gold stars at the end of the week received a piece of candy. In addition, any child who received an entire week of gold stars received a piece of candy. All children began the day without stars so that, with the exception of the stars placed on the wall chart, everyone entered the program at the same level.

Such a procedure was a form of a token reinforcement program, but there were important procedural differences between the experimental phases designated Token and Follow-up. The back-up reinforcers used during the Token Phases were more expensive than the two pieces of candy a child could earn each week during the Follow-up Phase. In addition, four daily ratings occurred at half-hour intervals in the afternoons during the Token Phases but not during Follow-up. On the other hand, stars, peer pressure, and a very small amount of candy were used in the Follow-up Phase. As mentioned previously, both stars and peer pressure had been used sporadically in the Base Period with little effect. Most importantly, it was felt that the procedures used in the Follow-up Phase could be implemented by any teacher. During this phase there were six observations over a four-week period.

Reliability of Observations

The reliabilities of child observations were calculated according to the following procedure: an agreement was scored if both observers recorded one or more disruptive behaviors within the same 20-sec interval; a disagreement was scored if one observer recorded a disruptive behavior and the other observer recorded none. The reliability of the measure of disruptive behavior was calculated for each child each day by dividing the number of intervals in which there was agreement that one or more disruptive behaviors occurred by the total number of agreements plus disagreements. An agreement was scored if both observers recorded the same behavior within the same 20-sec interval. A disagreement was scored if one observer recorded the behavior and the other did not. The reliability of a particular class of teacher behavior on any one day was calculated by dividing the total number of agreements for that class of behaviors by the total number of agreements plus disagreements for that class of behaviors. Reliabilities were calculated differently for child behaviors and teacher behaviors because different types of dependent measures were utilized for children and the teacher, and it was felt that reliability measures should be reported for the specific dependent measures used.

At least one reliability check was made during the afternoon on every child during the Base Period, and one child had three.[3] The average reliability of the measure of disruptive behavior during the afternoons of the Base Period for each of the seven children ranged from 88 to 100%. The following figures represent the number of reliability checks and the average of those reliability checks after the Base Period for each child: S1: 6, 86%; S2: 7, 94%; S3: 6, 94%; S4; 6, 93%; S5: 6, 87%; S6: 6, 84%; S7: 6, 97%. Because of the repeated high reliabilities, reliability checks were discontinued when the token and back-up reinforcers were reinstated; i.e., no reliability checks were made during or after the Withdrawal Phase.

Adequate morning reliabilities were not obtained until the Rules Phase of the study. The following figures represent the number of reliability checks and the average of these reliability checks during the Rules Phase: S1: 3, 93%; S2: 4, 68%; S4: 3, 91%; S6: 3, 88%. Morning reliability checks after the Rules Phase were made approximately every three observations (approximately seven occasions) through the first Token Period. Average reliabilities of the four children during the Rules, Educational Structure, Praise and Ignore, and Token I Phase ranged from 92 to 99%.

Eleven reliability checks for the various classes of teacher behavior before the Praise and Ignore Phase was introduced yielded average reliabilities as follows: academic instruction, 75%; social instruction, 77%; praise to individuals, 77%; praise to the class, 94%; criticism to individuals, 73%; criticism to the class, 72%; threats to individuals, 83%; and threats to the class, 83%.

---

[3]Before 10 of the 18 observation days during the Base Period were eliminated because movies were shown on those days, at least three reliability checks had been made during the afternoon on each child.

RESULTS

Child Behavior

Figures 16.1 and 16.2 present morning and afternoon data; some of the variability within conditions can be seen. Figure 16.3 presents data of individual children as well as an average of seven children across afternoon conditions. An analysis of variance was performed on the percentages of combined disruptive behavior, averaged within the eight afternoon experimental conditions, for the seven subjects (*see* Fig. 16.3). The analysis of variance for repeated measures (Winer, 1962, p. 111) indicated differences among the eight experimental conditions ($F = 7.3$; $df = 7$, 42; $p < 0.001$). On the other hand, the percentages of combined disruptive behavior of the four children observed in the morning, averaged within conditions, did not change during Rules, Educational Structure, Praise and Ignore, or Token I ($F = 1.0$; $df = 4$, 12). Differences among afternoon conditions were assessed by t-tests. Significant and nonsignificant differences are grouped individually in Table 16.1.[4]

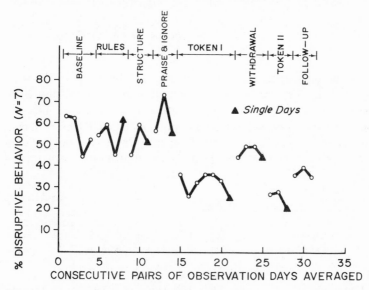

Fig. 16.1. Average percentage of combined disruptive behavior of seven children during the afternoon over the eight conditions: Base, Rules, Educational Structure, Praise and Ignore, Token I, Withdrawal, Token II, Follow-up.

---

[4]Two-tailed tests.

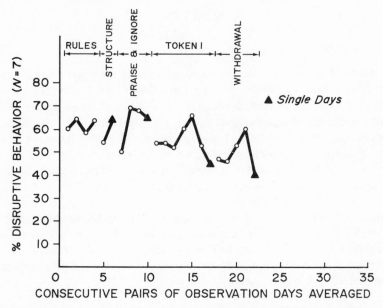

Fig. 16.2. Average percentage of combined disruptive behavior of four children during the morning over five conditions: Base, Rules, Educational Structure, Praise and Ignore, Token I, Withdrawal, Token II, Follow-up.

It should be emphasized that comparisons between Follow-up and Praise and Ignore are more meaningful than comparisons between Follow-up and Base, Rules, or Educational Structure. Praise and Follow-up were similar procedures; both included Rules, Educational Structure, and Praise and Ignore. The Base Period did not include any of these. Furthermore, after Rules and Educational Structure were

Table 16.1.

Significant		Non-Significant	
Token I vs. Withdrawal	t = 3.3**	Rules vs. Educational Structure	t = 0.8
Token II vs. Withdrawal	t = 2.9*	Educational Structure vs. Praise	t = 1.0
Token I vs. Praise	t = 3.4**	Base vs. Withdrawal	t = 1.2
Token II vs. Praise	t = 3.0*	Token I vs. Follow-up	t = 1.1
Base vs. Follow-up	t = 3.2**	Token II vs. Follow-up	t = 1.5
Praise vs. Follow-up	t = 3.3**		
Withdrawal vs. Follow-up	t = 3.2**		

**p < 0.02, df = 6, *p < 0.05, df = 6.

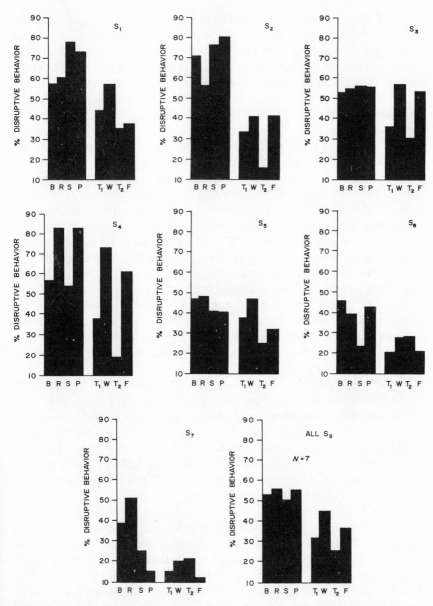

Fig. 16.3. Percentage of combined disruptive behavior for each of seven children during the eight conditions: Base, Rules, Educational Structure, Praise and Ignore, Token I, Withdrawal, Token II, Follow-up.

initiated, Mrs. A. stated that she required more academic work from the children than during Base Period. A statistical analysis of the group data suggests that a token reinforcement program can reduce disruptive behavior and that a token reinforcement program can be replaced with a variant of a token program without an increase in disruptive behavior. However, a more detailed analysis of the data for individual children indicated that the Token Reinforcement Program was more effective for some children than others.

The introduction of Rules, Educational Structure, and Praise and Ignore did not have any consistent effects on behavior (see Fig. 16.3). Praising Appropriate Behavior and Ignoring Disruptive Behavior deserve special mention. Although Mrs. A. used criticism occasionally during the Praise and Ignore Phase, she generally ignored disruptive behavior and used praise frequently. Initially, a number of children responded well to Mrs. A.'s praise, but two boys (S2 and S4) who had been disruptive all year became progressively more unruly during the Praise and Ignore Phase. Other children appeared to observe these boys being disruptive, with little or no aversive consequences, and soon became disruptive themselves. Relay races and hiding under a table contributed to the pandemonium. Several children were so disruptive that the academic pursuits of the rest of the class became impossible. The situation became intolerable, and the Praise and Ignore Phase had to be discontinued much earlier than had been planned.

The disruptive behavior of S7 was reduced to a very low level of 15% by a combination of Rules, Educational Structure, and Praise and Ignore. In the previous token program (O'Leary and Becker, 1967) in which a number of variables including rules, praise, educational structure, and a token program were simultaneously introduced, disruptive behavior during the token period was reduced to a level of 10%. Thus, the present Token Reinforcement Program probably would not be expected further to reduce disruptive behavior in this child.

During Token I, there was a marked reduction ($\geqslant 18\%$) in the disruptive behavior of five children (S1, S2, S3, S4, and S6) and a reduction of 3% in S5. Withdrawal of the Token Program increased disruptive behavior from 5% to 45% in these six children. Reinstatement of the Token Program led to a decrease in five of these six children (S1, S2, S3, S4, S5). The disruptive behavior of five children (S1, S2, S4, S5, and S6) ranged from 8% to 39% lower during the Follow-up than during the Praise and Ignore Phase of the study. Since on no occasion did the Follow-up procedures precede Token I and/or Token II, this study did not demonstrate that Token I and/or Token II were necessary conditions for the success of the Follow-up procedures.

In summary, Token I and Token II were definitely associated with a reduction of disruptive behavior, *and* the Follow-up procedure was effective with three of the six children (S1, S2, and S4) who had more than 15% disruptive behavior during the Praise and Ignore Phase (S7 had 15% disruptive behavior during the Praise and Ignore Phase). Token I and Token II were associated with marked reductions of disruptive behavior of S3, but the frequency of disruptive behavior during the Follow-up was not substantially lower than during the Praise and Ignore Phase. Definitive conclusions concerning the effects of the Token Program cannot be drawn for S5 and S6, although some reduction of disruptive behavior was associated with either Token I and Token II for both of these children. In addition, the disruptive behavior of S5 and S6 was 8% and 20% less respectively during Follow-up than during the Praise and Ignore Phase.

Teacher Behavior

On any one day, the percentage of each of the eight classes of teacher behavior was calculated by dividing the number of intervals in which a particular class of behavior occurred by the total number of intervals observed on that day. Percentages rather than frequencies were used because of slight variations from the usual 90-min time base.

The percentages of different classes of teacher behavior were averaged within two major conditions: (1) data before Praise and Ignore Phase, and (2) data in the Praise and Ignore and succeeding Phases. The data in Fig. 16.4 show that in the Praise and Ignore Phase, Mrs. A. increased use of praise to individual children from 12% to 31% and decreased use of criticism to individuals from 22% to 10%. Mrs. A. also increased use of praise to the class from 1% to 7% and decreased criticism directed to the class from 11% to 3%. Because the frequency of threats was quite low, threats to individuals and threats to the class were combined in one measure. Using this combined measure, Mrs. A.'s use of threats decreased from 5% to 1%. There were no differences in Mrs. A.'s use of academic or social instruction. Consequently, the changes in the children's disruptive behavior can probably be attributed to contingencies and not to Mrs. A.'s use of cues concerning the desired behaviors.

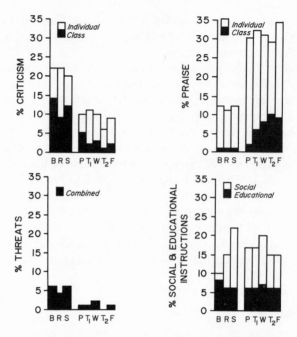

Fig. 16.4. Percentage of various teacher behaviors to individuals and to the class during the eight conditions: Base, Rules, Educational Structure, Praise and Ignore, Token I, Withdrawal, Token II, Follow-up.

DISCUSSION

Although a Token Reinforcement Program was a significant variable in reducing disruptive behavior in the present study, the results are less dramatic than those obtained by O'Leary and Becker, (1967). A number of factors probably contributed to the difference in effectiveness of the programs. The average of disruptive behavior during the Base Period in the 1967 study was 76%; in the present study it was 53%. The gradual introduction of the various phases of the program was probably less effective than a simultaneous introduction of all the procedures, as in the previous study. In the earlier study, the children received more frequent ratings. Five ratings were made each day at the introduction of the 1.5-hr token program, and they were gradually reduced to three ratings per day. In the present study, the children received four ratings per day during a 2-hr period. In the 1967 study, the class could earn points for popsicles by being quiet while the teacher placed ratings in the children's booklets;

in the present study, group points were not incorporated into the general reinforcement program. In the 1967 study, the teacher attended a weekly psychology seminar where teachers discussed various applications of learning principles to classroom management. An *esprit de corps* was generated from that seminar that probably increased the teacher's commitment to change the children's behavior. Although Mrs. A. received graduate credits for her extensive participation in the project, she did not attend a seminar in classroom management. A number of children in the present study had an abundance of toys at home and it was difficult to obtain inexpensive prizes which would serve as reinforcers; in the earlier study, selection of reinforcers was not a difficult problem, since the children were from disadvantaged homes.

Related Gains

Academic The 14 children for whom there were both pre- and post-measures on the California Achievement Test (including S1, S4, S5, S6, and S7) gained an average of 1.5 yr from October to June. The mean CAT score in October was 1.5 while the mean score in June was 3.0. Although there was no matched control group, such gains are greater than those usually obtained (Tiegs and Clark, 1963). While such gains are promising, conclusions about the effects of a token system on academic performance must await a more systematic analysis.

Attendance Comparisons of the attendance records of the seven children during the observational days of the token and non-token phases yielded the following results: the average attendance percentage during the 45 observation days of Base, Rules, Educational Structure, Praise and Ignore, and Withdrawal was 86%. The average attendance percentage during the 20 observation days of Token I and Token II was 98%; the average attendance percentage during the 26 observation days of Token I, Token II, and Follow-up (a variant of a token program) was 99%. These attendance records are very encouraging, but because of the usual seasonal variations in attendance and the small sample of children, more definitive evidence is needed before conclusions about the effects of a token program on attendance can be made.

Cost of Program

The cost of the reinforcers in the present study was approximately $125.00. It is estimated that 3 hr of consulting time per week would be essential to operate a token reinforcement program effectively for one class in a public school. The cost of such a program and the amount of consulting time seem relatively small when compared to the hours psychologists spend in therapy with children, often without producing significant behavioral changes (Levitt, 1963). Furthermore, as evidenced in the present study, control of behavior may be shifted from reinforcers, such as toys, to reinforcers existing within the natural educational setting, such as stars and peer prestige.

Generalization

During the morning, the majority of the children were engaged in independent seat work, while four or five children were in a reading group with the teacher in the back of the room. Although there were rules and frequent instructions during the morning, there was little reinforcement for appropriate behavior since Mrs. A. felt that it would be disruptive to the rest of the class to interrupt reading groups to praise children who were doing independent work at their seats. Ayllon and Azrin (1964) found that instructions without reinforcement had little effect on the behavior of mental patients. Similarly, Rules (instructions) without reinforcement did not influence the behavior of the children in this study.

Mrs. A. was instructed to praise appropriate behavior and ignore disruptive behavior in the morning as well as the afternoon. However, Mrs. A.'s criteria of appropriate behavior in the morning differed from her criteria in the afternoon. For example, in the morning she often answered questions when a child failed to raise his hand before speaking. In the afternoon, on the other hand, she generally ignored a child unless he raised his hand. In order to achieve "generalization" of appropriate behavior in a Token Program such as this one, the teacher's response to disruptive behavior must remain constant throughout the day. The percentage of disruptive behavior was reduced during the morning of the first few days of Token I, but the children presumably learned to discriminate that their appropriate behavior was reinforced only in the afternoon. The differences in the children's behavior between the morning and the afternoon help to stress the point that "generalization" is no magical process, but rather a behavioral change which must be engineered like any other change.

REFERENCES

Allen, K. Eileen; Hart, Betty M., Buell, Joan S., Harris, Florence R., and Wolf, M. M. Effects of social reinforcement on isolate behavior of a nursery school child. *Child Development*, 1964, **35**, 511–518.

Ayllon, T. and Azrin, N. H. Reinforcement and instructions with mental patients. *Journal of the Experimental Analysis of Behavior*, 1964, **7**, 327–331.

Becker, W. C., Madsen, C. H., Arnold, Carole R., and Thomas, D. R. The contingent use of teacher attention and praise in reducing classroom behavior problems. *Journal of Special Education*, 1967, **1** (3), 287–307.

Birnbrauer, J. S., Wolf, M. M., Kidder, J. D., and Tague, Celia. Classroom behavior of retarded pupils with token reinforcement. *Journal of Experimental Child Psychology*, 1965, **2**, 219–235.

Brown, P. and Elliot, R. Control of aggression in a nursery school class. *Journal of Experimental Child Psychology*, 1965, **2**, 103–107.

Hall, R. V., Lund, Diane, and Jackson, Deloris. Effects of teacher attention on study behavior. *Journal of Applied Behavior Analysis*, 1968, **1**, 1–12.

Harris, Florence R., Johnston, Margaret K., Kelley, C. Susan, and Wolf, M. M. Effects of positive social reinforcement on regressed crawling of a nursery school child. *Journal of Educational Psychology*, 1964, **55**, 35–41.

Harris, Florence R., Wolf, M. M., and Baer, D. M. Effects of social reinforcement on child behavior. *Young Children*, 1964, **20**, 8–17.

Kuypers, D. S., Becker, W. C., and O'Leary, K. D. How to make a token system fail. *Exceptional Children*, 1968, **35**, 101–109.

Levitt, E. E. Psychotherapy with children: A further evaluation. *Behaviour Research and Therapy*, 1963, **1**, 45–51.

O'Leary, K. D. and Becker, W. C. Behavior modification of an adjustment class: A token reinforcement program. *Exceptional Children*, 1967, **33**, 637–642.

Quay, H. C., Werry, J. S., McQueen, Marjorie, and Sprague, R. L. Remediation of the conduct problem child in a special class setting. *Exceptional Children*, 1966, **32**, 509–515.

Scott, Phyllis M., Burton, R. V., and Yarrow, Marian R. Social reinforcement under natural conditions. *Child Development*, 1967, **38**, 53–63.

Tiegs, E. V. and Clark, W. W. Manual, California Achievement Tests, Complete Battery. 1963 Norms. California Test Bureau, Monterey, California.

Winer, B. J. *Statistical principles in experimental design*. New York: McGraw-Hill, 1962.

Wolf, M. M., Giles, D. K., and Hall R. V. Experiments with token reinforcement in a remedial classroom. *Behaviour Research and Therapy*, 1968, **6**, 51–64.

Zimmerman, Elaine H. and Zimmerman, J. The alteration of behavior in a special classroom situation. *Journal of the Experimental Analysis of Behavior*, 1962, **5**, 59–60.

ARTICLE 17

Classroom Behavior of Retarded Pupils with Token Reinforcement*[1]

J. S. BIRNBRAUER,[2] M. M. WOLF,[3] J. D. KIDDER, and CECILIA E. TAGUE[4]

University of Washington and Rainier School

Abstract: It was the practice in an experimental programmed instruction classroom to reinforce correct responses with knowledge of results, verbal approval, and tokens. The tokens, check marks, were exchanged at the end of each class for an item from an array of edibles, inexpensive toys, and school supplies. To determine if the token reinforcement was essential to the relatively high levels of accuracy and rates of studying maintained by the retarded pupils, tokens were not dispensed for a period of at least 21 days and were then reinstated. Daily records of items completed, percentage of errors, and disruptive behavior were kept. During the no-token period three general patterns of results were obtained: (1) Five of the 15 pupils showed no measurable change in performance. (2) Six pupils increased either markedly in over-all percentage of errors or sufficiently to reduce progress in the programs. (3) Four pupils showed an increase in percentage of errors, a decline (or considerable variability) in amount of studying, and an increase in disruptive behavior. Baseline performance was recovered in these 10 pupils when token reinforcement was reinstated.

Recommendations for maintaining the motivation of pupils to study usually are limited to (1) preparing materials which are intrinsically reinforcing, i.e., are "interesting," "meaningful," and so on (e.g., Kirk and

*Reprinted from the *Journal of Experimental Child Psychology*, Vol. 2, No. 2, June 1965, pp. 219–235. Copyright © 1965 by Academic Press Inc.

[1]Paper read by the senior author at the American Psychological Association Convention, Los Angeles, September, 1964.

This research is part of a project sponsored by Rainier School (C. H. Martin, Superintendent), the White River School District (Paul Webb, Superintendent) located at Buckley, Washington, and the University of Washington. It was supported in part by NIMH project grant MH-01366 and research grant MH-2232.

[2]Now at the University of North Carolina, Chapel Hill.

[3]Now at the University of Arizona.

[4]We are indebted to Mrs. Eileen Argo and to Miss Josephine Grab for their services as assistant teachers, to Mr. John Nonnenmacher for collating the data, and to Dr. S. W. Bijou for his support and advice.

Johnson, 1951, pp. 270–271); (2) using materials and procedures which combine interest value and high probabilities of success, e.g., Montessori methods (Standing, 1962), Moore's "Responsive Environments" (Pines, 1963), and programmed instruction (Porter, 1957; Skinner, 1958); and (3) presenting social and/or symbolic reinforcers, e.g., teacher approval, grades, and stars. Although these methods may provide adequate incentives for many pupils, they probably do not for many others (Brackbill and Jack, 1958), for example, retarded readers (Walters and Kosowski, 1963), school drop-outs, and so-called chronic behavior problems. They did not appear adequate for the retarded pupils attending an experimental programmed instruction classroom (Birnbrauer, Bijou, Wolf, and Kidder, 1965). Had the pupils not been retarded, the poor classroom behavior and academic progress would have been attributed to the teachers, their methods, and/or low motivation.

In the experiment described here, it was assumed that the last of these was the case, and a token reinforcement system was introduced. Token reinforcers are tangible objects or symbols which in and of themselves probably have little or no reinforcing power. However, they may be exchanged for a variety of other objects which are reinforcing. Therefore, they should become generalized reinforcers (Skinner, 1953). The tokens in the present study were check marks which the teachers inserted in booklets that the pupils carried. When a pupil accumulated enough check marks in his booklet, he exchanged them for candy, a small toy, or other item of his choice immediately after he finished his work for the day. Thus, all of the pupils were reinforced in the same way during class and yet individual preferences were considered by maintaining a variety of items for exchange. The effectiveness of token systems has been demonstrated in laboratory studies by Staats, Staats, Schutz, and Wolf (1962) and by Heid (1964), and their practical advantages and other features have been discussed by Birnbrauer and Lawler (1964) and by Staats, Minke, Finley, Wolf, and Brooks (1964).

The purpose of this study was to determine the effects of discontinuing the token system for a relatively long period and subsequently reinstating it. Throughout the study, the teachers gave approval for appropriate behavior in the manners that were natural to them; they could remove a pupil from class for disruptive behavior; the pupils studied a variety of subjects in each session; and there were opportunities for peer interaction. These conditions made the experimental setting more like ordinary classrooms than laboratories for studies of reinforcement.

METHOD

Subjects

All of the 17 pupils enrolled in the Rainier School Programmed Learning Classroom took part in this study. Fourteen were residents (two were diagnosed as mongoloid; three, familial; and nine, brain-damaged) and three commuted (no clinical diagnoses available). They were all mildly or moderately retarded and were selected for this class because they performed at the first-grade level or below in academic achievement in spite of up to 5 years of previous education at Rainier School.

The characteristics of the pupils were: CA, 8 to 14 years; Peabody Picture Vocabulary Test Mental Age, 4–2 to 8–11; IQ, 50 to 72; California or Metropolitan Achievement Test Grade Equivalents, no score to 1.6 in reading and no score to 1.8 in arithmetic. Nine pupils were first enrolled in this class in September of the year in which this study was conducted; eight had been enrolled during the preceding academic year. Four of the second-year pupils and all of the first-year pupils attended in the morning; the other four second-year pupils attended in the afternoon.

Experimental Design

The study, a within-*S* design, consisted of three conditions: baseline (B), experimental (NT), and return to baseline (B2), in that order. Since a token reinforcement system had been used during the preceding academic year with eight of the *S*s, the baseline conditions (B and B2) included dispensing of tokens; the experimental condition (NT) did not. During B and B2, the following conditions were in effect: (1) Social approval and tokens followed cooperative behavior and correct responses to the instructional materials. (2) Social extinction—i.e., no teacher response—followed incorrect responses and inappropriate, but not disruptive, behavior. (3) A brief time-out period (removal from the classroom) followed disruptive behavior or refusal to comply with instructions. Although no tokens were dispensed during NT, the teachers continued to deliver approval and to administer the time-out procedure in the same fashion as in B and B2.

NT lasted 21 days for the 13 pupils who attended class in the morning and 35 days for the afternoon group of four. (Originally, the study was to be conducted with just the afternoon class to minimize the effects of the study upon other aspects of the research project.) Reinstatement took place on the same day, seven days after the Christmas vacation, for all pupils.

Although we use the expression "days," each pupil attended this class for one to two hours per day. The data include percentage of errors (accuracy), number of items completed on the academic programs (productivity), and the amount of time spent in time-out (index of disruptive behavior).

Classroom Description and General Procedures

Each pupil attended the experimental classroom for one to two hours according to a schedule which ensured that no more than six pupils were present at a time. There was no group instruction or classes as such. Instead, each pupil was given assignments in such areas as sight vocabulary, phonics, reading comprehension, cursive writing, addition, and time-telling. (Most pupils attended other classes in arts and crafts, music, and physical education. This study pertains to their performance in the programmed learning class, the only class in which token reinforcers were dispensed and data collected.) He completed his assignments independently of the activities of the other pupils, either in the classroom proper or in one of the three individual study rooms located at one end of the room.

All of the material was prepared by the staff and was constantly being evaluated and revised as necessary. The pupils' assignments were planned every day on the basis of the previous performance of each individual, with changes being made when the error rate exceeded about 10%. In some programs the pupil was required to repeat sets when this occurred; in others, a simpler form of the program was presented, or the program was dropped temporarily until the difficulty could be found and corrected. In all cases, the teachers attempted to increase the amount of work accomplished per day.

Immediate knowledge of results was built into most programs; in others, it was delayed until the assignment was completed. Assignments required from 5 to 45 minutes. Social reinforcement and token reinforcement (during B and B2 only) were dispensed in either of two ways: (1) When a child studied independently, he indicated that he was finished by raising his hand, and the appropriate reinforcers were given as the teacher scored the work with the pupil. (2) When the program required a teacher's being present—e.g., in sight vocabulary, at the beginning of all programs, and where the type of response or other aspect of a program was changed —a token reinforcer and a social reinforcer were dispensed as each item was completed *correctly*. In September, the second procedure was followed most often; the proportion of independent studying time was increased on an individual basis.

The teachers were one male certified teacher and three female assistants. One assistant had a B.A. in Psychology and had worked in this classroom during the previous year; the other two were recent high school graduates who were trained in the performance of classroom duties by the teacher and the experienced assistant. The teachers applied the contingencies quite skillfully and probably as nearly alike as four humans could. Ordinarily, all four teachers were in the classroom. When they were not working with pupils, they performed such duties as recording data and preparing instructional materials. Children were not assigned to a teacher; whoever was free at the moment scored the completed work and gave the next assignment.

Token Reinforcement Procedures

Each pupil had a folder containing three sheets of paper each divided into squares, his "mark book." The token value of the pages varied according to the number of squares on them, and each folder had a combination of pages, e.g., two 2¢ pages and one 5¢ page. (Three pages of different values were filled concurrently so that the pupil always had partial scores or credit toward a tangible reinforcer.) When the pupil completed his work for the day, completely filled pages were usually exchanged for items from the assortment of back-up reinforcers, which included a variety of edibles, bubble gum, balloons, "caps," stationery and pencils, and trinkets. A few of the pupils saved the value of the pages either toward a more expensive object, which was purchased specifically for them, or toward a trip to town to spend the money. The pupils earned about 2¢ a day in token value. In actual value, they earned about $7 each during the academic year.

The teachers gave a check mark for every correct response to an item, a bonus of 10 marks if an assignment was error-free, and a few marks for being especially cooperative or doing something extra. Marks were made unsystematically on the three pages. Simultaneously, the teachers made such verbal comments as "good," "right," "you did that well." These comments were continued but no tokens or other tangible reinforcers were given in NT.

No attempt was made to formally explain this system to the pupils. Primarily, actual contact with the system was relied upon; and the teachers, especially at the beginning, made a point of saying such things as "Good, you get a mark for that," "Your 2¢ page is almost full," or "You've completed your 5¢ page today—good for you." Also, the number of squares was manipulated to ensure contact even though a pupil might have relatively low productivity. There is no evidence that pupils were aware of this. In about two weeks, it appeared that obtaining marks and particularly completing a page were reinforcing to them.

Time-out Procedures

Talking out of turn, responding incorrectly, cursing, and similar offenses usually were ignored by the teachers. However, if a pupil's offensive behavior was disruptive, he was told to stop and return to work or go "to the hall." If the warning did not result in prompt compliance, the teacher carried out the threat. The pupil was sent to the time-out area, a bare 8×22-foot room in the hallway, for 10 minutes, at which time, provided he had been quiet for the preceding 30 seconds, he was given permission to resume his studies. If he did not enter the classroom within 2 minutes, the door was closed for an additional 10 minutes. This practice was also in effect during NT. Examples of behavior that resulted in the application of time-out were refusal to undertake or complete an assignment, talking to or "roughhousing" with another pupil, temper tantrums, and throwing or destroying objects.

(The term "time-out" is an abbreviation of "time-out from positive reinforcement" (Ferster and Appel, 1961). We prefer the term because it emphasizes that our rationale for using the procedure was to ensure that disruptive behavior was *not* reinforced by peers and/or inadvertently by the teachers.)

Change from Tokens to No-Tokens (B to NT)

On the first day of NT, a teacher made the following announcement: "I wanted you in here all at one time to tell you something. There will be no more marks given. We want you to continue your good work just as you have been doing but you will not get marks." The mark folders and exchange trays had been removed previously. In response to questions the teachers merely replied that "the rules had been changed." (To our own surprise, there was little immediate reaction to this announcement though the mood of the class that day might be described as unenthusiastic. One pupil said that it was not fair and that he would not work any more, but completed his assignments anyway. Others asked teachers later why marks were not being given, but the reply, "the rules have been changed," ended the enquiry. It was as if the announcement had not been comprehended until after the pupils had experienced not receiving marks. The lack of reaction may be attributable in part to the fact that most of these children were institutionalized and in part to the teachers' long-established tendency not to reply to complaints or non-study-oriented conversation.)

On the first day of B2, the mark folders were placed in the previously familiar location. No announcement was made.

Data

The teachers maintained a daily record sheet for each pupil. This showed the assignments that the pupil was to have and contained space for recording the time that the pupil entered class, when he left, the beginning and ending of time-out periods and of each assignment, the total number of items completed, and number of errors made per assignment. Since the time data, except for time-out periods, were only good approximations of how each pupil spent his time in class, we shall present just the items completed, percentage of errors, and the duration of time-out periods.

An item was defined as any question or task culminating in a response that was scored objectively either "correct" or "incorrect." This criterion was met by all of the assigned studies except the cursive-writing exercises. Examples of items were: a sentence and a fill-in question about it: a multiple-choice discrimination problem; $2 + 2 =$; a picture and a set of possible matching words; and the printed direction. "Put 2 spoons in box 4," and an array of objects and numbered boxes. Over the course of this study, items increased in difficulty and tended to become longer. Thus, 100 items in January should have required substantially more and different work than 100 items in September.

Obviously, whether or not a procedure or incentive is "adequate" depends upon one's criteria. In general, we regarded 10% errors as the maximum acceptable level of performance. Although arbitrary and perhaps higher than most teachers require, 10% errors was nevertheless the level that resulted in our revising a program or classroom procedure. To take a specific example, if S exceeded 9% errors on a set in the Sight Vocabulary Program (SVP), he was required to repeat that set. If several Ss "failed" the same set, it was revised. So that the implications of the percentage-of-errors data in this class may be better understood, we shall report the ratio of the number of times SVP sets were "passed" (errors were less than 10%) to the number of times sight vocabulary was included in the pupil's daily assignments. This will be referred to as the "SVP ratio."

RESULTS AND DISCUSSION

Although each pupil reacted to the removal and reinstatement of token reinforcement in a somewhat idiosyncratic way, three general patterns were obtained. (1) Five Ss showed, for all practical purposes, no adverse effects of NT. (2) Six Ss increased in percentage of errors in NT, but continued to cooperate and to complete the same or a greater number of items. (3) Four Ss increased in percentage of errors, accomplished less work, and became serious disciplinary problems during NT.[5] After tokens were reinstated, most of the Ss completed progressively more work and stabilized at levels of percentage of errors that were lower than at any previous time.

The four Ss described under (3) were those who attended class together in the afternoon and had been subjected to 35 days of NT. There were no discernible relationships between CA, IQ, or the type or amount of material being studied and the results obtained.

Figures 17.1, 17.2, and 17.4 to 17.6 show all of the applicable data for selected Ss. The total items completed (productivity), percentage of errors (accuracy), and time-out were compiled for each three-day period S attended class. The SVP ratios cover the experimental period in which shown. If the number of NT days was not divisible by three, the first NT point was obtained by counting backward from the end of NT and prorating the remainder. The B and B2 data were obtained by counting backward from the last day of B and forward from the first day of B2. Thirty days of B2 are shown. The B data includes all of the regular classes after an evaluation that required most of September but varied among

---

[5]The data of two Ss were discarded. One was ill during most of the NT period; the other received a change in assignments coincident with the beginning of NT that could not be eliminated as a factor in accounting for the observed changes.

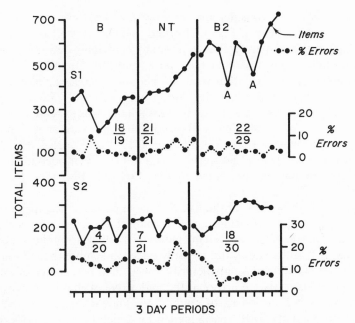

Fig. 17.1. Total items completed (left ordinate, solid line) and percentage of errors records (right ordinate, dotted line) of *S* 1 and *S* 2, who exemplify *S*s not affected by NT. The ratios are the number of times SVP errors were less than 10%, over the number of presentations of SVP in each period. Subject 2's short B period was due to an extended illness in September and October.

individuals. Otherwise, the variability in amount of data resulted from the fact that this study was conducted in a classroom. Pupils were absent and classes were shortened so that the pupils might attend special events. We also excluded a day if the records contained incomplete entries, or if a program ordinarily given was pre-empted by a test or other special activity, e.g., writing a letter. No more than five days was excluded for any pupil for these reasons.

The analysis performed was a visual comparison between each *S*'s performance in NT and that during B and B2. It was concluded that removing token reinforcement had an effect only when there was a change of some duration in either the percentage of errors or the time-out data that would not have been predicted from the B data, *and* when at least the level of performance obtained in B was recovered in B2. The productivity data are shown primarily to indicate that changes in percentage of errors were not due to increases in amount of work. Because of our definition of an item, there was considerable variation in productivity. For example, the sharp declines at A in Fig. 17.1 do not indicate that S1 was working less diligently, but merely that a program containing fewer but more time-consuming items was presented more frequently. In other words, S1 completed all of the work that was assigned on those days. On the other hand, the declines in productivity during NT in Figs. 17.5 and 17.6 do mean that the Ss were not completing the work that was expected.

The data of Ss which clearly showed that there was or was not an effect are presented in Fig. 17.1, S1; Fig. 17.2; Fig. 17.4, S3; Fig. 17.5, S6; and Fig. 17.6. Those that were difficult to classify or open to alternative interpretations are presented in Fig. 17.1, S2; Fig. 17.4, S4; Fig. 17.5, S7.

Figure 17.1 shows two of the five Ss whose performance appeared to be independent of token reinforcement. Subject 1, the more typical S of this subgroup, steadily increased in amount of studying from the middle of B through NT to the end of B2. He only once made more than 9% errors on SVP and maintained a satisfactorily low level of percentage of errors. Whether the slight rise in errors at the end of NT would have persisted with a longer NT period is, of course, not known. Note that the low point in productivity in B was preceded by a high percentage of errors. This reflects the teachers' efforts to adjust the assignments according to the pupil's performance.

Subject 2 differs from S1 in that she performed more poorly until about 12 days after the tokens were reinstated. Then, her percentage of errors

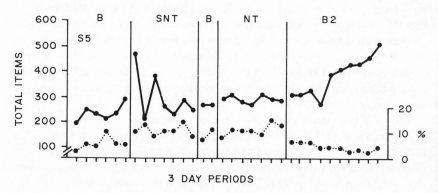

Fig. 17.2. Records of S5 prepared as Fig. 17.1. S5 exemplifies Ss whose percentage of errors increased in NT to the borderline satisfactory level. SNT denotes token reinforcement for all work except SVP.

stabilized at an acceptable level although the amount of work was increased. It is tempting to attribute this improvement to the reinstatement of tokens, but in the absence of an increase in percentage of errors in NT, the data are equivocal.

Subject 1 was 14-years-old, diagnosed as brain-damaged, and one of the second-year pupils. The results were consistent with our impression that S1 was quite sensitive to being correct and receiving approval. Subject 2, a first-year student, was an 11-year-old mongoloid who, in addition to SVP, was receiving primarily pre-reading and pre-arithmetic instruction.

Figures 17.2 and 17.4 contain three examples of decreased accuracy during NT, but show no effect upon productivity or degree of cooperation. None of the six Ss represented required the use of the time-out procedure. The NT percentage-of-error levels were from 2 to 6 times higher than those in B and B2.

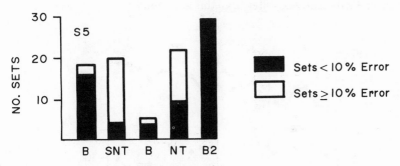

Fig. 17.3. A graphic representation of S5's SVP ratios for the experimental periods in Fig. 17.2. No token reinforcement was delivered for studying SVP in SNT and NT.

Subject 5 (Fig. 17.2) performed satisfactorily in B until he was subjected to a special no-token period (labeled SNT) during which he received tokens for all correct responses except while studying Sight Vocabulary. His percentage of errors immediately doubled and remained at the higher level through a six-day resumption of B and through NT. In B2, S5 attained a remarkably low and stable error rate. Note the attempts by the teachers to increase the amount of work at the beginning of SNT. They were deterred by the higher error rate.

While the percentage of errors shown in Fig. 17.2 during SNT and NT bordered upon our acceptable 10% level, the higher level of errors had considerable effect upon progress in SVP, as can be seen in Fig. 17.3.

When reinforced with tokens, $S5$ routinely made fewer than 10% errors on SVP sets. When no tokens were dispensed, he "failed" over 50% of the time.

Three other Ss showed changes in percentage of errors during NT of the order exhibited by $S5$. This subgroup may be thought of as borderline students. With token reinforcement they maintained at least passing records; without it, they did not.

Subject 3 and $S4$ (Fig. 17.4) yielded somewhat unique patterns. The accuracy record of each is distinctly worse during NT. There is virtually no overlap between error scores in B (B2) and NT. However, the inverted U-shape of $S4$'s NT data and the fact that much of the change occurred immediately suggest that $S4$ was affected most by the change in routine *per se* and not necessarily by the absence of token reinforcement. The possibility cannot be ruled out that baseline performance would have been regained without reinstating token reinforcement. Subject 3's data do not suffer from this ambiguity.

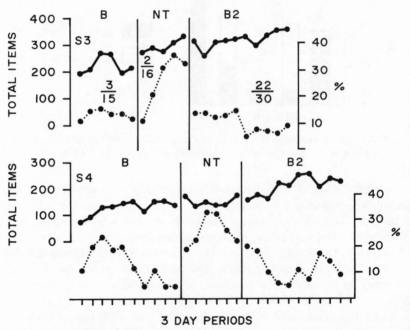

Fig. 17.4. Records of Ss whose percentage of errors increased markedly in NT. Subject 3's NT period is short because of periodic absences. Subject 4 was not studying SVP.

Subject 3 was 9-years-old and had the lowest IQ of the pupils, 50. Subject 4 was 10-years-old and had the highest IQ, 72. Subject 5 was 12-years-old and had an IQ of 60. All were diagnosed as brain-damaged.

Figures 17.5 and 17.6 show the performance of the four second-year pupils in the afternoon class. They were 10 to 12-years old; three were brain-damaged, and the other was a nonresident who probably would be

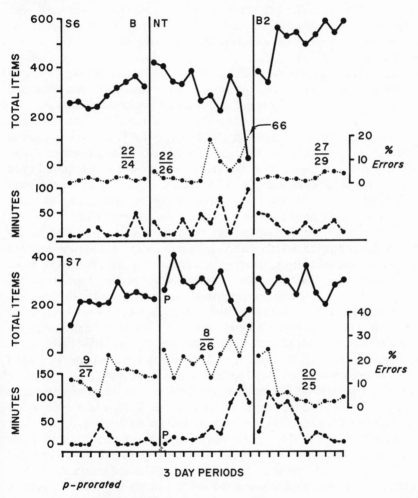

Fig. 17.5. Total items completed (left ordinate, solid line), percentage of errors (right ordinate, dotted line) and time-out (left ordinate, dashed line) records of *S*s 6 and 7. The final NT percentage of error level of *S*6 was 66%.

diagnosed as familial. This group had 35 days of NT. Time-out is plotted for each.

Subject 6, the nonresident, was one of the most capable pupils. This is reflected in (1) his stable 5% error rate except toward the end of NT, (2) his progress in SVP, and (3) the large number of items completed in B2. However, he occasionally required the use of the time-out procedure. During NT, he more often refused to cooperate, interacted with other pupils, particularly $S7$, and verbally abused the teachers. Consequently, he spent progressively more time in the time-out room and his productivity declined. During the last *three* days in NT, he completed six items, four incorrectly, yielding the terminal 66% error rate. As soon as tokens were reinstated, his former error rate was recovered and productivity increased. Time-out declined slowly to its former level.

Subject 7's data are presented because of their probable importance to the changes which occurred in $S6$ during NT. Token reinforcement evidently exerted little control over $S7$'s behavior. The amount of studying was not increased during the year, and time-out was required even beyond the data shown in Fig. 17.5. About 15 days after tokens were reinstated, $S7$ went through a period of refusing to attend class, although once he was brought to class his accuracy level was exemplary.

Without token reinforcement, his behavior became worse in all respects. He competed overtly with $S6$ to be removed from class and engaged in such behavior as hitting, chasing, and shouting at the other boys. Most often, $S6$ replied. That the disruptive interaction occurred mostly in NT suggests that token reinforcement provided a means whereby the teachers could effectively combat peer reinforcement. Subject 7's relatively good behavior when tokens were being given may *not* have been due to his being reinforced with tokens. Rather, the tokens were sufficiently strong to eliminate peer reinforcement of $S7$'s disruptive behavior. In fact, it was not uncommon for a pupil to tell another in effect to "Leave me alone — I've got work to do." In other words, although the token reinforcement system did not yield the degree of control over $S7$ that was expected, it did minimize the effects that his behavior had upon other pupils.

Subjects 8 and 9 (Fig. 17.6) share several common features. Each maintained satisfactory *over-all* accuracy levels in B and B2, often failed SVP sets, were cooperative during B, and performed erratically in NT. Subject 8's unpredictability is most evident in his NT time-out record, which varies cyclically from no time in three days to as much time as $S6$ and $S7$ spent. Subject 9 varied considerably in accuracy. Subject 8's offenses most often took the form of adamant refusals to study, with

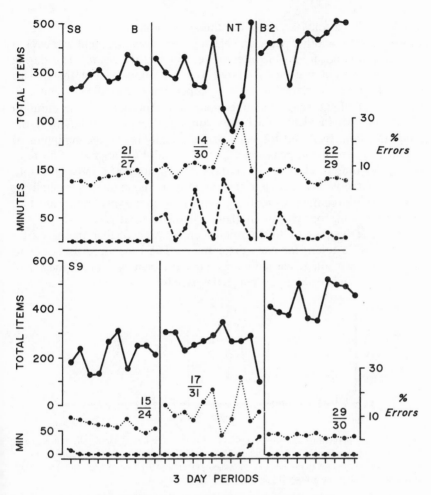

Fig. 17.6. Records of *S*s 8 and 9 prepared as Fig. 17.5.

unquotable verbal behavior. (During NT, the assistant teacher was reminded that *S* 8's behavior for an entire year in a former class had been this way — "he was either an angel or a hellion. You'd never know from one day to another what to expect of him.") Clearly, *S*s 8 and 9 were better students with token reinforcement than with only social and intrinsic reinforcement.

These data do not convey the entire picture of the conditions in the afternoon class during NT. The number of warnings increased; these usually sufficed for *S*9. Often, the time-out room was occupied when it was needed for another pupil, and placing more than one pupil in the room at a time was not a feasible alternative. Further, it became clear during NT that time-out was not aversive to some pupils and/or that it was losing its aversive properties. The competition between *S*s 6 and 7 to be sent out of the room was one indication. Another was the duration of time-out per incident, which was contingent upon *S*s behavior in the time-out room. In B and B2, each period usually lasted the minimum 10 minutes, whereas the peaks in Figs. 17.5 and 17.6 approach the total amount of time in class for three days. It appears that removing a child from a classroom is effective to the extent that it is, in fact, time-out from positive reinforcement. Complying with classroom expectations must be more reinforcing, one way or another, than the alternatives.

The effectiveness of token reinforcement was further increased by taking away a token for each error made. The procedure used was to cross out a previously earned mark. After the page was filled, these had to be re-earned in order to exchange the page for a back-up reinforcer.

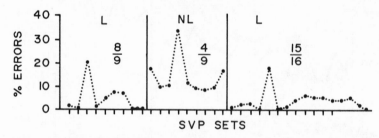

Fig. 17.7. Daily percentage of errors record of *S*9 with token loss (L) and without token loss (NL) for errors on the Sight Vocabulary Program (SVP), SVP ratios are shown for each period. The number of items per set increased systematically from 80 to 100. These data were obtained after the 30-day B2 data in Fig. 17.6.

Figure 17.7 shows *S*9's accuracy level while studying sight vocabulary with and without loss of a token for each error. With loss in effect, the percentage of errors was halved, and this reduction was sufficient for him to pass the 10% criterion for advancing to the next set almost every day. Like token positive reinforcement, however, loss of tokens for mistakes may not be considered a generally effective technique. Not all pupils showed a corresponding decrease in errors as did *S*9.

The variability in the findings is consistent with the results of studies comparing the strength of various reinforcers in children (Brackbill and Jack, 1958; Hollis, 1965; Terrell, 1958; Terrell, Durkin, and Wiesley,

1959; Terrell and Kennedy, 1957), and is a consequence of the inability to control the history of the pupils' experiences with the events employed as reinforcers. It is not expected that an unselected, captive group of people will be equally responsive to the same reinforcers when their individual performance is studied. Thus, for some pupils social reinforcement and/or success were sufficient; for S 7, both social *and* token reinforcement were weak. The proportions of Ss like S 1 and like Ss 6 and 7 undoubtedly differ widely from class to class and school to school.

There are two important points to take into account in interpreting these results. First, the teachers were accustomed to dispensing tokens and believed in their efficacy, for they had not encountered problems like those presented by Ss 6–9 since prior to the introduction of tokens a year earlier. During NT, the teachers reported that all pupils seemed to pay less attention to instructions and correction, and to react more slowly and less enthusiastically. The teachers' enthusiasm also seemed to have decreased. While it is believed that the pupils' behavior changed first, this belief cannot be documented. It would be valuable to replicate this study with teachers who do not routinely use tangible reinforcement and who do not have daily access to the data. However, we see no alternative that will preclude the teachers' changing in response to changes in the pupils' behavior. Indeed, the good teacher must behave this way.

The second factor to consider is that the pupils had received token reinforcement for studying for at least three months before NT started. One could argue that because of the frequent pairing of approval, being correct, and tangible reinforcement, the removal of tokens, i.e., extinction, should have relatively little effect for some time. This view is consistent with the fact that no effect was obtained in 21 days with five pupils, a progressive effect was observed in S 3, and a delayed effect was observed in Ss 6–9.

Finally, we should emphasize that the results pertain to a situation in which something that has been a part of the reinforcement complex is abruptly omitted.

To recapitulate: (1) Five of the 15 Ss included in this analysis gave no measurable indication in 21 days that token reinforcement was necessary to maintain their cooperation and level of accuracy (Fig. 17.1). (2) One S (S 3) steadily increased in percentage of errors during NT to a level four times that obtained in B and B2; another S (S 4) also increased markedly in percentage of errors during NT but may have been responding to the change in routine *per se*. The decreases in accuracy would have been alarming by most standards (Fig. 17.4). (3) Four Ss declined in accuracy in NT at least to the point where the effect was educationally significant as measured by their advancing in one program, sight vocabulary (Figs. 17.2 and 17.3). (4) Three *S*s (*S*s 6, 8, and 9), were clearly more cooperative and more accurate with token reinforcement than without it. In fact, their disruptive behavior in NT was such that dropping them from school would have been in order under ordinary circumstances (Figs. 17.5 and 17.6). (5) The token reinforcement system and programs were not sufficient to bring another *S*'s behavior under sufficient control for him to benefit from education (Fig. 17.5, *S* 7). (6) The tokens were sufficiently powerful to contain disruptive peer interactions, substantially reducing the need for time-out procedures. (7) The effects of loss of tokens for errors ranged from no apparent effect to a considerable increase in accuracy (Fig. 17.7).

REFERENCES

Birnbrauer, J. S., Bijou, S. W., Wolf, M. M., and Kidder, J. D. Programmed instruction in the classroom. In L. Ullmann and L. Krasner (Eds.), *Case studies in behavior modification*. New York: Holt, Rinehart, and Winston, 1965.

Birnbrauer, J. S., and Lawler, Julia. Token reinforcement for learning. *Ment. Retardation*, 1964, **2**, 275–279.

Brackbill, Yvonne, and Jack, D. Discrimination learning in children as a function of reinforcement value. *Child Develpm.*, 1958, **29**, 185–190.

Ferster, C. B., and Appel, J. B. Punishment of S^Δ responding in match to sample by time-out from positive reinforcement. *J. exp. Anal. Behav.*, 1961, **4**, 45–56.

Heid, W. H. Nonverbal conceptual behavior of young children with programmed material. Unpublished doctoral thesis, Univer. of Washington, 1964.

Hollis, J. H. Effects of reinforcement shifts on bent-wire performance of severely retarded children. *Amer. J. ment. Defic.*, 1965, **69**, 531–535.

Kirk, S. A., and Johnson, G. O. *Educating the retarded child*. Boston: Houghton-Mifflin, 1951.

Pines, Maya. How three-year-olds teach themselves to read—and love it. *Harpers*, May, 1963.

Porter, D. A critical review of a portion of the literature on teaching devices. *Harvard educ. Rev.*, 1957, **27**, 126–147.

Skinner, B. F. *Science and human behavior*. New York: MacMillan, 1953.

Skinner, B. F. Teaching machines. *Science*, 1958, **128**, 969–977.

Staats, A. W., Minke, K. A., Finley, J. R., Wolf, M. M., and Brooks, L. O. A reinforcer system and experimental procedure for the laboratory study of reading acquisition. *Child Develpm.*, 1964, **35**, 209–231.

Staats, A. W., Staats, Carolyn K., Schutz, R. E., and Wolf, M. M. The conditioning of textual responses using "extrinsic" reinforcers. *J. exp. Anal. Behav.*, 1962, **5**, 33–40.

Standing, E. M. *The Montessori method—A revolution in education.* Fresno: Academy Library Guild, 1962.

Terrell, G. The role of incentive in discrimination learning in children. *Child Develpm.*, 1958, **29**, 231–236.

Terrell, G., Durkin, Kathryn, and Wiesley, M. Social class and the nature of the incentive in discrimination learning. *J. abnorm. soc. Psychol.*, 1959, **59**, 270–272.

Terrell, G., and Kennedy, W. A. Discrimination learning and transposition in children as a function of the nature of the reward. *J. exp. Psychol.*, 1957, **53**, 257–260.

Walters, R. H., and Kosowski, Irene. Symbolic learning and reading retardation. *J. consult. Psychol.*, 1963, **27**, 75–82.

CHAPTER 7

Token Reinforcement Programs:
Intrinsic Reinforcers

Because of the increasing use of token programs in classrooms (O'Leary & Drabman, 1971), and because of the unfortunate general reliance on back-up reinforcers not readily available to most classroom teachers, this chapter will deal only with token reinforcement programs which utilized reinforcers available to most classroom teachers.

More specifically, we have given token reinforcement programs utilizing natural reinforcers a place of special import since programs using natural reinforcers should be tried before the programs using extrinsic reinforcers are implemented.

When extrinsic reinforcers are utilized in a classroom, one is faced not only with the problem of transfer of control from the extrinsic reinforcers to the natural reinforcers but also with the problem of the acquisition and payment of extrinsic reinforcers. The cost of reinforcers may vary with the age of the child, frequency of disruptive behavior, the frequency of the back-up reinforcers, and with the rapidity of the transfer from extrinsic to intrinsic reinforcers. Back-up reinforcers for classrooms have varied in cost from $7 (Birnbrauer, Wolf, Kidder, & Tague, 1965) to $250 per student per year (Wolf, Giles, & Hall, 1968) where the programs were in effect for the full academic year. With disruptive children in elementary schools, one could probably institute a token program and gradually decrease the frequency of back-up reinforcers from every day to every five days over a four month period, and then rely on intrinsic reinforcers – and thereby spend approximately

$20 per student per year (O'Leary, 1969). However, in many instances it may never be necessary to use extrinsic reinforcers, and the three articles in this chapter present a feasible alternative to their use, *viz.*, the use of free time, special activities, and allowances as back-up reinforcers.

The article by Osborne (1969) (*18*), describes how a teacher can record certain behaviors of the children in her class and simultaneously implement a treatment procedure. Osborne asked the teacher to reinforce in-seat behavior with free time — a reinforcer which may be particularly useful to teachers whose children attend for only short periods of time and seem particularly restless or hyperactive. Teachers who are on half-day sessions from 1 to 5 in the afternoon because of lack of classroom space may find it difficult to maintain the attention of their classes, and free time contingencies may prove useful in increasing the attending behavior of such young children. One might be inclined to think that giving children free-time would reduce the amount of effective teaching time. On the contrary, the increase in academic output more than compensates for the free-time periods and the teacher will have more time for teaching than when she was attempting to instruct restless, inattentive children. Also, as Osborne demonstrated, when the children's behavior improves, the response requirement (time required in-seat for 5 minutes of free time) can be increased without a decrease in the appropriate behavior (staying-in-seat).

The contingency reversal used by Osborne may appear puzzling to some. During the first free-time noncontingent period many of the children remained in their seats although the teacher told them that they could have a break even if they forgot to stay in their seats. It is possible that the children were reinforced for remaining in their seats even though they were not required to do so in order to obtain the break. As Osborne stated, "at free-time presentation the behavior most likely to be occurring was in-seat behavior, and, therefore, remaining seated may have been adventitiously maintained in strength by the subsequent presentation of the noncontingent free-time." Consequently, in order to more definitely evaluate whether making free time contingent upon in-seat behavior was critical in increasing the frequency of in-seat behavior, Osborne removed all reinforcement for in-seat behavior by having the teacher tell the children that if they remained seated, they would not receive a break.*

---

*Another study which effectively used access to free-time activities successfully was performed by Hopkins, Schutte, and Garten, 1970.

The study by Bushell, Wrobel, and Michaelis (1968) (*19*), is an example of the effective use of natural reinforcers in the form of special events such as a story, a gym class, or a short movie. As might be expected with children differing in age and sex, the effects of the contingent special events varied markedly even though the children generally showed more study behavior during the contingent than the noncontingent phase. As noted by Bushell *et al.*, some of the variability in study behavior may have been due to the practice of allowing children to accumulate tokens from day to day. With young children, the practice of requiring them to spend all or a large portion of the tokens until their behavior is under control would seem well advised. As their behavior improves, the children can be given more and more alternatives with regard to saving, lending, and banking. It is interesting that these pre-school children would borrow and lend tokens and hire the services of one another.

The McKenzie *et al.* (1968) article, (*20*), is an interesting documentation of the effectiveness of parent involvement in a token program. Most token programs have not involved the parents because of the possibility that parent involvement itself might confound the results of the study. However, since the success of token programs in classrooms is now well demonstrated (O'Leary & Drabman, 1971), it is probable that more investigators will include parent involvement in order to increase the long range effectiveness of such programs. McKenzie *et al.* point out that having grades serve as tokens is a procedure which can be implemented by any teacher, and that since the parents of the children in this study were accustomed to giving their children allowances, there was no added cost of back-up reinforcers for either the parents or the school. It should be strongly emphasized that the systematic use of the reinforcers intrinsic to the classroom such as recess, free-time activities, special privileges, group versus individual lunch, teacher attention, and weekly grades were associated with only 68% attending to reading but when the allowances (reinforcers intrinsic to many homes) were made contingent upon grades the attending increased to 86%. In short, the usual reinforcers available to the teacher had to be combined with reinforcers available to the parents to obtain optimal pupil performance.

Free-Time as a Reinforcer in the Management of Classroom Behavior*

J. GRAYSON OSBORNE[1]

New Mexico School for The Deaf

Abstract: Six subjects, comprising one class at a school for the deaf, were given reinforcement consisting of time free from school work for remaining seated in the classroom. As a result, the frequency of leaving their chairs was sharply reduced. A second procedure presented free-time not contingent on remaining seated. Little change was seen in the already lowered response rate. An extension of the time required to be seated with corresponding reduction in the number of daily free-time periods did not reduce the effectiveness of the procedure. A one-day observation after six weeks indicated that the procedure was still effective. A one-day contingency reversal, requiring subjects to leave their chairs at least once during each seated period in order to receive free-time, substantially raised the frequency of out-of-seat responses.

Recent studies have indicated that classroom behavior of humans can be successfully manipulated given proper application of the controlling environmental contingencies. Homme, C'deBaca, Devine, Steinhorst, and Rickert (1963) reported that preschool nursery children would engage in the low-probability behaviors of sitting quietly and looking at a blackboard if those behaviors were intermittently followed by the opportunity to engage in higher-probability behaviors such as running or shouting. Thomas, Becker, and Armstrong (1968) showed that disruptive behavior in the classroom can be manipulated as a function of teacher's behavior. They further suggested that one important classroom management device is the use of approval for appropriate behavior.

The usefulness of the token economy has also been proven in the classroom. Wolf, Giles, and Hall (1968) demonstrated that overall achieve-

---

*Reprinted from the *Journal of Applied Behavior Analysis*, Vol. 2, No. 2, Summer 1969, pp. 113–118. Copyright 1969 by the Society for the Experimental Analysis of Behavior, Inc.

[1]Reprints may be obtained from the author, New Mexico School for the Deaf, 1060 Cerrillos Road, Santa Fe, New Mexico 87501.

ment gains could be nearly doubled in a remedial classroom, using a token reinforcement system, over what was achieved in the regular classroom without the token system. Wolf *et al.* (1968) estimated the average cost of their token system at $250 for each of the 16 students for a year. Other investigators have produced gains in specific academic areas utilizing token systems. For example, Staats and Butterfield (1965) produced a large number of reading responses in a non-reading juvenile delinquent. The cost for that subject was $20.31 over 40 hr of work. Staats, Minke, Goodwin, and Landeen (1968) extended Staats' earlier work to 18 junior-high aged subjects. Reading responses were strengthened over 38.2 hr of training at a cost of approximately $22 per subject. In both studies, significant achievement gains in reading resulted.

Birnbrauer, Bijou, Wolf, and Kidder (1965) in their work with institutionalized retardates showed that the token economy need not be expensive to be effective. Extrapolation from their data, which indicate an average payoff of 5¢ per week per student for a regular school year, would suggest a financial cost of less than $20 for back-up reinforcers. In an extension of their earlier work, these same investigators were able to strengthen academic behavior within a similar token system. The costs averaged approximately $7 per student for the 15 students in the class over 1 yr (Birnbrauer, Wolf, Kidder, and Tague, 1965).

Studies utilizing the token economy have demonstrated its usefulness in education. However, in many cases the cost of providing back-up reinforcers is outside the financial ability of most institutions without special funding. In addition, most school administrations oppose paying their students for learning. The classroom management techniques propounded by Homme and Becker indicate that much behavior can be modified in the classroom without a token economy and its cost.

The present study illustrates a behavior management technique that can be used to control behavior in the classroom with no financial cost to the institution involved.

METHOD

A teacher approached the experimenter regarding her class's behavior. She was experiencing problems in maintaining students' attention. Discussion indicated that a major difficulty was the occurrence of behavior incompatible with academic behavior: students were often out of their chairs while the teacher was teaching. The teacher reported that this was disruptive to the entire class. Attempts to reseat students meant interruption of the teacher's presentation until calm was restored. The strong possibility existed that the behavior of students leaving their seats was being maintained by the time away from school work it provided.

Subjects

Six girls at the New Mexico School for the Deaf ranged in age from 11 yr 8 months to 13 yr 8 months; they were grouped in one class because of poor school achievement and less than average intelligence.

Table 18.1.

Subjects	Age	Achieve- ment*	I.Q.**	Hearing Loss
1	12-10	2.1	74***	Severe
2	13-8	2.0	63	Severe-Profound
3	13-3	2.5	62	Severe-Profound
4	11-8	2.4	65	Profound
5	13-4	2.1	53	Profound
6	12-10	2.1	53	Severe

*Stanford Achievement Test (Elementary), **Leiter International Performance Scale (1948 revision) except as noted, ***Wechsler Intelligence Scale for Children (Performance Scale).

Table 18.1 contains a complete description of the subjects. None of the girls was described by the staff as a behavior problem.

The class was in session in the same room from 8:05 A.M. until 12:10 P.M. Monday through Friday with no scheduled recess. A once-weekly session in the school library provided the only regular occasion on which a scholastic activity took place outside the classroom. Physical education, home economics, and other activities took place in the afternoon elsewhere on campus.

Procedures

Baseline measurement The overall procedure followed the standard single-organism, ABA design where each subject was her own control. Before instituting modification procedures, the frequency of occurrence of students leaving their seats was measured over five days. All data were recorded by the teacher on special data sheets, divided by subject, into successive time periods from 8:05 A.M. to 12:00 noon. The length of these periods was arbitrarily established at 15 min with each period separated from the former one by 5 min.

Response definition   The response was easily defined. A subject attaining an upright position without teacher permission constituted an out-of-seat response. Construction of the one-piece chair-desks made it impossible to assume this position within the plane of the chair-desk. Hence, a subject was literally out of her seat before the response criterion was met. (Without the help of elaborate timing apparatus, it was not feasible to measure the time spent seated; hence, the use of an easily definable response, the converse of remaining seated.) In "emergencies," an out-of-seat response was allowed with teacher permission. Sharpening pencils, getting a drink of water, going to the restroom and the like were allowed only on "free" time.

The teacher continued her usual policy with respect to all other negative behavior throughout the study. Generally, this involved verbal reprimands, turning a student's chair-desk toward the wall, or taking the student to the principal's office. These consequences generally followed severe disobedience, foul language, or temper outbursts.

Reliability   Responses were also recorded by the experimenter and a supervising teacher on separate occasions. The supervisor was largely unaware of the nature of the project. She was given a chart identical to the teacher's, told how the response was defined, and asked to note instances of the behavior when she visited the classroom during her regular observation periods. Generally, the length of the supervisor's stay was for one or two of the seated segments. The experimenter also occasionally recorded response occurrences. A total of 15 seated segments over the course of the study was observed by the supervisor or the experimenter in which the six subjects were present. Over these 90 observations the teacher's record was compared with the supervisor's or the experimenter's. Reliability was computed by dividing the sum of agreements and disagreements between teacher and observer into total agreements. In this way, reliability was checked in each phase of the study on approximately 18% of the days the study was in effect. On none of the 90 observations did the teacher's record differ from that of the supervisor or the experimenter.

First free-time contingent period   To begin the modification, the

teacher presented the following instructions to the class at 8:05 A.M.:
"From now on we will be doing something new. I want you all to sit in
your chairs. You must not leave them without asking me. If you can do
that, you will be given five minutes of your own time at 8:20."

The teacher announced each successive free-time period as it occurred.
If the teacher was engaging in a formal presentation to the class, this
presentation was halted during the free-time period. If a student left her
seat during a seated segment, the teacher said: "You forgot, no break."
Otherwise, her presentation of the ongoing seat work was continued.

Free-time was restricted to the interior of the classroom with the exception of trips to the restroom or water fountain. The subjects were not
forced to get up during free-time periods if they did not want to. Those
who had not earned the free-time were required to remain seated and
working and not allowed to interact with their peers during that period.
At the end of a free-time period, the teacher indicated that it was time to
begin again and when the next free-time period would come. Five days
were completed under this condition.

Free-time non-contingent period   To start this period the teacher
presented the following instructions at 8:05 A.M. of the eleventh day:
"I want you all to sit in your chairs. You must not leave them without
asking me; but if you forget, you will still be given your break." In this
section of the study if a student left her seat during a seated segment, the
response was noted but the teacher said nothing and the class activity
continued.

Five days were allowed under this condition.

Second free-time contingent period   The second modification period
began immediately after the non-contingent free-time condition was
terminated. To reinstate modification conditions the teacher repeated the
set of instructions delivered in the first modification period. Thirty-five
days were recorded under these conditions.

Pursuant to another modification in the class, a point system for completion of academic work was introduced on Day 28. Within this system,
the subjects could earn check marks and gummed stars on a chart, and
were occasionally given a field trip outside of school time. In all other
respects the class was conducted as usual.

Third free-time contingent period   The teacher noted that the students
did not always use all of their free-time periods. That is, for one or two of
these periods each day some students would remain seated and perhaps

working. Thus, it was thought likely that an increase in seated time and a corresponding decrease in the number of free-time periods would not lessen the effectiveness of the procedure. Beginning on the fifty-first day of the study at 8:05 A.M., the teacher presented the following instructions to the class: "Starting today we will work until 8:30 before we take our break. Remember you must not leave your chairs without asking me. If you can do that, you will be given five minutes of your own time at 8:30."

For the remainder of the study seated segments were 25 min in length. Free-time periods remained 5-min long; however, lengthening each seated segment by 10 min reduced the number of free-time periods per morning from 12 to 8.

Post-check   Approximately six weeks after the termination of data collection, a single day's post-check was made. The contingencies of the third free-time contingent period had been left in effect by the teacher throughout the intervening time.

Contingency reversal   In the week following the post-check the teacher was asked to reverse the response requirement for a single day. At 8:05 A.M. that day she presented the following instructions to the class: "Today we will do something different. If you remain seated, you will not be allowed to take your break. You must get out of your seat at least once each period in order to have your break."

RESULTS

Figure 18.1 shows the rate of out-of-seat responses for each subject under the different procedures. The different procedures are separated by the vertical dashed lines. Omitted data points comprise days when a given subject was absent.

Before the reinforcement contingency was introduced (Days 1 to 5) the students engaged in slightly more than one out-of-seat response per 15-min segment. After the modification procedure was introduced, responding decreased sharply (Days 6 to 10). During the first free-time contingent period, only 0.08 responses took place per student in the average 15-min period. That is, a response occurred approximately once each 30 min. The difference between baseline and first modification periods was highly significant ($t = 47.35$; $p < 0.001$ one-tailed).

While the shapes of premodification baselines were dissimilar for the

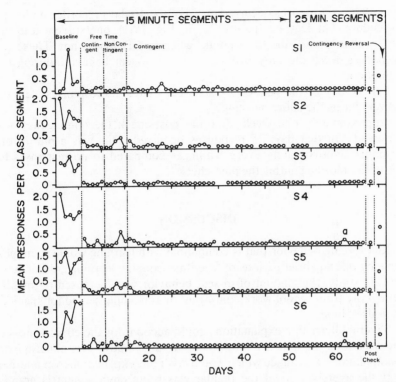

Fig. 18.1. The average number of out-of-seat responses for each subject per class segment for each day of the study.

six subjects, Fig. 18.1 shows that the effect of the procedure, a sharply reduced response rate, was similar for all.

When free-time periods were awarded non-contingently (Days 11 to 15), little change was noted in the lowered response rate (Fig. 18.1).

Making free-time periods again contingent on remaining seated produced another decrease in the frequency of the response. The difference between the free-time non-contingent period and the second free-time contingent period was significant (t = 1.86; p < 0.05 one-tailed).

Free-time periods contingent on remaining seated for 15-min segments were left in effect through Day 50. Inspection of the individual performances (Fig. 18.1) indicates that fewer responses occurred as that point was approached.

On Day 51 the seated segments were lengthened to 25 min. It can be seen that no responses occurred on 15 of the 16 days recorded under this procedure. On Day 62 (points "a" in Fig. 18.1), one student told two others that it was time for a break, when in fact it was not. These two responses were the only instances of out-of-seat behavior during this condition.

On the day of the post-check six weeks later, no responses were observed during the entire morning.

Approximately one week after the post-check the contingency was reversed. On that day, 25 responses occurred. This was a rate of one response approximately every 8 min, as compared to no responses for the entire morning during the post-check.

DISCUSSION

Reinforcing behavior that is compatible with learning would seem possible by offering brief periods of free-time from the learning environment. In this study, the amount of in-seat behavior was increased by making time away from school work contingent on remaining seated for specified periods of time.

Several alternative explanations could account for the effectiveness of the free-time periods as reinforcers in this study. No experimental manipulations were made which would favor one explanation over another.

If the aversiveness of the regular classroom environment is granted (Skinner, 1968), the presentation of free-time may have constituted an escape conditioning procedure. That is, by remaining seated for a given period of time, the subjects could escape seat work and the teacher's formal presentation for a 5-min period, while those who had been out of their seats in the preceding segment had to continue working.

On the other hand, the free-time periods afforded the subjects the opportunity to engage in positively reinforcing activities such as obtaining a drink of water, talking with classmates, or talking with the teacher about favored subjects; the free-time periods may, therefore, have been positive reinforcers. If that was in fact the case, the present procedure constituted operant conditioning of desirable classroom behavior by positive reinforcement.

Finally, the present results can be explained in terms of the Premack reinforcement principle. That principle states that one event is capable of reinforcing another event if the reinforcing event has a higher probability of occurrence and its occurrence is made contingent upon emission of a lower-probability behavior (Premack, 1959). In the present study, the high-probability behavior (*i.e.*, reinforcing event) was non-academic behavior which could be emitted during the free-time period contingent upon prior emission of the lower-probability behavior of remaining seated for a given time.

The possibility exists that the students came under instructional control when procedural changes were instituted. This is unlikely, however, in view of the fact that instructions were presented only once at the beginning of each procedural change. Hence, long-term maintenance of the behavior was probably due to the modification procedures.

The lack of clear change in the response rate when free-time (*i.e.*, reinforcement) was presented non-contingently may have been due to "adventitious" reinforcement. At the start of that procedure (Day 11), all subjects had attained nearly perfect performances in remaining seated to obtain free-time. That is, more in-seat behavior was occurring than its converse, out-of-seat behavior. Hence, at free-time presentation the behavior most likely to be occurring was in-seat behavior and, therefore, remaining seated may have been adventitiously maintained in strength by the subsequent presentation of the non-contingent free-time. The literature presents a similar case with pigeons (Herrnstein, 1966).

The use of the point system to increase academic output that began on Day 28 may have contributed to keeping the subjects seated. However, inspection of Fig. 18.1 shows that in the 10 days before Day 28, nearly 80% of the 60 subject-days in that period contained no out-of-seat responses.

In terms of financial outlay, the study provided a "cost-free" technique for managing classroom behavior available to most teachers. At the end of the study, total free-time per day equalled 40 min—a time approximately double a standard recess in the public school—but seemingly a reasonable payment to maintain the behavior of a special population. Although not attempted in the present study, it is conceivable that a further lengthening of the time required to be seated, and consequent reduction in the number and total daily duration of free-time periods, could have been successfully implemented.

REFERENCES

Birnbrauer, J. S., Wolf, M. M., Kidder, J. D., and Tague, C. E. Classroom behavior of retarded pupils with token reinforcement. *Journal of Experimental Child Psychology*, 1965, **2**, 219–235.

Birnbrauer, J. S., Bijou, S. W., Wolf, M. M., and Kidder, J. D. Programmed instruction in the classroom. In L. Ullmann and L. Krasner (Eds.), *Case studies in behavior modification*. New York: Holt, Rinehart & Winston, 1965. Pp. 358-363.

Herrnstein, R. J. Superstition: a corollary of the principles of operant conditioning. In W. K. Honig (Ed.), *Operant behavior: areas of research and application*. New York: Appleton-Century-Crofts, 1966. Pp. 33-51.

Homme, L. E., C'deBaca, P., Devine, J. V., Steinhorst, R., and Rickert, E. J. Use of the Premack principle in controlling the behavior of nursery school children. *Journal of the Experimental Analysis of Behavior*, 1963, **6**, 544.

Premack, D. Toward empirical behavior laws: I. Positive reinforcement. *Psychological Review*, 1959, **66**, 219-233.

Skinner, B. F. *The technology of teaching*. New York: Appleton-Century-Crofts, 1968.

Staats, A. W. and Butterfield, W. H. Treatment of non-reading in a culturally deprived juvenile delinquent: an application of reinforcement principles. *Child Development*, 1965, **36**, 925-942.

Staats, A. W., Minke, K. A., Goodwin, W., and Landeen, J. Cognitive behavior modification: 'motivated learning' reading treatment with subprofessional therapy-technicians *Behaviour Research and Therapy*, 1965, **5**, 283-299.

Thomas, D. R., Becker, W. C., and Armstrong, M. Production and elimination of disruptive classroom behavior by systematically varying teacher's behavior. *Journal of Applied Behavior Analysis*, 1968, **1**, 35-45.

Wolf, M. M., Giles, D. K., and Hall, R. V. Experiments with token reinforcement in a remedial classroom. *Behaviour Research and Therapy*, 1968, **6**, 51-64.

ARTICLE 19

Applying "Group" Contingencies to the Classroom Study Behavior of Preschool Children*

DON BUSHELL, Jr., PATRICIA ANN WROBEL, and MARY LOUISE MICHAELIS[1]

University of Kansas and Webster College

Abstract: A group of 12 children were enrolled in a preschool class. During the first experimental stage they participated in special events contingent on token earning. Tokens were acquired by engaging in a variety of study behaviors. After a level of study behavior was established under this contingency, the special events were provided noncontingently. Study behavior declined throughout the noncontingent stage. Reestablishing the original contingencies produced an immediate return to the initial level of study behavior. Noncontingent special events reduced the amount of independent study, group participation, and cooperative study. The study behavior of each child was altered in the same direction, though differences in the magnitude of effects from child to child were observed.

The experimental analysis of behavior has concentrated on the examination of responses emitted by a single subject. Recently, extensions of this research have begun to deal with groups of individuals. Behavioral research with adult psychiatric patients (Ayllon and Azrin, 1965), and retarded children (Birnbrauer, Wolf, Kidder, and Tague, 1965) has indicated that certain operant techniques can be applied effectively well beyond the "artificial" conditions of the experimentally isolated subject.

*Reprinted from the *Journal of Applied Behavior Analysis*, Vol. 1, No. 1, Spring 1968, pp. 55–61. Copyright 1968 by the Society for the Experimental Analysis of Behavior, Inc.

[1]This study was carried out as a part of the program of the Webster College Student Behavior Laboratory, and preparation of the report was supported in part by the Institute for Sociological Research, The University of Washington. The authors gratefully acknowledge the able assistance of the observers who made this study possible: Alice Adcock, Sandra Albright, Sister Eleanor Marie Craig, S. L., Jim Felling, and Cleta Pouppart. We are particularly indebted to Donald M. Baer who encouraged us to commit this study to paper and subsequently gave thoughtful criticism to the manuscript. Reprints may be obtained from Don Bushell, Jr., Dept. of Human Development, University of Kansas, Lawrence, Kansas 66044.

In most group situations it is not practical to program individually special contingencies for the responses of each group member. Uniform criteria must be designed according to which a number of individuals are to be rewarded or punished. Schools, prisons, hospitals, business, and military organizations all maintain systems of response contingencies which are quite similar for all the individuals of a certain category within the organization. The objective of this research was to determine whether operant techniques may be applied to a group of individuals with effects similar to those expected when a single subject is under study. The specific behavior under analysis was the study behavior of a group of preschool children.

The dependent variables were behaviors such as attending quietly to instructions, working independently or in cooperation with others as appropriate, remaining with and attending to assigned tasks, and reciting after assignments had been completed. Counter examples are behaviors such as disrupting others who are at work, changing an activity before its completion, and engaging in "escape" behaviors such as trips to the bathroom or drinking fountain, or gazing out the window. To the extent that the first constellation of behaviors is present and the second is absent, a student might be classified as industrious, highly motivated, or conscientious; in short, he has good study habits.

METHOD

Children and Setting

The subjects were 12 children enrolled in a summer session. Three other children were not considered in this report because they did not attend at least half of the sessions due to illness and family vacations. Four of the 12 children were 3-yr old, two were 4-yr old, five were 5-yr old, and one was 6-yr old. These 10 girls and two boys would be described as middle class; all had been enrolled in the preschool the preceding spring semester, all scored above average on standardized intelligence tests, and all had experienced some form of token system during the previous semester.

Classes were conducted from 12:45 to 3:30 p.m., five days a week for seven weeks. A large room adjoining the classroom afforded one-way sight and sound monitoring of the class. The program was directed by two head teachers who were assisted for 25 min each day by a specialist who conducted the Spanish lesson. All of the teachers were undergraduates.

Daily Program

Data were collected in three phases during the first 75 min of each of the last 20 class days of the summer session. During the first 20 min, individual activities were made available to the children for independent study, and the amount of social interaction, student-student or student-teacher, was very slight. The next 25 min were devoted to Spanish instruction. The interaction pattern during this period was much like that of a typical classroom, with the teacher at the front of the assembled children sometimes addressing a specific individual but more often talking to the entire group. The remaining 30 min were given over to "study teams", with the children paired so the one more skilled at a particular task would teach the less skilled. Composition of the groups and their tasks varied from day to day according to the developing skills of the children.

Following this 75 min, a special event was made available to the children. Special events included: a short movie, a trip to a nearby park, a local theater group rehearsal, an art project, a story, or a gym class. The special event was always 30 min long and was always conducted outside the regular classroom. The children were not told what the activity would be for the day until immediately before it occurred.

Token Reinforcement

The tokens, colored plastic washers about 1.5-in. in diameter, served as a monetary exchange unit within the classroom. As the children engaged in individual activities, Spanish, and study teams, the teachers moved about the room giving tokens to those who appeared to be actively working at their various tasks, but not to those who were not judged to be attending to the assignment at the moment.

To minimize unproductive talking about the tokens, the teachers avoided mentioning them. Tokens were never given when requested. If a child presented a piece of work and then asked for a token, the request was ignored and additional work was provided if needed. Similarly, the presentation of tasks was never accompanied by any mention of tokens, such as "If you do thus and so, I will give you a token." The tokens were simply given out as the children worked and, where possible, the presentation was accompanied by such verbal statements as "good", "you're doing fine, keep it up", "that's right", etc. The teachers avoided a set pattern in dispensing the tokens so that their approach would not become discriminative for studying. They would watch for appropriate behavior, move to that child, present a token and encouragement, then look for another instance not too nearby. During Spanish, the two teachers were able to present tokens for appropriate responding to the children who were assembled in front of the Spanish teacher. During study teams the teachers presented tokens as they circulated from group to group, and also at a checking session at the end of the period. Here, the student-learner recited what had been learned and both children were given tokens according to the performance of the learner. Each teacher distributed from 110 to 120 tokens during the 75 min.

The tokens could be used to purchase the special-event ticket. The price varied from 12 to 20 tokens around an average of 15 each day so the children would not leave their study activities as soon as they acquired the necessary amount. Children who did not earn enough to purchase the special-event ticket remained in the classroom when the others left with the teachers. There were no recriminations or admonishments by either the teachers or the students, and the one or two children left behind typically found some toy or book to occupy themselves until the rest of the class returned. After the special event, additional activities enabled the children to earn tokens for a 3:00 p.m. snack of cookies, ice cream, milk, or lemonade, and a chair to sit on while eating. Tokens could be accumulated from day to day.

As tokens became more valuable, theft, borrowing, lending (sometimes at interest), hiring of services and a variety of other economic activities were observed. No attempt was made to control any of these except theft, which was eliminated simply by providing the children with aprons which had pockets for the tokens.

Observation and Recording Procedures

The four principal observers were seated in an observation room. Each wore earphones which enabled audio monitoring of the class and also prevented inter-observer communication. On a signal at the beginning of each 5-min period, each observer looked for the first child listed on the roster and noted that child's behavior on the data sheet, then looked for the second child on the list, and noted its behavior; and so on for each child. All observers were able to complete the total observational cycle in less than 3 min. During the 75 min of observation, the children's behavior was described by noting what the child was looking at, to whom he was talking, and what he was doing with his hands. Fourteen daily observations of each child by each observer produced 672 items of data each day.

Criteria were established by which each behavioral description on the data sheets could be coded as either "S", indicating study behavior, or "NS", indicating nonstudy behavior. Behaviors such as writing, putting a piece in a puzzle, reciting to a teacher, singing a Spanish song with the class, and tracing around a pattern with a pencil were classified as "S", if they were observed in the appropriate setting. Descriptions of behaviors such as counting tokens, putting away materials, walking around the room, drinking at the fountain, looking out the window, rolling on the floor and attending to another child, were classified as "NS". Singing a Spanish song was scored "S" if it occurred during the Spanish period when called for, but "NS" if it occurred during an earlier or later period. Similarly, if one child was interacting with another over instructional materials during the study teams period, the behavior was labeled "S", but the same behavior during another period was classified "NS".

If a given child's behavior was described 14 times and eight of these descriptions were coded "S", then the amount of study time for that child was 8/14 for that day. The amount of study behavior for the entire class on a given day was the sum of the 12 individual scores.

Time-Sampling Validity Check

Time-sampling assumes that, in a given situation, the behavior observed at fixed spacings in time adequately represents the behavior occurring during the total interval. To check the validity of this assumption, a fifth observer described the behavior of only three children much more frequently. At the beginning of each 15-sec interval an automatic timing device beside the fifth observer emitted a click and flashed a small light. The observer then described the ongoing behavior of the first of the three target children of the day, noting essentially the child's looking, talking, and hand behaviors. The procedure was repeated for the second child, then the third. At the onset of the next 15-sec interval, the sequence was repeated. The tape ran continuously. Consequently, during the same interval when the principal observers made 14 observations, the fifth made slightly more than 300 observations of each of the three children. This procedure was used during nine of the 20 experimental sessions, and the three children chosen for this type of observation varied.

The data sheets completed by the four regular observers and the tapes recorded by the fifth observer were coded each day by the four principal observers who assigned either an "S" or "NS" to each description. Coding was accomplished independently by each observer without consultation. The fifth observer did not participate in classifying any of the tape descriptions.

Design

The study, a within-group design, consisted of three stages. During the first stage, participation in the special event was contingent upon the purchase of the necessary ticket with tokens. After nine days under these conditions, participation in the special event was made noncontingent. During the seven days of the noncontingent stage, the children were presented with special-event tickets and snack tickets as they arrived for school. Tokens and verbal statements of praise and encouragement were still given for the same behaviors as during the first phase, but the tokens no longer had any purchasing power. All the privileges of the classroom were available to every child regardless of how much or how little study behavior he or she displayed.

The decision to continue dispensing tokens but devalue them by providing everything free was made in order to retain all of the original procedures except the contingent special event. Had the tokens been given on a noncontingent basis at the beginning of each session, or eliminated entirely, this might have altered the behavior of the teachers toward the children throughout the remainder of the session.

After the sixteenth day of the study, the aprons containing the accumulated tokens were "sent to the cleaners" and all of the tokens were removed. As the children arrived the next day and asked where their tickets were, they were told they would have to buy them. When the children noted that they couldn't because they had no tokens, the teachers responded by saying: "Perhaps you can earn some. Your (activity— name) is over there." Thus, for the final four days, the last days of the summer session, the initial conditions were restored with special-event and snack tickets again being made contingent upon tokens acquired by the students for study behavior.

RESULTS

Figure 19.1 shows that study behavior was influenced by whether or not the special event was contingent upon it. During the first nine-day stage, offering the special event contingent on study behavior resulted in an average score for the class as a whole of 67%. During the noncontingent stage, the observed study behavior declined 25 percentage

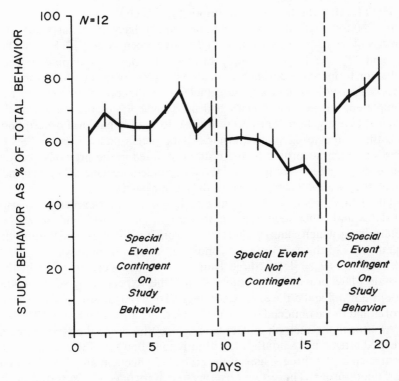

Fig. 19.1. Mean per cent of 12 children's study behavior over 20 school days. Vertical lines indicate the range of scores obtained by the four observers each day.

points over seven days to a low of 42%. Restoring the original contingencies on Day 17 was associated with a 22% increase in study behavior over that of the previous day.

Because the study behavior data were derived from observational measures, a number of checks were made to establish the reliability of the procedures. First, the total class score obtained by each observer for each day was compared to the scores of the other three observers. The vertical lines at each point in Fig. 19.1 describe the range of group scores obtained by the four observers each day. Inspection of these lines indicated that the same pattern was described even if the summary class score for any given day was drawn at random from the four available scores. Indeed, the data of any one, or any combination, of the four observers presented the same pattern with respect to the effects of contingent reinforcement upon study behavior.

The fact that the behavior descriptions of each day were coded within a few hours after they were obtained might have been an additional source of error. A description might have been coded "NS" on Day 15 and "S" on Day 19 simply because the observer expected study behavior to increase during the final contingent stage. To check for such effects, four new coders were empaneled nine months after the study was completed. These new coders had no knowledge of the details of the original investigation. They were trained to read behavioral descriptions like those appearing on the original data sheets and assign an "S" or "NS" to each according to the criteria outlined in the previous section. Once they agreed within 5% on the independent scoring of a given data sheet, they were each given nine of the original sheets.

The data sheets given to the new coders were in scrambled order with all dates and other identifying marks obscured so they had no way of determining which stage a sheet came from even if they understood the significance of the experimental conditions. Sheets from Days 3, 4, 5, 12, 13, 14, 18, 19, and 20 (three from each stage) were recoded in this fashion. The procedure guaranteed that the expectations of the coder would not influence the scores obtained. The comparison of the original scores and those obtained by the new coders are shown in Fig. 19.2.

As a further check on coding bias, two of the original observers were recalled after a nine-month interval to recode one set of four data sheets from each of the three stages of the study, 12 sheets in all, also presented in random order. These two observers each recoded the descriptions of one of the other observers and their own data sheets completed at the time of the original study. The results are also shown in Fig. 19.2 for Days 2, 11, and 17. These points, marked △, indicate that the results obtained by having the original observers recode their own and someone else's data do not differ from those obtained when newly trained coders score the original data. In all cases the scores obtained described the effects of contingent and noncontingent reinforcement in the same way.

The comparison of the total score for the three target children obtained by the regular method and the tapes is shown in Fig. 19.3 and supports the validity of the 5-min time-sampling technique.

The data describing the effects of the different contingencies upon each of the three instructional styles (individual activities, group instruction, teams), failed to demonstrate that this was an important dimension in the present study. Day-to-day variability was greater for these smaller periods than for the entire session, but in all cases the proportion of study behavior dropped similarly in the absence of the contingent special event and rose during the final four days.

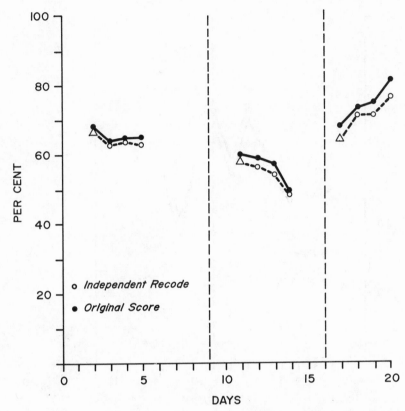

Fig. 19.2. Mean study behavior scores obtained by original observers compared with scores obtained by a panel of coders nine months after the completion of the study. △ indicates scores obtained by two of the original observers who recoded the original data sheets nine months after the completion of the study.

Just as the day-to-day variability increased as the analysis moved from the whole class to periods within each day's class, individual study behavior was more variable than the aggregate data for all 12 children. It is to be expected that students of different age, sex, and educational background will perform differently in comparable settings, but all 12 records shown in Fig. 19.4 indicate that noncontingent reinforcement was less effective in sustaining study behavior than contingent reinforcement. There was no case in which an individual student displayed more study behavior during the second stage of the study than was displayed during the first and third stages.

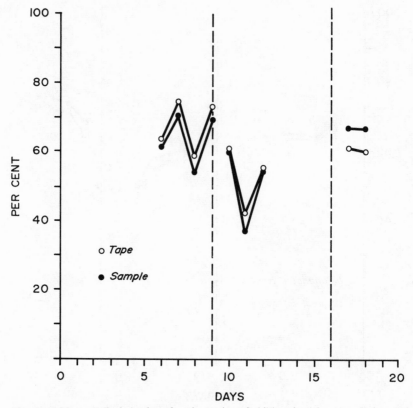

Fig. 19.3. Mean study behavior of various trios of children based on taped observations each day compared with written time-samples during the same period.

DISCUSSION

The results indicate that the contingent special event controlled much of the study behavior. In the time available it was not possible to continue the noncontingent stage until study behavior stabilized. With such an extension, study behavior might have gone lower.

A token system has much to recommend it from a practical standpoint, for there are many school activities (recess, early dismissal, extra-curricular events) which might be employed to develop and maintain higher levels of study behavior. Further, the classroom teacher responsible for the behavior of many students can manage a token system, but

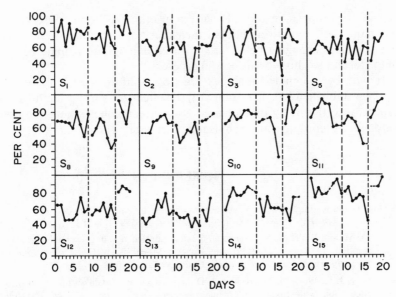

Fig. 19.4. Per cent of each individual child's behavior classified as study behavior under all conditions. Dotted lines without points indicate absence.

faces some difficulty in relying solely on verbal praise and attention as reinforcers. Behavior modification with social reinforcement requires constant monitoring of the subject's responding (Baer and Wolf, 1968). This can be done only on a very limited scale in a classroom by a single teacher.

The day-to-day variability in individual records requires further study. At first glance it would appear that the individual fluctuations could indict the smoother curve of the group as resulting from the canceling effect of numerous measurement errors at the individual level. However, the several measurement checks suggest that other factors may have been more important in explaining the variability. For example, the practice of allowing the children to accumulate tokens from day to day may have produced some variability. It allowed the children to work hard and lend one day, and loaf and borrow the next; work hard and save one day, loaf and spend their savings the next. This would tend to produce a smooth curve for the group, since not everyone could lend at the same time nor could all borrow at once. The present practice in the preschool is to remove all tokens from the children's pockets after each day's session.

The next approximation toward a useful classroom observational technique will require additional measures to determine the effects of the students' changing behavior on the attending and helping behavior of the teachers. This work is now in progress.

It may be concluded that: (1) practical reinforcement contingencies can be established in a classroom; (2) the effects of various contingencies can be ascertained by direct observational techniques where the use of automated recording equipment is not practicable.

REFERENCES

Ayllon, T. and Azrin, N. H. The measurement and reinforcement of behavior of psychotics. *Journal of the Experimental Analysis of Behavior*, 1965, **8**, 357–383.

Baer, D. M. and Wolf, M. M. The reinforcement contingency in preschool and remedial education. In Robert D. Hess and Roberta Meyer Baer (Eds.), *Early education: current theory, research, and practice*. Chicago: Aldine, 1968, pp. 119–130.

Birnbrauer, J. S., Wolf, M. M., Kidder, J. D., and Tague, C. E. Classroom behavior of retarded pupils with token reinforcement. *Journal of Experimental Child Psychology*, 1965, **2**, 219–235.

Behavior Modification of Children with Learning Disabilities Using Grades as Tokens and Allowances as Back up Reinforcers*

HUGH S. MCKENZIE, MARILYN CLARK, MONTROSE M. WOLF, RICHARD KOTHERA, and CEDRIC BENSON[1]

Abstract: The modification of academic behaviors of children in a learning disabilities class was undertaken by arranging for events such as amount of teacher attention, recess, and quality of weekly grade reports to be consequences for academic progress. As academic behaviors achieved with these consequences stabilized at less than an optimal level, the children's parents agreed to have the children earn their allowances on the basis of the weekly grade reports. This token reinforcement system, with grades as tokens and with allowances as added back up reinforcers, significantly increased the children's academic behaviors.

A number of investigations have indicated that behavior modification techniques can be highly effective in the beneficial change of social and academic behaviors of both normal and exceptional children. Recent research has applied these techniques to bright, preschool children (Bushell, Wrobel, and McCloskey, 1967); to school dropouts (Clark, Lackowicz, and Wolf, 1968); to emotionally disturbed children (O'Leary

---

*Reprinted from *Exceptional Children*, Vol. 34, 1968, pp. 745–752.

[1]Hugh McKenzie is Assistant Professor of Education, University of Vermont, Burlington; this research was conducted when he was Research Fellow, Bureau of Child Research, University of Kansas. Marilyn Clark is Special Education Teacher, Skyline School, Shawnee Mission, Kansas. Montrose M. Wolf is Associate Professor of Human Development and Research Associate in the Bureau of Child Research, University of Kansas, Lawrence. Richard Kothera is Superintendent of Schools, Roesland District 92, Shawnee Mission, Kansas. Cedric Benson is Director of Special Education, West Suburban Association for Special Education, Oak Park, Illinois; this research was conducted when he was Director of Special Education, NEJC Cooperative Program in Special Education, Johnson County, Kansas. This study was supported in part by grants 5 T01 NB05362-05 and 3 P01 HD00870-04SI from the National Institutes of Health.

and Becker, 1967); and to low achieving culturally deprived children (Wolf, Giles, and Hall, 1968). More extensive reviews of this growing body of experimental literature may be found in Anderson (1967) and Whelan (1966). The approach that these investigations have taken has been to employ token reinforcers such as colored chips or point cards to improve and maintain improvement of social and/or academic behaviors. Items such as candy, gum, toys, and money have served as back up reinforcers to these tokens, since tokens are exchanged for them.

The problems which can be created, even by an effective token reinforcement system, may be numerous. Not only can token systems be costly in terms of teacher time, but they also may involve an additional burden to already strained school budgets. The administration of tokens such as colored chips and the overseeing of the exchange of tokens for back up reinforcers such as toys may be an unfamiliar role for teachers. Also, parents may be given no function in a token system, although it is recognized that parents can play an integral part in an effective program for children with special needs (Cruickshank, 1967).

These considerations mean that a token system must make a contribution to the amelioration of the children's learning difficulties which is significantly greater than that possible with less costly procedures. As O'Leary and Becker (1967) have indicated, the rationale usually offered for employing token systems is that other incentives available to the school, such as teacher attention and grades, have not been effective, since the children involved still exhibit a high frequency of asocial and nonacademic behaviors.

The primary goal of the present research was to assess whether a pay for grades token reinforcement system could increase academic behavior to levels higher than those achievable with the usually available school incentives. Another aim was to reduce the problems often associated with token systems. By employing grades as tokens, the teacher was not subjected to an unfamiliar role. With weekly allowances as back up reinforcers for grades, parents were able to administer the exchange aspect of the system and were consequently involved in the program. Because parents managed the exchange of tokens for back up reinforcers, and because corrections and some form of grades are an integral part of almost any instructional program, the teacher spent little extra time in the execution of this system. Since the parents of the children of the present study were accustomed to giving their children allowances, neither parents nor school assumed added costs.

METHOD

Subjects The subjects were ten students in a learning disabilities class which was held in Skyline Elementary School, Roesland School District #92, Shawnee Mission, Kansas, during the 1966–1967 school year. This class was one of several special classes operated by the Northeast Johnson County Cooperative Program in Special Education, Johnson County, Kansas.

These ten students, eight boys and two girls, ranged in age from ten to 13 years and were selected for a learning disabilities class on the basis that although their ability levels were above the educable mentally retarded range, their achievement levels were retarded by at least two years in one or more academic areas. All students had received medical and/or psychological evaluations which had suggested minimal brain damage with accompanying emotional disturbance. Case histories reported all students to be highly distractible and prone to engage in disruptive behaviors.

Data are reported on eight of the ten students, as data were incomplete on two students who returned to regular classes after the first week of the pay for weekly grades period.

Teacher Prior to teaching the Skyline special class, the teacher had had five years of full time teaching and five years of teacher substitute work in grades K-8. She had obtained her M.Ed. in Special Education from the University of Kansas, with the major part of the academic work for this degree involving courses in behavior modification and operant psychology. Her master's thesis dealt with a basic education program for school dropouts employing a token reinforcement system (Clark, Lackowicz, and Wolf, 1968).

Volunteers from a women's service organization also participated in the program as teacher aides. These aides served mainly to correct and grade the children's academic work.

Classroom The Skyline special classroom is similar to self contained classrooms found in many elementary schools. With the exception of desk shields extending about 20 inches above and on three sides of a desk's writing surface, no effort was made to reduce stimuli in the room to a bare minimum, as is sometimes recommended (Cruickshank, 1967). Decorative curtains served as window drapes; different colors surfaced walls, floor, and ceiling; books, teaching materials, and art supplies were always in full view. Walls served as display areas for the children's art work and construction projects. The room often had a festive air as the children decorated it for the various seasons.

Instructional Materials and Programming   The commercially available academic materials used were those which might be found in any elementary classroom. Where possible, the children worked on programmed instructional materials (e.g., the SRA reading series). Otherwise, children did workbook assignments (e.g., Ginn's arithmetic workbooks). Such materials were used because they require overt responses.

Prior to the beginning of school and during the first two days of school, the teacher tested the children with the Durrell Analysis of Reading Difficulty and the SRA Achievement Tests. On the basis of these measures, children were placed at academic levels in each of the five instructional areas of the class: reading, arithmetic, spelling, penmanship, and English composition and grammar.

Children were given weekly assignments in each of these five instructional areas, with one assignment sheet for each area. Assignment sheets listed the materials to be worked on each day and the total number of responses assigned, and provided space for the child to record his starting and finishing time and for the teacher (or aide) to record daily the number of responses completed, the number correct, and the child's grade. In each academic area, children were required to complete all previous assignments before going on to new work. If any work was not completed by the week's end, it was assigned for the following week as a new assignment.

Observations and Recording Procedures   Children were observed by a research assistant through the one way mirror of a room adjacent to the classroom. A sound system was arranged so that the assistant could hear what occurred.

Observation time covered the first three hours of every morning: the reading and arithmetic periods, together with a short break between these periods in which the children had physical education or recess. Attending was defined as direct orientation toward work materials, i.e., a child was scored as attending if he was sitting at his desk with materials open and before him, and eyes directed toward these materials. Any contact with teacher or aide (raising hand for teacher help or discussion of assignment) was likewise scored as attending. In group work, a child was scored as attending if he was oriented toward work materials, to a reciting fellow student, or to the teacher, or if he himself was responding orally to a lesson. All behaviors other than those specified above were scored as nonattending.

An attending score was obtained for each child once every three minutes. From 90 to 120 seconds were required to observe and score the entire class. The remaining 60 to 90 seconds of the three minute period were used to note teacher and aide behaviors and prepare for the next group of observations.

The reading period lasted about 80 minutes and the arithmetic 60, so that approximately 26 and 20 measures of attending to reading and arithmetic, respectively, could be made on each child on each school day. A child would at times finish an assignment early, resulting in fewer observations of that child for that assignment period. The observer stopped recording the behavior of a child when he had turned his materials in to the teacher or aide and these materials had been certified as complete.

Although the observer was aware of the general orientation of the investigation, he was informed neither of the details of the pay for grades procedure, nor of when it was put into effect.

Baseline Period Incentives available in the school were employed as described below.

1. *Recess.* The children earned recess by the successful completion of all of their assignments for the given assignment week up to the point of a given recess period. Children were required to work through recess if their work was not complete.
2. *Free Time Activities.* When a child had completed all of his assigned work before a given academic period had ended, he was free to go to a free time table to draw, paint, or construct, or he could read a book of his choice at his seat. Free time activities were not available to children until all work was complete.
3. *Special Privileges.* School errands were run by those children who were working hard and well, or who had shown recent improvement in the quality of their work. Line leaders and monitors were chosen on the same basis.
4. *Group versus Individual Lunch.* Children who had all of their work complete by lunchtime earned the privilege of eating in the school cafeteria with the rest of the school. Those whose work was incomplete ate at their desks, in silence.
5. *Teacher Attention.* The attention of the teacher was contingent upon appropriate working behaviors of the children. For example,

the teacher would say to a hard working child, "Good for you, you're working well, and that's the way you'll become smart in arithmetic and return to regular class sooner." Inappropriate behavior was either ignored or, if disruptive, was punished.

6. *Weekly Grades.* Every week children were given grades to take home to their parents. The parents signed the grade sheets, which the children then returned to the teacher. Both daily and weekly grades were included on these grade sheets. *A* grades indicated that a child had finished his work with 90 percent correct, *B* indicated 80 to 90 percent, *C* indicated 79 percent and below, and *Incomplete* indicated that a child had failed to finish his assigned work.

The teacher conducted group parent conferences once a month at the school, during which time the parents were instructed to praise grades of *A* and *B* and to compliment children for their hard work. Grades of *C* were acceptable, while brief expressions of sorrow were to be paired with grades of Incomplete (e.g., "That's too bad you didn't finish all your work in reading this week"), and children were to be encouraged to finish all work for the next week.

Discussions about academic behaviors and their reinforcers were undertaken by the teacher with individual children as well as with the entire group. These discussions were kept brief and never were held when a child was emotionally upset. Through these discussions it was hoped that the children would gain a further awareness of how they could succeed academically and what rewards would accompany such achievement.

To be maximally effective, reinforcers must be consistently applied. In this case, academic behaviors were consistently reinforced, while nonacademic behaviors were extinguished (not reinforced) or punished (resulting in the removal of some reinforcer). To ensure consistency, both the observer and the first author observed the teacher (and aides, where appropriate) and made at least one report a day to the teacher concerning her application of behavior modification techniques. For example, a tally sheet was kept of the number of times the teacher attended to academic behaviors during the school day and of the number of times she incorrectly attended to inappropriate, nonacademic behaviors. By daily discussion of this tally sheet, the teacher was able to increase her frequency of attending to good behaviors and could virtually ignore the unacceptable ones.

The teacher was likewise informed if a child had earned but not been awarded the opportunity to run a school errand, and if a child should not have been allowed recess because of incomplete work. With this information feedback, the teacher appeared to increase her behavior modification skills.

Pay for Weekly Grades Period All procedures employed during the baseline period were continued in identical fashion during the pay period. However, the weekly grades of the baseline period now acquired an additional back up reinforcer: the payment of a weekly allowance to children by their parents on the basis of the children's grades for all subject areas. All the children had received some allowance previous to this period, but the amount received had not depended on their weekly grades. Children were paid for the average weekly grade of each subject area.

At a parent teacher conference toward the end of the baseline period, parents were instructed in the pay for grades procedures. As an example, parents were told that a child might be paid ten cents for *A*'s, five cents for *B*'s, and one cent for *C*'s, while *Incompletes* would lead to a subtraction of the *A* amount, or minus ten cents. The parents determined the precise amounts on the basis of how much money their child was accustomed to having and the cost of the items he would be expected to purchase from his earnings. Amounts actually paid by parents for the weekly grades ranged from the values in the above example up to five times each grade amount in the example. Thus, with the five areas of the special class, plus physical education and music which the children took with the other children in the school, children's maximum earnings varied from $0.70 to $3.50. With *Incompletes* being subtracted from earned allowance, it was possible for a child to owe his parents money. Toward this eventuality, parents were told to allow such an indebted child to perform some household chores over the weekend to square his debt. No money beyond the debt was to be earned, however. One indebted child, during the early part of the pay period, settled the debt by cleaning the garage.

Parents were asked to sit down with their child each Friday afternoon when the child brought home his weekly grades, calculate with the child the amount earned, and then pay him this amount. This was to be made an important weekly event. Parents were also asked to see that a large portion of the allowance be immediately consumed, and that the child be expected to pay with his earnings for all items he valued highly. Such things as movies, sweets, models, dolls, horseback riding, the purchase and care of pets, makeup, and inexpensive clothes were to be the children's financial responsibility. The children were not allowed to earn other money about the home, and any added money which came as presents or which was earned outside the home was to be banked. Such procedures helped to maintain the child's need and desire for money at high levels so that money would continue to serve as an effective reinforcer for academic behavior.

Parents informed their children of the pay procedure on the day before the start of the week which would lead to the first payment for weekly grades. Parents also told their children what items the child would be expected to purchase with his earned allowance.

The pay procedure was continued for the remainder of the year for all children, including children who returned to regular classes. Regular classroom teachers were instructed to give these children grades of *D* and *F*, as well as higher grades, when their work was at these levels. A grade of *D* subtracted the *B* amount from a child's allowance, while a grade of *F* subtracted the *A* amount. When a child had successfully made the transition to regular class and had performed well for an extended period of time, the length of grade periods was increased, e.g., from once a week to once every two weeks, with appropriate increases in amounts paid for grades. In this way it was hoped to strengthen the child's academic behavior further and to prepare him for the longer grading periods he would encounter in his future schooling.

RESULTS

A marked increase in attending to reading occurred in the pay period compared with the baseline period (*see* Fig. 20.1). Overall medians increased from 68 percent in the baseline period to 86 percent in the pay period.

It is necessary to be certain that the increases in the pay period cannot be attributed to progressive, though perhaps gradual, increases during the baseline period, since the consequences employed during the baseline period may have been increasing attending. Since the most powerful test for such trends was desired, an analysis of variance, rather than a nonparametric test, was performed on the baseline data, yielding an *F* ratio of less than one (*see* Table 20.1) which allows the retention of the hypothesis that the baseline procedures had no tendency to increase attending to reading. By computing eta square, it was estimated that

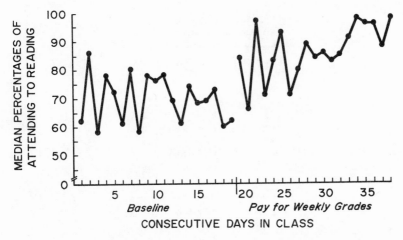

Fig. 20.1. Patterns of medians in attending to reading.

trends accounted for only 6 percent of the variance of the baseline period.

The increase in attending to reading from the baseline period to the pay period was significant (*see* Table 20.2); $p < 0.005$, one tailed Wilcoxon Matched Pairs Signed Ranks Test (Siegel, 1956). The data for each student conformed very closely to the pattern of medians shown in Fig. 20.1. Thus, it can be inferred that the token reinforcement system led to substantial gains in attending to reading for all students.

Similar results were obtained in arithmetic (*see* Fig. 20.2). Overall medians increased from 70 percent in the baseline period to 86 percent in the pay period. The analysis of variance for trends during the arithmetic baseline period also yielded an insignificant F ratio (*see* Table 20.3; $F = 1.154$, $p > 0.25$). Through eta square, it was estimated that only 8 percent of the baseline arithmetic variance could be accounted for by trends.

Table 20.1. Analysis of Variance for Baseline Trends of Percentages of Attending to Reading

Source	SS	df	MS	F
Between Subjects	32345.368	7		
Within Subjects	36351.684	144		
Trends	4337.302	18	240.96	< 1
Residual	32014.382	126	254.08	

Table 20.2. Subjects' Median Percentages of Attending to Reading

Subjects	Baseline	Pay	Increase
S1	71	89	18
S2	82	95	13
S3	23	77	54
S4	83	93	10
S5	72	83	11
S6	72	79	7
S7	75	83	8
S8	62	75	13

Note: Wilcoxon $T = 0$; $p < 0.005$ (one tailed test)

Attending to arithmetic also showed significant increases for the pay period over the baseline period (*see* Table 20.4; $p < 0.005$, one tailed Wilcoxon Test). Six subjects' graphs showed the same general form as the median graph in Fig. 20.2. Thus, it can be inferred that the token system led to substantial gains in attending to arithmetic for these six subjects. The remaining two subjects (Subjects 2 and 7) showed gradual but steady increases in attending to arithmetic for the last ten days of the

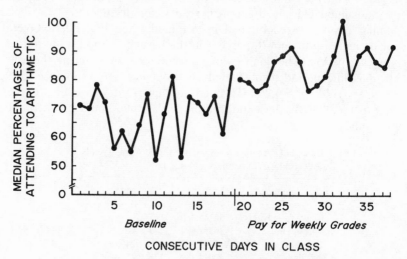

Fig. 20.2. Patterns of medians in attending to arithmetic.

Table 20.3. Analysis of Variance for Baseline Trends of Percentages of Attending to Arithmetic

Source	SS	df	MS	F
Between Subjects	36957.158	7		
Within Subjects	51337.684	144		
Trends	7265.842	18	403.678	1.154*
Residual	44071.842	126	349.776	

*$p > 0.25$.

baseline period. Consequently, it cannot be concluded that the increases in attending to arithmetic shown by these two subjects for the pay period over the baseline period can be attributed solely to the pay for weekly grades procedure.

Percentages of attending were determined in the following way: if a total of 20 observations were made on a child in arithmetic, and if, of these, ten were scored as attending, the child's percentage of attending to arithmetic on that day was $10/20 \times 100$ or 50 percent. Reliability checks were made between the first author and the observer on four occasions, two for reading and two for arithmetic. Reliability coefficients, estimated by the Pearson product moment formula and calculated across subjects with day and academic area held constant, were 0.91 and 0.95 for reading and 0.88 and 0.90 for arithmetic.

Table 20.4. Subjects' Median Percentages of Attending to Arithmetic

Subjects	Baseline	Pay	Increase
S1	67	88	21
S2	89	94	5
S3	36	79	43
S4	80	94	14
S5	83	88	5
S6	63	76	13
S7	64	81	17
S8	53	68	15

Note: Wilcoxon $T = 0$; $p < 0.005$ (one tailed test)

The attending data were obtained during October, November, and part of December, 1966. The month of September was used to refine the observational techniques and to ensure that instructional procedures and materials were adequate to meet each child's needs.

Although the observations were stopped after Christmas vacation, the number of *Incompletes* (with the exception of Subject 8) and the percentages of correct responses indicated that subjects maintained for the remainder of the school year the level of academic behavior attained during the pay period. Students' earnings varied from week to week and ranged from 30 to 85 percent of maximum possible earnings.

As the working efficiency of the students increased, larger assignments were given. At the end of the school year, all ten students were working successfully one to four levels above their starting levels in all academic areas. Six of the ten students were returned full time to regular classes to one grade higher than the ones they had been in during the previous school year. For two of these six, grading periods were extended to four weeks and for one, to two weeks, while the other three remained on the one week period since they were returned to regular classes with only two months of the school year left. In spite of the fact that regular classroom teachers were instructed to give grades of *D* and *F* when appropriate, half of the returned students consistently earned *B* averages and half earned *C* averages. At the close of the school year, all six of the returned students were again promoted, this time by their regular classroom teachers.

DISCUSSION

The present study demonstrated that a token reinforcement system with grades as tokens and allowances as back up reinforcers can significantly increase levels of academic behavior beyond those maintained by the systematic application of other reinforcers available to a school.

All students, with the exception of Subject 8, maintained these increased levels of academic behavior. This subject, with the pay still in effect, would alternate several weeks of complete work and high grades with several weeks of incomplete work. His parents reported that they had never reached agreement on the proper administration of the pay procedures and were, consequently, very inconsistent in its application. The subject was originally required to purchase his weekly movie and a construction model, yet his parents said that they gave him these rewards even when his earnings were insufficient to purchase them. One parent, on several occasions, had claimed all of his earnings as payment for misdemeanors committed at home. In the spring of the year he acquired a high level of social and academic behavior which was maintained for the remainder of the school year. This change in his behavior was coincidental with the death of one of his parents.

Grades have long been the token reinforcement system of schools. But as a reinforcer's effectiveness is directly proportional to its immediacy of presentation (Bijou and Baer, 1961), an apparent weakness of this grade system has been that grade reports are presented to children every six to nine weeks, a long delay of reinforcement for a child of elementary school age.

Teachers must correct children's work to ensure learning, and it is but a small step from corrections to grades. Although the teacher of the present study had volunteer aides to assist in the grading, the teacher felt that she could carry out the daily grading and weekly reports, and actually did for the many days that aides were absent.

No test was made to test the effect of the allowance back up reinforcer in the maintenance of high levels of academic behavior for the remainder of the school year. This effect could have been tested by paying the children their allowances independently of their weekly grades. If attending to academic materials had decreased significantly with this change, evidence would have been provided for a maintaining effect for this back up reinforcer. The risk of returning students to their less efficient levels of the baseline period overruled the possible gains in scientific information, and this analysis was not made.

CONCLUSION

The token reinforcement system used in the present study increased levels of academic behavior with highly distractible and disruptive children. Several additional advantages are inherent in this token system. First, teachers need not spend valuable time in overseeing the exchange of tokens for back up reinforcers. Parents can manage this task at home. Secondly, parents are frequently able to bear the cost of the allowance back up reinforcer, as many parents provide allowances for their children anyway. For parents unable to bear this cost, it seems likely that a service organization could be found which would contribute funds which parents could then pay to their children on the basis of weekly grades. Finally, the present system can open, as it did in this case, an effective channel of communication and cooperation between parents and teachers of children with special educational needs.

REFERENCES

Anderson, R. C. Educational psychology. In P. R. Farnsworth (Editor), *Annual Review of Psychology*. Volume 18. Palo Alto, California: Annual Reviews, 1967. Pp. 129–164.

Bijou, S. W., and Baer, D. M. *Child development*. Volume 1. New York: Appleton-Century-Crofts, 1961.

Bushell, D., Wrobel, P. A., and McCloskey, M. L. Some effects of normative reinforcement on classroom study behavior. Unpublished manuscript, Webster College, 1967.

Clark, M., Lackowicz, J., and Wolf, M. A pilot basic education program for school dropouts incorporating a token reinforcement system. *Behaviour Research and Therapy*, 1968, **6** (2), 183–188.

Cruickshank, W. M. *The brain-injured child in home, school, and community*. Syracuse, New York: Syracuse University Press, 1967.

O'Leary, K. D., and Becker, W. C. Behavior modification of an adjustment class: a token reinforcement system. *Exceptional Children*, 1967, **33**, 637–642.

Siegel, S. *Nonparametric statistics*. New York: McGraw-Hill, 1956.

Whelan, R. J. The relevance of behavior modification procedures for teachers of emotionally disturbed children. In P. Knoblock (Editor), *Intervention approaches in educating emotionally disturbed children*. Syracuse, New York: Syracuse University Press, 1966. Pp. 35–78.

Wolf, M. M., Giles, D. K., and Hall, R. V. Experiments with token reinforcement in a remedial classroom. *Behaviour Research and Therapy*, 1968, **6**, 51–64.

CHAPTER 8

The Effects of Peers as Therapeutic Agents in the Classroom

The influence of peers on a child's academic and social development is frequently discussed but rarely documented by research. Peers are influential in several ways. First, they serve as models of both appropriate and inappropriate behavior. Children model the dress, language, and social behavior of their peers in varying degrees. A withdrawn child may become more outgoing by observing his socially confident friends. Unfortunately, inappropriate behavior such as drug abuse, cheating, and aggression may also be increased as a result of modeling a peer.

Second, peers influence a child by responding contingently to the child's behavior. For example, peers offer and withdraw their friendship dependent upon the child's behavior. A disruptive child may "shape up" in response to his peer's aversive admonitions. On the other hand, children may "shape up" the behavior of their peers through positive controls. For example, membership in a street gang may be made contingent upon the child's demonstration of courage and skill of fighting.

A third important aspect of peer influence is competition. "Doing better than one's peers" seems to function as a reinforcer for many children. The successful use of competition for modifying behavior is dramatically demonstrated in the Soviet educational process (Bronfenbrenner, 1970, pp. 51–69). Beginning in the first grade, Soviet children compete with each other in systematic ways with the competition first being controlled by the teacher and gradually by the classmates themselves. Competition occurs between rows or other groupings rather than between individuals. The Soviet approach is a direct attempt to utilize peer influence for modifying the behavior problems of all children. Although one might not wish to use competition as frequently and systematically as the Soviets, occasional use of competition could probably be very effective in many classrooms.

Teachers and psychologists have sought to harness peer influence and use it to benefit the class in at least three ways.

1. The most indirect procedure is to praise a target child's peers for appropriate behavior with the intention that the target child will behave more appropriately. Investigators differ in their explanation of this effect. Target children may behave better by modeling better behaved peers. Target children may behave better because they have heard the teacher specify what behaviors she will reward — praising another child acts as a discriminative stimulus. Finally, seeing another child being reinforced may serve as a reinforcer (vicarious reinforcer) for the target child. The evidence for modeling or vicarious reinforcement is contradictory (Broden, Bruce, Mitchell, Carter, & Hall, 1970; Becker, Thomas, & Carnine, 1969), and it may be that the effect is found only when the peer receiving reinforcement is seated very near the target child (*see* comment at end of Chapter 5).

2. The procedure most frequently employed by the investigators whose work appears in this chapter consists of the following basic elements. One or more target children are selected by the teacher. The entire class receives a variety of rewards dependent upon how well the target children behave. The fundamental assumption of this procedure is that the peers will exert influence on the target children to improve their behavior. Unfortunately, there has been no attempt to measure the extent to which this peer pressure exists or influences the target children.

3. The third procedure for utilizing peer influence to deal with problem children is one which may yield more useful information than the first two methods since the processes are more apparent and peer influence is more direct. In this case the peer is directly responsible for contingency management. More specifically, the peer observes and records the target behaviors and dispenses the reinforcers according to a specific procedure outlined by the teacher or other professional personnel.

The articles in this chapter represent some initial attempts to examine the effectiveness of peer influence in modifying the behavior of children in the classroom. Evans and Oswalt (1968) (*21*), successfully influenced the academic progress of five out of six children by rewarding the entire class when the target child answered questions correctly. The experimenters assumed that the class would reward the target child for his appropriate responses and that as a consequence, the target child would show academic progress. As mentioned above, neither of these assumptions were corroborated with observations of the peers' responses to the target child. One important possibility which Evans and Oswalt do not consider is that the target child may have shown just as much improvement if only he and not the entire class were rewarded for his successes.

The study by Barrish, Saunders, and Wolf (1969) (*22*), is one of the few attempts to use a punishment or loss of privileges procedure. A fourth grade class was divided into two teams. Each time any member of the team disobeyed the classroom rules, the entire team received a point which could lead to a loss of privileges if enough points were accumulated. Another departure from common procedure was the statement of the classroom rules in a negative manner, e.g., "No one was to be out of his seat" versus the more usual "Sit in your seats." Barrish *et al.* also suggest that one approach to dealing with the child who attempts to thwart the system is to withdraw him from the class "game" and place him on an individual point system. The general success of the program should alert us to the probability that punishment or loss procedures can be effective and should not be disregarded without a thorough evaluation.

Carlson, Arnold, Becker, and Madsen (1968) (*23*), devised a multiple component treatment program for reducing the frequency of classroom tantrums displayed by an eight-year-old girl. The main elements of the program consisted of restraining Diane in her chair during a tantrum (punishment), rewarding Diane for each tantrum-free half-day with stars which were accumulated and which led to a class party (reinforcing the target child and her peers when the target child behaved well), and rewarding each peer who paid no attention to Diane when she was having a tantrum (reinforcing peers for appropriate peer behavior – in this case for the appropriate use of contingencies with respect to the target child). The Carlson, *et al.* (1968) study is basically a case report. Observations were made continuously and the teacher consulted frequently with experienced personnel, but there was no attempt to alter the procedures in order to determine which of the components was primarily responsible for the change in the frequency of Diane's tantrums. This report is a good example of the manner in which teachers can and should apply the principles and procedures outlined in this book.

Surratt, Ulrich, and Hawkins (1969) *(24)*, demonstrated how a peer successfully altered the study behavior of four target children. A fifth grader recorded the amount of time the four first graders were working appropriately by using four timers mounted in a console. A set of counters provided visible evidence of the working time accumulated by each child each day. The first graders were rewarded with extra privileges for increasing amounts of working time. Although the apparatus used in this study was rather expensive, it would not be difficult to adapt an inexpensive paper and pencil recording system to accomplish the same task. Surratt *et al.* also point out some problems which can arise when a child receives individual attention from someone other than the teacher. For example, the presence of the peer may have become a cue to the target child that he was in a situation where he would receive extra rewards for his efforts. Consequently, the child may have improved in the presence of the contingency manager but shown little improvement in the peer's absence. Again, the question is raised of how to generalize the skills the child acquires in the special situation to the rest of the day when he is following a normal classroom routine (*see* chapters on Intrinsic Token Programs and Self-Management for discussions of procedures for achieving generalization).

The aid of peers to execute a token program was investigated by Winett, Richards, Krasner, and Krasner (1970). Second grade children in a public school dispensed tokens during a period when the teacher was giving special attention to individual children. Tokens (poker chips) were placed in each child's milk carton by a child monitor. The tokens were later exchangeable for inexpensive trinkets, school supplies, and tickets to a local movie. As mentioned on a number of occasions in this book, and as Winett *et al.* imply, it would have been wise to use natural "back-up" reinforcers such as free time or special privileges rather than the trinkets. Nonetheless, this study is important in that (1) it demonstrated how young children can monitor their own program with minimal supervision, (2) it provided evidence that children can significantly increase the appropriate behavior of other children, and (3) it documented how peers might execute a token program without any unusual machines or devices — simply poker chips, milk cartons, and the contingent scheduling of desired activities.

When children evaluate the behavior of other children, there always is the possibility of a child occasionally being very harsh in his or her evaluations of others and there is the possibility with older children that they might exert pressure on a child in or out of class to have that child give him good evaluations. In order to eliminate ratings which are unduly lenient or harsh, one might have the evaluator or monitor be an elected position. Phillips, Bailey, and Wolf (1969) found that having an elected manager who was allowed both to give and take away points in a token program was not only an effective method of increasing the work behavior of juvenile offenders it also was a highly preferred system. In order to decrease the possibility of undue pressure being exerted on children — as might be the case with children in a class for very disruptive children in hospitals — severe fines could be levied for placing undue pressure on children to give them good or high evaluations.

In sum, child monitored programs have very distinct advantages and they seem to offer an interesting method of teaching a child to pay closer attention not only to the behavior of others but also to his own behavior. In addition, they could teach a child to participate at an early age in a democratically governed system rather than an autocratic one. We believe that such training is not only in keeping with our basic historical traditions, it is good training in self-management.

The area of peer influence is a very significant one. In the natural environment peers are one of the greatest sources of reinforcement and punishment for other children. In a sense, peers are natural behavior modifiers. Consequently, if peer influence can be used systematically and to appropriate ends, fewer children should require special attention from professionals.

Acceleration of Academic Progress through the Manipulation of Peer Influence*[1]

GARY W. EVANS and GAYLON L. OSWALT[2]

Bureau of Child Research, University of Kansas

and

Parsons State Hospital and Training Center

Abstract: Discontinuance of regular classroom duties for the entire class (early dismissal or story reading) was made contingent upon the performance of under-achieving children in two sections of a fourth-grade class and two sections of a sixth-grade class. Experimental Ss' weekly test scores increased to a statistically significant extent in relation to the test scores of control Ss.

Behavior modification techniques have been successfully applied to a variety of behavior problems associated with the classroom, e.g. hyper-activity (Homme, *et al.*, 1963; Patterson, *et al.*, 1965), peer isolation (Allen, *et al.*, 1965; Patterson and Brodsky, 1966), and school phobia (Patterson, 1965). In spite of the successes in these areas, few attempts to manipulate academic achievement have been reported. Zimmerman and Zimmerman (1962) reported a case study of academic progress obtained by selective teacher-approval of correctly spelled words. The study by Patterson, *et al.* (1965), indicates that peer influence is helpful in reducing hyperactivity in the classroom, but its effect on academic achievement was not investigated.

This paper reports an attempt to accelerate academic progress of selected individuals by arranging contingencies in such a manner that peer

*Reprinted from *Behaviour Research and Therapy*, Vol. 6, 1968, pp. 189–195.

[1]This study was conducted and supported under NICHHD Grant No. 00870 04.

[2]The authors wish to thank Mis Joella Ragan, Mrs. Linda Ney, Mrs. Nancy Thompson and Mr. Gordon Huggins of the Parsons, Kansas Public School System for their cooperation during the course of this study.

influence is brought to bear on the subjects' academic performance. The specific procedures used in the following experiments resulted from the assumptions that: (a) most grade-school children will approve of behavior which leads to a story period or early dismissal from class: (b) peer approval has reinforcing properties for the underachieving child.

EXPERIMENT 1

Subjects

The Ss were 22 students from a fourth-grade spelling class. Two experimental Ss (S_1 and S_2) were selected by the classroom teacher and the other 20 students served as control Ss. Experimental Ss were students who were, according to the teacher, "capable of doing considerably better work than they are presently doing."

Procedure

This experiment was conducted over a 13-week period. On the final day of each school week during this period, the teacher constructed and administered a 10-word spelling test covering words that had been presented during that school week.

The first four weeks (Phase 1) was a baseline period in which weekly test scores were recorded but no treatment was introduced. During weeks five through nine (Phase 2), the teacher announced daily, 5 min prior to the morning recess, that the class would be dismissed for recess immediately if S_1 could correctly spell a specified word (or words). The teacher then presented a word for S_1 to attempt to spell (the word was selected from those covered during the preceding period). If S_1 spelled the word correctly, the class was dismissed immediately. If his spelling of the word was incorrect, classwork was continued until the customary dismissal time. During weeks ten through thirteen (Phase 3), the procedure was identical to that of Phase 2, with the exception that early dismissal was made contingent on S_2's responses rather than S_1's. No questions were asked of S_1 in Phase 3.

Results

The results are illustrated in Fig. 21.1. The results clearly show that the test performance of both S_1 and S_2 showed considerable improvement

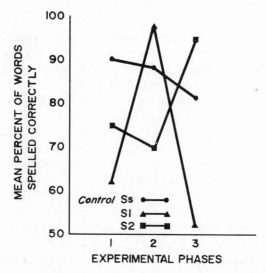

Fig. 21.1. Mean percent of correctly spelled words on weekly tests under Phase 1 (baseline), Phase 2 (experimental treatment applied to S_1), and Phase 3 (experimental treatment applied to S_2).

when the experimental treatment was in effect. Once the experimental condition was discontinued however, S_1's performance declined to its previous level relative to the control Ss. The control Ss showed a slight decline in test performance throughout the experiment. Whatever the reason was for this decline (e.g. more difficult tests, spring weather), it does serve to illustrate that the improvement manifested by S_1 and S_2 during the experimental phases was not due to the presence of elements common to the class as a whole.

EXPERIMENT 2

Subjects

The Ss were 20 students from a fourth-grade arithmetic class. Two experimental Ss (S_3 and S_4) were selected by the classroom teacher (the teacher of this class also taught the spelling class described in Experiment 1). Again, the two experimental Ss were students who the teacher believed were performing below their capabilities. The remaining 18 students in the class served as control Ss.

Procedure

This experiment was conducted over a 14-week period. On the final day of each school week during this period, the teacher constructed and administered a ten-problem arithmetic examination covering material that had been presented during the school week.

Again, the first 4 weeks (Phase 1) was a baseline period in which weekly test scores were recorded but no treatment was introduced. During weeks five through nine (Phase 2), the teacher announced daily, 5 min before the class was scheduled to be terminated, that she (the teacher) would read a story to the class for the remainder of the period if S_3 could solve a specified arithmetic problem. The teacher then presented a problem, selected from material presented during the period, for S_3 to attempt to solve. If S_3's solution were correct, the teacher read aloud to the class for the remainder of the period. If S_3's solution were incorrect, normal classwork was continued until the end of the period. During weeks ten through fourteen (Phase 3), story reading was made contingent on S_4's responses, rather than S_3's. Daily questions were asked of S_3 in Phase 3, but no experimental consequences were associated with her answers.

Results

The results are illustrated in Fig. 21.2. Again, the results clearly show that the experimental Ss showed considerable improvement when placed under the experimental condition. Notice, however, that S_3's performance did not deteriorate in Phase 3 when the treatment discontinued. This finding differs from that of Experiment 1 where S_1 failed to maintain his improved performance when the treatment was discontinued. The control Ss' test performance remained quite stable over the three phases of the experiment illustrating that improvement manifested by S_3 and S_4 was not due to the presence of elements in the situation common to the class as a whole.

EXPERIMENT 3

Subjects

The Ss were 24 students from a sixth-grade, social-science class. One experimental S (S_5) was selected by the teacher on the basis that he had not been doing as well as he should have been doing in his classwork. The remaining 23 students served as control Ss.

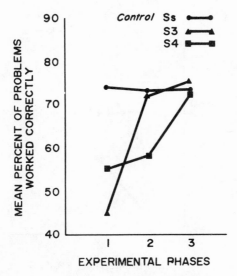

Fig. 21.2. Mean percent of correctly solved arithmetic problems on weekly tests under Phase 1 (baseline), Phase 2 (experimental treatment applied to S_3), and Phase 3 (experimental treatment applied to S_4).

Procedure

This experiment was conducted over a 10-week period. On the final day of each week, the teacher administered a ten-item test covering material presented during the week.

Again the first four weeks (Phase 1) was a baseline period in which weekly test scores were recorded but a treatment was not introduced. During weeks five through ten (Phase 2), the teacher announced daily, 5 min prior to the customary noon dismissal time, that the class would be dismissed 5 min early if S_5 could correctly answer a question over material covered during the class period. The teacher than asked S_5 a question and, if he responded correctly, the class was dismissed. If he responded inappropriately to the question, classwork was continued until the customary dismissal time.

Results

The results are illustrated in Fig. 21.3. The results show that S_5 showed some improvement relative to the control Ss, but the extent of the improvement was considerably less than that manifested by experimental Ss in the first two experiments.

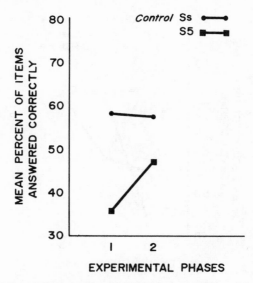

Fig. 21.3. Mean percent of correctly answered items on weekly social science tests under Phase 1 (baseline) and Phase 2 (experimental treatment applied to S_5).

EXPERIMENT 4

Subjects

The Ss were 24 students from a sixth-grade, general-science class. An experimental S (S_6) was selected by the teacher (the teacher of this class also taught the social-science class described in Experiment 3). Again, the experimental S was a student who the teacher believed should be doing better work than he was currently doing. The remaining 23 students served as control Ss.

Procedure

The procedure and time periods were identical to those employed in Experiment 3 with the exception that dismissal time was contingent on a correct response from S_6 5 min prior to afternoon recess, rather than noon hour.

Results

Figure 21.4 illustrates that the test performance of both S_6 and the control group declined during Phase 2. Since there was little change in S_6's

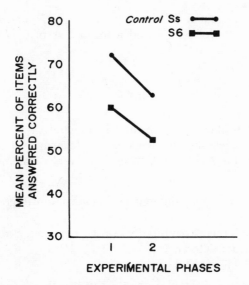

Fig. 21.4. Mean percent of correctly answered items on weekly science tests under Phase 1 (baseline) and Phase 2 (experimental treatment applied to S_6).

standing relative to the control group, the decline was probably due to an environmental element (such as more difficult examinations) other than the experimental treatment.

ANALYSIS OF RESULTS

A mean change score was obtained for each experimental S by subtracting his mean test score during the preceding baseline phase(s) from his mean test score during the treatment phase. Thus, the mean change score for S_1 was his mean test score in Phase 2, minus his mean test score in Phase 1. The mean change score for S_2 was his mean test score in Phase 3, minus his mean test score in Phases 1 and 2 combined. Mean change scores were also obtained for the control groups so that mean change scores for each experimental S could be compared with an appropriate group change score.

The difference between each experimental S's change score and the change score of the appropriate control group was obtained. These six difference scores were analyzed statistically by means of the paired t-test. The mean difference was found to be statistically significant beyond the 0.02 level of confidence ($t = 3.678$; df $= 5$). Whereas the experimental

Ss showed a mean gain of 1.73 items per test (17.3%) under the treatment conditions, the control Ss showed a mean loss of 0.37 items per test (3.7%) under these conditions.

DISCUSSION

The results of these experiments demonstrate that the procedures described can accelerate the academic performance of underachieving grade-school children. The lack of uniformity of results may have been due to:

1. Age or educational differences between fourth-grade and sixth-grade children.
2. Teacher differences in attitude toward or execution of the program.
3. Subject matter differences.
4. Individual differences among subjects.

The question of the relative effects of these different variables cannot be answered by the data obtained in these experiments. A confounding of effects is present due to the fact that one teacher taught both fourth-grade classes and the other teacher taught both sixth-grade classes. The difference in responsiveness to the treatment may have been due to certain attitudinal differences between the teachers, or the fact that the program was more effective with fourth-grade Ss than with sixth-grade Ss may have led to attitudinal differences between the teachers.

Anecdotal reports by the teachers indicate there was a difference in the manner in which the fourth-grade and sixth-grade children reacted to the program. The fourth-grade teacher reported several attempts by peers to influence the experimental Ss' success (e.g. urging S to study his material and offering assistance). No such attempts by peers was noticed by the sixth-grade teacher. Both teachers reported, however, that their classes were pleased when early dismissal occurred. Differences in teacher attitudes toward the program were indicated by their verbal reports. The fourth-grade teacher spoke very favorably of the program, while the sixth-grade teacher was unimpressed. Further experimentation to isolate teacher, grade, and subject matter differences is planned.

Experimentation is also planned to identify procedures which will prevent relapses after the treatment is discontinued, such as the one exhibited by S_1. At least two possibilities suggest themselves. One possibility is to continue to ask the child questions but eliminate the consequences of his answer. This treatment was applied to S_3 in Phase 3 (Experiment 2) and her performance did not deteriorate. A second possible preventative of severe deterioration after the treatment condition is removed is gradually to decrease the treatment frequency until the desired behavior comes under the control of positive natural consequences.

A comment on the generalization of learned behavior seems appropriate at this point. Note that the dependent variable employed in this study, weekly test performance, was not the behavior that was actually reinforced. The finding that reinforcing daily performance will affect behavior on weekly tests which is not reinforced, though not particularly surprising, demonstrates that behavioral generalization does occur under the conditions of these experiments.

Acquisition of control over an individual's behavior by making a class-reinforcer contingent on the behavior of the individual is a treatment technique that lends itself to a variety of behavior and learning problems in the classroom. In addition to its versatility, the technique has the advantage of requiring very little of the teacher's time or energy. Tests and records are necessary only to evaluate the effectiveness of the procedure. Once the conditions under which the procedure is effective are established, tests and records are not a necessary part of the program. Hopefully, these features will serve to make the technique both effective and practical for general use in the classroom situation.

REFERENCES

Allen K. E., Hart B. M., Buell J. A., Harris F. R. and Wolf M. M. (1965) Effects of social reinforcement on isolate behavior of a nursery school child. In *Case studies in behavior modification* (Eds. Ullmann and Krasner), pp. 307–312.

Homme L. E., C'deBaca P., Devine J. V., Steinhorst R. and Rickert E. J. (1963) Use of the Premack principle in controlling the behavior of nursery school children. *J. exp. Analysis Behav.* **6**, 544.

Patterson G. R. (1965) A learning theory approach to the treatment of the school phobic child. In *Case studies in behavior modification* (Eds. Ullmann and Krasner), pp. 279–285.

Patterson G. R. and Brodsky G. (1966) A behavior modification program for a child with multiple problem behaviors. *J. Child Psychol. Psychiat.* **7**, 277–295.

Patterson G. R., Jones J. W., Whittier J. and Wright M. A. (1965) A behavior modification technique for the hyperactive child. *Behav. Res. & Therapy* **2**, 217–226.

Zimmerman E. H. and Zimmerman J. (1962) The alteration of behavior in a special class-room situation. *J. exp. Analysis Behav.* **5**, 59–60.

ARTICLE 22

Good Behavior Game: Effects of Individual Contingencies for Group Consequences on Disruptive Behavior in a Classroom*[1]

HARRIET H. BARRISH, MURIEL SAUNDERS, and MONTROSE M. WOLF

University of Kansas

Abstract: Out-of-seat and talking-out behaviors were studied in a regular fourth-grade class that included several "problem children". After baseline rates of the inappropriate behaviors were obtained, the class was divided into two teams "to play a game". Each out-of-seat and talking-out response by an individual child resulted in a mark being placed on the chalkboard, which meant a possible loss of privileges by all members of the student's team. In this manner a contingency was arranged for the inappropriate behavior of each child while the consequence (possible loss of privileges) of the child's behavior was shared by all members of this team as a group. The privileges were events which are available in almost every classroom, such as extra recess, first to line up for lunch, time for special projects, stars and name tags, as well as winning the game. The individual contingencies for the group consequences were successfully applied first during math period and then during reading period. The experimental analysis involved elements of both reversal and multiple baseline designs.

*Reprinted from the *Journal of Applied Behavior Analysis*, Vol. 2, No. 2, Summer 1969, pp. 119–124. Copyright 1969 by the Society for the Experimental Analysis of Behavior, Inc.

[1]This study is based upon a thesis submitted by the senior author to the Department of Human Development in partial fulfillment of the requirements for the Master of Arts degree. The research was supported by a Public Health Service Fellowship IFI MH-36, 964-01 from the National Institute of Mental Health and by a grant (HD 03144) from the National Institute of Child Health and Human Development to the Bureau of Child Research and the Department of Human Development, University of Kansas. The authors wish to thank Drs. Donald M. Baer and Don Bushell, Jr., for helpful suggestions in preparation of the manuscript; Mr. Rex Shanks, Mr. Frank A. Branagan, and Mrs. Betty Roberts for their invaluable help in conducting the study; and Mrs. Susan Zook, Mrs. Sue Chen, and Mr. Jay Barrish for their contributions of time for reliability checks. Reprints may be obtained from the authors, Department of Human Development, University of Kansas, Lawrence, Kansas 66044.

Researchers have recently begun to asses the effectiveness of a variety of behavioral procedures for management of disruptive classroom behavior. Some investigators have arranged token reinforcement contingencies for appropriate classroom behavior (Birnbrauer, Wolf, Kidder, and Tague, 1965; O'Leary and Becker, 1967; Wolf, Giles, and Hall, 1968). However, these token reinforcers often have been dependent upon back-up reinforcers that were unnatural in the regular classroom, such as candy and money. On the other hand, several investigators have utilized a reinforcer intrinsic to every classroom, *i.e.*, teacher attention (Zimmerman and Zimmerman, 1962; Hall and Broden, 1967; Becker, Madsen, Arnold, and Thomas, 1967; Hall, Lund, and Jackson, 1968; Thomas, Becker, and Armstrong, 1968; Madsen, Becker, and Thomas, 1968). Even so, at least one group of investigators (Hall *et al.*, 1968) encountered a teacher who apparently did not have sufficient social reinforcers in her repertoire to apply social reinforcement procedures successfully. The present study investigated the effects of a classroom behavior management technique based on reinforcers natural to the classroom, other than teacher attention. The technique was designed to reduce disruptive classroom behavior through a game involving competition for privileges available in almost every classroom. The students were divided into two teams and disruptive behavior by any member of a team resulted in possible loss of privileges for every member of his team.

METHOD

Subjects and Setting

The study was conducted in a fourth-grade classroom of 24 students. Seven of the students had been referred several times by the teacher to the school principal for such problems as out-of-seat behavior, indiscriminate noise and talking, uncooperativeness, and general classroom disruption. Further, the school principal reported that a general behavior management problem existed in the classroom. According to the teacher, she frequently had informed the class of the rules of good classroom behavior.

Definition of the Behavior

One and sometimes two observers visited the classroom for approximately 1 hr each Monday, Wednesday, and Friday. Observation took place during the last half of the reading period and the first half of the math period. During both of these periods, similar types of activities such as individual assignments, oral lessons and discussion, chalkboard work, and short quizzes were assigned to the students; only the subject matter varied—*i.e.*, reading or math. Recording was discontinued during the brief transition from the reading to the math period.

Observers sat at the side of the classroom and avoided eye contact and interactions both before and during recording. Observers used recording sheets similar to those used in other studies (Hall *et al.*, 1968). These were divided into rows of squares for each behavior. Each square represented an interval of 1 min. If any child in the classroom emitted the behavior, a check was made in the row assigned to the behavior, in the square representing that particular interval of time. Teacher attention to inappropriate behavior was marked in the corresponding square by an asterisk.

Inter-observer agreement was analyzed by having a second observer periodically (at least once during each of the experimental conditions) make a simultaneous but independent observation record. Agreement was measured by comparing the two records for agreement, interval by interval. The percentage of agreement between the two records was calculated (number of agreements × 100 ÷ the total number of intervals). In addition, by indicating teacher attention to inappropriate behavior by an asterisk, intervals could be compared asterisk against check in the appropriate square to yield a percentage of agreement between the observer and the teacher during the phases that the game was in affect.

While the behavioral definitions were constructed by the experimenter, they were formulated with the help of the principal and the classroom teacher on the basis of what they considered to be the disruptive classroom behaviors.

Out-of-seat behavior was defined as leaving the seat and/or seated position during a lesson or scooting the desk without permission. Exceptions to the definition, and instances not recorded, included out-of-seat behavior that occurred when no more than four pupils signed out on the chalkboard to leave for the restroom, when pupils went one at a time to the teacher's desk during independent study assignment, and when pupils were merely changing orientation in their seat. Also, when a child left his seat to approach the teacher's desk, but then appeared to notice that someone else was already there or on his way and consequently quickly returned to his seat, the behavior was not counted. Permission was defined throughout the study as raising one's hand, being recognized by the teacher, and receiving consent from her to engage in a behavior.

Talking-out behavior was defined as talking or whispering without permission. It included, for example, talking while raising one's hand, talking to classmates, talking to the teacher, calling the teacher's name, blurting out answers, or making vocal noises such as animal-like sounds, howls, cat calls, *etc.*, all without permission.

Introduction of the Game

Immediately after the reading period and before the math period in which the system was initially used, a presentation closely following the points listed below was made by the teacher to her class. She explained that: (a) what they were about to do was a game that they would play every day during math period only. (b) The class would be divided into two teams. (She then divided the class by rows and seats of the center row.) (c) When a team or teams won the game, the team(s) would receive certain privileges. (d) There were certain rules, however, that the teams had to follow to win. (These rules were based on the behavior categories as previously defined.) (1) No one was to be out of his seat without permission (except that four pupils were allowed to leave their seats without permission in order to sign out on the chalkboard to leave for the restroom). Permission could be obtained only by raising the hand and being called on by the teacher. (2) No one was to sit on top of his desk or on any of his neighbor's desks. (3) No one was to get out of his seat to move his desk or scoot his desk. (4) No one was to get out of his seat to talk to a neighbor. This also meant that there was to be no leaning forward out of a seat to whisper. (5) No one was to get out of his seat to go to the chalkboard (except to sign out for the restroom), pencil sharpener, waste basket, drinking fountain, sink, or to the teacher without permission. (6) When the teacher was seated at her desk during study time, students could come to her desk one at a time if they had a question. (7) No one was to talk without permission. Permission could again be obtained only by raising the hand and being called on by the teacher. (8) No one was to talk while raising his hand. (9) No one was to talk or whisper to his neighbors. (10) No one was to call out the teacher's name unless he had permission to answer. (11) No one was to make vocal noises. (e) Whenever she saw anyone on a team breaking one of these rules, that team would get a mark on the chalkboard. (f) If a team had the fewest marks, or if neither team received more than five marks, the team(s) would get to (1) wear victory tags, (2) put a star by each of its members' names on the winner's chart, (3) line up first for lunch if one team won or early if both teams won, and (4) take part at the end of the day in a 30-min free time during which the team(s) would have special projects. (g) The team that lost would not get these privileges, would continue working on an assignment during the last half-hour of the day, and members would have to stay after school as usual if they did not do their work during the last half-hour period. (h) If a team or teams had not received more than 20 marks in a week, it would get the extra weekly privilege of going to recess 4 min early.

Whenever the experimental conditions were changed, point "a" was again presented to the class by the teacher with a new explanation about when the game would be played. All the above points were presented before the initial use of the program and then once again after a week-long period of achievement testing during which time the game had not been in effect. The victory tags were commercially prepared circular convention tags. Each tag was of the same color and was threaded with a uniform length of wool yarn of a contrasting color. Tags were worn around the neck. They allowed the teacher to identify easily the winners during the rest of the day. The star chart consisted of a 22-in by 28-in piece of white poster board labeled "Winners". The chart was divided into two portions designated "Team One" and "Team Two" and ruled off with team members (names) by dates (month and day). The stars were commercially manufactured with gummed backs. The special projects consisted of educational activities in the areas of science or arts which were done as a team or individually.

During the first period in which the game was applied, the teacher stipulated that the team with the fewest marks, or 10 or less, would win. The criterion for the second observed session, and for all other sessions except the last one, was set at five marks or fewer. The last session was also the last full day of school. The teacher expected the children to be very excited, and she wanted to be sure that both teams would win, since she had treats planned for the special project period. For this session the criterion was the fewest marks, or eight or less.

Experimental Phases

The experimental design included both reversal and multiple baseline phases. The data were recorded separately during the reading and math periods providing the two baselines. The study was divided into four corresponding phases. A session in one class period corresponded to a session in the other class period in that they were recorded consecutively and on the same day.

I. MATH-Baseline, READING-Baseline For 10 sessions, the normal (baseline) rates of out-of-seat and talking-out behaviors of the class were recorded during the math and reading periods. The teacher carried out her classroom activities in her usual manner.

II. MATH-Game₁, READING-Baseline During the second phase, the game was introduced during math but not during reading.

III. MATH-Reversal, READING-Game In the third phase, the game was introduced during reading and withdrawn during math.

IV. MATH-Game₂, READING-Game Lastly, the game was reintroduced in math period and remained in effect during reading period. Both periods were treated as one extended period, thus using the same initial criteria of the least number of marks or five or fewer marks.

RESULTS

Figure 22.1 shows the extent to which out-of-seat and talking-out behaviors were influenced by the game. These data indicate that the game had a reliable effect, since out-of-seat and talking-out behaviors changed maximally only when the game was applied. In the math and reading baselines, the median intervals scored for talking-out was approximately 96% and for out-of-seat it was approximately 82%.

When the game was applied during math period, there was a sharp decline in the scored intervals to medians of approximately 19% and 9% respectively. Meanwhile, during reading period where the game was not applied, talking-out behavior remained essentially at baseline levels and out-of-seat behavior declined somewhat.

During the third phase, the game was withdrawn during math period, and the baseline rates of the behaviors recovered; in the same phase during the reading period, the game was introduced for the first time, and a decline in the per cent of scored intervals for both behaviors resulted. Finally in the fourth phase, the game was applied during math and reading periods simultaneously. The disruptive behaviors again declined during math and continued low in reading.

Both teams almost always won the game. Of the 17 class periods that observations were made both teams won on all but three occasions, or 82% of the time.

The reliability of the measurement procedures was analyzed during the reading and math periods on six occasions. Three different reliability

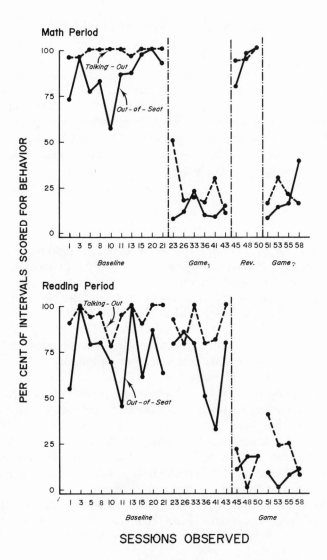

Fig. 22.1. Per cent of 1-min intervals scored by an observer as containing talking-out and out-of-seat behaviors occurring in a classroom of 24 fourth-grade school children during math and reading periods. In the baseline conditions the teacher attempted to manage the disruptive classroom behavior in her usual manner. During the game conditions out-of-seat and talking-out responses by a student resulted in a possible loss of privileges for the student and his team.

observers were used. Agreement for out-of-seat behavior ranged from 74% to 98% and averaged 91%. Agreement for talking-out behavior ranged from 75% to 98% and averaged 86%.

Agreement between the observer and the teacher was measured during each class period that the game was played. Agreement about the occurrence of out-of-seat behavior ranged from 61% to 100% and averaged 92%. Agreement about the occurrence of talking-out behavior ranged from 71% to 100% and averaged 85%. Thus, the levels of agreement between the observer and the teacher, and the observer and the reliability observers were approximately the same.

DISCUSSION

The game significantly and reliably modified the disruptive out-of-seat and talking-out behavior of the students. The experimental design involving elements of both multiple baseline and reversal strategies, demonstrated that the effect could be replicated across subject matter periods and that the game had a continuing role in maintaining the reduced level of disruptive behavior. On the other hand, no analysis was carried out to determine the roles of the various components of the game. An analysis of exactly what components contributed to the effectiveness of the procedure is left to future research.

As in the present study, the subject-matter periods of the typical school day lend themselves perfectly to a multiple baseline experimental design. Simultaneous baselines of the behavior of one student or of an entire class can be obtained simultaneously in two or more subject-matter periods. The modification technique can then be introduced successively into each of the periods. If in each instance there is a change in behavior (and the behavior during the remaining baseline periods remains essentially unchanged), the investigator will have achieved a believable demonstration of the effectiveness of his technique. And he will have done so without having depended upon or required a reversal of the behavior (Baer, Wolf, and Risley, 1968).

Some problems arose which should be noted. The preparation of the special projects required the time and ingenuity of the teacher. This sometimes placed an extra burden on her, since she had also to prepare regular lessons. Another problem that was perhaps not as serious concerned teacher observation of behaviors. No signaling system was used. The teacher had to become alert to out-of-seat and talking-out behaviors in addition to continuing to conduct regular classroom activities. Spotting the target behaviors did not appear to be difficult for the teacher except when she faced the chalkboard or talked with individual students.

The greatest problem with the game involved two students who, before the study began, had been referred to the principal on a number of occasions for disruptive behavior. Both were on the same team and consistently gained a number of marks for their team. Usually they engaged in talking-out behavior. In most instances only one of the students was involved. In one session, one of these students emphatically announced that he was no longer going to play the game. Both the other children and the teacher expressed the opinion that it was not fair to penalize further an entire team because one member would not control himself. The teacher, therefore dropped the student from the game and the marks that normally would have been imposed on the entire team were imposed just on him. During the free time, he also refused to work so he was kept after school. The same individual-consequence procedure was used for one or both students on six occasions. Each time, the marks that they had accumulated were subtracted from the team score. It is possible that the numerous peer comments that appeared to be directed toward these students may have served as social reinforcement for their disruptive behavior. It is important to note, however, that when the students were dropped from their team the observer continued to record their behavior as before.

Some reactions to the program were gathered from the children, teacher, and school officials. The program was apparently popular with students and school officials. Every professional involved in the study who directly observed the classroom situation during the game stated that in general the students seemed to enjoy playing the game. The teacher stated that some students went so far as to request that the game be played every period. After the last session in which the game was played, the teacher requested that each child briefly write whether they liked or disliked the game and why. Of the 21 comments turned in, 14 indicated that they liked the game and seven indicated that they did not. Of those who indicated that they liked the game, some made comments such as: "I like the game because I can read better when it is quiet", "I liked it. Cause it was fun", "You give us free time", "I like the morning game because it helps keep people quiet so we can work", and, "I like the team game because we win all the time". Of those who indicated that they disliked the game, some made comments such as: "No I hate being quiet", "I didn't like it because you didn't make good rules", "Because when your team loses the team that won will make fun of your team", and "Its not fair because we have the guys that talk a lot". The teacher stated that she was pleased with the method because "it was an easy program to install since it did not change any of the rules or daily activities in the classroom." All of the back-up reinforcers, with the possible exception of the victory tags, naturally occurred in the classroom setting. Only the structure of the free-time period at the end of the day changed, but it, of course, involved projects of an educational nature.

While game-like techniques are certainly not new to the classroom (Russell and Karp, 1938), an experimental analysis of their effects on behavior is unique. It may follow that an understanding of the mechanisms of the game, *e.g.*, peer competition, group consequences *vs.* individual consequences, *etc.*, together with research designed to enhance the significance of winning, by pairing winning with privileges, could lead to a set of effective and practical techniques of classroom behavior management based on games.

REFERENCES

Baer, D. M., Wolf, M. M., and Risley, T. R. Some current dimensions of applied behavior analysis. *Journal of Applied Behavior Analysis*, 1968, **1**, 91–97.

Becker, W. C., Madsen, C. H., Jr., Arnold, C. R., and Thomas, D. R. The contingent use of teacher attention and praise in reducing classroom behavior problems. *Journal of Special Education*, 1967, **1**, 287–307.

Birnbrauer, J. S., Wolf, M. M., Kidder, J. D. and Tague, C. E. Classroom behavior in retarded pupils with token reinforcement. *Journal of Experimental Child Psychology* 1965, **2**, 219–235.

Hall, R. V. and Broden, M. Behavior changes in brain-injured children through social reinforcement. *Journal of Experimental Child Psychology*, 1967, **5**, 463–479.

Hall, R. V., Lund, D., and Jackson, D. Effects of teacher attention on study behavior. *Journal of Applied Behavior Analysis*, 1968, **1**, 1–12.

Madsen, C. H., Becker, W. C., and Thomas, D. R. Rules, praise, and ignoring: elements of elementary classroom control. *Journal of Applied Behavior Analysis*, 1968, **1**, 139–150.

O'Leary, K. D. and Becker, W. C. Behavior modification of an adjustment class: a token reinforcement program. *Exceptional Children*, 1967, **33**, 637–642.

Russell, D. H. and Karp, E. E. *Reading aids through the grades*. New York: Bureau of Publications, Columbia University, 1938.

Thomas, D. R., Becker, W. C. and Armstrong, M. Production and elimination of disruptive classroom behavior by systematically varying teacher's behavior. *Journal of Applied Behavior Analysis*, 1968, **1**, 35–45.

Wolf, M. M., Giles, D., and Hall, R. V. Experiments with token reinforcement in a remedial classroom. *Behaviour Research and Therapy*, 1968, **6**, 51–64.

Zimmerman, E. H. and Zimmerman J. The alteration of behavior in a special classroom situation. *Journal of Experimental Analysis of Behavior*, 1962, **5**, 59–60.

ARTICLE 23

The Elimination of Tantrum Behavior of a Child in an Elementary Classroom*

CONSTANCE S. CARLSON, CAROLE R. ARNOLD, WESLEY C. BECKER,
and CHARLES H. MADSEN

2506 McDivitt Road, Madison, Wisconsin, Iowa State University, University of Illinois,
and Florida State University

Abstract: Temper tantrums in children produce considerable distress for parents and other adults responsible for their training. Informal observation has suggested that such tantrums are maintained by attention and other forms of reinforcement which typically follow them. Williams (1959) has described an extinction procedure he used with a 21-month-old child who tantrumed when left at bedtime. The procedure essentially involved placing the child in bed and not responding to his outburst. Tantrums were readily eliminated in seven days. Wolf, Risley and Mees (1964) have reported a related procedure. A $3\frac{1}{2}$-yr-old autistic child was placed in a room by himself when he tantrumed, and was allowed to come out only after the tantrum ceased. This particular procedure combined extinction with mild punishment (time out from positive reinforcement). In the case to be reported, no facilities were available for isolating an 8-yr-old when she had a tantrum in the classroom, and an alternative procedure was devised.

CASE REPORT

Diane was an 8-yr-old Negro child from a family of five children. An older sister died with sicle-cell anemia and a younger sister has the same difficulty. Both parents work and were in debt because of high medical bills. Diane attended a neighborhood school which was 95 per cent Negro. Her IQ was average on the Stanford-Binet (LM). On the Wide Range Achievement Test given in January 1966 (mid-second grade) Diane scored 1.8 grades in reading, 1.2 in spelling, and 1.5 in oral math.

She began the year in one adjustment class (16 children), but was moved

---

*Reprinted from *Behaviour Research and Therapy*, Vol. 6, 1968, pp. 117–119.

at Christmas to another class in an attempt by the school to establish better social relationships. She was described as being quite fearful and timid, and the children in the first grade disliked her and fought with her frequently. In her new class (Mrs. C.'s) she displayed no unusual behavior at first, perhaps because she was frequently ill and had little chance to interact with the children. Then, in February, severe tantrums started and occurred as often as three a week. When the first few tantrums occurred, Diane was taken to the office. Although Diane was isolated from her peers, she received immediate attention from her teacher, the secretaries, the social worker, the principal, and on two occasions, from her mother when she was summoned to the school. Mother reported that tantrums were quite frequent at home and that the younger siblings were isolated from Diane when a tantrum was in progress. Diane received her mother's undivided attention.

On March 1, 1966, Mrs. C. let a tantrum run its course in the room. The tantrum was actually too long and too intense to be handled in the room. Such behavior as profane screaming, running wildly from place to place, picking up chairs, and actually throwing them, attacking other children, etc. were displayed. At this point, Mrs. C., who was attending a seminar on behavior modification with the co-authors, requested help.

PROCEDURES

The following program was established

1. It was explained to Diane and the class than when Diane was behaving badly, Mr. Z., a teacher aide, would hold her down in her chair. Diane resented being touched or held, so holding served as punishment.

2. Diane's chair was placed in the back of the room so that the other children could not see her.

3. It was explained to the other children that everyone who did not turn around at all to watch Diane would receive a candy treat. A treat was passed out to demonstrate what would happen as the explanation was given. The aim was to withdraw peer attention from the tantrum behavior. To prevent the children from provoking tantrums to get a treat, candy was given intermittently at times when Diane was not tantruming.

4. A positive incentive for non-tantrum behavior was established. Her teacher decided that an obtainable goal would be to give Diane a star (on the board) for each half-day of non-tantrum behavior. When

four stars *in a row* were received there would be a little class party, with Diane passing out the treats. The latter provision was designed with the thought of increasing Diane's acceptance by her peers.

The program was begun on March 14th and continued through June 10th. On May 9th, Mrs. C. suggested extending the required stars to six, but Diane said "Let me try for ten". Ten became the new goal.

RESULTS

Diane had a tantrum on Monday, March 14th, the morning the program was explained to the class. There were none the rest of the week. She earned the treat for the class and had a chance to "feel important".

During the next week, tantrums occurred on Monday, Thursday, and three times on Friday. Two of the tantrums on Friday were recorded by two observers whose notes are summarized below.

First tantrum

1.35 pm.   Apparently it started in the hall while the class was returning from the bathroom. Mrs. C. was restraining Diane as the class came back. Mr. Z. took Diane to her seat and sat her down while continuing to hold her. Diane struggled and shouted repeatedly, "let me go", "stinking rat, you let me go". She attempted to hit Mr. Z. Mrs. C. passed out candy to those who were not turning, and took candy away from a child who turned to look after receiving candy. Yelling continued at a high volume. "Black dog, let me go". Objects were thrown at a neighboring girl. The rest of the class was very good at ignoring her. Finally she started crying and shouting, "stinking rat, black dog, let me go, can't you hear?" "Let me go. You hate me and I hate you" (repeated).

1.43 pm.   Lesson started for rest of class. Diane was shaking her desk and screaming. She kicked herself out of her chair on to the floor. Mr. Z. sat her back in the chair and continued to hold her. "Stinking rat". She tried to spit on teacher.

1.46 pm.   Diane was quiet and the restraint was stopped. She started looking in her desk, rattling papers. Mrs. C. put a *Weekly Reader* in front of her. She threw it off her desk.

1.48 pm.   Mr. Z. was not holding her. In a low voice she said to him "let me go". She got her glue and some papers. Mr. Z. moved to the back of the room. This activity continued for 5–10 minutes. She ignored the class activity.

Second tantrum

2.10 pm.   The class started out to recess, which Diane was denied. She went out with the class and Mr. Z. had to go after her and bring her back.

2.25 pm.   Mr. Z. brought her in and blocked the door. She got her glue and said "if you don't let me go, I'll throw glue on you". She tried to push through. Mr. Z. took her to her seat and told her he would have to hold her until she was quiet. "I'll throw glue on you". Mr. Z. told her he would have to take the glue away from her. "I don't care. I'll have my father buy more. You black bitch, let me go". Threw several objects from desk. "You black bitch, you let me go". Threw books. Mr. Z. said, "Sit still". "I'm gonna drop everything in my desk on this floor. I ain't gonna pick none of it up".

2.28 pm.   Tried to bite Mr. Z. several times. 'I'll bite the shit out of you". She turned the desk over with her feet. "I can do so much with my foot that you will be surprised". She called for mother, "Oh, Mama", and in a half cry, "You let me go". "I'm gonna turn everybody's desk over". "Let me go". . . . "I'll make all the racket I can".

2.32 pm.   "You black dog, you don't have to hold me". She settled down and Mr. Z. turned her loose. "I'm getting my desk". She turned her desk up on its legs. "I'm getting me something to clean it with". She went to the sink and brought back a wet sponge and started washing the inside of her desk.

2.36 pm.   The rest of the class returned from recess. She ignored the rest of the class and continued to wash her desk. She then started to put the items from the floor neatly back into her desk. Diane received no attention from other students. By 2.45 things were all cleaned up and Diane was walking around the room quietly.

The observers felt that the "peak of the extinction curve" had been reached. No tantrums occurred the following week. Diane's reactions were notably changed. At first, she covered her ears so that she could not hear the children enjoying the candy (given periodically for ignoring Diane). Then she was very sullen and expressed a desire to change schools, move away, etc. During periods when no tantrums occurred, she looked noticeably happier. She began to play and take part in group activities with the girls on the playground.

During the next week she had one tantrum (Tuesday, April 14th). Her attitude seemed to be continually improving. More and more chances to praise her for success were found. On April 15th, Mrs. C. added a new component to the program. At noon, before coming in the building for the afternoon session, Diane went after Hope. In Mrs. C.'s words:

> I could see that this behavior would continue if Diane came in so I told her that she'd really goofed. She had 3 x's in a row and all she needed was four, and if she was going to act like that, she couldn't come in the building. Previously she would have reacted to this by saying "I'm going home". This time, however, she stayed outside by the fence for a while, then entered the building and stood outside our classroom door. We ignored her. After the class's bathroom break, I said, "Come on in, Diane". She broke into tears and said, "I'm sorry, Mrs. C., I won't do it again". I now knew that the room and the school were positive for her.

On April 18th in the presence of observers, Diane was called on in math. She did not answer correctly and a moment later spoke out saying "Hope, don't you dare call me stupid". From her tone and actions it looked like a tantrum was coming. Mrs. C. ignored Diane's speaking out and praised her neighbor for not speaking out of turn. By the careful use of praise of other children for appropriate behavior, Diane was drawn back to the class and Hope was led to turn around and ignore Diane. Both girls were then praised for properly answering questions about the lesson.

Mild tantrums, requiring Mr. Z.'s aid occurred on April 19th and 29th. They consisted mainly of crying, without profanity, and lasted less than 5 min. A mild eruption occurred on May 2nd, but was controlled by comments such as "Oh dear, I hope we don't lose our x," or "I'll be glad when everyone is in his seat".

School was out June 10th. Between May 2nd and the end of the school year, no other tantrums occurred. During the final month of school, Diane's attitudes continued to improve. She learned to make friends and to react to the school and her teacher in positive ways. Mrs. C. described her as a happy, cheerful child during the last month.

SEQUEL

In the fall Diane was moved to another school. With the changed situation, tantrums re-occurred. They were handled by sending Diane to the principal's office. This often required the principal to remain in the office through lunch until he could return her to class. In the middle of the year, Diane was "staffed" at the new school. Mrs. C. attended the staffing and described the procedures used to control Diane the previous year. Both the principal and the new teacher were convinced that some "deep-down disturbance" was causing the tantrums and that talking about "how she feels" would help. They could not see the behavior as being maintained by the attention it received or by escape from the classroom. An attempt was made to place Diane in a special research classroom for emotionally disturbed children, but she was not accepted. She was placed on daily tranquilizers. A report from the school social worker in April, 1967 indicated that Diane's behavior had "deteriorated to a level worse than it had ever been the previous year". Diane was re-staffed and was scheduled to enter the special research class for emotionally disturbed children in September.

On May 22, 1967, Diane came back to visit Mrs. C. at her old school. She chatted for about 5 min and gave Mrs. C. a piece of gum "for being such a nice teacher last year". She was smiling and happy, and had several friends with her. Mrs. C. commented, pointedly, that she saw "no signs of inner conflict".

ARTICLE 24

An Elementary Student as a
Behavioral Engineer*[1]

PAUL R. SURRATT, ROGER E. ULRICH, and ROBERT P. HAWKINS

Kalamazoo Valley Intermediate School District
and Western Michigan University

Abstract: Four first-grade public school students exhibited non-study behaviors during a period when all children were to study individually. A fifth-grade student modified the maladaptive behaviors of the four first-grade students. Lights on the four students' desks, which were associated with opportunity for reinforcement, rapidly brought study behavior under stimulus control. Differential reinforcement of other behaviors dramatically decreased studying. Reinforcement was reinstituted and studying returned to a high and stable rate. Surreptitious post-experimental observation using closed-circuit TV indicated that the behavioral changes effected during the experimental phases were partially maintained by the regular classroom environment. A replication of the baseline phase with the observer in the classroom produced an increase in the rate of study behavior, indicating that the observer's presence acted as a discriminative stimulus for studying. An additional contingency requiring improved academic behavior was imposed before the fifth grader was given the opportunity to engage in the behavior modification experiment.

*Reprinted from the *Journal of Applied Behavior Analysis*, Vol. 2, No. 2, Summer 1969, pp. 85–92.
Copyright 1969 by the Society for the Experimental Analysis of Behavior, Inc.
[1]This research was supported by a grant from the Michigan Department of Mental Health entitled In-School Treatment Program. The authors wish to express their gratitude to Mr. Kenneth Otis, Superintendent, Vicksburg Community Schools, and to Mrs. Francis Smink, Principal; Mrs. Judy Berghuis, First-Grade Teacher; Mr. Brent Lehmkuhl, Student Engineer; and entire staff of Indian Lake Elementary School for their cooperation and support throughout this experiment. Appreciation is also extended to Dr. Donald Whaley and Mr. Marshall Wolfe for their comments and criticisms throughout the study and in preparation of the manuscript. Gratitude is also expressed to Miss Lois Huey, Miss Brigette Symannek, Mr. Richard Cole, Miss Cheri Yeager, Miss Madeline Lewis, Miss Marilyn Arnett, and Miss Sylvia Delaney for their aid in preparation of the manuscript and graphs.

Reprints may be obtained from Paul R. Surratt, Rehabilitation Institute, Southern Illinois University, Carbondale, Illinois 62901.

The use of behavior modification techniques in regular public school classrooms has recently received considerable attention (Hall, Lund, and Jackson, 1968; Thomas, Becker, and Armstrong, 1968; Madsen, Becker and Thomas, 1968). In each of these cases, the teacher was utilized as a behavioral engineer, which necessitated that he or she selectively observe the behavior of each of the children in question. Within a normal classroom, there are times when such observations are not practical. For example, when a teacher is working intensively with a small reading group, it is frequently not possible to attend closely to the behaviors of other class members located in another part of the room.

If time, personnel, and adequate funds were available, the optimal condition within a school would be for a trained behavioral therapist to work with children who are exhibiting mild problems. Because of the prohibitive cost involved in hiring special personnel and the lack of individuals with sufficient training, many problems are allowed to exist and to develop until it is only after a severe behavioral problem is well established that any student is given professional attention.

In a setting where the teacher is unable to work with the behaviors in question, he or she must utilize the resources at hand. In the typical school setting, an abundant resource available for the modification of student behavior, is other students.

It has been shown that nurses and hospital attendants (Ayllon and Michael, 1959), parents (Zeilberger, Sampen, and Sloane, 1968; Hawkins, Peterson, Schweid, and Bijou, 1966), as well as many other diverse populations can be trained effectively in a short period of time to modify the behavior of others (Ulrich, Stachnik, and Mabry, 1966; Homme, 1969). Ulrich and Kent (1966) have suggested the use of college students as instructors for less advanced students.

Many behavior modification studies (*i.e.*, Hawkins *et al.*, 1966) have attempted to assess the long-term effects of their experimental manipulations by returning the observer to the setting in which the manipulations took place. That observer then records the behavior that is occurring and these data are presented as the residual effect of the experimental manipulations. It would seem feasible that in varying degrees an observer-modifier could become a discriminative stimulus for the behavior in question. The validity of standard post-check methodologies would be in some doubt if such a discriminative function could experimentally be attributed to the presence of the observer-manipulator within the classroom.

The present study investigated the behaviors of four first-grade students in response to controls exerted by a fifth grader functioning as a student engineer. In addition, the effect of the presence of the student engineer during post-check was assessed.

METHOD

Subjects

Four students, enrolled in the first grade of a rural public school, had been described by the teacher as students who did not complete work assignments during study times, but engaged in incompatible behaviors such as talking, walking around the room, and "day dreaming". All four of these children were reported to be experiencing some trouble with their classwork. Two of the four had repeated at least one grade and were being considered by school personnel as candidates for a special remedial classroom. The behavioral engineer in the present study was a fifth grader from the same school.

Apparatus

The experiment was conducted in the first-grade room of a public school which was equipped with the usual classroom facilities and accommodated 29 students and a teacher.

The apparatus consisted of a console designed and constructed to record the behaviors in question and to give feedback to the subjects as to whether they were meeting criterion for those behaviors. Power to the entire console was controlled by a Gra-Lab Session Timer, Model 176, that determined session length. Four silent, single throw, mercury switches each controlled a Cramer Running Timer Meter, Model 636, as well as current to an outlet on the back of the console. When a subject engaged in the behavior being monitored, the console operator would place that student's switch in the "ON" position, which would activate the running-time meter and provide current to the outlet for that particular student. During Phases II through VI, electric lights were plugged into the outlets on the console which were illuminated when the student's switch was in the "ON" position.

Throughout all phases, the student engineer wore dark sunglasses with narrow eye openings to prevent direct eye-to-eye contact between the engineer and the pupils being observed.

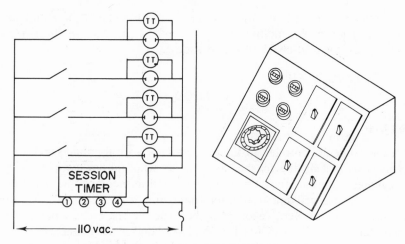

Fig. 24.1. A schematic and line drawing of console.

Procedure

Sessions were conducted each weekday morning between 9:40 and 10:00. During this time the teacher conducted a small reading group in one corner of the room and the remaining students were assigned arithmetic problems to be completed individually at their desks.

"Working" was the behavior recorded and was operationally defined as any of the following: (1) looking at the blackboard; (2) counting on fingers, pencils, crayons, *etc.*; or (3) writing on paper. When the student was engaged in any of these behaviors, his or her timer was turned "ON", and recorded "time working". When the student was engaged in behaviors other than "working", the switch was kept in the "OFF" position. These data were converted into "per cent time working" by dividing total number of minutes spent working by the total session length in minutes, times 100.

For several days before the first session, the student engineer operated the console within the classroom without lights in order to become proficient in its use and to allow the students to adapt to the observer's presence.

The study was conducted in eight phases, which will be discussed in order. During the first phase, baseline data were collected to determine the amount of time spent "working" during each session. In the second condition, lights were placed on the desks of Ricky and Dennis which were individually illuminated when either of the students met criterion for "working". Tim and Lisa, without lights, continued in the baseline phase. This phase allowed an assessment of: (1) the effect of response-contingent lights (with Ricky and Dennis) and (2) the effect of seeing another student receive response-contingent light (with Tim and Lisa).

During Phase III, Ricky and Dennis were told: "If you study a great deal during class today, you will get a little blue ticket. On that ticket you may write anything that you want to do tomorrow morning such as ___." In this blank the students could have written any activity in which they desired to engage, such as going to the gym, going to the playground, performing janitorial tasks around the school building, or any other activity that could be arranged by the experimenter. The duration of each of these activities was 15 min. On the first day, criterion for reinforcement for Dennis or Ricky was 12 min of work out of a total session length of 20 min. For the next three days, criterion was raised 2 min per day and on the fourth day was raised 1 min; thus, the successive criteria were 12, 14, 16, 18, and 19 min. From that point on, criterion remained at 19 min. That is, Ricky and Dennis had to emit working behaviors during 95% of the session in order to receive a blue ticket exchangeable for a chosen activity. At the onset of this phase, lights were placed on Tim's and Lisa's desks, but no reinforcement contingencies were stated; nor were reinforcements given for increased study time. This allowed for the assessment of the effects of response-contingent lights where reinforcement was not available and where the behaviors of the two other subjects were being reinforced for increased study time.

At the onset of the fourth condition, Tim and Lisa were told: "If you study a great deal during class today, you will get a little blue ticket. On that ticket you may write anything that you want to do tomorrow morning such as ___." The same increasing sequence of reinforcement criteria, beginning with 12 min of working behavior, was utilized with Tim and Lisa as had been used with Ricky and Dennis.

During the fifth phase, a differential reinforcement of other behavior (DRO) contingency (Bijou and Baer, 1966) was put into effect for all four children. Under this contingency, all behaviors except "working" were reinforced.

Following the DRO condition, the reinforcement contingencies for appropriate "working" behaviors that had been in effect, were reinstated. When this phase was completed, the students and the student engineer were told that the study was completed. They were thanked for their help and participation, and the experimenters, with their equipment, left the building. After this phase and before the onset of the post-check

TV condition, a time lapse of 37 days occurred. During this period, the four children, along with remaining class members, continued to work individually on arithmetic problems while the teacher was working with a reading group.

Before the post-check TV condition, a closed-circuit television camera, which scanned the seats of the four subjects, was installed in the classroom. This installation was accomplished on a weekend when classes were not in session. The camera and tripod were so concealed that the only portion visible to the class was an opening for the lens. The morning after the camera was installed, the teacher told the class that it was a piece of scientific apparatus to be used in a night class held in the room, and it was generally disregarded thereafter. In a small enclosed booth outside the classroom, a television monitor was installed whereby the student engineer, utilizing the console, again monitored time spent "working" by the four children for six consecutive school days without their knowledge.

In the final condition, a replication of baseline was conducted by having the student engineer walk into the room with the console and measure time "working". No lights were on the subjects' desks.

At the end of each session during phases when reinforcement was available, the students would gather around the console and compare their timer against their criterion time, which was written on the data sheet. If they met or exceeded criterion for reinforcement, they were given the small blue ticket. The following morning, immediately after classes began, the children who had tickets from the day before were allowed 15 min in which to engage in the activity that they had chosen. To avoid social isolation, the children were given the option of taking a friend with them for the 15-min reinforcement periods. If, at the end of the daily sessions, the students had not met criterion, they were told: "I'm sorry, you did not keep your light on long enough today. Please take your seat." Thus, the following morning, they would not have the necessary blue ticket to be excused from class. After the four students returned from their reinforcing activity, the class was instructed in the daily arithmetic session and the experimental session commenced.

The student engineer was a fifth-grader whose own classroom was operated on a token economy. The student engineer evidenced a great deal of interest in his role in this study, which led the experimenters to speculate that the Premack Principle (Premack, 1965) could be utilized to modify his academic behavior. Thus, before each of the experimental sessions, each of his teachers was consulted about his academic performance for the previous day. If his performance was above average in all classes, he was given a token by the experimenter for good academic achievement and at the end of the session was given an additional token for operating the console. If, on any occasion, his work was not above average in any of his classes, he was not given a token for academic performance but was given a token for operation of the console. The student engineer was told also that he would not be allowed to operate the console if his teachers reported that his academic performance in any classes was less than above average for any two consecutive days. The latter situation never occurred.

Reliability checks were conducted throughout the study by having a second observer record "time working" for one of the four subjects. These observations were made by the classroom teacher and the experimenters. The larger of the two "times" thus derived was then divided into the smaller and the quotient multiplied by 100, yielding per cent agreement. Reliability checks for the entire study averaged 95% agreement, with a range of 89% to 99%.

RESULTS AND DISCUSSION

Figure 24.2 shows the percentage of time spent "working" for each of the four subjects. The results of the study will be presented and discussed in the successive order of the eight phases.

During the baseline, "working" time ranged from 15% to 78%, with a mean of 52.8%. In all four subjects there is a downward trend in "working" time as the baseline progresses. A possible explanation for this decline is that the introduction of the student engineer and the console into this classroom a few days before the baseline produced a "Hawthorne effect" on working behavior; that is, the mere change in the stimuli of the classroom brought on a temporary increase in productive behaviors. The baseline data of Fig. 24.2 would then represent the decline of this effect, or the gradual return to "normal" productivity as the subjects adapted to the new stimuli. The fact that the student engineer was in the classroom for less than an hour per day would be likely to make this adaptation gradual, as the data show the change to be.

The introduction of the lights for Ricky and Dennis, in the second phase, and their response-contingent operation appears to have produced a slight (and perhaps transient) increase in Ricky's working behavior and little or no effect on Dennis'. However, the effect on Ricky's behavior

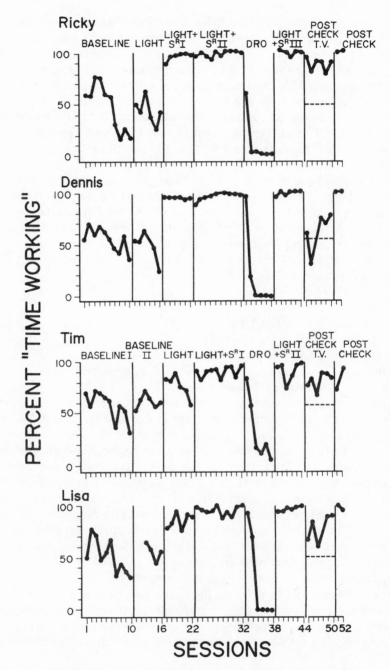

Fig. 24.2. Graph showing per cent "time working" for all students.

cannot readily be interpreted as evidence that the light's operation had a reinforcing function for this subject, because there was also an apparent increase in Tim's and Lisa's working behavior, even though there were no lights on their desks.

In the third phase, Tim and Lisa were given lights that were turned on when the subjects emitted "working" behaviors. This resulted in a clear increase in these behaviors from Lisa and a smaller (perhaps temporary) increase from Tim. It seems unlikely that all of this increase was due to the simple introduction of a novel stimulus. First, the lights could not be very novel because similar ones had been on Ricky's and Dennis' desks for six days. Second, it is improbable that the high performance produced in Tim and Lisa above their baseline performance in both cases would result from such a minor stimulus change. Therefore, it appears that at least part of the increase in Tim's and Lisa's performance in the third phase could be due to the response-contingent nature of the lights' operation. The turning on of the lights may have been a reinforcer in this phase for Tim and Lisa because they observed Ricky and Dennis being recognized and receiving reinforcements for increased "working" time, via the same light system. Thus, seeing Ricky and Dennis receive a reinforcing consequence may have served as a setting event (Bijou and Baer, 1966) that increased the reinforcing function of response-contingent lights alone for Tim and Lisa.

Before and during this study, these four students were seated together in one portion of the room. Another plausible explanation, which might partially account for the increase in time "working" on the part of Tim and Lisa, is that Ricky and Dennis, who were now working, provided fewer distractions. Typically, during the baseline phase when any one student began emitting deviant behavior, it appeared as if the other students attended to that behavior. In addition, many of the nonworking behaviors, such as conversation, required two or more individuals. It could be that part or all of the increase in time "working" on the part of Tim and Lisa could be attributed to: (1) the fact that Ricky and Dennis no longer provided distractions, (2) that Ricky and Dennis did not attend to Tim or Lisa when they emitted some distracting behavior, or (3) a combination of these two.

For Ricky and Dennis, the response-contingent lights combined with the special privileges for studying "a great deal" clearly served to increase their working behavior during the third phase. They averaged 95.8% and 95.5% working time, respectively, in this phase.

In the fourth phase, the same conditions were continued for Ricky and Dennis and their high level of performance continued. The same conditions were also applied to Tim and Lisa, and their performance improved as well.

The DRO contingency, applied to all four subjects in the fifth phase, produced a rapid decline in "working" time for each child. In the last three sessions of this phase, the mean "working" time for the four subjects combined was 2.8%. This effect, combined with the effect of the conditions of the next phase, when lights and special activities were again contingent upon "working" behaviors, suggests that the reinforcement contingencies were highly effective and were indeed responsible for the high performance attained by the four subjects during reinforcement phases. In addition, the results of the DRO condition suggest that neither the presence of novel stimuli in the room nor the status of being singled out as subjects for special treatment were variables powerful enough (at this time in the study) to exert much control over the behaviors being measured. Any tendency of these variables to increase (or decrease) the behaviors was clearly overridden by the control exerted by the reinforcement contingency.

When the subjects were surreptitiously observed via closed-circuit TV approximately six weeks after the last application of the contingent lights and special activities, their performance was generally better than it had been during the baseline. Mean "time working" was 76.7%.

To facilitate comparison between baseline performance and performance during the post-experimental follow-up, each subject's mean working time from the baseline is presented as a dashed line in the segment of Fig. 24.2 depicting the results of the TV follow-up. According to the data collected by TV, three of the four children showed a better performance six weeks after the experiment than during the baseline, suggesting that the brief application of special reinforcement contingencies during the experiment produced a lasting improvement in working behaviors.

Evidently the conditions existing before the experiment were insufficient to produce a high level of performance in these four children; but once sufficient contingencies were applied to strengthen working behaviors, the pre-experimental contingencies were adequate to maintain those working behaviors in moderate strength. This conclusion assumes, of course, that the environment after the experiment was essentially the same as it had been before. It is possible that the experiment inadvertently changed some important behavior of the teacher's, or of the subjects' peers, and that these new behaviors served to maintain the subjects' performance after the experimental contingencies were removed; however, no such changes were observed by the experimenters. Others in this class, who were described by the teacher as "good" students, were observed to be studying a comparable amount of time.

Patterson, Jones, Whittier, and Wright (1965) suggest that schedules of reinforcement and punishment on the part of parents and peer group can be critically important in maintaining behaviors of students within classrooms. It could also be that very subtle interactions were occurring along these lines that were not apparent to the experimenters.

In the second post-check, "time working" was generally found to be as high as it had been during the phases when "working" behaviors were being systematically reinforced. As is evident in Fig. 24.2, "time working" was lower during the TV post-check than during the post-check when the observer was present in the classroom. There are at least two possible explanations for the difference between the results of the two follow-up phases, and both explanations would seem to hold implications for behavior modification research that utilizes observers to obtain data.

The first explanation is that the student engineer and his console were discriminative stimuli whose presence occasioned working behaviors. The student engineer served both as an observer and a dispenser of consequences for the subjects, and would thus be likely to acquire a discriminative function. As each child took readings from the console at the end of the session to determine whether or not he or she had met criterion, it also seems feasible that the console itself could have acquired a discriminative function. If this explanation of the difference in the data of the last two phases is valid, it raises a question regarding the interpretation of certain previous studies. For example, Hawkins *et al.* (1966), in order to teach a mother to be therapeutic toward her own child, had the observer signal the mother when to reward or punish the child. In addition, they instructed the mother to limit the therapeutic procedures to the times when the experimenter-observer was present. These conditions could have resulted in the observer becoming a discriminative stimulus for appropriate behaviors, in which case the favorable data obtained by the same observer in a later follow-up may not have represented the child's "usual" behavior. These follow-up data may reflect, at least partially, the appropriate behavior occasioned by the observer's presence. This interpretation can be made of any follow-up data obtained by an observer whose presence has been (or may have been) correlated with experimental procedures (as in Hall *et al.*, 1968). Certainly it is highly probable that the student engineer in the present study would become a discriminative stimulus for the behavior in question, as he was directly connected with both the observation of the behavior in question and its subsequent reinforcement. While these data do not suggest that a more passive observer (*i.e.*, no direct contact with subjects) would become an equally strong discriminative stimulus in another setting, they do seem to raise some question as to whether and to what degree such events might occur. In order to separate the effects of observer presence, not only during post-check but throughout studies of this nature, the ideal observational medium would seem to be one where the subject is unaware of the observer's presence. The TV method of obtaining data in the present study may be one solution to this problem.

The second explanation of the difference between the findings of the two post-experimental checks is that "working" behaviors may have been more difficult to discriminate via TV than by direct observation. To determine the feasibility of this hypothesis, additional data were recorded in a similar classroom by both TV and direct observation, allowing comparison between data obtained through these two media. The subject was an adult imitating the kind of behavior exhibited by the four subjects in the experiment. A TV camera was located in the room at approximately the same distance from the subject as had been employed in the experiment. Four sessions of approximately 5 min each were held and were recorded on videotape for later viewing. The subject's behavior was also recorded by an observer located approximately 10 ft away. At the end of a session, the observer did not look at the stopwatch on which he recorded "working" time, but handed it to the experimenter who made a record of the time. The observer then watched the videotape recording of the same session and again recorded the subject's "working" time, making it possible to determine intra-observer reliability. In addition, a second observer later viewed this same recording, making it possible to assess inter-observer reliability. This second measure of accuracy of data recording was considered important to control for any "practice effect" or retention of how a particular response had been recorded during the intra-observer reliability phase.

The four sessions, each with a new observer, all yielded intra-observer reliabilities above 99%. Inter-observer reliabilities in the four sessions were obtained with four different pairs of observers and were all above 97%. These results suggest that the "working" behaviors defined in the present experiment could be recorded as accurately via TV as they could be by direct observation. Thus, it appears that the performance of the four children in the second follow-up was actually better than during the TV follow-up, rather than an artifact of the difference in media of observation.

The "working" behaviors modified in the present experiment are assumed to be correlated with the actual accomplishment of assigned work and ultimately with academic achievement. Some evidence was obtained that this assumption may be valid. The teacher reported that the four children completed a greater number of problems, and that a higher proportion of problems completed were correct during the phases of the study when "working" behaviors were reinforced than during other phases (except the follow-up phase); and that these gains were at least partially maintained after the study terminated. She also reported that the subjects exhibited more "working" behavior and less disruptive behavior throughout the day than during the experiment. Surprisingly, Tim was considered by the teacher to have shown the greatest improvement outside the arithmetic period, even though his "working" behavior in this experiment showed the least improvement and he appeared rather apathetic about the blue tickets and the special activities obtained in exchange for them.

In general it appears that the present technique has considerable promise for helping some children in school settings. It is capable of modifying the behavior of several children at one time and yet involves very little professional time. In fact, it should tend to release the teacher from some of the time she spends attempting to stop disruptive behavior for the acceleration of more adaptive behaviors. Techniques based on this one should be useful to teachers, principals, school psychologists, school social workers, and others faced with the problem of helping children more consistently to exhibit more adaptive classroom behavior.

REFERENCES

Ayllon, T. and Michael, J. The psychiatric nurse as a behavioral engineer. *Journal of the Experimental Analysis of Behavior*, 1959, **2**, 323–334.

Bijou, S. W. and Baer, D. M. Operant methods in child behavior and development. In W. Honig (Ed.), *Operant behavior: areas of research and application*. New York: Appleton-Century-Crofts, 1966. Pp. 718–789.

Hall, R. V., Lund, D., and Jackson, D. Effects of teacher attention on study behavior. *Journal of Applied Behavior Analysis*, 1968, **1**, 1–12.

Hawkins, R. P., Peterson, R. F., Schweid, E., and Bijou, S. W. Behavior therapy in the home: amelioration of problem parent-child relations with the parent in a therapeutic role. *Journal of Experimental Child Psychology*, 1966, **4**, 99–107.

Homme, L. Contingency management. *Educational Technology Monographs*, Vol. II, No. 2, 1969.

Madsen, C. H., Jr., Becker, W. C., and Thomas, D. R. Rules, praise, and ignoring: elements of elementary classroom control. *Journal of Applied Behavior Analysis*, 1968, **1**, 139–150.

Patterson, G. R., Jones, R., Whittier, J., and Wright, Mary A. A behavior modification technique for the hyperactive child. *Behaviour Research and Therapy*, 1965, **2**, 217–226.

Premack, D. *Reinforcement theory*. Paper read at the Nebraska Motivation Symposium, Lincoln, 1965.

Thomas, D. R., Becker, W. C., and Armstrong, M. Production and elimination of disruptive classroom behavior by systematically varying teacher's behaviors. *Journal of Applied Behavior Analysis*, 1968, **1**, 35–45.

Ulrich, R. and Kent, N. D. *New tactics for the education of psychologists*. Paper presented at the American Psychological Association, New York, 1966.

Ulrich, R., Stachnik, T., and Mabry, J. *Control of human behavior*. Glenview, Ill.: Scott, Foresman and Company, 1966.

Zeilberger, J., Sampen, S., and Sloane, H., Jr. Modification of a child's problem behaviors in the home with the mother as therapist. *Journal of Applied Behavior Analysis*, 1968, **1**, 47–53.

CHAPTER 9

Programmed Instruction and Teaching Machines

Every teacher has the responsibility to provide instruction which maximizes the probability that her children will learn. The use of programmed instruction (PI) and teaching machines (TM) may contribute significantly to the ease and efficiency of teaching. PI is a way of arranging academic materials in logically sequenced small steps. Each step or frame of the program provides information, requires the student to respond to the information, and gives feedback to the student regarding the correctness of his response. This is a very simplified description of PI, and the reader should keep in mind the facts that PI can be presented to the student in many formats (one of which is TM's) and that some educational materials may look like and be labeled "PI" without meeting even the most basic criteria of PI.

The developers of PI materials cite many potential advantages of individualized instruction. The child can learn the material at his own rate. The slow child is not lost as his teacher and classmates forge ahead. Similarly, the bright child can avoid the boredom of waiting while others catch up. Unlike the child whose "learning rate" is determined by the teacher, the child who learns at his own individual rate experiences less failure and consequently may develop better attitudes toward his teacher and his school work. The child using PI may also learn better, e.g., he may learn faster and retain the material for a longer period of time. In addition to these advantages for the student, PI offers several possible advantages to the teacher. She can effectively teach more children. The teacher or teacher-aide can circulate among a large class providing help when needed. If small group work is still necessary, the remainder of the class can be working on PI materials rather than becoming bored, fidgety, or disruptive. Another consequence of independent seat work on PI materials is that children learn individual responsibility, i.e., they become less dependent on the teacher's directions. Second, when the class is a heterogeneous one with a wide range of achievement levels, PI has the advantage of allowing the teacher to deal with each child at his own level rather than requiring her to teach to the average child and to lose the rest of the class. Finally, PI may be a partial solution to the problems of some disruptive children. As mentioned elsewhere in this book, behavior problems are often correlated with academic problems. A child who is experiencing a great deal of failure in his academic work may occupy his time disrupting the class. If a teacher can supply such a child with PI, she will avoid embarrassing him by singling him out for remedial work and at the same time allow him to work at a level where he can succeed and learn.

While PI has yet to prove itself clearly superior to regular classroom instruction in all of the above-mentioned ways, the obvious disadvantages of PI are few. Probably the most serious problem is that much of what is called PI is so poorly conceived and produced that any observant educator could visualize six old men, sitting around a table, each writing his own section regardless of what the others are doing and just possibly without having seen a child in years. The poor quality of many programs is due in part to a lack of research evaluating the extent to which the programs accomplish their goals. The number of satisfactory evaluative studies has been quickly exceeded by the quantity of TM's and PI materials, leaving the educator to trudge through a morass of artistically designed and enthusiastically sold books, machines, pamphlets, workbooks, and other assorted gimmicks of varying quality. In addition to the disadvantages of quantity without quality, certain forms of PI are unreasonably expensive. Perhaps some communities and educators associate expense with quality. In the case of TM's, it is our opinion that the quality of the product usually fails to match the cost when the cost drastically exceeds that of the average elementary school textbook series. Thus, the additional cost of PI is probably not warranted unless the effectiveness of the PI has been clearly documented with research evidence — not just with testimonials and advertising brochures.

As alluded to above, quantities of PI materials have been developed over the past 10 years. There is considerable variety in format, medium of presentation, type of programming, and subject matter. The following discussion will describe some of the more widely used programs, but it is not intended to be exhaustive. Perhaps the first distinction that should be made is between PI in book or workbook form and PI which is presented by a TM.

Two frequently used reading programs in workbook form are "Programmed Reading" (Buchanan, 1968) and "Reading" (Sullivan, 1968). These two series are often confused, but there are some major differences which should be pointed out. The Buchanan series is in color but requires many pre-reading or reading readiness skills such as discrimination of words from letters, letter writing, and letter recognition. It is probably best suited for first graders who have had extensive training in reading readiness or for older children who need the additional motivation provided by color and full sentences. The Sullivan program is not in color but does have some advantages over the Buchanan series. It requires relatively few pre-reading skills, and it seems to be more carefully written than the Buchanan series. The Sullivan series seems most appropriate for beginning readers who have had little reading readiness experience. Both series are based primarily on phonics as are all the reading programs discussed here.

There are two well written PI series which offer reading in addition to material in other subject areas. The "Individual Prescribed Instruction" (IPI) series published by Appleton-Century-Crofts includes reading and mathematics. These programs are in small booklets which are stored in a central clerical office. The teacher or aide writes the child a "prescription" based on completed work. The child takes the "prescription" to the supply center and receives the booklet containing the appropriate pages. One appealing aspect of the IPI material is that it is being continually revised; and since the program is in small booklet form, revisions are uncomplicated and inexpensive. One comment on the reading program — there is little reading readiness material at present and some additional instruction at this level would be advantageous for most students.

The Englemann-Becker program includes reading, mathematics and language arts. Programs in social studies and science are being developed. This series is being used primarily in Head Start/Follow-Through programs although SRA has published some of the material under the label DISTAR. Englemann and Becker will publish new programs themselves. This series is designed for children through approximately third grade in contrast to the previously described programs which are written at least through the sixth grade level. It should be noted that the Englemann-Becker program includes detailed teacher manuals which have been successfully used by paraprofessionals and that the program incorporates small group along with individual instruction.

The most well known writing program is Skinner and Krakower's "Write and See" (1968). As the child traces progressively more incomplete figures with a special pen, color appears on the page where the child has moved his pen out of the accepted boundaries. There are two difficulties with this program. First, it advances too rapidly for most beginners, e.g., the letters are smaller than most kindergarten children can handle. Second, the program is based on tracing with helping cues being gradually dropped out. Unfortunately, many teachers have found that tracing skills are not equivalent to copying skills and in fact the generalization from tracing to copying is often unsatisfactory.

Teaching machines come in many shapes and sizes. One of the simplest and least expensive is the Min-Max, a plastic box with a roller and a display window. A page of material — handwritten, typed, or professionally produced — is inserted in the box and rolled forward. The child sees the question and writes his answer in the display opening, rolls the sheet forward, observes both his and the correct answer simultaneously, and rolls the sheet to the next question.

The cost of teaching machines rises rapidly from the $15 Min-Max to the $50,000 Talking Typewriters designed by O. K. Moore and the Suppes and Atkinson Computer Assisted Instruction which is composed of a central computer facility in Stanford, California and individual consoles in schools as far away as New York and Washington, D.C. The Talking Typewriter is manufactured by Edison Responsive Environments (ERE) and consists of a completely enclosed, soundproof cubicle and a small computer. In the cubicle, the child sits before a typewriter, a display area, and a slide projection screen. The teacher inserts an ERE program or one of her own into the computer. ERE can supply an adaptation of the Sullivan reading program, and almost any other subject matter can be presented on the typewriter. The child then hears and sees a coordinated series of instruction. He types his answers on the typewriter which by freezing its keys allows him to type only the correct answers. While the Talking Typewriter is a very impressive system, there is some question regarding the benefits gained by using such expensive equipment. Only one child at a time can use the Talking Typewriter. While paraprofessionals have been used successfully as monitors who insert the programs and attend to repairs, trained teachers are required to adjust the programs for each child's particular needs. Unlike PI in book form, the Talking Typewriter provides the teacher with no information regarding the number and nature of the errors which the child makes — information which is essential to good programming and teaching. In short, the Typewriter appears to have few advantages over PI presented in book form other than attention-getting devices which require frequent and expensive repair.

Suppes and his associates (Suppes & Ihrke, 1970) have developed computer assisted mathematics and reading programs which have been used in some very interesting ways. In addition to implementation in regular classrooms, Computer Assisted Instruction (CAI) has been used in schools for the deaf where the visual computer materials have a distinct advantage over the usual teaching techniques. In New York City some 2,400 students receive CAI Dial-A-Drill arithmetic lessons at home via telephone. CAI differs in one important aspect from previously discussed programs — it responds to the nature of the child's errors automatically by presenting remedial materials specific to the error before permitting the child to proceed through the main program. Although CAI uses sophisticated computer equipment, there is only one main computer center which is connected by telephone to the many individual units and relatively inexpensive consoles around the country.

There are some obvious differences between PI presented in book form and PI presented on teaching machines. Certainly teaching machines can be expensive, especially when only one student at a time can use the machine — as is the case with the ERE Talking Typewriter. Suppes' Computer Assisted Instruction can be used by many students at once since many individual units can be connected with the central computer facility simultaneously. Thus certain teaching machines have the potential for teaching students for less than it would cost to hire teachers. Another advantage cited by proponents of teaching machines is that the machine itself may increase the students motivation to learn. It may be that students who have experienced long term failure in school will benefit from a new method of presenting material, but a carefully written program in book form accompanied by the occasional use of a tape recorder or typewriter may supply as much incentive as a more expensive apparatus. It should be pointed out that in all cases, the quality of the PI will do more to determine the success of a teaching machine than will the machine itself.

A teacher may find it useful to write her own small programs to guide students through difficult sections of material or to give the slower students an extra boost. Because of the poor quality of some PI, she may wish to adapt and improve the program for her own situation. The following discussion will outline briefly the essential components of the two basic forms of programming. Most text books on PI will have more detailed discussions of programming and there is a good programmed text on programming available by Markle (1964).

There are two theoretical approaches to programming. Skinner advocates the use of a straight line program. In an ideally written straight line program, prompts and careful fading of cues enable every student to proceed through the program, responding to every step or frame without error. Crowder (*see* Morrill, 1961, (26) proposes a branching program under the assumption that students are bound to make errors and that the program should be responsive to the nature of these errors. Thus, when a student makes an error in a branching program, he is directed to a particular section of the program designed to deal with the specific error being made. While there are advantages to both types of programming, most teachers will find the straight line program easier to write. The development of a straight line program includes the following steps:

1. Specify precisely the terminal behavior, i.e., what you expect the child to know or be able to do at the completion of the program. For example, you might want the child to be able to add numbers 1 through 9.
2. List all the specific behaviors which you do not wish to teach but which are prerequisites for beginning the program, e.g., counting from 1 to 18. Pretests should be given to assess whether the child does in fact have all of these prerequisite behaviors.
3. List all the specific behaviors which the child must learn in order to perform the terminal behavior. One example of a behavior which is necessary for adding is associating the correct quantity with the written number.
4. For each specific behavior you wish to teach the child, compose a sequential series of frames which: (a) present a small amount of information, (b) require the child to make a response to this information either by composing a response or by selecting a response from several which you provide, and (c) make it highly probable that the child will make the correct response. For example, two initial frames for teaching the relation between quantity and the written number might look something like this

While the response of A, filling in 2 triangles, and B, circling the 2, may appear obvious, these frames illustrate two skills the child should have before beginning the program. First, the child must be able to follow the instructions: "Fill in the blank" and "circle the correct answer." Second, the child must be able to supply himself with the correct instruction when he sees the frames. Each frame should require the child to move slightly closer to the specific terminal response.

5. Provide the correct answer to each frame immediately.
6. Gradually remove all help or prompts so that the child can produce the terminal behavior unaided at the completion of the program.

By now you may be harboring serious doubts about the desirability of using PI. The following quotation succinctly expresses our attitude regarding programmed instruction:

> One of the main differences between a textbook and a program is that a textbook teaches only when students have been given some extraneous reason for studying it. A program contains its own reasons. Fortunately for us, the human organism is reinforced by many things. Success is one of them. A baby shakes a rattle because the production of noise is reinforcing, and adults put jigsaw puzzles together and work crossword puzzles for no more obvious reason than they come out right. In a good program, the student makes things come out right; he makes things work; he brings order out of chaos. A good program helps him do so. It makes right responses highly probable—just short of telling him what they are ... Many people resist making a student's task easy, and the beginning programmer may find himself unwilling to give a response away. As a teacher he has felt the need to keep students under aversive control, and he may not yet be fully aware of his power to control them in other ways.
>
> A program is also reinforcing because it clarifies progress. It has a definite size. The student knows when he is half-way through, and when he has finished. Because of all this a good program pulls the student forward. He may feel exhausted when he has finished, but he does not need to force himself to work (Skinner, 1969, p. 4).*

The best advice we can give is this. If you feel your present material is inadequate—give PI a try. It probably won't be any worse than what you're using and it may be better—especially if you use a little ingenuity in adapting and improving the program and if you are discriminating in your selection of a program. Companies that produce the better programs can often supply you with research information regarding the success of the program. Take particular note of the types of children participating

---

*Reprinted with permission of the Editor, from B. F. Skinner's "Contingency management in the classroom," in *Education*, 1969, **90**, 2, 93–100. Published by Cassel & Hoye, Milwaukee, Wisconsin. Copyright © 1969 by Managing Editor, *Education*, University of Wisconsin, Milwaukee, Wisconsin 53201.

in the research and compare them to your own. Some programs may be successful with bright middle class children but are too advanced for the same aged children who have had very little training and encouragement in academic pursuits. Also note the performance of the research children on standardized achievement tests. These data will allow you to make some comparisons with other academic materials. Finally, if you decide to use PI, keep careful records of the errors your children make — how many they make and where they occur. This information will quickly disclose the weak spots in any program and will indicate where the teacher can use her programming skills to provide supplementary materials. No program is perfect for all children. PI should not be viewed as a way for teachers to get out of teaching, but rather as a way to provide better instruction. It is the teacher's responsibility to make adjustments in her program just as it is the publisher's obligation to continually evaluate and revise the program. For this reason the publisher of your program may be interested in your error rates as he plans for revisions of the program.

The first two articles reprinted in this chapter were included to provide the reader with additional background material and a discussion of some of the problems confronting the rapidly expanding area of programmed instruction and teaching machines. Morrill (1961) (26), presents a particularly good outline of the programming process. Special attention should be given to Skinner's (1963) (25), discussion of the potential misuse of teaching machines as well as his reply to those who are skeptical about the effectiveness of programmed materials.

Williams, Gilmore, and Malpass (1968) (28), describe an experiment in which usual classroom routine, programmed instruction in textbook form, and programmed instruction presented on a teaching machine were compared with respect to their influence on certain reading skills. It should be emphasized that the findings reflect the contribution of PI over and above usual classroom instruction and not the relative effectiveness of the various procedures.

The Reese and Parnes (1970) article, (27), is especially interesting in light of the criticism that PI may inhibit the creativity of the students. While the control classroom curricula did not include teaching creativity, it is clear that PI can be effective in developing the creative behaviors of students.

In the final article (Atkinson, 1968) (29), the Stanford Computer Assisted Instruction (CAI) system is described. The student responds to the CAI by writing with a light pen on a television screen or cathode ray tube. This article differs slightly from many of the others in the book in terms of the language and concepts which are used. However, it is well written and the last section on the results of the first year of operation clearly points out the success of the program.

ARTICLE 25

Reflections on a Decade
of Teaching Machines*

B. F. SKINNER

Harvard University

To the general public, and to many educators as well, the nature and scope of teaching machines are by no means clear. There is an extraordinary need for more and better teaching, and any enterprise which may help to meet it will not be left to develop normally. The demand for information about teaching machines has been excessive. Articles and books have been published and lectures given; symposia have been arranged, and conferences and workshops have been held and courses taught. Those who have had anything useful to say have said it far too often, and those who have had nothing to say have been no more reticent.

Education is big business. Teaching machines were soon heralded as a growth industry, and fantastic predictions of the sales of programmed texts were circulated. Devices have been sold as teaching machines which were not well built or designed with any understanding of their function or the practical exigencies of their use. No author was ever more warmly received by a publisher than the author of a programed text. Many programs, to be used either with machines or in textbook form, have been marketed without adequate evaluation.

TEACHERS AND DEVICES

The "mechanizing of education" has been taken literally in the sense of doing by machine what was formerly done by people. Some of the so-called computer-based teaching machines are designed simply to dupli-

---

*Reprinted with the permission of the author and the publisher from *Teachers College Record*, Vol. 65, 1963, pp. 168–177.

cate the behavior of teachers. To automate education with mechanical teachers is like automating banking with mechanical tellers and book-keepers. What is needed in both cases is an analysis of the functions to be served, followed by the design of appropriate equipment. Nothing we now know about the learning process calls for very elaborate instrumentation.

Educational specialists have added to the confusion by trying to assimilate the principles upon which teaching machines are based to older theories of learning and teaching.

In the broadest sense, teaching machines are simply devices which make it possible to apply our technical knowledge of human behavior to the practical field of education (Skinner, 1954). Teaching is the expediting of learning. Students learn without teaching, but the teacher arranges conditions under which they learn more rapidly and effectively. In recent years, the experimental analysis of behavior has revealed many new facts about relevant conditions. The growing effectiveness of an experimental analysis is still not widely recognized, even within the behavioral sciences themselves, but the implications of some of its achievements for education can no longer be ignored.

An important condition is the relation between behavior and its consequences; learning occurs when behavior is "reinforced." The power of reinforcement is not easily appreciated by those who have not had firsthand experience in its use or have not at least seen some sort of experimental demonstration. Extensive changes in behavior can be brought about by arranging so-called contingencies of reinforcement. Various kinds of contingencies are concealed in the teacher's discussions with his students, in the books he gives them to read, in the charts and other materials he shows them, in the questions he asks them, and in the comments he makes on their answers. An experimental analysis clarifies these contingencies and suggests many improvements.

SHAPING BY PROGRAM

An important contribution has been the so-called "programing" of knowledge and skills — the construction of carefully arranged sequences of contingencies leading to the terminal performances which are the object of education. The teacher begins with whatever behavior the student brings to the instructional situation; by selective reinforcement, he changes that behavior so that a given terminal performance is more and more closely approximated. Even with lower organisms, quite complex behaviors can be "shaped" in this way with surprising speed; the human organism is presumably far more sensitive. So important is the principle of programming that it is often regarded as the main contribution of the teaching machine movement, but the experimental analysis of behavior has much more to contribute to a technology of education.

The direct contact which often exists between teacher and student favors the construction of programed sequences, and the teacher who understands the process can profit from the opportunity to improvise programs as he goes. Programs can be constructed in advance, however, which will successfully shape the behavior of most students without local modifications, and many of them can conveniently be mediated by mechanical devices. Laboratory studies have shown that contingencies emphasizing subtle properties of behavior can often be arranged *only* through instrumentation. There are potentially as many different kinds of teaching machines as there are kinds of contingencies of reinforcement.

Teaching machines which present material to the student and differentially reinforce his responses in well constructed programs differ in several ways from self-testing devices and self-scoring test forms, as well as from the training devices which have long been used by industry and the armed services. As Pressey (1926) pointed out many years ago, a student will learn while taking a multiple-choice test if he is told immediately whether his answers are right or wrong. He learns not to give wrong answers again, and his right answers are strengthened. But testing has traditionally been distinguished from teaching for good reason. Before using a self-testing device, the student must already have studied the subject and, presumably, learned most of what he is to learn about it. Tests usually occupy only a small part of his time. Their main effect is motivational: A poor score induces him to study harder and possibly more effectively. Materials designed to be used in self-testing devices have recently been programed, but the contingencies which prevail during a test are not favorable to the shaping and maintaining of behavior.

Conventional training devices arrange conditions under which students learn, usually by simulating the conditions under which they eventually perform. Their original purpose was to prevent injury or waste during early stages of learning, but attention has recently been given to programing the actual behaviors they are designed to teach. To the extent that they expedite learning, they are teaching machines. Terminal performances have usually been selected for practical reasons, but a more promising possibility is the analysis and programing of basic motor and perceptual skills—a goal which should have an important place in any statement of educational policy.

In arranging contingencies of reinforcement, machines do many of the things teachers do; in that sense, they teach. The resulting instruction is not impersonal, however. A machine presents a program designed by someone who knew what was to be taught and could prepare an appropriate series of contingencies. It is most effective if used by a teacher who knows the student, has followed his progress, and can adapt available machines and materials to his needs. Instrumentation simply makes it possible for programer and teacher to provide conditions which maximally expedite learning. Instrumentation is thus secondary, but it is nevertheless inevitable if what is now known about behavior is to be used in an effective technology.

THE NEW PEDAGOGY

Any practical application of basic knowledge about teaching and learning is, of course, pedagogy. In the United States at least, the term is now discredited, but by emphasizing an analysis of learning processes, teaching machines and programed instruction have been responsible for some improvement in its status. The significance of the teaching machine movement can be indicated by noting the astonishing lack of interest which other proposals for the improvement of education show in the teaching process.

Find Better Teachers

In his *Talks to Teachers*, William James (1899) insisted that there was nothing wrong with the American school system which could not be corrected by "impregnating it with geniuses." It is an old formula: If you cannot solve a problem, find someone who can. If you do not know how to teach, find someone who knows or can find out for himself. But geniuses are in short supply, and good teachers do not come ready-made. Education would no doubt be improved if, as Conant (1963) has repeatedly pointed out, good teachers who know and like the subjects they teach could be attracted and retained. But something more is needed. It is not true that "the two essentials of a good teacher are (a) enthusiasm and (b) thorough knowledge of and interest in his subject" (Helwig, 1960, p. 845). A third essential is knowing how to teach.

Emulate Model Schools

Rickover's (1959) criticism of the present American school system is well known. His only important positive suggestion is to set up model schools, staffed by model teachers. The implication is that we already have, or at least can have for the asking, schools which need no improvement and whose methods can be widely copied. This is a dangerous assumption if it discourages further inquiry into instruction.

Simplify What is to be Learned

Unsuccessful instruction is often blamed on refractory subject matters. Difficulties in teaching the verbal arts are often attributed to the inconsistencies and unnecessary complexities of a language. The pupil is taught manuscript handwriting because it more closely resembles printed forms. He is taught to spell only those words he is likely to use. Phonetic alphabets are devised to help him learn to read. It may be easier to teach such materials, but teaching itself is not thereby improved. Effective teaching would correct these pessimistic estimates of available instructional power.

Reorganize What is to be Learned

The proper structuring of a subject matter is perhaps a part of pedagogy, but it can also serve as a mode of escape. Proposals for improving education by reorganizing what is to be learned usually contain an implicit assumption that students will automatically perceive and remember anything which has "good form"—a doctrine probably traceable to Gestalt psychology. Current revisions of high school curricula often seem to lean heavily on the belief that if what the student is to be taught has been "structured," he cannot help understanding and remembering it (Bruner, 1960). Other purposes of such revisions cannot be questioned: Materials should be up to date and well organized. But a high school presentation acceptable to a current physicist is no more easily taught or easily remembered than the out-of-date and erroneous material to be found in texts of a decade or more ago. Similarly, the accent of a native speaker encountered in a language laboratory is no more easily learned than a bad accent. No matter how well structured a subject matter may be, it must still be taught.

Improve Presentation

Pedagogy can also be avoided if what is to be learned can be made memorable. Audio-visual devices are often recommended for this purpose. Many of their other purposes are easily defended. It is not always easy to bring the student into contact with the things he is to learn about. Words are easily imported into the classroom, and books, lectures, and discussions are therefore staples of education; but this is often an unfortunate bias. Audio-visual devices can enlarge the student's nonverbal experience. They can also serve to present material clearly and conveniently. Their use in attracting and holding the student's attention and in dramatizing a subject matter in such a way that it is almost automatically remembered must be questioned, however. It is especially tempting to turn to them for these purposes when the teacher does not use punitive methods to "make students study." But the result is not the same. When a student observes or attends to something in order to see it more clearly or remember it more effectively, his behavior must have been shaped and maintained by reinforcement. The temporal order was important. Certain reinforcing events must have occurred *after* the student looked at, read, and perhaps tested himself on the material. But when colored displays, attractive objects, filmed episodes, and other potentially reinforcing materials are used to attract attention, they must occur *before* the student engages in these activities. Nothing can reinforce a student for *paying* attention if it has already been used to *attract* his attention. Material which attracts attention fails to prepare the student to attend to material which is not interesting on its face, and material which is naturally memorable fails to prepare him to study and recall things which are not, in themselves, unforgettable. A well prepared instructional film may appear to be successful in arousing interest in a given subject, and parts of it may be remembered without effort, but it has not taught the student that a subject may *become* interesting when more closely examined or that intensive study of something which is likely to be overlooked may have reinforcing consequences.

Multiply Contacts between Teacher and Student

Audio-visual devices, particularly when adapted to television, are also used to improve education by bringing one teacher into contact with an indefinitely large number of students. This can be done, of course, without analyzing how the teacher teaches, and it emphasizes a mode of communication which has two serious disadvantages: The teacher cannot see the effect he is having on his students, and large numbers of students must proceed at the same pace. Contributions to pedagogy may be made in designing programs for educational television, but the mere multiplication of contacts is not itself an improvement in teaching.

Expand the Educational System

Inadequate education may be corrected by building more schools and recruiting more teachers so that the total quantity of education is increased, even though there is no change in efficiency.

Raise Standards

Least effective in improving teaching are demands for higher standards. We may agree that students will be better educated when they learn more, but how are they to be induced to do so? Demands for higher standards usually come from critics who have least to offer in improving teaching itself.

The movement symbolized by the teaching machine differs from other proposals in two ways. It emphasizes the direct improvement of teaching on the principle that no enterprise can improve itself to the fullest extent without examining its basic processes. In the second place, it emphasizes the implementation of basic knowledge. If instructional practices violate many basic principles, it is only in part because these principles are not widely known. The teacher cannot put what he knows into practice in the classroom. Teaching machines and programed instruction constitute a direct attack on the problem of implementation. With appropriate administrative changes, they may bridge the gap between an effective pedagogical theory and actual practice.

EDUCATIONAL GOALS

An effective technology of teaching calls for a re-examination of educational objectives. What is the teacher's actual assignment? Educational policy is usually stated in traditional terms: The teacher is to "impart knowledge," "improve skills," "develop rational faculties," and so on. That education is best, says Dr. Hutchins (1963), which develops "intellectual power." The task of the teacher is to change certain inner processes or states. He is to improve the mind.

The role of the teacher in fostering mental prowess has a certain prestige. It has always been held superior to the role of the trainer of motor skills. And it has the great advantage of being almost invulnerable to criticism. In reply to the complaint that he has not produced observable results, the teacher of the mind can lay claim to invisible achievements. His students may not be able to read, but he has only been trying to make sure they wanted to learn. They may not be able to solve problems, but he has been teaching them simply to think creatively. They may be ignorant of specific facts, but he has been primarily concerned with their general interest in a field.

Traditional specifications of the goals of education have never told the teacher what to do upon a given occasion. No one knows how to alter a mental process or strengthen a mental power, and no one can be sure that he has done so when he has tried. There have been many good teachers who have supposed themselves to be working on the minds of their students, but their actual practices and the results of those practices can be analyzed in other ways. The well educated student is distinguished by certain characteristics. What are they, and how can they be produced? Perhaps we could answer by redefining traditional goals: Instead of imparting knowledge, we could undertake to bring about those changes in behavior which are said to be the conspicuous manifestations of knowledge, or we could set up the behavior which is the mark of a man possessing well developed rational power. But mentalistic formulations are warped by irrelevant historical accidents. The behavior of the educated student is much more effectively analyzed directly as such.

Contrary to frequent assertions, a behavioristic formulation of human behavior is not a crude positivism which rejects mental processes because they are not accessible to the scientific public (Skinner, 1963a). It does not emphasize the rote learning of verbal responses. It does not neglect the complex systems of verbal behavior which are said to show that a student has had an idea, or developed a concept, or entertained a proposition. It does not ignore the behavior involved in the intellectual and ethical problem solving called "thinking." It does not overlook the value judgments said to be invoked when we decide to teach one thing rather than another or when we defend the time and effort given to education. It is merely an effective formulation of those activities of teacher and student which have always been the concern of educational specialists (Skinner, 1961).

Not all behavioristic theories of learning are relevant, however. A distinction is commonly drawn between learning and performance. Learning is said to be a change in some special part of the organism, possibly the nervous system, of which behavior is merely the external and often erratic sign. With modern techniques, however, behavior can be much more successfully studied and manipulated than any such inner system, even when inferences about the latter are drawn from the behavior with the help of sophisticated statistics. An analysis of learning which concentrates on the behavior applies most directly to a technology, for the task of the teacher is to bring about changes in the student's behavior. His methods are equally conspicuous: He makes changes in the environment. A teaching method is simply a way of arranging an environment which expedites learning.

MANAGING CONTINGENCIES

Such a formulation is not easily assimilated to the traditional psychology of learning. The teacher may arrange contingencies of reinforcement to set up new *forms* of response, as in teaching handwriting and speech or nonverbal forms of behavior in the arts, crafts, and sports. He may arrange contingencies to bring responses under new kinds of *stimulus control*, as in teaching the student to read or draw from copy, or to behave effectively upon other kinds of occasions. Current instructional programs designed to fulfill such assignments are mainly verbal, but comparable contingencies generate nonverbal behavior, including perceptual and motor skills and various kinds of intellectual and ethical self-management.

A second kind of programing maintains the student's behavior in strength. The form of the response and the stimulus control may not change; the student is simply more likely to respond. Some relevant methods are traditionally discussed under the heading of motivation. For example, we can strengthen behavior by introducing new reinforcers or making old ones more effective, as in giving the student better reasons for getting an education. The experimental analysis of behavior suggests another important possibility: Schedule available reinforcers more effectively. Appropriate terminal schedules of reinforcement will maintain the student's interest, make him industrious and persevering, stimulate his curiosity, and so on; but less demanding schedules, carefully designed to maintain the behavior at every stage, must come first. The programing of schedules of reinforcement is a promising alternative to the aversive control which, in spite of repeated reforms, still prevails in educational practice.

In neglecting programing, teaching methods have merely followed the lead of the experimental psychology of learning, where the almost universal practice has been to submit an organism immediately to terminal contingencies of reinforcement (Skinner, 1963b). A maze or a discrimination problem, for example, is learned only if the subject acquires appropriate behavior before the behavior he brings to the experiment has extinguished. The intermediate contingencies are largely accidental. The differences in behavior and in rate of learning which appear under these conditions are often attributed to inherited differences in ability.

In maximizing the student's success, programed instruction differs from so-called trial-and-error learning where the student is said to learn from his mistakes. At best, he learns not to make mistakes again. A successful response may survive, but trial-and-error teaching makes little provision for actually strengthening it. The method seems inevitably committed to aversive control. For the same reason, programed instruction does not closely resemble teaching patterned on everyday communication. It is usually not enough simply to tell the student something or induce him to read a book; he must be told or must read and then be questioned. In this "tell-and-test" pattern, the test is not given to measure what he has learned, but to show him what he has not learned and thus induce him to listen and read more carefully in the future. A similar basically aversive pattern is widespread at the college level, where the instructor assigns material and then examines on it. The student may learn to read carefully, to make notes, to discover for himself how to study, and so on, because in doing so he avoids aversive consequences, but he has not necessarily been taught. Assigning-and-testing is not teaching. The aversive by-products, familiar to everyone in the field of education, can be avoided through the use of programed positive reinforcement.

Many facts and principles derived from the experimental analysis of behavior are relevant to the construction of effective programs leading to terminal contingencies. The facts and principles are often difficult, but they make up an indispensable armamentarium of the effective teacher and educational specialist. We have long since passed the point at which our basic knowledge of human behavior can be applied to education through the use of a few general principles.

PRINCIPLE AND PRACTICE

The difference between general principles and an effective technology can be seen in certain efforts to assimilate the principles of programed instruction to earlier theories. Programed instruction has, for example, been called "Socratic." It is true that Socrates proceeded by small steps and often led his students through an argument with a series of verbal prompts, but the example often cited to illustrate his method suggests that he was unaware of an important detail—namely, that prompts must eventually be "vanished" in order to put the student on his own. In the famous scene in the *Meno*, Socrates demonstrates his theory that learning is simply recollection by leading an uneducated slave boy through Pythagoras's Golden Theorem. The boy responds with the rather timid compliance to be expected under the circumstances and never without help. Although Socrates himself and some of those among his listeners who were already familiar with the theorem may have understood the proof better at the end of the scene, there is no evidence whatsoever that the boy understood it or could reconstruct it. In this example of Socratic instruction, at least, the student almost certainly learned nothing.[1]

A seventeenth-century anticipation of programed instruction has also been found in the work of Comenius, who advocated teaching in small steps, no step being too great for the student who was about to take it. Programing is sometimes described simply as breaking material into a large number of small pieces, arranged in a plausible genetic order. But size of step is not enough. Something must happen to help the student take each step, and something must happen as he takes it. An effective program is usually composed of small steps, but the whole story is not to be found in Comenius's philosophy of education.

Another venerable principle is that the student should not proceed until he has fully understood what he is to learn at a given stage. Several writers have quoted E. L. Thorndike to this effect, who wrote in 1912,

> If, by a miracle of mechanical ingenuity, a book could be so arranged that only to him who had done what was directed on page one would page two become visible, and so on, much that now requires personal instruction could be managed by print.

In commenting on this passage, Finn and Perrin (1962) have written, "... Here are the insights of a genius. History can very often teach us a lesson in humility—and it does here. The interesting question is: Why couldn't we see it then?" We might also ask, why couldn't Thorndike see it then? He remained active in education for at least 30 years, but he turned from this extraordinarily promising principle to another and—as it proved—less profitable approach to educational psychology.

---

[1]The program of the *Meno* episode constructed by Cohen (1962) is an improvement in that the student responds with less prompting.

It is always tempting to argue that earlier ideas would have been effective if people had only paid attention to them. But a good idea must be more than right. It must command attention; it must make its own way because of what it does. Education does not need principles which will improve education as soon as people observe them; it needs a technology so powerful that it cannot be ignored. No matter how insightful the anticipation of modern principles in earlier writers may seem to have been, something was lacking or education would be much further advanced. We are on the threshold of a technology which will be not only right but effective (Skinner, 1968).

CRITERIA OF RESEARCH

A science of behavior makes its principal contribution to a technology of education through the analysis of useful contingencies of reinforcement. It also suggests a new kind of educational research. Thorndike never realized the potentialities of his early work on learning because he turned to the measurement of mental abilities and to matched-group comparisons of teaching practices. He pioneered in a kind of research which, with the encouragement offered by promising new statistical techniques was to dominate educational psychology for decades. It led to a serious neglect of the process of instruction.

There are practical reasons why we want to know whether a given method of instruction is successful or whether it is more successful than another. We may want to know what changes it brings about in the student, possibly in addition to those it was designed to effect. The more reliable our answers to such questions, the better. But reliability is not enough. Correlations between test scores and significant differences between group means tell us less about the behavior of the student in the act of learning than results obtained when the investigator can manipulate variables and assess their effects in a manner characteristic of laboratory research. The practices evaluated in studies of groups of students have usually not been suggested by earlier research of a similar nature, but have been drawn from tradition, from the improvisations of skillful teachers, or from suggestions made by theorists working intuitively or with other kinds of facts. No matter how much they may have stimulated the insightful or inventive researcher, the evaluations have seldom led directly to the design of improved practices.

The contrast between statistical evaluation and the experimental analysis of teaching has an illuminating parallel in the field of medicine.

Various drugs, regimens, surgical procedures, and so on must be examined with respect to a very practical question: Does the health of the patient improve? But "health" is only a general description of specific physio-logical processes, and "improvement" is, so to speak, merely a by-product of the changes in these processes induced by a given treatment. Medicine has reached the point where research on specific processes is a much more fertile source of new kinds of therapy than evaluations in terms of improvement in health. Similarly, in education, no matter how important improvement in the student's performance may be, it remains a by-product of specific changes in behavior resulting from the specific changes in the environment wrought by the teacher. Educational research patterned on an experimental analysis of behavior leads to a much better understanding of these basic processes. Research directed toward the behavior of the individual student has, of course, a long history, but it can still profit greatly from the support supplied by an experimental analysis of behavior.

This distinction explains why those concerned with experimental analyses of learning are not likely to take matched-group evaluations of teaching machines and programed instruction very seriously. It is not possible, of course, to evaluate either machines or programs *in general* because only specific instances can be tested, and available examples by no means represent all the possibilities; but even the evaluation of a given machine or program in the traditional manner may not give an accurate account of its effects. For example, those who are concerned with improvement are likely to test the student's capacity to give right answers. Being right has, of course, practical importance, but it is only one result of instruction. It is a doubtful measure of "knowledge" in any useful sense. We say that a student "knows the answer" if he can select it from an array of choices, but this does not mean that he could have given it without help. The right answer to one question does not imply right answers to all questions said to show the "possession of the same fact." Instructional programs are often criticized as repetitious or redundant when they are actually designed to put the student in possession of a number of different responses "expressing the same proposition." Whether such instruction is successful is not shown by any one right answer.

CORRECT OR EDUCATED?

A preoccupation with correct answers has led to a common misunder-standing of programed materials. Since a sentence with a blank to be filled in by the student resembles a test item, it is often supposed that the response demanded by the blank is what is learned. In that case, a student could not be learning much because he may respond correctly in 19 out of 20 frames and must therefore already have known 95 per cent of the answers. The instruction which occurs as he completes an item comes from having responded to other parts of it. The extent of this instruction cannot be estimated from the fact that he is right 19 out of 20 times, either while pursuing a program *or on a subsequent test*. Nor will this statistic tell us whether other conditions are important. Is it most profitable for the student to execute the response by writing it out, by speaking it aloud, by speaking it silently, or by reading it in some other way? These procedures may or may not have different effects on a selected "right-answer" statistic, but no one statistic will cover all their effects.

Research in teaching must not, of course, lose sight of its main objective — to make education more effective. But improvement as such is a questionable dimension of the behavior of either teacher or student. Dimensions which are much more intimately related to the conditions the teacher arranges to expedite learning must be studied even though they do not contribute to improvement or contribute to it in a way which is not immediately obvious.

The changes in the behavior of the individual student brought about by manipulating the environment are usually immediate and specific. The results of statistical comparisons of group performances usually are not. From his study of the behavior of the individual student, the investigator gains a special kind of confidence. He usually knows what he has done to get one effect and what he must do to get another.

Confidence *in* education is another possible result of an effective technology of teaching. Competition between the various cultures of the world, warlike or friendly, is now an accepted fact, and the role played by education in strengthening and perpetuating a given way of life is clear. No field is in greater need of our most powerful intellectual resources. An effective educational technology based upon an experimental analysis will bring it support commensurate with its importance in the world today.

REFERENCES

Bruner, J. S. *The process of education*. Cambridge: Harvard Univer. Press, 1960.

Cohen, I. S. Programed learning and the Socratic dialogue. *Amer. Psychologist*, 1962, **17**, 772–75.

Conant, J. B. *The education of American teachers.* New York: McGraw-Hill, 1963.

Finn, J. D. and Perrin, D. G. *Teaching machines and programmed learning: A survey of the industry, 1962.* Washington, D.C.: U.S. Office of Education, 1962.

Helwig, J. Training of college teachers. *Sci.,* 1960, **132**, 845.

Hutchins, R. M. *On education.* Santa Barbara: Center for the Study of Democratic Institutions, 1963.

James, W. *Talks to teachers.* New York: Holt, 1899.

Pressey, S. J. A simple device for teaching, testing, and research in learning. *Sch. & Soc.,* 1926, **23**, 373–76.

Rickover, H. G. *Education and freedom.* New York: Dutton, 1959.

Skinner, B. F. The science of learning and the art of teaching. *Harvard Educ. Rev.,* 1954, **24**, 86–97.

Skinner, B. F. Why we need teaching machines. *Harvard Educ. Rev.,* 1961, **31**, 377–98.

Skinner, B. F. Behaviorism at fifty. *Sci.,* 1963 a, **140**, 951–58.

Skinner, B. F. Operant behavior. *Amer. Psychologist,* 1963 b, **18**, 503–15.

Skinner, B. F. *The technology of teaching.* New York: Appleton-Century-Crofts, 1968.

Thorndike, E. L. *Education.* New York: Macmillan, 1912.

ARTICLE 26

Teaching Machines: A Review*[1]

CHARLES S. MORRILL[2]

The same forces which have characterized the evolution of general educational practices are inherent to the history of the new science of automated teaching. As a result of the expansion and multiplying complexities of political, economic, and social interests, there developed an ever increasing need for the rapid education of large numbers of people. New educational objectives demanded new methods of instruction, and the history of education is marked by many diverse attempts at establishing more efficient teaching procedures. Once again teaching methods must be reevaluated. Rigid adherence to the principle of personal teacher-student relationships no longer seems feasible — an instructional system more appropriate for present-day needs must be established. It is probable that the use of automated teaching devices can fill this need in the method of education. As Corrigan (1959) has suggested:

> The automated teaching method has grown out of a pressing need. This need has been created by a two-fold technical training problem. As advances in science and technology have beem made, there has been an ever increasing demand for well-trained instructors; at the same time the availability of these trained persons has been diminishing. This situation is aggravated further by the increased scope and complexity of subjects, and the ever increasing ratio between number of instructors and students (p. 24).

*Reprinted from the *Psychological Bulletin*, Vol. 58, 1961, pp. 363–375, by permission of the American Psychological Association.

[1]The research reported in this document was supported by the Department of the Air Force under Air Force Contract AF-33-(600) 39852.

[2]The author wishes to acknowledge the valuable editorial assistance of Sylvia Pilsucki.

CURRENT TRENDS IN AUTOMATED
TEACHING MACHINES

Current interest in the area of automated teaching machines is well illustrated by the simple index of frequency-per-year of published teaching machine articles. Fry, Bryan, and Rigney (1960) report that for the years prior to 1948 there are only 6 references, whereas through 1959 there were more than 50 reports published.

The grandfather of automated teaching machines is Sydney L. Pressey (1926, 1927), who designed machines for automated teaching during the mid-1920s. His first device was exhibited and described at the American Psychological Association (APA) meetings in 1924; an improved device was exhibited in 1925 at the APA meetings. Both forms of the apparatus automatically performed simultaneous administration and scoring of a test and taught informational and drill material. Pressey's device, about the size of a portable typewriter, presented material to the subject via a small window. Four keys were located alongside the apparatus. If the student activated a key corresponding to the correct answer, the machine advanced to the next item. If his response was incorrect, the machine scored an error and did not advance to the next item until the correct answer was chosen. The capacity of the drum was 30 two-line typewritten items; the paper on which the questions appeared was carried as in a typewriter.

In 1927, Pressey summarized his effort as follows:

> The paper reports an effort to develop an apparatus for teaching drill material which (a) should keep each question or problem before the learner until he finds the correct answer, (b) should inform him at once regarding the correctness of each response he makes, (c) should continue to put the subject through the series of questions until the entire lesson has been learned, but (d) should eliminate each question from consideration as the correct answer for it has been mastered (p. 552).

In 1930, Peterson devised a self-scoring, immediate feedback device. The Chemo Card, as this device was later called, utilized the technique of multiple choice. A special ink was used by the student in marking his answer. The mark appeared red if the answer was incorrect; a dark color resulted if the answer was correct. Although Pressey's notions and the Chemo Card might have stimulated an interest in automated teaching techniques in the twenties, educators and researchers obviously were not at that time ready for this advanced concept of teaching. Automated teaching did not take hold.

In 1932, Pressey published an article describing a kind of answer sheet which could be scored by an automatic scoring device. This apparatus recorded errors by item and thus provided the instructor with clues as to what questions needed further instruction. In 1934, Little experimented with this device as well as with the device originated by Pressey in 1926. His results favored the use of automated devices in contrast to regular classroom techniques.

The next appearance of automated teaching literature came a considerable number of years later. During World War II, the Automatic Rater was used by the Navy for training. This device projected a question on a small screen; the subject's response consisted of pushing one of five buttons.

In 1950, Pressey described a new automated device called the Punchboard. Multiple-choice questions were presented to the student. The key answer sheet inside the Punchboard contained holes opposite the correct answers only. If the answer was correct, the student's pencil penetrated deeply; if incorrect, the pencil did not penetrate the paper significantly. Angell and Troyer in 1948 and Angell in 1949 reported the results of using the Punchboard. Both studies suggested the superiority of this method over traditional classroom procedures.

In 1954, Skinner published "The Science of Learning and the Art of Teaching," which provided the basis for the development of his teaching machines. In this article, he stressed the importance of reinforcement in teaching and suggested teaching machines as a method of providing this needed reinforcement for the learner.

Reports concerning the Subject-Matter Trainer began to appear in 1955 (Besnard, Briggs, Mursch, & Walker, 1955; Besnard, Briggs, & Walker, 1955). This electromechanical device is a large multiple-choice machine used essentially for training and testing in the identification of components and in general verbal subject matter. Extensive research has been done with this device because of its considerable flexibility, i.e., it allows several modes of operation for self-instruction: variety of programmed subject matter, drop-out feature after items have been mastered, etc.

The Pull-Tab, used experimentally by Bryan and Rigney in 1956, was a device in which the subject received not only a "right" or "wrong" indication after his choice but also a somewhat detailed explanation of "why" a response was incorrect. In 1949, Briggs had found in experimenting with the Punchboard that learning is significantly enhanced by immediate knowledge of results. Bryan and Rigney's data illustrated that the combination of immediate knowledge of results plus explanation, if the student is in error, produced significantly higher scores on a criterion test than if no explanation had been given. The importance of this research from a historical point of view is that it investigated immediate knowledge of results as a factor existing on a continuum with varying degrees of effect. Up to this point any comparison involving the effectiveness of teaching machines had been one between classroom instruction and the "new" machine under consideration. In Briggs' and in Bryan and Rigney's research, however, we see the beginning of a concern, to become greater in the next few years, with the possible effects of specific variables and their interactions on learning.

The years 1957–58 mark the beginning of the period in which resurgent interest in teaching machines was initiated. Ramo's arguments (1957) reopened the consideration of automated techniques for classroom use. His article served as one of the more forceful attempts to alert educators to the needs and requirements for automated techniques in education. Skinner's continued interest (1958) served as the major catalyst in this area. In his article, he reviewed earlier attempts to stimulate interest in teaching machines and further explained that the learning process was now better understood and that this increased sophistication would be reflected in teaching machine technology. Skinner suggested that the most appropriate teaching machine would be that which permits the student to *compose* his response rather than to select it from a set of alternatives. On the basis of this philosophy and in conjunction with other principles of learning theory to which Skinner adheres, he designed a teaching machine with the following characteristics. The questions, printed on a disk, are presented to the student through a window. The student's response is written on a paper tape, which is advanced under a transparent cover when the student lifts a lever. At this point the correct answer appears in the window. If the student is correct, he activates the lever in one manner, which eliminates the item from the next sequence. If he is incorrect, the lever is activated in a different manner, thus retaining the item in the next sequence.

Holland (1960), a co-worker of Skinner's, has suggested several well-known learning principles that should be applied to teaching machine technology: immediate reinforcement for correct answers is a must, learned behavior is possible only when it is *emitted* and reinforced, gradual progression (i.e., small steps in learning sequences and reducing wrong answers) is necessary to establish complex repertoires, gradual withdrawal (fading or vanishing) of stimulus support is effective, it is necessary to control the student's observing and echoic behavior and to train for discrimination, the student should write his response. The Skinner machine does in fact employ these principles.

Ferster and Sapon (1958) described the Cardboard Mask, a most simple teaching machine which employs the principles which Skinner and Holland outline so clearly. This device is a cardboard folder containing mimeographed material which is presented one line at a time. The student, after writing his response on a separate sheet of paper, advances the paper in the mask, thereby exposing the correct response.

In 1958, a number of investigators interested in teaching machines recommended that the programmed material be a function of the student's response. This idea suggests that a "wrong" response may not necessarily be negative reinforcement and that both the "right" and "wrong" responses should modify the program. Rath and Anderson (1958) and Rath, Anderson, and Brainerd (1959) have suggested the use of a digital computer which automatically adjusts problem difficulty as a function of the response. Crowder's (1955, 1958, 1959) concept of "intrinsic programming" permits the response to alter the programming sequence.

During the last few years, researchers have been focusing their attention on investigating many of the variables which are pertinent to the design and use of teaching machines. The seemingly simple task of defining a teaching machine has been a serious problem to many authors (Day, 1959; Silberman, 1959; Weimer, 1958). Some definitions have made more extensive demands on teaching devices than others. Learning theorists (Kendler, 1959; Porter, 1958; Skinner, 1957; Spence, 1959; Zeaman, 1959) are now most outspoken concerning the application of theoretical concepts to teaching machine technology. Transfer of training, mediational processes, reinforcement, motivation, conditioning, symbolic processes, and language structure are but a few of these areas of interest.

There are indeed many other variables about which there is a divergence of opinion and about which experimental evidence is completely lacking or controversial. The reports of Skinner (1958), Israel (1958), Coulson and Silberman (1960), Fry (1959), and Stephens (1953) are all focused, at least in part, on questions related to response modes, e.g., multiple choice, construction of the response, responses with reinforcement, etc. Briggs, Plashinski, and Jones (1955) investigated self-paced vs. automatically paced machines. The importance of motivation in connection with teaching machines has been explored by Holland (unpublished), Mayer and Westfield (1958), and Mager (1959).

Essentially, the history of automated teaching is short – it started in the mid-twenties and was strenuously reactivated by the appearance of

Skinner's 1958 article. Empirical investigations of many important issues in this field are just now beginning to appear. However, the necessity of developing automated teaching methods has been evident for many years.

GENERAL PROBLEM AREAS

Definition As in any new field, the first problem is one of definition. What is a teaching machine? Silberman (1959) says that a teaching device consists of four units: an input unit, an output unit, a storage unit, and a control unit. As such, this definition includes a broad category of devices, from the most simple to the most complex. Weimer (1958) goes beyond the device itself, stating that a teaching machine must present information to the student as well as test the student by means of a controlled feedback loop. Crowder (1960) insists that a teaching machine

> must in some way incorporate two-way communication. That is, the student must respond to the information presented by the machine, and the machine must in turn recognize the nature of the student's response and behave appropriately (p. 12).

Perhaps the most inclusive definition is one given by Day (1959):

> A teaching machine is a mechanical device designed to present a particular body of information to the student. . . . Teaching machines differ from all other teaching devices and aids in that they require the active participation of the learner at every step (p. 591).

Although the emphasis in some of the above concepts is different, together they give a rather complete description and, if you will, definition.

Programming The programming of subject matter for teaching machines is the most extensive and difficult problem in this new technology. Beck (1959) describes specific concepts which he thinks appropriate for programming a Skinner-type machine:

> A student's responses may be restricted and guided in a great number of ways. These range from all types of hints . . . to simply presenting the response which it is desired a student acquire (p. 55).

Carr (1959) discusses in some detail the importance of programming in terms of learning efficiency and retention. Much of what he says remains open for empirical verification. Rothkopf (1960) has suggested that the development of programmed instruction suffers from two difficulties: a weak rational basis for program writing and inadequate subject-matter knowledge among program writers.

The extent to which any initial program needs revision is perhaps exemplified by the program in Harvard's course Natural Sciences 114. Holland points out that the first program of material included 48 disks, each containing 29 frames, whereas a revision and extension of the program the following year included 60 disks of 29 frames each. Holland's objective was to extend the program and decrease the number of student errors. Crowder's (1960) programming objectives are different from Holland's. He states:

> By means of "intrinsic programming" it [the program] recognizes student errors as they occur and corrects them before they can impede understanding of subsequent material or adversely affect motivation (p. 12).

Crowder considers it almost impossible to write a program which completely avoids error, and therefore he structures the program requirements on the probability of error. When an error is made, the next presentation explains the subject's mistake. Depending on the nature of the error and when it occurs, the subject may either return to the original question or enter a program of correctional material.

Another concept for programming is known as *branching* (Bryan & Rigney, 1959). Through branching, many possible routes are provided through which the subject can proceed, depending on the response. The subjects are allowed to skip certain material if they have demonstrated a knowledge of it. One study (Coulson & Silberman, 1960) suggests that under branching conditions subjects require less training time than under nonbranching conditions; however, results on the criterion test were not significantly different.

For certain kinds of subject matter, *vanishing* is still another concept for programming (Skinner, 1958). A complete or nearly complete stimulus is presented to the subject. Subsequent frames gradually omit part of the stimulus until all of it is removed. The subject is then required to reconstruct the stimulus.

To program verbal learning sequences, Homme and Glaser (1959) suggest the Ruleg. With this method, the written program states a rule and provides examples for this rule. In each case, either the rule or the example is incomplete, requiring the subject to complete it.

In a recent study Silverman (1960b) investigated methods of presenting verbal material for use in teaching machines. He recommended that further research involving the design and use of teaching machines should take into consideration the possible use of context cues as a means of facilitating serial rote learning. At the same time, however, he stated that continuous use of context cues as ancillary prompts should be avoided, since such prompts can interfere with learning.

The optimum size of steps and the organization of the programmed material are two formidable problems. Skinner (1958) states:

> Each step must be so small that it can always be taken, yet in taking it the student moves somewhat closer to fully competent behavior (p. 2).

In order to determine the value of steps in a program, Gavurin and Donahue (1961) investigated the effects of the organization of the programmed material on retention and rate of learning. They state that the assumption that optimum teaching machine programs are those in which items are presented in a logical sequence has been validated for acquisition but not retention. The results of a study carried out by Coulson and Silberman (1959) indicated that small steps were more time consuming but resulted in statistically significant higher test scores on one of the criterion tests. Pressey (1959) in principle disagrees with Skinner's notion of short and easy steps, and he strongly suggests an experimental investigation of this question. Both rate of learning and retention (recall or recognition) are of critical concern.

The above discussion suggests several areas which are directly applicable to programming and which are under investigation and/or need further experimentation. Indeed, there are a number of unanswered questions in the programming complex, some of which have been suggested by Galanter (1959):

1. What is the correct order of presentation of material?
2. Is there an optimum number of errors that should be made?
3. How far apart (in some sense) should adjacent items be spaced?
4. Is experimentally controlled pacing more effective (in some sense) than self-spacing?
5. Is one program equally effective for all students?
6. What are the effects of using different programming techniques (branching, intrinsic programming, vanishing) in various subject-matter areas?
7. What criteria are most appropriate in the evaluation of student learning?

The questions are but a few of the intriguing and complex problems facing investigators in the new field of programming material for teaching machines. Answers to these questions will help not only the educator but also the engineer who is concerned with writing adequate specifications for the construction of teaching machines.

Response Mode The kind of response that should be given by a subject has been a controversial question in the teaching machine field. Pressey's original machine (1926) required the subject to press a lever corresponding to his choice of answer. The format of the answers was multiple-choice. Skinner (1958) emphasized the necessity of having the subject *compose* (construct) the response. Skinner states:

> One reason for this is that we want him to recall rather than recognize — to make a response as well as see that it is right. Another reason is that effective multiple-choice material must contain plausible wrong responses, which are out of place in the delicate process of "shaping" behavior because they strengthen unwanted forms (p. 2).

Coulson and Silberman (1960) investigated this question of multiple-choice vs. constructed response by using *simulated* teaching machines — human beings were used instead of automatic control mechanisms. Their results indicated that the multiple-choice response mode required significantly less time than the constructed response mode and that no significant difference was obtained between response modes on the criterion test. Further, they reported that no significant differences were obtained among the experimental groups on the multiple-choice criterion subtest or on the total (multiple-choice plus constructed respose) criterion test. Fry (1959) has discussed this response-mode question along with other variables, and he has carried out extensive research concerning constructed vs. multiple-choice response modes. The results of his study favor the use of constructed response when recall is the objective of the learning.

In addition to the basic controversy (which needs much more investigation) between multiple-choice and constructed responses, there are several "variations on the theme" which are evident. Stephens (1953) has recommended that every wrong answer in a multiple-choice question appear as a correct choice for another item. He calls this program "inside alternatives." His data indicate that there was no difference between control and experimental groups on a criterion test using either nonsense syllables or Russian unless each right choice appeared as a wrong alternative for the three subsequent items. The use of prompts in general has been shown to be an effective technique in automated teaching (Cook, 1958; Cook and Kendler, 1956; Cook & Spitzer, 1960).

Using learning booklets, Goldbeck (1960) investigated the effect of response mode and learning material difficulty on automated instruction. The three response modes used were: overt response (the subject was required to construct a written response), covert response (the subject was permitted to think of a response), and implicit response (the subject read the response which was underlined). Goldbeck states:

> Learning efficiency scores, obtained by dividing quiz scores by learning time, showed that the implicit (reading) response condition produced significantly more efficient learning than the overt response condition. The covert response condition fell between the other conditions in learning efficiency (p. 25).

Concerning quiz-score results, the overt response group

> performed significantly poorer than the other response mode groups at the easy level of difficulty. Performance of the overt response group improved significantly at the intermediate difficulty level to the extent that it exceeded the performance of all other groups (pp. 25–26).

Goldbeck concludes that

> doubt is cast upon the assumption that the best learning is achieved by use of easy items and requiring written constructed responses (p. 26).

To the author's knowledge, the use of an oral response in conjunction with the Skinner teaching machine and its effect on learning rate and retention have not been reported in the literature. Furthermore, the importance of response mode as a function of reinforcement must be specified. Israel (1958) has suggested that natural and artificial reinforcement may affect the subjects' learning. A most comprehensive analysis of response-mode and feedback factors has been reported by Goldbeck and Briggs (1960).

The general area of reinforcement suggests problems related to the drop-out feature of teaching machines. Pressey's (1927) original machine dropped items after the correct answer had been given twice. Skinner's machines at the Harvard Psychological Laboratory also have the drop-out feature, although the commercially available machines based on Skinner's design do not incorporate this feature. With reference to a study carried out at Harvard, Holland (unpublished) reported significantly superior performance when the drop-out feature was used.

If items are dropped, the sequence of items is of course changed. How important is the sequence? If items should be dropped, by what criterion of learning can one justify omitting an item from the sequence? If items are not dropped and the criterion for the learning procedure is a complete run (i.e., once through the sequence without error) what is the effect upon retention? Being correct is positive reinforcement; thus, some items under these circumstances will receive a greater amount of positive reinforcement than others. What would be the effect of additional reinforcements with or without drop-out? Again, a plethora of problems and a paucity of answers!

Response time, another important variable, has been investigated by Briggs, Plashinski, and Jones (1955). Their study suggests that there is no difference between self-paced and automatically paced programs as determiners of response time. However, the problem of pacing for individual items is still a recent one and needs further research. Another aspect of response time—the distribution of practice—has been studied extensively since Ebbinghaus' investigation in 1885. For example, Holland (unpublished) states that in an experiment at Harvard "a few students completed all the disks in a small number of long sessions while others worked in many short sessions. . . . Apparently the way practice was distributed made little difference" (p. 4). Nevertheless, the distribution of practice, like the problem of pacing, is yet a subject of controversy, with most investigations favoring some form of distributed practice (Hovland, 1951).

The above section outlines briefly some of the major problems associated with the variable affecting response mode. Although some of the variables have already been investigated, these and others, together with their interactions, need further research.

Knowledge of Results   There are many peripheral problems related to teaching machines, one of which is the effect of immediate knowledge of results on learning. Angell (1949), using a multiple-choice punchboard technique, found that "learning is significantly enhanced by immediate knowledge of results." Briggs (1949), also using the Punchboard, confirmed these results. Bryan and Rigney (1956) noted superior performance when subjects were given knowledge of results, specifically, an explanation if the answer was incorrect. This last study was later expanded by Bryan, Rigney, and Van Horn (1957), who investigated differences between three kinds of explanation given for incorrect response. None of the three types of explanation proved to be superior in teaching the subjects. Because of their controvertible results, the above studies demonstrate that, although immediate knowledge of results appears to be effective in the learning process, this problem contains many facets which need more empirical data.

Motivation   One of the many reasons given for the effectiveness of teaching machines is that the student's motivation is increased. Psychologists and educators have realized for some time that the motivation variable ranks very high among those variables pertinent to learning. In 1958 and 1959, Holland surveyed the use of the teaching machine in classes at Harvard. He found that most students felt that they would have gotten less out of the course if the machines had not been used, that most students preferred to have machines used for part of the course, and finally that most students felt that the teaching machine was used by the instructor "to teach me as much as possible with a given expenditure of my time and effort. During a field tryout of the Subject-Matter Trainer in the Semiautomatic Ground Environment System, Mayer and West-field (1958) observed that "motivation to work with the trainer is high." The supervisory as well as the operational personnel encouraged the use of this training technique.

Mager (1959) suggests that motivation and interest are a function of the percentage of correct responses. He observed that in two young subjects negative feelings for learning mathematics in the usual classroom situation did not transfer to learning mathematics by means of a teaching machine.

The cause of this phenomenon is perhaps best explained by the subjects' statement that, because they were able to understand the programmed material, it did not seem to be mathematics at all. This interesting relationship between comprehension and motivation needs further investigation.

Equipment   There are many inexpensive models of teaching machines which will soon hit the consumer market. For much of this equipment, there is very little experimental evidence which supports the various designs. As previously pointed out, Holland has collected data which support the efficiency of the drop-out feature in a teaching machine; yet commercial models presently available do not incorporate this feature, presumably because of its high cost. Generally, it seems that production is now and will continue to be out of phase with much of the research which has provided necessary teaching machine specifications. Moreover, because of their expense, it is likely that some very important features will be omitted in manufacture.

The methods of displaying programmed material, another unexplored problem area, must be investigated so as to provide the design engineer with requirements based on empirical findings. The display problem is less acute, perhaps, with material for the elementary school than it is with programs designed to teach maintenance procedures and aspects of the biological sciences.

The use of computer controlled teaching machines has been recommended by many authors (Coulson & Silberman, 1959; Skinner, 1958). Utilizing a central computer, with many programs capable of adapting to individual needs and of providing stimulus materials to 50 or more students simultaneously, is a feasible notion for large-scale training programs. With a computer, the display problem again becomes a major issue. Training in pattern recognition, information handling, and display interpretation are but a few appropriate areas which should be studied.

The alternate modes of presentation become more extensive as computer capacity increases. In the case of certain kinds of subject matter, a computer generated, pictorial display of information may be a more effective presentation than any other display techniques. Future research must solve these problems in equipment design.

Teaching Machines and Other Techniques   The use of automated teaching devices may be optimized, perhaps, if there is a proper balance between this technique and other compatible teaching methods. What percentage of a course should be machine taught? What subject matter is best suited to automated devices? If classroom courses were as carefully and thoughtfully programmed as some of the programs currently being prepared for teaching machines, might some of the advantages of teaching machines diminish? Perhaps some of the apparent advantages of teaching machines are no more than methods of illustrating correctable classroom techniques! It might well be that the instructor's enthusiasm and inspiration, a factor supposedly dominant in higher education, is vital in mastering a particular subject-matter area. Will creativity in certain students be harmed by extensive education via the machine? Again, consideration of the use of a teaching machine, the subject matter, the program, the level of education, and the techniques used in combination with the teaching machine provide a fertile field for experimentation. As of now, questions in this area remain unanswered. Silverman (1960a) has presented an excellent, detailed discussion of problems inherent in this new technology of automated teaching and the current trends in the field.

PROBLEMS OF APPLICATION

The most obvious problems in the attempt to use automated teaching techniques have been outlined in the previous section. There is still much of the unknown associated with techniques, machines, programming, etc. to be eliminated before a direct solution to a particular training problem can be specified. Many alternatives exist, the best of which has not yet been determined. In addition to these voids, there is a serious lack of definition in the objectives of many training programs.

What is the objective of a particular automated course or program? From a pragmatic point of view, what are the criteria by which a specific educational program can be evaluated? For example, the objectives might range from the teaching of rote tasks to the presentation of more abstract material. Needless to say, the techniques for both teaching and evaluating learning could be substantially different in each case. The purpose of teaching, the objective of an educational program, must be initially defined. Only then will the concepts *learning* and *teaching* be meaningful in a particular context.

After definition, the next step is to determine what subject matter will provide the student with the necessary information. It is at this point that the major pitfall in education is likely to appear. Even though many training programs do not have a defined objective, their course content is nonetheless prescribed, and the text and/or materials used in previous, nonautomated courses become the prime source of material for an automated teaching program. To program an automated teaching machine with presently available materials might well result only in a more efficient method of teaching the wrong material!

The third step requires decisions in the selection of appropriate teaching techniques. Answers to questions involving programming, choice of teaching machine, learning procedures, pacing, and response modes are still not known.

The fourth and last step requires an evaluation of the selected automated teaching method in terms of the originally established objectives. Conventional methods of instruction should be compared with the innovative methods by means of a specific set of criteria, e.g., in terms of training time, job performance, retention of learned information, etc.

The questions confronting the researcher in teaching machine technology are one example of the broader questions of man-machine interrelation. Data pertinent to the principles of human engineering, the optimum man-machine interaction, the degree to which the machine can perform functions formerly allocated to man, and the appropriate allocation of functions between man and machine will be provided by a research program investigating teaching machines. Inadequate attention to any of the above-mentioned steps will result in failure to provide the needed answers in a field which may increase training effectiveness and reduce training costs.

REFERENCES

Angell, G. W. The effect of immediate knowledge of quiz results on final examination scores in freshman chemistry. *J. educ. Res.*, 1949, **42**, 391–394.

Angell, G. W., and Troyer, M. E. A new self-scoring test device for improving instruction. *Sch. Soc.*, 1948, **67**, 84–85.

Beck, J. On some methods of programming. In E. H. Galanter (Ed.), *Automatic teaching: The state of the art.* New York: Wiley, 1959. Pp. 55–62.

Besnard, G. G., Briggs, L. J., Mursch, G. A., and Walker, E. S. Development of the subject-matter trainer. *USAF Personnel Train. Res. Cent. tech. Memo.*, 1955, No. ASPRL-TM-55-7.

Besnard, G. G., Briggs, L. J., and Walker, E. S. The improved subject-matter trainer. *USAF Personnel Train. Res. Cent. tech. Memo.*, 1955, No. ASPRL-TM-55-11.

Briggs, L. J. The development and appraisal of special procedures for superior students and an analysis of the effects of knowledge of results. *Abstr. Doctoral Dissertations, Ohio State U.*, 1949, No. 58.

Briggs, L. P., Plashinski, D., and Jones, D. L. Self-pacing versus automatic pacing of practice on the subject-matter trainer. *USAF Personnel Train. Res. Cent. lab. Note*, 1955, No. ASPRL-LN-55-8.

Bryan, G. L., and Rigney, J. W. An evaluation of a method for ship-board training in operations knowledge. *U. Sth. Calif. Electronics Personnel Res. Group tech. Rep.*, 1956, No. 18.

Bryan, G. L., and Rigney, J. W. Current trends in automated tutoring and their implications for naval technical training. *U. Sth. Calif. Dept. Psychol. tech. Rep.*, 1959, No. 29.

Bryan, G. L., Rigney, J. W., and Van Horn, C. An evaluation of three types of information for supplementing knowledge of results in a training technique. *U. Sth. Calif., Electronics Personnel Res. Group tech. Rep.*, 1957, No. 19.

Carr, W. J. Self-instructional devices: A review of current concepts. *USAF WADC tech. Rep.*, 1959, No. 59–503.

Cook, J. O. Supplementary report: Processes underlying learning a single paired-associate item. *J. exp. Psychol.*, 1958, **56**, 455.

Cook, J. O., and Kendler, T. S. A theoretical model to explain some paired-associate learning data. In G. Finch and F. Cameron (Eds.), *Symposium on Air Force human engineering, personnel, and training research.* Washington, D.C.: National Academy of Sciences-National Research Council, 1956. Pp. 90–98.

Cook, J. O., and Spitzer, M. E. Supplementary report: Prompting versus confirmation in paired-associate learning. *J. exp. Psychol.*, 1960, **59**, 275–276.

Corrigan, R. E. Automated teaching methods. *Automated teach. Bull.*, 1959, **1**(2), 23–30.

Coulson, J. E., and Silberman, H. F. Proposal for extension of automated teaching projects. *Sys. Develpm. Corp. field Note*, 1959.

Coulson, J. E., and Silberman, H. F. Effects of three variables in a teaching machine. *J. educ. Psychol.*, 1960, **51**, 135–143.

Crowder, N. A. The concept of automatic tutoring. *USAF Personnel Train. Res. Cent. organizational Pap.*, 1955.

Crowder, N. A. *An automatic tutoring book on number systems.* Vol. 1. Timonium, Md.: Hoover Electronics Co., 1958.

Crowder, N. A. Automatic tutoring by means of intrinsic programming. In E. H. Galanter (Ed.), *Automatic teaching: The state of the art.* New York: Wiley, 1959. Pp. 109–116.

Crowder, N. A. The "tutor." *J. Amer. Soc. Train. Dir.*, 1960, **14**(5), 12–17.

Day, J. H. Teaching machines. *J. chem. Educ.*, 1959, **36**, 591–595.

Ferster, C. B., and Sapon, S. M. An Application of recent developments in psychology to the teaching of German. *Harv. educ. Rev.*, 1958, **28**, 58–69.

Fry, E. B. Teaching machine dichotomy: Skinner versus Pressey. Paper presented at American Psychological Association, Cincinnati, September 1959.

Fry, E. B., Bryan, G. L., and Rigney, J. W. Teaching machines: An annotated bibliography. *Audio Visual commun. Rev.*, 1960, **8**, Suppl. 1, 1–80.

Galanter, E. H. The ideal teacher. In E. H. Galanter (Ed.), *Automatic teaching: The state of the art*. New York: Wiley, 1959, Pp. 1–11.

Gavurin, E. I., and Donahue, V. M. Logical sequence and random sequence. *Automated teach. Bull.*, 1961, **1**(4), 3–9.

Goldbeck, R. A. The effect of response mode and learning material difficulty on automated instruction. *Amer. Inst. Res. tech. Rep.*, 1960, No. AIR-328-60-IR-124.

Goldbeck, R. A., and Briggs, L. J. An analysis of response mode and feedback factors in automated instruction. *Amer. Inst. Res. Tech. Rep.*, 1960, No. AIR-328-60-IR-133.

Holland, J. G. Teaching machines: An application of principles from the laboratory. In Proceedings of the Educational Testing Service Invitational Conference, October 1959. *The impact of testing on the educational process*. Princeton, N. J.: Educational Testing Service, 1960.

Homme, L. E., and Glaser, R. Problems in programming verbal learning sequences. Paper presented in symposium on research issues in study of human learning raised by developments in automated teaching methods, American Psychological Association, Cincinnati, September 1959.

Hovland, C. I. Human learning and retention. In S. S. Stevens (Ed.), *Handbook of experimental psychology*. New York: Wiley, 1951. Pp. 613–689.

Israel, M. L. Skinnerian psychology and educational redesign. Paper read in symposium, American Psychological Association, Washington, D. C., September 1958.

Kendler, H. H. Teaching machines and psychological theory. In E. H. Galanter (Ed.), *Automatic teaching: The state of the art*. New York: Wiley, 1959. Pp. 177–185.

Little, J. K. Results of use of machines for testing and for drill upon learning in educational psychology. *J. exp. Educ.*, 1934, **3**, 45–49.

Mager, R. F. Preliminary studies in automated teaching. *IRE Trans. Educ.*, 1959, **E-2**, 104–107.

Mayer, S. R., and Westfield, R. L. A field tryout of a teaching machine for training in SAGE operations. *USAF Cambridge Res. Cent. tech. Memo.*, 1958, No. OAL-TM-58-16.

Peterson, J. C. A new device for teaching, testing, and research in learning. *Trans. Kans. Acad. Sci.*, 1930, **33**, 41–47.

Porter, D. Teaching machines. *Harv. Grad. Sch. Educ. Ass. Bull.*, 1958, **3**(1), 1–5.

Pressey, S. L. A simple apparatus which gives tests and scores—and teaches. *Sch. Soc.*, 1926, **23**, 373–376.

Pressey, S. L. A machine for automatic teaching of drill material. *Sch. Soc.*, 1927, **25**, 549–552.

Pressey, S. L. A third and fourth contribution toward the coming "industrial revolution" in education. *Sch. Soc.*, 1932, **36**, 668–672.

Pressey, S. L. Development and appraisal of devices providing immediate automatic scoring of objective tests and concomitant self-instruction. *J. Psychol.*, 1950, **29**, 417–447.

Pressey, S. L. Certain major psycho-educational issues appearing in the conference on teaching machines. In E. H. Galanter (Ed.), *Automatic teaching: The state of the art.* New York: Wiley, 1959. Pp. 187–198.

Ramo, S. A new technique of education. *Engng. sci. Mon.*, 1957, **21** (October), 17–22.

Rath, G. J., and Anderson, Nancy S. The IBM research center teaching machine project: I. The teaching of binary arithmetic. II. The simulation of a binary arithmetic teaching machine on the IBM 650. Paper presented at USAF Office of Scientific Research symposium on teaching machines, University of Pennsylvania, December 8–9, 1958.

Rath, G. J., Anderson, Nancy S., and Brainerd, R. C. The IBM research center teaching machine project. In E. H. Galanter (Ed.), *Automatic teaching: The state of the art.* New York: Wiley, 1959. Pp. 117–130.

Rothkopf, E. Z. A do-it-yourself kit for programmed instruction. *Teach. Coll. Rec.*, 1960, **62**, 195–201.

Silberman, H. F. Introductory description of teaching machines (physical characteristics). Paper read in symposium on automated teaching, Western Psychological Association, San Diego, California, April 1959. (Abstract).

Silverman, R. E. Automated teaching: A review of theory and research. USN Training Device Center, 1960. (ASTIA AD-241 283) (a)

Silverman, R. E. The use of context cues in teaching machines. USN Training Device Center, 1960. (ASTIA AD-238 777) (b)

Skinner, B. F. The science of learning and the art of teaching. *Harv. educ. Rev.*, 1954, **24**, 86–97.

Skinner, B. F. *Verbal behavior.* New York: Appleton-Century-Crofts, 1957.

Skinner, B. F. Teaching machines. *Science*, 1958, **128**, 969–977.

Spence, K. W. The relation of learning theory to the technology of education. *Harv. educ. Rev.*, 1959, **29**, 84–95.

Stephens, A. L. Certain special factors involved in the law of effect. *Abstr. Doctoral Dissertations, Ohio State U.*, 1953, No. 64.

Weimer, P. K. A proposed "automatic" teaching device. *IRE Trans. Educ.*, 1958, **E-1**, 51–53.

Zeaman, D. Skinner's theory of teaching machines. In E. H. Galanter (Ed.), *Automatic teaching: The state of the art.* New York: Wiley, 1959. Pp. 167–176.

ARTICLE 27

Programming Creative Behavior*

HAYNE W. REESE and SIDNEY J. PARNES

State University of New York at Buffalo

Abstract: Creativity, as measured by standard tests, can be increased by training in creative problem solving. To determine whether training with the programmed materials developed by the junior author is effective, high school students were given a 1-semester course with (a) the program alone (2 schools) or (b) the program taught by an instructor (2 schools). (c) Control students in 2 other schools were given no training. (d) Additional control groups within the 4 experimental schools were also included. A battery of creativity tests was given to all Ss at the beginning and end of the semester. In general, the instructor-taught group appeared to improve more on the tests than the program-alone group, and both improved more than the control groups.

Numerous experiments have been conducted to evaluate deliberate methods of developing creative behavior. In a review of the literature reporting such research, Parnes and Brunelle (1967) concluded that the evidence overwhelmingly indicates that creative ability, as measured by existing tests, can be increased.

The purpose of the present study was to evaluate the effects of a *programmed* course in creative problem solving. Research suggests that incremental teaching of subject matter can be more efficient than conventional teaching methods. For example, the findings of Porter (1959)

---

*Reprinted from *Child Development*, Vol. 41, No. 2, June 1970, pp. 413–423. Copyright 1970 by The Society for Research in Child Development, Inc.

The research reported herein was supported by Title VII, project no. 5-0716, from the Office of Education, U.S. Department of Health, Education, and Welfare. We wish to thank the Consulting Psychologists Press, Inc., Palo Alto, California, for permission to reproduce the Dominance Scale of the California Psychological Inventory. The set of booklets prepared for this research may be secured through the ERIC Document Reproduction Service, 4936 Fairmont Avenue, Bethesda, Maryland 20014. Most of the programmed material has been integrated into the *Creative Behavior Guidebook* (Parnes 1967) and a companion *Creative Behavior Workbook* of the same date by the same author and publisher. Dr. Reese's present address: Department of Human Development, University of Kansas, Lawrence, Kansas 66044. Dr. Parnes is now at State University College at Buffalo.

showed that students could master a programmed course in spelling four times faster than a conventionally taught course. Schramm's (1964) annotated bibliography cited 36 studies, of which 17 showed significant superiority for students who completed programs as compared with those in conventional classes. In all but one of the remaining 19 studies, no significant differences appeared. In the one exception, the classroom students proved superior to the programmed ones.

Authorities emphasize the value of creative thinking in programming but give much less attention to programming deliberately for creative development. Only a small number of the studies of programming dealt with development of creative thinking (Anderson 1965; Barlow 1960; Day 1961; Olton 1966).

The objective of the present research, at the high school senior level, was to determine whether or not subjects receiving creative problem-solving training with programmed materials alone show increases in creative ability to the same extent as subjects receiving the same error-free programmed materials in an instructor-taught procedure, and whether or not either or both of these groups show a significant gain in creative ability when compared with control subjects receiving no training.

METHOD

Subjects

Six academic high schools from the Buffalo School District were included in the study. In each school, all senior students who indicated that they intended to continue their formal education after graduation were assembled and, after being fully informed about the nature of the experiment, were asked to volunteer to participate. They were told, before being asked to volunteer, that one-quarter unit of high school credit would be given for participation and that attendance at the training sessions would be required of volunteers who were selected to be included. Of some 1,384 apparently eligible students, 957 volunteered.

Subjects included in the study were selected on the basis of IQ and probability of regular attendance at training sessions. The acceptable IQ range was set at 105 to 130. Lorge-Thorndike scores, obtained from school records, were used to evaluate IQ. Volunteers with 10 or more absences per semester in the previous year were excluded as poor risks, except for a few with one or two extra absences who were included in order to fill particular groups. These two criteria, and scheduling problems, reduced the number of students initially included to 193. Five students did not complete the course, leaving 188 subjects.

Materials

The criterion measures were obtained from a battery of eight tests, seven designed to assess five aspects of creative behavior, and one designed to assess a personality characteristic presumably associated with creativity. The tests were the Dominance Scale of the California Psychological Inventory (Gough 1957), the Product Improvement Test (Torrance 1962), and AC (1960) Test of Creative Ability ("Other Uses"), abbreviated forms of four of Guilford's (1966) tests (Apparatus, Planning Elaboration, Alternate Uses, and Consequences), and the unabbreviated form of a fifth Guilford test (Associational Fluency). All tests were administered with the standard instructions and were scored by two independent raters using standard scoring instructions provided by the authors of the tests. The possibility of rater bias and halo effect in the scoring was eliminated by coding the protocols. The raters could not tell what subject, school, or treatment condition any protocol came from, nor whether it was from a pretest or a posttest when the same form was used in both testing sessions. Interrater scoring agreement was computed for random samples of protocols from all of the subjectively scored tests (all except the Dominance Scale of the California Psychological Inventory [CPI], which is objectively scored). The obtained interrater scoring reliabilities are given in Table 27.1. (Intercorrelations among the scores are given in appendix 1 of Parnes 1966.)

The experimental material was a programmed sequence of 28 booklets designed to teach the principles of creative problem solving described by Parnes (1967). The preparation, preliminary testing, and revision of the programmed booklets required about 2 years (*see* Parnes 1966, pp. 17–20).

Procedure

Pretests The subjects initially selected were given the battery of criterion tests in two 40-minute sessions, 2 days apart. The Associational Fluency, Alternate Uses, Planning Elaboration, Apparatus, and Other Uses tests were given in the first session, and the Consequences, CPI Dominance, and Product Improvement tests were given in the second

Table 27.1. Interrater Agreement for Criterion Measures

Creative Behavior and Measure	Pretest Form	Pretest Scoring Agreement	Posttest Form	Posttest Scoring Agreement
Fluency:				
Associational Fluency	[a]	0.94	–	–
Other Uses, quantity	[b]	0.99	–	–
Consequences, total	Items 1–3	0.97	–	–
Product Improvement, Fluency	Toy dog	1.00	Toy monkey	1.00
Flexibility:				
Alternate Uses	Parts I and II	0.96	–	–
Product Improvement, Flexibility	Toy dog	0.82	Toy monkey	0.74
Originality:				
Consequences, Remote	Items 1–3	0.68	–	–
Product Improvement, Originality	Toy dog	0.78	Toy monkey	0.81
Elaboration:				
Planning Elaboration	Part A	0.88	Part B	0.99
Sensitivity:				
Apparatus	Items 1–9	0.80	Items 10–18	0.78

Note: Dash means that same form was used in posttest as in pretest; reliability computed only on pretest.
[a]Complete unabbreviated form used.
[b]One item, wire coat hanger, from Part V used.

session. The tests were administered by members of the experimental staff, but no "program-proctor" or "instructor" tested any subjects who were to be in his group.

Treatments   "Program" and "Instructor" groups were given two 40-minute training sessions per week for 13 weeks, beginning after the pretest sessions. The students in the Program groups were given a new booklet from the sequence at the beginning of each training session (and a second booklet in two sessions), and worked through the booklet during the session without interaction with other students. A program-proctor was present but served only to distribute the materials and to answer administrative kinds of questions.

The Instructor groups were given *exactly* the same material as in the booklets, with no deviations allowed; but the material was presented by instructors in the conventional classroom fashion. During each training session, the subjects in the Instructor groups were encouraged to discuss the material and to interact with one another in developing the kinds of creative responses that the subjects in the Program groups had to develop alone.

Subjects who were absent from a session were given makeup work to do at home. For the Program groups, the makeup assignment consisted of working through the appropriate booklet. For the Instructor groups, the assignment was to read equivalent material.

Control groups had no contact with the experiment except in the pretest and posttest sessions.

Posttests   The posttests were given with the same procedures as the pretests, and were given to any one group by the same person who had given the pretests.

Design

The six schools included in the study were divided into two levels on the basis of ratings by three professional members of the experimental staff. The characteristics rated were the extent to which both the school and the neighborhood showed an academic interest and an interest in education as a whole, including cultural and enrichment opportunities. The three schools rated lowest were designated "Level I" schools, and the three rated highest were designated "Level II" schools.

In order to eliminate discussion among subjects given different treatments, and hence to eliminate contamination of the treatment effects, each of the three treatment conditions (Program, Instructor, and Control) was given in separate schools. Two schools, one from each level, were assigned to each condition, using a table of random numbers. The basic design, then, was a 2×3 factorial, with two school levels and three treatments.

The Level I schools had ratings that were highly similar to one another, but the Level II schools were less homogeneous. Therefore, additional control groups were included to provide a check on possible sampling errors in the between-school comparisons. These additional control groups were "in-school" controls. Within each of the two Program schools and the two Instructor schools, an in-school control group was selected at random from the eligible volunteers. The in-school control groups were treated exactly like the groups in the two Control schools. Since the results of comparisons with in-school control groups were essentially the same as comparisons with the control groups from separate schools, only the latter comparisons are given in the present report. (*See* Parnes 1966 for the other comparisons.)

For the analyses of the data, the number of subjects was reduced by excluding subjects who had been absent from an excessive number of training sessions and by omitting others at random to balance the group sizes. The group sizes for the final analyses are given in Table 27.2.

Table 27.2. Sample Sizes for Statistical Analyses

Group	All Tests Except Other Uses		Other Uses	
	Level I Schools	Level II Schools	Level I Schools	Level II Schools
Program	31	31	31	31
Instructor	31[a]	31	17	17[b]
Control	31	31	27[b]	27

[a]Includes one "fictitious subject" (group means) (*see* Lindquist 1956, p. 148).

[b]Data lost because of expiration of available testing time. (Other Uses was last test in battery.)

RESULTS

Analyses of variance of the pretest scores indicated that the School Levels by Treatments interaction was significant on every measure except

Other Uses and Dominance. The interactions indicated that there were differences among schools within each school level and that the directions of the differences were not the same in both school levels. The differences, besides being statistically significant, were fairly large; and therefore posttest scores were examined with analysis of covariance techniques.

Table 27.3. Adjusted Posttest Means on Criterion Measures

Test	Level I Schools			Level II Schools		
	Program	Instructor	Control School	Program	Instructor	Control School
Assoc. Fluency	15.9	13.4	14.1	16.3	16.1	12.1
Other Uses	12.6	13.3	11.3	13.3	17.2	11.1
Conseq., Total	17.8	19.1	16.1	18.0	21.0	15.3
P.I., Fluency	14.7	17.1	12.4	14.7	17.9	13.7
Alternate Uses	18.9	19.1	15.9	20.3	19.1	15.7
P.I., Flexibility	7.5	8.5	6.9	8.0	8.7	6.1
Conseq., Remote	7.2	8.1	6.3	7.6	8.6	7.1
P.I., Originality	4.8	4.6	3.9	4.9	6.5	3.1
Planning Elab	12.8	14.0	11.7	13.0	14.2	10.6
Apparatus	8.3	8.5	7.2	8.4	8.6	7.3
CPI Dominance	28.4	27.9	27.1	28.2	27.3	26.9

Table 27.3 presents the means of the adjusted posttest scores, Table 27.4 summarizes the results of the analyses of covariance of these scores, and Table 27.5 summarizes the results of *t* tests of differences between pairs of treatments. There were no significant differences in the adjusted posttest scores of the personality scale (Dominance); but, in general, the analyses of the adjusted posttest measures of creative behavior indicated that the Instructor groups were significantly superior to the Program groups, and both were significantly superior to the Control groups.

Exactly this pattern of results was obtained on three of the four fluency measures, on one of the two flexibility measures, and on the elaboration measure. A similar pattern, with no significant difference between the experimental groups but with both significantly superior to the Control groups, was obtained on the other fluency measure in one school level, on the other flexibility measure, on one of the two originality measures, and on the sensitivity measure. The other originality measure and the Associational Fluency measure in one school level yielded uninterpretable results.

Table 27.4. Summary of Analyses of Covariance of Posttest Scores

| | | F Ratios | | |
Measure	Error Mean Square[a]	School Levels ($df=1$)	Treatments ($df=2$)	S × T ($df=2$)
Associational Fluency	14.85	< 1.00	9.07***	5.73***
Other Uses	16.56	2.53	10.49***	2.66
Consequences, Total	16.29	< 1.00	17.80***	1.75
Product Improvement, Fluency	18.98	1.11	16.23***	< 1.00
Alternate Uses	18.83	< 1.00	14.01***	< 1.00
Product Improvement, Flexibility	2.97	< 1.00	22.98***	2.24
Consequences, Remote	11.51	1.32	3.69*	< 1.00
Product Improvement, Originality	9.22	< 1.00	6.99***	2.95
Planning Elaboration	10.79	< 1.00	12.52***	< 1.00
Apparatus	7.06	< 1.00	4.00**	< 1.00
Dominance	19.81	< 1.00	1.32	< 1.00

[a]Error $df=143$ for Other Uses, 178 for all other tests.
*$p < 0.05$, **$p < 0.025$, ***$p < 0.01$.

DISCUSSION

The data clearly establish that working alone through a programmed sequence of booklets designed for the purpose can yield significant gains on standard measures of creative behavior, but that working through the same material presented in conventional fashion by an instructor, with class participation and interaction, generally yields larger gains. This finding has important implications not only for the researcher interested in the theoretical problem of creativity but also for the researcher interested in possible classroom applications.

It is important to point out that no discussion at all was allowed between the proctor and the students who took the program on their own. The proctor merely greeted the students on arrival and handed out and collected the booklets. Any questions were related back to the booklets. In classroom usage, the programs could be dealt with much more flexibly.

The junior author observed informally that the students who worked on their own appeared to exert more effort than did the instructor-taught students but appeared to be less interested in the course. This observation, the conclusion of James, Guetzkow, Forehand, and Libby (1962),

Table 27.5. Comparisons of Pairs of Treatments

Creative Behavior and Measure	Instructor vs. Program	Instructor vs. Control	Program vs. Control
Fluency:			
Associational Fluency:			
Level I schools	− 2.57*	< 1.00	1.79
Level II schools	< 1.00	4.05**	4.17**
Other Uses	2.58**	4.70**	2.34*
Consequences, Total	3.04**	5.96**	2.90**
Product Improvement, Fluency	3.04**	5.64**	2.08*
Flexibility:			
Alternate Uses	< 1.00	4.24**	4.86**
Product Improvement, Flexibility	2.74**	6.74**	3.99**
Originality:			
Consequences, Remote	1.53	2.71**	1.19
Product Improvement, Originality	1.29	3.67**	2.39*
Elaboration:			
Planning Elaboration	2.05*	4.98**	2.93**
Sensitivity:			
Apparatus	< 1.00	2.58*	2.30*

Note: Body of table gives value of t computed with denominator based on within-cells variance of appropriate analysis of covariance; df of $t = df$ of within-cells variance (Lindquist 1956, p. 327). School levels combined except on Associational Fluency (only measure with significant interaction).

$*p < 0.05$, $**p < 0.01$.

and pilot work which has already been conducted in other classes, suggest that the best approach may be to combine programmed instruction with classroom participation directed by an instructor.

REFERENCES

AC test of creative ability. Chicago: Education-Industry Service, Industrial Relations Center, University of Chicago, 1960.

Anderson, R. C. Can first graders learn an advanced problem-solving skill? *Journal of Educational Psychology*, 1965, **56**, 283–294.

Barlow, J. A. Aspects of programming, learning, and performance. Paper presented at the meeting of the American Psychological Association, Chicago, September 1960.

Day, W. F. Programming a teaching machine course in thinking and problem solving. Unpublished manuscript, University of Nevada, 1961.

Gough, H. C. *Manual for the California Psychological Inventory*. Palo Alto, Calif.: Consulting Psychologists Press, 1957.

Guilford, J. P. Report No. 36 from the Psychological Laboratory. University of Southern California Laboratory, Photoduplication Services Department, Los Angeles, 1966.

James, B. J.; Guetzkow, H.; Forehand, G. A.; and Libby, W. L. Education for innovative behavior in executives. Cooperative Research Project no. 975, Office of Education, U.S. Department of Health, Education, and Welfare, August 1962.

Lindquist, E. F. *Design and analysis of experiments in psychology and education*. Boston: Houghton Mifflin, 1956.

Olton, R. M. A self-instructional program for the development of productive thinking in fifth and sixth grade children. In F. E. Williams (Ed.), *First seminar on productive thinking in education*. St. Paul, Minn.: Creativity and National Schools Project, Macalester College, 1966.

Parnes, S. J. Programming creative behavior. Final Report, Office of Education, U.S. Department of Health, Education, and Welfare, Title VII, Project No. 5-0716, State University of New York at Buffalo, 1966.

Parnes, S. J. *Creative behavior guidebook*. New York: Scribner's, 1967.

Parnes, S. J., & Brunelle, E. A. The literature of creativity. Part 1. *Journal of Creative Behavior*, 1967, **1**, 52–109.

Porter, D. Some effects of year long teaching machine instruction. In E. Galanter (Ed.), *Automatic teaching, the state of the art*. New York: Wiley, 1959. Pp. 85–90.

Schramm, W. *The research on programmed instruction*. Washington: U.S. Department of Health, Education, and Welfare, 1964.

Torrance, E. P. *Guiding creative talent*. Englewood Cliffs, N.J.: Prentice-Hall, 1962.

ARTICLE 28

Programmed Instruction for Culturally Deprived Slow-Learning Children*[1]

CHARLES F. WILLIAMS, M.S., ALDEN S. GILMORE, M.A., and
LESLIE F. MALPASS, Ph.D.

American Institutes for Research, University of South Florida,
and Virginia Polytechnic Institute

Deutsch (1964) has estimated that forty to seventy per cent of the school populations in America's twenty largest cities consists of children from marginal social and economic circumstances. Others, reported by Kirk (1962), have estimated that over thirty per cent of school age children from low socio-economic circumstances may be classified as slow learners. By the time these children reach junior high school, approximately sixty per cent of them are retarded one to four years in reading performance. These and similar reports (e.g., Kennedy, Van De Reit, & White, 1963) have suggested that social and economic deprivation is related to retardation in school achievement, and that this retardation tends to increase with age, at least through early adolescence.

Both the educable mentally retarded and the slow learner frequently demonstrate motivational problems in regard to academic performance (Dunn, 1963). A "failure syndrome" often exists which involves lack of attention, lack of interest in school work, and regression in social behavior. This may be due, in part, to teachers' lack of opportunity to give individual attention to these children's learning problems.

Other studies (e.g., Malpass, Hardy, Gilmore, & Williams, 1964;

*Reprinted from *The Journal of Special Education*, Vol. 2, No. 4, 1968, pp. 421–427.

[1]This research was supported by the U.S. Office of Education, Bureau of Research, OE Project 6-8438. It was completed while Mr. Williams and Mr. Gilmore were colleagues at MacDonald Training Center, Tampa, Florida, and Dr. Malpass was at the University of South Florida. The assistance of Dr. Robert Dwyer as consultant and of Mrs. Elizabeth Schmidt as research assistant is gratefully acknowledged.

Birnbrauer, Kidder, & Tague, 1964; Blackman, 1965) have suggested that, for mentally retarded children, programmed instruction (PI) can overcome some of the disadvantages of the typical classroom learning situation, although they do not indicate that PI should be used as a total substitute for class-room experience. These studies have indicated that teaching machines tend to stimulate attention and interest in learning materials, and that they contribute to higher performance in word acquisition, arithmetic, and simple reading skills. It seemed reasonable to assume that such conditions would eventuate if PI were used to supplement the ordinary classroom activities of slow-learning children as well. Certainly, studies by Vernon (1958) and others (*op. cit.*) have suggested that conventional classroom procedures have not been maximally effective in helping such children to acquire the skills involved in reading.

STATEMENT OF THE PROBLEM

The purpose of this study was to evaluate the effects of programmed instruction on the acquisition and retention of word recognition, phrase recognition, sentence reading, and concomitant reading skills by slow-learning children. Specifically, it was decided to compare the efficiency of learning these skills by means of two types of programmed instruction and standard classroom instruction.

Lumsdaine & Glaser (1960), Stolurow (1961), and Becker (1963) have reported that both teaching machine and programmed textbook presentations have been effective with normal children. Smith & Quackenbush (1960), Malpass, *et al.* (1964), and Blackman (1965), among others, have demonstrated the utility of automated instruction for retarded children. Examination of the literature, however, revealed no extensive studies of the effectiveness of linear PI, using either machine or programmed textbook, for the slow-learning group (Malpass, 1967). Neither have there been any studies comparing the effectiveness of teaching machines versus programmed textbooks for such children.

The problem for this study, then, was to evaluate the usefulness of programmed verbal materials for slow-learning children from marginal socioeconomic backgrounds. A corollary problem was to compare the effectiveness and feasibility of two types of programmed presentation, i.e., teaching machine and programmed textbooks, in contrast to conventional classroom learning.

SUBJECTS

The subjects were required to meet two major criteria: they had to fall into operationally-defined categories of "slow-learning" and "culturally deprived." To meet the first criterion, the child had to have a tested IQ between 76 and 90 and be retarded at least six months in school achievement. To meet the second, he had to come from a home and neighborhood classified by professional social workers as "marginal in economic circumstances" (annual family income no higher than $4,000), as well as "culturally deprived" (little conventional intellectual stimulation in terms of number of books and magazines in the home, little encouragement of academic achievement by parents or siblings, and no utilization of community libraries or other "cultural" outlets).

Approximately 200 subjects (Ss) were initially investigated to see if they met the foregoing and the following criteria: age, sex, IQ, and reading achievement. Forty-eight of them, who seemed to constitute a relatively homogeneous group, were selected. They were randomly divided into three groups of 16 each. Subsequently, one S from each group was eliminated, leaving three groups of 15, which were used for comparison of instructional techniques.

Table 28.1 summarizes the descriptive variables used to identify Ss as a function of their random assignment to the groups. The mean chronological ages, mental ages, Gates Primary Reading Test scores, and number of programmed words recognized (out of a possible 93) were all reasonably congruent.

Table 28.1. Summary of Descriptive Variables about Subjects

	Group M		Group W		Group C	
Sex	Boys	Girls	Boys	Girls	Boys	Girls
Number	6	9	10	5	9	6
	Mean	Range	Mean	Range	Mean	Range
Chronological Age	7.8	6.8 to 10.2	7.3	6.8 to 8.8	7.3	7.8 to 8.6
Mental Age[1]	6.7	4.9 to 8.1	6.4	4.7 to 8.1	6.0	5.3 to 7.3
Programmed Words Known	18.3	7 to 34	17.3	0 to 32	18.6	0 to 36
GPRT[2] – Grade Placement	1.47	1.3 to 1.9	1.56	1.3 to 1.9	1.56	1.3 to 2.2
GPRT – Raw Score	2.3	0 to 8	4.2	0 to 8	3.7	0 to 11

[1]Mental ages were calculated from scores in the Peabody Vocabulary Test (Dunn, 1959)

[2]Gates Primary Reading Test, Type PPR, Paragraph Reading (Gates, 1958)

Each S was in the second grade in one of the three schools located in the lowest socio-economic districts of Tampa, Florida; all of them met the criteria for "slow-learning" and "culturally deprived" children given above. Each of the three groups of Ss was to be exposed to one instructional method.

PROCEDURE

The group taught by the teaching machine was designated as Group M, the programmed text book group as Group W, and the conventional classroom group as Group C.

Instructional methods

Group M received instruction from the Mast Teaching Machine, a mechanical optical device which provides rear projection of prepared filmstrips on a ground glass screen. The S examines the exposed top three-quarters of a frame presenting an individual item in a linear sequence; he then notes his response on a mechanically-actuated strip of adding machine tape located directly beneath the screen. Then he presses a button marked "Answer," which actuates a mechanical slide, revealing the correct response. At the same time, the adding machine tape is moved forward approximately one inch to a position beneath a lucite shield. The S thus cannot alter his response, but he may view it in relationship to the correct response. Having examined the two responses, he then presses a button marked "Advance" and the upper portion of a new frame is exposed.

Preparation of daily materials, as well as loading and focusing of the machine, were done by a research assistant. The relatively simple mechanical operation of the machine was learned rapidly by all subjects.

Group W received instruction from a workbook of linear programmed printed material, prepared by a lithographic plate process from the original printed material and art work used to make the filmstrips for the Mast Teaching Machine. Each workbook consisted of 19 pages; each page contained four sequential frames of programmed material, arranged vertically. The S used a 4×6 file card to screen off part of the page, exposing only one frame and a three-part multiple-choice question. Using a pencil, he indicated his choice of answer by circling it or marking it through with an "X." He then exposed the answer portion of the frame by sliding his card approximately one-half inch further down the page, thus having an opportunity to compare his answer choice with the exposed correct answer. This provided immediacy of feedback similar to that in the machine presentation.

The sequence of frame presentations, the art work and all other aspects of the program were exactly the same as those used in the machine method. The major difference for the two PI groups, then, was in the format, not in the substance, of the program.

Subjects in Group C were enrolled in the same classrooms as the experimental subjects and were exposed to the regular classroom routine, but not to the programmed instructional materials. The investigators recognized that Group C could not be considered a "control group"; rather, these Ss were selected to provide a basis for measuring the amount of learning which might be attributable solely to classroom enrollment.

As anticipated, some progress was shown by Group C during the instructional period. However, the magnitude of difference between the two groups of PI subjects and the classroom group indicates that much of this difference can be attributed to the programmed instruction.

This research program was not intended to study programmed instruction versus classroom instruction, since the experimental subjects were exposed to both conditions. Rather, the intent was to see to what extent programmed instructional materials would be effective in supplementing regular classroom instruction. Since ninety percent of the programmed words were drawn from basic sight vocabulary lists, it was anticipated that there would be considerable overlap between the programmed words and the material being presented in the classroom.

Presentation conditions

The 93 words used in the study were drawn for the most part from vocabulary lists found in most basic reading series. They included commonly-used nouns, pronouns, verbs, prepositions and articles which are usually presented in first and second grade classes. The machine and textbook programs were identical, except for the mechanics of presentation. The 93 words were presented in 16 lesson units, each designed to take up one instructional period. Programmed words were presented singly, in two-to-four-word phrases, and in simple sentences. The Paragraph Reading Test was composed wholly of words from the program, but none of the sentences in the PRT was used in the instructional program.

Individual instruction rooms were provided in each of the three schools and a regular schedule of instruction periods was maintained. Pupils were sent to the "special teaching room" at designated times each day. A project assistant was in attendance with them during instruction. The assistants prepared the materials for the *S*s and reviewed the new words to be presented, so that *S*s were familiar with their pronunciation; they also answered any questions that arose. The assistants were instructed to keep their interactions with *S*s to an absolute minimum during the instructional periods. They supervised three to five *S*s at a time. (They later reported that, if space and equipment were available, six to ten *S*s could be supervised by one person.)

For both machine and workbook presentations, individual sessions averaged approximately forty minutes; the range was from twenty minutes to one hour. All *S*s completed the program within one month.

Evaluation of instruction

Pupil progress was evaluated just before and immediately after the instructional period. To measure retention, a retest was given thirty days after completion of instruction. The evaluation instruments were (1) the Peabody Picture Vocabulary Test (Dunn, 1959), (2) a sight recognition test of programmed words, (3) the Gates Primary Paragraph Reading Test (GPRT, Gates, 1958), and (4) the Paragraph Reading Test (PRT), constructed wholly of programmed words described earlier. All measures except the PPVT were used for post-instruction evaluation. The 30-day follow-up evaluation consisted only of the sight recognition test. (The GPRT was not included in the 30-day test because of its observed lack of sensitivity.)

Data from the GPRT were reported as raw scores and grade equivalencies. The former gave a more precise index of progress achieved. Data from the sight recognition list and the PRT were also presented as raw scores. No attempt was made to assign grade equivalencies for the PRT.

RESULTS

Pre-instruction information is presented in Table 28.1, which provides a reference point for analysis of gains made in word recognition and GPRT scores. "Gains" are defined simply as differences between words known prior to instruction and those known afterwards.

Table 28.2 presents the mean gains made by each of the groups on the relevant assessment measures. The average word gains for the three

Table 28.2. Gains in Word Recognition and Reading

	Instruction Groups					
	Group M		Group W		Group C	
Assessment Criteria	Mean	Range	Mean	Range	Mean	Range
Programmed Words (N = 93)						
Pre-instruction to						
Post-Test	30.7	8 to 50	33·1	10 to 55	4.5	− 1 to 10
Pre-instruction to 30						
days Post-Test	30.9	11 to 58	30.1	11 to 50	10.9	1 to 34
Paragraph Reading						
(Programmed Words:						
N = 177)						
Pre-instruction to						
Post-Test	75.2	24 to 144	79.6	20 to 145	25.5	3 to 64
Gates Primary Reading Test						
Raw Scores						
Pre-instruction to						
Post-Test	3.2	− 3 to 7	2.1	− 1 to 7	1.4	− 4 to 7
Grade Placement						
Pre-instruction to						
Post-Test	0.19	− 0.30 to 0.55	0.16	− 0.05 to 0.50	0.08	− 1.50 to 0.65

groups were 30.7 words (Group M), 33.1 words (Group W), and 4.5 words (Group C). These represent percentage gains of 166 per cent, 191 per cent, and 24 per cent. Another way of comparing group differences is to point out that Group M gained 41.0 per cent of the total number of "unknown" words during instruction and Group W gained 43.6 per cent. However, Group C gained only 6.1 per cent of the words not initially recognized.

The Paragraph Reading Tests constructed from the 93 programmed words consisted of 177 words. The two PI groups demonstrated significantly higher recognition scores on the post-instruction "tests" than did Group C. The mean word recognition gain was 75.2 words for Group M, 79.6 words for Group W, and 25.5 words for Group C. Although fluency was not measured objectively, project assistants reported "reasonable" fluency in paragraph reading for both PI groups, but not for the classroom group. That is, most Ss in the PI groups pronounced enough words consecutively to convey the impression that they were "reading," not merely recognizing individual words.

On the Gates Primary Reading Test, mean word gains were 3.2 (Group

M), 2.1 (Group W), and 1.4 (Group C). The equivalent grade-level advances for the three groups were 0.19, 0.16, and 0.08, respectively. The range of scores showed that some Ss in each group actually recognized fewer individual words on the test following instruction, although the majority showed increases in word recognition. Children in both PI groups did better than those in the classroom group; however, the magnitude of difference was not as great as on the other assessment techniques.

In our previous work with retarded children (Malpass, *et al.*, 1964) one of the most significant findings was the high level of retention of word-recognition several weeks after termination of programmed instruction. A similar finding is indicated in Table 28.2 for slow-learning, culturally deprived children. In a follow-up evaluation, thirty days after completion of the study, over ninety per cent of words acquired during instruction were retained by Ss in both teaching machine and programmed textbook groups. An interesting corollary was that the Ss in Group C actually gained in numbers of words recognized over this period. The post-instruction and 30-day follow-up test scores represent very high levels of "retention" for slow-learning children taught by both PI methods. They indicate that the effects of programmed instruction continue well after it is terminated.

Calculation of t-ratios between each group demonstrated no significant differences between the two PI groups in word gains on any of the measuring instruments. There were large and significant differences between both of these groups and the classroom group, however. They are reported in detail in the investigators' report to the U.S. Office of Education (Williams, Gilmore, & Malpass, 1967).

In summary, Ss in both the teaching machine and programmed text-book groups demonstrated dramatic gains in word-recognition and paragraph reading during the study, and maintained high levels of performance more than four weeks later. The classroom group also showed gains in both types of verbal performance, but they were of much lower magnitude. The dramatic differences between groups taught by programmed instruction and those taught by conventional classroom procedures are reflected not only in raw score gains, but also in the range of scores for each of the assessment procedures (*see* Table 28.2).

DISCUSSION

The consistency of differences in post-instruction word recognition and Paragraph Reading Test scores between the two PI groups and the classroom group is notable. However, the results of the Gates Paragraph Reading Test do not reflect the same magnitude of raw-score differences between PI and classroom learning as do the other tests. On the one hand, this suggests a lack of sensitivity of the instrument for the purpose of this study. On the other, it may mean that the words selected for the study were too restricted in number or difficulty to be useful for generalizations about paragraph reading ability. On the basis of results of the PRT (composed only of programmed words), however, it seems reasonably certain that contextual reading, utilizing words presented via PI, is improved greatly by exposure to either teaching machine or programmed textbook.

The teaching machine presentation was by far the most appealing to the children, according to observations of the project assistants and the investigators. Other studies (e.g., Birnbrauer, et al., 1964) have suggested that there may be a diminution in motivational appeal after a month or two of working at the machines. For the period of this study (one month), there appeared to be little decrease in interest by Ss in this learning process.

While the programmed workbook did not seem to have the same attractiveness for the Ss as the teaching machine, progress of the children in Group W was highly similar to that of those using the machine. However, several cases were reported of casual treatment of the workbooks, with episodes of random marking, "cheating" by looking ahead in the book, and a lower general motivational level than for Group M.

All classroom teachers involved in the project reported that both programmed methods had marked salutary effects on the interest of Ss in reading in the classroom. They also reported increases in self-confidence.

These findings and reports suggest that, for slow-learning children, both teaching machine and programmed textbook presentations facilitate learning of verbal material and increase motivation for other aspects of school work. Presentation of verbal materials of the type and amount used in this study definitely seems feasible for slow-learning children of similar ages and socio-economic circumstances.

REFERENCES

Becker, J. L. *A Programmed guide to writing autoinstructional programs.* Camden: Radio Corp. America, 1963.

Birnbrauer, J. S., Kidder, J. K. & Tague, C. E. Programming reading for the teacher's point of view. *Programmed Instruction,* **3**, 1964, 1–2.

Blackman, L. S. & Capobianco, R. J. An evaluation of programmed instruction with the mentally retarded utilizing teaching machines. *Amer. J. ment. Defic.*, September, 1965.

Deutsch, M. Social and psychological prospectives on the development of the disadvantaged learner. *Merrill-Palmer Quarterly*, Spring, 1964.

Dunn, L. M. *The Peabody Picture Vocabulary Test*. American Guidance Service, Inc., 1959.

Dunn, L. (Ed.), *Exceptional children in the schools*. New York: Holt, Rinehart and Winston, 1963. Chapter 2.

Gates, A. I. *Gates Primary Reading Test, Type PPR, Paragraph Reading*. New York: Bureau of Publications, Teachers College, Columbia Univer., 1958.

Kennedy, W. A., Van De Reit, V. & White, J. C., Jr. A normative sample of intelligence and achievement of Negro elementary school children in the southeastern United States. *Monographs of the Society for Research in Child Development*, 1963, **28**, No. 6.

Kirk, S. A. *Educating exceptional children*. Boston: Houghton Mifflin, 1962.

Lumsdaine, A. A. & Glaser, R. *Teaching machines and programmed learning*. Washington, D.C.: National Education Assn. of the U.S., 1960.

Malpass, L. F. Programmed instruction for retarded children. In A. Baumeister (Ed.), *Mental retardation: Selected problems in appraisal, education, and rehabilitation*. Chicago: Aldine Pub. Co., 1967.

Malpass, L. F., Hardy, M. W., Gilmore, A. S. & Williams, C. F. Automated instruction for retarded children. *Amer. J. ment. Defic.*, **69**, 3, November, 1964.

Smith, E. A. & Quackenbush, J. Devereux teaching aids employed in presenting elementary mathematics in a special education setting. *Psychol. Rep.*, **7**, 1960, 333–336.

Stolurow, L. M. *Teaching by machine*. U.S. Dept. Health, Education, and Welfare, Office of Education, OE-34010, Cooperative Research Monograph No. 6, U.S. Government Printing Office, Washington, D.C., 1961.

Vernon, M. D. *Backwardness in reading*. Cambridge Univer. Press, 1958.

Williams, C. F., Gilmore, A. S. & Malpass, L. F. *Programmed reading instruction for culturally deprived slow learners*. Washington, D.C.: U.S. Dept. Health, Education, and Welfare, Office of Education; OE Project 6-8438, 1967.

ARTICLE 29

Computerized Instruction and The Learning Process*

RICHARD C. ATKINSON

Stanford University

In recent years there has been a tremendous number of articles and news releases dealing with computer-assisted instruction, or as it has been abbreviated, CAI. One might conjecture that this proliferation is an indicant of rapid progress in the field. Unfortunately, I doubt that it is. A few of the reports about CAI are based on substantial experience and research, but the majority are vague speculations and conjectures with little if any data or real experience to back them up. I do not want to denigrate the role of speculation and conjecture in a newly developing area like CAI. However, of late it seems to have produced little more than a repetition of ideas that were exciting in the 1950s but, in the absence of new research, are simply well-worn cliches in the late 1960s.

These remarks should not be misinterpreted. Important and significant research on CAI is being carried on in many laboratories around the country, but certainly not as much as one is led to believe by the attendant publicity. The problem for someone trying to evaluate developments in the field is to distinguish between those reports that are based on fact and those that are disguised forms of science fiction. In my paper, I shall try to stay very close to data and actual experience. My claims will be less grand than many that have been made for CAI, but they will be based on a substantial research effort.

In 1964 Patrick Suppes and I initiated a project under a grant from the Office of Education to develop and implement a CAI program in initial

*Invited address presented at the meeting of the Division of Educational Psychology, American Psychological Association, Washington, D.C., September 1967.

Reprinted from the *American Psychologist*, Vol. 23, No. 4, April 1968, pp. 225–239, by permission of the American Psychological Association.

reading and mathematics. Because of our particular research interests, Suppes has taken responsibility for the mathematics curriculum and I have been responsible for the initial reading program. At the beginning of the project, two major hurdles had to be overcome. There was no lesson material in either mathematics or reading suitable for CAI, and an integrated CAI system had not yet been designed and produced by a single manufacturer. The development of the curricula and the development of the system have been carried out as a parallel effort over the last 3 years with each having a decided influence on the other.

Today I would like to report on the progress of the reading program with particular reference to the past school year when for the first time a sizable group of students received a major portion of their daily reading instruction under computer control. The first year's operation must be considered essentially as an extended debugging of both the computer system and the curriculum materials. Nevertheless, some interesting comments can be made on the basis of this experience regarding both the feasibility of CAI and the impact of such instruction on the overall learning process.

Before describing the Stanford Project, a few general remarks may help place it in perspective. Three levels of CAI can be defined. Discrimination between levels is based not on hardware considerations, but principally on the complexity and sophistication of the student-system interaction. An advanced student-system interaction may be achieved with a simple teletype terminal, and the most primitive interaction may require some highly sophisticated computer programming and elaborate student terminal devices.

At the simplest interactional level are those systems that present a fixed, linear sequence of problems. Student errors may be corrected in a variety of ways, but no real-time decisions are made for modifying the flow of instructional material as a function of the student's response history. Such systems have been termed "drill-and-practice" systems and at Stanford University are exemplified by a series of fourth-, fifth-, and sixth-grade programs in arithmetic and language arts that are designed to supplement classroom instruction. These particular programs are being used in several different areas of California and also in Kentucky and Mississippi, all under control of one central computer located at Stanford University. Currently as many as 2,000 students are being run per day; it requires little imagination to see how such a system could be extended to cover the entire country. Unfortunately, I do not have time to discuss these drill-and-practice programs in this paper, but there are several recent reports describing the research (Fishman, Keller, & Atkinson, 1968; Suppes, 1966; Suppes, Jerman, & Groen, 1966).

At the other extreme of our scale characterizing student-system interactions are "dialogue" programs. Such programs are under investigation at several universities and industrial concerns, but to date progress has been extremely limited. The goal of the dialogue approach is to provide the richest possible student-system interaction where the student is free to construct natural-language responses, ask questions in an unrestricted mode, and in general exercise almost complete control over the sequence of learning events.

"Tutorial" programs lie between the above extremes of student-system interaction. Tutorial programs have the capability for real-time decision making and instructional branching contingent on a single response or on some subset of the student's response history. Such programs allow students to follow separate and diverse paths through the curriculum based on their particular performance records. The probability is high in a tutorial program that no two students will encounter exactly the same sequence of lesson materials. However, student responses are greatly restricted since they must be chosen from a prescribed set of responses, or constructed in such a manner that a relatively simple text analysis will be sufficient for their evaluation. The CAI Reading Program is tutorial in nature, and it is this level of student-interaction that will be discussed today.

THE STANFORD CAI SYSTEM

The Stanford Tutorial System was developed under a contract between the University and the IBM Corporation. Subsequent developments by IBM of the basic system have led to what has been designated the IBM-1500 Instructional System which should soon be commerically available. The basic system consists of a central process computer with accompanying disc-storage units, proctor stations, and an interphase to 16 student terminals. The central process computer acts as an intermediary between each student and his particular course material which is stored in one of the disc-storage units. A student terminal consists of a picture projector, a cathode ray tube (CRT), a light pen, a modified typewriter keyboard, and an audio system which can play prerecorded messages (*see* Fig. 29.1).

The CRT is essentially a television screen on which alpha-numeric characters and a limited set of graphics (i.e., simple line drawings) can

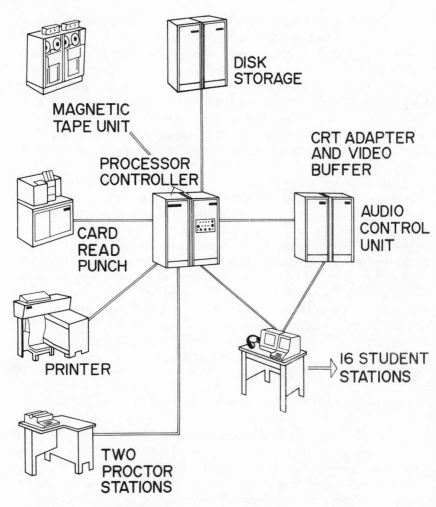

Fig. 29.1. System configuration for Stanford CAI System.

be generated under computer control. The film projector is a rear-view projection device which permits us to display still pictures in black and white or color. Each film strip is stored in a self-threading cartridge and contains over 1,000 images which may be accessed very quickly under computer control. The student receives audio messages via a high-speed device capable of selecting any number of messages varying in length from a few seconds to over 15 minutes. The audio messages are stored in tape cartridges which contain approximately 2 hours of messages and, like the film cartridge, may be changed very quickly. To gain the student's attention, an arrow can be placed at any point on the CRT and moved in synchronization with an audio message to emphasize given words or phrases, much like the "bouncing ball" in a singing cartoon.

The major response device used in the reading program is the light pen, which is simply a light-sensitive probe. When the light pen is placed on the CRT, coordinates of the position touched are sensed as a response and recorded by the computer. Responses may also be entered into the system through the typewriter keyboard. However, only limited use has been made of this response mode in the reading program. This is not to minimize the value of keyboard responses, but rather to admit that we have not as yet addressed ourselves to the problem of teaching first-grade children to handle a typewriter keyboard.

The CAI System controls the flow of information and the input of student responses according to the instructional logic built into the curriculum materials. The sequence of events is roughly as follows: The computer assembles the necessary commands for a given instructional sequence from a disc-storage unit. The commands involve directions to the terminal device to display a given sequence of symbols on the CRT, to present a particular image on the film projector, and to play a specific audio message. After the appropriate visual and auditory materials have been presented, a "ready" signal indicates to the student that a response is expected. Once a response has been entered, it is evaluated and, on the basis of this evaluation and the student's past history, the computer makes a decision as to what materials will subsequently be presented. The time-sharing nature of the system allows us to handle 16 students simultaneously and to cycle through these evaluative steps so rapidly that from a student's viewpoint it appears that he is getting immediate attention from the computer whenever he inputs a response.

THE CAI READING CURRICULUM

The flexibility offered by this computer system is of value only if the curriculum materials make sense both in terms of the logical organization of the subject matter and the psychology of the learning processes involved. Time does not permit a detailed discussion of the rationale behind the curriculum that we have developed. Let me simply say that our approach to initial reading can be characterized as applied psycholinguistics. Hypotheses about the reading process and the nature of learning to read have been formulated on the basis of linguistic information, observations of language use, and an analysis of the function of the written code. These hypotheses have been tested in a series of pilot studies structured to simulate actual teaching situations. On the basis of these experimental findings, the hypotheses have been modified, retested, and ultimately incorporated into the curriculum as principles dictating the format and flow of the instructional sequence. Of course, this statement is somewhat of an idealization, since very little curriculum material can be said to have been the perfect end product of rigorous empirical evaluation. We would claim, however, that the fundamental tenets of the Stanford reading program have been formulated and modified on the basis of considerable empirical evidence. It seems probable that these will be further modified as more data accumulate.

The introduction of new words from one level of the curriculum to the next is dictated by a number of principles (Rodgers, 1967). These principles are specified in terms of a basic unit that we have called the vocalic center group (VCG). The VCG in English is defined as a vowel nucleus with zero to three preceding and zero to four following consonants. The sequencing of new vocabulary is determined by the length of the VCG units, and the regularity of the orthographic and phonological correspondences. Typical of the principles are the following:

1. VCG sets containing single consonant elements are introduced before those containing consonant clusters (*tap* and *rap* before *trap*).
2. VCG sets containing initial consonant clusters are introduced before those containing final consonant clusters (*stop* before *post*).
3. VCG sets containing check (short) vowels are introduced before those containing letter name (long) vowels (*met* and *mat* before *meat* or *mate*).
4. Single VCG sequences are introduced before multiple VCG sequences (*mat* before *matter*, *stut* before *stutter*).

More detailed rules are required to determine the order for introducing specific vowels and consonants within a VCG pattern, and for introducing specific VCG patterns in polysyllabic words. These rules frequently represent a compromise between linguistic factors, pattern productivity, item frequency, and textual "usefulness," in that order of significance.

The instructional materials are divided into eight levels each composed of about 32 lessons.[1] The lessons are designed so that the average student will complete one in approximately 30 minutes but this can vary greatly with the fast student finishing much sooner and the slow student sometimes taking 2 hours or more if he hits most of the remedial material. Within a lesson, the various instructional tasks can be divided into three broad areas: (*a*) decoding skills, (*b*) comprehension skills, (*c*) games and other motivational devices. Decoding skills involve such tasks as letter and letter-string identification, word list learning, phonic drills, and related types of activities. Comprehension involves such tasks as having the computer read to the child or having the child himself read sentences, paragraphs, or complete stories about which he is then asked a series of questions. The questions deal with the direct recall of facts, generalizations about main ideas in the story, and inferential questions which require the child to relate information presented in the story to his own experience. Finally, many different types of games are sequenced into the lessons primarily to encourage continued attention to the materials. The games are similar to those played in the classroom and are structured to evaluate the developing reading skills of the child.

Matrix construction   To illustrate the instructional materials focusing on decoding skills let me describe a task that we have called matrix "construction." This task provides practice in learning to associate orthographically similar sequences with appropriate rhyme and alliteration patterns. Rhyming patterns are presented in the columns of the matrix, and alliteration patterns are presented in the rows of the matrix as indicated in Fig. 29.4.

The matrix is constructed one cell at a time. The initial consonant of a CVC word is termed the initial unit, and the vowel and the final consonant are termed the final unit. The intersection of an initial unit row and a final unit column determines the entry in any cell.

The problem format for the construction of each cell is divided into four parts: Parts A and D are standard instructional sections and Parts B and C are remedial sections. The flow diagram in Fig. 29.2 indicates that remedial Parts B and C are branches from Part A and may be presented independently or in combination.

To see how this goes, let us consider the example illustrated in Fig. 29.3. The student first sees on the CRT the empty cell with its associated initial and final units and an array of response choices. He hears the audio

---

[1]For a detailed account of the curriculum materials see Wilson and Atkinson (1967) and Rodgers (1967). See also Atkinson and Hansen (1966) and Hansen and Rodgers (1965).

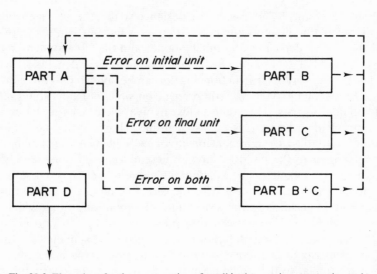

Fig. 29.2. Flow chart for the construction of a cell in the matrix construction task.

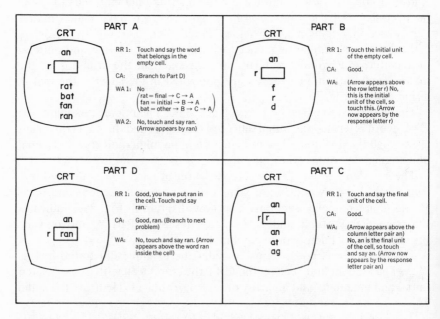

Fig. 29.3. First cell of the matrix construction task.

message indicated by response request 1 (RR 1) in Part A of Fig. 29.3. If the student makes the correct response (CA) (i.e., touches *ran* with his light pen), he proceeds to Part D where he sees the word written in the cell and receives one additional practice trial.

In the initial presentation in Part A, the array of multiple-choice responses is designed to identify three possible types of errors:

1. The initial unit is correct, but the final unit is not.
2. The final unit is correct, but the initial unit is not.
3. Neither the initial unit nor the final unit is correctly identified.

If, in Part A, the student responds with *fan* he is branched to remedial Part B where attention is focused on the initial unit of the cell. If a correct response is made in Part B, the student is returned to Part A for a second attempt. If an incorrect response (WA) is made in Part B, an arrow is displayed on the CRT to indicate the correct response, which the student is then asked to touch.

If, in Part A, the student responds with *rat*, he is branched to remedial Part C where additional instruction is given on the final unit of the cell. The procedure in Part C is similar to Part B. However, it should be noted that in the remedial instruction the initial letter is never pronounced (Part B), whereas the final unit is always pronounced (Part C). If, in Part A, the student responds with *bat*, then he has made an error on both the initial and final unit and is branched through both Part B and Part C.

When the student returns to Part A after completing a remedial section, a correct response will advance him to Part D as indicated. If a wrong answer response is made on the second pass, an arrow is placed beside the correct response area and held there until a correct response is made. If the next response is still an error, a message is sent to the proctor and the sequence is repeated from the beginning.

When a student has made a correct response on Parts A and D, he is advanced to the next word cell of the matrix which has a problem format and sequence identical to that just described. The individual cell building is continued block by block until the matrix is complete. The upper left-hand panel of Fig. 29.4 indicates the CRT display for adding the next cell in our example. The order in which row and column cells are added is essentially random.

When the matrix is complete, the entries are reordered and a criterion test is given over all cell entries. The test involves displaying the full matrix with complete cell entries as indicated in the lower left-hand panel of Fig. 29.4. Randomized requests are made to the student to identify cell

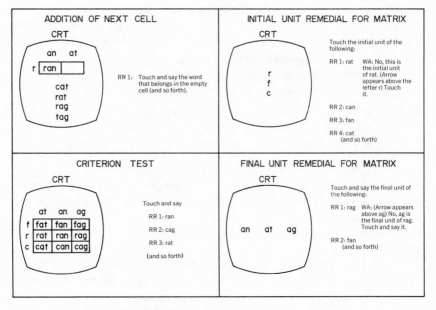

Fig. 29.4. Continuation of matrix construction task.

entries. Since the first pass through the full matrix is viewed as a criterion test, no reinforcement is given. Errors are categorized as initial, final, and other; if the percentage of total errors on the criterion test exceeds a predetermined value, then remedial exercises are provided of the type shown in the two right-hand panels of Fig. 29.4. If all the errors are recorded in one category (initial or final), only the remedial material appropriate to that category is presented. If the errors are distributed over both categories, then both types of remedial material are presented. After working through one or both of the remedial sections, the student is branched back for a second pass through the criterion matrix. The second pass is a teaching trial as opposed to the initial test cycle; the student proceeds with the standard correction and optimization routines.

An analysis of performance on the matrix task is still incomplete, but some preliminary results are available. On the initial pass (Part A) our students were correct about 45% of the time; however, when an error did occur, 21% of the time it involved only the final unit, 53% of the time only the initial unit, and 26% of the time both initial and final units. The pattern of performances changed markedly on the first pass through the criterion test. Here the subject was correct about 65% of the time; when an error occurred, 32% of the time it involved only the final unit, 33% of the time only the initial unit, and 35% of the time both units. Thus performance showed a significant improvement from Part A to the criterion test; equally important, initial errors were more than twice as frequent as final errors in Part A, but were virtually equal on the criterion test.

The matrix exercise is a good example of the material used in the curriculum to teaching decoding skills. We now consider two examples ("form class" and "inquiries") of tasks that are designed to teach comprehension skills.

Form class   Comprehension of a sentence involves an understanding of English syntax. One behavioral manifestation of a child's syntactic sophistication is his ability to group words into appropriate form classes. This task provides lesson materials that teach the form-class characteristics of the words just presented in the matrix section of a lesson. The following type of problem is presented to the student (the material in the box is displayed on the CRT and below are audio messages; the child answers by appropriately placing his light pen on the CRT):

	tan	
Dan saw the	fat man	hat.
	run	

Only one of the words in the column will make sense in the sentence. Touch and say the word that belongs in the sentence.

CA: Yes, Dan saw the tan hat. Do the next one.

WA: No, tan is the word that makes sense. Dan saw the tan hat. Touch and say tan. (An arrow then appears above tan.)

The sentence is composed of words that are in the reading vocabulary of the student (i.e., they have been presented in previous or current lessons). The response set includes a word which is of the correct form class but is semantically inappropriate, two words that are of the wrong form class, and the correct word. A controlled variety of sentence types is employed, and the answer sets are distributed over all syntactic slots within each sentence type. Responses are categorized in rather broad terms as *nouns*, *verbs*, *modifiers*, and *other*. The response data can be examined for systematic errors over a large number of items. Examples of the kinds of questions that can be asked are: (*a*) Are errors for various form classes in various sentence positions similarly distributed? (*b*) How are response latencies affected by the syntactic and serial position of the response set within the sentence? Answers to these and other questions should provide information that will permit more systematic study of the relationship of sentence structure to reading instruction.

Inquiries Individual words in sentences may constitute unique and conversationally correct answers to questions. These questions take the interrogative "Who ......? What ......? How ......?" etc. The ability to select the word in a sentence that uniquely answers one of these questions demonstrates one form of reading comprehension. The inquiry exercises constitute an assessment of this reading comprehension ability. In the following example, the sentence "John hit the ball" is displayed on the CRT accompanied by these audio messages:

Touch and say the word that answers the question.

RR 1 Who hit the ball?
CA: Yes, the word "John" tells us who hit the ball.
WA: No, John tells us who hit the ball. Touch and say John. (An arrow then appears on the CRT above John.)
RR 2 What did John hit?
CA: Yes, the word "ball" tells us what John hit.
WA: No, ball tells us what John hit. Touch and say ball. (An arrow then appears above ball.)

As in the form-class section, each sentence is composed of words from the student's reading vocabulary. A wide variety of sentence structures is utilized, beginning with simple subject-verb-object sentences and progressing to structures of increasing complexity. Data from this task bear on several hypotheses about comprehension. If comprehension is equated with a correct response to an inquiry question, then the following statements are verified by our data: (*a*) Items for which the correct answer is in the medial position of the sentence are more difficult to comprehend than items in the initial or final positions; final position items are easier to comprehend than items in the initial position. (*b*) Items for which the correct answer is an adjective are more difficult to comprehend than items in which the correct answer is a noun or verb; similarly nouns are more difficult than verbs. (*c*) Longer sentences, measured by word length, are more difficult to comprehend than shorter sentences.

These are only a few examples of the types of tasks used in the reading curriculum, but they indicate the nature of the student-system interaction. What is not illustrated by these examples is the potential for long-term optimization policies based on an extended response history from the subject. We shall return to this topic later.

PROBLEMS IN IMPLEMENTING THE CURRICULUM

Before turning to the data from last year's run, let me consider briefly the problem of translating the curriculum materials into a language that can be understood by the computer. The particular computer language we use is called Coursewriter II, a language which was developed by IBM in close collaboration with Stanford. A coded lesson is a series of Coursewriter II commands which causes the computer to display and manipulate text on the CRT, position and display film in the projector, position and play audio messages, accept and evaluate keyboard and lightpen responses, update the performance record of each student, and implement the branching logic of the lesson flow by means of manipulating and referencing a set of switches and counters. A typical lesson in the reading program, which takes the average student about 30 minutes to complete, requires in excess of 9,000 coursewriter commands for its execution.

Table 29.1. Audio Scrip and Film Chips with Hypothetical Addresses

Address	Message
	Audio information
A01	Touch and say the word that goes with the picture.
A02	Good. Bag. Do the next one.
A03	No.
A04	The word that goes with the picture is bag. Touch and say bag.
A05	Good. Card. Do the next one.
A06	No.
A07	The word that goes with the picture is card. Touch and say card.
	Film strip
F01	Picture of a bag.
F02	Picture of a card.

Table 29.2. Computer Commands Required to Present Two Examples of the Problem Described in the Text

Commands	Explanation
PR	Problem: Prepares machine for beginning of new problem.
LD 0/S1	Load: Loads zero into the error switch (S1). The role of switches and counters will be explained later.
FP F01	Film Position: Displays frame F01 (picture of a bag).
DT 5,18/bat/	Display Text: Displays "bat" on line 5 starting in column 18 on the CRT.
DT 7,18/bag/	Displays "bag" on line 7 starting in column 18 on the CRT.
DT 9,18/rat/	Displays "rat" on line 9 starting in column 18 on the CRT.
AUP A01	Audio Play: Plays audio message A01. "Touch and say the word that goes with the picture."
L1 EP 30/ABCD1	Enter and Process: Activates the light-pen; specifies the time limit (30 sec.) and the problem identifier (ABCD1) that will be placed in the data record along with all responses to this problem. If a response is made within the time limit the computer skips from this command down to the CA (correct answer comparison) command. If no response is made within the time limit, the commands immediately following the EP command are executed.
AD 1/C4	Add: Adds one to the overtime counter (C4).
LD 1/S1	Loads one into the error switch (S1).
AUP A04	Plays message A04. "The word that goes with the picture is bag. Touch and say bag."
DT 7,16/→/	Displays arrow on line 7, column 16 (arrow pointing at "bag").
BR L1	Branch: Branches to command labeled L1. The computer will now do that command and continue from that point.
CA 1,7,3,18/C1	Correct Answer: Compares student's response with an area one line high starting on line 7 and three columns wide starting in column 18 of the CRT. If his response falls within this area, it will be recorded in the data with the answer identifier C1. When a correct answer has been made, the commands from here down to WA (wrong answer comparison) are executed. Then the program jumps ahead to the next PR. If the response does not fall in the correct area, the machine skips from this command down to the WA command.
BR L2/S1/1	Branches to command labeled L2 if the error switch (S1) is equal to one.
AD 1/C1	Adds one to the initial correct answer counter (C1).
L2 AUP A02	Plays audio message A02. "Good. Bag. Do the next one."
WA 1,5,3,18/W1 WA 1,9,3,18/W2	Wrong Answer: These two commands compare the student response with the areas of the two wrong answers, that is, the area one line high starting on line 5 and three columns wide starting in column 18, and the area one line high starting on line 9 and three columns wide starting in column 18. If the response falls within one of these two areas, it will be recorded with the appropriate identifier (W1 or W2). When a defined wrong answer has been made, the commands from here

Table 29.2 (*continued*)

Commands	Explanation
	down to UN (undefined answer) are executed. Then the computer goes back to the EP for this problem. If the response does not fall in one of the defined wrong answer areas, the machine skips from this command down to the UN command.
AD 1/C2	Adds one to the defined wrong answer counter (C2).
L3 LD 1/S1	Loads one into the error switch (S1).
AUP A03	Plays message A03. "No."
AUP A04	Plays message A04. "The word that goes with the picture is bag. Touch and say bag."
DT 7,16/→/	Displays arrow on line 7, column 16.
UN	Undefined Wrong Answer: If machine reaches this point in the program, the student has made neither a correct nor a defined wrong answer.
AD 1/C3	Adds one to the undefined answer counter (C3).
BR L3	Branches to command labeled L3. (The same thing should be done for both UN and WA answers. This branch saves repeating the commands from L3 down to UN.)
PR	Prepares the machine for next problem.
LD 0/S1 FP F02 DT 5,18/card/ DT 7,18/cart/ DT 9,18/hard/	These commands prepare the display for the 2nd problem. Notice the new film position and new words displayed. The student was told to "do the next one" when he finished the last problem so he needs no audio message to begin this.
L4 EP 30/ABCD2	Light-pen is activated.
AD 1/C4 LD 1/S1 AUP A07 DT 5,16/→/ BR L4	These commands are done only if no response is made in the time limit of 30 seconds. Otherwise the machine skips to the CA command.
CA 1,5,4,18/C2	Compares response with correct answer area.
BR L5/S1/1 AD 1/C1 L5 AUP A05	Adds one to the initial correct answer counter unless the error switch (S1) shows that an error has been made for this problem. The student, is told he is correct and goes on to the next problem. These commands are executed only if a correct answer has been made.
WA 1,7,4,18/W3 WA 1,9,4,18/W4	Compare response with defined wrong answer.
AD 1/C2 L6 LD 1/S1 AUP A06 AUP A07 DT 5,16/→/	Adds one to the defined wrong answer area and the error switch (S1) is loaded with one to show that an error has been made on this problem. The student is told he is wrong and shown the correct answer and asked to touch it. These commands are executed only if a defined wrong answer has been made.
UN	An undefined response has been made if the machine reaches this command.
AD 1/C3 BR L6	Adds one to the undefined answer counter and we branch up to give the same audio, etc. as is given for the defined wrong answer.

A simple example will give you some feeling for the coding problem. The example is from a task designed to teach both letter discrimination and the meaning of words. A picture illustrating the word being taught is presented on the projector screen. Three words, including the word illustrated, are presented on the CRT. A message is played on the audio asking the child to touch the word on the CRT that matches the picture on the film projector. The student can then make his response using the light pen. If he makes no response within the specified time limit of 30 seconds, he is told the correct answer, an arrow points to it, and he is asked to touch it. If he makes a response within the time limit, the point that he touches is compared by the computer with the correct-answer area. If he places the light pen within the correct area, he is told that he was correct and goes on to the next problem. If the response was not in the correct area, it is compared with the area defined as a wrong answer. If his response is within this area, he is told that it is wrong, given the correct answer, and asked to touch it. If his initial response was neither in the anticipated wrong-answer area nor in the correct-answer area, then the student has made an undefined answer. He is given the same message that he would have heard had he touched a defined wrong answer; however, the response is recorded on the data record as undefined. The student tries again until he makes the correct response; he then goes on to the next problem.

To prepare an instructional sequence of this sort, the programmer must write a detailed list of commands for the computer. He must also record on an audio tape all the messages the student might hear during the lesson in approximately the order in which they will occur. Each audio message has an address on the tape and will be called for and played when appropriate. Similarly a film strip is prepared with one frame for each picture required in the lesson. Each frame has an address and can be called for in any order.

Table 29.1 shows the audio messages and film pictures required for two sample problems along with the hypothetical addresses on the audio tape and film strip. Listed in Table 29.2 are the computer commands required to present two examples of the problems described above, analyze the student's responses, and record his data record. The left column in the table lists the actual computer commands, and the right column provides an explanation of each command.

While a student is on the system, he may complete as many as 5 to 10 problems of this type per minute. Obviously, if all of the instructional material has to be coded in this detail the task would be virtually impossible. Fortunately, there are ways of simplifying coding procedure if parts of the instructional materials are alike in format and differ only in certain specified ways. For example, the two problems presented in Table 29.2 differ only in (*a*) the film display, (*b*) the words on the CRT, (*c*) the problem identifier, (*d*) the three audio addresses, (*e*) the row display of the arrow, (*f*) the correct answer area, and (*g*) the correct answer identifier. This string of code can be defined once, given a two-letter name, and used later by giving a one-line macro command.

The use of macros cuts down greatly the effort required to present many different but basically similar problems. For example, the two problems presented in Table 29.2 can be rewritten in macro format using only two lines of code: Problem 1: CM PW]F01]bat]bag]rat]A01] ABCD1]A04]A02]A03]7]1,7,3,18]C1]; Problem 2: CM PW]F02]card] cart]hard]]ABCD2]A07]A05]A06]5]1,5,4,18]C2]. The command to call a macro is CM, and PW is an arbitrary two-character code for the macro involving a picture-to-word match. Notice that in Problem 2 there is no introductory audio message; the "]]" indicates that this parameter is not to be filled in.

The macro capability of the source language has two distinct advantages over code written command by command. The first is ease and speed of coding. The call of one macro is obviously easier than writing the comparable string of code. The second advantage is increase in accuracy. Not only are coding errors drastically curtailed, but if the macro is defective or needs to be changed, every occurrence of it in the lesson coding can be corrected by modifying the original macro; in general, the code can stay as it is. The more standard the various problem formats, the more valuable the macro capability becomes. Apart from a few non-standard introductory audio messages and display items, approximately 95% of the reading curriculum has been programmed using about 110 basic macros.

The macro command feature of the language has significant implications for psychological research. By simply changing a few commands in a particular macro, one can alter the flow of the teaching sequence whenever that macro is called in the program. Thus, the logic of an instructional sequence that occurs thousands of times in the reading curriculum can be redesigned by adding or modifying a few lines of code in a given macro. If, for example, we wanted to change the timing relations, the type of feedback, or characteristics of the CRT display in the task described above, it would require only a few lines of code in the PW macro and would not necessitate making changes at every point in the curriculum where the picture-to-word exercise occurred. Thus, a range of experimental manipulations can be carried out using the same basic program and display materials, and requiring changes only in the command structure of the macros.

As indicated in Table 29.2, a bank of switches and counters is defined in the computer and can be used to keep a running record on each student. There is a sufficient number of these registers so that quite sophisticated schemes of optimization and accompanying branching are possible. Thus, one is in a position to present a series of words and to optimize the number of correct responses to some stipulated criteria, for example, five consecutive correct responses for each of the words. Or one can select from an array of phrases choosing those phrases for presentation that have the greatest number of previous errors. As a consequence of these decisions, each student pursues a fundamentally different path through the reading materials.

SOME RESULTS FROM THE FIRST YEAR OF OPERATION

The Stanford CAI Project is being conducted at the Brentwood School in the Ravenswood School District (East Palo Alto, California). There were several reasons for selecting this school. It had sufficient population to provide a sample of well over 100 first-grade students. The students were primarily from "culturally disadvantaged" homes. And the past performance of the school's principal and faculty had demonstrated a willingness to undertake educational innovations.

Computerized instruction began in November of 1966 with half of the first-grade students taking reading via CAI and the other half, which functioned as a control group, being taught reading by a teacher in the classroom. The children in the control group were not left out of the project, for they took mathematics from the CAI system instead. The full analysis of the student data is a tremendous task which is still under-way. However, a few general results have already been tabulated that provide some measure of the program's success.

Within the lesson material there is a central core of problems which we have termed main-line problems. These are problems over which each student must exhibit mastery in one form or another. Main-line problems may be branched around by successfully passing certain screening tests, or they may be met and successfully solved; they may be met with in-correct responses, in which case the student is branched to remedial material. The first year of the project ended with a difference between the fastest and slowest student of over 4,000 main-line problems completed. The cumulative response curves for the fastest, median, and slowest students are given in Fig. 29.5. Also of interest is the rate of progress during the course of the year. Figure 29.6 presents the cumulative number of problems completed per hour on a month-by-month basis again for the fastest, median, and slowest student. It is interesting to note that the rate measure was essentially constant over time for increase for the fast student.

From the standpoint of both the total number of problems completed during the year and rate of progress, it appears that the CAI curriculum is responsive to individual differences. The differences noted above must not be confused with a variation in rate of response. The difference in response rate among students was very small. The average response rate was approximately four per minute and was not correlated with a student's rate of progress through the curriculum. The differences in total number of main-line problems completed can be accounted for by the amount of

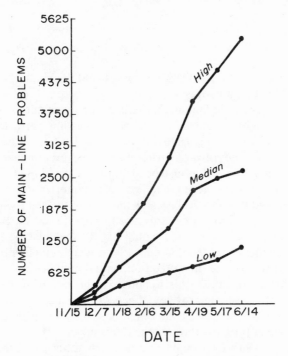

Fig. 29.5. Cumulative number of main-line problems for fastest, median, and slowest student.

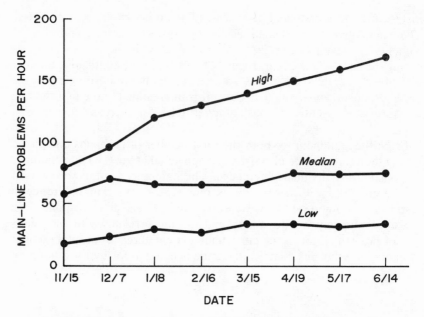

Fig. 29.6. Cumulative rate of progress for fastest, median, and slowest student.

remedial material, the optimization routines, and the number of accelerations for the different students.

It has been a common finding that girls generally acquire reading skills more rapidly than boys. The sex differences in reading performance have been attributed, at least in part, to the social organization of the classroom and to the value and reward structures of the predominantly female primary grade teachers. It has also been argued on developmental grounds that first-grade girls are more facile in visual memorization than boys of the same age, and that this facility aids the girls in the sight-word method of vocabulary acquisition commonly used in basal readers. If these two arguments are correct, then one would expect that placing students in a CAI environment and using a curriculum which emphasizes analytic skills, as opposed to rote memorization, would minimize sex differences in reading. In order to test this hypothesis, the rate of progress scores were statistically evaluated for sex effects. The result, which was rather surprising, is that there was no difference between male and female students in rate of progress through the CAI curriculum.

Sex differences however might be a factor in accuracy of performance. To test this notion the final accuracy scores on four standard problem types were examined. The four problem types, which are representative of the entire curriculum, were Letter Identification, Word List Learning, Matrix Construction, and Sentence Comprehension. On these four tasks, the only difference between boys and girls that was statistically significant at the 0.05 level was for word-list learning. These results, while by no means definitive, do lend support to the notion that when students are removed from the normal classroom environment and placed on a CAI program, boys perform as well as girls in overall rate of progress. The results also suggest that in a CAI environment the sex difference is minimized in proportion to the emphasis on analysis rather than rote memorization in the learning task. The one problem type where the girls achieved significantly higher scores than the boys, word-list learning, is essentially a paired-associate learning task.

As noted earlier, the first graders in our school were divided into two groups. Half of them received reading instruction from the CAI system; the other half did not (they received mathematics instruction instead). Both groups were tested extensively using conventional instruments before the project began and again near the end of the school year. The two groups were not significantly different at the start of the year. Table 29.3 presents the results for some of the tests that were administered at the end of the year. As inspection of the table will show, the group that received reading instruction via CAI performed significantly better on all of the posttests except for the comprehension subtest of the California

Table 29.3. Posttest Results for Experimental and Control Groups

Test	Experimental	Control	p value
California Achievement Test			
Vocabulary	45.91	38.10	< 0.01
Comprehension	41.45	40.62	—
Total	45.63	39.61	< 0.01
Hartley Reading Test			
Form class	11.22	9.00	< 0.05
Vocabulary	19.38	17.05	< 0.01
Phonetic discrimination	30.88	25.15	< 0.01
Pronunciation			
Nonsense word	6.03	2.30	< 0.01
Word	9.95	5.95	< 0.01
Recognition			
Nonsense word	18.43	15.25	< 0.01
Word	19.61	16.60	< 0.01

Achievement Test. These results are most encouraging. Further, it should be noted that at least some of the factors that might result in a "Hawthorne phenomenon" are not present here; the "control" group was exposed to CAI experience in their mathematics instruction. While that may leave room for some effects in their reading, it does remove the chief objection, since these students also had reason to feel that special attention was being given to them. It is of interest to note that the average Stanford-Binet IQ score for these students (both experimental and control) is 89.[2]

Owing to systems and hardware difficulties, our program was not in full operation until late in November of 1966. Initially, students were given a relatively brief period of time per day on the terminals. This period was increased to 20 minutes after the first 6 weeks; in the last month we allowed students to stay on the terminal 30 to 35 minutes. We wished to find out how well first-grade students would adapt to such long periods of time. They adapt quite well, and next year we plan to use 30-minute periods for all students throughout the year. This may seem like a long session for a first-grader, but our observations suggest that their span of attention is well over a half hour if the instructional sequence is truly responsive to their response inputs. This year's students had a relatively small number of total hours on the system. We hope that by beginning in the early fall and using half-hour periods, we will be able to give each student at least 80 to 90 hours on the terminals next year.

I do not have time to discuss the social-psychological effects of introducing CAI into an actual school setting. However, systematic observations have been made by a trained clinical psychologist, and a report is being prepared. To preview this report, it is fair to say that the students, teachers, and parents were quite favorable to the program.

Nor will time permit a detailed account of the various optimization routines used in the reading curriculum. But since this topic is a major focus of our research effort, it requires some discussion here. As noted earlier, the curriculum incorporates an array of screening and sequencing procedures designed to optimize learning. These optimization schemes vary in terms of the range of curriculum included, and it has been convenient to classify them as either short- or long-term procedures. Short-term procedures refer to decision rules that are applicable to specific problem formats and utilize the very recent response history of a subject to determine what instructional materials to present next. Long-term

---

[2]More details on these and other analyses may be found in Atkinson (1967) and Wilson and Atkinson (1967).

optimization procedures are applicable to diverse units of the curriculum and utilize a summarized form of the subject's complete response record to specify his future path through major instructional units.

As an example of a short-term optimization procedure, consider one that follows directly from a learning theoretic analysis of the reading task involved (Groen & Atkinson, 1966). Suppose that a list of m words is to be taught to the child, and it has been decided that instruction is to be carried out using the picture-to-word format described earlier. In essence, this problem format involves a series of discrete trials, where on each trial a picture illustrating the word being taught is presented on the projector screen and three words (including the word illustrated) are presented on the CRT. The student makes a response from among these words, and the trial is terminated by telling him the correct answer. If x trials are allocated for this type of instruction (where x is much larger than m), how should they be used to maximize the amount of learning that will take place? Should the m items be presented an equal number of times and distributed randomly over the x trials, or are there other strategies that take account of idiosyncratic features of a given subject's response record? If it is assumed that the learning process for this task is adequately described by the one-element model of stimulus sampling theory, and there is evidence that this is the case, then the optimal presentation strategy can be prescribed. The optimal strategy is initiated by presenting the m items in any order on the first m trials, and a continuation of this strategy is optimal over the remaining $x - m$ trials if, and only if, it conforms to the following rules:

1. For every item, set the count at 0 at the beginning of trial $m + 1$.
2. Present an item at a given trial if, and only if, its count is *least* among the counts for all items at the beginning of the trial.
3. If several items are eligible under Rule 2, select from these the item that has the smallest number of presentations; if several items are still eligible, select with equal probability from this set.
4. Following a trial, increase the count for presented item by 1 if the subject's response was correct, but set it at 0 if the response was incorrect.

Even though these decision rules are fairly simple, they would be difficult to implement without the aid of a computer. Data from this year's experiment establish that the above strategy is better than one that presents the items equally often in a fixed order.

This is only one example of the type of short-term optimization strate-gies that are used in the reading curriculum. Some of the other schemes are more complex, involving the application of dynamic programming principles (Groen & Atkinson, 1966), and use information not only about the response history but also the speed of responding. In some cases the optimization schemes can be derived directly from mathematical models of the learning process, whereas others are not tied to theoretical analyses but are based on intuitive considerations that seem promising.[3]

Even if short-term optimization strategies can be devised which are effective, a total reading curriculum that is optimal still has not been achieved. It is, of course, possible to optimize performance on each unit of the curriculum while, at the same time, sequencing through the units in an order that is not particularly efficient for learning. The most signifi-cant aspect of curriculum development is with regard to long-term opti-mization procedures, where the subject's total response history can be used to determine the best order for branching through major instructional units and also the proper balance between drill and tutorial activities. It seems clear that no theory of instruction is likely to use all the information we have on a student to make instructional decisions from one moment to the next. Even for the most sophisticated long-term schemes, only a sample of the subject's history is going to be useful. In general, the problem of deciding on an appropriate sample of the history is similar to the problem of finding an observable statistic that provides a good esti-mate of a population parameter. The observable history sample may be regarded as an estimate of the student's state of learning. A desirable property for such a history sample would be for it to summarize all in-formation concerning the current learning state of the student so that no elaboration of the history would provide additional information. In the theory of statistical inference, a statistic with an analogous property is called a sufficient statistic. Hence, it seems appropriate to call an observ-able sample history with this property a "sufficient history."

In the present version of the reading curriculum, several long-term optimization procedures have been introduced with appropriate sufficient histories. As yet, the theoretical rationale for these procedures has not been thoroughly worked out, and not enough data have been collected to evaluate their effectiveness. However, an analysis of long-term optimiza-tion problems, and what data we do have, has been instructive and has suggested a number of experiments that need to be carried out this year.

---

[3]The learning models and optimization methods that underlie much of the reading curriculum are dis-cussed in Atkinson and Shiffrin (1968), Groen and Atkinson (1966), Rodgers (1967), and Wilson and Atkinson (1967).

It is my hope that such analyses, combined with the potential for educational research under the highly controlled conditions offered by CAI, will lay the groundwork for a theory of instruction that is useful to the educator. Such a theory of instruction will have to be based on a model of the learning process that has broad generality and yet yields detailed predictions when applied to specific tasks.

In my view, the development of a viable theory of instruction and the corresponding learning theory will be an interactive enterprise, with advances in each area influencing the concepts and data base in the other. For too long, psychologists studying learning have shown little interest in instructional problems, whereas educators have made only primitive and superficial applications of learning theory. Both fields would have advanced more rapidly if an appropriate interchange of ideas and problems had existed. It is my hope that prospects for CAI, as both a tool for research and a mode of instruction, will act as a catalyst for a rapid evolution of new concepts in learning theory as well as a corresponding theory of instruction.

REFERENCES

Atkinson, R. C., & Hansen, D. N. Computer-assisted instruction in initial reading: The Standord Project. *Reading Research Quarterly*, 1966, **2**, 5–25.

Atkinson, R. C., & Shiffrin, R. M. Human memory: A proposed system and its control processes. In K. W. Spence & J. T. Spence (Eds.), *The psychology of learning and motivation: Advances in research and theory*. Vol. 2. New York: Academic Press, 1968, 89–195.

Fishman, E. J., Keller, L., & Atkinson, R. C. Massed vs. distributed practice in computerized spelling drills. *Journal of Educational Psychology*, 1968, **59**, 290–296.

Groen, G. J., & Atkinson, R. C. Models for optimizing the learning process. *Psychological Bulletin*, 1966, **66**, 309–320.

Hansen, D. N., & Rogers, T. S. An exploration of psycholinguistic units in initial reading. Technical Report 74, 1965, Stanford University, Institute for Mathematical Studies in the Social Sciences.

Rodgers, T. S. Linguistic considerations in the design of the Stanford computer-based curriculum in initial reading. Technical Report 111, 1967, Stanford University, Institute for Mathematical Studies in the Social Sciences.

Suppes, P. The uses of computers in education. *Scientific American*, 1966, **215**, 206–221.

Suppes, P., Jerman, M., & Groen, G. J. Arithmetic drills and review on a computer-based teletype. *Arithmetic Teacher*, 1966, April, 303–308.

Wilson, H. A., & Atkinson, R. C. Computer-based instruction in initial reading: A progress report on the Stanford project. Technical Report 119, August 25, 1967, Pp. 1–83. Stanford University, Institute for Mathematical Studies in the Social Sciences.

CHAPTER 10

The Effective Use of Paraprofessionals

This chapter concerns the use of paraprofessionals in the classroom. The term "paraprofessional" describes the people who work beside or along with professional personnel but who are not trained in all aspects of the profession or who do not have a professional degree. Paraprofessionals such as housewives and college students have been working for some time in various mental hospital volunteer programs. Parents are now working as teacher aides in many schools on both a salaried and volunteer basis. The increased importance of paraprofessionals parallels the increased recognition that professionals are in very short supply and that involvement of community members in the schools can benefit the community, the children, and the paraprofessionals (*see* Pearl & Riessman, 1965, Chapters 3 and 4).

The articles presented here demonstrate the usefulness of parents and college students as paraprofessionals in the classroom. In addition, peers have been successfully used as paraprofessionals in the classroom; but because the problems involved are unique, we have devoted Chapter 8 to the topic. Although interest in the community mental health field is expanding, research on the effectiveness of paraprofessionals is scarce. Most of the literature on community mental health is concerned with discussions of issues such as: role blending of existing professions, the development of new community agencies, new uses for existing agencies, the extension of consultation services to teachers and parents, and demographic information on the need for expanded community services. Controlled experimentation on the contribution of paraprofessionals is nearly nonexistent.

There are several ways in which the paraprofessionals can aid the class-room teacher. Grading papers is perhaps the most obvious way. Additional areas of potential usefulness include: administering and scoring achievement tests; actual participation in behavior modification programs, e.g., observing and recording the frequencies of various behaviors, dispensing tokens and other reinforcers; the preparation of individualized or programmed instruction materials; tutoring individual children; setting up science experiments; showing films; and perhaps teaching in circumscribed areas. The usefulness of a paraprofessional is limited only by the imagination and willingness of the school system and the supervising teacher.

Paraprofessionals have some special advantages over professional personnel. (1) Many parents and housewives will work in the classroom at little or no cost. Certainly the cost is far less than the cost of hiring extra teachers and school psychologists. (2) They can be used on a temporary basis, when needed. For example, a housewife might be able to carry out a testing program which requires her to spend one or two weeks every semester—although she would not want the responsibility of even a half time job. (3) Since paraprofessionals may work with only a limited aspect of the classroom routine, their training may be intensive rather than extensive. (4) Often a *new* person in the classroom can be effective because he may have a fresh way of presenting materials; he does not have a history of difficulty with the children and no reputation, good or bad, to impede him. (5) The paraprofessional can provide a vital link with the community—with benefits for all. Parents gain a new understanding of school procedures and problems. People working in their own communities usually have more motivation to succeed and more ability to develop rapport with the students than non-community members. Participation in the educational process can encourage the development of leadership skills and can increase the community's concern for maintaining and up-grading their school system and allied educational and cultural institutions. (6) Finally, and perhaps needless to say, the paraprofessional can save the teacher valuable time—time in which she can use her own professional skills to maximum effectiveness.

The use of paraprofessionals involves more than depositing a naive adult in the midst of 30 first graders and telling her to "go to it". A school system may encounter a variety of difficulties which must be overcome if a paraprofessional is to be successful. Some teacher unions may oppose paraprofessionals on the grounds that they are displacing teachers, performing duties for which they are not prepared or certified, or even lowering the quality of education. The unions can be presented with the following counter-arguments: (1) paraprofessionals should be used to aid, not replace teachers, by doing things the teacher herself would not ordinarily have time for; (2) paraprofessionals should receive training in the specific area in which they will function; (3) and as such, they may in fact become more skilled in this specific area than the teacher and will contribute to improving the quality of education – not lowering it.

Even if unions can be convinced of the advantages of aides or paraprofessionals, the individual teachers may find it very difficult to adjust to the presence of paraprofessionals. Teachers may view the aide as a threat to their own prestige and authority and consequently may fail to utilize the aide effectively. A well-planned introduction of paraprofessionals into the school system and proper training programs may help to alleviate the teacher's fears. It is possible that the source of the fears may be the teacher's own inadequacies – a problem with which this book is designed to cope. The necessity for high quality training programs cannot be overemphasized. The teachers themselves should play an important part in the development of training programs. Written instructions which are specific, filled with examples, practically-oriented, and designed for naive readers facilitate both the training and evaluation phases of such programs. Another consideration is the need for supervision and evaluation. While this requires some time on the part of professional personnel, adequate guidance can prevent the occurrence of unfortunate mistakes; and constant revision of training and instructional manuals will only improve the program. Some people have raised the question of whether a paraprofessional can command the respect and gain control of the children. Again, the quality of the training and supervisory programs and the manner in which the paraprofessional is introduced to the children will determine the extent of this difficulty.

The first article (Allerhand, 1967), (*30*), in this chapter demonstrates one function parents can perform as paraprofessionals in the schools. Results indicated that parents were as effective as psychology graduate students in administering two standardized intelligence tests. Training was completed in three sessions. The parents worked on a volunteer basis.

Thomas, Nielsen, Kuypers, and Becker (1968), (*31*) compared the effects of what might be called "behavioral consultation" with the teacher and tutoring by a college student on the reading skills and disruptive classroom behavior of a first grade boy. While the design of the study leaves some questions unanswered, it seems reasonable to conclude that tutoring by a paraprofessional was valuable over and above the changes the teacher was able to make through her own methods of handling the child. We might point out that the comparison of tutoring and high approval would have been more complete if the experimenter had been able to return to a high approval-no tutoring phase after tutoring had been in effect for a period of time. It would also have been desirable to have some ongoing measures of the boy's reading skills throughout the entire study. Finally, the fact that the boy began wearing his glasses more regularly coincident with the onset of the tutoring programs may have contributed to the increase in his reading skills.

The third article (Ryback & Staats, 1970), (*32*), describes a procedure for training parents to teach reading to their children. The financial advantages gained by replacing professionals with paraprofessionals is clearly demonstrated; and the effectiveness of the SMART program is reflected in significant improvement on standardized achievement tests as well as on the SMART reading materials.

Effectiveness of Parents of Head Start Children as Administrators of Psychological Tests*[1]

MELVIN E. ALLERHAND

Western Reserve University

Abstract: The purpose of this study was to assess the effectiveness of parents of Head Start children as administrators of psychological tests. 7 parents independently tested a group of children who were also evaluated by psychology graduate students. The individually administered tests involved were the Caldwell Pre-School Inventory and the Peabody Picture Vocabulary Test. The correlation between the 2 groups of testers was 0.88 on the Pre-School inventory and 0.64 on the Peabody Picture Vocabulary Test. On the strength of these correlations and other methods of examining the data, it is suggested that less sophisticated individuals with high motivation may be adequate in performing certain professional tasks, such as the administration and scoring of individual tests.

In very recent years, much consideration has been given to the area of training nonprofessionals in tasks currently viewed as being in the professional range (Hallowitz & Riessman, 1965; Pearl & Riessman, 1965; Rioch, Elkes, & Flint, 1965). The end products of such studies and demonstration projects suggest a range of clearly defined, specific tasks that, with appropriate training and supervision, may very effectively be carried out by individuals indigenous to the situation.

A recent paper by Blum (1965) points to the importance of defining service jobs relevant to the services required, rather than primarily considering the professional training—in this case, of the social worker. He further indicates that to accomplish a certain task, it may be necessary

*Reprinted from the *Journal of Consulting Psychology*, Vol. 31, No. 3, 1967, pp. 286–290, by permission of the American Psychological Association.

[1]This work was supported by the Office for Economic Opportunity under Contract OEO-512. Evelyn Century, research associate, has aided the author in the analysis of the data and the preparation of this report.

to have a variety of people with a variety of expertise and special emotional qualifications. Schwartz (1962) has implemented these ideas in a project with professionals and nonprofessionals within a public assistance agency. Such thoughts and efforts come out of the clear recognition that there are considerable manpower shortages and that there may be particular tasks that can be handled more effectively by individuals either closer to the actual locus of application of the service or better equipped to carry out specific aspects of a larger function. This position regarding the poor person has been forcefully expressed by Pearl and Riessman (1965).

There is another argument presented by proponents of training poor people to carry out services within their own community. This is an effort to upgrade the level of functioning and permit the development of leadership within the group of people who are seeking to gain an economically more desirable position in society. This orientation has been central in such programs as Head Start—the inclusion of poor people on various boards for planning an assault on poverty, etc.

Although we have indications that nonprofessional people can be trained for certain professional tasks (Hallowitz & Riessman, 1965), there is still a general feeling of doubt, and, understandably, within professional ranks there are rather specific questions as to the performance of nonprofessionals in particular professional tasks. It is the intent of this investigator to: (*a*) evaluate the potentialities of previously untrained people for filling service roles within their own primary groups, (*b*) locate and define the areas of service for which nonprofessional people can be trained, (*c*) investigate whether it is feasible to establish a training and supervisory program which will effectively produce such service workers, and (*d*) to measure the impact of such trained people on their families and communities.

If it is determined that people with limited formal education could be used in handling certain services which previously had been performed only by trained professionals, a dual benefit could be realized—a benefit to those being serviced and to those doing the servicing. Underlying this approach is the belief that individuals who are part of a group may have greater effectiveness in performing services within that group. This study is one effort in that direction.

The purpose of this study was to assess the effectiveness of parents of Head Start (HS) children as administrators of psychological tests. Particular consideration was given to such factors as identification with the poor community and similarity of ethnic and skin-color characteristics which might contribute to differential test success of the HS children in the sample. Katz (1964) referred to the impact of such variables as the kind of tester, circumstances of the testing situation, etc., on the level of functioning, particularly of the Negro child. He concluded that Negro children are more vulnerable to stress in a predominantly white situation and thus are likely to have lowered achievement. Thus, we wondered whether the poor child in an urban center such as Cleveland would respond differently to a white sophisticated tester as contrasted with a Negro unsophisticated tester.

Further, we reflected on the question of sophistication as a variable; there are indications that unsophisticated testers at times enable a subject to achieve a higher score because of inadvertent clueing, and, on other occasions, that the novice tester may cause a lowered test score because of inexperience in manipulating the test items.

METHOD

The study is primarily concerned with comparing a group of parents of Head Start children selected to administer psychological tests with a group of experienced graduate student testers.

Seven parents (four Negro and three white)[2] of Head Start children were trained in the administration of the Pre-School Inventory Test[3] (PI) and the Peabody Picture Vocabulary Test (PPVT). The parents were paid $2.00 per hour during their period of participation. A counterbalanced order of test administration was established. Thus, there was an equal number of children initially tested by the parents and graduate students. The child was tested on two different occasions with a maximum of 5 intervening days. Fifty-seven Negro Head Start children were evaluated during this study.[4] The age range was 5 years, 2 months to 6 years, 3 months, with a mean age of 5 years, 4 months.

The seven parent testers were female, ranged in formal education from

---

[2]The size of the sample only permits for reasonable indications, especially in the comparison of white and Negro testers.

[3]This test was developed by Bettye M. Caldwell for the evaluation of the Head Start Program, summer 1965. In the original form, the 161-item test purportedly measured the academic achievement of young children as expected by nursery and kindergarten teachers. Item analysis has suggested the following categories which the 1966 revision (85 items) reflects: personal-social responsiveness, associative vocabulary, concept activation-numerical, and concept activation-sensory (Caldwell & Soule, 1966).

[4]All the children received both administrations of the Pre-School Inventory; however, 13 children were not given the PPVT by the graduate students because of time pressures.

the 9th to 12th grade, and were 28–39 years of age. They were selected randomly from a group of 30 volunteers.

The three graduate students were female, white, had a minimum of 1 year of graduate study in psychology, including training in test administration, and had administered at least 100 PIs and 60 PPVTs.

Training Procedure

The parent testers experienced an intensive 3-session training in test administration. The first session involved a description of the pilot study and an acquaintance with the PI. After a discussion of the construction of the test, there was an examination of the series of items included. Whenever there was some question about the phrasing of the item or the particular method of categorizing and scoring, this was discussed in some detail. The involvement of the parents became increasingly evident. It was strongly recommended that the parents try out any of the items on available children in the community. It was further indicated that during these training sessions attempts would be made to point out the kinds of errors that unsophisticated testers may make in the application of test items. This seemed to set the stage for a good-natured and frank exchange on known errors which had considerable payoff in subsequent training sessions, as it became much more tolerable to hear criticism. The joys of success and accomplishment seemed to increase tolerance for such critical exchanges and resulted in an application of the suggestions in the testing approach.

The second session, which was 3 days later, was primarily devoted to discussing the particular questions that parents had regarding the PI and further centered on the experiences they had had in practice administrations. The questions they raised paralleled those previously raised by sophisticated testers during an earlier training experience. For example, in Item 30 on the PI the child is asked how many broken arms he has, and in order to get some type of a "none" or "not any" response, the parents suggested some stimulus phrases for this question which they had found effective in gaining the response. One of the suggestions was "How many tails do you have?"

The remainder of the second training session involved role-playing some of the items on the PI and the introduction of the administration of the PPVT. There was a demonstration of the PPVT followed by each of the parent tester's attempting to administer portions of the test. A critical discussion of the testing approaches ensued. It was then recommended that the parents administer as many PIs and PPVTs to community children as they could prior to the final training session.

During the final session, the majority of the time was used in discussing particular problems that the parents experienced in the administration of both tests. Some of the interfering characteristics were brought to the attention of the parent testers. For example, one of the parents tended to use the testing situation as a teaching medium. She persisted in probing for the "correct" answer. The group became aware of the testing as an assessing technique. In the final role-play that concluded the third session, this particular parent showed a decided decrease in the probing approach.

Testing Procedure

The tests were actually administered in two Head Start child-development centers. A member of the research team acted as coordinator in making arrangements for rooms and the selection of the group of children to be tested. Except for these administrative matters, the parents carried out the entire testing procedure, escorting the child from his classroom to the testing room and from the testing room back to his classroom. As indicated earlier, each child was independently tested on different occasions by both a parent tester and graduate student.

Method of Analysis

Similarity of results of parent and graduate student testers was compared by (*a*) deriving percentages of the total number of agreements on answers to items in the PI by the group of Head Start children, (*b*) correlating raw scores of the children obtained for the PI and PPVT, and (*c*) obtaining significance of difference tests based on the group means for the PI and the PPVT. In addition, a significance test was calculated for the test series, comparing the first with the second test administration to determine possible discrepancies relating to the test-retest process. A more detailed analysis of the categories within the PI was made comparing the content and concepts involved in the test.

RESULTS

Table 30.1 shows an overall examination of the amount of agreement between the parent testers and the graduate student testers. The total

Table 30.1. Percentage of Agreement between Individual Parent and Graduate Student Testers on the PI

Parent tester	Percentage of agreement on individual tests[a]									N	Average percentage agreement on individual tests
				Student tester							
W₁	0.67	0.92	0.63	0.76	0.76	0.80	0.68	0.78		8	0.76
W₂	0.76	0.77	0.86	0.78	0.77	0.65	0.81			7	0.77
N₃	0.82	0.77	0.85	0.71	0.77	0.73	0.72	0.80		8	0.77
N₄	0.82	0.67	0.78	0.64	0.85	0.79	0.75	0.71	0.76	9	0.75
W₅	0.87	0.71	0.82	0.80	0.76	0.59	0.71			7	0.75
N₆	0.73	0.80	0.76	0.84	0.77	0.78	0.84	0.78		8	0.79
N₇	0.87	0.67	0.81	0.76	0.79	0.74	0.70	0.69	0.62 0.72	10	0.74
Total										57	0.76

Note: Abbreviated: W = white; N = Negro.

[a]Columns 1–3 – one student tester for all Ss; Columns 4–10 – panel of student testers was used with these Ss.

average of agreement was 76% for the PI. It is also evident from the table that there was a high degree of general consistency among the parent testers, as reflected by the 74–79% range. Further, there is no apparent difference between the results obtained by the Negro and white parent examiners. Thus, the remainder of the analysis treats the parents as a group.

Table 30.2 shows the degree of relationship between the children's test scores achieved by the parent and graduate student testers. The correlation for the PI was 0.88 and for the PPVT was 0.64. Both of these relationships are significant ($p < 0.01$).

Table 30.2. Relationship between Combined Parents and Sophisticated Testers on PI and PPVT

Test	N	
PI	57	0.88**
PPVT	44	0.64**

**$p < 0.01$.

Table 30.3 is an attempt to detect whether the parents were systematically affecting performances upwards or downwards. Testing the differences after combining the scores (whether the parent administered the test first or second), we find no significant difference between the means of parents and students for either PI or PPVT. On the PI, significant

Table 30.3. Differences between Test Results Relative to Order of Testing by the Parents

Test	N	D	SD
PI			
Parent (combined, first & second)	57	0.97	1.62
Parents first	25	3.09	2.27*
Parents second	32	4.12	2.04*
PPVT			
Parents (combined, first & second)	44	2.1	1.05
Parents first	25	1.79	1.60
Parents second	19	0.32	1.32

*$p < 0.05$.

differences were found in favor of the second testing, whether the second tester was parent or student. Either the test-retest condition or the passage of 5 days seemed to increase the score on this test. However, with the PPVT there was no significant change in the score when the tests were administered within approximately 5 days of one another, regardless of who the tester was.

DISCUSSION

Two factors have clearly emerged from this study. First, we have seen a demonstration of effective administering of psychological tests by the parents. It must be kept in mind that the parents were compared with a sophisticated group of students who were trained in manipulating test techniques and keenly aware of the need for objectivity in testing situations. Despite these factors, very significant correlations, particularly on the PI, were obtained. It should be noted that the test-retest reliability coefficients (Dunn, 1965) for the PPVT in the age range 4 years, 6 months to 7 years are very similar to the intertester coefficient established in this study. Thus, it is suggested that both results demonstrate the comparable effectiveness of the parents and students in these test administrations. It must be recognized that the parents were only performing the testing and scoring functions — not the interpretation of the results.

Second, there was evidence of the efficiency of the parent group, as shown by their high level of agreement with graduate students on the PI (74–79%). Such effectiveness was present considering both educational background and skin-color variables within the limits of the sample. The fact that there was a significant difference resulting from the order in which the PI was given, regardless of which group tested last, suggests even greater similarity in effectiveness between the students and parents and demonstrates that the children learned to be more accurate through either the passage of time and/or more exposure to the test items. The PPVT scores evidently were not so affected.

In summary, then, the effectiveness revealed by the parents in this study supports the findings of Reiff and Riessman (1964) that there is a potential corps of untrained people who may be used for services requiring some areas of testing skill. Highly motivated individuals indigenous to the particular setting may very well provide the traits needed for negating the handicaps inherent in lack of professional training. Their motivation may well be related to the special recognition associated with these professional tasks. In fact, one mother referred to a neighbor's comments: "Who do you think you are with your tests, a psychologist or something?" The mother reported with obvious pride, "I'm learning how to do something — something important."

Additional training of the parents for building-in objectivity and test manipulative skill is indicated and would help to reduce some of the differences found in this study. It is likely that the qualities demonstrated by the parents as testers may also be used in other aspects of professional service, such as the observation and handling of data. Each utilization is being examined in an ongoing study by the author.

Beyond the testing-research fields, Pearl and Riessman (1965) have studied and suggested a wide range of "new careers for the poor," including direct care services, counseling, teacher assisting, etc. It is essential that careful study associated with immediate social needs guide us in the further development of the handling (under appropriate control) of professional tasks by people with limited formal education. No doubt this approach raises some dangers. The necessary selection, training, and continued supervision must be assumed by the broadly educated and trained professionals. There may well be a necessity for reexamination of the graduate preparation of psychologists, with a view toward such evolving manpower solutions. Some examination has been given to this direction (Allerhand, 1965).[5] No doubt much more is required.

REFERENCES

Allerhand, M. E. Convergence – a moment of role fixing in the development of the clinical child psychologist. Paper read at American Psychological Association, Chicago, September 1965.

Blum, A. Manpower utilization – Wishful thinking unfulfilled. Paper read at Council on Social Work, Denver, January 1965. (Available through Western Reserve University, School of Applied Social Sciences, Mimeo.)

Caldwell, B. M., & Soule, D. The Pre-School Inventory: Administration and scoring. Rochester: University of Rochester, 1966. (Mimeo)

Dunn, L. M. *Expanded manual, Peabody Picture Vocabulary Test*. Minneapolis: American Guidance Service, 1965.

Hallowitz, E., & Riessman, S. Progress report on neighborhood service center program. Report to the Office of Economic Opportunity. New York: New York University, 1965. (Mimeo)

Katz, I. Review of evidence relating to effects of desegregation on the intellectual performance of Negroes. *American Psychologist*, 1964, **19**, 381–389.

Pearl, A., & Riessman, D. *New careers for the poor*. New York: Free Press, 1965.

Reiff, R., & Riessman, F. The indigenous non-professional. New York: New York University, Nile Mental Health Program, 1964. (Mimeo)

Rioch, M. J., Elkes, C., & Flint, A. *Pilot project in training mental health counselors*. (USPHS Publ. No. 1254) Washington, D. C.: United States Government Printing Office, 1965.

Schwartz, E. Organization and utilization of public assistance personnel. Chicago: University of Chicago, School of Social Work, 1962. (Mimeo)

---

[5]A mimeographed copy of this paper may be obtained from the author.

ARTICLE 31

Social Reinforcement and Remedial Instruction in the Elimination of a Classroom Behavior Problem*[1]

DON A. THOMAS,
LORETTA J. NIELSEN,
DAVID S. KUYPERS
and WESLEY C. BECKER, Ph.D.[1]

University of Illinois

Teachers often encounter children who are apparently unresponsive to attempts to control their disruptive behavior. Sometimes they seem to "deliberately do the opposite" when attempts are made to correct them. Often such children are labeled "emotionally disturbed" and their failure to perform academically is attributed to this. A careful evaluation of the reasoning involved in the proposition that "emotional disturbance" is a *cause* of poor classroom learning indicates that what is observed is a child who acts in a way which is incompatible with working on an assigned task (such as getting out of seat, talking out of turn, hitting and pushing peers, making unusual noises, and the like). This behavior is used to infer the presence of "emotional disturbance."

Two propositions then follow: *Emotional disturbance causes observed disruptive behavior;* and *emotional disturbance causes the observed failure to perform academically.* The first proposition substitutes a description for an explanation. It says nothing about the manipulable variables which increase or decrease the frequency of such behavior. We have simply said that A is A. Reasoning of this sort has been labeled circular

*Reprinted from *The Journal of Special Education*, Vol. 2, No. 3, 1968, pp. 291–305.
[1]The authors are indebted to Richard A. Sturgeon, school principal, for his cooperation and to the administration of School District #116, Urbana, Illinois. We are also greatly indebted to the classroom teacher, who would prefer to remain anonymous, for her very important contribution to the study. The observers were Diane Hays, Sandra Beldin, and Rita Politzer. This research was supported by Grant No. HD-00881-05 from the National Institutes of Health.

505

reasoning, tautological reasoning, the substitution of description for explanation, or the giving of a pseudo-explanation. Given the above, the proposition that *emotional disturbance causes the observed failure to perform academically* can be transformed to the proposition that *the observed disruptive behavior causes the observed failure to perform academically*. This transformed statement also contains a logical fallacy. What has been observed are two classes of behavior (disruptive activities and poor academic performance) which tend to occur together with some frequency. But there is no basis in the observations for knowing *whether* or *how* they are "causally" related.

Modern behavior theory and experimental studies indicate that both disruptive behavior and academic performance are a function of their consequences (e.g., positive reinforcing consequences, punishing consequences, or an absence of them). If this is so, the observed high frequency of disruptive behavior and low frequency of academic behavior could be due to: (a) classroom conditions which strengthen or maintain the disruptive behavior and are incompatible with academic work; (b) an academic program which is unable to provide positive consequences, either because it demands responses which the child is unable to perform (failure), or because appropriate academic responses are not reinforced if they do occur; or (c) any combination of *a* and *b* above, since disruptive and academic behavior are incompatible. This view suggests that remedial procedures need to consider ways of strengthening appropriate academic, *as well reducing disruptive*, behavior. It might be that for some children poor learning conditions "cause" the behavior labeled emotional disturbance.

Recent work in public schools (Becker, Madsen, Arnold & Thomas, 1967; Madsen, Becker & Thomas, 1968) has indicated that teachers can be trained to use consequences such as praise and approval to strengthen on task behavior, and to remove strengthening consequences for disruptive behavior (by ignoring it). In the study by Becker *et al.* (1967) seven of ten children in five different classes showed remarkable improvement in on task behavior when the teachers made their rules clear, ignored disruptions, and praised appropriate classroom behavior. For two children, additional incentives were required to bring about a change. Of major interest for the present study was the final boy, Dan, a fourth grader functioning at a second grade reading level. Using rules, ignoring disruptive behavior, and praising appropriate behavior resulted in a small improvement in on task classroom behavior. However, it improved dramatically with the addition of a half-hour of remedial reading training each day. The results suggest that improvement in reading increased the possibility of positive consequences for academic work. Praise and approval from the teacher were relatively ineffective in establishing appropriate classroom behavior until the child was able to do the work.

The present study attempts to replicate and refine the previously reported results by assessing the effects of a combination of remedial tutoring in reading and social reinforcement. The plan was to introduce the social reinforcement procedures and remedial tutoring one at a time, and to assess their effects on classroom behavior and academic performance. To provide a more stringent test of the effectiveness of the program, classroom behavior was assessed at a time of the day when there was no reading.

METHOD

Subjects

Child Rich was a 6-year-old Negro boy who had recently been transferred to a school in a predominantly middle-class Caucasian neighborhood. He was the older of two children. His mother had been divorced twice, and his father, after spending several years in the Air Force, was attending classes at the University. The mother attended church each day and took Rich with her. She did not allow him to play with Negro children in his neighborhood, and she had been heard to say that they "act like animals and should be treated like animals and locked up." In the classroom (of 23 students) there was only one other Negro child.

Rich's teacher, Mrs. Y., reported that he was a "holy terror." She had attempted to control his behavior for approximately six months. Since she felt that his behavior was growing progressively worse, she anticipated that she would soon be unable to effectively teach the rest of the class. She reported that Rich caused so much trouble in the room that the other children were unable to do their work, and she could not give them the attention they deserved because much of her time was spent keeping Rich out of trouble. At this time an observation during the morning (when Rich was supposed to be on his best behavior) revealed a large repertoire of disruptive behavior.

It was impossible to determine from observation alone whether Rich had academic deficiencies. He rarely paid attention when material was presented. He was in the lowest of three reading groups, and his progress was extremely slow. In six months, he had completed only the three pre-primers in the Ginn basic reading series. This included 56 vocabulary words and supplementary workbook exercises. Intelligence testing indicated that he was functioning in the average range with an I.Q. of 93 (Stanford-Binet, Form L-M); however, he was a member of an accelerated first-grade class whose average level of intelligence was 116.5, with a range of 147 to 92 (California Test of Mental Maturity, Short Form). Rich's I.Q. on the California test was 95.

Before tutoring (mid-March), Rich scored 1.4 in reading on the Wide Range Achievement Test, and had a total Language Age of 6 years and 4 months on the Illinois Test of Psycholinguistic Abilities. While these scores indicated only a mild educational retardation, they constituted a more severe deficit in the classroom of bright children with whom he was competing. One would also expect this deficit to increase unless appropriate steps were taken.

Teacher   Mrs. Y. had more than ten years experience, but this was her first year with an accelerated class. She spent much time responding to disruptive behavior with reprimands, scolding, and explanations of what children should and should not do. When asked to specify the precise behavior she wanted changed (i.e., disruptive behavior to be eliminated and appropriate behavior to be increased) she wrote out a list of 16 behaviors which she didn't like (e.g., being out of seat, talking, etc.), but she had difficulty specifying appropriate behavior she wanted increased. She wanted "the children to do what they are supposed to do."

Observations of Child Behavior

The categories for recording Rich's behavior were constructed according to the procedures reported by Becker *et al.* (1967). Eight categories of *Disruptive Behavior* were specifically defined, and a ninth category (Other Task) was established to include behavior not specifically listed which in the rater's judgment appeared to be incompatible with classroom learning. The categories of Disruptive Behavior were as follows:

Gross Motor   Getting out of seat, standing up, walking around, running, hopping, skipping, jumping, rocking chair, moving chair, arm flailing, and rocking body without moving chair.

Kneeling   Kneeling in seat, sitting on feet, and lying across desk.

Aggression Hitting, pushing, shoving, pinching, slapping, poking, or using an object to strike another child.

Disturbing Others Grabbing objects or work belonging to another child, knocking objects off a neighbor's desk, destroying property of other children, throwing objects.

Talking Conversing with other children, calling teacher, blurting out answers or questions, and singing.

Vocalization Crying, screaming, coughing, sneezing, whistling, and other non-verbal vocalizations. (Both Talking and Verbalization were rated only when the observers could hear the response as well as see its source.)

Noise Rattling or tearing papers, throwing books or other objects onto his desk, tapping feet, clapping, slamming desk top, tapping desk with objects, kicking or scooting desk or chair. (Again, the action had to be seen and the noise heard.)

Orienting While seated, the child turns head or both head and body toward another person, shows objects to others, looks at others. (Looking less than four seconds was not rated unless accompanied by a turn of more than 90% from desk. Whenever an Orienting response overlapped two time intervals, and could not be rated in the first, it was rated in the second interval if the total response met the time criterion.)

Other Tasks The child is doing things other than those prescribed by teacher which are not included in the above categories (e.g., playing with objects, looking at the floor, untying his shoe laces, wringing his hands, ignoring questions).

In addition to the nine categories of Disruptive Behavior, one class of *Relevant* or On Task behavior was recorded. Relevant Behavior was recorded whenever Rich was working on the assigned task for a full ten seconds.

Observers were undergraduates who had been trained in the use of the categories. They used a clipboard, stop watch, and a special recording sheet. They recorded every class of Disruptive Behavior which occurred in a 10-second interval. However, each category of Disruptive Behavior could be rated only once during a 10-second interval. Observation periods were 20 minutes in length. During each minute, the observers would record behavior in the first five 10-second intervals and make notes during the last one. Percentage of Disruptive Behavior was defined as the percentage of observation intervals in which Disruptive Behavior occurred. Frequent checks on the reliability of the observations were made by including a second observer (*see* Fig. 31.1). Reliabilities were computed by dividing the number of exact agreements on behavior category and time interval by the number of agreements plus disagreements.

Observations were made during the afternoon, at a time when activities varied from day to day, including TV, science, workbook activities, show and tell, and occasional movies. This period was selected because it did not involve reading and was reportedly Rich's worst period of the day. Since the observers had been trained not to respond to the children, the class soon came to ignore them (see Becker *et al.*, 1967, for details).

Observations of Teacher Behavior

Three categories of teacher behavior were recorded:

Approval to Relevant Behavior   Relevant Behavior was defined by the child behavior code. Teacher Approval included subcategories of *Praise* (that's good, I like that, you are doing well, etc.), *Physical Contact* (embracing, holding hand, sitting child on lap, etc.), *Head Reactions* (nodding, smiling, winking, etc.), and *Granting Privileges* (allowing to help her, choosing an activity, etc.).

Approval to Disruptive Behavior   This category was rated if the teacher showed any of the Approval Reactions listed above *following* Disruptive Behavior as defined by the child code.

Disapproval to Disruptive Behavior   Teacher Disapproval included *Criticism* (stop that, I don't like that, shouting, etc.), *Physical Contact* (holding, grabbing, spanking, slapping, etc.), *Head Reactions* (grimacing, frowning), *Threats of Punishment* (you'll have to go to the office if you don't stop that, you'll lose recess unless you behave), and *Withholding Privileges* (denying recess, isolating from the group, etc.).

Disapproval Reactions to Relevant Behavior did not occur often enough to report, although they were initially included in the recordings.

Each occurrence of a teacher behavior (directed toward any child) falling into the defined categories was recorded. The teacher measures, therefore, reflect the frequency of occurrence of such behavior in a 20-minute observation interval. Frequent reliability checks were made.

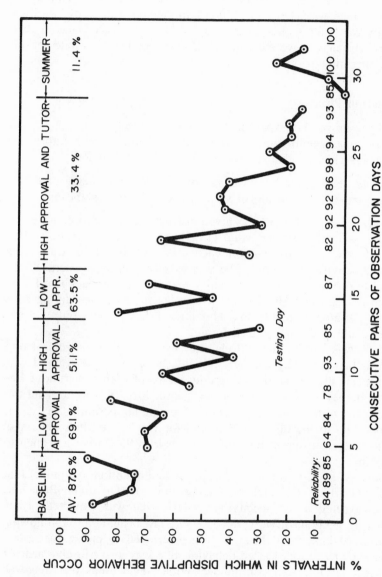

Fig. 31.1. Percentage of intervals in which Disruptive Behavior occurred as a function of experimental conditions.

511

Teacher reliability was calculated by dividing agreements on category and time interval by agreements plus disagreements. Reliability of teacher ratings was checked 22 times throughout the study. Average reliability was 0.89, with a range from 0.77 to 1.00. Recordings of child and teacher behavior were usually made in successive 20-minute periods rather than simultaneously.

Experimental Phases

The phases of the experiment included a Baseline period, several levels of social reinforcement (Approval and Disapproval), tutoring in reading plus a high level of Approval, and a Follow-Up period.

Baseline   Eight days of Baseline observations were made of Rich's behavior in the classroom and of Mrs. Y.'s behavior toward the class.

Low Approval$_1$ Mrs. Y. was given instructions to reinforce Relevant Behavior as in the Becker *et al.* (1967) study. She was instructed to make the rules very explicit for each class period and for transitions from one activity to another. She was asked to place a general set of rules (4 to 6 rules worded in a positive manner) on the blackboard. The children read through the entire list of rules at least twice during both morning and afternoon sessions. This procedure was repeated until the children could read and repeat each rule.

Mrs. Y. was also instructed to ignore Disruptive Behavior unless one child was being hurt by another. Initially, behavior to be ignored was made specific by having Mrs. Y. produce a list of Rich's Disruptive Behaviors. If they were too extreme to ignore, Mrs. Y. was to send the child directly to the office, saying only, "you are not permitted to ____ in this room, go to the office until I send for you." The office personnel were instructed to direct the child to a chair in the corner and then to ignore him.

Finally, Mrs. Y. was told to give praise and attention to conduct that facilitated learning and which was incompatible with Disruptive Behavior. She constructed a list specifying exactly what was expected of the children. In general, these were academic, prosocial, and rule-following responses. Additionally, Mrs. Y. was instructed to praise successive approximations to the desired behavior. She was to try to give at least one Approval Reaction per minute. While some focus on Rich was expected (when he showed improvement), the teacher was to spread her approval around the class.

During the first eight days, Mrs. Y. was unable to increase her approval for Relevant Behavior to the desired level or to eliminate Disapproval to Disruptive Behavior. Therefore, this period actually constituted a *Low Approval* condition.

High Approval In order to increase Mrs. Y.'s Approval Reactions, she was provided with a small counting machine which served two purposes: it provided a cue to remind Mrs. Y. to use Approval; and it also provided constant feedback so that the amount of Approval being given might be constantly compared to the target rate of one Approval Reaction per minute.

Low Approval$_2$ After ten days of High Approval, Mrs. Y. was instructed to attempt to control the children in the same way she had before the study began. She was so distressed by the increase in Disruptive Behavior that she could not withdraw Approval Reactions to the Baseline level. Thus, the withdrawal condition actually constituted a return to the Low Approval situation.

High Approval and Tutoring Tutoring in remedial reading was instituted in conjunction with a return to the High Approval condition in the classroom. High Approval and Tutoring were maintained until the end of the school year. Since Rich was far behind his classmates, and only six weeks of school remained when the tutoring program was started, no further experimental manipulations were attempted.

Follow-Up Rich went to summer school and although observations there were confounded by the difference in environment, teacher, peers, time of observation (AM vs. PM), etc., an estimate of the continued effects of remedial tutoring and differential social reinforcement was obtained.

During the summer term, Rich was observed eight times over a period of five weeks. The teacher and child categories were identical with those used during the spring semester. However, the rating procedure was somewhat different. During the summer term there were some students who appeared to be much more disruptive than Rich, and in order to obtain data on these students a random sampling procedure was used. Each student in the class was given a number, drawn each day to determine the sequence of observations. Observations were taken three times a week and each child was observed three to four minutes a day.

Remedial Tutoring

The remedial program followed procedures developed by Staats and Butterfield (1965). It was conducted by a college junior majoring in psychology who had not had previous experience in remedial reading work. A brief training period was used to introduce her to the Staats and Butterfield procedure.

Materials   The books involved were the three pre-primers and the next two readers in the Ginn Basic Reading Series, which were being used in Rich's classroom. The 358 vocabulary words included were each typed on a $3'' \times 5''$ card, and reading passages were broken down into small units of paragraphs or pages and placed on $5'' \times 8''$ cards. There were 75 words per unit in the pre-primers, 175 in *The Little White House* and in the first 20 units of *On Cherry Street*, and 120 words per unit in the remainder of *On Cherry Street*. "Back-up," or unconditioned reinforcers, consisted of edibles (candy, gum, etc.) and manipulables (small toys and games).

Tutoring Procedure   The three pre-primers which Rich had already completed in class were used to begin the tutoring program for two reasons. First, since there was a high probability of his emitting a correct response on this material, he could earn many tokens (marks on a card) and would therefore be likely to receive a back-up reinforcer at the end of each of the first few sessions. The initial pairing of tokens with back-ups without extended periods of delay would result in the tokens rapidly becoming conditioned reinforcers. Secondly, because the early material was quite easy, Rich would have many opportunities to receive social reinforcement or praise. Praise was also paired with other reinforcers, and soon became strong enough to be used alone to shape on task behavior. Such shaping would become more important as the material became more difficult.

For each reading unit, the new words (those not introduced at lower levels of the Ginn series) were presented first, six to twelve at a time. Rich was given two points for a correct response on the first try. If he did not know the word, *E* told him what it was and had him repeat it. Missed words were re-presented later and when Rich got one correct, he received one point.

After correctly reading a group of words, Rich read a story which contained them and old words (those presented earlier in the sequence). If he completed a unit (one or more paragraphs as defined earlier) of a story correctly, he was given four points. If he made one or two errors, he had to repeat the sentences in which they occurred. If he made three errors, he repeated the paragraph; four or more errors meant a repetition of the entire unit. As soon as he read a unit without error, he received two points. Later, when Rich began to study units that he had not yet read in class, the number of points for completed units was raised from 4 and 2 to 5 and 3.

All words missed during contextual reading were noted and were presented again at the start of the next session. Rich received ten points as soon as he went through all of these words consecutively without error.

Social reinforcement was given intermittently and was paired with the earning of points.

At the beginning of each session, Rich chose the prizes for which he intended to exchange his points at the end of it. He received a 10–15 cent prize for 50 points, a 25–30 cent prize for 100 points, and a 50 cent prize for 200 points. He was also given points for completing workbook assignments in class. He received five points for a perfect page, and three points for a corrected page or one finished with the teacher's aid.

Oral comprehension questions were asked after each story toward the end of the program. Two points were given for a correct response.

Rich was also given ten points if he wore his glasses, which he had usually left at home.

RESULTS

In interpreting the results, the reader should keep in mind two aspects of the procedure. First, the recordings of teacher behavior reflect her responses to the whole class, although she focused considerably on Rich. Unfortunately, our resources were inadequate for obtaining stable measures of teacher behavior toward one child in a 20-minute observation. However, it will be seen that changes in the teacher's approach to the class as a whole is systematically related to changes in Rich's behavior. Secondly, the experiment involves removing Disapproval Reactions of the teacher following Disruptive Behavior and increasing Approval Reactions for Relevant Behavior. The effects of these changes in reinforcement can be shown by graphing either percentage of Relevant Behavior or percentage of Disruptive Behavior, since one is the inverse of the other. We have elected to focus on Disruptive Behavior in the graphs.

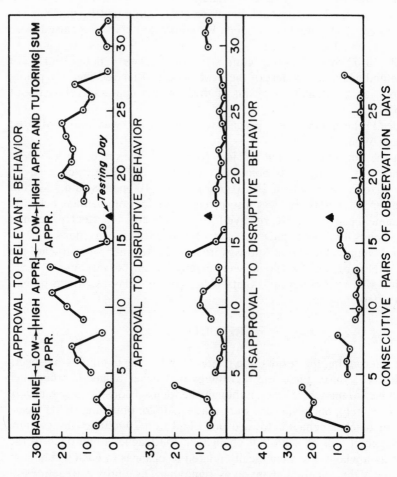

Fig. 31.2. Frequency of categories of teacher behaviors per 20-minute observation.

Changes in Disruptive Behavior

During Baseline, Rich displayed Disruptive Behavior in 87.6% of the observation intervals (Fig. 31.1) and he spent an average of 15 minutes each day in the principal's office. During this period, the teacher showed a high rate of Disapproval to Disruptive Behavior and Approval Reactions were infrequent (Fig. 31.2).

When the teacher began to ignore Disruptive Behavior and to Praise Relevant Behavior (Low Approval$_1$), the former declined to an average of 69.1%. However, Rich still averaged 22 minutes per day in the principal's office.

During the High Approval phase, Disruptive Behavior dropped to 51.1%, sometimes going as low as 30%. Mrs. Y. closely approached the objective of one Approval Reaction per minute, but there were also many occasions when Approval Reactions followed Disruptive Behaviors (Fig. 31.2). No time was spent in the principal's office.

Low Approval$_2$ (an attempt to return to Baseline conditions) brought an increase in Rich's Disruptive Behavior to an average of 64% (Fig. 31.1). One day, he spent 30 minutes in the office.

Point 17 in Figs. 31.1 and 31.2 deserves special mention. On this day, prior to the introduction of the tutoring program, the morning was spent testing Rich. He received a prize for working hard during the testing program and much praise was given. Following this, he behaved extremely well in class even though the teacher used more Disapproval and less Approval than usual.

During the High Approval and Tutoring period, Mrs. Y. was very consistent in ignoring Disruptive Behavior and praising Relevant Behavior. The level of Disruptive Behavior decreased consistently, and although the average was 33.4%, the average for the last six days of observation was 17%. No time was spent in the office.

During the summer school observation, the teacher's behavior was similar to that in the Low Praise$_2$ condition. Rich's Disruptive Behavior, however, remained low, averaging 11%.

Changes in Specific Categories of Disruptive Behavior

Analysis of specific categories of Disruptive Behavior revealed some expected and some unexpected changes (Table 31.1). In general, a decline is found in all categories of Disruptive Behavior from the Baseline to the High Approval and Tutoring condition, except for Orienting and Noise

Table 31.1. Average Percentage by Subcategories of Disruptive Behavior as a Function of Conditions

		Experimental Conditions			
Behavior Categories	Baseline	Low Approval$_1$	High Approval	Low Approval$_2$	High Approval and Tutoring
Gross Motor	34.5	11.9	12.8	10.5	6.9
Kneeling	10.7	11.9	3.0	4.0	7.5
Aggression	0.6	0.9	2.6	0.2	0.3
Disturbing Others	2.0	0.4	1.3	1.3	0.1
Talking	40.3	27.7	23.7	23.3	13.6
Vocalization	9.4	3.4	6.5	6.3	1.5
Noise	0.4	0.3	3.6	4.0	0.7
Orienting	2.9	1.5	3.8	3.0	3.8
Other Task	29.5	30.5	7.6	21.8	7.2

which had always occurred infrequently. The greatest percent of change occurred in Other Task (29.5% to 7.2%), Gross Motor (34.5% to 6.9%), and Talking (40.3% to 13.6%). Gross Motor showed the greatest decline from Baseline to Low Approval$_1$ (34.5% to 11.9%) and did not decline further until the High Approval and Tutoring condition. Praise was effective in motivating Rich to stay in his seat more often. However, Other Task behavior continued at a high rate through Low Approval$_1$ (Baseline = 29.5%, Low Approval$_1$ = 30.5%). Additional praise made Rich stay in his seat, but did not help him to work academically. With High Approval, a marked decrease in Other Task behavior occurred (7.6%). The return to Low Approval$_2$ showed an increase in Other Task (19.8%) and the final High Approval and Tutoring condition once again produced a sharp decrease in it (7.2%). In fact, during the last 10 days of Tutoring, Other Task activity was essentially zero. The Other Task category was the primary behavior to show expected response to the Low Approval-High Approval manipulation.

Three other behaviors, which were initially low in frequency, actually increased during the High Approval condition. Noise rose from 0.3% with Low Approval$_1$ to 3.6% with High Approval. Aggression went up from 0.9% to 2.6%, and Disturbing Others (property) rose from 0.4% to 1.3%. These findings suggest that Disapproval, which was markedly reduced during the High Approval phase, was probably suppressing these responses during Low Approval. The ignoring of this behavior (which is probably maintained by peer reactions) initially led to an increase in their frequency. At the same time, it should be noted that Other Task behavior decreased markedly as the teacher attempted to praise *on task* behavior. Rich could obtain praise by showing *on task* behavior, but could still get peer reinforcement for occasional Aggressive and Disturbing Others activities. As the reinforcement for Relevant Behavior continued over a longer period of time (High Approval plus Tutoring), each of these three categories of Disruptive Behavior decreased to essentially zero.

Remedial Tutoring

The remedial program lasted six weeks, during which 21 hours were spent in 30 tutoring sessions. The cost of the back-up reinforcers was $5.50.

Rich read on the first try 63% of 358 words. This included 56 words from the pre-primer, among which he made only one error. Of the 130 words presented more than once, 74 were read correctly on second trial, 34 on third trial, and 22 required four or more presentations. A final vocabulary test including all 358 words was administered at the end of the program. He made only 26 errors, reading 93% of the words correctly.

In oral reading (contextual reading) Rich made excellent progress. Out of a total of 156 units (not including pre-primer material) 50 units had to be recycled. Rich made a total of 98 errors involving 54 different words.

Performance on comprehension questions was remarkable. He made no errors on any of the comprehension questions, even though some of them were quite difficult.

How did Rich's progress during tutoring compare with the class in general? When Rich completed the pre-primers, 87% of the children in his classroom were reading *We Are Neighbors*, the third reader following the pre-primers in the Ginn series. At the end of the program Rich had completed the first two readers in the series and was ready to begin reading *We Are Neighbors*. At this time 70% of the children had finished the third reader and were beginning the next one.

Token reinforcement for completed workbook assignments also proved to be effective. One-fourth of the points Rich earned were for workbook pages. His progress in class was so rapid toward the end of the program that he was completing workbook assignments and corresponding reading materials in class on an equal level with his work in the tutoring program. He sometimes explained proudly to the tutor that he had worked on his assignments at home as well as in class.

Rich also wore his glasses more often when he was reinforced with tokens. The teacher reported that she and Rich's mother had frequently attempted to convince him to wear his glasses. He rarely brought them to school and almost never wore them even when he did. After the token procedure was instituted, he wore his glasses to every tutoring session but one, and was observed wearing them in class.

Test Results

Rich's reading grade on the Wide Range Achievement Test was 1.4 before tutoring and 2.0 afterward. On the Illinois Test of Psycholinguistic Abilities his total language age increased from 6 years, 4 months to 6 years, 10 months. The results are presented graphically in Fig. 31.3. Gains of a year or more occurred on four subtests. Rich also improved in responding to concept words by saying "yes" or "no" (Auditory Decoding), responding to concept pictures (Visual Decoding), demonstrating the functions of objects (Motor Encoding), and repeating visually presented sequences (Visual-Motor Sequential). However, his ability to describe the properties of objects (Vocal Encoding) decreased. In terms of the training procedures used, there is no clear explanation of the gains or loss of the "psycholinguistic functions" tested by the ITPA. They could reflect the unreliability of the test or a re-test practice effect. No specific attempt was made to work on the "capacities" tested by the ITPA. Whatever the explanation, the results support an interpretation of improved functioning in the use of some communication skills. Three of Rich's low points at retest involved speech (Vocal) and suggest a continuing deficiency in the use of language, often found in Negro children from disadvantaged backgrounds.

DISCUSSION

The results demonstrate that the teacher's use of differential social reinforcement played an important role in reducing some of Rich's Disruptive Behavior. We do not know whether a continued use of High Approval might have reduced Disruptive Behavior further, but the results of related studies (Becker *et al.*, 1967; Madsen *et al.*, 1968) have indicated that changes to be accomplished by differential social reinforcement usually occur within the first week or two.

The rapid progress made in remedial reading with an "untrained"

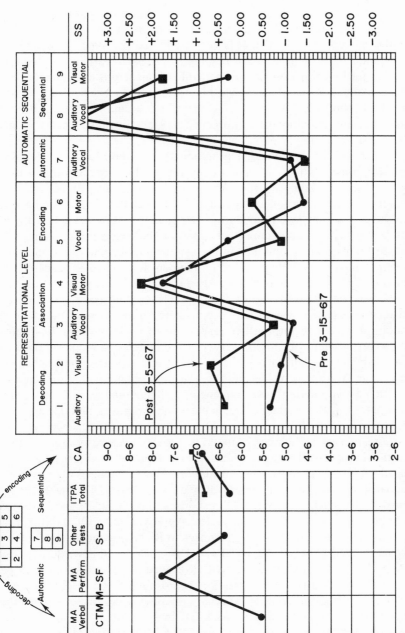

Fig. 31.3. Age-normed scores on the Illinois Test of Psycholinguistic Abilities before and after tutoring.

tutor is consistent with results reported by Staats & Butterfield (1965) and Staats (1967), and indicates that a token reinforcement procedure is both practical and efficient. It is very likely that the remedial procedures did much more than improve reading skills. Rich learned that working harder for longer periods of time paid off. The generous praise he received very likely did much to change his attitudes about school and school work. Technically, "success," completed work, and reading itself probably became conditioned reinforcers for Rich. In other words, he had been taught to "like to learn."

The effect of the remedial program on classroom behavior requires careful consideration. It is commonly reported by teachers that a child given special reading instruction learns to work well with his remedial teacher in the one-to-one situation, but still does not function on his own in the classroom. Two procedures were used to insure that gains in work skills would show up in improved classroom behavior. First, tokens were given for workbook activities in the classroom. Second, the teacher had been trained to provide social reinforcement for improved academic behavior. This combination of procedures proved to be very effective.

It was emphasized earlier that the primary measure taken of the teacher's behavior was of her responses to all members of the class. In addition, any time the teacher responded to Rich following Disruptive or Relevant Behavior, the observers would circle the response code for Rich's behavior. This measure does not indicate whether the teacher was giving an Approving or Disapproving reaction, but only that she attended to Rich. By comparing these frequencies with those in Fig. 31.2 some rough estimates of the probable frequencies of Approval and Disapproval Responses to Rich are possible. During Baseline, the teacher averaged 13.3 responses to Rich per 20 minutes. Most of these responses had to be in the Disapproval category. During Low Approval$_1$, the teacher averaged 8.9 responses to Rich per 20 minutes. These responses were probably equally divided between Approval and Disapproval. During High Approval, the teacher averaged 9.8 responses to Rich per 20 minutes. Most of these responses had to be in the Approval category. During Low Approval$_2$, an average of 5.9 responses to Rich were made. Again, these were divided between Approval and Disapproval. Finally, during High Approval and Tutoring, the teacher averaged 5.3 responses to Rich per 20 minutes. Most of this behavior would have to be in the Approval category. This last figure is especially interesting because it implies that the teacher was attending to Rich $2\frac{1}{2}$ times as often during Baseline, where Disruptive Behavior averaged 87.6%, as during High Approval and Tutoring where Disruptive Behavior averaged 33.4% (and 17% for the last six days). In other words, an effective program actually reduced the amount of time required in coping with Rich.

Observation of an incident at summer school provides evidence on the change in Rich's attitude toward school. Summer school children were registered either for an 8-to-10 o'clock reading program, a 10-to-12 o'clock arithmetic program, or both. Rich's mother registered him for reading, but not arithmetic. When she came to pick him up the first day, he begged to stay at school. On the second day, he broke into tears when his mother came to take him home and she allowed him to stay. Rich's teacher told him that she would be glad to have him if his mother and the principal agreed. His mother said he could stay if he would ask the principal for permission. With a history of being sent to the principal's office, this was a difficult thing for Rich to do. He entered the office by himself and asked for an appointment. The principal later reported that Rich "appeared quite frightened. Tears were still on his cheeks, and he seemed to have difficulty talking." But he went through with it and obtained permission to stay all morning. School attendance had definitely become a positive, desirable behavior for him.

REFERENCES

Becker, W. C., Madsen, C. H. Jr., Arnold, Carole Revelle, & Thomas, D. R. The contingent use of teacher attention and praise in reducing classroom behavior problems. *Journal of Special Education*, 1967, **1**, 287–307.

Madsen, C. H., Jr., Becker, W. C., & Thomas, D. R. Rules, praise and ignoring: elements of elementary classroom control. *Journal of Applied Behavior Analysis*, 1968, **1**, 139–150.

Staats, A. W. Cognitive behavior modification: methods of research and treatment with problem learners. Paper presented at the convention of the American Educational Research Association, New York, February, 1967.

Staats, A. W., & Butterfield, W. H. Treatment of nonreading in a culturally-deprived juvenile delinquent: An application of reinforcement principles. *Child Development*, 1965, **36**, 925–942.

Parents as Behavior Therapy-Technicians in Treating Reading Deficits (Dyslexia)*[1]

DAVID RYBACK and ARTHUR W. STAATS

University of Hawaii

Abstract: The present experiment was an attempt to discover whether parents of children with reading deficits could act successfully as therapy-technicians in helping their own children to overcome these deficits. Four children with reading problems were reinforced for appropriate reading behaviors with tokens backed up by monetary value. The children's parents administered the learning material following a 4-hr training period. All four Ss showed a positively accelerated rate of reading responses and made from 49,303 to 95,906 single word reading responses during the 35–65 hr of training. The number of new words learned ranged from 458 to 1040. At least 63 per cent of these words were retained on a short-term retention test and at least 53 per cent were retained on a long-term retention test administered 10–15 days later. The ratio of reinforcers to reading responses decreased markedly for all Ss despite the increasing difficulty of the material. Pre- and post-test comparisons indicated an increase (significant at the 0.05 level) in the children's reading ability. The results support the feasibility of parents providing complex behavior therapy to their children when they have standard procedures to follow and some supervision.

In 1963 it was suggested that parents must be considered to be the trainers of their children. "Whether the parent intends to or not, he manipulates many conditions of learning that will determine to a large extent the behaviors the child will acquire. As long as the child's behavioral development consists of innumerable training experiences, the parent has many of the controlling variables in his hands and cannot relinquish them regardless of his philosophy of child development ... Faced with a training task of such imposing responsibilities, it would seem that the

---

*Reprinted from the *Journal of Behavior Therapy and Experimental Psychiatry*, Vol. 1, No. 2, 1970, pp. 109–119.

[1]Portions of the data presented herein constituted a part of the Ph.D. dissertation of the first author at the University of Hawaii, 1969, done under the direction of the second author. The paper was jointly written.

parent would need an understanding of the principles of behavior by which children learn ... This suggests that the parent could be an active participant in arranging circumstances to produce most effectively an abundant, rich, adjustive, behavioral repertoire using a minimum of aversive stimulation and a' maximum of positive reinforcement ..." (Staats, 1963, pp. 412–413.)

Since this behavioral analysis of parent–child interactions, a number of studies have extended learning principles to childhood behavior problems, employing the parent as trainer or behavior therapist. Wahler, Winkel, Peterson and Morrison (1965) worked with mothers in the clinic and taught them to discriminate target behaviors of their children and to respond according to certain contingencies. In a subsequent step the mothers discriminated without cues from the experimenter but received feedback on their accuracy. The behaviors dealt with were commanding vs. co-operative behavior.

In their work with parent–child relationships, therapists have in several cases also moved out of the clinic and into the home setting. Russo (1964) demonstrated that parents can serve as trainers in both home and clinical settings, while Straughan (1964) conducted the therapy sessions at home. Straughan worked with the child in a playroom and served as a model while the parent observed. In a similar fashion, Rickard and Munday (1965) served as models in shaping non-stuttering in a 9-year-old while the mother observed. Subsequent to this, the mother acted as a model while the father observed. Similar modeling techniques were used by Ryback (1966) in training parents in the shaping of speech behaviors in mute schizophrenic children.

Walder (1966) and Wetzel, Baker, Roney and Martin (1966) have also used parents to treat their autistic children. Other behavior problems which have been treated by parents as trainers include emotional disturbances (Andronico and Guerney, 1967), destructive behaviors (O'Leary, O'Leary and Becker, 1967), aggressive behavior (Zeilberger, Sampen and Sloane, 1968), hyperactivity in the classroom (Patterson, 1965a) and at home (Hawkins, Peterson, Schweid and Bijou, 1966), school phobia (Patterson, 1965b) and excessive scratching (Allen and Harris, 1966). Zeilberger *et al.*, have generally concluded that "the most efficient way to modify deviant behavior may be to change the reactions of the natural milieu to that behavior" (1968, p. 47).

Of all the studies dealing with parents as subprofessional behavior modifiers only one deals with language training although this study (Ryback, 1966) lacked precise criteria for measuring behavior changes.

All other studies involved behaviors that could be altered in a relatively brief period of time. However, many deficits of human behavior are usually overcome only on the basis of learning over lengthy time periods (Staats, 1969). Simple instructions to reinforce or not reinforce a behavior will not suffice in such cases. It would seem necessary to develop, through research, methods and procedures for the standard application of behavioral principles in the treatment of complex cognitive deficits. It would be important to demonstrate that complex behavior therapy procedures could be successfully employed by the parent, under the supervision of the psychiatric or psychological professional.

One cognitive deficit that has been of perennial concern to medicine and psychology is the failure to learn to read normally, a deficit called dyslexia, displayed by a considerable percentage of children. Staats began the study of reading learning and of token-reinforcer methods for treating dyslexia in 1959 and has continued this work in a series of studies (Staats, Finley, Minke and Wolf, 1964; Staats, Minke, Finley, Wolf and Brooks, 1964; Staats, Staats, Schutz and Wolf, 1962). (His token-reinforcer system has spread widely, see Ayllon and Azrin, 1969.) Part of this project has involved the development of methods by which subprofessional personnel, under professional supervision, could successfully treat children who had severe problems of learning to read (Staats and Butterfield, 1965; Staats, Minke, Goodwin and Landeen, 1967a; Staats, Minke and Butts, 1970).

The purpose of the present experiment was to determine whether the same set of methods and materials could be successfully utilized by parents in the treatment of their own children's cognitive deficits. The behavioral deficit of dyslexia is ordinarily not easily treated and requires long-term treatment efforts by professionals. This study is the first to test the possibility that behavioral methods, when made standard and explicit, can be employed by the parent in individual treatment of complex behavioral deficits.

METHOD

Subjects and parents

One child was selected from the University of Hawaii Laboratory School. Three were chosen from the waiting list for the Reading Clinic at the University of Hawaii. These children were chosen from a population of students described as poor readers on the basis of standard achievement tests and teacher referrals. Final selection for participation in the experiment was on the basis of a 100-word test developed from the reading material. All children reading fewer than 80 out of the 100 words but no less than 20 were selected for the experiment.

S_1 was a 13-year-old boy of Japanese descent, an only child and had been diagnosed as mentally retarded by the State Psychologist of the Department of Public Instruction as well as by a clinical psychologist in private practice. S_1 was in a special non-graded class because of his learning difficulties and read 43 out of the 100-word test. At the onset of the program, Parent$_1$ had recently quit her job as librarian because of somatic manifestations of tension. She was unaware of the source of her tension since events in her life, including her marriage, were satisfactory. A 41-year-old woman, P_1, was below average in arithmetic and spelling skills, but was very superior in reading skills according to the Wide Range achievement Test (WRAT) by Jastak, Bijou and Jastak.

S_2 was an 11-year-old fifth-grade girl of Caucasian descent; the oldest of four children, her siblings were $9\frac{1}{2}$, 7 and 4 years old. S_2 had been diagnosed as an emotional problem by a clinical psychologist as well as by her teachers, her reading problem was thought to stem from her emotional problems. She read 61 words on the 100-word test. Parent$_2$ was a 31-year-old housewife. One of P_2's chief concerns during the experimental period was an ailing mother who made sporadic demands on her and this was sometimes a drain on her energy. P_2 was well below average in arithmetic, spelling and reading skills.

S_3 was a $10\frac{1}{2}$-year-old fifth-grade boy of Hawaiian descent; the second of four children, his siblings were $11\frac{1}{2}$, $8\frac{1}{2}$ and 7 years old. He had been described by the Department of Education as a learning disability and he had been diagnosed by a pediatrician, on the basis of neurological tests, as a learning disability with minimal cerebral dysfunction. He read 50 words on the 100-word test. Parent$_3$ was a 31-year-old clinic clerk at a hospital near her home. She was above average in arithmetic and spelling skills and was at a superior level in reading skills.

S_4 was an $8\frac{1}{2}$-year-old third-grade boy of Hawaiian descent; the youngest of four children, his siblings were 12, 11 and 10 years old. No problems were reported other than his learning disabilities and a heart ailment. He read 29 words on the 100-word test. Parent$_4$ was a 41-year-old woman who worked as a cashier at a cafeteria. P_4 was below average in her arithmetic, spelling and reading skills. The parents were given the Wide Range Achievement Test and the results are summarised in Table 32.1.

Table 32.1. Wide Range Achievement Test Scores of Parents

Sub-test	Parent$_1$	Parent$_2$	Parent$_3$	Parent$_4$	Mean
Reading					
Grade level	16.5	7.9	14.4	7.7	11.62
Percentile	99.4	34	96	37	66.60
Spelling					
Grade level	10.8	6.5	12.0	5.8	8.77
Percentile	77	19	84	23	50.75
Arithmetic					
Grade level	6.7	7.1	10.1	5.3	7.30
Percentile	23	25	63	12	30.75
Derived IQ	114.0	90.3	115.7	88.7	102.2

The combined income of each family ranged from $11,000 to $15,000 per annum. Each mother had completed a high school education while 2 fathers had completed high school, one had completed 8th grade and one had completed a year of college. The IQ's of the mothers ranged from 89 to 116, as the Table indicates, on the estimated scores which were derived from the WRAT results by averaging the Reading, Arithmetic and Spelling Standard Scores.

Training materials

The stimulus materials and procedures employed in the study have been described in detail elsewhere (Staats & Butterfield, 1965; Staats *et al.*, 1967a), and a manual further elaborates the techniques of recording the data and supervising the therapy-technicians (Staats, Van Mondfrans & Minke, 1967b). The procedures and token-reinforcer system will be called herein the Staats Motivation-Activating Reading Technique (SMART), based upon the evidence that the procedures ensure continuous motivation of the child throughout a complex training program. The materials are based upon the Science Research Associates Reading Laboratory. These stories are graded and involve a somewhat controlled introduction of new words in each lesson. The present methods require a list made of all of the new words added in each story, beginning with the first story. The training for each lesson thus begins with the individual presentation to the child of the new words to be learned, printed on 5×8 in. cards. Each new word is presented as a stimulus; if the child cannot read the word he is prompted. The children learn to read each word to a criterion of one correct unprompted reading, each word being deleted from the series as criterion is reached. Following this the paragraphs of the story are read by the child (the story is printed on $8\frac{1}{2} \times 11$ in. paper). The child is prompted on any words he cannot read, and the paragraph is re-read, if necessary, until it is done perfectly. Following the reading each paragraph of the story to criterion, the child is presented with the whole story to read silently.

The S.R.A. stories also include questions in each of the stories to test the comprehension. Thus, following the silent reading of the story the child is presented with the questions. Whenever a question is missed the child rereads the relevant paragraph in the story and responds to the question again.

Thus, each lesson consists of the following phases: The Individual Word Learning Phase, the Oral Paragraph Reading Phase, the Silent Reading Phase and the Comprehension Question Phase. A Vocabulary Review is presented following every 20 lessons, to test the extent to which the words previously learned in those lessons have been retained. The test thus occurs several weeks following for most of the words.

Token-reinforcer system

The motivational system consists of token-reinforcers of different value. The tokens are plastic discs of three different colors. A blue token is worth $\frac{1}{10}$ of a cent (or one point on the graph of reinforcement accrual described below), a white token is worth $\frac{1}{5}$ of a cent (or 2 points), a red token is worth $\frac{1}{2}$ cent (or 5 points). The daily recording of the child's progress is demonstrated to him with positive comment and approval from the parent. The parents were instructed in the use of positive social reinforcement and in avoiding the use of disapproval of any kind, including urging to do well, or to do better.

The child received in exchange for his tokens, when a sufficient number had been accrued, a cash account with the parent by which the child could purchase any item of his choice limited only by the amount of money he earned to date. The child had the opportunity of purchasing inexpensive items such as candy bars (within the customs of the family) as well as more expensive items. For the latter he would have to save his accumulating tokens for a longer period.

The different values of tokens were presented contingent upon the child's reading behaviors. According to plan the higher value reinforcers were delivered contingent upon the most valuable behaviors, thus, for example, the child was reinforced more heavily for reading a word correctly in his first attempt than after prompted learning trials and he was reinforced more highly for correctly answering the comprehension questions than for the silent reading itself (to ensure that the silent reading had occurred). However, the child was reinforced for all of his effortful behaviors in the reading task.

Behavior recording

The major source of data for the present type of study consists of the effects of the training upon the behavior of the subject during the extended experimental period. This methodology calls for a detailed recording of the stimuli presented to the subject and his responses to those stimuli. Thus, every single word stimulus presented to the child was recorded as was the response to that stimulus. When the paragraph reading task was presented each response to a word stimulus was recorded. If the child missed a word more than once this was also recorded. The number of token-reinforcers received was recorded, and so on. For these purposes data sheets (*see* Staats *et al.*, 1967b) were employed by the parents. Part of the training of the parents consisted of instruction in how to perform the recording duties.

Parent training and supervision

The training of parents involved approximately 4 hr. During this time they received a demonstration of the procedures by E (the first author) and were given a basic outline of the procedures. Then detailed instructions concerning the administration of the procedures and the collection of data were given. Questions were handled as they arose. Finally, the parents were given actual practice in administering the materials, taking turns playing the role of the child.

During the first couple of weeks, direct supervision of parents' participation was periodically maintained in the manner described (Staats *et al.*, 1967b). Following this, E's supervision was phased out gradually until the parents were working on their own except for the review tests which were administered by E.

One of the central aspects of E's supervision of the parents' behaviors in the training situation involved the use of a checklist (*see* Staats *et al.*, 1967b). This checklist related to two aspects of the parents' behaviors: firstly, to the mechanics of the therapy-technicians' task and, secondly, to the more subtle concerns of the behavior modification training techniques. On the one hand some checklist items called attention to such things as filling out the data sheets, recording time, writing down words missed for later review, counting tokens, filling out the token graph and so on. On the other hand the checklist contained items referring, for example, to the parent's pause in presenting single word stimuli before prompting, to re-presenting the missed words, delivering tokens, presenting paragraphs until the child had them entirely correct, use of pointing to direct the child's attention, checking occasionally on child during silent reading, correcting comprehension questions and having child reread relevant paragraphs in case of error, and so on. There were additional items that directed attention to aspects of the parents' training characteristics and to the behavior of the child; for example, to the parent watching to see if the child looked at the word when repeating it after prompting or if the child practiced interfering rehearsals in trying to learn the words, giving positive social reinforcement and avoiding any negative social reinforcement (especially on errors), and so on. Besides the specific check list E observed the quality of the training in general—especially with respect to insuring the absence of any negative social reinforcement, either direct or implied. When any procedures were erroneously handled or when the training included undesirable elements, corrective measures were immediately discussed with the parent following the session.

Half-hour group meetings of the parents and E were held at the end of the first, third and eighth weeks of the program to discuss any problems which may have arisen, technical or otherwise, and to discuss the motivation of the children as well as the parents' own motivation.

Testing materials

The 100 item single word reading test consisted of words randomly selected from the universe of 4253 words of the reading materials. Twenty words were selected from each of the five grade levels (1.2, 1.7, 2.3, 3.0, 4.0). The words were presented individually on 3 by 5 in. cards and had to be correctly pronounced for receipt of credit. Two alternate forms of the test were developed. The words of these were matched for difficulty according to the Thorndike–Lorge word count (Thorndike & Lorge, 1944), and across reading grade levels. One form of the test was used as a pre-test and the other as a post-test. The original form was also administered as an additional post-test. Evidence has shown the 100-word test to be a valid indicator of Ss' performance on the SMART (Staats *et al.*, 1967b; 1969).

The Wide Range Achievement Test (WRAT) (Jastak, Bijou & Jastak, 1965) was employed to characterise the academic achievement of each of the parents working with the children. The Diagnostic Reading Scales (Spache, 1963) were individually administered before and after the behavior therapy training procedures.

RESULTS AND CONCLUSIONS

Over a 5- to 7-month period, four mothers administered the Staats Motivation-Activating Reading Technique (SMART) to their children. During this period, Ss made many reading responses. They cooperated in the experiment with good attention and diligent work habits. The production of this type of behavior for such children in training conducted by the parent is of primary significance in itself. That is, it is only with procedures that yield such attention and work responses that the thousands of learning trials for complex learning can occur.

In this context it is interesting to consider the numbers of learning trials that did occur. That is, the total number of words the child read in the various types of training (including the comprehension and review tests) were tabulated as the training progressed. In the present study, the four Ss made an average of 74,730 single word reading responses during an average of 51.25 hr of training. During 65 hr of training, S_1 made 82,466 single word reading responses; during 50 hr of training, S_2 made 71,244; during 55 hr of training, S_3 made 95,906; and during 35 hr of training, S_4 made 49,303 single word reading responses. Cumulative records of the words read over the period of training are depicted in Fig. 32.1.

As Fig. 32.1 shows, the reading rates of the four Ss accelerated positively over the training sessions, although the acceleration was slight for S_2. This acceleration in response rate may be considered typical in these procedures since it has already occurred with a number of subjects (Staats *et al.*, 1967a, 1969). The typical curve is like that of S_1 and S_3 where an early acceleration is shown followed by a high linear response rate. These results indicate the high quality of the children's attention and work behaviors during training, resulting in the many learning trials, a prerequisite for any complex skill acquisition. It should also be noted that the acceleration occurred even though the reading material became increasingly difficult and was extended over a long period.

Before reading each story, Ss were presented with individual cards for all the words in that story which had not been previously presented. When these words were presented, Ss read a certain proportion correctly,

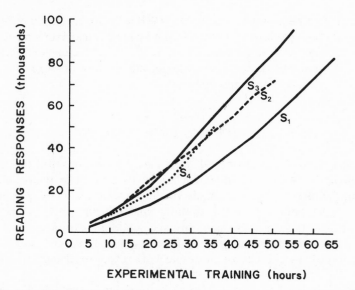

EXPERIMENTAL TRAINING (hours)

Fig. 32.1. Cumulative number of single word reading responses as a function of the time in experimental training.

the other words being missed on first presentation. The missed words were considered to be new words. Records were kept of the number of words the children missed on first presentation, the number of these words which were then later missed in the oral reading of the paragraphs, as well as the number of words originally missed that the Ss could not read on the review tests presented at a later time. S_1 learned 910 new words; S_2 learned 591; S_3 learned 1040; and S_4 learned 450 during training.

Although the Ss missed these new words on initial presentation, they were given training trials on these words and then read them again in the oral reading of the paragraphs. The number of errors made on this second presentation provided a measure of short-term retention of the words that had been previously learned. Thus, S_1 retained 576 (about 63%) of these words during the Oral Reading Phase; S_2 retained 504 (about 85%); S_3 retained 917 (about 88%); and S_4 retained 431 (about 94%). These results indicate that the criterion of one correct unprompted trial in the original vocabulary-learning phase produced considerable learning when the words were read in context.

A measure of long-term retention was obtained by individually presenting the words that had been first learned in the preceding 20 lessons. This test was given 10–15 days after training occurred. The training included the previous single word presentations of the words as well as the reading of the words in context both orally and silently. In addition, however, many new additional words had been learned in the interim. According to this measure, S_1 retained 478 of the 910 words (53%) on the long-term retention test; S_2 retained 404 of the 591 words (68%); S_3 retained 585 of the 1040 words (56%) and S_4 retained 340 of the 458 words (74%). These results indicate that the children covered a considerable amount of reading material, that they learned to read a large number of new words whether presented individually or in context and that even after a considerable intervening period they retained a good proportion of what they learned.

The 100-word reading test was administered to the Ss at the onset of the program and an alternate form of the test was administered at the termination of the program. Subject$_1$ made an increase of 31 per cent on the post-test over the pre-test, while S_2, S_3, and S_4 made increases of 44 per cent, 66 per cent and 224 per cent respectively. The pre-test mean was 45.75 while the post-test mean was 85.75. A one-tailed correlated t test indicated a significant increase at the 0.01 level of probability.

The results of the original form of the 100-word test, when administered at the completion of the program, were very similar to those of the alternate form. Subjects 1–4 scored 89, 86, 87 and 95, respectively, on the original form, as compared with the results on the other post-training form of the test, as shown in Table 32.2. Thus, the two forms were very

Table 32.2. Pre- and Post-Test Results in Reading Ability

Subject	Time of administration	Spache Diagnostic Reading Scales Reading Grade Level			100-Word test	
		Word recognition	Instructional level	Independent level	Score	Gain (%)
S_1	Pre	2.8	2.5	2.5	43	81
	Post	4.5	4.5	4.5	78	
S_2	Pre	3.8	3.0	3.75	61	44
	Post	5.0	4.5	5.0	88	
S_3	Pre	3.3	2.75	3.5	50	66
	Post	3.5	4.5	4.5	83	
S_4	Pre	2.3	2.25	2.25	29	224
	Post	5.0	4.5	5.0	94	
	t	2.786	11.719	4.434	4.655	
	p	< 0.05	< 0.005	< 0.025	< 0.01	

similar and may be considered to be representative samples of the universe of 4253 words. In the comparison of the two post-training tests three of the four scores deviate by four points or less. Only one score deviates as much as 11 points.

In addition to the above, the Spache Diagnostic Reading Scales were administered both at the onset and termination of the program. The pre- and post-test results are also shown in Table 32.2. On the Word Recognition subtest (in which Ss read single words aloud) the pre-test mean score indicated a 4.5 grade reading level (GRL), an increase significant at the 0.05 level. On the Instructional subtest in which Ss read stories aloud, the pre-test mean score indicated a 2.6 GRL while the post-test mean score indicated a 4.5 GRL, an increase significant at the 0.005 level. On the Independent subtest in which Ss read silently and were tested for comprehension, the pre-test mean score indicated a 3.0 GRL while the post-test mean score indicated a 4.7 GRL, an increase significant at the 0.025 level. For all Ss and in all subtests save one (Word Recognition for S_3), an increase of at least one grade level was obtained on the independent, standardized test. These are very important findings because they indicate that the training is not only specific to the particular materials involved. The children showed consistent increases on the standardized test—and the increases were larger than expected on the basis of the length of training involved.

One aspect of the SMART concerns the ratio of reinforcers to reading responses. The procedures were designed to reduce progressively the number of reinforcers given per reading response as the training progresses or, conversely, to require more reading responses per unit of reinforcement. Demonstration that this is possible in a long-term training program "is in part an answer to the question whether the use of extrinsic reinforcers in training will produce a child who is dependent upon those reinforcers" (Staats & Butterfield, 1965, p. 941). Figure 32.2 shows the ratio of reinforcers to the number of reading responses over the course of the training. The results support the earlier demonstrations in that the ratio of reinforcers to reading responses can be seen to decrease as a function of number of training sessions. This is especially interesting in light of the acceleration in rate of reading responses as shown in Fig. 32.1.

The mean cost of the reinforcers per child was $18.34. Subject$_1$ earned $17.36, S_2 earned $18.79, S_3 earned $20.89 and S_4 earned $16.32. Training of the parents took merely 4 hr. Since the parents were trained in a group setting, the average time for training was 1 hr per parent. Hence, the

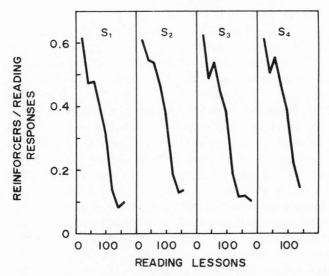

Fig. 32.2. Ratio of the monetary value of the tokens received to the number of reading responses made as a function of the number of lessons read.

cost of reinforcers required in the SMART and the expense of training parents were minimal. In addition, of course, there was time involved in the supervisory visits. However, these totaled roughly 5 hr per parent. Much of this could probably be shortened. It is quite evident that widespread medical or psychological treatment is not possible with a ratio of one highly-trained professional per child. The present methods, and their extension to other areas, could offer a method of extending treatment to larger numbers of children — with greater economy than is presently possible.

DISCUSSION

This study is the fourth in a sequence of experiments demonstrating the application of the Staats Motivation-Activating Reading Technique. Previous studies have involved children in the 14- to 16-year age range. The present study showed the procedures to work effectively with 4 children whose ages averaged 10.7 years.

One reason for which many, if not most, professionals are unwilling to venture into the area of parent-child therapeutic interaction is that the previous history of the dyadic interplay between child and parent prevent the therapist's approach from being effective. Thus, the customary parent–

child interaction in the context of complex skill acquisition is apt to be aversive for both participants. The situation is even more likely to occur with the child who has learning problems (or emotional, social, or cognitive problems). Any training program to be successfully conducted by the parent must overcome these past experiences of both parent and child.

In this context it is important to discuss the types of problems the various children treated with the SMART have had, in addition to reading deficits. In the previous experiments in which training was conducted by non-professional therapy-technicians (although not by parents) the children included a minority group juvenile delinquent, children from special classes for the retarded, children with emotional problems and ghetto black children who were severe educational problems. A number of these children were disturbed and delinquent children. In the present study the children's problems — mental retardation, emotionally disturbed, and cerebral dysfunction — would indicate the children to present serious treatment cases. Despite the severity of the diagnoses, the children responded well and the acquisition of reading skills did take place. Thus, utilizing the present procedures, it appeared that parents could serve as therapists for their children in an area in which only specialized professionals would ordinarily become involved.

As a side interest two of the siblings of the experimental Ss were given the pre- and post-tests at the same time that they were administered to the experimental Ss, S_2's $9\frac{1}{2}$-year-old sister obtained a pre-test score of 80 and a post-test score of 84 on the matched versions of the 100-word reading test, and this despite the fact that she had special tutoring in reading by a retired remedial reading specialist throughout the duration of her sister's SMART program. During this time, S_2 attained a 44 per cent increase on the post-over the pre-test. On the Spache Diagnostic Reading Scale, S_2's sister obtained scores of 4.5, 4.0 and 4.5 on both pre- and post-test scores of the three subtests. Again, no progress was shown. Although S_2 was a year ahead of her sister in school, she was quite a bit behind her sister in reading level at the beginning. But by the termination of the SMART administration, S_2 had caught up with her sister as indicated by the pre- and post-tests.

In a similar fashion S_3's $8\frac{1}{2}$-year-old brother, a third grader who also had a severe reading disability, was given the pre- and post-tests. Although S_3 attained a 66 per cent increase on the post- over the pre-test of the 100-word reading test, his younger brother, who received no help during this time, scored 7 and 11 on the pre- and post-tests respectively. On the subtests of the Spache Diagnostic Reading Scales the control sibling scored

1.6, 1.0 and 1.5 on the pre-test while scoring 1.8, 1.0 and 2.0 on the post-test, again indicating very little gain during the 6-month period. These results are important in providing some partial control data, and are also interesting methodologically. That is, use of siblings in this manner can be seen to have general implications for providing controls in behavior modification where one employs relatively few children.

It should be noted that despite the instruction of the parents, a problem in the training interaction did occur with the P_1S_1 dyad. Thus, P_1 sometimes inadvertently punished S_1 whenever he made a reading error. This was not done by what she said (merely a prompt of the erred response) but rather by how she said it; that is, with an annoyed, disappointed tone of voice. The parent was informed about this problem and the procedures were improved. This indicates the advantage of having professional supervision in some cases as was also shown in one of 18 therapy-technicians in an earlier study (Staats *et al.*, 1967a). It may be suggested, however, that sub-doctoral professionals can also be trained in the techniques and provide the supervision.

In conclusion, the importance of the present research findings lies in the fact that the SMART can be used by parents to teach their own children who have learning disabilities or other problems that result in cognitive deficits. Moreover, it is not necessary that the parents have previously had any special training nor that they be above average in intelligence, nor, for that matter, that they be educated beyond high school. Thus, the four parents with only 4 hr training in the SMART administration and subsequent supervision (notably in the one case) were able to successfully administer the materials. Moreover, training was administered in the everyday context of ongoing family demands on the mothers, in the homes of the respective families, while two of the mothers were holding full-time jobs. Even the very busy parent can administer the SMART with success if motivated and able to read.

REFERENCES

Allen K. E. and Harris F. R. (1966) Elimination of a child's excessive scratching by training the mother in reinforcement procedures. *Behav. Res. & Therapy* **4**, 79–84.

Andronico M. P. and Guerney B., Jr. (1967) The potential application of filial therapy to the school situation. *J. Sch. Psychol.* **6**, 2–7.

Ayllon T. and Azrin A. H. (1969) *The Token Economy: A Motivational System for Therapy and Rehabilitation*. Appleton, New York.

Hawkins R. P., Peterson R. F., Schweid E. and Bijou S. W. (1966) Behavior therapy in the home: amelioration of problem parent-child relations with parent in a therapeutic role. *J. Exp. Child Psychol.* **4**, 99–107.

Jastak, J. F., Bijou S. W. and Jastak S. R. (1965) Wide Range Achievement Test. Wilmington, Delaware: Guidance Associates.

O'Leary K. D., O'Leary S. and Becker W. C. (1967) Modification of deviant sibling interaction pattern in the home. *Behav. Res. & Therapy* **5**, 113–120.

Patterson G. R. (1965a) An application of conditioning techniques to the control of a hyperactive child. *Case Studies in Behavior Modification* (Eds. L. P. Ullmann and L. Krasner), pp. 370–375. Holt, New York.

Patterson G. R. (1965b) A learning theory approach to the treatment of the school phobic child. *Case Studies in Behavior Modification*. (Eds. L. P. Ullmann and L. Krasner), pp. 279–285. Holt, New York.

Rickard H. C. and Munday M. B. (1965) Direct manipulation of stuttering behavior: an experimental-Clinical approach. *Case Studies in Behavior Modification*. (Eds. L. P. Ullmann and L. Krasner), pp. 268–274. Holt, New York.

Russo S. (1964) Adaptations in behavioral therapy with children. *Behav. Res. & Therapy* **2**, 43–47.

Ryback D. (1966) M&M's and behavior modification. *J. Council except. Child.* **16**, 3–7.

Ryback D. (1969) Cognitive behavior modification: Motivated learning reading treatment with parents as therapy-technicians. Unpublished doctoral dissertation, University of Hawaii.

Spache G. D. (1963) Diagnostic Reading Scales. California Test Bureau.

Staats A. W. (1963) (with contributions by C. K. Staats), *Complex Human Behavior*. Holt, Rinehart and Winston, New York.

Staats A. W. (1968) *Learning, Language, and Cognition*. Holt, Rinehart and Winston, New York.

Staats A. W. (1969) Development, use and social extensions of token-reinforcement systems. Paper presented at the *Conference on Progress in Behavior Modification*, Honolulu.

Staats A. W. and Butterfield W. H. (1965) Treatment of nonreading in a culturally deprived juvenile delinquent: an application of reinforcement principles. *Child Dev.* **36**, 925–942.

Staats A. W., Finley J. R., Minke K. A. and Wolf M. M. (1964a) Reinforcement variables in control of unit reading responses. *J. exp. Analysis Behav.* **7**, 139–149.

Staats A. W., Minke K. A. and Butts P. (1970) A token-reinforcement remedial reading program administered by black instructional technicians to backward black children. *Behav. Ther.*, **1**, 331–353.

Staats A. W., Minke K. A., Finley J. R., Wolf, M. M. and Brooks L. O. (1964b) A reinforcer system and experimental procedure for the laboratory study of reading acquisition. *Child Dev.* **35**, 209–231.

Staats A. W., Minke K. A., Goodwin W. and Landen J. (1967a) Cognitive behavior modification: 'motivated learning' reading treatment with sub-professional therapy technicians. *Behav. Res. & Therapy* **5**, 283–299.

Staats A. W., Staats C. K., Schutz R. E. and Wolf M. M. (1962) The conditioning of reading responses utilizing 'extrinsic' reinforcers. *J. Exp. Analysis Behav.* **5**, 33–40.

Staats A. W., Van Mondfrans A. P. and Minke K. A. (1967b) *Manual of administration and recording methods for the Staats 'Motivated Learning' Reading Procedure.* Wisconsin Research and Development Center for Cognitive Learning, Madison.

Straughn J. H. (1964) Treatment with child and mother in the playroom. *Behav. Res. & Therapy,* **2**, 37–41.

Thorndike E. L. and Lorge I. (1944) *The Teacher's Word Book of 30,000 Words.* Columbia University, New York.

Wahler R. G., Winkel G. H., Peterson R. F. and Morrison D. C. (1965) Mothers as behavior therapists for their own children. *Behav. Res. & Therapy* **3**, 113–124.

Walder L. O. (1966) Teaching parents to modify the behaviors of their autistic children. Paper presented at the meeting of the American Psychological Association.

Wetzel R. J., Baker J., Roney M. and Martin M. (1966) Out-patient treatment of autistic behavior. *Behav. Res. & Therapy* **4**, 169–177.

Wolf M. M., Giles D. K. and Hall V. R. (1968) Experiments with token reinforcement in a remedial classroom. *Behav. Res. & Therapy* **6**, 51–64.

Zeilberger J., Sampen S. E. and Sloane H. N., Jr. (1968) Modification of a child's problem behaviors in the home with the mother as therapist. *J. Appl. Behav. Analysis* **1**, 47–53.

CHAPTER 11

Self-Management

The previous readings in this book have repeatedly demonstrated that a child's behavior is influenced by its consequences when those consequences are administered by an adult or a peer. Similarly, the chapter on programmed instruction included research citing the usefulness of carefully sequenced presentation of materials for influencing academic behavior. One might then ask if a child can learn to present materials or rewards to himself in a manner that will facilitate the acquisition of appropriate academic and social behavior. One might also ask whether the recording or evaluating of one's behavior alters that behavior in a significant way. Although knowing how a teacher can influence a child is extremely useful, one must address himself to problems of self-management if one is interested in long term behavior change. It is true that nobody's behavior is independent of the reactions from others, but as behavior modifiers, part of our job is to decrease the amount of dependence a child has on adults. If children can be taught self-management skills, the decline in appropriate behavior, often seen when adult approval or tangible reinforcers are withdrawn, may be avoided. More importantly, a child with self-management skills will presumably be able to learn a great deal when the teacher or parent is completely absent.

It is significant that we could find only several articles demonstrating the use of self-control procedures in the classroom. This dearth of evidence is probably the result of the notion that the principles of self-control are somehow different from the principles which govern other behavior. Equally important is the problem of readily identifying behaviors which are covert yet presumably critical in the development of self-control. Even if one could somehow identify covert or private behaviors such as self-instruction, there is the problem of regulating the frequency of their occurrence. Before considering some of these issues, let us consider what is meant by self-control in more detail. If one considers general problems usually subsumed under the self-control rubric as problems of "inter-response control," the behaviors involved can be considered like any other behaviors which are subject to principles of learning (Bijou, 1965b). Inter-response control refers to the manner in which a behavior of an individual controls other behaviors of that individual. That is, one is referring to the control which behaviors have over one another and thus the term inter-response (or between-response) control. Viewing self-control as inter-response control, one can look to research on how a behavior or a sequence of behaviors can increase or decrease the frequency of another behavior when all behaviors are made by the same individual. For example, how does counting to ten decrease the frequency of aggressive behavior? How does placing oneself in a quiet room with few distracting stimuli influence study behavior?

The following five articles demonstrate how behavioral principles can be applied to problems of self-control. As mentioned previously, the area of self-control suffers from the absence of research which clearly demonstrates the efficacy of self-control procedures in naturalistic settings. However, the three non-classroom studies in this chapter have implications for research and practice concerning self-control procedures in a classroom, and it is our opinion that research on self-control in naturalistic or non-contrived settings should be one of the most important areas of concern in the next decade.

Bandura and Perloff (1967) (*33*), demonstrated that self-administered consequences can in fact serve a reinforcing function. A child was given complete control over tokens which were exchangeable for prizes, and when he made the tokens contingent upon his behavior, they served to maintain it. Equally important, they demonstrated that it made relatively little difference whether the child or the adult delivered the tokens (reinforcers). One can infer from such data that it would be possible to establish conditions in which children prescribe their own standards of behavior in a classroom and have some or complete control over their reinforcers. That is, one could establish a token system in which the children were given free access to tokens and told to avail themselves of them only when they thought they deserved them. They would be told to take a token only after they had displayed the behavior which *they felt* warranted a token. Similarly, a teacher could teach children to go to recess or a special activity only after the children felt they had completed the behaviors (assignments) worthy of recess. A variation of teaching such self-control behavior was studied by Kaufman and O'Leary (1971) who effectively demonstrated that teenage boys institutionalized in a mental hospital could be taught to evaluate their own behavior in a token program. Even when the boys had complete freedom to assign themselves any rating despite their frequency of disruptive behavior or their academic progress, they behaved exceptionally well! (While these boys did not have free access to the back-up reinforcers, they could give themselves any rating which was exchangeable for back-up reinforcers and independent of their frequency of disruptive behavior or academic progress.) Such results combined with those of Bandura and Perloff document the effectiveness of both self-evaluative and self-reinforcing behaviors. Note that such behaviors must be taught; they do not occur spontaneously. However, if a child can be taught self-evaluative and self-reinforcing behaviors, the teacher's job ultimately will become much easier and the child will probably learn much more on his own in the future.

The precision with which self-control can be taught to young children is well illustrated by the Bem article, (*34*). She showed how a particular aspect of speech, namely self-instruction, can aid a child in performing certain motor tasks. Most importantly, she demonstrated in a step-by-step fashion how certain aspects of her training procedure influenced the child's behavior. The systematic evaluation of this training procedure should serve as an exemplary model for teachers who wish to critically evaluate what they do. The use of fading or gradual withdrawal of prompts as a teaching procedure should also be noted. The fading procedure should become a part of every teacher's repertoire and its use should be particularly helpful to those who are dealing with children with low frustration tolerances. Fading can be especially effective with such children because it minimizes the number of errors a child will make as he is being taught a new skill.

Self-instruction has been shown to be of aid in both initiating and suppressing behavior (Meichenbaum & Goodman, 1969; O'Leary, 1969) but the teacher may ask how self-instruction relates to classroom management. Most children of school age already have developed some control of their motor behavior through verbal means. However, some children may have little control of their own behavior; they may not use self-instructions to guide their behavior or even if they do, their self-instructions may be ineffective. In such cases, elementary teachers may tell their children to remind themselves about how to approach a problem by using a mnemonic device such as "i before e except after c." It is also possible to teach a child to use self-instruction with respect to social behaviors. In order to develop appropriate social skills, it may be helpful to teach the child to prompt himself to engage in appropriate behavior by teaching him to self-instruct. For example, a child can be taught to say to himself "Stop, look and listen" when he approaches a curb. Similarly, a child could be taught to say "Count to ten" or "Walk five steps" when he is angry. Older children also could be taught to say "relax" and in fact to relax when they are tense. Even if a child uses self-instructions, they may have only a negligible effect on his behavior. In order to maximize the influence of self-instruction, a teacher should reinforce the child not only for giving himself the appropriate self-instruction (e.g. "i before e except after c") but also for his subsequent appropriate behavior (correct spelling of the word).

The Bandura and Kupers (1964) article, (*35*), is significant since it shows how exposure to adults influences the manner in which a child rewards or reinforces himself. Their results should be of interest to both teachers and parents for they clearly show that a child will adopt either low or high standards for his own behavior depending upon the extent to which the adult models adopt high or low standards. Such patterns of behavior or standard setting is evidenced by teachers who scribble some assignments on the board and then erase the writing saying "That's not written very well." When a teacher is working with a group on a collaborative project where the teacher's contribution is an essential part of the project, she might say "I know we can do better than that; let's keep working until we get this part perfect." Possibly even more salient is the example of a band director who not only directly reinforces children for good performances but who also emphasizes his role in the cooperative effort of performing and who stresses the importance of his own behavior as well as that of his students.

It is particularly interesting to note in the Lovitt and Curtiss (1969) article, (*36*), that when a child was allowed to specify the number of points he received for a certain number of pages read or problems completed, he worked faster (responses/min.) than when his teacher specified the points he would receive for a given number of pages read or problems completed. While such results should be replicated and the correctness of the children's answers checked, this research addresses itself to an important topic and one which should definitely receive additional attention. Lastly, the Broden, Hall, and Mitts (1971) article, (*37*), documents the beneficial effects of recording one's own behavior. As the authors imply, self-recording may be particularly useful where a teacher cannot find time to attend to a child frequently—as often is the case where a teacher is lecturing to a class of thirty children. While research on smoking with adults (Bernstein, 1970) has shown that recording a behavior such as smoking is ineffective in the reduction of such behaviors, the Broden article demonstrates that with two eighth grade children, self-recording definitely was influential in increasing study behavior or in reducing talking-out behavior. However, with one student the slips and the self-recording procedures eventually lost their effectiveness presumably because no contingencies were ever applied to differential rates of talking out. As mentioned earlier, with teenagers who were asked to evaluate their own behavior in a token program, their disruptive behavior did not increase during a two week period when the teacher told them they could evaluate their own behavior. Like the student in the Broden *et al.* study for whom self-recording eventually lost its effectiveness these teenagers' disruptive behavior presumably would eventually increase if contingencies were not applied to both their self-evaluative *and* their disruptive behavior. With a class of disruptive first grade children, having children evaluate and record such evaluations was not effective in reducing disruptive behavior when such recording and evaluations had no consequences. However, when paired with consequences, such self-recording did reduce disruptive behavior (O'Leary, Kass, Schneider, & Romanczyk, study in progress).

Relative Efficacy of Self-Monitored and Externally Imposed Reinforcement Systems*[1]

ALBERT BANDURA and BERNARD PERLOFF

Stanford University

Abstract: This experiment was designed to test the behavior maintenance capabilities of self-monitored reinforcement and to compare it to that of an externally-imposed system of reinforcement. One group of children selected their own performance standards and rewarded themselves whenever they attained their self-prescribed level. For a 2nd group of children the same behavioral standards were imposed and the reinforcers were externally administered. Ss in the control groups performed either without any incentives, or received rewards on a non-contingent basis. The results disclose that self-monitored and externally applied reinforcement were equally efficacious, but both reinforcement systems sustained substantially more responsivity than did the control conditions. Contrary to expectation from reward-cost theories, most of the children imposed upon themselves highly unfavorable schedules of reinforcement which incurred high effort costs at minimum self-reward.

It has been abundantly documented by research that behavior is governed to some extent by its consequences. However, investigations of reinforcement processes have involved limited forms of reinforcing feedback, characteristically produced by externally controlled operations in which an experimenter imposes a particular contingency upon an organism and delivers reinforcing stimuli whenever the appropriate responses are displayed. While this system of behavioral control may be adequate in accounting for responsivity in infrahuman organisms, it is considerably less efficacious when applied to human functioning which is

*Reprinted from the *Journal of Personality and Social Psychology*, Vol. 7, No. 2, 1967, pp. 111–116, by permission of the American Psychological Association.

[1]This research was supported by Public Health Research Grant M-5162 and by Predoctoral Fellowship FI-MH-34,248 from the National Institute of Mental Health.

self-regulated to a greater degree. Unlike rats or chimpanzees, persons typically set themselves certain standards of behavior, and generate self-rewarding or self-punishing consequences depending upon how their behavior compares to their self-prescribed demands.

In recent years there have been numerous investigations of the conditions governing the acquisition of behavioral standards and self-reinforcing responses (Bandura, Grusec, & Menlove, 1967; Bandura & Kupers, 1964; Bandura & Whalen, 1966; Marston, 1965; Mischel & Libert, 1966). Although these studies have shown that after persons adopt a self-monitoring system their performances arouse positive and negative self-evaluative reactions, there has been no adequate demonstration that self-administered consequences do, in fact, possess reinforcing capabilities. The major purpose of the present study was therefore to test the efficacy of self-monitored reinforcement, and to compare it to that of an externally imposed system of reinforcement.

A self-reinforcing event includes several subsidiary processes, some of which have been extensively investigated in their own right. First, it involves a *self-prescribed standard of behavior* which serves as the criterion for evaluating the adequacy of one's performances. The standard-setting component has received considerable attention in studies of aspiration level.

In the case of most performances, objective criteria of adequacy are lacking and hence, the attainments of other persons must be utilized as the norm against which meaningful self-evaluations can be made. Thus, for example, a student who achieves a score of 120 points on an examination, and whose aspirations are to exceed modal levels, would have no basis for either positive or negative self-reactions without knowing the accomplishments of others. A self-reinforcing event, therefore, often involves a *social comparison process*.

Third, the *reinforcers are under the person's own control*; and fourth, *he serves as his own reinforcing agent*. These various defining characteristics guided both the form of the self-monitored reinforcement system and the types of controls that were instituted.

The capacity to maintain effortful behavior over time is perhaps the most important attribute of a reinforcement operation, and consequently it was this property that was tested in the present investigation. Children performed a task in which they could achieve progressively higher scores by turning a wheel on a mechanical device. Subjects in the self-monitored reinforcement condition selected their own performance standard and rewarded themselves whenever they attained their self-prescribed criterion. Children assigned to an externally imposed reinforcement condition were yoked to the self-reward group so that the same performance standard was set for them and the reinforcers were automatically delivered whenever they reached the predetermined level.

In order to ascertain whether subjects' behavioral productivity was due to the operation of contingent self-reinforcement or to gratitude for the rewards that were made available, children in an incentive-control group performed the task after they had received the supply of rewards on a noncontingent basis. A fourth group worked without any incentives to estimate the response maintenance value of the task itself.

It was predicted that both self-monitored and externally imposed reinforcement systems would sustain substantially more behavior than conditions in which rewards were bestowed noncontingently or were absent altogether. No hypothesis was put forward concerning the relative efficacy of the two systems of reinforcement, since there exists no adequate theoretical basis for a differential prediction.

METHOD

Subjects

The subjects were 40 boys and 40 girls drawn from two elementary schools in a lower middle-class area. The children's ages ranged from 7 to 10 years.

Apparatus

The apparatus consisted of a rectangular box, the front face of which contained a vertical plastic-covered aperture $\frac{1}{2}$ inch wide by 16 inches high divided into four equal sections. Contained within this upright column were four score-indicator lamps, each one capable of illuminating one and only one of the translucent sections. Directly adjacent to the sections were mounted, in ascending order, the corresponding numbers 5, 10, 15, and 20, signifying four performance levels.

The score indicator lamps were activated in an ascending order by turning a wheel located at the bottom of the apparatus. It required eight complete rotations of the wheel to advance 5 points, so that a total of 32 cranking responses was necessary to attain a 20-point score.

A criterion-selector switch, which could be turned to any one of four positions corresponding to the scores next to the lights, was mounted on the front panel of the apparatus. The electrical circuit was so designed that whenever the selected performance standard was attained a chime sounded and the lights were automatically extinguished, signifying the completion of the trial. For example, in the case where a 20-point standard was chosen, the lamps adjacent to the numbers 5, 10, 15, and 20 would be illuminated after 8, 16, 24, and 32 rotations of the wheel, respectively, and then all of them would simultaneously extinguish.

Contained within the upright section was an automatic chip dispenser which delivered plastic tokens into a bowl mounted in front of the apparatus. The bountiful supply of tokens was hidden from view since their public display would not only provide children with a basis for comparing their earned rewards with the maximum possible, but it might also produce erroneous hypotheses about normative performance on this task. These factors, if uncontrolled, could have served as extraneous determinants of responsivity in the contingent-reinforcement conditions.

Located above the chip receptacle was a button which, when pressed, released a token into the bowl. A remote control device was constructed that was capable of performing the same operations as the selector switch and the token delivery button, and when necessary, rendering them inoperative.

Procedure

The introductory phase of the experiment was the same for all subjects. The children were brought individually to a mobile laboratory, ostensibly to test some game equipment. After the experimenter explained and demonstrated the operation of the apparatus, the children were given a practice trial to familiarize themselves with the task.

Small plastic tokens served as the reinforcers or incentives in those treatment conditions that required them. Children who received contingent reinforcement — either self-administered or externally applied — were informed that the tokens would later be exchanged for prizes, and the more tokens they obtained the more valuable the redeemable prizes. The incentive control subjects, who were given tokens on a noncontingent basis, were also informed that the chips they possessed would be traded later for prizes.

Several procedures were instituted in order to remove any extraneous social influences on subjects' responsivity. It was explained to children in all groups that they would perform the task alone in the room because the experimenter had some other work to do, and they might work at it as long as they wished. They were asked to notify the experimenter, who was in another room of the mobile laboratory, after they no longer wished to continue the activity. Moreover, children in the self-reinforcement condition selected their performance standard after the experimenter had departed. To remove any concern that the experimenter might evaluate their behavioral productivity from the number of tokens accumulated, the children were instructed to place the banks in which they deposited their tokens in a sealed paper bag; a second experimenter would collect the banks later that day and return with the prizes in a few weeks. Finally, to control for the possibility that children's response output might be partly determined by the classroom activities they were missing, subjects in all four conditions were tested during the same instructional periods.

Children in the *self-monitored reinforcement condition* were informed that they would have to decide which performance standard they wished to set for themselves, and then to turn the selector switch to that level. In addition, they were instructed to treat themselves to tokens whenever they attained their self-imposed standard. Since these subjects had full control over the token rewards, they were free to choose their own magnitude of self-compensation on any given trial.

The children were further told that after they had selected the performance level they desired to attain, they could, if they wished, change it once, but only once, during the remainder of the session. This procedure was employed for two reasons: first, observation of self-reinforcing behavior occurring under naturalistic conditions reveals that individuals rarely shift their behavioral standards capriciously. Rather, persons usually adhere to their adopted standards and change them only as a result of cumulative feedback experiences. Therefore, an effort was made to elicit from children criterion-selection behavior which could be somewhat analogous to that occurring in everyday life.

The second reason for allowing the self-reinforcement group only one modification in their standards was related to the yoking requirement of the experiment. In order to control for the influence of behavioral standards upon responsivity across the four treatments, the performance requirements adopted by a child in the self-reward group were applied to the subject paired with him in each of the remaining conditions. Thus, for example, if a particular child in the self-monitoring group initially selected a criterion of 15 and after 20 trials lowered it to 10, this same pattern of standard was set for his yoked counterpart in each of the three comparison groups.

It is possible that any one of the children in the other conditions might persist longer than the self-reward subject to whom he was matched. If the standard selection had been highly changeable, there would be no basis for deciding that criterion to impose upon him for the remainder of the session. The limitation that standards be modified only once created a situation in which most self-reward children effected their allotted change before terminating the session, thus establishing the final performance requirement. In fact, 16 of 20 subjects had made the change before discontinuing the task. Therefore, it was meaningful to apply the standard last employed by the self-reward subject to children in the other conditions who might display more endurance than their matched partner.

After the instructions were completed, the children were handed a token bank, and left alone to perform the task as long as they wished.

Children in the *externally imposed reinforcement* system were yoked according to the procedure described above, so that the performance standard was fixed for them and the tokens were automatically delivered by the machine whenever they reached the prescribed performance level. They also received the same magnitude of reward as children in the self-reinforcement condition, that is, if a subject in the self-reward group treated himself to two tokens on a given trial, the machine would dispense two chips on the same trial to the paired counterpart in the external-reinforcement condition.

Subjects in this group were told that the machine determined the performance standard, and upon reaching it the tokens were automatically delivered. The token dispenser and the standard setting were, in fact, controlled by the experimenter from a remote console in an adjoining observation room.

Children in the "inheritance" or *incentive-control* condition were given at the beginning of the session the entire amount of tokens accumulated by their partner in the self-reward group. As in the previous treatment, the children were told that the machine regulated the performance standards operative at any given time. Another *control group of* subjects performed the task without receiving any tokens whatsoever to evaluate the response maintenance capacity of the game itself.

There are two important elements within a self-reinforcing event whose independent effects must be assessed before persistence of self-reinforced behavior can be meaningfully interpreted. These are (*a*) the self-imposition of an achievement standard, and (b) the self-administration of rewards. In order to examine the performance increments, if any, due to imposing a standard alone, a second study was conducted. The behavioral output of 10 children allowed to select the performance standard for which they endeavored was compared to that of 10 yoked subjects for whom the same standard was externally imposed; neither group, however, received any token rewards.

Dependent Measures

The number of cranking responses performed by the children, which constitutes the major dependent variable, was mechanically recorded. In addition, the experimenter recorded the performance standards selected by the self-reward children, and the number of reinforcers that they administered to themselves on each trial. A second observer, who scored independently the latter responses of 15 subjects, was in perfect agreement with the experimenter.

RESULTS

Behavioral Productivity

Figure 33.1 presents the mean number of effortful cranking responses performed by boys and girls in each of the four conditions of the main experiment. Analysis of variance of these data disclosed a highly significant main effect due to reinforcement conditions ($F = 15.56$; $p < 0.001$).

In order to determine the specific differences contributing to the overall treatment effect, separate t tests were computed for pairs of conditions. These analyses revealed that self-monitored and externally imposed reinforcement were equally efficious ($t = 1.62$), but both reinforcement systems sustained substantially more behavior than either noncontingent rewards or a nonreward condition. Children who reinforced their own behavior generated significantly more responses than children in the incentive-control group ($t = 3.91$; $p < 0.001$), or the no-incentive condition ($t = 3.87$; $p < 0.001$). The corresponding t values for comparisons between external reinforcement and the incentive-control and no-incentive-control groups were $t = 5.53$ ($p < 0.001$) and $t = 5.49$ ($p < 0.001$), respectively. It is also interesting to note that rewarding subjects noncontingently did not produce a significant incre-

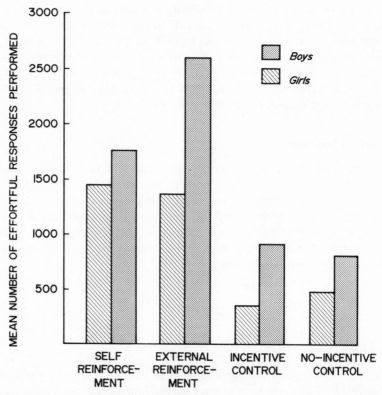

Fig. 33.1. Mean number of responses performed as a function of sex and type of reinforcement system.

ment in performance as revealed by comparison with the behavior of children who performed the task without any external incentives ($t = 0.04$).

The analysis also revealed that boys generated more responses than girls ($F = 13.09$; $p < 0.001$). Although no significant interaction effect was obtained between sex and treatment conditions, external reinforcement produced more behavior in boys ($t = 2.45$; $p < 0.05$) than the self-monitored system.

Children who set their own performance standards without engaging in self-reinforcement produced a mean number of 369 cranking responses, whereas the corresponding mean for the yoked controls was 586. Statistical analysis of these scores yielded no significant difference ($F = 1.56$) between the groups, thus indicating that self-imposition of a standard alone has no response maintenance value.

Self-Imposition of Performance Demands

The four performance standards employed in the present experiment essentially correspond to advancing fixed-ratio schedules of 8, 16, 24, and 32 responses for each self-reinforcement. Table 33.1 presents the standards initially adopted by children in the self-monitoring condition, the performance demands that they imposed upon themselves in later phases of the experiment, and the average magnitude of self-reward associated with the achievement of each standard.

It is apparent from these data that the children did not behave in ways that would maximize rewards. Not a single child chose the lowest ratio schedule, and approximately half the children self-prescribed the most austere schedule for self-reinforcement (i.e., 32 responses for each self-reward). Moreover, a third of the children subsequently altered their initial standard to a higher level, without a significant commensurate increase in amount of self-reward, thereby imposing upon themselves a more unfavorable work-to-reinforcement ratio.

Table 33.1. Self-Imposed Standards and Associated Magnitude of Self-Reward

Ss	1st standard	Mean no. rewards	2nd standard	Mean no. rewards
Boys				
1	10	1.00	No change	
2	10	1.00	5	1.09
3	15	1.00	20	1.18
4	15	1.00	20	1.00
5	15	0.98	No change	
6	20	1.11	5	1.02
7	20	1.00	10	1.06
8	20	1.00	10	0.90
9	20	1.00	15	1.00
10	20	1.00	No change	
Girls				
1	10	1.00	15	1.00
2	10	1.11	20	1.14
3	15	1.00	5	1.04
4	15	1.00	20	1.00
5	15	1.04	20	1.12
6	15	1.00	No change	
7	20	1.00	5	1.05
8	20	1.00	5	0.93
9	20	1.21	5	1.02
10	20	1.00	10	1.00

It is also interesting to note that three children occasionally did not reward themselves after attaining their chosen criterion. In two of the three cases this occurred after they had reduced their performance standard drastically. At times these children apparently did not regard their low performances as sufficiently meritorious to warrant self-reward.

DISCUSSION

Results of this study disclose that self-monitored reinforcement possesses considerable behavior maintenance value. Moreover, the high response productivity engendered by this system was not due to merely the self-imposition of a performance standard, or availability of positive incentives.

Although self-regulated and externally imposed reinforcement did not differ in their capacity to sustain behavior, there was some suggestive evidence that, within the age range studied, boys might be more responsive under conditions of externally determined than of self-governed reinforcement, while for girls both systems are equally efficacious. These findings are consistent with those of developmental studies (Sears, Rau, & Alpert, 1965), showing that sex differences in adult-role behavior and various indexes of self-control generally favor the girls. The obtained sex difference in response productivity under all treatment conditions is most likely due to the fact that the task required some physical effort, and consequently the boys' higher output simply reflects their greater strength.

A supplementary finding of considerable interest is the prevalence with which children imposed upon themselves highly unfavorable schedules of reinforcement. This behavior is all the more striking considering that the self-imposition of high performance demands occurred in the absence of any social surveillance and under high permissiveness for self-reward. Evidence obtained from experiments investigating the acquisition of self-reinforcing behavior (Bandura & Kupers, 1964; Bandura & Whalen, 1966; Bandura et al., 1967) throws some light on the probable mechanism governing this apparently irrational behavior.

The above studies demonstrate that after a person has adopted a standard of what constitutes a worthy performance, attainments that fall short of self-prescribed norms generate negative self-evaluative reactions, whereas those that match or exceed the guiding standard give rise to positive self-evaluations. Hence, under conditions where persons are provided with ample opportunities to optimize their material outcomes by engaging in behavior which has low self-regard value, strong conflicting tendencies are likely to be aroused. On the one hand, individuals are tempted to maximize rewards at minimum effort costs to themselves, but on the other hand, low quality performances produce negative self-evaluative consequences which, if sufficiently strong, may inhibit generous self-compensation. Indeed, many of the children in the experiment set themselves performance requirements that incurred high effort costs at minimum material recompense. These findings are at variance with predictions from reward-cost theories unless these formulations are extended to include the self-esteem costs of rewarding devalued behavior.

The foregoing discussion has been primarily concerned with conflicts that might arise between two forms of self-reinforcing tendencies and how their resolution results in selective self-reinforcement under the discriminative control of performance standards. Of equal importance is the recurring phenomenon in which self-generated consequences conflict with externally occurring outcomes, as when certain behaviors are reinforced by particular social agents, but if carried out would give rise to self-critical reactions. Conversely, response patterns may be effectively maintained by self-reinforcement operations under conditions of minimal external support. It is perhaps due to the stabilizing effects of self-reinforcement that persons do not ordinarily behave like weathervanes in the face of conflicting patterns of external contingencies which they repeatedly encounter in their social environment.

In view of the demonstrated efficacy of self-monitored systems, it would be of interest to explore further the extent to which self-reinforcement may substitute for, supplement, or override the effects of externally occurring outcomes. It would likewise be of considerable import to determine the degree to which overt behavior can be regulated by covert self-reinforcing operations which rely upon self-generated symbolic consequences in the form of self-satisfaction, esteem-enhancing reactions, or self-deprecation.

Although many children selected unusually high performance standards for themselves and did not lower them to enhance their fortunes, other children self-imposed equally lofty standards of achievement but later settled for a relatively mediocre level of productivity. Further research is needed to establish the conditions determining both the initial imposition of behavioral requirements for self-reward, and the direction in which self-reinforcement contingencies might subsequently be altered.

REFERENCES

Bandura, A., Grusec, J. E., & Menlove, F. L. Some social determinants of self-monitoring reinforcement systems. *Journal of Personality and Social Psychology*, 1967, **5**, 449–455.

Bandura, A., & Kupers, C. J. The transmission of patterns of self-reinforcement through modeling. *Journal of Abnormal and Social Psychology*, 1964, **69**, 1–9.

Bandura, A., & Whalen, C. K. The influence of antecedent reinforcement and divergent modeling cues on patterns of self-reward. *Journal of Personality and Social Psychology*, 1966, **3**, 373–382.

Marston, A. R. Imitation, self-reinforcement, and reinforcement of another person. *Journal of Personality and Social Psychology*, 1965, **2**, 225–261.

Mischel, W., I Liebert, R. M. Effects of discrepancies between observed and imposed reward criteria on their acquisition and transmission. *Journal of Personality and Social Psychology*, 1966, **3**, 45–53.

Sears, R. R., Rau, L., & Alpert, R. *Identification and child rearing.* Stanford: Stanford University Press, 1965.

Verbal Self-Control: The Establishment of Effective Self-Instruction*[1]

SANDRA L. BEM

University of Michigan

Abstract: 3- and 4-yr.-old Ss were required to press a lever that number of times corresponding exactly to a number of lights displayed and then covered. The mean percentage of correct responses for 4-yr.-olds was 94%, while that for 3-yr.-olds was only 28% ($p = 0.002$). Once 3-yr.-olds had been trained to respond correctly in the presence of external feedback, control of their behavior was shifted to their own self-instruction by means of a fading procedure. The success of fading indicates (a) that failures by 3-yr.-olds represent a learning deficit, not a developmental deficiency, and (b) that verbal self-control can be established experimentally by means of a learning procedure analogous to that used for establishing both external stimulus control and non-verbal self-control.

The present experiment is an investigation of the ontogenetic origins of verbal self-control, the ability to generate a self-instruction, and to respond to it appropriately. Earlier research has suggested that young children are not able to regulate their own behavior by means of self-instruction. Luria (1960) reports that the typical child under 4 yr. of age is not able to respond correctly when instructed to squeeze a rubber bulb twice at the onset of a particular signal. The child "gives two, three, four, even five or six reactions, but he cannot reach a real control of pressing only twice to each signal [p. 377]."

The same child can respond correctly, however, if he is given an external signal for response termination, if, for example, he is told to

---

*Reprinted from the *Journal of Experimental Psychology*, Vol. 74, No. 4 1967, pp. 485–491, by permission of the American Psychological Association.

[1]This research was supported in part by the Language Development Program, Center for Human Growth and Development, University of Michigan, with funds from National Institute of Mental Health Grant HD 01368-02, and in part by a summer fellowship granted to the author by the National Science Foundation. The author is grateful to David Birch for serving as advisor and to Daryl J. Bem for critical comments on the manuscript.

terminate his behavior at the sound of a bell. He can also respond appropriately to the motor components of his own speech as signals for response termination; if, for example, he is instructed to say "Toot, toot" at the onset of each signal, each of his verbal responses activates a single corresponding motor response, and his resulting behavior pattern is correct. As soon as these *E*-induced stimuli for response termination are removed, however, the child returns to his old pattern of failure. Using the pressing of a spring-loaded lever as the dependent variable, Birch (1966) reported similar failures by American children on a number of related tasks. Luria (1961) concluded that this absence of self-control was due to a poorly developed interoceptive cue system, a system of self-generated stimuli that could provide signals for response termination in the absence of external stimuli, but which does not emerge until the child's fourth or fifth yr.

The present experiment attempts to demonstrate that such a system of self-generated cues can be established experimentally in 3-yr.-old children whose pretest performance indicates an absence of verbal self-control. If effective self-instruction can be established during an experimental period of 3 wk., the absence of verbal self-control would appear to result not from a developmental deficiency, but from a learning deficit. The task designed to measure verbal self-control requires the child to press a lever that number of times corresponding exactly to the number of lights presented on a display; because the child is not permitted to respond until after the lights have been covered, he must make use of self-generated stimuli, i.e., counting responses, if he is to respond correctly.

METHOD[2]

Subjects

Six 3-yr.-old and six 4-yr.-old nursery school children served as *S*s; four were male and eight were female. Two of these *S*s participated in a pilot experiment which used a slight variation of the present procedure. Three additional 3-yr.-old *S*s left the nursery school before training could be completed; only their pretest data are reported.

---

[2]The invaluable assistance of Mary Burns of Little Farm Nursery School and Margaret Towsley of Children's Play School is gratefully acknowledged.

Apparatus

The apparatus included a panel of 12, 6-w. lights, each of which could be turned on and off independently; a rheostat which enabled E to dim all lights to zero simultaneously; a wooden box decorated as the face of a clown with a spring-loaded lever designed as the clown's tongue protruding from it. An $8\frac{1}{2} \times 11$ in. cardboard was used to cover the lights.

Tootsie rolls, cinnamon candy, and gold stars were given to each child at the end of an experimental session. When each child completed his final session, he was given a small toy.

Procedure[3]

The E spent 1 day at the nursery school in order to meet the children and to become a familiar adult to them. Each S was then brought to a private room of the nursery school and was seated at a small table. He was shown a basket from which he was told to choose one toy to be taken home "not today, but when the game is all finished." The S was also told that he would be given a piece of candy and a gold star at the end of every session, that he would be able to take his toy home when he had won "a lot of stars."

After demonstrating that the lever could be manipulated, E instructed S to press it down and to let it up. The E then demonstrated that each lever press turned off one light. At this time, however, S was not given the opportunity to turn lights off.

Pretests I and II One, two, three, four, or five of the 12 lights were illuminated, and S was asked to count them, that is, to generate one number for each. The lights were then covered, and S was asked to repeat all of his counting responses in the absence of the lights. His performance was considered correct if he correctly repeated his prior count, whether or not that count had itself been correct. The lights were again displayed, and S was asked to count them once more. Finally E again covered them, and S was asked to turn them off, that is, to press the lever until he thought all the lights were off and then to stop. The S was given no feedback at any time during the pretests; each behavior was demonstrated before E asked S to perform it. Three behaviors were thus measured: counting in the presence of the lights, counting in the absence of the lights, and pressing in the absence of the lights. The pretest was

---

[3]Complete instructions to Ss can be found in Bem (1966).

repeated a second time. It was expected that performance would not improve from the first administration to the second, that is, taking the test would not itself be responsible for successful test performance.

Only Ss who failed the pretest were to be eligible for training. Therefore, to insure that no amount of prompting could induce successful test performance, E explicitly demonstrated how successful test performance could be achieved; after counting the lights and covering them, E pressed and counted aloud that number of times corresponding exactly to the number of lights previously shown and asked S to do likewise. This procedure followed immediately after the second pretest.

Each pretest consisted of 15 trials, three presentations each of one, two, three, four, or five lights. The order of presentation was randomized, as well as the selection of lights to be illuminated during any single trial. Pretests were separated by at least 1 day.

The Ss were assigned to the various training procedures described below on the basis of their pretest performance. An S assigned to a given training procedure completed its requirements as well as those of all subsequent training procedures, in the order specified. Each S remained in a given phase of training until he reached a criterion of perfect performance for 15 consecutive trials. The Ss who reached criterion (93% correct) on all parts of the pretest were not trained further. Each phase of training was followed by a test identical to the pretest.

Each S attended as many sessions as necessary for his training to be completed. The number of sessions ranged from 2, for those Ss who required no training, to 16, for those Ss who required all training. A session typically lasted 10–15 min., ending when S showed signs of fatigue or boredom. It will be noted that each S is his own control, and that each S provides a complete replication of the experiment.

Verbal training   The Ss who did not reach a criterion of 14/15 or 93% correct on any of the three behaviors measured on the pretest were assigned to verbal training. Each of these Ss was instructed to count the lights presented on the display, that is, to generate one counting response for each, and his response was designated by E as either right or wrong. If the response was wrong, E gave the correct response and required that S repeat it. Training continued until S reached criterion. At this point, all Ss could count perfectly in the presence of the lights.

Verbal fading   The Ss who could count, but whose counting behavior in the absence of the lights did not reach criterion on the pretest, were assigned to verbal fading; this includes Ss who had just learned to count as a result of the above procedure. Each of these *S*s was asked to count the lights presented on the display and then to repeat those same numbers. Before the second sequence of counting responses was emitted, however, *E* reduced the light intensity slightly. On each succeeding trial, the light intensity was reduced further after *S*'s initial count until the lights were no longer discriminable. Because self-generated cues, i.e., the initial sequence of counting responses, were present along with the external ones during these trials, control of the second sequence of responses should shift from the disappearing external stimuli to the available self-generated stimuli. Verbal fading should thus enable all *S*s to repeat their prior counting in the absence of the lights.

Motor training The *S*s whose counting behavior reached criterion both in the presence and the absence of the lights were assigned to motor training. Lights were shown to *S*, and he was asked to count them; he was further instructed to press the lever repeatedly until all the lights were off. During this phase of training, *S* could see each lever press turn off one light; since external stimuli were present throughout, this phase of training was not expected to enhance self-control.

Verbal-motor training Each *S* was required to count the lights and then to turn them off by counting and pressing simultaneously. Following this procedure, all *S*s have been trained to emit all the behaviors appropriate to successful test performance, but those behaviors are still controlled only by external stimuli.

Verbal-motor fading Each *S* was required to count the lights on the display and then to turn the lights off by counting and pressing simultaneously. Before *S* turned off the lights, however, *E* reduced the light intensity slightly. On each succeeding trial, the light intensity was reduced further after *S*'s initial count until, eventually, the intensity of the lights was so low that no discriminable environmental change accompanied *S*'s motor behavior. Because the self-generated cues were present along with the external ones during these trials, control of the motor response should shift from the disappearing external stimuli to the available self-generated stimuli, i.e., *S*'s second sequence of counting responses. Because both his verbal and his motor behavior should now be under the control of self-generated stimuli, *S* should be able to respond correctly on the test.

Pilot variations The pilot apparatus was identical to that of the major experiment with the exception that a panel of only four lights was used. The *S* was exposed to all phases of training in the order specified with the exception of verbal fading; during verbal-motor fading, control of both his verbal and his motor behavior was shifted simultaneously from the lights to the available self-generated stimuli. Only three tests were administered: one before training had begun, one following verbal training, and one following the completion of all training. Each test consisted of 16 trials. Two behaviors were measured, i.e., counting in the presence of the lights and pressing in their absence.

RESULTS

Pretest Data — Developmental Trends

Counting—lights present   Three-yr.-old children are able to count. Five out of seven *S*s responded correctly on more than 93% of the trials. The number of correct responses by 4-yr.-olds was not significantly greater according to a two-tailed Mann-Whitney *U* test ($U = 10.5$, $p < 0.18$), although five out of six *S*s responded perfectly on all trials.

Counting—lights absent   In the absence of external stimuli, 4-yr.-olds remained able to generate the appropriate number of counting responses. As Table 34.1 indicates, they correctly repeated their prior verbal responses after the lights had been covered on 95.6% of the pretest trials. Their performance was significantly better than that of the 3-yr.-olds ($U = 3$, $p = 0.008$) who were able, nevertheless, to respond correctly on 74.3% of the trials.

Table 34.1. A Comparison of 3-yr.-olds vs. 4-yr.-olds: Mean Number and Percentage of Correct Responses out of 15 on the Pretest

	3-yr.-olds (N = 7)[a]		4-yr.-olds (N = 6)		U	p (two-tailed)
	Number	Percent	Number	Percent		
Counting—Lights Present	13.9	92.4%	14.7	97.8%	10.5	
Counting—Lights Absent	11.1	74.3%	14.3	95.6%	3	0.008
Pressing—Lights Absent	4.4	29.5%	9.0	60.0%	8.5	
Pressing—Lights Absent (After Prompting)	4.1	27.6%	14.2	94.4%	0	0.002

[a]The *S*s from the pilot study are not included because not all four measures were taken.

Pressing—lights absent Prior to any training, neither group was consistently able to terminate its motor behavior appropriately in the absence of external cues for response termination, that is, when the lights were covered. Three-yr.-olds pressed the lever the correct number of times on 29.5% of the trials, while 4-yr.-olds did so on 60% of them. The difference between the groups was not significant ($U = 8.5, p = 0.10$).

Thus, most *S*s remained unable to control their motor behavior appropriately, despite the fact that they were able to repeat their previous counting responses in the absence of external stimuli. This indicates that *S*s do, in fact, have available the responses that could serve as mediators of their subsequent motor behavior, but that these responses do not yet function as controlling variables.

Pressing and counting—lights absent Explicit demonstration by *E* enabled 4-yr.-olds to perform appropriately on the test. After *E* prompted them by pressing and counting aloud the correct number of times, these *S*s responded correctly on 94.4% of the trials. Because correct performance could be induced, none of the six 4-yr.-olds participated in training. The new instruction was not able, however, to effect improved performance in the 3-yr.-olds who responded correctly on only 27.6% of the trials. The pretest data considered alone, then, are consistent with the hypothesis that verbal self-control is a developmental phenomenon. It remains to be demonstrated that correct performance by the 3-yr.-olds depends crucially not upon a particular developmental level, but upon a learning procedure.

Results of Training

Effects of entire procedure At the completion of training, all *S*s were able to respond correctly. The solid lines in Fig. 34.1 indicate that five out of six *S*s responded perfectly, pressing the lever the correct number of times on every trial.[4] Only one error was made out of a total of 92 trials.

These data clearly indicate that the training procedure is sufficient for successful test performance, for self-control of response termination. They further demonstrate that the reported absence of mediation is not due to a developmental deficiency, but to a learning deficit. If an *S* is trained to respond to the self-generated stimuli of his own responses,

---

[4]Figure 34.1 does not include the data of 3-yr.-olds whose pretest data have been reported, but who left the nursery school before training could be completed.

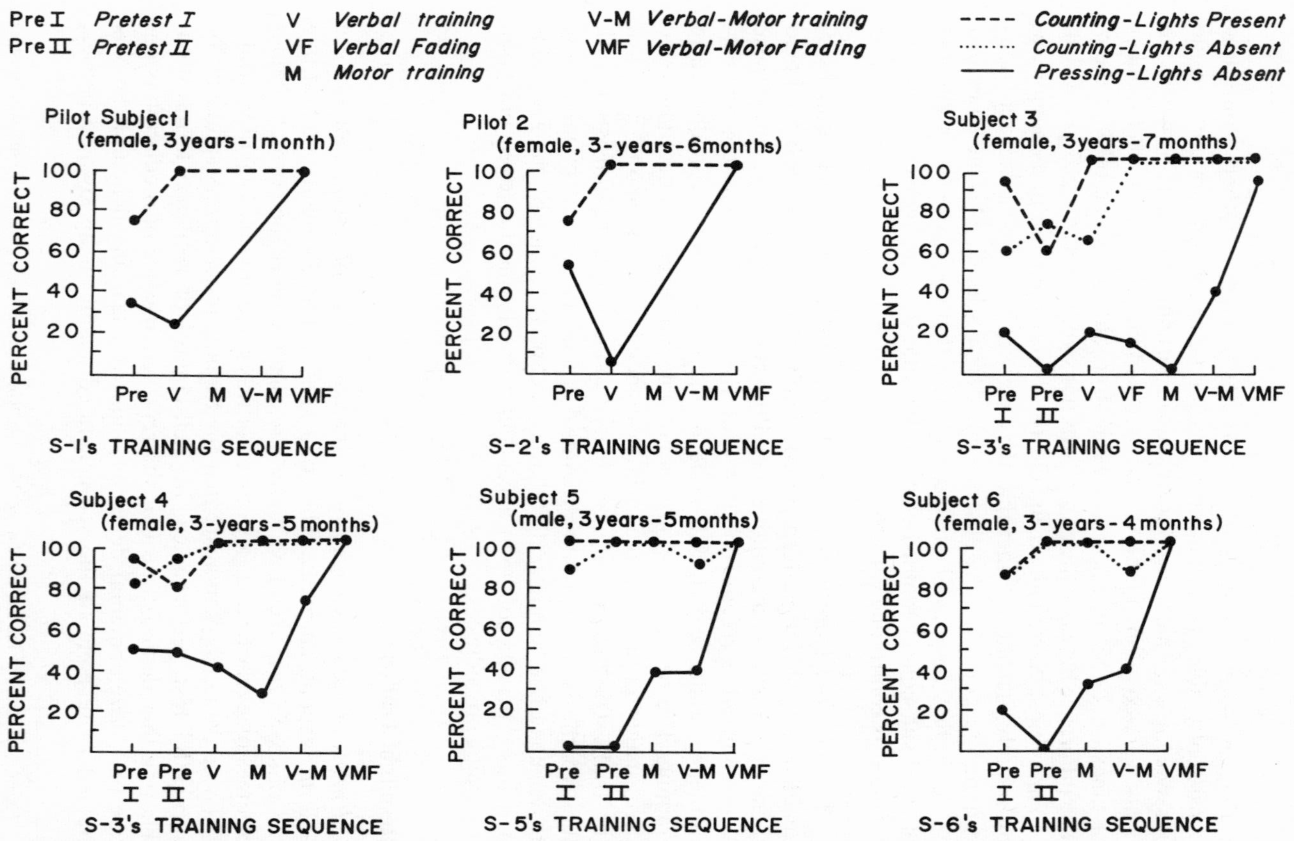

Fig. 34.1. Effects of all phases of training on counting-lights present, counting-lights absent, and pressing-lights absent.

that is, if his responses are forced to function as discriminative stimuli, that *S* is able to control his own behavior.

Effects of pretesting   Figure 34.1 indicates that taking the pretest is not itself responsible for correct responding; none of the four *S*s who took both pretests improved from the first administration to the second (*S*s 3, 4, 5, & 6).

Effects of verbal training   Training *S*s only to count the lights presented on the display did not effect improved test performance; the performance of three out of four *S*s declined (*S*s 1, 2, & 4), while that of the fourth improved, but only to a previously achieved level (*S* 3). Out of 15 trials, the mean-percentage correct was only 22.6% following verbal training. Clearly, verbal training does not itself produce successful performance on the test. As the dashed lines in Fig. 34.1 indicate, however, it did enable *S*s 1, 2, 3, & 4 to count perfectly. Because *S*s 5 and 6 reached criterion on the pretest, they did not participate in verbal training.

Effects of verbal fading   Because three out of four nonpilot *S*s were able to repeat their prior counting responses on the pretest, whether or not those responses had themselves been correct, only *S* 3 underwent verbal fading; as indicated by the dotted line in Fig. 34.1, that training did enable her to repeat her prior counting responses in the absence of the lights. Like the other *S*s, who could already generate the second sequence of counting responses, *S* 3 was still unable to perform correctly on the test. This demonstrates that the ability to emit appropriate self-generated stimuli is not itself sufficient for self-control of response termination.

Effects of motor training   No training was necessary to enable *S*s to respond correctly when they could see each lever press turn off one light. During the first 25 trials of motor training, the total number of incorrect responses by all nonpilot 3-yr.-olds was only five out of a possible 125; that is, 96% of their responses were correct. These results replicate Luria's finding that 3-yr.-olds are able to terminate their motor behavior appropriately when external stimuli are provided. They further suggest that *S*s must learn to replace those stimuli with self-generated ones if they are to respond correctly on the test.

It will be noted that motor training improved the test performance of *S* 5 and *S* 6. Prior to motor training, both of these *S*s had been emitting a number of responses for each trial far in excess of the number of lights presented. Motor training did not teach them to respond with the appropriate number of responses, but only to approximate the appropriate range. Accordingly, the percentage of correct responses for these Ss increased, but only to 36.7%. Seventy-five percent of all Ss' responses remained incorrect; these data clearly indicate that the entire procedure up to and including motor training is not sufficient for self-control of response termination.

Effects of verbal-motor training   In verbal-motor training, S turns lights off by pressing and counting simultaneously; he is still permitted to watch the lights as they go off. It will be noted that such training does effect some improvement in performance for Ss 3, 4, & 6; this is not unexpected since all the behaviors appropriate for final test performance are being consistently acknowledged as correct. The mean percentage of correct responses for all nonpilot Ss was only 48.3%, however, indicating that self-control had not yet been established.

Effects of verbal-motor fading   As previously reported, verbal-motor fading was sufficient for verbal self-control. Performance was virtually perfect for all Ss.

DISCUSSION

The results of the present experiment indicate that verbal self-control can be produced experimentally in 3-yr.-old children. The fact that its absence was found to result not from a developmental deficiency, but from a learning deficit indicates that speech can gain new functional significance by means of a learning procedure and, further, that a learning procedure may be necessary for the natural emergence of verbal self-control. While this does not imply that a child of any age can be trained to obey his self-instruction, it does emphasize the importance of learning in the establishment of effective self-instruction, and it therefore has direct bearing on the traditional question of the relative contributions of development and learning toward the natural emergence of verbal self-control.

The crucial component of the learning procedure used in the present experiment has become known as a fading procedure and was clearly demonstrated in an experiment by Terrace (1963). In his experiment, control of a pigeon's discrimination was shifted with no errors from the background color of a pecking disc to the orientation of a line on that disc. This was accomplished by superimposing the noncontrolling stimulus, the line, onto the controlling stimulus, the colored background, and then by gradually fading out the colored background; in this way, the functional characteristics of the controlling stimulus were transferred to the noncontrolling stimulus. Hefferline and Perera (1963) used a fading procedure with humans in order to transfer control from an external stimulus to a nonverbal response. Each *S* was required to press a key at the onset of a particular tone. The onset of the tone was made contingent upon the occurrence of a nondiscriminable thumb twitch, and the intensity of the tone was then gradually faded to zero. In this way, nonverbal self-control was effected without the awareness of *S*s.

The fact that a fading procedure was able to shift control in the present experiment from an external stimulus to a verbal self-instruction indicates not only that speech can gain new functional significance by means of a learning procedure, but also that functionally similar procedures are effective in establishing external-stimulus control, nonverbal self-control, and verbal self-control. Further, the fact that fading appears to be effective for establishing self-control in the laboratory suggests that some analogue to it may be the real world mechanism whereby speech becomes "interiorized" (Luria, 1960, p. 382) and verbal self-control emerges.

REFERENCES

Bem, S. L. Verbal self-control: The establishment of effective self-instruction. *Technical Report No.* 12, 1966 University of Michigan, Grant HD 01368-02, Center Human Growth Dev., National Institute of Mental Health.

Birch, D. Verbal control of nonverbal behavior. *J. exp. Child Psychol.*, 1966, **4**, 266–275.

Hefferline, R. F., & Perera, T. B. Proprioceptive discrimination of a covert operant without its observation by the subject. *Science*, 1963, **139**, 834–835.

Luria, A. R. Verbal regulation of behavior. In M. A. B. Brazier (Ed.), *The central nervous system and behavior*. New York: Josiah Macy, Jr., Foundation, 1960. Pp. 359–423.

Luria, A. R. The genesis of voluntary movements. In N. O'Connor (Ed.), *Recent Soviet psychology*. New York: Liveright, 1961. Pp. 165–185.

Terrace, H. S. Errorless transfer of a discrimination across two continua. *J. exp. Anal. Behav.*, 1963, **6**, 223–232.

ARTICLE 35

Transmission of Patterns of Self-Reinforcement Through Modeling*[1]

ALBERT BANDURA and CAROL J. KUPERS

Stanford University

Abstract: In a test of the hypothesis that patterns of self-reinforcement are acquired imitatively, 1 group of children observed either peer or adult models who adopted a high criterion for self-reinforcement, a 2nd group was exposed to models who exhibited a similar pattern of self-reward and self-disapproval, except they adopted a relatively low criterion, while children in a control group observed no models. A postexposure test revealed that the children's patterns and magnitude of self-reinforcement closely matched those of the model to whom they had been exposed. Adults generally served as more powerful modeling stimuli than peers in transmitting self-reinforcing responses.

According to current social-learning theories, new responses are acquired and existing behavioral repertoires are maintained or modified through positive or negative reinforcements administered by external agents. Although the controlling power of external reinforcing stimuli cannot be minimized (Ferster, 1958; Skinner, 1961), self-administered primary and conditioned rewards may frequently outweigh the influence of external stimuli in governing social behavior, particularly in the case of older children and adults.

The latter phenomenon, however, has been virtually ignored both in psychological theorizing and experimentation, perhaps due to the preoccupation with infrahuman learning. Unlike human subjects, rats or chimpanzees are disinclined to pat themselves on the back for commend-

---

*Reprinted from the *Journal of Abnormal and Social Psychology*, Vol. 69, No. 1, 1964, pp. 1–9, by permission of the American Psychological Association.

[1]This investigation was supported in part by Research Grant M-5162 from the National Institutes of Health, United States Public Health Service. The study was conducted while the junior author was the recipient of an undergraduate National Science Foundation research fellowship.

The authors are grateful to Robert Grant, Jefferson Union School District, and to Herbert Popenoe, Los Angeles City School Districts, for their assistance in arranging the research facilities.

able performances, or to berate themselves for getting lost in cul-de-sacs. By contrast, people typically make self-reinforcement contingent on their performing certain classes of responses which they have come to value as an index of personal merit. They often set themselves relatively explicit criteria of achievement, failure to meet which is considered undeserving of self-reward and may elicit self-denial or even self-punitive responses; on the other hand, they tend to reward themselves generously on those occasions when they attain their self-imposed standards. Since self-administered rewards may serve both as powerful incentives for learning and as effective reinforcers in maintaining behavioral repertoires in humans, it is of considerable interest to determine the manner in which self-reinforcing responses are acquired.

It is likely that self-rewarding responses are to some extent directly conditioned through differential reinforcements administered initially by external agents. In this learning process the agent adopts a criterion of what constitutes a worthy performance and consistently rewards the subject for matching or exceeding the adopted criterion level, while performances that fall short of it are non-rewarded or punished. When subsequently the subject is given full control over the self-administration of reinforcers, he is likely to utilize the rewards in a contingent manner, with achieved performance levels serving as the primary discriminative stimuli.

Some recent evidence for the direct conditioning of self-reinforcing responses is provided by Kanfer and Marston (1963a) who found that when subjects were generously rewarded on an ambiguous noncontingent task they not only increased their rate of self-reinforcement, but also rewarded themselves frequently on a new learning task; in contrast, when subjects participated with an agent who grudgingly parted with limited token rewards and cautioned against excessive self-reward, the subjects exhibited considerably less self-reinforcement on both the training and generalization tasks. In addition, the incidence of self-reinforcement has been found to be partly dependent on the correctness of the subjects' responses and on the similarity between training and generalization tasks (Kanfer, Bradley, & Marston, 1962; Kanfer & Marston, 1963b; Marston & Kanfer, 1963).

While the studies quoted above demonstrate the role of direct reinforcement in the acquisition of self-rewarding tendencies, it is doubtful that people receive much direct training in self-reinforcement on the majority of tasks they encounter, nor can performances in most situations be evaluated meaningfully independent of the accomplishments of others. Consequently, a person's self-evaluations may be importantly dependent upon the degree to which he matches the behavior of models whom he has chosen for comparison, and the self-reinforcement schedules which the models have adopted with respect to their own achievements. Some evidence for the influential role of vicarious learning is provided in recent demonstrations that social behavior may be rapidly acquired or modified as a function of observing the behavior and attitudes exhibited by models (Bandura, 1962). The present experiment, therefore, studied self-reinforcing responses as products of imitative learning.

Children participated in a task with an adult or a peer model, the scores being controlled by the experimenter. Under one experimental condition the model set a high criterion for self-reinforcement; on trials in which the model obtained or exceeded the standard he rewarded himself, while on trials in which he failed to meet the adopted standard he displayed self-denial and self-critical behavior. In a second experimental condition the model displayed a similar pattern of self-reward and self-disapproval, but adopted a relatively low self-reinforcement criterion. After exposure to their respective models the children received a wide range of scores and the performances for which they rewarded themselves were recorded.

It was predicted that children would imitate the self-reinforcement patterns exhibited by their respective models, whereas control-group subjects who were not exposed to the models would display no consistent pattern of self-reinforcement. On the assumption that children are apt to have been repeatedly positively reinforced for imitating models of the same sex and nonrewarded or negatively reinforced for opposite-sex imitation, it was also predicted that the subjects would match the self-reinforcement patterns of a same-sex model to a greater degree than that of a model of the opposite sex.

Finally, the relative effectiveness of models in shaping self-reinforcing responses may vary as a function of their prestige, competence, age status, or social power (Bandura, Ross, & Ross, 1963; Jakubczak & Walters, 1959; Miller & Dollard, 1941; Rosenbaum & Tucker, 1962). Because of differential competencies, adults are likely to exhibit more successful and rewarding responses than peers and, therefore, to the extent that children are differentially rewarded for matching adult and peer models, adults would eventually become the more powerful modeling stimuli. On the other hand, it might be argued that children would view adults as too divergent in ability to serve as meaningful models for self-evaluation (Festinger, 1954), whereas the self-reinforcement patterns exhibited by peers would be considered more realistic and, therefore, would be adopted more readily. In the present experiment, however, the adults displayed considerable variability in performance and a given subject would readily notice, from his own similarly wide range of scores, that there were little or no adult-child ability level differences on the particular task employed. Consequently, it was predicted that children would match the self-reinforcement patterns of adult models more closely than those of peer models.

METHOD

Subjects

The subjects were 80 boys and 80 girls ranging in age from 7 to 9 years. The children were drawn from six public schools participating in the Los Angeles Board of Education summer recreation program.

A male and female adult and two 9-year-old children served in the role of models. None of the subjects was acquainted with either the adult or the peer models.

Experimental Design

The children were subdivided into male and female subjects and randomly assigned to 16 experimental subgroups of 8 subjects each, and a control group consisting of 16 boys and 16 girls. Half the experimental children observed adult models, and half were exposed to peer models. In addition, half the children in both the adult and peer model conditions observed same-sex models, while the remaining children in each group witnessed models of the opposite sex. The control children had no prior exposure to the models and were tested only on the self-reinforcement task.

Procedure

A male assistant to the experimenter contacted the children individually on the playground and invited them to participate in the study. The assistant escorted each child to the experimental room and introduced him to the female experimenter and to the model, who supposedly had arrived early and was waiting for the session to commence.

In order to enhance the credibility of the experimental situation, the instructions were given to both the child and the model simultaneously, thus creating the set that the model was simply another naive subject. The experimenter explained that the purpose of the study was to collect normative data on the psychomotor abilities of a large sample of people. In the adult-model conditions, the experimenter added that data from adults as well as from children were desired, and that it was more convenient to test the adults in school than to transport the test apparatus from place to place. The experimenter further explained that subjects were being tested in pairs so as to expedite collection of the normative data. The same explanations were given to children in the peer-model condition, except the subjects were led to believe that their partner was selected at random from the participants in the recreation program. Following these preliminary instructions, the child and the model were introduced to the bowling task that provided a means for modeling self-reinforcement responses.

Apparatus

The bowling apparatus used in this experiment was the one employed by Gelfand (1962). The equipment consisted of a miniature bowling alley with a 3-foot runway at the end of which there were three upright doweled target markers. The middle marker was labeled 10 points while the two adjacent ones were each labeled 5 points. The subjects were informed that whenever a bowling ball hit a target, the corresponding marker would drop. The target area, however, was carefully screened from view by fiberboard shields which covered the end-zone area of the runway and encircled the targets; consequently, the children had no knowledge of whether or not the bowling balls were in fact striking the targets. The experimenter further explained that occasionally the balls might bounce off the sides of the alley and, therefore, there may at times be little correspondence between the observed route of the bowling balls and the markers that drop. Actually, the experimenter sat behind the apparatus and controlled the scores by pulling appropriate strings that dropped the point markers. The models thus obtained identical scores with each subject and, similarly, all children received the same pattern of performance scores. Since the experimenter had to reset the markers after each trial and to return the bowling balls to the children from the back of the apparatus via an inclined trough, her position and activities appeared quite natural and justified.

After acquainting the child and the model with the bowling apparatus, the experimenter explained the rules of the game. The subjects would be allowed three balls per game and each would have a chance to play quite a few games. In the adult-model condition, the experimenter asked the child if he would mind letting the model take the first turn since he had to return to his work shortly, while in the peer-model condition, the experimenter's decision to let the model perform first appeared to be arbitrary.

The experimenter then called the subject's attention to a large bowl of M & M candies positioned beside the starting point of the alley within easy reach of the bowler. The subjects were given highly permissive instructions to help themselves to the candy whenever they wished, but if they did not feel like eating all the M & Ms during the session they could save them in the containers provided. M & M candies were selected as reinforcers because of their high attractiveness value and low satiation properties.

Before commencing the trials, the subjects were asked to treat themselves to some candy while the experimenter set the targets. This procedure, in addition to enhancing permissiveness for self-reward, was primarily designed to identify those children who would refuse to take candy because of parental prohibitions or for other reasons. If a child refused to take any candy he was, therefore, excluded from subsequent phases of the experiment. This occurred very infrequently, affecting only approximately 5% of the children.

Patterns of Self-Reinforcement

The model performed for 10 trials of three balls each and obtained scores ranging from 5 to 30 points.

In the *high criterion for self-reinforcement* condition the model rewarded himself with candy and positive self-evaluative verbalizations only when he obtained or exceeded a score of 20. On such trials the model took one or two M & Ms and commented approvingly, "I deserve some M & Ms for that high score." "That's great! That certainly is worth an M & M treat." In contrast, on trials in which he failed to meet the adopted criterion of 20, the model denied himself candy and remarked self-critically, "No M & Ms for that." "That does not deserve an M & M treat."

In the *low criterion for self-reinforcement* condition the model, while exhibiting a similar pattern of self-reward and self-disapproval, adopted a criterion of 10 points, a relatively low level of performance. On trials in which he obtained or exceeded a score of 10, he rewarded himself with candy and made self-approving comments, while on trials in which he failed to meet the adopted standard he took no candy and criticized himself.

There was some minor variation in the magnitude of self-reinforcement; the model generally took one M & M when he performed at or slightly above criterion, and two M & Ms when he scored well above the adopted minimum level.

While the model performed his trials the child, seated next to the bowling apparatus, was engaged to help in the scoring process. The assistant stood at a nearby blackboard, recorded the appropriate number whenever a marker dropped, totaled the scores at the end of each game, and then announced them to the bowler. The child was asked to call out the number each time the marker dropped. His participation was solicited in this manner for two reasons: First, to reinforce the three-balls-per-game set so that his scores would be meaningful to him, and second, to insure that he was attending to the model's performances and self-reinforcing responses.

After completing his 10 trials the model departed, the assistant generously refurnished the candy supply, and the experimenter asked the child to take his turns. The postexposure test was conducted with the models absent in order to remove any situational pressures on the children to adopt the model's patterns of self-reinforcement.

The child then performed 15 trials of three balls each. He received scores similar to those of the model, ranging from 5 to 30 points, according to a prearranged program.

It was found during pretesting that children occasionally forgot their subscores or made errors in addition. Therefore, in the experiment proper the assistant recorded the scores on the blackboard for the child and announced the total number of points at the completion of each trial.

For the purpose of testing our hypotheses the scores were divided into three critical levels: 5, 10–15, and 20–30. Since even the model who adopted a low criterion for self-reinforcement had to reach a minimum level of 10 points before rewarding himself, and since pretest data revealed that children rewarded themselves relatively infrequently when they obtained the lowest possible score, only two 5-point trials were included. Similarly, it was not expected that scores of 20 or higher would elicit differential self-reinforcing behavior from control and experimental children since all subjects would be inclined to reward themselves for such commendably high levels of performance. For this reason, in only 5 of the 15 programed trials did children receive scores of 20 or higher. It was assumed that the 10–15 performance level would be the most crucial one in differentiating the groups and, therefore, the children obtained a score of 10 or 15 on approximately half of the total trials.

Measures of Self-Reinforcement

The assistant recorded on data sheets the trials for which the child rewarded himself with candy and the total number of M & Ms taken in each self-reinforced trial. The frequency of positive and negative self-evaluative remarks by the child that matched precisely the model's verbal responses was also recorded.

RESULTS

In order to provide a picture of the children's distribution of self-reinforcement as a function of treatment conditions, the number of times each child rewarded himself with candy for 5, 10–15, and for 20–30 point performances, respectively, was divided by his total number of self-reinforced trials. The mean percentages of self-reinforcing responses displayed by the experimental and control groups at each of the three performance levels are shown in Table 35.1 and summarized graphically in Figs. 35.1 and 35.2.

It should be noted that compared to the programed distribution the control children and those exposed to low-criterion models engaged in a slightly disproportionate frequency of self-reinforcement at the low or intermediate performance levels. The reason for this discrepancy is that some of the children displayed midtrial self-reinforcement; e.g., on a 20-point trial in which a child secured a score of 10 on the first roll, he might reward himself immediately rather than wait until he had completed the trial by rolling the two remaining bowling balls. In such cases the children were scored as having rewarded themselves for a 10-point performance and thus some children accumulated more 5- and 10-point trials than had been intended in the original programing.

Midtrial self-reinforcement occurred relatively frequently in the control group (23% of the total self-reinforced trials), but rarely in groups of children who observed a model exhibit either high (5%) or low (9%) standards for reinforcement. The difference between percentages of

Table 35.1. Distribution of Mean Percentage of Self-Reinforcement as a Function of Sex of Subjects, Sex and Age of Models, and the Self-Reinforcement Criteria Exhibited by the Models

| | Performance level | | | | | |
| | Adult models | | | Peer models | | |
Experimental treatment	5	10–15	20–30	5	10–15	20–30
High criterion						
Male model						
Boys	0	0	100	0	11	89
Girls	0	13	87	8	25	67
Female model						
Boys	0	8	92	0	23	77
Girls	0	5	95	6	16	78
Total	0	7	93	4	19	77
Low criterion						
Male model						
Boys	3	59	38	7	57	36
Girls	0	67	33	2	58	40
Female model						
Boys	0	75	25	3	67	30
Girls	0	60	40	7	60	33
Total	1	66	33	5	61	34
No model control	24	47	28			
Programed distribution	14	53	33			

midtrial self-reinforcement for the control children and those in the combined-model conditions is highly significant ($Z = 2.53$, $p < 0.02$). Considering that the models consistently postponed self-reward until the completion of a trial, these intergroup differences provide some evidence that the behavior of models is influential in transmitting self-control in the utilization of readily available rewarding resources.

Evaluation of Group Differences

The fact that the majority of children seldom rewarded themselves following performances that fell short of their models minimum criteria precluded the use of parametric tests of significance. Consequently, in group comparisons where the obtained frequencies of self-reinforcing responses were relatively low, chi-square tests were employed based on the number of children in a condition who reinforced themselves at all

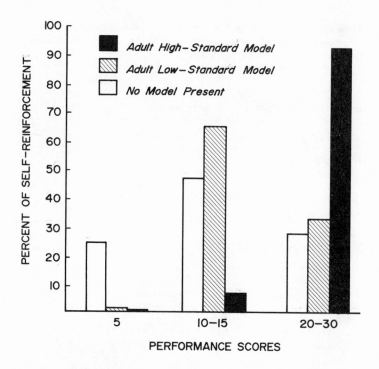

Fig. 35.1. The distribution of self-reinforcement as a function of performance level by control children and those exposed to adult models adopting high and low criteria for self-reinforcement.

after a given level of performance. The median test was utilized to evaluate the significance of differences at performance levels that resulted in a higher incidence of self-reward.

Since the results failed to reveal any significant sex-of-model or sex-of-subject influences on self-reinforcing responses, the data yielded by these subgroups were combined in testing the principal hypotheses.

Age Status of the Model

As predicted, children matched the self-reinforcement patterns of the adult models more precisely than their peer counterparts. Relative to the children who observed the high-criterion adult model, children in the high-criterion peer condition displayed a slightly greater tendency to reward themselves for 10–15 point performances ($\chi^2 = 7.06$, $p < 0.01$).

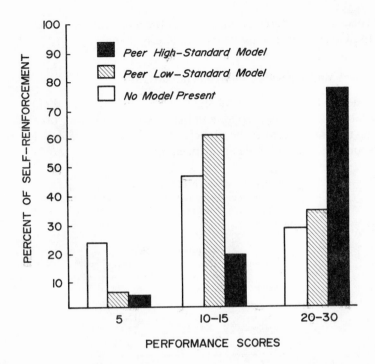

Fig. 35.2. The distribution of self-reinforcement as a function of performance level by control children and those exposed to peer models adopting high and low criteria for self-reinforcement.

The corresponding percentages of children in these two groups were 10% and 37%, respectively.

For the high-criterion subjects a score of 5 points fell well below the model's minimum standard. Consequently, very few of these children rewarded themselves at this performance level and no significant differences between peer- and adult-model conditions were obtained. On the other hand, in the low-criterion condition, where a score of 5 approached but did not quite reach the model's minimum criterion, more of the children who observed the peer model rewarded themselves at least once for a 5-point performance (37%) than did children who were exposed to the adult model (3%). This difference yielded a chi-square value of 11.68 that is significant beyond the 0.001 level. At the high performance levels, of course, the children engaged in frequent self-reinforcement regardless of the age status of the model.

Because of the differential influence of the adult and peer models, data from these treatment groups were analyzed separately.

Influence of Modeled Self-Reinforcement Patterns

In order to test the statistical significance of the obtained differences attributable to modeling, separate chi-square analyses were obtained for each of the three performance levels. The chi-square values and their corresponding level of significance appear in Table 35.2.

Table 35.2. Significance of the Differences in Self-Reinforcing Responses between Children in the Modeling Conditions and Those in the Control Group

Performance level	Adult-model condition χ^2	Peer-model condition χ^2
5 points	36.50*	15.79*
10–15 points	63.21*	33.33*
20–30 points	49.95*	40.53*

*$p < 0.001$.

These group differences may be summarized as follows: Children exposed to models adopting either low or high standards for self-reinforcement rarely rewarded themselves when performing at the lowest possible level, whereas a relatively high proportion of the control children engaged in self-reinforcement after obtaining identically low scores. At the intermediate performance level most of the children in the control and the low-criterion groups rewarded themselves, while self-reinforcement by children exposed to high-criterion models was relatively infrequent. Finally, at the high performance level children who observed the high-criterion model engaged in an exceedingly high proportion of self-reward relative to the controls and to the low-criterion model groups.

Imitation of Self-Approving and Self-Critical Verbal Responses

Since the incidence of imitative verbal self-reinforcement was essentially the same irrespective of the sex, age status, and criterion level of the models, the experimental subgroup data were combined in the statistical analysis.

Twenty-seven percent of the experimental children reproduced precisely the models' self-approving or self-critical verbalizations in response to their own performances. In contrast, not a single child in the control group expressed any positive or negative self-evaluative statements, imitative or otherwise. This difference yielded a chi-square value of 8.12, which is significant beyond the 0.01 level.

Magnitude of Self-Reinforcement

The children displayed some variability in the mean number of candies taken per self-reinforced trial. Chi-square analyses revealed that generosity in self-reward was not attributable to sex-of-subjects, sex-of-models, or to differential modeling treatments. The age status of the model, however, appeared to be a significant source of variance ($\chi^2 = 10.10$, $p < 0.01$). On the average, a higher percentage of the children in the peer-model condition (41%) rewarded themselves in excess of their model's maximum of two candies, than did either the control children (31%) or those who observed adult models (16%).

It will be recalled that the models rewarded themselves with two candies when they obtained high scores relative to their adopted standard, but took only one candy for criterion-level performances. In order to test for any modeling effects in the distribution of magnitude of self-reinforcement the mean number of M & Ms taken per trial after scores of 20 or lower were compared by the Wilcoxon test with the means for scores of 25 and 30 points.

While the control-group children did not engage in differential amounts of self-reinforcement as a function of performance level, subjects in each of the experimental subgroups, irrespective of whether they observed adults or peers modeling high or low standards, displayed greater self-reinforcement at the higher achievement levels. In each experimental condition the Z value was significant well beyond the 0.01 level.

DISCUSSION

The overall results of this experiment provide strong support for the hypothes s that patterns of self-reinforcement can be acquired imitatively through exposure to models without the subjects themselves being administered any direct differential reinforcement by external agents.

This is shown clearly by the fact that children in the experimental conditions made self-reinforcement contingent on their achieving performance levels that matched the self-reward criteria of their respective models, whereas children in the control group administered rewards to themselves more or less independently of their task accomplishments. The influence of models is further reflected in the finding that a number of the children reproduced precisely the content of their model's self-approving and self-critical verbal behavior. Not only did the children adopt the model's self-rewarding standards and verbal reinforcements, but they even matched the minor variations in magnitude of self-reinforcement exhibited by the models.

There are several possible reasons for the surprisingly precise matching of the models' self-reinforcing response patterns. First, the bowling task scores did not have much absolute value, consequently they provided the subjects little basis for judging what might constitute an inadequate or a superior performance independent of some reference norm. Even if relevant normative data were available, since the subjects' performances varied widely and unpredictably the children still had no basis for evaluating their own abilities. Thus the combination of performance ambiguity and instability would tend to enhance the patency of the model's standard-setting and self-reinforcing behavior. On the other hand, had the subjects' performances been consistently low and markedly discrepant from the model's achievements, the children might very well have rejected the model's relatively high self-reinforcement standards. In order to investigate this variable systematically, a study of imitative learning of self-reinforcement patterns is planned in which groups of children will obtain relatively stable scores at varying degrees of discrepancy from the performance levels and self-reinforcement criteria displayed by the models.

In accord with prediction and findings from other investigations cited earlier, adults served as more powerful modeling stimuli than peers in transmitting both standards and magnitude of self-reinforcement. Contrary to hypothesis, however, the study failed to yield any significantly Sex-of-Model × Sex-of-Subject interaction effects. This is particularly surprising since bowling might be considered a partially masculine-typed activity and, therefore, boys should at least be more prone than girls to imitate the male model (Bandura, Ross, & Ross, 1961). While the data from the high-standard condition suggest such a trend, the differences are not of statistically significant magnitude, perhaps because of the small number of cases in the cells.

Although the children acquired positive and negative self-reinforcing responses without the mediation of direct external reinforcement, it is probable that the evaluative properties of performances which fall short of, match, or exceed a reference norm are the resultant of past discriminative reinforcements. Through the repeated pairing of performance deficits with aversive consequences and successfully matched behavior with rewards, differential achievement levels per se eventually acquired positive and negative valence. It should be noted, however, that performance-produced cues have relatively little evaluative significance apart from a selected reference norm. Once the evaluative properties of differential accomplishments are well established, adequate or inadequate matches are likely to elicit similar self-evaluative responses irrespective of the specific behavior being compared. At this stage the whole process becomes relatively independent of external reinforcement and the specific contingencies of the original training situations. As demonstrated in the present experiment, subjects will adopt the particular criteria for self-reinforcement exhibited by a reference model, evaluate their own performances relative to that standard, and then serve as their own reinforcing agents.

Theory and research relating to the process of internalization and self-control have generally focused on *resistance to deviation* and the occurrence of *self-punitive responses* following transgression. Perhaps, an even more prevalent and important behavioral manifestation of self-control is the manner in which a person regulates the self-administration of highly rewarding resources. Thus in the experiment rewarding resources were readily available and their use was socially permissible; nevertheless, the groups of children differed markedly in the extent to which they utilized the reinforcers to obtain self-gratification. Children presented with low-criterion models were highly self-indulgent, rewarding themselves on the average more than twice as frequently as children in the high-criterion condition who displayed considerable self-denial. In the case of the control children, self-rewards were apparently freely dispensed and not made contingent on meeting or surpassing any minimum standard of achievement. These group patterns may be regarded as prototypic of cultures in which the majority of adults consistently display self-denying (Eaton & Weil, 1955) or self-indulgent (Hughes, Tremblay, Rapoport, & Leighton, 1960) behavior and, having limited opportunity to observe other behavioral examples, the children tend to model themselves after the prevalent self-reinforcement patterns.

In discussions of psychopathology and psychotherapy attention is frequently directed to the presence of behavioral deficits or to anxiety-

and guilt-motivated inhibitory tendencies. A large proportion of the clients seeking psychotherapy, however, present relatively competent repertoires and are not excessively inhibited in their social behavior. These clients experience a great deal of self-generated aversive stimulation and self-imposed denial of positive reinforcers stemming from their excessively high standards for self-reinforcement, often supported by comparisons with historical or contemporary models noted for their extraordinary achievement. This process frequently gives rise to depressive reactions, a lessened disposition to perform because of the unfavorable work to self-reinforcement ratio, and efforts to escape the self-generated aversive stimulation through alcoholism, grandiose ideation, and other modes of avoidant behavior. In these cases, the modification of standards for self-reinforcement would clearly constitute a principal psychotherapeutic objective (Bandura, 1969).

REFERENCES

Bandura, A. Social learning through imitation. In M. R. Jones (Ed.), *Nebraska symposium on motivation: 1962.* Lincoln: Univer. Nebraska Press, 1962. Pp. 211–269.

Bandura, A. *Principles of behavioral modification.* New York: Holt, Rinehart, & Winston, 1969.

Bandura, A., Ross, Dorothea, & Ross, Sheila A. Transmission of aggression through imitation of aggressive models. *J. abnorm. soc. Psychol.,* 1961, **63**, 575–582.

Bandura, A., Ross, Dorothea, & Ross, Sheila A. A comparative test of the status envy, social power, and secondary reinforcement theories of identificatory learning. *J. abnorm. soc. Psychol.,* 1963, **67**, 527–534.

Eaton, J. W., & Weil, R. J. *Culture and mental disorders.* Glencoe, Ill.: Free Press, 1955.

Ferster, C. B. Reinforcement and punishment in the control of human behavior by social agencies. *Psychiat. res. Rep.,* 1958, **12**, 101–118.

Festinger, L. A theory of social comparison processes. *Hum. Relat.,* 1954, **7**, 117–140.

Gelfand, Donna M. The influence of self-esteem on rate of verbal conditioning and social matching behavior. *J. abnorm. soc. Psychol.,* 1962, **65**, 259–265.

Hughes, C. C., Tremblay, M., Rapoport, R. N., & Leighton, A. H. *People of cove and woodlot: Communities from the viewpoint of social psychiatry.* New York: Basic Books, 1960.

Jakubczak, L. F., & Walters, R. H. Suggestibility as dependency behavior. *J. abnorm. soc. Psychol.,* 1959, **59**, 102–107.

Kanfer, F. H., Bradley, Marcia A., & Marston, A. R. Self-reinforcement as a function of degree of learning. *Psychol. Rep.,* 1962, **10**, 885–886.

Kanfer, F. H., & Marston, A. R. Conditioning of self-reinforcing responses: An analogue to self-confidence training. *Psychol. Rep.*, 1963, **13**, 63–70. (a)

Kanfer, F. H., & Marston, A. R. Determinants of self-reinforcement in human learning. *J. exp. Psychol.*, 1963, **66**, 245–254. (b)

Marston, A. R., & Kanfer, F. H. Human reinforcement: Experimenter and subject controlled. *J. exp. Psychol.*, 1963, **66**, 91–94.

Miller, N. E., & Dollard, J. *Social learning and imitation.* New Haven: Yale Univer. Press, 1941.

Rosenbaum, M. E., & Tucker, I. F. The competence of the model and the learning of imitation and nonimitation. *J. exp. Psychol.*, 1962, **63**, 183–190.

Skinner, B. F. *Cumulative record.* New York: Appleton-Century-Crofts, 1961.

ARTICLE 36

Academic Response Rate as a Function of Teacher- and Self-Imposed Contingencies*

THOMAS C. LOVITT and KAREN A. CURTISS[1]

University of Washington

Abstract: The purpose of this study was to assess the effects of the contingency manager (teacher or pupil) on a pupil's academic response rate. The results of two such experiments disclosed that higher academic rates occurred when the pupil arranged the contingency requirements than when the teacher specified them. A third study manipulated only reinforcement magnitude to ascertain whether amount of reinforcement had interacted with pupil-specified contingencies to produce the increase in academic response rate. The latter findings revealed that the contingency manager, not reinforcement magnitude, accounted for this subject's gain in performance.

The management of one's own behavior has often been expressed as one of the prime objectives of our educational system. The problem in programming toward such an end has been one of definition – specifying those variables that constitute self-management. Until the skills or traits that lead to a self-managing individual are clearly detailed and explicitly defined, the objective of self-management may never be realized. If, however, certain subproperties of self-management can be determined, sequentially ordered, and systematically presented, the probability of realizing this objective is greatly increased.

An individual who can control or manage his own behavior may be a person who has the ability to assess his own competencies, set his own behavioral objectives, and specify a contingency system whereby he might obtain these objectives. Translated to a school situation, this

*Reprinted from the *Journal of Applied Behavior Analysis*, Vol. 2, No. 1, Spring 1969, pp. 49–53. Copyright 1969 by the Society for the Experimental Analysis of Behavior Inc.

[1]Reprints may be obtained from Thomas C. Lovitt, Mental Retardation and Child Development Center, University of Washington, 4701 24th Ave. N.E., Seattle, Washington 98105.

would be an individual who knew his academic capabilities in terms of skill levels and rate of performance, could arrange a series of activities or steps to achieve a variety of self-imposed objectives, and could grant himself reinforcers on a prearranged schedule to accomplish certain behavioral sequences.

This last behavior, self-specification of contingencies, has been a neglected area of investigation. Traditionally, it is the teacher who arranges the contingencies in the classroom, saying to the pupil: "If you do these arithmetic problems, you will receive a gold star", or, "If you correctly answer these questions you will be allowed to go out for recess". Infrequently is the student allowed to arrange his own educational environment.

The purpose of this study was to analyze functionally the effects of self-imposed *versus* teacher-imposed contingencies on the behavior of a particular pupil. In this study the specification of contingencies was the independent variable, while academic response rate was selected as the dependent variable.

METHOD

Student and Conditions

The student was a 12-yr-old member of a class for children with behavioral disorders at the Experimental Education Unit, University of Washington. The student had been a member of this class, whose management system was based on the Premack design of high- and low-probability behaviors (Haring and Kunzelmann, 1966; Haring and Lovitt, 1967), for two academic years. Contingent upon academic responses (low-probability behaviors), the students in this class were given points in each of the academic areas. These points were later converted to minutes of time in the high-interest (high-probability behavior) room. The ratios of points-per-answer were individually specified, not only among class members but also among subject matter areas for any one student.

Procedures

This investigation consisted of three separate experiments; two manipulated the contingency manager and one manipulated magnitude of reinforcement. During Exp. I, baseline data relevant to the student's academic response rate were obtained for nine days. Each day a response rate figure was calculated that represented the student's performance in all of his scheduled subject matter areas. Throughout this period no attempt was made to explain to the student the response-per-point ratio in each academic area.

After this baseline period, Stage 1 was instituted. It was the intent at this time to instruct the student as to the relationship between correct answers and contingent points. Each day in this 12-day stage the teacher verbally explained the contingencies and placed a written copy of them on the student's desk. Table 36.1 outlines the contingency system in effect throughout Exp. I. The contract was composed of nine agreements, each of which had a response-per-point ratio. For example, the student was granted two points for each page read (Sullivan Associates Program, 1963) and one point per 10 mathematics problems (Singer Mathematics Program, 1965). As the student completed each academic assignment, he was shown how many responses had been made and was asked to calculate the corresponding points he had earned.

In Stage 2, which extended for 22 days, the copy of the response-point requirements was removed from the student's desk. He was now asked to specify verbally his own payment in each of the nine areas and to

Table 36.1. Contingency Specifications During Experiment I

| | Contingency Manager | |
Subject Area	Teacher-Specified	Child-Specified
Math	10 problems: 1 min of free time	10 problems: 1 min of free time
Supplementary Math	10 problems: 1	10 problems: 1
Reading		
(No errors)	1 page: 2	1 page: 2
(Errors)	1 page: 1	1 page: 1
Spelling	18 words: 1	*10 words: 2
Writing	20 letters: 1	*10 letters: 2
Library Reading	1 story: 3	*1 story: 10
Cyclo-Teacher		
Multiplication	1 side: 1	1 side: 1
Spelling	1 side: 2	1 side: 2

*Indicates where the child-imposed requirements differ from those imposed by the teacher.

record his decisions, which were then attached to his desk. As in Stage 1, when each assignment was completed the student was asked to calculate the points he had earned. Finally, in Stage 3, which lasted for seven days, the teacher-imposed contingencies were again in effect.

In Exp. I, as in all experiments of this study, the sequencing of academic areas was basically the same each day; reading was followed by math, then spelling, English, and writing. Furthermore, the time allotted to each subject was about the same each day: 2 hr for reading, 1 hr for math, and a total of 1.5 hr for spelling, English, writing, and library reading.

Regardless of any variability in the ordering of the subject areas or the time allotted to them, the teacher, not the student, always arranged the day's academic program. Thus, the subject could work only on each academic activity as it was scheduled, math during the math period and reading during the reading period. He could not switch freely from one academic area to another, regardless of the contingencies in effect from one activity to another, or who had imposed the contingencies.

After a period of four weeks, which separated the academic quarters at the University of Washington, Exp. II was begun. No baseline data were obtained during this second experiment, since the student was now fully acquainted with the response-per-point contingencies. Other procedures were carried out as detailed above, for the purpose of replicating Exp. I.

Teacher contingencies were explained, written out, and attached to the student's desk in Stages 1 and 3, while during Stage 2 the student's contingencies were in operation. The only difference between Exp. I and II was that in the first experiment, nine specific agreements were involved; in the latter investigation, eight were included. In both experiments, however, the student's complete program was included in the study. The response-per-point requirements of Exp. II are presented in Table 36.2.

Following this replication study, Exp. III was conducted. Since during Exp. II the student had altered all of the teacher-imposed requirements to grant himself more points per response, it was necessary to determine whether self-contingencies had affected the academic rate increase or whether this increase was due to increased payoff. Experiment III, therefore, consisted of three stages: (1) the teacher specified the response-per-point requirements she had placed in effect throughout Exp. I and II; (2) the teacher specified the requirements that the student had instituted during Exp. II; and (3) the teacher again specified her original requirements. These requirements were identical to those listed in Table 36.2. The only difference between Exp. II and III was that in Exp. III,

Table 36.2. Contingency Specifications During Experiment II

	Contingency Manager	
Subject Area	Teacher-Specified	Child-Specified
Math	10 problems: 1 min of free time	*10 problems: 2 min of free time
Reading		
(No errors)	1 page: 2	*1 page: 3
(Errors)	1 page: 1	*1 page: 2
Spelling	18 words: 1	*5 words: 1
Writing	20 letters: 1	*10 letters: 2
Language Arts	10 answers: 1	*10 answers: 2
Library Book	1 story: 3	*1 story: 6
	3 questions: 1	*3 questions: 2

*Indicates where the child-imposed requirements differ from those imposed by the teacher.

the teacher imposed the contingency requirements throughout, whereas in Exp. II the student set his own contingencies during Stage 2.

RESULTS

Experiment I

During the baseline period (unspecified contingencies), the student's median rate of response was 1.8 while its median rate during Stage 1 was 1.65. The response range during the baseline observations, which lasted for nine days, extended from 1.1 to 2.7; during the 12 days of Stage 1 it extended from 1.1 to 2.4. Stage 2 consisted of 22 daily sessions; in this stage the student's median rate of response was 2.5, ranging from 1.4 to 3.6. A median of 1.9 was obtained in the final stage of the experiment, which consisted of seven daily sessions, while the student's performance extended from 1.0 to 2.2 responses per minute. The data from this experiment are displayed in Fig. 36.1.

Experiment II

Throughout the 13 days of the first stage, the student's rate of response ranged from 0.8 to 2.1, with a median response rate of 1.6. During the

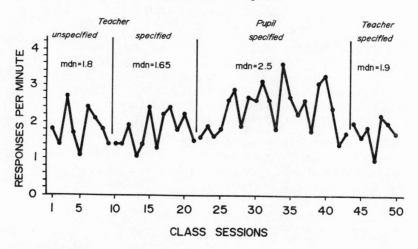

Fig. 36.1. Daily response rate throughout Exp. I.

second stage of this experiment, which also lasted for 13 days, the student's median rate was 2.3 responses per minute. His range at this time was 2.0 to 2.6 responses per minute. In the nine days of the final stage, return to teacher contingencies, the student's median rate of response was 1.5; the range, 1.2 to 1.7. The results of Exp. II are shown in Fig. 36.2.

Experiment III

The data from the final experiment are presented in Fig. 36.3. The student's median response rate was 1.5 for the 16 days of Stage 1. During Stage 2, which also lasted for 16 days, his median response rate was 1.2; and during the final stage, which consisted of 15 sessions, it was 1.4. The range during Stage 1 was from 1.1 to 2.1; from 0.6 to 1.7 during Stage 2; and from 0.6 to 1.6 during Stage 3.

DISCUSSION

The data from these experiments indicated that, for this student, self-imposed contingencies were associated with an increased academic

EXPERIMENT II
Teacher vs. self-contingencies

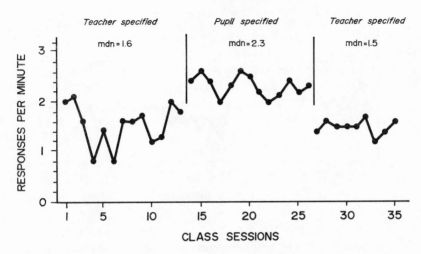

Fig. 36.2. Daily response rate throughout Exp. II.

response rate. This was evidenced in Exp. I and II; during Stage 2 of each experiment, the period of self-contingencies, the student's median performance was higher than during Stages 1 and 3, the periods of teacher-imposed contingencies.

That this response rate increase was attributed to the manipulation of the contingency manager, not to the contingency system being explained or not explained, was demonstrated in Exp. I. Although the latter manipulation might alter the response rate of some students, the data relevant to this variable indicated that, for this student, explaining or not explaining the contingencies produced nearly equal effects (*see* Fig. 36.1).

In addition, the data from Exp. III revealed that the response rate increase was due to manipulation of the contingency manager, and not to reinforcement magnitude. As mentioned earlier, although two experiments had demonstrated that during periods of self-specified contingencies the student responded at rates higher than during teacher-specified contingencies, this increased rate may have been due to mere magnitude of reinforcement. Indeed the contrary seemed to be the case; when the reinforcement ratios were increased by the teacher during Stage 2 of Exp. III, the student's response rate decreased, while it increased during Stage 3 when the original payment was in effect.

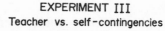

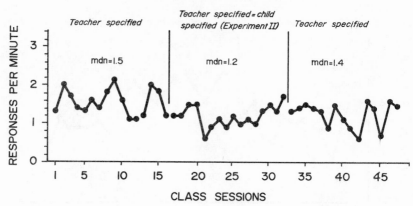

Fig. 36.3. Daily response rate throughout Exp. III.

Throughout this study, response units from the various areas of reading, math, and spelling were grouped under a single category, "academic response". It may be, therefore, that the effects of the student specifying his own contingencies were more pronounced in certain academic areas than in others. It might also occur that a student, when allowed to specify his contingencies in one area but not in another, would, in fact, respond at an accelerated rate in both areas. Research is currently being conducted in which the effects of self-imposed contingencies are being analyzed within separate areas of academic responding in order to specify more precisely the effects of self-contingency management.

The evidence from the present experiment, that self-scheduling of events is associated with accelerated performance, is supported, in part, by a recent experiment (Lovitt and Curtiss, 1968). In order to investigate the effects of choice as an independent variable, students were given a number of daily sessions, each comprising three phases. One phase consisted of assigned mathematics, one of assigned reading, and one of a choice period in which the students could select either reading or mathematics. The results revealed that the students' rates of responding were greater during choice periods than during no-choice periods. It appeared that, for the students in this study, being allowed to choose (even between two academic tasks) was the critical variable.

If continued explorations with self-contingency management reveal similar findings, the educational implications appear rather obvious, for not only does the individual begin to develop self-managing skills by arranging certain aspects of his own environment, but in so doing his academic performance increases.

Research is now in progress to specify other components of self-management. Once these elements have been detailed, not only can they be scheduled sequentially, but each can be independently manipulated to evaluate its effect on academic responding. One study currently being conducted is comparing differences in student performance when a child has available a graph showing his daily performance rates *versus* when he is not provided a graph of these data. A second investigation is designed to evaluate the effects on academic performance when a student plots his own performance data *versus* when the teacher does the plotting. Another study is concerned with the function of specifying academic requirements. During certain phases of this study, the teacher sets the program limits, while during other portions, the student specifies the limits for daily performance.

Self-management no doubt involves behaviors other than those specified in this report. The fact remains, however, that if education is committed to educate students so that they can not only discriminate a number of teacher-arranged stimuli, but also arrange their own environment – hence control their own behavior – we must conceive of these self-controlling behaviors as capable of being taught and learned. The behaviors leading toward self-management, therefore, must be independently investigated and sequentially arranged to formulate a self-management curriculum.

REFERENCES

Haring, N. G. and Kunzelmann, H. P. The finer focus of therapeutic behavioral management. *Educational therapy*, Vol. 1. Seattle: Special Child Publications, 1966. Pp. 225–251.

Haring, N. G. and Lovitt, T. C. Operant methodology and educational technology in special education. In N. G. Haring & R. L. Schiefelbush (Eds.), *Methods in special education*. New York: McGraw-Hill, 1967. Pp. 12–48.

Lovitt, T. C. and Curtiss, K. A. Choice as an independent variable. Unpublished manuscript, University of Washington, 1968.

Sullivan Associates Program, *Programmed reading*. Cynthia Buchanan, Director. New York: Webster Division, McGraw-Hill, 1963.

Singer Mathematics Program. *Sets and Numbers*. Patrick Suppes, Director. New York: L. W. Singer Company, 1965.

ARTICLE 37

The Effect of Self-Recording on the Classroom Behavior of Two Eighth Grade Students*

MARCIA BRODEN, R. VANCE HALL and BRENDA MITTS[1]

University of Kansas

Abstract: The effects of self-recording on classroom behavior of two junior high school students was investigated. In the first experiment study behavior of an eighth grade girl in history class was recorded. Following baseline observations her counselor provided slips for the girl to record whether or not she studied in class. This resulted in an increase in study. When slips were withdrawn study decreased and then increased once self-recording was reinstated. After teacher praise for study was increased, self-recording was discontinued without significant losses in study behavior. In the final phase increased praise was also withdrawn and study remained at a high level. In the second experiment the number of talk-outs emitted by an eighth grade boy were recorded during math period. Following baseline slips for recording talk-outs were issued for the first half of the period, for the second half, and then for the entire period. Talk-outs decreased when self-recording was in effect and increased again when self-recording was discontinued. When self-recording was reinstituted in the final phase there was a slight, though not significant decrease in talking out when compared to the Baseline$_2$ condition.

Helping a student acquire appropriate study behaviors has probably been a problem since schools began. Various techniques including counseling, special classes and use of the leather strap have been tried. Very

*Reprinted from the *Journal of Applied Behavior Analysis*, Vol. 4, No. 3, 1971. Copyright by the Society for the Experimental Analysis of Behavior Inc.

[1]The authors wish to express appreciation to observer Betty Smith and to Kenneth Tewell, Robert Clark, Larry Odom and Leo Richter of the Bonner Springs, Kansas Public Schools for their complete cooperation in making this study possible.

This study is part of the research conducted at the Juniper Gardens Children's Project and is partially supported by the National Institute of Child Health and Human Development (HD-03144-03) Bureau of Child Research and Department of Human Development and Family Life, University of Kansas.

Reprints may be obtained from R. Vance Hall, Juniper Gardens Children's Project, 2021 North Third Street, Kansas City, Kansas 66101.

often these approaches have been ineffective and parents, teachers and students have resigned themselves to a year of problems and frustration.

Since the 1960's a concerted effort has been made to systematically apply behavior modification principles in the public school classroom. In a number of studies it was shown that giving attention for a behavior immediately after it occurred caused this behavior to increase in strength while consistently ignoring a behavior frequently resulted in a decrease in strength. Broden and Hall (1968), Hall, Lund and Jackson (1968), and Thomas, Becker, and Armstrong (1968) successfully used this technique to affect study behavior in the classroom by having teachers attend only to study or non-disruptive behaviors while ignoring non-study or disruptive ones, Hall, Fox, Willard, Goldsmith, Emerson, Owen, Davis and Porcia (1971) used teacher attention, feedback, praise and other available reinforcers to control disputing and talking out behaviors in various classrooms.

The use of behavior modification principles was expanded to include varied techniques by other experimenters. Madsen, Becker, and Thomas (1968) assessed the effect of rules as well as ignoring and praising behaviors. Peer control of arithmetic and spelling scores was demonstrated in a study by Evans and Oswalt (1967). Barrish, Saunders and Wolf (1969) used a loss of classroom privileges to reduce out-of-seat and talking-out behaviors in a fourth grade class. Hall, Panyan, Rabon and Broden (1968) showed that teacher attention, a study game, and loss of time for a between period break were effective in increasing the study behavior of an entire class.

McKenzie, Clark, Wolf, Kothera and Benson (1968) used a token system backed by privileges and allowances to increase academic performance in a special education classroom. Broden, Hall, Dunlap and Clark (1970) increased study behavior in a junior high special education class using a point system in which points were redeemable for privileges available in the class and school. They demonstrated that while praise was effective in modifying behaviors, praise coupled with points issued contingently for acceptable behaviors seemed more effective on the junior high level.

Each of the methods listed, while successful, involved a relatively systematic effort on the part of the teacher to initiate the behavior change or to monitor and reinforce the desired behaviors. None of these studies dealt with the problem of what to do with a student in a room where the teacher doesn't want to or "can't" work with a specific student. Such situations are often found in secondary level classrooms where teacher lectures are a primary form of instruction.

The method used in the present study was self-recording. It was initially an effort to assess whether a subject's recording of his own behavior would help increase or decrease its occurrence, and whether someone not in the classroom could modify classroom behavior. It was also an attempt to assess a procedure whereby self-recording could be withdrawn with no significant decrease in study once higher study rates had been established.

EXPERIMENT I

Subject and Setting

Liza was an eighth grade girl enrolled in a history class at Bonner Springs Junior High, Bonner Springs, Kansas. She was doing poorly in history (her grade was a D—) and had told the counselor she was interested in doing better in school. The counselor set up weekly counseling sessions with Liza but found that according to the teacher and to Liza, just talking over a problem had not carried over into the class setting.

Liza's history class met daily immediately after lunch for 40 minutes. The teacher, a young man, stood near the front of the room throughout most of the period. Liza sat toward the back of the room. Classes were primarily lecture sessions in which the teacher talked as he stood in the front of the class. There was some class discussion when the teacher interspersed questions within the lecture.

The counselor and the experimenter had approached the teacher about giving increased attention to Liza for study. The teacher expressed a willingness to cooperate but felt that due to the lecture format of the class and the amount of material he had to cover each day he could not consistently attend to Liza for studying. For this reason it was decided to use self-recording with the counselor as the agent for initiating and carrying out the experimental procedures.

Observation

An observer entered the classroom during a five-minute break preceding the class and took a seat at the back of the room. She observed for 30 minutes of the 40 minute session, beginning when the bell rang signifying the start of class. She left during a break at the end of the class session. Pupil behaviors were recorded at the end of each ten seconds of observation. Teacher attention to Liza was recorded whenever it occurred. Liza was not told she was being observed.

Pupil behaviors were dichotomized into study and non-study behaviors. "Study" was defined as attending to a teacher-assigned task and meant that when it was appropriate, Liza should be facing the teacher, writing down lecture notes, facing a child who was responding to a teacher question or reciting when called upon by the teacher. "Non-study" behaviors meant Liza was out of her seat without permission, talking out without being recognized by the teacher, facing the window, fingering non-academic objects such as her makeup, comb, purse, or working on an assignment for another class.

Data were recorded on sheets composed of double rows of squares with each square representing the passage of ten seconds of time (*see* Hall, Lund, & Jackson, 1968). The top row was used to record teacher attention which was recorded whenever the teacher called on or spoke to Liza. The bottom row was used to record Liza's study or non-study behaviors.

Reliability checks were made at least once during each phase of the study. During these checks another observer made simultaneous and independent observations. After the observation the sheets were compared and scored interval by interval for the number of intervals of agreement. The total number of intervals of agreement were divided by the total number of intervals observed and this figure was multiplied by 100 to obtain a percentage figure. Agreement of the records for this study ranged from 87 to 96% for study behavior and 100% for teacher attention.

Method

Baseline$_1$ Baseline data were recorded for seven days prior to experimental procedures. The counselor saw the subject twice during this time for a weekly conference (a procedure followed prior to recording data and continued throughout the study).

Self-Recording$_1$ On the eighth day of observation the counselor met the subject in conference and gave her a slip containing three rows of ten squares (*see* Fig. 37.1) and directed her to record her study behavior "when she thought of it" during her history class sessions. Some aspects of study behavior were discussed at this time including a definition of what constituted studying.

Liza was instructed to take the slip to class each day and to record a "+" in the square if she was studying or had been doing so for the last

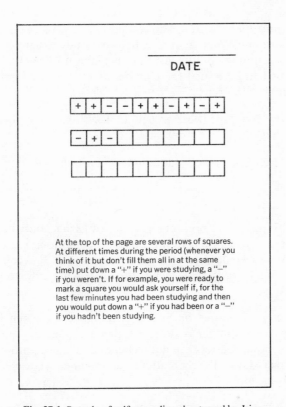

At the top of the page are several rows of squares. At different times during the period (whenever you think of it but don't fill them all in at the same time) put down a "+" if you were studying, a "−" if you weren't. If for example, you were ready to mark a square you would ask yourself if, for the last few minutes you had been studying and then you would put down a "+" if you had been or a "−" if you hadn't been studying.

Fig. 37.1. Sample of self-recording sheet used by Liza.

few minutes, and a "−" if she wasn't studying at the time she thought to record. Sometime before the end of the school day she was to turn it in to the counselor. The slips were available each day from the counselor and could be obtained during breaks between classes. At the weekly pupil-counselor conference the self-recording slips were discussed and the counselor praised Liza's reports of study behavior emphasizing the days when the per cent of plus marks was high.

Baseline₂ Slips were not issued for five days (days 14 through 18). When, on the second day of Baseline₂ Liza requested one, the counselor stated that she was out of slips and would tell her when she got more.

Self-Recording₂ Slips were once again handed to the subject by the counselor at some time prior to history period and Liza was instructed to record her study and non-study behavior.

Self-Recording Plus Praise   The teacher was asked to attend to Liza "whenever he could" and to praise her for study whenever possible. Slips for self-recording continued to be available to Liza and counselor praise continued to be issued for plus marks on the self-recording slips during the weekly conference.

Praise Only   No slips were issued to Liza. Teacher attention continued at a higher rate than during Baseline.

Baseline₃   Increased teacher attention was withdrawn.

Results

Baseline₁   Figure 37.2 presents a record of Liza's study behavior and of teacher verbal attention. During Baseline conditions Liza had a low rate of study (30%) despite two conferences with the counselor and promises to "really try." The mean rate of teacher attention was two times per session.

Self-Recording₁   During the Self-Recording₁ phase when Liza began to record her classroom behavior, a significant change in study behavior was noted. It increased to 78% and remained at that approximate level for the next six days. Teacher attention remained at a mean level of two times per session.

Baseline₂   On the fourteenth day of observation Liza was told by the counselor there were no more recording slips available. The first day under these conditions the rate of study was 70%. It then dropped to an average of 27% for the next four days. Teacher attention averaged 2.5 times per session.

Self-Recording₂   When recording slips were again issued to Liza her study rate increased to an average of 80%. However, when on two days no slips were issued (on days 20 and 27) the rate declined to 30% and 22% respectively. During this phase the teacher gave Liza attention approximately 1.7 times per class session.

Self-Recording Plus Praise   On day 30 the teacher was again asked to praise Liza or give her increased attention when she studied. At this point the teacher agreed to do so since Liza was now engaging in a higher rate of study and he felt it would be easy and justified to do so. In this phase teacher attention increased to 3.5 times per session. Liza continued

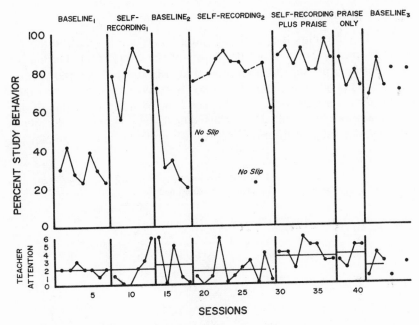

Fig. 37.2. A record of Liza's study behavior and/or teacher attention for study during: *Baseline₁* — Prior to experimental procedures; *Self-Recording₁* — Liza recorded study or non-study on slips provided by counselor; *Baseline₂* — Self-recording slips withdrawn; *Self-Recording₂* — Self-recording slips reinstated; *Self-Recording Plus Praise* — Self-recording slips continued and teacher praise for study increased; *Praise Only* — Increased teacher praise maintained and self-recording withdrawn. *Baseline₃* — Teacher praise decreased to baseline levels.

to carry slips to class, sometimes filling them out and sometimes not. Under these conditions study increased to 88%.

Praise Only On day 38 the Praise Only phase was begun and slips were discontinued. Teacher attention was observed to be at a mean rate of 3.7 times per session. Liza's study rate averaged 77%.

Baseline₃ The teacher was then asked to decrease the amount of attention to Liza. During this Baseline₃ phase no marked decrease in study rate was evident, though there was some decline. The first three joined points of the Baseline₃ phase represent consecutive days following the Praise Only phase. The three separated points represent post check days with approximately one week intervals between observations which further indicates increased study was being maintained.

Subject's Record Vs. Observer's Record

Table 37.1 presents the levels of study recorded by Liza and the observer during the Self-Recording phases of the experiment. During the Self-Recording$_1$ phase, Liza recorded study or non-study on the average of 12 times per session. There was very little correlation between Liza's and the observer's estimates of the per cent of study on a day-to-day basis. Variations between records ranged up to 29%. However, the means of the overall subject-observer records were similar. For example, the

Table 37.1. A record of per cent of study recorded by the observer and by Liza during self-recording phases of Experiment I

Experimental phase	Observer	Liza
Self-Recording$_1$	78%	80%
	54%	70%
	79%	—
	92%	63%
	82%	79%
	80%	90%
Mean	78%	76%
Self-Recording$_2$	75%	60%
	Probe "A"	
	78%	100%
	87%	80%
	90%	Forgot
	84%	Forgot
	84%	Forgot
	79%	75%
	Probe "B"	
	83%	90%
	59%	Forgot
Mean	80%	81%
Self-Recording$_3$	89%	Forgot
Plus Praise	93%	Forgot
	83%	Forgot
	92%	Forgot
	81%	66%
	81%	100%
	96%	Forgot
	88%	100%
Mean	88%	89%

mean of Liza's estimate of her study behavior during Baseline was 76%. The observer's record revealed that Liza actually studied an average of 78% of the time.

During the Self-Recording$_2$ phase there was a decrease in the number of times Liza recorded to 11 marks per class. On four days she did not record at all. Liza's mean estimate of her study was 81%, the observer's was 80%. Again there was little correlation, however, between Liza's record and the observer's record on a day-to-day basis.

The number of times Liza recorded during the Self-Recording Plus Praise condition declined markedly to 2.3 times per session and Liza recorded on only three of the nine days during this experimental phase. Liza's mean estimate of study was 89%, that of the observer was 88%.

There was, of course, no self-recording during the other phases of the experiment.

EXPERIMENT II

Subject and Setting

The second subject, Stu, was an eighth grade boy enrolled in a fifth period math class at the same school. He was referred by his teacher, a man, who expressed a desire to find some means to "shut Stu up." He reportedly talked out in class continually, disturbing both the teacher and his classmates. The class was composed of 28 "low" achieving students. It met for 25 minutes and then students went to lunch, returning afterward for another 20 minutes of class.

Observation

Observation records of Stu's behavior were made on sheets identical to those used in the previous experiment. The category of "talking out" was added, however, to the observation code. A talk-out was defined as "any verbalization which occurred during class which had not been recognized by the teacher and was recorded if it occurred at any time within each 10 second interval. Since some of Stu's talk-outs were not audible to the observer, both audible talk-outs and instances when Stu's lips moved while facing another student and while another student was facing him were considered as talk-outs. Study behavior and teacher attention to the subject were also recorded. Reliability of observation during each experimental phase was assessed in a manner similar to that used in the first study. Agreement of the records on the number of talk-outs ranged from 84 to 100%.

Method

Baseline₁   For nine days prior to initiation of experimental procedures data were recorded during the first half (Session A) of the period. On days 1, 4, 5, 6, and 8 data were recorded during the second half of the period (Session B) as well.

Self-Recording, Session A   During the first experimental phase the teacher handed a slip of paper to Stu at the beginning of class with the instructions to use it and that it would be collected during lunch. A facsimile of the slip is shown in Fig. 37.3. On it was printed a rectangular

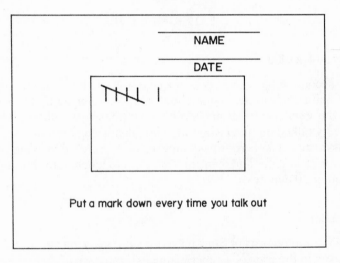

Fig. **37.3**. Sample of self-recording sheet used by Stu.

box about two inches by five inches and the statement "record a mark every time you talk out without permission." At the top of the slip was a place for the subject's name and the date. No further instructions were given to him.

Self-Recording, Session B   Slips were not issued during Session A but were given to Stu just before Session B began. No contingencies were in effect during Session A.

Self-Recording (Sessions A and B)₁ Stu was given the slip at the beginning of class and told to record all period (both Session A and Session B). He was told the slip would be collected at the end of class.

Baseline₂ Self-recording slips were not issued for any part of the math period.

Self-Recording (Sessions A and B)₂ Self-recording slips were issued and Stu was told to record talk-outs for the entire period and that the slips would be collected at the end of class.

Results

Baseline₁ During the Baseline phase Stu talked out on the average of 1.1 times per min. for the first half of the period and 1.6 times a min. during Session B (*see* Fig. 37.4).

Self-Recording, Session A When the teacher began issuing slips to Stu for Session A, the frequency of his talk-outs declined during Session

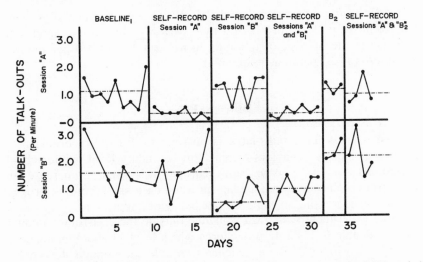

Fig. 37.4. A record of Stu's talking-out behavior during Sessions A and B of fifth period math class: *Baseline₁* – Prior to experimental procedures; *Self-Record, Session A* – Stu recorded his talk-outs during Session A only; *Self-Record, Session B* – Stu recorded his talk-outs during Session B only; *Self-Record, Sessions (A and B)₁* – Stu recorded his talk-outs during both math class sessions; *Baseline₂* – Return to Baseline conditions, self-recording slips withdrawn; *Self-Record (A and B)₂* – Stu recorded his talk-outs for both A and B Sessions.

A to 0.3 times a min. The frequency of these talk-outs during Session B, however, remained at 1.6 times a min.

Self-Recording, Session B   After giving Stu the sheet seven days for Session A the teacher commented that "it is the second half of the period which has always been the problem," so contingencies were reversed. Slips were issued only during the second half of the period. The rate of verbalizing without permission during Session B declined to 0.5 times a min. However, the rate of talking out during Session A, which was not under self-recording contingencies increased to 1.2 times a min.

Self-Recording (Sessions A and B)₁   When slips were issued for both A and B Sessions the mean talk-out rate during A was 0.3 times per min. while that for B was 1.0 per min., both well below baseline rates.

Baseline₂   When slips were no longer furnished Stu during a second baseline phase the rate of talk-outs increased to a mean of 1.3 during Session A and 2.3 per min. during Session B.

Self-Recording (Sessions A and B)₂   When self-recording slips were again issued for the entire period there was a slight but not significant decrease in the number of talk-outs to a mean rate of 1.0 per min. in Session A and 2.2 per min. in Session B.

DISCUSSION

These studies indicated that it is possible to use self-recording procedures to modify behaviors of pupils in secondary level public school classrooms. In Liza's case, self-recording was used to increase an appropriate behavior (study) while in Stu's case self-recording proved effective in decreasing an inappropriate behavior (talking out).

In the experiment with Liza someone outside the classroom, a counselor, was able to institute procedures which brought about an increase in study to a point that the teacher was able to maintain it with his attention and/or the other reinforcers already available in the classroom. Previous research has shown that systematic teacher attention can be used to increase study rates of elementary pupils (Hall, Lund, *et al.*, 1968; Hall, Panyan, *et al.*, 1968). Broden and Hall (1968) demonstrated that teacher attention was also effective at the junior high school level. There were indications, however, that secondary level teachers were sometimes reluctant to carry out procedures which did not seem to fit their teaching style.

In Liza's case initially the teacher did not feel he could systematically increase his attention for study due to the lecture-discussion format he used. On the first day of Baseline$_2$, however, when the self-recording slips had been withdrawn Liza's study behavior had remained at a high level. An analysis of the data showed that she had received an uncharacteristically high rate of attention from the teacher on that day (5 times). This indicated that it might eventually be possible to withdraw the slips and maintain high study rates and that the teacher might willingly increase his attention to Liza for study if her study rate was already at a high level. The drop in study rate on the second day and subsequent days of Baseline$_2$ indicated that Liza was still very much under the control of self-recording.

The effects of issuing self-recording slips was further confirmed in the Self-Recording$_2$ phase. When probes were inserted and she was given no slips on days 20 and 27 there were accompanying drops in study rates on those days. It is of interest to note that study dropped on day 27 despite the fact that by this second probe, Liza had begun "forgetting" to record her study and non-study behavior on some days. This would indicate the possibility that the slip itself had become a cue or discriminative stimulus (S^D) for study whether or not it was used for self-recording. Liza's record of her study behavior did not correlate with the observer's record. However, it is important to note that correlation between Liza's estimate and her actual behavior was not necessary to achieve or maintain high study rates.

When the slips were withdrawn in the Praise Only phase, study was maintained at an acceptable level. Even when increased praise was withdrawn in the Baseline$_3$ phase, study remained at acceptable levels. Although it would have been interesting to have continued the Baseline$_3$ phase for a longer period the experiment was terminated due to the close of the school term. Even so, the data indicated that once higher study levels were achieved and maintained for a period of time that slips and high rates of teacher attention could be withdrawn without significant reductions in study. There was some subjective evidence that Liza's increased study may have resulted in increased academic performance since her report card grade in history increased from D— to C.

Although the experiment with Stu was in many ways a replication of the first study there were several important differences. Liza had expressed a desire, in fact had requested help, to improve her study behavior.

Her counselor praised her when she reported high study rates on the self-recording slips. Later her teacher began attending to her and praising her for study once higher rates were achieved.

Stu, on the other hand, had not expressed concern or asked for help in decreasing his talking-out behavior. The teacher rather than a counselor was the agent for dispensing the self-recording slips to Stu. Another difference was that no attempt was made to differentially reinforce him with praise or attention for the decreases in talking out that were observed. Previous research (Hall, Fox, Willard, Goldsmith, Emerson, Owen, Davis, & Porcia, 1971) indicates that doing so would have increased the effectiveness of the procedures used. In spite of these factors it seems that initially issuing slips and having Stu record on them did affect his talking-out behavior. As in Liza's case this was true even though there was very little correlation between the number of talk-outs recorded by Stu and the observer's record. This is illustrated by the fact that on days 10, 11, and 12, the observer's record showed that Stu's talk-outs were occurring at 0.4, 0.3 and 0.3 times per min. On the same days however, Stu recorded 1.5, 0.5 and 0.8 talk-outs per min. That self-recording had little effect during the final phase of the experiment may have been due to the fact that no contingencies were ever applied to differential rates of talking out and the slips thus lost their effectiveness. Further research, however, will be necessary to determine if this is the case. Furthermore, the records kept of his study behavior indicated that initially self-recording of talk-outs may have affected his overall study rate. However, this effect was not conclusive or lasting. When self-recording was instituted for Session A, study increased from 30% to 55%. When self-recording was instituted for Session B, study increased from 24% to 42% while it decreased to 32% in Session A. When self-recording was instituted for the entire period, however, study decreased to 24%.

Perhaps the most promising feature of self-recording will be to use it as a procedure for initiating desirable levels of appropriate behavior to a point where the teacher can more easily reinforce the desired behavior with attention, praise, grades or other reinforcers available in the classroom.

REFERENCES

Barrish, H., Saunders, M., and Wolf, M. M. Good behavior game: Effects of individual contingencies for group consequences on disruptive behavior in a regular classroom. *Journal of Applied Behavior Analysis*, 1969, 2, 119–124.

Broden, M., & Hall, R. V. Effects of teacher attention on the verbal behavior of two junior high school pupils. Paper presented at Council for Exceptional Children Convention, New York, 1968.

Broden, M., Hall, R. V., Dunlap, A., & Clark, R. Effects of teacher attention and a token reinforcement system in a junior high school special education class. *Exceptional Children*, 1970, **36**, 341-349.

Evans, G., & Oswalt, G. Acceleration of academic progress through the manipulation of peer influence. *Behaviour Research and Therapy*, 1967, **5**, 1-7.

Hall, R. V., & Broden, M. Behavior changes in brain-injured children through social reinforcement. *Journal of Experimental Child Psychology*, 1967, **5**, 463-479.

Hall, R. V., Fox, R., Willard, D., Goldsmith, L., Emerson, M., Owen, M., Davis, F., Porcia, E. The teacher as observer and experimenter in the modification of disputing and talking out behaviors. *Journal of Applied Behavior Analysis*, 1971.

Hall, R. V., Lund, D., & Jackson, D. Effects of teacher attention on study behavior. *Journal of Applied Behavior Analysis*, 1968, **1**, 1-12.

Hall, R. V., Panyan, M., Rabon, D., & Broden, M. Teacher applied contingencies and appropriate classroom behavior. *Journal of Applied Behavior Analysis*, 1968, **1**, 315-322.

Madsen, C., Jr., Becker, W., & Thomas, D. Rules, praise, and ignoring: Elements of elementary classroom control. *Journal of Applied Behavior Analysis*, 1968, **1**, 139-150.

McKenzie, H., Clark, M., Wolf, M., Kothera, R., & Benson, C. Behavior modification of children with learning disabilities using grades as tokens and allowances as back up reinforcers. *Exceptional Children*, 1968, **34**, 745-752.

Thomas, D., Becker, W., & Armstrong, M. Production and elimination of disruptive classroom behavior by systematically varying teacher's behavior. *Journal of Applied Behavior Analysis*, 1968, **1**, 35-45.

Zimmerman, E., & Zimmerman, J. The alteration of behavior in a special classroom situation. *Journal of the Experimental Analysis of Behavior*, 1962, **5**, 59-60.

CHAPTER 12

The Implementation of Behavioral Principles in Your Classroom

ASSESSMENT

The previous chapters have presented a general introduction to behavior modification and provide examples of classroom demonstrations of behavioral approaches to classroom management. This chapter presents and discusses many of the practical aspects of employing behavioral procedures in the classroom. The practical problems the teacher must deal with will be discussed in the order in which she usually considers such issues when she is faced with a possible "problem child." A typical decision-making process might proceed as follows: The teacher first identifies the problem child and then consults other teachers and professional staff members who are familiar with the child, and makes decisions regarding the possible referral of the child to a consultant or agency. If she decides to deal with the problem herself, she becomes concerned with making a more detailed assessment of the problem situation, with implementing procedures to alleviate the problem, and with relating her approach to parents and other school personnel. Let us consider each of these decision areas in more detail.

Identification of Problem Children

For a number of reasons children are often not identified as problem children until they reach school age. Behaviors which are tolerated at home may not be tolerated in the classroom. Problems which go unnoticed or ignored in the pre-school years may become more obvious when the child is in school. Finally, the school situation may exacerbate or produce difficulties in relatively problem-free children. Early detection of problem children is clearly advantageous. Many problem behaviors become more difficult to change the longer they are left untreated, and more and more areas of a child's life are affected if a problem is allowed to continue. For example, if a child has poor vision, the parents may not be aware of the problem before the child enters school partly because the pre-school child isn't usually presented with situations which require normal visual acuity e.g., reading small print. Once he is in school, his reading will be affected. If his vision is not corrected, he will experience a considerable amount of failure and may become disruptive since he receives little approval for academic success, but can gain attention by disrupting the class. Fortunately, most vision and hearing problems are detected by the school's health personnel who routinely examine all children. However, many problems are not so easily and routinely detected by student service personnel. The responsibility of identifying existing or potential social and academic problems rests with the teacher because she has a unique opportunity to observe the child in many diverse situations. Several studies have investigated the degree to which teachers, psychologists, psychiatrists, and children have similar attitudes towards children's problems. Approximately 30 years ago, teachers tended to rate disruptive behavior more seriously than withdrawn behaviors while psychologists considered the withdrawn behaviors more serious than the disruptive ones (Wickman, 1928). Over the years (Beilin, 1959; Bower, 1966), agreement between teachers and clinicians has improved. Interestingly, children rank classroom problems more like teachers rank them than do psychologists (Zin, 1970). It is important to emphasize that differences between teachers' and clinicians' evaluations of children's problems do not imply that the teacher is wrong about her evaluations. After all, the teacher observes the child's reactions to peers and other adults, to success and failure, to both academic and social demands, and in both structured and unstructured settings. In essence, the teacher often knows the child better than anyone else—certainly better than the psychologist and occasionally even better than his parents know him. In fact, long term studies of children referred to child guidance clinics indicate that the teachers may have been right in their greater concern for the disruptive child than for the withdrawn child. Robbins (1966) found that the disruptive or "acting-out" child was referred for psychiatric aid in his adult life more frequently than was the withdrawn or nervous child.

While it may be true that the excessively withdrawn child is less likely to be a problem when he grows up than is the "acting-out" child, there are some special difficulties in identifying the withdrawn child who is a problem in elementary school. The withdrawn child whose academic work is adequate does not usually disrupt either the teacher or the rest of the class. As a consequence, the teacher may not realize that such a child is deficient in social skills or is unhappy. Even when she is aware of these problems she may ignore them, perhaps because she feels she must deal with disruptive children in the class first.

Granting that early detection is desirable and that the teacher is in a particularly good position to identify problems, what are the types of problems that the teacher may expect to encounter? First there are problems which occur infrequently and which are usually identified in the pre-school years but which sometimes go unnoticed or untreated until the child is in school. Included in this group are autism, mental retardation, childhood schizophrenia, minimal brain damage, enuresis (bed wetting), physical handicaps (severe hearing or vision loss), speech difficulties (stuttering or stammering), and epilepsy. Autism occurs in a very small percentage of the population and is characterized by behaviors such as extreme aloneness, speech disturbances (mutism or parrot-like speech), obsession for sameness, idiosyncratic eating patterns, and purposeless and repetitive activity. Retardation is often noticed when a child who enters nursery school, kindergarten or first grade, is particularly slow in language development or self-help skills. Approximately 2.5% of all children have IQ's below 70 and are called retarded. Thus a retarded child of 10 years may be expected to behave most like a 7-year-old child. Childhood schizophrenia is identified with behaviors such as little interest in daily activities, hyper- or hypo-activity, extreme fearful reactions, and peculiar thinking or verbal behavior. Children with minimal brain damage are usually hyperactive, impulsive, distractible, poor in arithmetic and have a short attention span. Epilepsy occurs in 7 out of every 100,000 children of school age (Bakwin & Bakwin, 1967). The epileptic seizure or attack varies from often unnoticed petit mal attacks to violent grand mal seizures. Enuresis (day or night wetting or both) occurs in about 15% of all 4-year-old children, in 10% of all 6-year-olds, and in 4% of all 12-year-olds (Lovibond, 1964).

A regular classroom teacher may rarely be faced with children who fit into any of the problem areas above, but she should certainly be aware of their existence. However, we can say with certainty that she will frequently encounter problems like those discussed in the previous chapters of the book. Briefly, this group of problem behaviors includes hyperactivity, distructive behaviors, aggression, isolation, disobedience, short attention span, fears, lieing, frequent physical complaints, unhappiness, and truancy.

Given the broad range of behaviors which are at least potential problems and the varying degree to which any particular child will display problem behaviors, the teacher needs some guidelines by which to make an initial evaluation of a child's problem. One can be fairly certain that the child requires some special attention (1) if his social behavior interferes significantly with his academic work, (2) if he interferes with the other children's academic work or social behavior, (3) if he interferes with the teacher's ability to operate effectively, or (4) if the child is unusually withdrawn.

At this point we offer a word of caution. There is a general tendency to label problem children as emotionally disturbed, retarded, brain damaged, or even schizophrenic. Almost any experienced educator will attest to the fact that once a child is labeled "abnormal" he will have considerably more difficulty regaining a "normal" label than he had in acquiring the "abnormal" label. We can see no advantage in hastily applied labels. The assumption "if we can classify or label the problem child, then we know how to treat him," is unjustly optimistic considering the state of our knowledge regarding the relationship between diagnosis and treatment. Premature labeling not only allows us to fool ourselves into thinking that the problem is nearly solved but also may have the effect of *creating* a child who lives up to his label. Teachers, parents, and other children convey to the "emotionally disturbed" child their expectations of how an "emotionally disturbed" child should behave, e.g., unpredictably, disruptively, or incompetently. Believing that this is how he should behave, the problem child often is surprisingly adept at fulfilling our expectations. Because of the problems inherent in the labeling process, some teachers prefer not to read any of their children's folders until they have spent six or eight weeks with the children. Children do respond differently to various teachers, and since a teacher who reads that a child was a "problem child" might respond to him as such, it is probably a good practice to avoid reading case records or reports about pupils until the teacher has formed his own opinion of the child.

Referral decisions

Since teachers are not expected to deal with all types of children's problems entirely on their own, most school systems hire a number of professional personnel who provide special services to the teachers and children. While the particular service personnel vary from school to school, a full complement would include school counselors, school psychologists, school social workers, nurses, doctors, reading specialists, speech therapists, and people trained to diagnose hearing and vision problems. A new teacher should quickly (1) become acquainted with her school's general referral policies and procedures, (2) locate the service personnel in her school, and (3) determine the responsibilities, capabilities, and limitations of these individuals. In addition to the services provided by the school, there are often a number of community agencies to which a child may be referred, e.g., child guidance clinics, speech and hearing centers, tutoring services, community or university psychological clinics, medical clinics, and specialists in private practice. The school may provide the teacher with information about agencies to whom she can refer a parent in conjunction with in-service teacher training programs, but the teacher should be prepared to acquire some of the information on her own or to encourage the school to take a more active role by inviting people from the community to describe their facilities.

The functions normally performed by school service personnel vary considerably from school to school and from individual to individual. However, a brief general description of the typical activities of the school psychologist, counselor, and social worker is useful for emphasizing the responsibility of the teacher in assessing and treating problem children. Traditionally the school psychologist spends most of his time administering intelligence and personality tests which he uses as the basis for a report to the teacher. The report is likely to contain the psychologist's general reaction to the child, a description of the child's intellectual abilities relative to those of other children of his age, and a judgement regarding the personality factors which may be relevant to the child's problem. The school psychologist usually does not take an active part in treating the child but may make referral suggestions. It has been our experience that teachers find an intellectual and achievement assessment useful, especially when the child is young or new to the school. Unfortunately, the remainder of the psychologist's assessment report usually contains much information about the dynamics of the child's personality but few practical suggestions for a teacher.

In a number of states, a psychologist cannot assess a child's social or intellectual functioning without parental permission. This policy was adopted because of public concern about the validity of testing and fear that the psychologist would pry into a child's family life and family problems. Unfortunately the child with the most problems in the classroom is often the child whose parents will not approve any assessment or therapeutic endeavors of the psychologist. However, as has been evidenced in this book, children's behavior can be altered significantly without taking the child out of class for individual psychotherapy. That is, a psychologist can observe a child directly in the classroom, consult with the teacher, and aid the teacher in the evaluation of changes in the child's behavior in the classroom without parental permission.

In contrast to the diagnostically-oriented traditional psychologist, the school counselor typically takes an active part in treatment. At the junior or senior high school level the emphasis is likely to be on educational and vocational guidance. For instance, a counselor may give students advice concerning curricula, the types of vocational training facilities, or colleges best suited for the individual. In addition, the school counselor may offer individual or group counseling regarding emotional or behavioral problems. While clear evidence regarding the efficacy of group counseling is lacking, the school counselor may successfully use such an approach in teaching a person social skills — particularly where the counselor takes a directive role and where there is a decided emphasis on teaching social skills. It is generally assumed that these once-a-week sessions in the counselor's office will lead to changes in the child's personality which will be evident not only in the counselor's office but also at home or in the classroom. This assumption has questionable validity, particularly with respect to elementary school children who have considerable difficulty translating the counselor's suggestions into improved classroom behavior. As mentioned throughout this book, children's behavior is notoriously situation specific. Johnny may be no problem in the classroom and on the same day be a disruptive bully on the playground (Wahler, 1969).

The school social worker is also subject to the difficulties of situation specific behavior. She typically assumes, and often rightly so, that the source of school behavior problems is in the home. However, she also assumes that by focusing her attention on changes in the family situation, she will effect changes in the child's behavior at school. Just as they may behave differently in different school situations, children may be a problem at school without being a problem at home. In fact, it is likely that a large number of school problems develop as a result of factors which are unique to the school environment, e.g., competition with other children for the teacher's attention or difficulty with academic material. However, one should not overlook the fact that parent cooperation in a treatment program being conducted in the classroom can greatly facilitate its success, and by working in conjunction with the classroom teacher, the school social worker can encourage such parent cooperation and involvement. A social worker can probably be of most help by assuring the school or a family that they are getting all the social services that are due them under current law. For example, a social worker can acquaint the parent with available medical care, nursing care, food allowances, and home-based tutorial programs and should help the parent in acquiring such services. A social worker also may make home visits to insure that children are receiving proper food, clothing, and living facilities and to determine whether there is any evidence of physical or psychological neglect or abuse of a child.

Let us assume that the teacher has a good understanding of the nature of referral sources which are available to her and that she has identified a problem situation. Her next decision should be whether to deal with the problem herself or to involve her referral sources and if so, to what degree. It is difficult to outline a decision-making process which clearly prescribes the best solution for every problem. However, in cases where physical or medical factors are suspected of being major contributors to the problem, as in the case of hearing and vision problems and epilepsy, it is reasonable to say that referral to the appropriate persons is always advisable. Similarly, referrals to the school psychologist and/or the family doctor should be made routinely in cases of extremely bizarre behavior of the kind generally associated with autism and childhood schizophrenia and in cases of possible retardation. As mentioned earlier, the teacher should consider seeking consultation if (1) a child's social behavior interferes significantly with his academic behavior, (2) he interferes with the other children's academic or social behavior, (3) he interferes with the teacher's ability to operate effectively, or, (4) the child is unusually withdrawn. The extent to which a teacher will use referral sources for these cases will vary according to the teacher's competence and limitations, the nature of the particular problem, and the skill of available referral personnel.

If you are beginning to suspect that we believe the teacher can be competent enough to handle a significant number of classroom problems almost entirely on her own—you are correct. This is certainly not to say that we would advise against consultation. A discussion with service personnel or with another particularly skilful teacher can be extremely useful. However, teachers often overestimate the success and skills of service personnel while underestimating the importance and often the necessity of treating the problem within the classroom situation. The teacher should be aware of her own limitations, but she should be willing to take some responsibility for social behavior problems just as she takes responsibility for her students' academic progress.

We have already discussed the approach generally adopted by some of the traditional service personnel. If the teacher seeks help from a behaviorally-oriented psychologist, she should be prepared for a slightly different approach. A behavioral consultant is likely to begin by observing the problem child in the classroom on several occasions. He may then ask the teacher to assist in the assessment of the problem by recording certain aspects of the child's behavior and perhaps the behavior of his peers or her own behavior. He may decide to see the child on his own for a short time and gradually introduce his behavior change procedures into the classroom. Alternately he may suggest that the teacher implement a procedure in the classroom directly, often asking the teacher to take responsibility for the implementation with more and more intermittent consulting on his part.

At present, the availability of behaviorally-oriented school personnel is limited. There are very few university departments of education, special education, school counseling and psychology, and school social work which have a behavioral emphasis. Most of the research in the area of behavior modification in the schools is carried out in psychology departments. If a teacher or psychologist wishes to locate a behavioral consultant, we would suggest that he first contact the psychology department of nearby universities. If he is unable to obtain help there, he might write the members of the editorial boards of journals such as "Journal of Applied Behavior Analysis"[1] and "Behavior Research and Therapy."[2] It would be best to write to editorial board members who are in your own geographical area since they presumably would be most aware of the research and treatment programs within their own area. In contacting these people, you should be specific about the kind and frequency of consultation you wish.

If the teacher decides to seek help from professionals, there are several ways in which she can facilitate the treatment process. The problem should be specifically and objectively described. If the problem behavior is discrete and easily observable, e.g., hitting other children, the teacher can count the number of times the behavior occurs over a four- or five-day period, noting the situation at the time the behavior occurs and her

---

[1]Published by Department of Human Development, University of Kansas, Lawrence, Kansas 66044.
[2]Published by Pergamon Press, Maxwell House, Fairview Park, Elmsford, New York 11003.

reaction to it (*see* the discussion of more detailed assessment procedures below). The teachers can also provide the professional source with a synopsis of the child's school history and the opinions of other teachers the child has had. If the onset of the problem was sudden, any information the teacher can provide regarding changes in the classroom routine or the child's social and family environment would be useful. After the referral has been made, the teacher should continue to provide any information which she considers relevant regarding the problem behavior. Active and voluntary participation on her part will give the service personnel useful feedback concerning their effectiveness and will probably encourage direct and more effective treatment.

Assessment Measures

When the teacher elects to deal with the problem herself or when she is collaborating with a behavioral consultant, she will find that a detailed assessment of the problem situation is indispensible, not only prior to any treatment decisions but also during treatment and periodically following treatment. A variety of assessment techniques have been used in the classroom, and they are designed to serve any of several purposes: (1) to clearly and objectively describe the problem, (2) to clarify factors influencing the problem, (3) to aid in making decisions concerning treatment, (4) to evaluate the effects of treatment, (5) to provide information regarding the possible reappearance or increase in the severity of the problem following treatment, and (6) to provide information for teachers the child may have in the future. The anecdotal record (*see* Table 1) is the simplest procedure, but it has many disadvantages. Typically it consists of a short paragraph in which the teacher notes her general evaluation of the problem situation and any factors she feels may be relevant. An ancedotal record is useful in the initial stages of assessment because it focuses the teacher's attention on the specific behaviors which constitute the problem and some of the variables which may be contributing to

Table 1. Anecdotal Record

Sam has become increasingly difficult to handle in my 1st grade class. He picks fights almost every day. Although he has no real friends, he is interested in the other children. This concern about what everyone else is doing often leads to general disruption in the class. Sam ignores all pleas to return to his seat and work, but is constantly seeking my attention.

the problem. For example, from her sample ancedotal record we know that Sam's problem behaviors include fighting, inappropriate concern for the other children's activities, and attention seeking. There is the implication that he lacks adequate skills to make friends. Unfortunately, the ancedotal record yields a description of the problem behaviors which is general and which is unlikely to reflect gradual changes over time. Since the record is the teacher's personal subjective reaction to the situation, her own biases, emotions, and attitudes can easily influence the objectivity of the record and make it improbable that another observer would produce an equivalent evaluation of the situation. To the extent that the record is subjective, the usefulness of the record for reflecting treatment changes and aiding consultants or other teachers is limited.

A second classroom assessment tool is the checklist (*see* Table 2) which consists of a list of adjectives (Scarr, 1966) or, as exemplified here, descriptions of children's behaviors — usually problem behaviors. The teacher simply checks the behaviors which apply to the child in question. The checklist is potentially more objective than the ancedotal record if the items are well defined and cover a wide range of behaviors. The teacher's own biases have less influence on the checklist than on the anecdotal record and agreement between observers is easier to achieve. Since the checklist makes reliable observations of children's behavior possible, one can investigate the relation between the pattern of behaviors checked and such variables as treatment effectiveness and prognosis. Gross changes in the child's behavior over time may be reflected on the checklist. An additional advantage of the checklist is that it may alert the teacher to important behaviors which she had not focused on pre-

Table 2. Checklist

Child: *Sam*　　Date: *11/9/70*　　Teacher: *Mrs. A.*

_____	1. bites nails
✕	2. bites other children
✕	3. talks out of turn
_____	4. prefers to play by himself
_____	5. fails to complete assignments
✕	6. gives orders to other children
✕	7. is restless
✕	8. jealous of attention paid to other children
_____	9. has feelings of inferiority
✕	10. lack of interest — bored

viously. Some of the major disadvantages of the checklist are that it provides little information on the frequency of the problem behaviors, it is not very sensitive to gradual changes over time, it does not indicate in any way factors which may be influencing to problem behaviors, and it gives no information on the relative importance of the behaviors checked. It should be noted that there are big differences among checklists with respect to the specificity of the adjectives or behavior descriptions. The more specific and less global the items are, the more useful and meaningful the checklist will be.

The behavior rating scale is an adaptation of the checklist (*see* Table 3). In addition to checking the behaviors the problem child displays, the teacher notes the degree to which each behavior applied to the child (Peterson, 1961). Like the checklist, the rating scale is relatively objective, allows for reliability checks between two or more raters, and can be used as an indicator of behavior change. Its primary advantage over the checklist is that the rating scale provides some information, albeit crude, regarding the frequency and relative importance of the child's behaviors. Most of the checklist's shortcomings also apply to the rating scale.

The last assessment technique we shall discuss is the one used by the majority of investigators represented in this book—the assessment of target behaviors (O'Leary, Becker, Evans, & Saudargas, 1969; Barrish, Saunders, & Wolf, 1969; Becker, Madsen, Arnold, & Thomas, 1967). As will become apparent in the following discussion, target assessment has all the advantages of the anecdotal record checklist, or rating scale but few of their disadvantages. Target assessment can very objectively

Table 3. Rating Scale

Child: *Sam*　　Date: *11/9/70*　　Teacher: *Mrs. A.*

⓪	1	2	1. bites nails
0	①	2	2. bites other children
0	1	②	3. talks out of turn
0	①	2	4. prefers to play by himself
0	①	2	5. fails to complete assignments
0	①	2	6. gives orders to other children
0	1	②	7. is restless
0	1	②	8. jealous of attention paid to other children
⓪	1	2	9. has feelings of inferiority
0	1	②	10. lacks interest, is bored

Note: 0 = no problem, 1 = mild problem, 2 = severe problem.

describe problem behaviors, can suggest and evaluate factors influencing the problem situation, has implications for treatment, can be used to evaluate both short and long term effects of treatment, and is clearly meaningful to other people interested in the child's problem. After completing an anecdotal record and perhaps a checklist or behavior rating scale, the teacher has fairly well identified the behaviors which require modification, that is, the target behaviors.

She should also attempt to ascertain whether there are problems in the child's home which may be directly contributing to his classroom difficulties. Parent involvement both in the assessment and treatment stages can be extremely beneficial to all concerned.

The first step in proceeding with a target assessment is the careful specification of the target behaviors. See the behavior descriptions in Table 4. The behavior description or code should include all the behaviors the teacher wishes to observe and should specifically mention behaviors to be excluded from the category such as behaviors which are similar to the disruptive behaviors but which the teacher does not wish to include as disruptive (*see* especially the description of out-of-seat behavior). A good guideline for writing behavior descriptions is to make the descriptions as complete and unambiguous as possible so that another person could use the descriptions to produce observations of the child's behavior that would agree very closely with the teacher's ratings.

In Sam's case, the teacher might decide to focus on hitting other children, restlessness, and attention-seeking. Although Sam's boredom seems to be an important behavior, it is very difficult to specify the behaviors from which the teacher makes the conclusion that Sam is bored. One obvious factor related to boredom which can easily be assessed by the teacher is the level of Sam's academic performance. There are two possibilities. Sam may be doing poorly and is bored because he doesn't

Table 4. Behavioral Descriptions of Aggression, Vocalization, and Out-of-Seat for O'Leary. Kaufman. and Balsam

Symbol	Title	Description
A	Aggression	Child makes an intense movement directed at another person so as to come into contact with him, either directly or by using a material object as an extension of the hand.
		Includes: Blocking others with arms or body from attaining goal (e.g., while walking up aisle), Tripping, Kicking, Throwing.

Table 4 (*continued*)

Symbol	Title	Description (continued)
V	Vocalization	Any non-permitted "audible" behavior emanating from the mouth.
		Includes: If vocalization is obvious, but can't be heard (obvious—if another child responds), Answering without being called on, Moaning, Yawning, Belching, Crying, Shouting, "Operant" coughs.
		Excludes: Vocalization in response to teacher's question, Sneezing, Automatic coughing.
O	Out-of-Seat	Observable movement of the child from his seat when not permitted or requested by teacher. None of the child's weight is to be supported by his seat.
O	Out-of-Seat	*Includes:* Time limits on the following: Pencil sharpening—$1\frac{1}{2}$ minutes, Getting a drink—$1\frac{1}{2}$ minutes (fountain in room), Getting a book—$1\frac{1}{2}$ minutes, Going to the bathroom: (a) 2 minute limit, beginning with teacher's permission, (b) 30 second limit beginning when child leaves the bathroom.
		Note: If the child returns to his seat after $1\frac{1}{2}$ (or 2 minutes, where applicable), but during the 10 second inter-interval period, the "O" will be recorded in the 20 second interval just prior to the 10 second.
		Going to get a reading book during a math lesson, When child is fully standing and the back of legs touch his seat, Going to the teacher's desk when not permitted, Throwing away papers, Stretching.
		Excludes: Retrieval of an accidentally dropped task-related object, Leaning forward to pick up an object even if all contact with the seat is momentarily lost, providing the child is not standing fully erect on feet.
		Note: If teacher asks children to sit on the floor, then point of reference changes from seat to floor.

understand the assignments, or he may be doing well and is bored because he is not challenged. While this chapter focuses on social behavior problems, the teacher should be aware of the influence academic problems can have on social behaviors and take appropriate action with respect to academic problems as quickly as possible either by seeing that the child receives extra help or by providing him with more stimulating material.

  As mentioned above, Sam's teacher had decided to focus on hitting, restlessness, and attention-seeking. In writing the behavioral descriptions she must ask herself exactly what she means by hitting, restlessness, and attention-seeking. The only difficulty with observing hitting is the question of intention, e.g., was it a friendly tap or a punch; otherwise the description of aggression in Table 4 is easily developed. By restlessness the teacher may mean any number of things (*see* descriptions of out-of-seat, modified out-of-seat, touching other's property, playing and orienting in Appendix). For the purposes of our example, let us assume that Sam's most disruptive restless behavior seems to involve getting out of his seat. Attention-seeking may include coming to the teacher's desk frequently and talking out of turn. Since getting out of seat includes coming to the teacher's desk, no new category is required. Talking out of turn might best be described as vocalization (Table 4). Note that by focusing on aggression, out-of-seat, and vocalization, the teacher is directing her attention at only a few of Sam's behaviors and no attempt is made to achieve a comprehensive record of the entire range of his behaviors.

  Once the teacher has written descriptions of the disruptive behavior she is concerned about, she will use these codes to record the frequency of the behaviors. There are several procedures for recording behaviors. If teacher aides or volunteers are available, they can observe the behaviors. More frequently, the teacher will need to make the observations herself. It would be difficult for the teacher to make daily 20-minute observations as is typical of many of the studies in this book. There are at least two other options open to her. Event recording (Table 5) is appropriate if the behavior occurs infrequently (e.g., 0 to 5 times per day), or is of particularly short duration (e.g., talking out). The teacher can simply make a tally on a sheet of paper every time the behavior occurs. If duration is an important aspect of behavior (e.g., temper tantrums) she should record the duration of each behavioral event. The frequency or average duration of each behavior should be calculated each day. For more frequently occurring behaviors, a time sampling procedure (Table 6) is useful. The teacher might select two or three 15–30 minute intervals

Table 5. Event Recording: Number of Events/Day

	Monday	Tuesday	Wednesday	Thursday	Friday	Weekly Average
Aggression	///	𝄠𝄠	𝄠𝄠	////	////	
	3	5	6	4	4	4.4
Vocalization	𝄠𝄠 ///	𝄠𝄠 𝄠𝄠	𝄠𝄠 /	𝄠𝄠 𝄠𝄠 //	𝄠𝄠 𝄠𝄠 /	
	8	10	6	12	11	9.4

during the day when she will record the target behaviors. The interval selected, e.g., 30 min., should be divided into smaller segments, e.g., ten 3 min. segments. Every three minutes the teacher should look at the child and note whether the behavior is occurring (*see* Table 4). It is advisable to make observations in a variety of situations initially, e.g., small reading groups, lectures to the entire class, independent seat work, recess, or the first half-hour of the day, since some behaviors may occur in one or two situations but not in others. The situations in which the behavior occurs with the highest frequency should be selected for continued observation. At the end of each day, the teacher should calculate the average frequency of each behavior she is observing (Table 6). Plotting these daily averages on a graph provides a good visual description of the child's behavior changes.

Whenever possible, the teacher should have someone else make simultaneous observations in order to determine the reliability of the teacher's

Table 6. Time Sampling

Monday 10:00–10:30 – Independent seat work									
Minutes									
3	6	9	12	15	18	21	24	27	30

	3	6	9	12	15	18	21	24	27	30
Out-of-Seat										
Teacher	×	—	—	×	×	×	×	×	—	×
Reliability Checker	×	—	—	—	—	×	×	×	×	×

%Out-of-Seat = 7(×)/10(intervals) = 70% (Use teacher ratings).
%Reliability = Agreements/Agreements + Disagreements

$$= \frac{5(\times/\times)}{5(\times/\times) + 2(\times/\mathord{-}) \mp 1(\mathord{-}/\times)} = 5/8 = 62\%.$$

observations. Reliability or agreement between observers using continuous recording or time sampling is calculated for each behavior by dividing the total number of agreements by the number of agreements plus disagreements. An agreement is scored if both the teacher and the observer recorded the same behavior for the same 3-minute interval. A disagreement is scored if one observer recorded the behavior and the other observer did not. The reliability of an overall measure of disruptive behaviors should also be calculated (Table 6). If the reliability of each behavior is over 70%, the teacher can have some confidence that her observations fairly accurately represent the child's behavior. The importance of obtaining a regular estimate of reliability cannot be overemphasized. There are a number of variables which tend to decrease reliability and consequently the meaningfulness of the observations. For example, the teacher may have strong positive or negative feelings toward the child which could affect her observations. During the treatment phase, the teacher's expectations of how the child will respond to treatment can influence her observations. Finally, if the behavior descriptions are imprecise, reliability will be poor, and the teacher cannot justifiably say that the changes in the child's behavior, as evidenced by her observational records, are either real or are due to the treatment procedure the teacher has used.

There are several other kinds of observations which the teacher will find especially useful in the assessment of children's problem behaviors. By systematically observing behaviors such as the frequency with which other children in the class are out of their seats, the teacher may be better able to judge the severity of Sam's behavior. Sometimes a child's disruptive behavior, e.g., punching other children, is maintained by the way his peers respond. It is possible that the only attention some children receive from their peers occurs during or immediately after a fight. When the teacher suspects that peer attention to the target behavior is important, she should systematically observe peer reactions to the target behaviors. Similarly, the teacher herself may inadvertently be attending to or reinforcing disruptive behavior, she may be failing to provide sufficient rewards for appropriate behaviors, or she may be unduly criticizing or harshly reprimanding the child. By systematically recording her own reactions to the disruptive child — or by having someone else observe her behavior — the teacher can make better judgements regarding treatment and is made more directly aware of the influence she has over the child.

To summarize the important elements of target assessment mentioned above, the teacher should:

1. Select 1–4 behaviors on which she will focus her attention.
2. Write a detailed behavior description which is as complete and unambiguous as possible.
3. Decide which type of recording system to use. If the teacher can have someone else do the observing, continuous recording is preferred. If she is making the observations herself, she can choose either event recording or time sampling.
4. Record the behaviors in as many situations as possible as frequently as possible ($\frac{1}{2}$ hr./day minimum for time sampling).
5. Arrange for regular reliability checks (at least once a week).
6. Obtain similar observations of her own behaviors and possibly of some other children in the class.
7. Make daily summaries of her observations and record them graphically.

As you have seen from the articles in this book, target assessment is integrally tied to behavioral treatment procedures. The choice of the term "assessment" is not accidental. Rather than providing a "diagnosis" of the child before treatment, target assessment provides not only ongoing evaluation of the child's behavior but also an evaluation of other important aspects of the problem situation including the teacher's behaviors and the effects of treatment. Target assessment is objective when the reliability of the observations is high; it provides detailed information on the frequency and relative importance of the behaviors observed; it provides unambiguous information to consultants, parents, and other teachers; and it has direct implications for treatment.

When teachers and students are presented with a description of target assessment, the usual reaction is that they see the advantages and understand the rationale but question the feasibility of making regular observations, checking the reliability of their observations, and continuing their assessment through treatment and follow-up. Most of the research in this book was conducted by the teacher with rather constant supervision by the experimenter, who usually provided observers and reliability checkers. However, a recent article by Hall, Fox, Willard, Goldsmith, Emerson, Owen, Porcia, and Davis (1971) presents six excellent responses to the question of feasibility. Six teachers who were taking a course in classroom management employed target assessment and primarily praise and ignore procedures to modify talking-out-of-turn behaviors in their respective classes. In each case, the teacher systematically recorded the relevant behaviors, arranged for reliability checks, conducted a treatment procedure, and evaluated the effectiveness of the treatment by temporarily withdrawing the treatment procedure. Methods used to record the behaviors included paper and pencil tallies, mechanical counters similar to those used in keeping golf scores, and tape recorders. Similarily, the teachers were able to obtain reliability checks by using existing school resources, e.g., a pupil, a teacher aide, a tape recorder, and a fellow teacher. The generality of their success is exemplified by the wide variety of classes and children dealt with: a 15-year-old boy in a class of 15 junior high schools educable mentally retarded, a 10-year-old boy in a class for educable mentally retarded, a 13-year-old boy in a class of 6 junior high school emotionally disturbed children, a boy in a regular class of 27 third graders, 30 children in a poverty area regular first grade class, and 27 children in a poverty area regular second grade class.

So the answer to the question of feasibility is yes, when the teacher has the kind of background outlined in this book. We might add that it is not uncommon for a teacher to feel under less pressure and to spend less time dealing with a problem when she uses target assessment and actively initiates a solution to the problem than when she worries extensively about what to do and is unsuccessful in receiving help from an outside source.

IMPLEMENTATION

It would be difficult to find a substitute for good common sense when it comes to putting into practice the behavioral principles and procedures described in this book, but we can offer a few general guidelines which should be useful. To reiterate a point, a good, thoughtful teacher with a bit of courage should be able to implement a number of the behavioral techniques by herself. Among those procedures which each teacher should make a part of her natural interactions with her children are: praising desirable behavior, ignoring minor disruptions, making classroom rules clear to all children, modeling desirable behaviors herself, shaping both academic and social behaviors, praising and shaping behavior incompatible with disruptive behavior, and using soft reprimands. With consultation or after some supervised experience with the procedures, a teacher should be able to use cost and other simple punishment techniques, self-instruction, self-reinforcement, and self-specification of contingencies, and peers and other paraprofessionals as behavior modifiers. Ongoing and active consultation should accompany the implementation of most types of token programs, time-out for reinforcement, fear elimination procedures, and complex programmed instruction (especially when teaching machines are used).

In selecting a procedure to employ with a problem child, the teacher should first decide whether she wants to increase and/or decrease the frequency of certain behaviors. If she wants to decrease the frequency of some behavior, she must always develop another behavior to take its place. Children are always behaving and if the frequency of a disruptive behavior is decreased (e.g., aggression), the child will do something else on the occasions that he was aggressive. It behooves the teacher to develop appropriate social behavior to replace aggressive behavior since a child left to his own devices will replace aggression with other behaviors already in his repertoire and these may not always be the most desirable (e.g., swearing).

As another general rule, we would advice a teacher to use "hard" procedures such as token programs only after she has made a concerted effort to deal with the problem using "soft" procedures such as systematically praising appropriate behaviors and ignoring disruptive ones. Regular observations of the child's and the teacher's behavior will be the best indicator of when to try another procedure and any procedure adopted should be in effect for at least one week before the teacher can make a judgement regarding its efficacy.

Finally, some special comments should be made concerning what is the most basic and, on the surface, the simplest procedure discussed in this book—the contingent use of teacher's praise and affection. It is our experience that there is a wide range of individual differences regarding the ease and spontaneity with which teachers are physically affectionate and verbally encouraging toward their students. On occasion, even the most naturally rewarding and affectionate teacher will find it difficult to maintain her spontaneity. This seems to be especially true when teachers are implementing behavioral techniques for the first time and when they are faced with a particularly obstreperous child. There are several reasons why some teachers may feel unnatural or mechanical when they first use behavioral procedures. If the teacher is systematically observing her own behavior, she will be aware of exactly what she is doing to a much greater degree than usual. In deciding to praise a child more frequently, the teacher will be continuously noticing when and how often she praises or is affectionate toward the child. Thus, closely observing one's own behavior may lead to feelings of artificiality and a lack of spontaneity—although the behavior may look completely natural to an outside observer.

There are occasions when a teacher will not only feel unnatural but will in fact look uncomfortable, forced, or stilted in her attempts to praise a child. Even the most experienced teacher may have difficulty in reacting positively when she is faced with a child who is a great deal of trouble, who seems to respond adversely to her attention, or who may even present a real threat to her. Some teachers—like many other people—find it difficult to be affectionate in public. Such a teacher might undoubtedly function very well with older children but would be handicapped in dealing with first or second graders.

Unfortunately, simply instructing a teacher to be more positive does not always work, but we can make some suggestions which a consultant or the teacher herself might find useful. All the suggestions we will make are based on the principle of shaping. That is, the teacher should not expect herself to become instantly and appropriately positive to all children—she must train herself to be affectionate and to praise as gradually and systematically as she would teach a child to read.

In general, a teacher should begin with a child whom she likes and gradually change her behavior toward more difficult children. It will be easier to concentrate first on verbal praise and then to focus on physical affection. Give praise or affection as soon as possible following an appropriate behavior. *Smile* when you praise a child. Vary the volume and intensity of your voice. Become excited when appropriate. The use of stars may be helpful since the occasion for attention is specified and since the child will usually respond positively to the tokens even if he would not respond to teacher-attention by itself. Remember, the teacher's behavior must be rewarded and a positive response from a child is a very effective reinforcer. A positive response from a child is more likely if the teacher mentions the child's name when praising him or plans other activities which will make the teacher and the school more positive in the child's eyes, e.g., individual tutoring sessions, compliments on the child's appearance, active interest in something the child likes, or special projects with the child.

The teacher may ask someone to observe her either in individual sessions or in the classroom and to give her immediate feedback regarding how and when she used her attention to children more effectively. It would be useful for the teacher to observe a teacher or consultant who skilfully uses praise and affection. The teacher may also make use of tape recorders, video tape recorders, and role playing sessions to change her behavior. A teacher might list a variety of praise comments, decide to praise a child a certain number of times a day, and monitor her own behavior by making a tally each time she praises a child. In addition, she could make notes to herself in her instructional material to remind her to praise more frequently and be affectionate.

Since it is difficult for some teachers to develop examples of praise and affection, we include the following list:

Johnny, that's the *right* answer!
The class is so quiet, I can hear myself think.
Mary, you're working very well today.
Tom, that's a good looking shirt.
Your handwriting is much better today, Judy.
Bill, thank you very much for helping Joe.
You read that whole paragraph perfectly, John.
Look at how well Carol is paying attention.
Touch the child's hand when he comes to your desk.
Hug the child when he is standing close to you on the playground.
Put your hand on his back when you're at his desk.
Pat a well-behaved child on the back as you pass him.

With practice the teacher will gradually find herself feeling more spontaneous and natural and her children will respond accordingly.

Who Should Change the Child's Behavior?

As evidenced in the majority of articles in this book, the person primarily responsible for changing the behavior of children in the classroom is the teacher. Usually, the teacher herself is in the best position to change the child's behavior, but occasionally it may be very helpful to utilize a teacher aide (paraprofessional), consultant, or a peer in bringing about change in the classroom. Decisions about who should be the primary instrument of change should be based upon the degree of disruptive behavior the child displays and the degree of the child's academic deficit. If either of these is marked, then it is wise to seek aid. On the other hand, if a child displays disruptive behavior which is not unusually serious or has only slight academic deficits, the teacher should attempt to bring about change herself. As demonstrated in the articles in the praise chapter, the use of contingent teacher attention can be very effective in changing a child's disruptive behavior—even where the rates of disruptive behavior are quite high. On the other hand, consider a child who has an academic deficit in addition to displaying high rates of disruptive behavior. Until he is given special aid or tutoring in the particular subject, it is folly to expect dramatic changes in disruptive behavior (Becker, Madsen, Arnold, & Thomas, 1967).

Deciding who should bring about change in a classroom should also be based upon the number of children in the class who have severe academic deficits or who display high rates of disruptive behavior. One or two children with high rates of disruptive behavior can probably be handled by the teacher (Becker, *et al.*, 1967). If more than two or three children display very high rates of disruptive behavior, it is certainly wise to enlist the help of a consultant, teacher aide, or a peer in bringing about classroom change. If three children display very high rates of disruptive behavior, they are probably hindering the academic progress of other children since a great deal of the teacher's time is spent in simply trying to control the disruptive behavior of the three troublesome children. Where no assistance is available to the teacher who has a number of very disruptive children, she should also consider special class placement for one or more of those children. However, since the quality and staff of special classes varies so drastically from one school system to another, we would advise the teacher to visit the special class in which the child is to be placed before such a referral is made. A referral to a special class must be made in light of the advantages and disadvantages of such place-ment *both* to the child's regular class *and* to the child himself.

A child with severe academic deficits who does not display disruptive behavior can often be aided immensely by special tutoring or special attention from a teacher without assigning him to a special class. Since such a child is usually not hindering the academic progress of others, the assistance of an older child or high school student could be of help in providing the child with approval and corrective feedback concerning his academic progress.

Where the total class is plagued by high rates of disruptive behavior and gross academic deficits, obviously assistance of some sort is needed and should be demanded to conduct both special instruction and special incentive systems. Similarly where academic deficits are severe in a group of children, the more personnel available the greater the likelihood of change. As evidenced in the incentive system described by O'Leary and Becker (1967), where someone other than the teacher introduces and helps initiate a token program, the program can be extremely effective. Nonetheless, there is also ample evidence that the teacher herself can introduce and execute a token program under supervision (O'Leary & Drabman, 1971). However, because of the frequency of failures in the implementation of token programs using extrinsic reinforcers, it is strongly advised that such programs be implemented only with psychological consultation. Where stars and special privileges instead of candy and prizes are used as back-up reinforcers, often the teacher acquainted with behavioral principles may well be successful in implementing a token system on her own.

Where personnel are scarce or where it is difficult to schedule such personnel, the teacher should avail herself of any instrumentation which could be useful in teaching the child new academic skills. For example, where human personnel are not readily available to assist in behavior change, an *instrument* or machine can assist in the teaching. The Language Master (Bell & Howell) is a simplified tape recorder which records and plays back single words and short sentences on strips of magnetic tape which are attached to cards. The teacher can record any sort of lesson on a series of cards and the child can respond by writing or recording his answers. Earphones allow the child to work privately and without disturbing others. Alternatively, a tape recorder could be used to have a child listen to a classmate or teacher recite the ABCs. The child himself could record the alphabet and then later listen to his own voice. During the next decade, undoubtedly, inexpensive teaching machines will be developed which may be used in any classroom just as tape recorders and Language Masters are now used. While none of these machines or instruments are a panacea, they can be very helpful in providing some individualized instruction which is so necessary for children with academic and social deficits.

In deciding which person should change a child's behavior, it is also necessary to consider who or what is maintaining the child's inappropriate behavior. If it is likely that the teacher herself is somehow maintaining the child's inappropriate behavior, she should try to assess what she is doing and modify her own behavior. On the other hand, if a child's inappropriate behavior is being maintained by his peers, it is useful to consider various ways of changing the peers' behavior. On occasion, it may be very clear to a teacher that various ways in which she reacts to a child hinders progress with that child. For example, if a child has created a great deal of trouble for the teacher, she may hold a grudge against the child, and in such instances it is useful to get an aide or a peer to modify the child's behavior. As mentioned in Chapter 10, if a paraprofessional is to be a change agent it is necessary to have a well-defined goal and method by which the aide can reach that goal.

When is Consultation Required?

In addition to the referral issues discussed earlier in this chapter, a number of factors should be noted about the necessity of consultation in various instances.

Consultation usually should be sought:

1. When a token reinforcement program utilizing extrinsic back-up reinforcers is being considered because of the unusual types of prizes, because of the frequent failures in implementations of token programs by inexperienced personnel and because such token programs are *not* necessary in many instances although they are occasionally seen as the only answer by teachers, principals, and hospital directors.
2. When there is a systematic use of frequent reprimanding or time-out from reinforcement. Again such procedures are often not indicated, and because of their possible negative side-effects, they generally should be avoided. Furthermore, as evidenced earlier in this book, some forms of reprimands actually may lead to increases in inappropriate behavior. Time-out from reinforcement in the form of placing a child at the side or back of the room is a procedure occasionally used by a number of teachers. On the other hand, the use of a small room (Time-out Booth) should probably be reserved for hospitals and classrooms for emotionally disturbed children—*after* other more positive methods of behavior change have been tried.
3. When precise evaluation of a procedure for research purposes is sought. A teacher obviously can't record the host of critical factors which are simultaneously operating in a classroom; and even if she could, because of her own opinions, her data might be biased.
4. When a teacher is attempting to implement a large scale behavior modification program for the *first* time—e.g., a token program.
5. When it is unclear whether the particular program being implemented will be powerful enough to change the child's problem behavior.
6. When it is thought that problems or hardships in the home are impeding the progress of a program (e.g., frequent fighting among

family members, death of a parent, absence of adequate food or clothing), or when there may be some physical impediment which would hamper progress of the program (e.g., epilepsy or brain damage).
7. When it is unclear whether the teacher should place her major emphasis on academic or social behavior.

Evaluating the Success of Treatment

As has been emphasized repeatedly in this book, objective evaluations of treatment should always be made. A teacher might feel, however, that since she is not engaging in research but rather is aiding the child in a practical fashion, objective evaluations need not be made. While a teacher need not engage in evaluations which are as extensive as those of the researcher, some evaluation is necessary if she wants to know whether her methods are effective. Such evaluations have the advantage of:

1. Making the teacher more attuned to her own behavior and its effects or lack of effects on her class,
2. Providing the teacher with objective evaluations of procedures that were tried with a child to aid in any referral process,
3. Providing the teacher with some indication of gradual changes in a child that would be difficult to detect by simple anecdotal records or retrospective reports of what the child was like,
4. Providing the teacher with critical information concerning the necessity for changing certain aspects of a particular treatment program, and
5. Prompting teachers to become critical consumers of research since after engaging in evaluations themselves, they will be in a better position to evaluate how other research is done.

It should now be evident to the reader that objective observations alone are not enough to assess whether a treatment is successful. To clearly demonstrate that the treatment employed led to the observed behavior change there must be some *manipulation* of the treatment procedure; it must be withdrawn, intensified, or diminished. Alternatively, the treatment procedure might be applied in a sequential fashion to different behaviors; it could be applied to one behavior during a particular period, but not applied in another period (multiple baseline). Later the treatment could be applied in both periods as was illustrated in the article by Barrish,

Saunders and Wolf (1969) *(22)*. The ABAB design and the multiple baseline illustrated in this book are methods of evaluating the effectiveness of a procedure within a single class. Because the withdrawal of successful procedures is sometimes difficult for a teacher to implement and sometimes difficult to justify to parents, let us re-examine the use of a multiple baseline as it is applied in the classroom. Assume that the teacher (1) has particular difficulty with a child talking out of turn during reading and arithmetic classes and (2) wants to examine the effectiveness of increasing her praise to the child when he raises his hand. First, she or an observer would record the frequency of talking out of turn during both classes. Next, she would increase the number of praise comments during one of the classes, e.g., reading, while continuing to respond in her usual manner during arithmetic. Later she would increase the number of praise comments during both classes. If a decline in the frequency of talking out of turn during each class period was observed when the use of praise was increased during that class period, the teacher could probably feel confident in saying that her praise reduced the frequency of talking out of turn.

Follow-Through

As mentioned in Chapter 1, the term Follow-Through has been used recently by the Office of Education and the Department of Health Education and Welfare in Washington to designate the continuation of special teaching or special programs which follow a child's Head-Start Program. The government rightly recognized that a child could be taught certain skills in Head Start but that such skills often were not maintained several years later. Children who were in Head Start were not distinguishable from those children who did not have a Head-Start experience by the time they reached third grade. Similarly, because psychologists are recognizing the clear relation between a child's everchanging environment and thus everchanging behavior, there is a greater focus on the child's environment following particular treatment programs. As evidenced many times in this book by ABAB experimental designs, when different classroom treatment programs were withdrawn or dramatically changed, the behavior of the children usually deteriorated. Let us again restate that when a child's behavior is not reinforced, it will extinguish or decrease in frequency. Thus when one withdraws a particular program which helped prompt and maintain or reinforce a child's behavior, one must make sure that there are different reinforcers that can be scheduled less frequently than those used in the special program but which will maintain the child's behavior. In short, someone must see that there is some follow-through! In a few instances, when a new skill is taught, its mastery will be reinforcing enough to maintain a child's behavior when the special program is withdrawn. However, for the large majority of children with social problems, the new mastery or new competence will not be sufficiently reinforcing to maintain the appropriate behavior, and one must do all he can to insure that the new skill is prompted and reinforced in whatever new environments the child enters. This is especially true in the case of social behavior since the natural school environment does not provide regular and immediate feedback regarding social behavior as it does for academic behavior.

Generalization

Intimately related to the problem of Follow-Through is the issue of generalization. Generalization refers to extent to which a particular program will have long range or far-reaching effects. That is, if a treatment focuses on a particular behavior or group of behaviors, will the treatment influence other groups of behaviors? In addition people wish to know how long the effects of a program will last, or how long the good behavior will be maintained when the treatment program is stopped. People also want to know whether a treatment program will influence a child in situations where the treatment has not been instituted. Actually a teacher might be interested in several variations of the types of generalization discussed above but in every case the question hinges around the issue of producing a behavior change which will not be limited to the treatment situation. That is, to be maximally effective one must teach behavior which will have wide-ranging effects. As mentioned in Chapter 1, when one teaches a mute child to speak by using food or token reinforcement, such reinforcement can later be withdrawn; and the child will continue to speak in a variety of times and places. He probably will start saying things that were not taught to him in his special speech program. However, speech is a very special behavior in that it will always be reinforced by one's natural environment. On the other hand, teaching a ghetto child mathematics will not have such naturally occurring positive consequences. For example, a ghetto child's gang, his parents, and sometimes even his teachers will do little to reinforce any newly acquired mathematics skill. Similarly, one may teach a hospitalized adolescent child a number of social skills which most adults would call appropriate, polite behavior;

however, when such polite behavior is displayed on the ward it may not be reinforced by the child's peers or even by the attendants and his behavior would thus decline. Because of this problem of maintaining behavior, Ayllon and Azrin (1968) have developed the following general rule or guideline for use in developing goals of programs in hospital settings which we feel has relevance for any training program: "Teach only those behaviors that will continue to be reinforced after training." The implications of such a rule are clear for a teacher. She should try to teach skills which will be rewarded by the child's natural environment, and if she doubts that such rewards will be forthcoming she should talk to the parents of the child, the child's new teacher, or the child's other teachers and specifically enlist their cooperation in reinforcing the newly acquired skill.

Because of the apparent situation-specificity of many of the behaviors that have been discussed in this book, we hope that research during the next decade will concentrate on teaching children skills in a manner that will diminish the problem of the rapid extinction of such skills. Until such research is completed, however, there are a number of behavioral principles which can be followed to maximize such generalization. Let us assume that being polite is a behavior or group of behaviors which one would like to increase. First one can teach general rules of conduct which specify what polite behaviors a child should exhibit in a wide variety of situations. For example, one should usually teach a child to be polite with everyone, not just with a particular teacher or a particular parent. A number of people should be asked to reinforce the skill being taught, e.g., parents, teachers (Wahler, 1969), and peers (a teacher can prompt a single child or several children to respond positively to polite behaviors of a particular peer). The teacher should also describe to the child the *various* kinds of behaviors which are considered polite, e.g., saying please, thanking, asking for a toy instead of grabbing it, sharing toys, etc. That is, if we wish to see some generalization across different kinds of behaviors, the child must know what sorts of different behaviors to display. If such behaviors cannot be easily practiced in the classroom where a child or adult can reinforce them, the teacher might role-play a number of interactions with the child to practice behaving politely in a *variety* of ways. The teacher may also take advantage of other children's polite behaviors and reinforce them so that such behavior can serve as a positive model for the child who is being taught to be polite. Similarly, a teacher should monitor her own behavior and see that she does in fact display polite behavior toward the children in her own class lest she be a victim of the adage "Children do as you do, not as you say."

PUBLIC RELATIONS ISSUES

Behavior Modification Programs to be Discussed with the Public

Whenever a teacher is considering the implementation of a program which might be viewed negatively by other teachers, parents, or community members, both the principal and the parents should be alerted to the program and their approval should be obtained before such a program is instituted. For example, if a child is being considered for a program where extrinsic reinforcers are to be used, or where a high school or older elementary school child will be used as a tutor, the parents should be consulted. If explained carefully, the use of either extrinsic reinforcers or peer tutoring can be easily justified to parents of very disruptive children. An explanation of any procedures which are not ordinarily part of a teacher's routine and which might be viewed negatively by parents will not only aid in the execution of such procedures, it may also prevent a great deal of misunderstanding. In this endeavor as in many others, "An ounce of prevention is worth a pound of cure."

How will other Personnel React to Behavior Modification?

Ten years ago when behavior modification was known and practiced by very few people, it was viewed with skepticism by many professionals. Today, almost all universities and many hospitals and community mental health centers are searching for people skilled in the use of behavior modification techniques. The *Journal of School Psychology* is being deluged with manuscripts dealing with behavior modification (personal communication, Jack Bardon, October, 1970) and *Exceptional Children* recently published an issue (October, 1970) in which all its articles were solicited manuscripts from people engaged in behavior modification with children. That is, journals which deal with problems of children sense a need to publish behavior modification research, and as this research is published, the demand for consultation by people versed in behavior modification will become greater and greater. This is certainly not to say that there is no opposition to behavior modification, but all indications reveal a growing acceptance of behavioral procedures. Most reluctance comes from psychologists, psychiatrists, and social workers who have been trained in the psychoanalytic tradition, since the behavioral approach is an obvious threat to their professional status. However, the opposition can be minimized by avoiding the use of complicated technical terminology, by emphasizing the similarities of the behavior modification approach to the approach good parents and teachers naturally take, and by noting that behavioral techniques are very useful for improving the good behaviors the child already has. Rather than simply telling others how a behavioral approach might work, it is best to demonstrate its application. Here as in many areas "Actions speak louder than words." It is especially convincing to demonstrate the effectiveness of behavioral procedures with children who have been unsuccessfully treated by other approaches, and of course when you are successful with such children, you should inform others of your successes.

Problems of Dealing with Powerful Procedures

Very frequently when a behavior modification approach is initiated in a hospital or school setting, one hears comments such as "You are manipulating the lives of children," or "You are controlling a child instead of allowing him to develop freely." Whether we wish to admit it or not, we are all being controlled and exerting control in various ways in our daily lives. However, the application of behavior modification principles makes this control very apparent. When one can see behavior change dramatically before his very eyes, the issues of control and its various ramifications cannot be ignored. An important consequence of dealing with a powerful procedure is that one must consider whether it is really advisable to change a behavior. That is, one can easily be duped into maintaining a poor educational system when in fact he ought to be revamping the system. In short, the application of any principles of behavior cannot be divorced from social values. The classrooms and the goals of education in the year 2000 may be very unlike the classrooms and goals of 1970, but the *principles* of behavior modification described in this book will still apply to changing children's behaviors. The behavior modification approach provides a set of rather well-defined procedures to change behavior, but the procedures do not spell out the goals or the behaviors which *ought* to be taught or changed. It is always the duty of every educator, scientist, and citizen to evaluate the aims of our educational systems. Whether the goals of education in the year 2000 involve a structured class or an unstructured class, a class which emphasizes affective or cognitive development, it is our opinion that the types of principles and procedures described in this book will be helpful in reaching whatever goals our educational systems choose.

References

Allerhand, M. E. Effectiveness of parents of Head Start children as administrators of psychological tests. *Journal of Consulting Psychology*, 1967, **31**, 286–290.

Aronfreed, J., & Reber, A. Internal behavioral suppression and the timing of social punishment. *Journal of Personality and Social Psychology*, 1965, **1**, 3–16.

Atkinson, R. C. Computerized instruction and the learning process. *American Psychologist*, 1968, **23**, 225–239.

Ayllon, T., & Azrin, N. H. *A motivating environment for therapy and rehabilitation.* New York: Appleton-Century-Crofts, 1968.

Ayllon, T., Smith, D., & Rogers, M. Behavioral management of school phobia. *Journal of Behavior Therapy and Experimental Psychiatry*, 1970, **1**, No. 2, 125–128.

Azrin, N. H., & Lindsley, O. R. The reinforcement of cooperation between children. *Journal of Abnormal and Social Psychology*, 1956, **52**, 100–102.

Baer, D. M. The consultation process model as an irrational state of affairs. *Psychology in the Schools*, 1970, **7**, No. 4, 341–344.

Baer, D. M., Peterson, R. F., & Sherman, J. A. The development of imitation by reinforcing behavioral similarity to a model. *Journal of the Experimental Analysis of Behavior*, 1967, **10**, 405–416.

Bailey, J., Phillips, E., & Wolf, M. Modification of predelinquents' classroom behavior with home-based reinforcement. Paper presented to American Psychological Association, Miami, September, 1970.

Bakwin. H., & Bakwin, R. M. *Clinical management of behavior disorders in children.* New York: Saunders, 1967.

Bandura, A. Modeling approaches to the modification of phobic disorders. Paper presented to Ciba Foundation Symposium, London, 1968.

Bandura, A. *Principles of behavior modification.* New York: Holt, Rinehart, & Winston, 1969.

Bandura, A., Grusec, J. E., & Menlove, F. L. Vicarious extinction of avoidance behavior. *Journal of Personality and Social Psychology*, 1967, **5**, 16–23.

Bandura, A., & Kupers, C. J. Transmission of patterns of self-reinforcement through modeling. *Journal of Abnormal and Social Psychology*, 1964, **69**, 1-9.

Bandura, A., & Perloff, B. Relative efficacy of self-monitored and externally imposed reinforcement systems. *Journal of Personality and Social Psychology*, 1967, **7**, 111-116.

Bandura, A., Ross, D., & Ross, S. A. Imitation of film-mediated aggressive models. *Journal of Abnormal and Social Psychology*, 1963, **66**, 3-11.

Bandura, A., & Walters, R. H. *Social learning and personality development*. New York: Holt, Rinehart, & Winston, 1963.

Barrett, B. H. Acquisition of operant differentiation and discrimination in institutionalized retarded children. *American Journal of Orthopsychiatry*, 1965, **35**, 862-885.

Barrett, B. H., & Lindsley, O. R. Deficits in acquisition of operant discrimination and differentiation shown by institutionalized retarded children. *American Journal of Mental Deficiency*, 1962, **67**, 424-436.

Barrish, H. H., Saunders, M., & Wolf, M. M. Good behavior game: Effects of individual contingencies for group consequences on disruptive behavior in a classroom. *Journal of Applied Behavior Analysis*, 1969, **2**, 119-124.

Becker, W. C., Madsen, C. H., Arnold, C. R., & Thomas, D. R. The contingent use of teacher attention and praise in reducing classroom behavior problems. *Journal of Special Education*, 1967, **1**, 287-307.

Becker, W. C., Thomas, D. R., & Carnine, D. *Reducing behavior problems: An operant conditioning guide for teachers*. National Laboratory on Early Childhood Education, Urbana, Illinois, 1969.

Beilin, H. Teachers' and clinicians' attitudes toward the behavior problems of children: A reappraisal. *Child Development*, 1959, **30**, 9-25.

Bem, S. L. Verbal self-control: The establishment of effective self-instruction. *Journal of Experimental Psychology*, 1967, **74**, 485-491.

Berkowitz, H. A preliminary assessment of the extent of interaction between child psychiatric clinics and public schools. *Psychology in the Schools*, 1968, **5**, 291-295.

Bernstein, D. A. The modification of smoking behavior: A search for effective variables. *Behaviour Research and Therapy*, 1970, **8**, 133-146.

Bijou, S. W. Experimental studies of child behavior, normal and deviant. In L. Krasner & L. P. Ullmann (Eds.), *Research in Behavior Modification*. New York: Holt, Rinehart, & Winston, 1965. a

Bijou, S. W. Social variables and the beginnings of self-control. Paper presented to Society for Research in Child Development, Bowling Green, Ohio, March, 1965. b

Birnbrauer, J. S., Wolf, M. M., Kidder, J. D., & Tague, Cecilia E. Classroom behavior of retarded pupils with token reinforcement. *Journal of Experimental Child Psychology*, 1965, **2**, 219-235.

Bower, E. M. *Technical report: A process for in-school screening of children with emotional handicaps*. Princeton, New Jersey: Educational Testing Service, 1966.

Bregman, E. O. An attempt to modify the emotional attitudes of infants by the conditioned response technique. *Journal of Genetic Psychology*, 1934, **45**, 169-198.

Broden, M., Bruce, C., Mitchell, M. A., Carter, V., & Hall, R. V. Effects of teacher attention on attending behavior of two boys at adjacent desks. *Journal of Applied Behavior Analysis*, 1970, **3**, 199-203.

Broden, M., Hall, R. V., & Mitts, B. The effect of self-recording on the classroom behavior of two eighth grade students. *Journal of Applied Behavior Analysis*, 1971, in press.

Bronfenbrenner, U. *Two Worlds of Childhood: U.S. and U.S.S.R.* New York: Russell Sage Foundation, 1970.

Brown, P., & Elliot, R. Control of aggression in a nursery school class. *Journal of Experimental Child Psychology*, 1965, **2**, 103-107.

Bryan, J. H., & Walbek, N. H. Preaching and practicing generosity: Children's actions and reactions. *Child Development*, 1970, **41**, 329-353.

Buchanan, C. D. *Programmed reading.* St. Louis: Webster Division, McGraw-Hill, 1968.

Bushell, D., Wrobel, P. A., & Michaelis, M. L. Applying "group" contingencies to the classroom study behavior of preschool children. *Journal of Applied Behavior Analysis*, 1968, **1**, 55-61.

Carlson, C. S., Arnold, C. R., Becker, W. C., & Madsen, C. H. The elimination of tantrum behavior of a child in an elementary classroom. *Behaviour Research and Therapy*, 1968, **6**, 117-119.

Cheyne, J. A., & Walters, R. H. Punishment and prohibition: Some origins of self-control. In T. M. Newcomb (Ed.), *New Directions in Psychology.* New York: Holt, Rinehart, & Winston, 1970, pp. 281-366.

Circirelli, V., Cooper, W., & Granger, R. The impact of Head Start: An evaluation of the effects of head start and children's cognitive and affective development. Westinghouse Learning Corporation, June 12, 1969.

Cohen, H. L. Motivationally oriented designs for an ecology of learning. Paper presented to American Education Research Association, New York, February, 1967.

Conners, C. K. A teacher rating scale for use in drug studies with children. *American Journal of Psychiatry*, 1969, **126** No. 6, 152-156.

Conners, C. K., Eisenberg, L., & Barcai, A. Effect of dextroamphetamine on children. *Archives of General Psychiatry*, 1967, **17**, 478-485.

Curry, D. R. Case studies in behavior modification. *Psychology in the Schools*, 1970, **7**, 330-335.

Despert, J. L. *The emotionally disturbed child—then and now.* New York: Vantage, 1965.

Engelmann, S., & Becker, W. C. Engelmann-Becker Follow-Through Project. University of Oregon, Eugene, Oregon, 1970.

English, H. B. Three cases of the "conditioned fear response." *Journal of Abnormal and Social Psychology*, 1929, **24**, 221-225.

Eron, L. D. Relationship of TV viewing habits and aggressive behavior in children. *Journal of Abnormal Psychology*, 1963, **67**, 193-196.

Evans, G. W., & Oswalt, G. L. Acceleration of academic progress through the manipulation of peer influence. *Behaviour Research and Therapy*, 1968, **6**, 189-195.

Eysenck, H. J. The effects of psychotherapy: An evaluation. *Journal of Consulting Psychology*, 1952, **16**, 319-325.

Ferster, C. B., & DeMyer, M. K. A method for the experimental analysis of the behavior of autistic children. *American Journal of Orthopsychiatry*, 1962, **32**, 89-98.

Freud, A. *The psychoanalytical treatment of children*. New York: Schocken, 1964.

Fromm-Reichmann, F. *Principles of intensive psychotherapy*. Chicago: University of Chicago Press, 1950.

Gewirtz, J. L., & Baer, D. M. Deprivation and satiation of social reinforcers as drive conditioners. *Journal of Abnormal and Social Psychology*, 1958, **57**, 165–172.

Hall, R. V., Alexrod, S., Foundopoulos, M., Shellman, J., Campbell, R. A., & Cranston, S. The effective use of punishment to modify behavior in the classroom. *Educational Technology*, April, 1971, 24–26.

Hall, R. V., Fox, R., Willard, D., Goldsmith, L., Emerson, M., Owen, M., Porcia, E., & Davis, F. Modification of disputing and talking out behaviors with the teacher as observer and experimenter. *Journal of Applied Behavior Analysis*, 1971, in press.

Harris, F. R., Johnston, M. K., Kelley, C. S., & Wolf, M. M. Effects of positive social reinforcement on regressed crawling of a nursery school child. *Journal of Educational Psychology*, 1964, **55**, 35–41.

Holland, J. G., & Skinner, B. F. *The Analysis of Behavior*, New York: McGraw-Hill, 1961.

Homme, L. E. Perspectives in psychology: XXIV. Control of coverants, the operants of the mind. *Psychological Record*, 1965, **15**, 501–511.

Homme, L. E., DeBaca, P. C., Devine, J. V., Steinhorst, R., & Rickert, E. J. Use of the Premack principle in controlling the behavior of nursery school children. *Journal of the Experimental Analysis of Behavior*, 1963, **6**, 544.

Hopkins, B. L., Schutte, R. C., & Garten, K. The effects of access to a playroom on the rate and quality of printing of first and second grade students. Unpublished manuscript, University of Kansas, 1970.

Jacobsen, E. *Progressive relaxation*. Chicago: University of Chicago Press, 1938.

Jones, E. *The life and work of Sigmund Freud*: New York: Basic Books, 1955.

Jones, M. C. The elimination of children's fear. *Journal of Experimental Psychology*, 1924, **7**, 383–390.

Kaufman, K. F., & O'Leary, K. D. Reward, cost, and self-evaluation procedures with schizophrenic children. Unpublished manuscript, State University of New York, 1971.

Krumboltz, J. D., & Thoresen, C. E. The effect of behavioral counseling in group and individual settings on information-seeking behavior. *Journal of Counseling Psychology*, 1964, **11**, 324–333.

Lawler, E. E., & Hackman, J. R. Impact of employee participation in the development of pay incentive plans: A field experiment. *Journal of Applied Psychology*, 1969, **53**, No. 6, 467–471.

Lazarus, A. A. The elimination of children's phobias by deconditioning. *Medical Proceedings of South Africa*, 1959, **5**, 261–265.

Lazarus, A. A., Davison, G. C., & Polefka, D. A. Classical and operant factors in the treatment of a school phobia. *Journal of Abnormal and Social Psychology*, 1965, **70**, 225–229.

Lehrman, L. J., Sirluck, H., Black, B. J., & Glick, S. J. Success and failure of treatment of children in the child guidance clinics of the Jewish Board of Guardians, New York City. Jewish Board of Guardians Research Monograph, 1949, No. 1.

Levitt, E. The results of psychotherapy with children: An evaluation. *Journal of Consulting Psychology*, 1957, **21**, 189–196.

Levitt, E. Psychotherapy with children: A further evaluation. *Behaviour Research and Therapy*, 1963, **1**, 45–51.

Lindsley, O. R. Geriatric behavioral prosthetics. In R. Kastenbaum (Ed.), *New thoughts on old age*. New York: Springer, 1964, pp. 41–60.

Lovaas, O. I. A behavior therapy approach to the treatment of childhood schizophrenia. In J. P. Hill (Ed.), *Minnesota Symposium on Child Psychology*. Minneapolis, Minnesota: University of Minnesota Press, 1967, pp. 108–159.

Lovibond, S. H. *Conditioning and enuresis*. Oxford: Pergamon, 1964.

Lovitt, T. C., & Curtiss, K. A. Academic response rate as a function of teacher and self-imposed contingencies. *Journal of Applied Behavior Analysis*, 1969, **2**, 49–53.

Luria, A. R. Psychological studies of mental deficiency in the Soviet Union. In N. R. Ellis (Ed.), *Handbook on mental deficiency*. New York: McGraw-Hill, 1963, pp. 353–387.

Madsen, C. H., Becker, W. C., & Thomas, D. R. Rules, praise and ignoring: Elements of elementary classroom control. *Journal of Applied Behavior Analysis*, 1968, **1**, 139–150.

Mann, J., & Rosenthal, T. L. Vicarious and direct counterconditioning of test anxiety through individual and group desensitization. *Behaviour Research and Therapy*, 1969, **7**, 359–367.

Markle, Susan M. *Good frames and bad*. New York: Wiley, 1964.

Masserman, J. H. *Behavior and neurosis*. Chicago: University of Chicago Press, 1943.

McIntire, R. W., Jensen, J., & Davis, G. Control of disruptive behavior with a token economy. Paper presented to Eastern Psychological Association, Philadelphia, 1968.

McKenzie, H. S., Clark, M., Wolf, M. M., Kothera, R., & Benson, C. Behavior modification of children with learning disabilities using grades as tokens and allowances as back up reinforcers. *Exceptional Children*, 1968, **34**, 745–752.

Meichenbaum, D. H., Bowers, K. S., & Ross, R. R. A behavioral analysis of teacher expectancy effect. *Journal of Personality and Social Psychology*, 1969, **13**, 306–316.

Meichenbaum, D., & Goodman, J. The developmental control of operant motor responding by verbal operants. *Child Development*, 1969, **40**, 785–798.

Meyer, A. The role of mental factors in psychiatry. *American Journal of Insanity*, 1908, **65**, 39–56.

Miller, N. E. Learning of visceral and glandular responses. *Science*, 1969, **163**, 434–445.

Monohan, J. T. The effects of delay on the modification of rule-breaking behavior by self-instruction. Unpublished Master's thesis, University of Indiana, 1970.

Morrill, C. S. Teaching machines: A review. *Psychological Bulletin*, 1961, **58**, 363–375.

Mowrer, O. H., & Mowrer, W. A. Enuresis: A method for its study and treatment. *American Journal of Orthopsychiatry*, 1938, **8**, 436–447.

Obler, M., & Terwilliger, R. F. Pilot study on the effectiveness of systematic desensitization with neurologically impaired children with phobic disorders. *Journal of Consulting and Clinical Psychology*, 1970, **34**, 314–318.

O'Connor, R. Modification of social withdrawal through symbolic modeling. *Journal of Applied Behavior Analysis*, 1969, **2**, 15–22.

O'Leary, K. D. The effects of self-instruction on immoral behavior. *Journal of Experimental Child Psychology*, 1968, **6**, 297–301.

O'Leary, K. D. Establishing token programs in schools: Issues and problems. Paper presented to American Psychological Association, Washington, D. C., August, 1969.

O'Leary, K. D. Diagnosis of children's behavior problems. In H. C. Quay & J. S. Werry (Eds.), *Behavior Disorders of Children*, New York: Wiley, in press.

O'Leary, K. D., & Becker, W. C. Behavior modification of an adjustment class. *Exceptional Children*, 1967, **33**, 637–642.

O'Leary, K. D., & Becker, W. C. The effects of the intensity of a teacher's reprimands on children's behavior. *Journal of School Psychology*, 1968, **7**, No. 1, 8–11.

O'Leary, K. D., Becker, W. C., Evans, M. B., & Saudargas, R. A. A token reinforcement program in a public school: A replication and systematic analysis. *Journal of Applied Behavior Analysis*, 1969, **2**, 3–13.

O'Leary, K. D., & Drabman, R. Token reinforcement programs in the classroom: A review. *Psychological Bulletin*, 1971, **75**, 379–398.

O'Leary, K. D., Kaufman, K. F., Kass, R., & Drabman, R. The effects of loud and soft reprimands on the behavior of disruptive students. *Exceptional Children*, 1970, **37**, 145–155.

O'Leary, K. D., Poulos, R. W., & Devine, V. T. Tangible reinforcers: Bonuses or Bribes. *Journal of Clinical and Consulting Psychology*, December, 1971.

Osborne, J. G. Free-time as a reinforcer in the management of classroom behavior. *Journal of Applied Behavior Analysis*, 1969, **2**, 113–118.

Patterson, G. R. An application of conditioning techniques to the control of a hyperactive child. In L. P. Ullmann, & L. Krasner (Eds.), *Case studies in behavior modification*, New York: Holt, Rinehart, & Winston, 1965, pp. 370–375.

Paul, G. L. *Insight versus desensitization in psychotherapy*. Stanford: Stanford University Press, 1966.

Pearl, A., & Riessman, F. *New careers for the poor; the non-professional in human service*. New York: Free Press, 1965.

Pendergrass, V. Children and behavior modification: Time-out from positive reinforcement as a punishment procedure. Paper read at Florida Psychological Association, Miami, Florida, May 1, 1970.

Peterson, D. R. Behavior problems of middle childhood. *Journal of Consulting Psychology*, 1961, **25**, 205–209.

Phillips, E. L. Achievement place: Token reinforcement procedures in a home-style rehabilitation setting for "pre-delinquent" boys. *Journal of Applied Behavior Analysis*, 1968, **1**, 213–223.

Phillips, E., Bailey, J., & Wolf, M. M. Achievement place: A token economy in a home-style rehabilitation center for juvenile offenders. Paper presented to American Psychological Association, Washington, D.C., 1969.

Poser, E. G. The effect of therapist's training on group therapeutic outcome. *Journal of Consulting Psychology*, 1966, **30**, 283–289.

Reese, H. W., & Parnes, S. J. Programming creative behavior. *Child Development*, 1970, **41**, 413–423.

Reisman, J. M. *The development of clinical psychology*. New York: Appleton-Century-Crofts, 1966.

Rioch, M. J., Elkes, E., Flint, A. A., Usdansky, B. C., Newman, R. G., & Silber, E. National Institute of Mental Health pilot study in training mental health counselors. *American Journal of Orthopsychiatry*, 1963, **33**, 678–689.

Robbins, L. N. *Deviant children grown up*. Baltimore, Maryland: Williams & Wilkins, 1966.

Rosenthal, R., & Jacobsen, L. Teachers' expectancies: Determinants of pupils' IQ gains. *Psychological Reports*, 1966, **19**, 115–118.

Ryback, D., & Staats, A. W. Parents as behavior therapy-technicians in treating reading deficits (dyslexia). *Journal of Behavior Therapy and Experimental Psychiatry*, 1970, **1**, No. 2, 109–119.

Scarr, S. The Adjective check list as a personality assessment technique with children: Validity of the scales. *Journal of Consulting Psychology*, 1966, **30**, 122–128.

Schwitzgebel, R. *Street corner research: An experimental approach to the juvenile delinquent*. Cambridge: Harvard University Press, 1964.

Skinner, B. F. *Science and human behavior*. New York: Macmillan, 1953.

Skinner, B. F. Reflections on a decade of teaching machines. *Teacher's College Record*, 1963, **65**, 168–177.

Skinner, B. F. *The technology of teaching*. New York: Appleton-Century-Crofts, 1968.

Skinner, B. F. Contingency management in the classroom. *Education*, 1969, Cassel & Hoye, Milwaukee, Wisconsin.

Skinner, B. F., & Krakower, S.-A. *Handwriting with write and see*. Chicago: Lyons and Carnahan, 1968.

Snow, R. E. Unfinished pygmalion. *Contemporary Psychology*, 1969, **14**, 197–199.

Solomon, R. L. Punishment. *American Psychologist*, 1964, **19**, 239–253.

Solomon, R. L., Turner, L. H., & Lessac, M. S. Some effects of delay of punishment on resistance to temptation in days. *Journal of Personality and Social Psychology*, 1968, **8**, 233–238.

Staats, A. Development, use, and social extensions of reinforcer systems in the solution of human problems. Paper presented at a conference on behavior modification. January, 1969, Honolulu, Hawaii.

Sullivan, M. W. *The elementary school reading laboratory*. Palo Alto, California: Behavioral Research Laboratories, 1968.

Suppes, P., & Ihrke, C. Accelerated program in elementary school mathematics – The fourth year. *Psychology in the Schools*, 1970, **3**, 111–126.

Surratt, P. R., Ulrich, R. E., & Hawkins, R. P. An elementary student as a behavioral engineer. *Journal of Applied Behavior Analysis*, 1969, **2**, 85–92.

Thomas, D. A., Becker, W. C., & Armstrong, M. Production and elimination of disruptive classroom behavior by systematically varying teacher's behavior. *Journal of Applied Behavior Analysis*, 1968, **1**, 35–45.

Thomas, D. A., Nielsen, L. J., Kuypers, D. S., & Becker, W. C. Social reinforcement and remedial instruction in the elimination of a classroom behavior problem. *The Journal of Special Education*, 1968, **2**, 291–305.

Thorndike, R. L. Pygmalion in the classroom: A review. *Teacher's College Record*, 1969, **70**, 805–807.

Tunney, J. V. How smart do you want your child to be? *McCalls*, October, 1970.

Ulett, G. A., & Goodrich, D. W. *A synopsis of contemporary psychiatry.* St. Louis: C. V. Mosby Company, 1969.

Ullmann, L. P., & Krasner, L. *Case studies in behavior modification.* New York: Holt, Rinehart, & Winston, 1965.

Ullmann, L. P., & Krasner, L. *A psychological approach to abnormal behavior.* Englewood Cliffs, New Jersey: Prentice-Hall, 1969.

Ulrich, R., Wallace, F., & Dulaney, S. Pyramidal instruction: The use of elementary students as teachers of infants. Unpublished manuscript. Western Michigan University, 1970.

Wahler, R. G. Setting generality: Some specific and general effects of child behavior therapy. *Journal of Applied Behavior Analysis*, 1969, **2**, 239–246.

Walters, R. H., Parke, R. D., & Cane, V. A. Timing of punishment and the observation of consequences to others as determinants of response inhibition. *Journal of Experimental Child Psychology*, 1965, **2**, 10–30 (abridged).

Ward, M. H., & Baker, B. L. Reinforcement therapy in the classroom. *Journal of Applied Behavior Analysis*, 1968, **1**, 323–328.

Watson, J. B. Psychology as a behaviorist views it. *Psychological Review*, 1913, **20**, 158–177.

Watson, J. B., & Rayner, R. Conditioned emotional reactions. *Journal of Experimental Psychology*, 1920, **3**, 1–14.

Watson, L. Application of operant conditioning techniques to institutionalized severely and profoundly retarded children. *Mental Retardation Abstracts*, 1967, **4**, No. 1, 1–18.

Watson, L. Progress Report. Franklin County Behavior Modification Program, Columbus State Institute, Columbus, Ohio, 1970.

Webster's Third New International Dictionary. (unabridged) G. & C. Merriam Company, Springfield, Massachusetts, 1967.

Weiner, H. Controlling human fixed interval performance. *Journal of the Experimental Analysis of Behavior*, 1969, **12**, 349–373.

Wickman, E. K. *Children's behavior and teacher's attitudes.* New York: The Commonwealth Fund, 1928.

Williams, C. D. The elimination of tantrum behavior by extinction procedures: Case report. *Journal of Abnormal and Social Psychology*, 1959, **59**, 269.

Williams, C. F., Gilmore, A. S., & Malpass, L. F. Programmed instruction for culturally deprived slow-learning children. *The Journal of Special Education*, 1968, **2**, 421–427.

Winett, R. A., Richards, C. S., Krasner, L., & Krasner, M. Child monitored token reading program. 1970 Unpublished manuscript. State University of New York, Stony Brook, New York.

Witmer, H. *Psychiatric interviews with children.* Cambridge, Massachusetts: Harvard University Press, 1946.

Witmer, H. L., & Keller, J. Outgrowing childhood problems: A study in the value of child guidance treatment. *Smith Coll. Stud. Soc. Wk.*, 1942, **13**, 74–90.

Wolf, M. M., Birnbrauer, J. S., Williams, T., & Lawler, J. A note on apparent extinction of vomiting behavior of a retarded child. In L. P. Ullmann & L. Krasner (Eds.), *Case studies in behavior modification.* New York: Holt, Rinehart, & Winston, 1965.

Wolf, M. M., Giles, D. K., & Hall, V. R. Experiments with token reinforcement in a remedial classroom. *Behaviour Research and Therapy*, 1968, **6**, 51–64.

Wolpe, J. An approach to the problem of neurosis based on the conditioned response. Unpublished M.D. Thesis, University of the Witwatersrand, 1948.

Wolpe, J. *Psychotherapy by reciprocal inhibition.* Stanford: Stanford University Press, 1958.

Wolpe, J., & Rachman, S. Psychoanalytic "evidence": A critique based on Freud's case of Little Hans. *Journal of Nervous and Mental Diseases*, 1960, **130**, 135–148.

Yates, A. J. *Behavior therapy.* New York: Wiley, 1970.

Zimmerman, E. H., & Zimmerman, J. The alteration of behavior in a special classroom situation. *Journal of the Experimental Analysis of Behavior*, 1962, **5**, 59–60.

Zin, A. Children's behavior problems as viewed by teachers, psychologists, and children. *Child Development*, 1970, **41**, 871–879.

APPENDIX

Behavior Code

Symbol	Title	*Description*

Symbol   *Title*

(1) O   *Out of chair*   Observable movement of the child from his chair when not permitted or requested by teacher. None of the child's weight is to be supported by the chair.

Includes: Time limits on the following: Pencil sharpening—$1\frac{1}{2}$ minutes, Getting a drink—$1\frac{1}{2}$ minutes (Fountain in Room), Getting a book—$1\frac{1}{2}$ minutes (time limit starts from the second that the child gets out of seat), Going to the bathroom: (a) 2 minute limit, beginning with teacher's permission, (b) 30 sec. limit beginning when child leaves bathroom.

Note: If the child returns to the chair after $1\frac{1}{2}$ (or 2 minutes, where applicable), but during the 10 second inter-interval period, the "O" will be recorded in the 20 sec. interval just prior to the 10 sec.

Going to get a reading book during a math lesson, When child is fully standing and the back of legs touch chair, Going to teacher's desk when not permitted, Throwing away papers, Stretching.

Excludes: Retrieval of an accidentally dropped task-related object, Leaning forward to pick up an object even if all contact with the chair is momentarily lost, providing the child is not standing fully erect on feet.

Note: If teacher asks children to sit on the floor, then point of reference changes from chair to floor.

(2) θ   Modified out of chair   Movement of child from his chair, with some aspect of the body still touching the chair.

Includes: Leaning forward to pick up an object even if all contact with the chair is momentarily lost, providing the child is not

657

Symbol	*Title*	*Description*
		standing fully erect on feet, Standing near desk with one foot on the chair.

Excludes: When child is fully standing and the back of legs touch chair, Sitting on feet, One "cheek" off chair.

(3) T   Touching others' Property

Child comes into contact with another's property without permission to do so.

Includes: Grabbing, re-arranging, destroying the *property* of another, Using material object as extension of hand to touch others' property, Hand brushing on others' desk if this act is incompatible with learning (i.e., the child is attending to the act), Touching desk of another, whether other person is seated in it or not (this includes teacher's desk), Resting elbows on desk behind if this act is incompatible with learning or annoys the other child.

Excludes: Touching others on the back or any part of the body or clothing, Use of shared possessions such as rulers, erasers, art materials, Elbow resting on another's desk or hand brushing against it, if the desks are together and neighbor is not disturbed and such an act is not incompatible with learning.

(4) V   Vocalization

Any non-permitted "audible" behavior emanating from the mouth.

Includes: If vocalization is obvious, but can't be heard (obvious — if another child responds), Answering without being called on, Moaning, Yawning, Belching, Crying, Shouting, "Operant" coughs.

Excludes: Vocalization in response to teacher's question, Sneezing, Automatic coughing.

(5) P   Playing

Child uses his *hands* to play with his own or community property, so that such behavior is incompatible (or would be incompatible) with learning. Or reading non-task-related material.

Includes: Playing with toy car when assignment is spelling, Playing with comb or pocketbook, Poking holes in workbook, Cleaning nails with pencil, Drawing on self, Manipulating pencil in such a manner as to make the behavior *incompatible* with learning e.g., shoving pencil back and forth on desk, waving pencil through air as an airplane, Picking scabs, nails, or nose if the desired "object" is separated from the body and manipulated, Looking into desk and moving arms, but does not come out with a task-related object, Reading non-task-related material.

Symbol	*Title*	*Description*

Excludes: Touching others' property, Playing with own clothes, Lifting desk or chair with feet (rate N if this creates audible noise), Banging pencil on desk (rate N if audible), Simply twiddling pencil if it is not seen as being incompatible with learning, Picking scabs, nails, or nose if the desired "object" is *not* separate from the body.

(6) ♩ Orienting Response

The turning response is not rated unless the child is seated and the turn must be more than 90 degrees. The turning response is rated when the child is turned more than 90 degrees, using the desk as a reference point.

Includes: Turning to the person behind, Looking to the rear of the room.

Excludes: Orienting during class discussions when the teacher directs (either implicitly or explicitly) the class to attend to a child's explication of an answer.

(7) N Noise

Child creating any audible noise, without permission, other than vocalization.

Includes: Moving desk around, Pencil tapping, Banging of any object, Fishing in desk without coming out with anything or coming out with an inappropriate object, Shuffling feet more than once each way, Any noise made while getting out of chair without permission.

Excludes: Shuffling feet (if only once each way), Accidental dropping of a task-related object (book or pencil), Pushing chair back and forth *once* during a permitted act (Except to get a task-related object).

(8) A Aggression

Child makes an intense movement directed at another person so as to come into contact with him, either directly or by using a material object as an extension of the hand.

Includes: Blocking others with arms or body from attaining goal (Except while walking up aisle), Tripping, Kicking, Throwing.

Excludes: Brushing against another (*Include* if action is continually repeated).

(9) X Time-Off-Task

Child does not do assigned work for entire 20-second interval.

Includes: Child does not write when so assigned, Child does not read when so assigned, Daydreaming.

(10) Ab No inappropriate behavior as defined by the above categories.

Index

PERGAMON JOURNALS OF RELATED INTEREST . . .

JOURNAL OF BEHAVIOR THERAPY AND EXPERIMENTAL PSYCHIATRY
BEHAVIOUR RESEARCH AND THERAPY
JOURNAL OF CHILD PSYCHOLOGY AND PSYCHIATRY

PERGAMON GENERAL PSYCHOLOGY SERIES

Edited by **A.P. Goldstein & L. Krasner**

THE PRACTICE OF MANAGERIAL PSYCHOLOGY

Pergamon Management and Business Series, Volume 1

By **Andrew J. DuBrin**, *Rochester Institute of Technology, New York*

Innovative conceptual schemes are presented to show the practitioner, student, and manager what the underlying factors are that determine if intervention will be helpful, meaningless, or harmful to organizations. The Managerial Psychology Matrix, for example, specifies the proper conditions for applying such techniques as sensitivity training, performance appraisal, psychological assessment, team development meetings, organizational analysis, and superior-subordinate counseling.

Managerial psychology, according to DuBrin's conception, is the application of psychological concepts, techniques, approaches, methods, and interventions toward increasing the effectiveness of managers and organizations. Clinical-industrial, personnel, and organizational psychology constitute the three fields upon which managerial psychology is based.

The author's experience as a consultant provides many of the illustrations and examples presented in this book. Practice, research, and theory provide the knowledge base for the innovations and new conceptualizations offered.

HOMOSEXUAL BEHAVIOUR: THERAPY AND ASSESSMENT
International Series of Monographs in Experimental Psychology, Volume 14
By **Philip Feldman** and **Malcolm MacCulloch,** both of the
University of Birmingham, England

Including a review of the techniques and results of past treatment of homosexuals, the authors present a detailed account of their recent successful work in the field with the Anticipatory Avoidance Learning (AA) technique and compare this technique with Classical Conditioning and Psychotherapy.
CONTENTS: Treatment: A Review of Techniques and Results. The Development of a Treatment Technique. The Results of Aversion Therapy on a Series of Homosexual Patients. The Sexual Orientation Method. A Controlled Trial of Anticipatory Avoidance, Classical Conditioning, and Psychotherapy. Behavioural and Physiological Measures Within Treatment. The Assessment of Personality and its Influence on the Outcome of Treatment. Conclusions and Speculations. Appendix A: Case Histories. The Series. The Trial. Appendix B: Conditioning Experiment on Two Normal Volunteers. References.
1971   SBN 08-016244-4

PSYCHOTHERAPEUTIC ATTRACTION
Pergamon General Psychology Series, Volume 14
By **Arnold P. Goldstein,** *Syracuse University, New York*

Encompassing some twenty-five integrated investigations conducted over a five-year period, the research program reported in this volume extrapolates the procedures and findings from social-psychological research on interpersonal attraction to diverse clinical settings, and examines the usefulness of these procedures for enhancing the level of therapist-patient attraction in psychotherapy.
1971   SBN 08-016398-X

TEAM TEACHING AT THE COLLEGE LEVEL
Pergamon General Psychology Series, Volume 5
By **Horatio M. LaFauci** and **Peyton E. Richter,** both of the
Boston University College of Basic Studies

The first book in the educational field to be devoted solely to team teaching at the college level, this volume is based on the thesis that a skillfully taught, effectively administered team teaching program can stimulate active, productive dialogue between students and teachers and furnish students with unusual opportunities for personal growth and academic progress. Drawing on their experience at Boston University, where a team system was first developed in 1949 and where an entire two-year program of studies now successfully functions, the authors describe the nature, scope, and administration of selected team teaching programs and analyze their impact on developing curriculum. A survey of the various roles of faculty and students involved in teaching-learning teams, housing requirements of the programs, and the limitations and prospects of this emerging concept are also given.
1970   SBN 08-006946-0

THE PRACTICE OF BEHAVIOR THERAPY
Pergamon General Psychology Series, Volume 1
By **Joseph Wolpe,** *Temple University Medical School*

This volume systematically presents the most recent developments in both the theory and application of behavior therapy techniques. Professor Wolpe focuses on the practical approach to the neurotic personality, viewing the patient in his totality: an organism completely determined by his constitution, his environment, and his learning.
1969   PGPS-I   SBN 08-006390-X (softcover)
                                   SBN 08-006563-5 (hardcover)

SOCIOLOGY AND SOCIAL WORK
Perspectives and Problems

By **Brian J. Heraud**

From recent reviews. . .

"A British text, refreshingly free from jargon, that attempts to bring the two fields together by discussing what has kept them apart. The author describes the development of social work, its failure to become a profession, and its social function within the context of a sociological analysis of the structure of society. The final emphasis is on the possibilities and problems ahead for greater interaction between the two disciplines. Though written for the British arena, the book cites many American references and has applicability to the American scene."

—CHILD WELFARE

"This is an important, superbly written book. . . . It represents a major contribution to the sociology of social work."

—NEW SOCIETY

COLLEGE AND STUDENT
Selected Readings in the Social Psychology of Higher Education
Pergamon General Psychology Series, Volume 28

Edited by **Kenneth A. Feldman,** *State University of New York at Stony Brook*

The thirty-two readings that comprise this source book are concerned with the student in college and, in a sense, the college in the student. Focusing on the connections between students' *intra*personal and *inter*personal processes (whether these latter occur in a friendship dyad or among the members of a multiversity of 40,000 students), the selections in *College and Student* include recent, provocative theoretical efforts, scholarly analyses, and reports of recent research.

College and Student will also provide an excellent supplementary textbook for courses in social psychology, socialization, culture and personality, the sociology (psychology) of youth, and the numerous new courses devoted specifically to higher education that are currently being added to college curricula.

DATE DUE REMINDER

MAY 1 0

OCT 17

APR 2

JUL 1

DEC

Plea

th

DATE DUE REMINDER

DEC 13 2007

NOV 10 2009

DEC 2 0 2018

NOV 2 0

Please do not remove
this date due slip.